AN UNDERGROUND THEATRE

The author and publisher gratefully
acknowledge financial support from

Dublin City Council
&
Boston College

★

An Underground Theatre

Major Playwrights in the Irish Language
1930–80

PHILIP O'LEARY

UNIVERSITY COLLEGE DUBLIN PRESS
PREAS CHOLÁISTE OLLSCOILE
BHAILE ÁTHA CLIATH
2017

First published 2017
by University College Dublin Press
UCD Humanities Institute, Room H103
Belfield
Dublin 4
Ireland
www.ucdpress.ie

ISBN 978-1-910820-15-5 hb

CIP data available from the British Library

*The right of Philip O'Leary to be identified as the
author of this work has been asserted by him*

Typeset in Scotland in Plantin and
Fournier by Ryan Shiels
Text design by Lyn Davies
Printed in England on acid-free paper by
CPI Antony Rowe, Chippenham, Wiltshire

For Joyce

★

Contents

Abbreviations

AA	*Ar Aghaidh*
AC	*The Anglo-Celt*
ACS	*An Claidheamh Soluis*
CE	*The Cork Examiner*
CS	*The Connacht Sentinel*
CT	*The Connacht Tribune*
DP	*The Derry People and Donegal News*
EH	*Evening Herald*
EP	*Evening Press*
FH	*Fermanagh Herald*
FL	*Fáinne an Lae*
GA	*Galway Advertiser*
IG	*Irisleabhar na Gaedhilge*
II	*Irish Independent*
IMN	*Irisleabhar Mhá Nuad*
IN	*The Irish News*
IP	*The Irish Press*
IR	*The Irish Rosary*
IT	*Irish Times*
K	*The Kerryman*
LCC	*Léachtai Cholm Cille*
LL	*Limerick Leader*
LO	*Leitrim Observer*
MC	*Meath Chronicle*
ME	*The Munster Express*
MN	*The Mayo News*
NG	*The Nenagh Guardian*
NUIG	National University of Ireland, Galway
SF	*Sinn Féin*
SI	*Sunday Independent*
SS	*The Southern Star*
TH	*The Tuam Herald*
UCC	University College, Cork
UCD	University College, Dublin
UCG	University College, Galway
UH	*Ulster Herald*
WE	*Westmeath Examiner*
WP	*The Western People*

List of Illustrations

Every reasonable effort has been made to trace the copyright holders of these images. If there are any omissions UCD Press will be pleased to insert the appropriate acknowledgement in any subsequent printing or edition.

Foreword

Theatre in Irish has been a reality for more than a century, but it has always remained, as Críostóir Ó Floinn noted in 1967, an 'underground' art. Were one to ask the average reader of Irish to name ten plays in the language, the answer might be surprising – Douglas Hyde's *Casadh an tSúgáin* (The twisting of the rope) (1901), Micheál Mac Liammóir's *Diarmaid agus Gráinne* (1928), Brendan Behan's *An Giall* (The hostage) (1958), Máiréad Ní Ghráda's *An Triail* (The trial) (1964), perhaps works like Seán Ó Tuama's *Gunna Cam agus Slabhra Óir* (A pistol and a golden chain) (1956), Seán Mac Mathúna's *Gadaí Géar na Geamh Oíche* (The bitter thief of a winter's night) (1992), or Alan Titley's *Tagann Godot* (Godot turns up) (1995), and then silence. While poetry in Irish has now reached a sizeable audience, due in no small measure to translation into English, and fiction in Irish can count on a predictable if small readership, today's Gaelic playwrights face many of the same challenges as did their predecessors a century ago – a lack of theatres dedicated at least in part if not exclusively to the production of work in Irish, and a need to not only attract but also to create an audience for those plays. The fact that they have managed to accomplish so much deserves to be much better known, and thus we have this book.

An Underground Theatre: Major Playwrights in the Irish Language 1930–80 is not a history of theatre in Irish. For that we have Pádraig Ó Siadhail's *Stair Dhrámaíocht na Gaeilge 1900–1970* (A history of drama in Irish 1900–1970), although obviously a continuation of the work he did is urgently needed to bring the story to the present. Rather, this book is intended to pay overdue attention to the work created for the stage by the most significant and influential Gaelic playwrights up to the year 1980.[1] The opening date of 1930 corresponds with the first performances of plays by two of these playwrights, Máiréad Ní Ghráda and Séamus Ó Néill, although their early plays were very much apprentice efforts. The book ends in 1980 – although works by Críostóir Ó Floinn from the 1980s are discussed and an afterword provides a brief survey of developments since that end date.

I have tried throughout to deal with these plays as both works of dramatic literature and scripts for theatrical performance. To give a sense of how they were received by those who first saw them, I have quoted fairly extensively from reviews of premieres and major revivals in contemporary newspapers and periodicals. To suggest what popularity and/or influence plays may have had, I have provided lists (by no means necessarily complete) stating where, when, and by whom they were performed over the years. When available, the names of directors have been given, and on occasion the names of actors. The goal throughout has been to show that theatre in Irish has been a living if often invisible art form, with its companies, venues, prizes, and, of course, critics. In any work of this kind legitimate questions may be raised concerning inclusions and omissions. I am entirely confident that any proposed canon of modern theatre in Irish would have to include the five playwrights whose work is the focus here. The one additional dramatist who might have been included – and whose omission troubles me a bit – is Diarmaid Ó Súilleabháin (1932–85). However, none of his plays have been published, and few if any have had significant revivals, leaving him, albeit unjustly, a figure of limited influence on subsequent Gaelic theatre. Some readers might wonder why I did not begin at the beginning, going back to the work of Douglas Hyde. The plays of the earliest Gaelic dramatists, of whom Hyde, Patrick Pearse, and Pádraic Ó Conaire are probably the best, are, however, primarily of historic rather than literary interest. The sustained effort to create a serious Gaelic theatre does not begin until the founding of An Comhar Drámaíochta in Dublin in 1923 and Taibhdhearc na Gaillimhe in Galway in 1928. And while both of those groups produced some interesting and ambitious plays worthy of a book to themselves – most notably works by Piaras Béaslaí, Gearóid Ó Lochlainn, and Séamus de Bhilmot – none of it reaches the level achieved by the writers in this book.

Other readers might object to what they see as a failure to consider individual plays of merit, works like Liam O'Flaherty's *Dorchadas* (Darkness) (1926), Béaslaí's *An Danar* (The Dane) (1928), de Bhilmot's *Grádh níos Mó* (Greater love) (1938), Ó Lochlainn's *Na Fearachoin* (The dogs of war) (1938), Labhrás Mac Brádaigh's *An tÚdar i nGleic* (The author in a quandary) (1945), Walter Macken's *Oighreacht na Mara* (The heritage of the sea) (1944), Behan's *An Giall* (1958), or Siobhán Ní Shúilleabháin's *Cití* (Kitty) (1975). All of these plays and others not named are worthy of attention, but my aim here was to study the work of playwrights who created a body of significant work in Irish, rather than to examine a series of individual plays by disparate writers.

On a practical note, I should state that with a few exceptions duly noted, all translations in the text are my own. I have tried to keep them as literal as possible without violating the natural flow of the English. The Irish is, however, always provided. Short passages in Irish are usually integrated into the main text; longer passages are given in footnotes. For several of the plays I have used the typescripts provided by An Comhlachas Náisiúnta Drámaíochta. These are intended for use as scripts for Gaelic companies to perform, not as polished publications. As a result they often contain typographical errors or omit length marks over vowels. I have silently emended such obvious flaws. As I have noted in previous books, I am not entirely comfortable with the adjective 'Gaelic', as in 'Gaelic theatre'. I fully accept the prior claim of writing in Irish to the title 'Irish literature', but to so use it for a more general audience can only cause confusion, and the circumlocution literature, or plays, written in Irish soon become cumbersome. Therefore, in the interest of clarity, though with misgivings, I frequently use 'Gaelic' here.

Several people have been of invaluable assistance to me in the writing of this book. For 12 summers (1991–2002), I worked in Dublin as director of Boston College's Abbey Theatre Summer Workshop, where I had the opportunity to talk on a daily basis with Tomás Mac Anna, who, in his own idiosyncratic way, taught me more about theatre in Irish than I realised at the time. Críostóir Ó Floinn has been more than generous in answering my questions by email and by sending me a copy of his unpublished play *Taibhsí na Faiche Móire* (The ghosts of Eyre Square). Another of Ó Floinn's unpublished plays *An Spailpín Fánach* (The wandering farm labourer) was photocopied for me from the script in the Taibhdhearc na Gaillimhe papers at the National University of Ireland, Galway by Dr Louis de Paor of NUIG. Dr Éamon Ó Ciosáin of the National University of Ireland, Maynooth, provided me with a copy of the typescript of his grandmother Máiréad Ní Ghráda's unpublished one-act play *Rité*. I bought copies of other unpublished plays from An Comhlachas Náisiúnta Drámaíochta. Other individuals from whose expertise I have benefited are Professors Gearóid Denvir and Nollaig Mac Congáil of NUIG, Professor Alan Titley of University College, Cork, and especially Professor Brian Ó Conchubhair of the University of Notre Dame. Gratitude is also due to all the speakers and participants at the February 2016 conference 'Drámaíocht na Gaeilge' (Drama in Irish) organised by Professor Ó Conchubhair and myself and sponsored by Boston College. At Boston College, Anne Kenny and the staff of the Interlibrary Loan Office invariably provided me with what I needed in record time. Librarian Kathy Williams was also a great help. At UCD Press, Noelle Moran and Damien Lynam went beyond the call of duty in their work on this book, and I am always in the debt of Barbara Mennell, my first editor at UCD Press. For their help in sourcing images I am grateful to Mary Clarke, City Archivist, Dublin City Library and Archive; Kieran Hoare, Archivist, James Hardiman Library, NUIG; Darach Ó Tuairisg, Fíbín Teo; and Seán Walsh, Irish Photo Archive. Finally, the dedication of this book only begins to express my gratitude to Joyce Flynn for her constant support and incisive comments on theatre in general and Irish theatre in particular. It is altogether redundant to say that any errors or absurdities are my own doing.

PHILIP O'LEARY
South Yarmouth, Mass.
June 2017

AN UNDERGROUND THEATRE

Opening the 1967 Oireachtas Drama Festival in the new Peacock Theatre, the playwright Críostóir Ó Floinn made joking reference to the location of the Peacock beneath the Abbey Theatre, declaring: 'It is altogether appropriate that the place we are gathering for this Festival is this underground catacomb' (*Feasta*, May 1968, p. 5).[1] While Ó Floinn was thinking primarily here of the religious associations of the catacombs as particularly appropriate for an art form that had its roots 'in the ancient world as an aspect of religion' (sa seansaol mar ghné den religiún), the metaphor also captures the always marginal and frequently ignored role of theatre in Irish in the cultural life of the nation. Of course given the humble origins of that theatre at the end of the nineteenth and the beginning of the twentieth centuries, underground could be seen as a step up for Gaelic drama. Those origins are themselves rather mysterious – or at the very least obscure. The native Irish did not cultivate the genre at all, although in the early years of the language revival those who wanted to see a Gaelic drama stressed the theatrical potential of the performance style of traditional storytellers as well as of the dialogues between St Patrick and various revenants found in the tales of Fionn mac Cumhaill and his warrior band.[2] Both of these sources would be explored and exploited during the revival and after, but for the pioneers of the Gaelic theatre movement the native tradition offered little of immediate use. As Pádraig Ó Séaghdha ('Pádraig na Léime') lamented in 1909, 'It is a great source of regret for us that we lack native writing for the stage as a model for our task now' (*SF*, 23/10/09).[3]

The actual emergence of the genre in Irish is surprisingly hard to pin down. In 1899 *Irisleabhar na Gaedhilge/The Gaelic Journal* published a dialogue entitled 'Dúnlaing Óg agus a Leannán Sidhe' (Young Dúnlaing and his fairy lover), which had been collected by Séamus Ó Fiannachta (James Fenton) from Seán Chrocháin Ó Beirn of Sneem, Co. Kerry the previous year. The piece was performed by students from Patrick Pearse's Scoil Éanna (St

Enda's school) at the Theatre of Ireland in Dublin's Hardwicke Street in May 1915. According to the programme for this performance, 'Dúnlaing Óg agus a Leannán Sidhe' had been 'enacted among the people up to sixty or seventy years ago'.[4] Writing of the piece in the Gaelic League[5] weekly *An Claidheamh Soluis*, the poet and scholar Tadhg Ó Donnchadha ('Torna') stated that it was thought that the piece was 'at least three hundred years old' (trí chéad bliadhain d'aois ar a laighead), to which *An Claidheamh Soluis* added that its existence 'disproved . . . the accepted statement that native Irish literature had never evolved a drama' (*ACS*, 22/5/15). Unfortunately, neither Ó Donnchadha nor anyone else has ever offered authoritative support for such claims. Equally intriguing – and frustrating – are the three 'plays' (drámaí) or dramatic pieces collected by Fionán Mac Coluim from Tadhg Ó Conchubhair of Lispole, Co. Kerry and published in *An Lóchrann* in 1909–10, 1918, and 1918 again, respectively. Even the journal's editor, Pádraig Ó Siochfhradha ('An Seabhac'), who had been born within 20 miles of Ó Conchubhair, was startled by *Caismirt na gCearc* (The quarrel over the hens), *An Dá Dhrúncaer* (The two drunkards), and *Cleamhnas an Bhacaigh* (The tramp's matchmaking). Ó Siochfhradha wrote: 'There are not the same things in the head of anyone else in Ireland . . . The poetic anecdotes Tadhg has are a sort of form to themselves in the literature. Who first made them?'[6] We still do not have a good answer to that question. 'An Seabhac' attributed them to Ó Conchubhair, but Ó Conchubhair himself identified Muiris Ó Grifín as his source for at least *Caismirt na gCearc*.[7] Whoever put them together, they are, as originally published in *An Lóchrann* and recently in book form as *Drámaíocht ó Dhúchas ó Bhéalaithris Thaidhg Uí Chonchubhair* (Drama from the native tradition from the oral narration of Tadhg Ó Conchubhair), curious hybrid constructions, complete with rudimentary stage directions, whose source is also unclear.[8] It must, however, be acknowledged that whatever entertainment these little skits, others like them, or a piece like 'Dúnlaing Óg agus a Leannán Sidhe' provided Irish-speaking people in their own localities in the nineteenth century (or earlier), they contributed nothing to the development of a true dramatic literature in the language.

We are on much solider ground when we come to *An Bárd 'gus an Fó* (The poet and the prince), which was the first true play in Irish ever performed, improbably enough in the Steinway Hall in New York City in November 1884. This was a short work with music composed by Paul McSwiney, who also provided a libretto that was translated into Irish by Pádraig Ó Beirn.[9] Obviously a theatre movement in Irish could not be based 3,000 miles from Ireland, and it was again the trans-Atlantic Ó Beirn who provided actors at Donegal's Aonach Thír-Chonaill (The Donegal fair) in 1898 with an Irish translation of the 'St Patrick at Tara' scene in Father Eugene O'Growney's *The Passing of Conall*. Just weeks later there took place a Punch and Judy show for which Douglas Hyde and Norma Borthwick provided dialogue in Irish. With more than a touch of hyperbole, Lady Gregory, whose estate at Coole in Co. Galway provided the venue for this event, would later write: 'I hold that the beginning of modern Irish drama was in the winter of 1898, at a school feast at Coole, when Douglas Hyde and Miss Borthwick acted in Irish in a Punch and Judy show.'[10] A more convincing candidate for the first play in Irish staged in Ireland – short, translated, but not a part of something longer or a puppet show – was *An Fiaclóir*, Micheál Mag Ruaidhrí's translation of John Cannon's farcical sketch *The Dentist*, which was performed by the Blackrock branch of the Gaelic League in April 1900. The following month saw the production of the original play *Tadhg Saor* (Tadhg the craftsman) by An tAthair Peadar Ua Laoghaire in Cronin's Hall in Macroom, Co. Cork, and drama in Irish was on its way, finally reaching Dublin itself with the 1901 production in the Antient Concert Rooms of *Eilís agus an Bhean Déirce* (Eilís and the beggar woman). This play by Peadar Mac Fhionnlaoich ('Cú Uladh') was performed by the Fay Brothers' Ormonde Dramatic Society under the auspices of Maud Gonne's Inghinidhe na hÉireann (Daughters of Ireland). A few months later, in October 1901, the Irish Literary Theatre produced Hyde's *Casadh an tSúgáin* (The twisting of the rope) in the Gaiety Theatre to considerable acclaim. This was the first play in Irish ever staged in a professional theatre in Ireland. Unbeknownst at the time, the production was to be the high point for the Gaelic theatre movement for more than a decade.

Of course plays were still being performed, almost always by actors associated with branches of the Gaelic League. However, very few of those plays had any literary value at all. Most would-be Gaelic playwrights knew next to nothing about the theatre – indeed the priests who contributed so much to the Gaelic literary movement in the early revival were not even allowed to attend plays – so they were very much working in the dark, relying on what they knew from books or the contemporary commercial stage. That meant Shakespeare, as well as Dion Boucicault and his Irish and English imitators. Writing in 1904, 'Connla Caol' warned those interested in writing plays in Irish to choose their models carefully: 'Some of our Irish writers in drama have wasted effort in trying to breathe new life into the Elizabethan conventions, which are as dead to-day as their founders' (*Inis Fáil*, Dec. 1904, p. 6). For the most part those writers ignored him and other critics who urged them to reduce the number of scenes, set changes, subplots, characters, and long-winded bouts of purple rhetoric. Even a simple farce with a rural setting could create problems for anybody interested in producing it. Thus the editors of *Banba* were stupefied by the special effects called for in *Muinntear Chillmhuire nó Bó i bPoll* (The people of Cillmhuire, or a cow in a hole) by Séamus Ó Dubhghaill ('Beirt Fhear'):

3

We will present the first volume of *Banba* again to anyone who will tell us how a wave can be set in motion on stage, how seven men can gather around a bog-hole there and pull a cow out of it with ropes and sacks, how the cow can be kept on the stage with water and mud flowing from her sides, how she can be driven from there to the byre, how, – how, – how will the *play* be put on the stage, that is what we want to know. (*Banba*, June 1903, p. 214)[11]

If a trivial comedy could create such problems, it is not hard to imagine what challenges higher ambitions might bring on. For example, An tAthair Peadar Ua Laoghaire's *An Bealach Buidhe* (The yellow road), a one-act historical play about one of the exploits of Aodh Ó Néill, had eight scenes, all with different settings, and nine speaking parts, while the one-act historical play *Aodh Ó Néill* by Pádraig Ó Séaghdha ('Conán Maol') had seven scenes requiring six set changes, and a cast of more than 20 characters. And such excess was the norm even after the Gaelic League's annual Oireachtas introduced regular competitions for the writing of plays in 1901.[12]

Whatever their shortcomings with regard to stagecraft, most of these early Gaelic playwrights had a sound, often native, command of the Irish language. Their audiences, however, were all too often not so blessed. Writing of those who watched the 'St Patrick at Tara' scene at Aonach Thír-Chonaill in 1898, an anonymous contributor to *Fáinne an Lae* noted that 'the audience thoroughly enjoyed the piece, though it was presented in a vernacular foreign to probably most of them' (*FL*, 15/4/99). When *An Tobar Draoidheachta* (The magic well) by An tAthair Pádraig Ó Duinnín was per-formed in Dunmanway, Co. Cork in 1902, the critic for *An Muimhneach Óg* asserted that the play was 'generally enjoyed even by people who did not understand a word of Irish' (*Muimhneach Óg*, June 1903, p. 5). Apparently playgoers who saw Peadar Mac Fhionnlaoich's *Eilís agus an Bhean Déirce* in Belfast in 1900 also liked the play, although *An Claidheamh Soluis* reported that 'the audience as a whole could not follow the work' (*ACS*, 10/11/00). When the situation was different, that fact was newsworthy, as when *An Claidheamh Soluis* stated of a 1902 performance of Hyde's *Casadh an tSúgáin* in Ballaghaderreen, Co. Roscommon that 'the best thing is that many who were present understood Irish' (*ACS*, 22/2/02). It was an Irish playwright working in English, Padraic Colum, who best summed up the way things were in the early years of the revival:

For a long time there will be, in the general audience for Irish plays, many who do not know the language, or know it imperfectly, many who, in Mark Twain's phrase, 'average it up.' A play depending on subtlety of characterisation and refinement of nature could not be a success with such an audience. (*ACS*, 27/8/10)

He could not have imagined how long the long time he mentioned would turn out to be.

Actually, there was at the time little likelihood that Gaelic playwrights would produce plays 'depending on subtlety of characterisation and refinement of nature', or that the part-time, amateur, and entirely untrained Gaelic actors available would have known what to do with such plays were they to miraculously appear. Indeed one of the biggest worries about such actors was whether or not they could speak the language in which they were supposed to be acting. As 'Ardánach' wrote in 1904, 'It does great damage to the Gaelic drama to put people on stage who don't have an idea in the world what the words they say mean' (*IG*, Apr. 1903, p. 272).[13] Predictably enough, some argued that theatre in Irish should for the foreseeable future be a strictly Gaeltacht project. Thus as late as 1929, the acerbic native speaker Séamus Ó Grianna ('Máire') could write:

> But the first play one of them [native speakers] will write, even if it is just a disorganised, shapeless, unfinished thing – and even if they have no place to stage it but in a cowshed at the cow's rump with a candle in a porter bottle for lighting – it will have a virtue that the plays in the Abbey Theatre do not have. It will be a natural start and it will evolve with time. (*FL*, Nov. 1929, p. 7)[14]

As Ó Grianna himself was well aware, however, the problem was that the people of the rural Gaeltachtaí had had no experience whatsoever with theatre of any kind. Moreover, given the remote western areas in which they lived, they lacked any real opportunities to develop that experience and were thus unlikely to create a truly native school of acting and dramatic art in Irish. Most in the language movement with an interest in theatre understood that, as had been the case elsewhere in the western world, drama would have to emerge from the cities and towns.

It was, then, a development of considerable importance when within days of each other in 1913, two new Gaelic theatre companies appeared in Dublin. Na hAisteoirí (The actors), made up largely of people who had been involved in the theatrical productions of the militantly Munster-oriented Craobh an Chéitinnigh (Keating branch) of the Gaelic League, was the brainchild of Piaras Béaslaí, who would go on to provide the group with many of the plays they were to produce in their brief existence. Na hAisteoirí presented their first productions – *Beart Nótaí* (A bundle of banknotes) by Máire Ní Shíthe and Eilís Ní Mhurchadha and Béaslaí's *Cluiche Cártaí* (A game of cards), an adaptation of an eighteenth-century play in English by Arthur Murphy – at the Gaelic League's headquarters in Dublin in April 1913. Na Cluicheoirí (The players) were closely linked with the League's Ard-Chraobh

5

(Central branch), which had been at often vitriolic odds with the Keating branch over provincial sensitivities for nearly two decades.[15] The group's first appearance before the public was in May 1913 when its actors performed Pádraic Ó Conaire's *Bairbre Ruadh* (Red-haired Barbara) and a translation of Seamus O'Kelly's *The Shiuler's Child* at the Abbey. Na Cluicheoirí would have a rather spectacular inaugural year in 1913, with an excursion to Spiddal in the Conamara Gaeltacht in August and a return to the Abbey in November.

It would, however, be Béaslaí's Aisteoirí that would have the greatest inspirational and practical effect on Gaelic theatre in both Dublin and the provinces. According to a report on the group's activities in *An Claidheamh Soluis* in 1914, 'their greatest successes have been in the comparatively unspoiled country places' (*ACS*, 22/8/14), an opinion that seems to be confirmed by an account of their summer tour of Cork and West Kerry on their way to that year's Oireachtas in Killarney. Of course, Dublin was their base of operations, and there their preference for original plays – most by Béaslaí – set them apart from Na Cluicheoirí, the majority of whose productions were of Abbey Theatre plays translated into Irish.[16] Despite their differences, the two groups shared the stage at the Abbey in April 1915, when Na hAisteoirí performed Béaslaí's *Fear na Milliún Punt* (The millionaire) and Na Cluicheoirí put on Alphonsus Ó Labhra's *An tSnaidhm* (The knot). Unfortunately, like so much in Irish cultural life, theatre in Irish was a casualty of the 1916 Easter Rising and the struggle for independence that followed in its wake. As Béaslaí recalled in 1918, 'We were forging ahead nicely when Easter Week came and Na hAisteoirí were scattered, for there was not a single man amongst them who did not have some connection with the work of that week' (*FL*, 5/1/18).[17] That Na Cluicheoirí were no more fortunate is evident from a 1920 piece in *Misneach* stating that there had been no plays in Irish produced in Dublin for the past two years and that 'most likely the troubled times are the cause, but whatever is responsible it has been a great step back and a great detriment to the work for the Irish language' (*Misneach*, 8/5/20).[18]

With the return to an albeit uneasy peace after the War of Independence and the Civil War, it was possible to once again consider the potential for an active Gaelic drama movement in Dublin. Actually, the first step had already been taken by Gearóid Ó Lochlainn in late 1921. Perhaps because he had been away for 14 years acting in Denmark and thus had not been involved with either Na hAisteoirí or Na Cluicheoirí, Ó Lochlainn was the ideal man to step in and pick up the pieces. Drawing on all that he had learned in the professional theatre and film industry in Copenhagen, he gathered together his own company, Aisteoirí Átha Cliath (The Dublin actors) – although to be fair most of his players were former members of Béaslaí's Aisteoirí. Forced to disband when the Civil War erupted in Dublin in June 1922, Aisteoirí Átha

Cliath were back in June 1923 to perform plays in the Gaiety Theatre during a short festival that took the place of that year's cancelled Oireachtas.[19] More important, this group (and thus through it Na hAisteoirí) became the nucleus of An Comhar Drámaíochta (The drama society), which began life as a theatrical management and promotion organisation, and went on to become by far the most important force in Gaelic drama in Dublin for the next 20 years.[20] Writing as 'An Lochlannach' (The Scandinavian) in April 1923, Ó Lochlainn let those with an interest in seeing plays in Irish more regularly know that something important was in the works: 'According to what I hear there is at present a little group whose goal is to lay the foundation stone of the Irish-language stage and who will not stop working until Irish has its legitimate and proper place in the country's drama' (*II*, 10/4/23).[21] An Comhar Drámaíochta staged its first production in the Abbey in November 1923, performing three one-act plays, two of them original works. The company was back at the Abbey with three more one-act plays, all translations, the following week. These performances were to set the pattern for An Comhar for the rest of its active existence: short – often one-night – runs of a mix of original and translated plays, many of them one-acters, performed in a hired space that gave them inadequate time to rehearse, much less to develop a polished acting style. Ó Lochlainn and Béaslaí, along with León Ó Broin, would be the leading lights of An Comhar in its first decade, and they would over the years draw on the talents of such important figures in the history of Gaelic drama as Máiréad Ní Ghráda, Micheál Mac Liammóir, Pádraig and Micheál Ó Siochfhradha, Séamus de Bhilmot, and Cyril Cusack.

The handicaps noted above were significant, and throughout the 1920s and 1930s we find members of An Comhar lamenting the fact that they had no space of their own in which to rehearse or to stage productions for even the most modest of runs; that they found it very difficult to get new scripts and therefore had to rely on the much less popular translations; and that as a result they were never able to build a satisfactory and reliable audience for their work. Virtually all with an interest in Gaelic drama in Dublin saw this lack of a theatre dedicated to the production of plays in Irish as the most significant challenge An Comhar faced, the one that underlay most of the others. Again and again, we hear calls for such a theatre. Gearóid Ó Lochlainn made the case ambitiously in 1929: 'Nothing less will do than a theatre in which plays in Irish will be performed six nights a week during forty weeks in the year and in which the artistic standard will not be below that which is usual in the Abbey Theatre and the Gate Theatre' (*Leader*, 16/12/39). Instead, between 1923 and 1943, An Comhar would perform in the Abbey (1923–9), the Peacock (1929–30, 1934–5, 1936–41, and 1942) the Gate (1930–4, 1941–2), and the Torch (1935–6).

Those involved with An Comhar were quite well aware of their problems, but lest they forgot, they had a bevy of critics to remind them. In particular, some of those critics seized on two intractable failings that damned the group in their eyes. First of all, many prominent members of An Comhar, people like Béaslaí, Ó Broin, and Ní Ghráda, had well-known connections with the Free State government and the Cumann na nGaedheal party. Béaslaí had been a major-general and press censor, Ó Broin an army officer, and Ní Ghráda the secretary of Ernest Blythe, a government minister many saw as having the blood of 77 executed republicans on his hands. Critics with republican views and/or a later affiliation with Éamon de Valera's Fianna Fáil party were hardly likely to let this perceived apostasy pass unremarked. Even more important, the majority of those active in An Comhar were not native speakers of Irish, leaving the group open, sometimes with justification, to criticism of the quality of Irish spoken on stage. Once again, Séamus Ó Grianna expressed this criticism with characteristic acerbity. Beginning with his familiar argument that theatre in Irish must come from the Gaeltacht, he wrote: 'I will, of course, be told that the people of the Gaeltacht have no knowledge of that craft. I admit that. But however bad they are, they are as good as the crowd that has been in the Abbey Theatre for the past five years. In the first place they don't rely on Liverpool Irish' (*FL*, Nov. 1929, p. 1).[22] The following month he pronounced An Comhar's productions 'a great public disgrace' (mór an náire shaoghalta) and declared: 'It is bad enough for us that the Gaeltacht is vanishing without a flock of simple Yahoos without mouth or tongue stammering on stage and trying to convince us that they have the language of our ancestors' (*FL*, Dec. 1929, p. 1).[23] Through it all, the amateurs of An Comhar Drámaíochta carried on.

As noted above, An Comhar had started as a group of enthusiasts who wanted to encourage drama in Irish by dealing with administrative affairs like securing playing space, helping select plays, and providing publicity. The actual work on stage would be done by Ó Lochlainn's Aisteoirí Átha Cliath. With time, however, and certainly by 1928 when Béaslaí replaced Ó Lochlainn as the director of most of its productions, An Comhar had become a real theatre company, with not only its own board of directors, but also a group of actors on which it could draw, and a growing repertoire of plays both original and translated. Needless to say, this expansion of its activities put an increased burden on the company, as did its peripatetic trek through the theatres of Dublin and the pressing problem of attendance. There were, of course, successful shows that drew a crowd, but all too often reviews of An Comhar's productions drew attention to rows of empty seats. Indeed in 1937, 'S. Ó M.' could write: 'How many thousand Irish speakers are there in Dublin to-day? Yet what of the audience for Gaelic plays in the chief city of the Irish Nation? In the Peacock Theatre of 100 seats it is not an unusual thing for the Gaelic players to play to 50, 40, 30, aye, and sometimes to only 20 people' (*Leader*, 12/6/37).

It was to address this problem that in 1936 the board of An Comhar proposed a new policy, undertaking to act as what in effect would be a coordinating body for Gaelic drama nationwide, with a special emphasis on Dublin. When this idea was officially adopted the following year, An Comhar continued to perform plays with its own company – the former Aisteoirí Átha Cliath now known as Foireann Tofa an Chomhair (The select company of An Comhar) – and also hosted productions by affiliated groups, including Gaelic League branches like the still very active Craobh an Chéitinnigh, as well as Craobh na gCúig gCúigí, Craobh Moibhí, Craobh Liam Uí Mhaolrúnaidhe, Craobh na nGardaí, and Craobh Thomáis Dáibhis; Trinity College's Cumann Gaedhealach na hOllscoile; Cumann Gaedhealach na Stáitsheirbhíse; and various Dublin area school groups.[24] While this scheme may have boosted attendance as relatives and friends of the actors dutifully came to the theatre, it could only have lowered the general standard that it had taken An Comhar so long to develop.

In 1935, Ernest Blythe was appointed to the Abbey Theatre's board of directors, and by 1938 he had won over his fellow board members to the principle that the theatre had an obligation to stage plays in Irish. Yet despite the fact that he had been the minister responsible for securing a state subsidy of £600 for An Comhar in 1924, he did not see a band of amateur actors as the best way to Gaelicise the Abbey. Writing in 1938 he stated: 'Meantime Gaelic drama cannot continue to rest in the hands of amateurs. It has, for some time, been clear that there can be little real progress until Irish plays are performed by a permanent company of professional players working under a competent producer [i.e. director] who has had a sound technical training.'[25] To realise this vision, he set in motion his subsequently much-maligned scheme that required the professionals in the National Theatre to be able to perform bilingually.[26] Such a plan obviously rendered An Comhar largely irrelevant except as a source of Irish-speaking extras to back up the Abbey's lead players in Gaelic productions. An Comhar did, however, have one thing of value in Blythe's mind – its state subsidy – and he secured that by merging the group with the Abbey. Not surprisingly, there were members and supporters of An Comhar who were always suspicious of Blythe's intentions and worried about what a merger with the Abbey would mean for the future of their own long-suffering company. For example, the playwright and later Abbey director Séamus de Bhilmot, six of whose plays were produced by An Comhar, wrote of the proposed merger: 'The direct influence on the theatre of a language other than Irish is not, I think sincerely, for the ultimate advantage of Drama or Dramatists in the Irish language' (*Leader*, 23/5/42).[27] He would later see how right he was. The deal had, however, been done in the same month he was writing, and An Comhar's May 1942 production of Donn Piatt's translation of Joseph Bédier and Louis Artus's *Tristan et Iseult* marked the final appearance of An Comhar Drámaíochta as an independent company.[28]

After 1942, the group had a shadow existence, giving the Abbey its subsidy, providing Irish-speaking actors in mostly minor roles, and doubtless on occasions inspiring enough guilt in the National Theatre to get a play in Irish on stage. Ironically, however, An Comhar was still in the 1950s and 1960s given credit for the most successful productions ever mounted in Irish, the Abbey's *geamaireachtaí* or pantomimes, which began in 1945 and continued annually until 1969, drawing thousands of people, many with imperfect Irish at best, into the theatre to see these lavish, topical, funny, and easy to follow spectacles.[29] An Comhar actually remained in existence until 1967, when its subsidy was given directly to the Abbey, and the group quietly vanished.

It was an unworthy end to a brave experiment. The flaws of An Comhar were many, and some were serious. But for two decades it provided Dublin's Irish speakers with a chance to hear the language spoken regularly on stage during the theatre season. This contribution was made even more significant by the fact that from 1924 to 1939 the Gaelic League's Oireachtas, whose competitions had done much to encourage the writing of new plays and which had been one of the most important venues for their performance, was not held.[30] Over 20 years, An Comhar produced or assisted in the production of some 200 plays, if one includes revivals. The majority were one-act plays and a significant number were translations, but An Comhar also encouraged original work, staging more than 50 new plays in Irish, most of which might never have been written had it not been for the existence of the company. In addition, An Comhar's influence extended beyond Dublin, so that amateur companies throughout Ireland borrowed their name, and we find references to Comhar Drámaíochta Chorcaighe, Comhar Drámaíochta na Ceard-Scoile, and Comhar Drámaíochta na Scoile Tráchtála in Cork; Comhar Drámaíochta Phort Láirge in Waterford; Comhar Drámaíochta Luimnighe in Limerick; and Comhar Drámaíochta Átha Luain in Athlone; as well as Cumann Drámaíochta Bhaile an Fheirtéarigh and Cumann Drámaíochta na Feothanaighe, both in Co. Kerry. None of these groups were directly affiliated with the Dublin Comhar and the name An Comhar Drámaíochta itself is hardly original, but there can be little doubt that it was the example of the Dubliners that inspired most if not all of these amateur players and many others who named themselves with a bit more imagination.

The Abbey's highly successful experiment with *geamaireachtaí* was inspired in part by the public's response to similar entertainments at Taibhdhearc na Gaillimhe (The Galway theatre) in Galway, but much more by the Gaelic variety shows created by a new Dublin theatre group, Compántas Amharclainne na Gaeilge (The Irish-language theatre company). This company, which drew most of its members from the actors of the Keating branch, but also attracted former members of An Comhar Drámaíochta, was founded in 1943 by the playwrights Séamus de Bhilmot, Micheál Ó Siochfhradha, Annraoi Saidléar, and the ubiquitous Gearóid Ó Lochlainn. Its goal was at first to produce original plays in Irish, its initial performance being the March 1944 premiere of de Bhilmot's political play *Prólog don Réim Nua* (Prologue to the new order). This was followed by a revival of the same author's *Déamar agus a Bhean* (Damer and his wife) at the Oireachtas in October. The company's mission was, however, to change radically with the success of its bilingual variety show *Geamaí na Nollag*[31] in the Peacock in December 1944, followed quickly by a similar show, *Seamaí an Earraigh* in the Peacock two months later. This new direction was confirmed when in May 1945 An Compántas produced *Hot-Seadh*, the first of its so-called *Seadh-Seóanna* (Seadh-shows), variety shows that again mixed Irish and English and were to include titles like *Aith-Seadh* (1945), *Got-Seadh* (1946), *Hit-Seadh* (1947), *Nú-Seadh* (1947), *Gate-Seadh* (1948), *Sár-Seadh* (1948), *Gáir-Seadh* (1949), *More-Seadh* (1949), *Fun-Seadh* (1950), and the final one, *Star-Seadh* (1953), by which time both the imagination and the energy were largely gone from these entertainments. An Compántas did produce a few actual plays in the 1950s – translations of Eugene O'Neill's *Ile* and Eugène Ionesco's *La cantatrice chauve*, for example – before disbanding in 1958. But their initial goal of bringing new and original work in Irish to the stage was never realised, and the group will be remembered, if at all, for the startling success and popularity of their variety shows in the 1940s.

Throughout the 1930s, 1940s, and 1950s, schools,[32] universities, and amateur groups, in particular those associated with Gaelic League branches, continued to perform in Irish throughout the country, with the players of Craobh an Chéitinnigh and Craobh Moibhí being, as they had long been, the most active and accomplished of such groups in Dublin. The disappearance of An Comhar, the focus of An Compántas on the *Seadh-Seóanna*, and the return of the Oireachtas in 1939 with its competitions for both the writing and performance of plays made the work of such amateurs even more important. These circumstances also, of course, left the Abbey as the *de facto* home of Gaelic drama in the capital. For many at the time – and since – such a development seemed only natural. The Abbey was, after all, the state-subsidised National Theatre of a nation whose first official language was Irish. Moreover, it had just taken over what had been the most active Gaelic company (and its subsidy). Unfortunately, the Abbey has never met even the most modest expectations of those with an interest in Gaelic drama. With the takeover of An Comhar still a sore point, the Abbey did in 1942–3 stage six plays in Irish, but none of them were original works, and, with the exception of 1943–4 when three original full-length plays in Irish were produced – Micheál Ó hAodha's *Ordóg an Bháis* (The thumb of death), Eibhlín Ní Shúilleabháin's *Laistiar de'n Éadan* (Behind the face), and Peadar Ó hAnnracháin's *Stiana* – those first years after An Comhar's demise set the pattern for the Abbey's involvement with the Irish language. There would be a rare full-length premiere like that of Máiréad Ní Ghráda's *Giolla an tSolais* (Lucifer) in 1945 or Seán Ó Tuama's *Gunna Cam agus Slabhra Óir* (A pistol and a golden chain) in 1956, but these plays were only on the Abbey stage for a night or two. On occasion, a play that had been performed elsewhere would be given a night at the Abbey as was the case with, among a few others, Piaras Béaslaí's *An Bhean Chródha* (The brave woman) in 1943; Labhrás Mac Brádaigh's *An tÚdar i nGleic* (The author in a quandary) in 1945; Walter Macken's *Oighreacht na Mara* (The heritage of the sea), which was performed by the Taibhdhearc players in the Abbey in 1945; or Micheál Mac Liammóir's *Diarmaid agus Gráinne* in 1947. Once in a while, a translation might be performed, as were Blythe's own version of Molière's *Le bourgeois gentilhomme* as *Sodar i ndiaidh na nUasal* in 1944, Máire Ní Shíothcháin's translation of T. C. Murray's *Birthright* as *Oidhreacht* in 1946, or Liam Ó Briain's rendering of Henri Ghéon's *La joyeuse farce des 'encore'* as *Arís* in 1948.

While the Abbey over the years produced a number of new one-act plays, many of those were put on after the main attraction in English and without any advance publicity, in the apparent hope of trapping people into staying for the Gaelic show. When the original Abbey building burned down in 1951 and the company relocated to the considerably larger Queen's Theatre across the Liffey, it became even more financially unfeasible to produce work – and in particular full-length work – in Irish. When the new Abbey opened on the original site in 1966 and the new Peacock followed in 1967, plays in Irish were all but ignored on both stages.[33] This disregard for the language outraged some Irish speakers who believed that they had been promised more plays in the language in the Peacock at least in return for the final curtain's falling on An Comhar Drámaíochta. In the period between 1966 and the end-date of this study in 1980, the Abbey, excluding the Christmastime shows in Irish that replaced the *geamaireachtaí*, performed *no* new plays in Irish on its main stage, while the Peacock produced no more than a dozen.

Motivated by their frustration with the Abbey, as well as by the simple fact that in the 1950s there was no venue where one could expect to regularly see plays in Irish (not to mention new plays in Irish), a committee of Irish speakers with an interest in drama came together in 1954 to discuss the question of Gaelic theatre, with particular focus on Dublin. Among those on this committee were familiar names like Piaras Béaslaí, Gearóid Ó Lochlainn, and Máiréad Ní Ghráda from the days of An Comhar Drámaíochta. But there were also younger members as well as people involved with a new initiative founded the previous year to advance the cause of language revival.

While Gaelic theatre was not one of the initial concerns of Gael-Linn, which raised money for revival activities by running football pools, by 1954 it had expressed its awareness of the need for a dedicated theatre in Dublin for the production of plays in Irish and had also declared its willingness to finance such a venture. In the meantime, the broadcaster, journalist, and former Taibhdhearc na Gaillimhe actor and scriptwriter Seán Mac Réamoinn had suggested in the monthly magazine *Comhar* that Irish speakers in Dublin form a 'Club Drámaíochta' (Drama club) to build the base for a future audience for such a theatre (*Comhar*, Nov. 1954, pp 21–3). With the help of Cumann na Scríbhneoirí (The writers' association) and Comhdháil Náisiúnta na Gaeilge (The national congress of the Irish language), that club was soon a reality. In 1955 Gael-Linn found and rented a suitable space for a small theatre in the Damer Hall beneath the Unitarian church in St Stephen's Green, and appointed its own manager Riobard Mac Góráin to run the theatre.[34] Productions would be the responsibility of An Club Drámaíochta. Thus began what would for the next 15 years be the most productive and exciting venture in the history of theatre in Irish. As was true of An Comhar Drámaíochta, An Club Drámaíochta began as a production company that brought in actors and directors for each show. A big difference, however, was that the club had its own theatre and soon began to hire its own professional director for several shows each season. And those doing the hiring clearly had an eye for directorial talent. The first director chosen was Frank Dermody (Proinsias Mac Diarmada), followed by Tomás Mac Anna, and at various times, Niall Tóibín, Seán Ó Briain, Noel Ó Briain, and Dónall Farmer. Predictably, these developments attracted the interest of the most talented Irish-speaking actors and soon, for the first time ever, Gaelic theatre had not only a home, but a core of dedicated and talented directors and performers working together on a regular basis. Moreover, in a development that must have thrilled many in the language movement, in 1959 a group of native speakers resident in Dublin, most of them from Conamara, came together to form Aisteoirí na Gaeltachta (The Gaeltacht actors), with Frank Dermody as their director. The company was welcomed enthusiastically when it produced a programme of three translated one-act plays, two by Lady Gregory and Synge's *Riders to the Sea*, in February 1959. 'P. Mac A.' wrote in the *Irish Times*: 'Somehow, the natural acting of the performers, their grace of movement and their beautiful flow of language reminded one of what the early days of the Abbey Theatre must have been like' (*IT*, 10/2/59). A year later, the group performed Frank Dermody's own play *Oidhreacht Bhideog Mhóir* (Big Bideog's inheritance), directed by Séamus Páircéir. Unfortunately, that was to be the last appearance by the company, although several of its actors, most notably the poet Máirtín Ó Direáin, remained active in the theatre.

An Damer got off to an impressive start in its first season in 1955–6, offering audiences seven plays, three of them original new work, performed by, among others, Craobh an Chéitinnigh, Craobh na gCúig gCúigí, and, visiting from the Donegal Gaeltacht, Aisteoirí Ghaoth Dobhair (The Gweedore actors). The following year Compántas Chorcaí (The Cork company) brought Seán Ó Tuama's one-act historical play *Moloney* to An Damer, and the theatre would later produce the premiere of his play *Iúdás Iscariot agus a Bhean* (Judas Iscariot and his wife) in 1967. In addition, An Damer would host or stage productions of other works by this major playwright – *Ar Aghaidh leat, a Longadáin* (Onward, Longadán) in 1959 and again in 1976, *Corp Eoghain Uí Shúilleabháin* (The corpse of Eoghan Ó Súilleabháin) in 1964, *Gunna Cam agus Slabhra Óir* in 1964, and *Déan Trócaire ar Shagairt Óga* (Have mercy on young priests) in 1972. Other major plays that had their first performance at An Damer were Brendan Behan's *An Giall* (The hostage) (1958), Seán Ó Riada's *Spailpín a Rúin* (My darling wander farm labourer) (1960), Séamus Ó Néill's *Rún an Oileáin* (The secret of the island) (1961) and *An tSiúr Pól* (Sister Paul) (1964), Máiréad Ní Ghráda's *Stailc Ocrais* (Hunger strike) (1962) and *An Triail* (The trial) (1964), Diarmaid Ó Súilleabháin's *Macalla* (Echo) (1966), and Críostóir Ó Floinn's *Aggiornamento* (1968), *Cóta Bán Chríost* (The white coat of Christ) (1969), and *Homo Sapiens* (1975). Its two greatest successes were *An Triail*, still regularly revived, and *An Giall*, the simple and moving original version of what would become a very different play in the hands of Joan Littlewood. In addition, An Damer produced other original full-length works of interest, new one-act plays, revivals of important pieces previously performed at the theatre or by other companies, and a fair number of translations, some of plays never seen in Dublin in either Irish or English. Once again, however, despite its production of a fair number of fine new plays, the ever-prominent place of translations in every season's schedule was a source of ongoing frustration. In an interview with Liam Ó Lonargáin in 1968, Micheál Ó Ruairc, the manager of An Damer, acknowledged the theatre faced persistent problems but saw the lack of new work in Irish as the most significant of them: 'More money, more writers, more people attending the plays. The most important thing beyond all others is to encourage and nurture writers. If we had an abundance of writers the other things would come' (*Feasta*, Sept. 1968, p. 14).[35]

Those things did not come, and the resulting financial problems, problems that had more than once interfered with the work of An Damer, eventually led to the theatre's demise in 1976. A subsequent effort from 1979 to 1981 to revive the company on a professional basis was unsuccessful despite some interesting productions like Eoghan Ó Tuairisc's *Carolan* and a revival of *An Giall*.[36] This professional group, with Áine Uí Dhrisceoil directing, also did some touring in 1979, but much of its energy was spent trying to fill seats with *geamaireachtaí* like Maev Nic Giolla Íosa'a *Cinder Eile* (i.e. Cinderella, lit. 'Another cinder') (1980), *Fronnsa* (Farce) (1981), and *An Scadán Dearg* (The red herring) (1981), or Pádraig Ó Giollagáin's rock 'n' roll play *Clann Thomáis* (The Clan of Tomás) (1980).[37] However anticlimactic its end, An Damer offered Dublin audiences the most exciting and sophisticated seasons of Gaelic plays they had ever seen. Even a few moments of conversation with anyone who was a regular playgoer at An Damer in its heyday will make clear that the time it was in existence was a Golden Age for theatre in Irish.

Of course there will be many in Galway who will argue, and not without reason, that the real flowering of Gaelic drama took place – and is still, if sporadically, taking place – in the west. While An Comhar Drámaíochta was enjoying its subsidy and making its mark in Dublin, its benefactor, Ernest Blythe, was turning his attention to Galway, where some drama enthusiasts were talking about starting a theatre for plays in Irish. In January 1928 he met a delegation from Galway and told its members that the government could provide a subsidy of £600 per year. Almost immediately the Galwegians set to work, hiring a building that was later purchased and that has, with some repairs and renovations, remained their base of operations ever since, and employing Micheál Mac Liammóir as what we would now call their artistic director. On 27 August 1928, Taibhdhearc na Gaillimhe opened, its initial production being Mac Liammóir's *Diarmaid agus Gráinne*, with the author featuring as co-director (with Hilton Edwards), set designer, and male lead. Blythe, who had travelled to Galway for the opening, was impressed, calling the show 'a production in Irish that was incomparably more artistic than anything which had ever been given in the place [i.e. Galway] in English'.[38] *The Connacht Sentinel* expressed the local pride the production and events surrounding it had inspired: 'From every point of view the initial production last night was an unbounded success . . . Indeed, the committee, the author, the players, and all concerned have reason to be proud of their achievement' (*CS*, 22/8/28). Thus began a Gaelic theatrical initiative that continues in Galway to the present day.

Back in Dublin, An Comhar Drámaíochta must have envied their western counterparts their theatre, their access to both actors and audiences with good Irish – the Conamara Gaeltacht was at the city's doorstep, the nation's legally mandated Gaelic university was a 15 minute walk from the theatre, and the Irish army's Irish-speaking First Infantry Battalion was based just a few miles away. Moreover, Taibhdhearc na Gaillimhe had a director, designer, and actor of genius in Mac Liammóir (although from the start he was more interested in his new Dublin theatre, the Gate, than he was in An Taibhdhearc). Still, he directed all the plays the theatre produced in its first two seasons and was still involved on occasion in the third. To replace him, An Taibhdhearc's board brought in the Chicago-born soldier Frank Dermody (Proinsias Mac Diarmada), who after doing first-rate work in Galway went on to have a distinguished career at the Abbey and An Damer. The early Taibhdhearc seems to have been particularly fortunate in its directors, for when Dermody left for the Abbey in 1938, he was replaced after a few months, in which three members of the theatre filled in, by Walter Macken (Uaitéar Ó Maicín), who stayed until 1948, producing 76 plays before himself heading off to the Abbey. After his departure, the theatre's luck ran out and for eight years productions were often in the hands of guest directors and part-time appointees, although Seán Ó hÓráin directed many of the plays between 1950 and 1955. In 1956, Traolach Ó hAonghusa took over as artistic director, remaining in that post until 1969. Throughout the 1970s most of An Taibhdhearc's productions were directed by Risteárd Ó Broin, Seán Stafford, or Pádraig Ó hÉanaí. Guest directors at the time included Dermody, Alan Simpson, and Frank J. Bailey.

Despite having the benefit of its own theatre and the stability provided by a series of fine directors, the part-time amateur company at An Taibhdhearc was plagued by some of the same problems that beset An Comhar. Thus we read complaints of poor acting, wretched attendance, and even poor Irish spoken on stage. For example, a note in the minutes from a meeting of An Taibhdhearc's board declares of a 1930 production of Lady Gregory's *Hyacinth Halvey* in translation: 'Hy [*sic*] Halvey very bad – Mac Glla [*sic*] Cionnaith and Capt. Paor from Rinn Mór [*sic*] had bad Irish, Gill very bad as usual.'[39] On the whole, however, most playgoers who got to see the Galway company liked what they saw. Thus in 1943, Seán Ó Maolriamh [*sic*] wrote to *The Connacht Tribune* to praise An Taibhdhearc for 'the liveliest, most vigorous, sprightliest, most spirited, excellently performed stage acting a person could see or hear, even were he in Dublin at the Abbey or the Gate!' (an aicteáil stáitse is beodha, bríoghmhaire, bíogúila [*sic*] meanmach [*sic*] is a d'fhéadfadh duine d'fheiceáil nó do chloisteáil dá mbadh i mBaile Átha Cliath féin 'na [*sic*] mhainistreach [*sic*] nó an Geata dhó) (*CT*, 12/6/43). Galwegians must also have been delighted when the actors from An Taibhdhearc impressed Dublin audiences and critics like Sean O'Faolain, who though by no means favourably disposed to the language revival at the time, wrote of the Galway actors: 'The general level of the production is high: taking all in all at least as high as the average production at the Gate, if not at their best quite as high as those Gate productions at their best' (*Bell*, Jan. 1941, p. 86). A high point for An Taibhdhearc was its 1951 production of Shaw's *Saint Joan* as translated by Siobhán McKenna, who also played the lead. The play was directed by one of the theatre's guest directors, Ian Priestly Mitchell, who despite not knowing Irish and working on a production schedule that had him commuting back and forth between Dublin and Galway, managed to create a

genuine theatrical event in both cities. Writing of the Dublin production at
the commercial Olympia Theatre, 'C. Ní Mh.', having addressed McKenna
as 'Ireland's Golden Girl of 1951', stated: 'To say that you brought around
1,500 people together to listen to Irish for three hours on a winter's night
when one out of every four people in the capital had the flu! I have been
marvelling at your accomplishment ever since and I will not stop, for I
cannot cease being amazed' (*Aiséirghe*, Feb. 1951, p. 2).[40] Actually, those
involved with An Taibhdhearc may have been most gratified by the judgement of the notoriously captious editor of *Ar Aghaidh*, An tAthair P. Eric
Mac Fhinn, who, after seeing the Taibhdhearc players in Dublin in 1940, wrote:

> The Galway actors won fame for themselves as a result of the plays they performed
> in the Gate Theatre . . . An Taibhdhearc now has a fine company of actors; they
> have learned their craft as far as the gestures and the poses of the stage are
> concerned, they have all the knowledge involved with lighting and stage design.
> (*AA*, Dec. 1940, p. 5)[41]

Of course our main interest here is in the plays An Taibhdhearc produced,
and in that regard their achievement is noteworthy. From 1928 through
1980, not counting *geamaireachtaí* or one-act plays, the theatre introduced
its audiences to nearly 40 new full-length plays in Irish, including works by
Micheál Mac Liammóir, Séamus de Bhilmot, Walter Macken, Eoghan Ó
Tuairisc, Siobhán Ní Shúilleabháin, and Críostóir Ó Floinn. In addition, it
mounted major revivals of plays by Máiréad Ní Ghráda, Brendan Behan,
Ó Tuairisc, Ó Floinn, and Seán Ó Tuama, as well as dozens of translations by
playwrights as diverse as Shakespeare, Boucicault, Kaufmann and Hart,
Eugene O'Neill, Bertolt Brecht, Shaw, Agatha Christie, Brian Friel, Harold
Pinter, and Neil Simon. The regular recourse to translations was not, however, a good sign, and the years from 1950 to 1980 were troubled ones for An
Taibhdhearc. Indeed, in 1966 Colm Cronin, the drama critic for *The Irish
Press*, asked: 'Is Taibhdhearc na Gaillimhe an anachronism? . . . Is it fulfilling
its function, which by the way seems to be somewhat nebulous?' For Cronin,
'the Taibhdhearc, in theatrical terms, is working in a wilderness and in
isolation and also under very curious conditions. The more one considers it,
the more one becomes aware of how little it matters on a countrywide basis
and how slight its impact on theatre is generally.' Concluding his pessimistic
analysis, Cronin wrote: 'As the years go by it seems to be losing sight of itself.
Somehow or other a mantle of mediocrity has settled over it and it lacks
variety. Most people know of its existence but they all do not know why and
possibly care less' (*IP*, 6/5/66). As we will see in the afterword of this book,
some of these same points could be raised about An Taibhdhearc today, but

what is perhaps most important is the fact that despite all its problems it has survived and is still capable of mounting successful productions of important new plays in Irish when such are available.

As has been noted, the production of plays in Irish was not limited to Dublin and Galway. In addition to the groups in various Irish cities and towns that used the name An Comhar Drámaíochta, there were amateur companies and Gaelic League branches that occasionally staged such plays at drama festivals and *feiseanna*.[42] Aside from An Taibhdhearc, the most important of the companies outside of Dublin was doubtless Compántas Chorcaí, which was founded by Seán Ó Tuama and Dan Donovan (Dónall Ó Donnabháin) and first appeared on stage in Cork City in December 1953.[43] In addition to producing plays in the city, Compántas Chorcaí organised drama classes and occasionally toured in the Munster Gaeltacht. From the start, this company stood out for the quality of its productions. For example, it placed first in three straight Oireachtas drama festivals from 1954 to 1956, and was for many years a welcome guest at An Damer. Like other Gaelic theatre groups, Compántas Chorcaí was largely dependent on translations. Thus the first two of its three prizewinning productions at the Oireachtas were of translations. The third production, however, introduced the work of the playwright whose original plays would be the group's greatest contribution to theatre in Irish. That playwright was Seán Ó Tuama, and the 1956 production at the Oireachtas was of his one-act historical play *Moloney*. It would be followed by Compántas productions of Ó Tuama's full-length plays *Ar Aghaidh linn, a Longadáin* (1959), *Is É Seo M'Oileán* (This is my island) (1961), *Corp Eoghain Uí Shúilleabháin* (1963), and *Déan Trócaire ar Shagairt Óga* (1970). Moreover, in 1957 the company produced a major revival of Ó Tuama's masterpiece *Gunna Cam agus Slabhra Óir*, originally performed by the Abbey at the 1954 Oireachtas.[44] Other significant plays revived by Compántas Chorcaí were Behan's *An Giall* (1965), Diarmaid Ó Súilleabháin's *Bior* (Spike) (1965), and Seán Ó hEidirsceoil's *Tycoon* (1967).[45]

In 1963, Ó Tuama, Donovan, and John O'Shea founded the Everyman Theatre with the goal of mounting first-rate productions of modern and international plays in Cork. Compántas Chorcaí became the Gaelic wing of this new initiative. There can be little doubt that the quality of work done by An Compántas benefited from the group's association with Everyman. For example, reviewing the Compántas production of Behan's *An Giall* in 1965, 'R. Ó D.' wrote: 'Compántas Chorcaí . . . have a justifiable reputation in the city for their plays in Irish and for attempting drama entirely above the general level of local theatre' (*Evening Echo*, 2/2/65).[46] It is also true, however, that, as An Comhar Drámaíochta and its supporters at the Abbey had already discovered, the Gaelic lamb never benefited from lying down with the English lion in any joint theatrical venture. When Donovan stopped directing plays

for An Compántas to devote more of his time to the English plays at
Everyman, and when Ó Tuama left the theatre at around the same time, the
glory days of An Compántas were over. In an interview with Vera Ryan for
her book *Dan Donovan: An Everyman's Life*, Donovan offered a rather pessimistic account of how he and Ó Tuama left Compántas Chorcaí:

> Seán and I understood one another so well after all the years. We were a little bit
> defeated by all the difficulties. The basic team of Compántas Chorcaí was quite
> hard-worked . . . Our resources were few. There was the constant difficulty of
> getting good actors who had enough good Irish. Seán would be able to see what
> was around the University in any given year. That was a great help. He may have
> felt he had gone as far as he could in the eight plays. All the investment of hard work
> had insufficient fruit.[47]

One could well question that last statement. Compantás Chorcaí lived on
through our period into the twenty-first century, one amateur Gaelic company
among many, but the work it did in the 1950s and 1960s bringing those plays
by Ó Tuama alive for the playgoing public bore rich fruit and remains a
major contribution to the history of theatre in Irish.

A few words should also be said about the activities of Gaeltacht theatre
companies in our period. As noted above, from early in the revival there were
those who argued that Gaelic drama could only evolve naturally in the areas
where Irish was spoken as the first language of the people. However cogent such an argument might be in theory, in practice drama came to the
Gaeltachtaí from the cities and towns. That is not, however, to say that
amateur Gaeltacht companies did not make their own significant contribution to the theatre movement over the years, most importantly through
the training of actors – and eventually playwrights – thoroughly fluent in the
language. The two Gaeltacht groups about which we know most are Co.
Galway's Aisteoirí an Spidéil (The Spiddal actors), the subject of a recent
study by Máirín Breathnach Uí Choileáin,[48] and Co. Donegal's Aisteoirí
Ghaoth Dobhair, whose work attracted attention virtually from its inception
in 1931, leading to appearances at An Damer and other venues outside the
Gaeltacht.

Aisteoirí an Spidéil first took the stage in 1910, performing, as they still
do, in Coláiste Chonnacht. In their early days they staged the kind of short
simple comedies and language propaganda plays that comprised the bulk of
the minuscule Gaelic repertoire at the time, but over the years they came to
rely more and more on translations, some of them provided by members of
the company itself. Contrary to the experience of companies in the cities,
however, these translations seem to have been popular in Conamara. In the
1950s and 1960s the company travelled regularly and successfully to amateur

drama competitions, where they sometimes won despite being the only actors performing in Irish.[49] From the 1970s on, they have to some extent remade themselves, still producing mostly translations but also reviving a work like *De Réir na Rúibrící* (According to the rubrics) by Eoghan Ó Tuairisc in 1962, just a year after its premiere in An Taibhdhearc.

Eoghan Mac Giolla Bhríde and his sister Áine Nic Giolla Bhríde founded Aisteoirí Ghaoth Dobhair in Gaoth Dobhair in the Donegal Gaeltacht in 1931. The group's first production in January 1932 was the premiere of Mac Giolla Bhríde's own full-length history play *I nAimsir an Mháirtínigh* (In Martyn's time), and the company would perform his *An Fealltóir* (The traitor), another full-length history play, in 1937 (*IP*, 20/12/37).[50] It is likely that these plays as well as many if not most of the plays in the early days of the Aisteoirí were directed by Áine Nic Giolla Bhríde, who would be the leading figure in the company from the death of her brother in 1939 to her own retirement in 1981. From the start Aisteoirí Ghaoth Dobhair was a troupe willing to travel, regularly performing throughout the Donegal Gaeltacht and entering – and winning – drama competitions in the north-west and farther afield. In 1940, the group won no fewer than four trophies in different competitions, most notably Corn Chomhaltas Uladh (The Comhaltas Uladh trophy) and Craobh na hÉireann (The all-Ireland championship). The group also visited Derry, Belfast, Dundalk, Galway, Dublin, and, in 1954 and 1958, Glasgow. In Dublin, it appeared on the stage of the Abbey in 1946 and was a guest of An Damer in 1960 and 1961. Of its 1960 production of a translation of Joseph Tomelty's *All Souls' Night*, Dominic O'Riordan wrote: 'It is always an occasion when Aisteoirí Ghaoth Dobhair come to An Damer – the finest Irish in the distinctive accent that is rarely heard on the stage of the city . . . It is as if a clean wind from the north was blowing through Stephen's Green . . . I am delighted that the house was packed' (*IP*, 19/1/60).[51] It is also worth noting that Gearóid Ó Lochlainn took an active interest in the work of Aisteoirí Ghaoth Dobhair almost from the outset. As an inspector of drama for the state's Department of Education, he was able to keep a benevolent eye on the group and on more than one occasion he appeared on stage in Gaoth Dobhair in the summer months.[52]

In 1961 Siobhán McKenna officially opened Amharclann Ghaoth Dobhair (The Gweedore theatre), a modern, purpose-built home for the company. To celebrate the occasion, Aisteoirí Ghaoth Dobhair presented *Cor na Cinniúna* (The twist of fate), an new original play by Áine Nic Giolla Bhríde. Unfortunately, in this case the company's control of its own playing space does not seem to have been a spur to greater things. Indeed in 1965, Nóra Ní Cheoláin could write of Amharclann Ghaoth Dobhair that it was 'a white Elephant under a red roof' (ina Eilifint bhán faoi dhíon dearg) (*Inniu*, 16/7/65). The main complaint against Aisteoirí Ghaoth Dobhair is a familiar one. By far the majority of its productions right from the start in 1932 have been translations – and not always well-chosen ones. And as the years went by, the group put more and more of its time and energy into creating and performing *geamaireachtaí* to fill the seats. As Pádraig Ó Siadhail has pointed out, Aisteoirí Ghaoth Dobhair never availed themselves of the worthwhile scripts available from writers like Eoghan Ó Tuairisc, Máiréad Ní Ghráda, Seán Ó Tuama, Brendan Behan or Críostóir Ó Floinn – all of whom had proved that they could draw an audience. With regard to original plays of their own, by 1980 Aisteoirí Ghaoth Dobhair had produced virtually nothing beyond the two plays by Eoghan Mac Giolla Bhríde from the 1930s, Áine Nic Giolla Bhríde's *Cor na Cinniúna*, and Tomás Mac Giolla Bhríde's *Le Bánú an Lae* (At the dawning of the day).

Of necessity, this short sketch has overlooked the work of many dedicated and talented individuals and groups who kept the Irish language on stage around the country for decades, often in the face of apathy or worse.[53] They deserve better treatment than they have received here, for it was often their efforts that meant playwrights could have a chance to see and hear their work being performed before an audience. Still, however inadequate, this review of Gaelic theatre history should provide at least a sense of the cultural and performance context in which those playwrights of Críostóir Ó Floinn's underground theatre practised their craft during the first century of the Gaelic revival, and it is to the most accomplished of those playwrights we may now turn our attention.

ONE

UNLIKELY ICONOCLAST

MÁIRÉAD NÍ GHRÁDA (1896–1971)

When *On Trial*, the English-language version of Máiréad Ní Ghráda's *An Triail*, was produced at the Galway Drama Festival in 1959, Jim Fitzgerald, one of the adjudicators, sparked what a reporter for *The Connacht Tribune* termed 'a storming debate' when he called the work 'a nasty dirty play' and added that 'the play was a lie from the word go and it was the fault of the author that the audience laughed for the wrong reasons' (*CT*, 28/3/69). Such reservations were neither *sui generis* nor new, for, as John Horgan wrote in 1965, one of the judges for the play competition, sponsored by the Irish Life Assurance Company in 1964, stated not only that the brothel scene in *An Triail* should never have been written, but that the entire play should never be staged (*IT*, 19/4/65). While, as we will see, most of the controversy surrounding the play was inspired by its forthright treatment of sensitive subject matter, some of the uneasiness it caused may have been due to surprise that the author was not only a woman, but one that many in the Irish-language community would never have suspected of this kind of iconoclastic nerve. Certainly by the time that *An Triail* was produced at An Damer during the 1964 Dublin Theatre Festival, Ní Ghráda had been a prominent figure on the language scene for nearly 40 years.

Born in Kilmaley, Co. Clare in 1896, she would have had access to what Éamon Ó Ciosáin has called 'a rich heritage' (dúchas saibhir) through the elderly native speakers of the language still living in the neighbourhood and through her father, who could recite poems like 'An Siota agus a Mháthair' (The brat and his mother) and 'Cúirt an Mheán Oíche' (The midnight court).[1] After attending the local national school, she went on to secondary education at the Convent of Mercy in Ennis and then, having won a County Council scholarship, to University College, Dublin, where she took a BA in Irish, English, and French and then an MA in Irish. Her dissertation, directed by Douglas Hyde, was on 'An Aoir i n-Éirinn' (Satire in Ireland) and included her edition of the late Ulster Cycle tale *Táin Bó Geanainn* (The raid for

Geanann's cattle). During theWar of Independence she was active in both Cumann na mBan and the Gaelic League, was arrested for disrupting traffic while selling League badges, and spent a brief time in Mountjoy Jail.[2] During the war she also became Ernest Blythe's secretary, a position she retained after he became a minister in the first Cumann na nGaedheal government. After marriage in 1923 and a short initial spell as a teacher, she took a position in 1926 with the state's new broadcasting station 2RN (later Radio Athlone and then Radio Éireann), eventually becoming in 1929 the first female announcer in Ireland or Britain.[3] She left her full-time position at the station in 1935 when Fianna Fáil appointed many of its previously banned supporters to jobs in the station, and she could not resume full-time work later under Fianna Fáil legislation that denied civil service positions to married women. She did, however, work for the station part-time, and her voice would be one familiar on the radio for decades.

It was, then, over the airwaves that her compatriots in general and her colleagues in the language movement in particular first came to know her. She wrote, produced, and presented a wide range of programmes over the years, many of them directed at children, an audience she felt deserved entertainment and instruction of the highest quality. Writing of her weekly, hour-long show 'Uair i dTír na nÓg' (An hour in the Land of the Young), Maurice Gorham stated: 'Artists of eminence enjoyed broadcasting in the children's hour – Uair i dTír na nÓg, as it was billed in the published programmes. Sara Allgood and F. J. McCormick, who were amongst the greatest stars of the Abbey, often took part.'[4] Over the years she also presented programmes on classical music and musicians – she was in charge of the station's record collection – as well as popular quiz shows in both Irish and English; reviewed recent publications in Irish; debated with Ernest Blythe on what was wrong with the state's Irish-language publishing scheme An Gúm; spoke on a range of topics including 'Pillars of the Language', the literature of England, health and hygiene, and 'compulsory English in the Gaeltacht'; and read from her own works like *Tír na Deo* (Never-Never Land), her translation of *Peter Pan*, and *Manannán*, her pioneering science-fiction novel for young readers. Of particular importance is that her time at the station gave her a chance to work with a different kind of drama.[5] She prepared the scripts for at least three radio series: the children's programmes 'Saol na Tuaithe i bhFuirm Dráma' (The life of the country in dramatic form), which commenced broadcast in 1937, 'Saol na Cathrach i bhfuirm Dráma' (The life of the city in dramatic form), first broadcast in 1938, and what was called in the radio listings 'Dramatisation of ThisWeek's Historical Picture' or 'Our Historical Picture', which ran in 1946 and 1947 and may have attracted older as well as younger listeners.[6] She also wrote an undated and unpublished radio play in English entitled *William of Dublin* and several of her plays for children were broadcast from time to time.[7] It is interesting to note here that in comments made by her in 1962 on the challenges radio faced with the introduction of an Irish television station, Ní Ghráda saw the kind of programmes with which she was frequently and successfully involved as precisely those in which radio could excel:

> If RÉ is not to become the despised and neglected poor relation of TÉ, it must concentrate on doing the things which it can do as well, or better, than the latter. Religious ceremonies, music, lectures, art criticism, poetry, debates and discussions of current events – these are all things which sound radio can handle better than its rival . . . TV tends to make us unduly conscious of pretty faces, hair-dos and sleek and personable young men. Sound radio can help to adjust the balance by fostering the things of the spirit. (*IP*, 13/1/62)

If many knew Ní Ghráda as a broadcaster before they ever saw her plays (if they saw them at all), many more, especially but not exclusively the young, knew her from another of her professions. During the 1930s she began her long career in educational publishing, working first with Pádraig Ó Siochfhradha ('An Seabhac') at the Educational Company of Ireland and then succeeding Risteárd Ó Foghludha ('Fiachra Éilgeach') as an editor at Browne and Nolan. She seems to have authentically loved this work, and she was certainly good at it, editing books by others and writing or compiling widely used texts for students of Irish, English, history, geography, and maths at both primary and secondary level. As Ursula Ní Dhálaigh, herself a former executive at the Educational Company of Ireland, wrote, 'There are few Irish people above the age of 40 who did not have one of Máiréad's books at school.'[8] Among her best-known works of this kind are *Cúrsaí an Lae* (Daily events) (1932), *Foclóir Gaeilge–Béarla* (Irish–English dictionary) (1949), her editions of various works of An tAthair Peadar Ua Laoghaire in standardised spelling, and the still available and useful *Progress in Irish* (1960), a work directed at adult learners.[9] Her deep interest in education also led her to take on the additional task of editing the professional journal *The Teacher's Work* for many years.

Yet somehow with all of these demanding professional duties as well as her responsibilities as wife and mother of a boy and a girl, she managed to develop an early, abiding, and ever more accomplished involvement with the theatre, most notably the theatre in Irish. One might, of course, see her nine plays for children, plays like *Hansel agus Gretel* (1935), *An Rí a Bhí Breoite* (The king who was sick) (1936), *Cúchulainn* (1937), *Abracadabra* (1962), and *Alaidín* (1966), as part of her educational work, but while the writing of such plays was clearly important to her throughout her life, her interest in theatre extended well beyond its pedagogical potential. Thus, along with

Piaras Béaslaí, Gearóid Ó Lochlainn, andTadhg Ó Scannail, she was present at the foundation of An Comhar Drámaíochta in 1923,[10] even acting with the company before her marriage, although family responsibilities doubtless limited her involvement with An Comhar in its early years.[11] Nevertheless she still managed during the 1930s to write two one-act plays for the company as well as the previously noted plays for children.These would be followed by the full-length *Giolla an tSolais* (Lucifer) for the Abbey in 1945. In the 1950s and 1960s, with her children raised, she took a more active role in the development and promotion of Gaelic drama, working, as Siobhán Ní Bhrádaigh writes, with 'almost every group that was founded during her time to develop drama in Irish' (beagnach chuile chumann a bunaíodh lena linn chun drámaíocht na Gaeilge a fhorbairt).[12] For example, as a member, officer, and president of Cumann na Scríbhneoirí, she was a forceful advocate for theatre as a genre that had been unduly neglected by writers of Irish. Indeed it was under her presidency that, following a November 1954 symposium on the subject 'Ní Drámaíocht go hAmharclann' (There can be no drama without a theatre), Cumann na Scríbhneoirí decided 'to call for a meeting of all interested in the Gaelic drama to found a GaelicTheatre Club in Dublin' (*FH*, 20/11/54). She also immediately asked Comhdháil Náisiúnta na Gaeilge to support this initiative (*DP*, 27/11/54).A few days later, she became the chairperson of a theatre committee to explore the whole question, a committee whose membership reads like a who's who of Gaelic theatre at the time: Micheál Mac Liammóir, Gearóid Ó Lochlainn, Siobhán McKenna, Séamus de Bhilmot, Máirtín Ó Direáin, and Cyril Cusack among others. Also members were two representatives from the newly founded Gael-Linn, which immediately volunteered to find and hire an appropriate playing space.[13] And thus, with Ní Ghráda involved at all stages, was born Dublin's Damer Theatre, in which she herself was to see her greatest triumph.[14]

However central to her career, the creation of An Damer did not represent the extent of her active involvement with Gaelic theatre at this time. As we will see, during the 1950s and early 1960s she worked closely with directorTomás Mac Anna in the production of several fine one-act plays at the Abbey.[15] In addition, she was involved with the umbrella organisation An Chomhairle Náisiúnta Drámaíochta from its foundation in 1961, serving on its first board of directors (*IP*, 4/7/61). Over the years she supported An Cumann Scoildrámaíochta,[16] and opened or addressed various drama festivals and seminars.[17] Indeed the only theatrical activity she did not seem to engage in was the adjudication of drama competitions at local Gaelic League *feiseanna*.

All of these activities were motivated by her profound awareness of how serious were the challenges facing theatre in Irish, challenges to which she devoted a good deal more thought than did many of her colleagues.With the Abbey in effect slighting if not ignoring Irish, An Comhar Drámaíochta wandering homeless from temporary stage to temporary stage, and An Damer not yet even a dream, her assessment of the situation in the early 1930s was both blunt and accurate:

> With regard to drama in Irish, we must admit that the biggest gap has yet to be filled. We have no Gaelic Theatre. And when I say that, I am not talking about the house or the performance hall. Not at all. What I am talking about is the combination of the three things that are necessary in a Theatre, that is the plays, the actors, and the audience.[18]

Even after the decision to create a Gaelic theatre in Dublin, and despite the continuing contributions of Taibhdhearc na Gaillimhe, her analysis retained much of its cogency. Characteristically, Ní Ghráda was not content with merely bewailing the predicament in which she and her fellow Gaelic theatre enthusiasts found themselves. Instead, she set out to solve those problems she thought she could. Thus while she apparently felt incapable of actively taking on the task of improving the uneven quality of Gaelic acting (including the pronunciation of Irish on stage), she was certainly aware of it and willing to adapt her plays to the skills of the actors available. As Éamon Ó Ciosáin has written, 'If it was amateur actors who were most involved with theatre in Irish, she wrote plays for them, as had Douglas Hyde before her.'[19] Above all, she was confident that she could do much to provide new plays and to attract audiences. And those plays would be original creations, not the translations that had made up such a large share of the Gaelic repertoire from the start and that continued to be essential, even at An Damer.

It was not that she opposed translation on principle. She had tried her hand at the craft with considerable success with *Micheál*, her Irish version of Miles Malleson's *What Men Live By*,[20] staged at the Gate Theatre by An Comhar Drámaíochta in 1933, and with *Tír na Deo*, her translation of J. M. Barrie's *Peter Pan*, broadcast over Radio Éireann in 1937 and published by An Gúm the following year. As late as her opening address to Féile Náisiúnta na Drámaíochta (The national drama festival) at the 1967 Oireachtas she could state: 'It would be a good and profitable thing for us to have translations of the work of the great writers of the Continent. We have a great deal to learn from them and we should take an interest in their work.' To which, however, she added: 'But let us not have so many exotic plants that the weak, bending native shoot will be smothered.' Nor was her primary reservation about translation ever rooted in a narrow cultural nationalism, as she made clear in the same address:

> This also is noticeable about the translations: the people of Dublin are not interested in them; I don't know about the people outside the capital. But the

people of Dublin would prefer an original play however weak to a translation however excellent . . . If the translations are promoted too much I fear that two harmful things will be done, two things for which theatre in Irish will not be the better: the public will be put off attending the theatre and the growth of the native drama will be hindered. (*Feasta*, June 1967, p. 21)[21]

What she wanted was a Gaelic theatre that would be a writer's theatre and would do for playwrights working in Irish what the Globe had done for Shakespeare and the Abbey for Irish writers of English:

What I would like to see being done is . . . for the playwright to be a member of the theatre company as was Shakespeare in the Globe Theatre long ago – the playwright and the actors working cooperatively – the playwright always learning his craft through practising the craft . . . The Abbey Theatre was a theatre for writers in its early days, when Yeats and Synge and Lady Gregory were in charge there. (*Feasta*, June 1967, p. 20)[22]

Interestingly enough, she then uses as a good example of such a creative process her fellow Damer playwright Brendan Behan's collaboration with Joan Littlewood to transform *An Giall* into *The Hostage*, a transformation with which not all critics able to compare the two have been favourably impressed.[23] As we will see below, she could more justly have invoked her own long-running partnership with Tomás Mac Anna to illustrate the kind of creative synergy she had in mind.

The point was not, then, just to get plays in Irish, but rather to get good, stage-worthy plays in Irish that audiences would want to see. Ever since the beginning of the Gaelic dramatic movement, prize competitions had been held to encourage the writing of plays, with everyone from the Gaelic League to the Irish Life Assurance Company sponsoring contests for plays on a regular basis. And while some in the movement were sceptical that such competitions could inspire worthwhile plays that otherwise would not have been written, Ní Ghráda was unwilling to dismiss out of hand an idea of whose potential she had first-hand experience as the winner of a number of significant prizes. Thus in her 1967 address at Féile Náisiúnta na Drámaíochta, where prizewinning plays from the Oireachtas competitions were being staged, she stated: 'It was as a result of competitions that the best drama ever, the drama of ancient Greece, grew and blossomed. It was for the drama competitions in the City of Athens that Aeschylus, Euripides, and Sophocles wrote their tragedies and Aristophanes his comedies' (*Feasta*, June 1967, p. 19).[24] Of course, as she well knew, success in such competitions, even at the level of the national Oireachtas, was no guarantee of dramatic competence, much less excellence. Prizes might well spur a writer to attempt a play, but only talent joined with hard work and patience could make that play something worth seeing. In a world of Gaelic playwrights who, like herself, could only be part-time amateurs, Ní Ghráda demanded the dedication and sacrifice of the true artist, telling competitors to forget about judges or even audiences. Instead, they should concentrate entirely on 'the desire for perfection that the God of Glory put in your minds and hearts' (an mian chun foirfeachta a chuir Dia na Glóire in bhur aigne agus in bhur gcroí). Nor should these would-be playwrights expect much of anything in return for their efforts: 'But, of course, if a person is satisfied with himself that is the end of him as an artist. The striving for perfection, the eternal searching for what is highest – the things he never finds – the mixture of satisfaction and dissatisfaction that goes with the striving, that is the artist's reward' (*Feasta*, June 1967, p. 20).[25]

She must, however, have known that such ideals, however exemplary, could only be aspirational for Gaelic playwrights well into the future if not forever. Given the often dismal attendance at plays in Irish, no playwright could afford to ignore the question of how to attract playgoers, never mind enthusiastic and sophisticated ones. It should be remembered that outside of the Gaeltacht, people who could follow a play in Irish with some ease and pleasure were always in a distinct minority, even in Dublin. Moreover, the fact that a person could follow a play in Irish did not necessarily mean he or she would want to. In particular, Gaeltacht people living in the city might well find theatre a rather esoteric and off-putting way to spend their time and money. Nevertheless, as we have seen, many in the language movement argued that Gaelic drama would be best served by rooting it in the Gaeltacht and dealing with rural subjects and themes that would interest an audience of native speakers. Ní Ghráda would have none of this, as a correspondent for *The Irish Press* noted in a 1962 piece in which he wrote that Ní Ghráda did not agree 'at all' (olc ná maith) with such views, adding that her opinion was 'It is not right to restrict the drama' (*IP*, 10/2/62).[26]

Ní Ghráda was here trying to balance two of the guiding principles in her life. A committed cultural and linguistic nationalist – she was, for example, contemptuous of what she called 'the enemy . . . the cynic . . . the LFM-er' (an namhad . . . an fear ciniciúil . . . an LFM-er)[27] – she was keenly aware of the challenges facing the language in contemporary Ireland. Indeed her grandson Éamon Ó Ciosáin has written: 'She felt a bit of despair with regard to Irish. She once said that she was glad that she was not part of the generation that would lose Irish forever – the thought of Ireland without Irish depressed her.'[28] Despair was not, however, an option for her, and her whole professional career as broadcaster, as editor and author of schoolbooks, and as playwright was devoted to making sure that that kind of Ireland would never come into being. Not surprisingly, then, despite her exalted view of the artist's vocation, she was unable to see her work as a purely aesthetic pursuit.

Instead she believed that her mission was, in part at least, to aid the people who came to her plays to experience a transformative experience of their own true native culture through their true native language, even if their knowledge of that language was not all that it could be and their attention span was, as a result, relatively brief. As Ó Ciosáin has insightfully noted, 'she worked inside of the restraints of the context in which she found herself, but she wanted to improve the world.'[29]

She also had to work in a context that may have limited the topics seen as appropriate for work in Irish. Four of her one-act plays were successful for the Abbey company during its exile at the Queen's Theatre following the Abbey fire of 1951, a period during which Ernest Blythe often tried to get a hearing for plays in Irish by staging them after the featured play in English and before the audience could escape. However, two of her other short plays, *Rité* and *Stailc Ocrais* (Hunger strike) were never produced by the Abbey, perhaps due to the National Theatre's reluctance at the time to court controversy in the first national language. While it is difficult to imagine why Blythe would have objected to the politics of *Rité* in the fervently anti-communist climate of Ireland in the 1950s, his opposition to *Stailc Ocrais*, with its heroic treatment of republican hunger strikers in Mountjoy Jail, is easily comprehensible when one recalls his unrelenting hard-line position with regard to such prisoners when he was a member of the Cumann na nGaedheal government during the Civil War. At any rate, *Rité* and *Stailc Ocrais* would both have their first production at An Damer.

The restrictions and the possible censorship imposed by the Abbey could, then, be significant problems for Ní Ghráda prior to the opening of An Damer, which welcomed full-length plays and did not shy from controversy. But a bigger and more persistent challenge she and all other Gaelic playwrights had to overcome involved the difficulty of writing mature drama in Irish for playgoers who had learned – or at least studied – Irish at school and had forgotten much of it after leaving the classroom. While not herself a native speaker, Ní Ghráda had been exposed to older Irish speakers from childhood, had heard Irish poetry recited by her father, had taken an MA in Irish at University College, Dublin, and worked professionally with the language as broadcaster, editor, and author. Yet despite her own mastery of the language, she managed to write an Irish that was accessible without being simplistic or burdened with esoteric native idioms, unfamiliar neologisms, or Anglicised vocabulary or syntax. Reviewing the production of her play *Mac Uí Rudaí* (Ó Rudaí) at the Abbey in 1963, Bairtle Ó Brádaigh praised the natural flow of her Irish: 'The dialogue is genuine and alive, and ideas are not twisted to pull in odd speech, proverbs, or de Bhaldraithe's word-weaving' (*Feasta*, Oct. 1963, p. 24).[30] Furthermore, as a writer with a sound working knowledge of stagecraft, she availed herself of all the tricks available to her to make it easier for linguistically challenged audience members to follow her plays with enjoyment, claiming, 'By gestures and mime I make them self-explanatory.'[31]

Such an approach is evident in her very first play, the one-act *An Udhacht* (The will), originally written for her students in a domestic economy college in Kilmacud, Dublin, after she had failed to find any suitable existing play for them to act for St Patrick's Day. The play was originally staged at the school in 1930 or 1931, but reached a wider audience when, directed by Micheál Mac Liammóir, it was produced by An Comhar Drámaíochta at the Gate Theatre in April 1931. This play could not have intimidated spectators with any knowledge of Irish at all. Nor could anyone have predicted from it the future course of her dramatic career. *An Udhacht* is a broad farce that Ní Ghráda tells us was inspired by Puccini's *Gianni Schicchi*. Siobhán Ní Bhrádaigh sees early examples of the influence of expressionism on Ní Ghráda here, but this is surely reading history backwards, for the broad characterisations and exaggerated gestures here are those of knockabout farce and not borrowings from a sophisticated European dramatic theory.[32] With a good deal of comic stage business, various relatives and neighbours try to convince a man who pretends to be dying that he should will his worldly wealth to them. Just before he 'dies', he tells them all that he is leaving his estate to the St Vincent de Paul Society and that they will get nothing. Thwarted and disinherited, the 'survivors' decide that one of their number will pretend to be the 'dead' man and prepare a new will in their favour. Predictably, he makes himself the sole heir, only to have the others threaten him with the harsh penalties imposed on those who make fraudulent wills. When he responds that they are all in effect his accomplices in the proposed fraud, they grudgingly agree to witness the document for him, only to have their 'dead' kinsman and neighbour emerge from the chest into which they have stuffed him and throw them all out of his house and life for good.

There would seem to be little if anything to separate *An Udhacht* from the many other harmless comic skits that had been written in Irish since the turn of the twentieth century. However, unlike the work of almost all other Gaelic playwrights, it seems to have captivated producers, actors, and audiences, and has never left the Gaelic repertoire. It was, for example, revived by the Limerick Dramatic Society in 1936, with a local critic calling it 'a light comedy' and writing that 'the suggestions made to the old man as to what to do with his property are mirth-provoking in the extreme' (*LL*, 25/1/36). The same year saw a performance of the play by Co. Donegal's Derrybeg Players at a Gaelic festival in Letterkenny (*DP*, 8/8/36)[33] and by Co. Sligo's Cumann Drámaidheachta Chúl Bac at the Marian Arts Guild Festival in Dublin (*IP*, 3/6/36). In 1940, students at the Rathmines Technical School produced the play with acting that was 'amateurish' but also with 'an enthusiasm which carried it along' (*IP*, 24/6/40). Amateur groups continued to be attracted to the play over the years, with productions by, for example, the London branch of the Gaelic League in 1953 (*NG*, 24/10/53); the Waterford branch of the Catholic group An Réalt in 1956 (*ME*, 9/11/56); the Ballinaclough, Co. Tipperary branch of the Gaelic League in 1958 (*NG*, 30/8/58); students at Navan's St Martha's College, the Athboy Technical School, and the Navan branch of the Gaelic League, all at the Meath Drama Festival in 1959 (*MC*, 28/2/59); Co. Kerry's Aisteoirí Bhréanainn at Féile na Mumhan in 1968 (*LL*, 9/3/68); Charleville, Co. Cork's Aisteoirí an Rátha in 1970 (*K*, 28/3/70); Ballingeary, Co. Cork's Club na nÓg at the 1973 Oireachtas in Dublin (*II*, 7/5/73); Aisteoirí Mhagh-Culainn of Moycullen, Co. Galway in 1974 (*CT*, 12/4/74); the Castlebar, Co. Mayo branch of the Gaelic League at the Oireachtas in Dublin the same year (*CT*, 26/4/74); students of the Galway Regional College at the Gweedore Drama Festival in 1978 (*DP*, 4/3/78); the students of St Patrick's College, Drumcondra, in 1980 (*IP*, 6/12/80); Cumann Drámaíochta an Mhuileann Cearr at the National Drama Festival sponsored by An Comhlachas Náisiúnta Drámaíochta in Cornamona, Co. Mayo in 1985; and Co. Kerry's Aisteoirí Dhún Chaoin in 1996 (*K*, 16/2/96). It should also be noted that the text of the play, published by An Gúm in 1935, had gone through five printings by 1939. However trivial, *An Udhacht* has had a staying power that transcended both time and the borders of county and province, a longevity and appeal shared by very few other plays in Irish not written by Máiréad Ní Ghráda.

Her next play, *An Grádh agus an Gárda* (Love and the guard), is another farce, a comedy of errors and mistaken identities that does, however, involve more fleshed-out characters and complicated plot twists than does her pretty much single-joke first effort. Siobhán Ní Bhrádaigh believes, probably correctly, that it is its more realistic style and its greater emphasis on the story line that explains why *An Grádh agus an Gárda* was never as popular with amateur theatre companies as was *An Udhacht* and Ní Ghráda's other one-act plays over the years:

> The style to be seen in *An Uacht* is the style Máiréad used later in the short plays. Most likely she thought that this was the best and most appropriate style for audiences who didn't know Irish. *An Grá agus an Gárda* was not performed much when the short plays were most popular, but *An Uacht* and other plays by Máiréad written in the same style were often performed.[34]

An Grádh agus an Gárda did win a prize for one-act plays sponsored by Radio Athlone in 1936, although the adjudicator's verdict on the play and its fellow award-winners was hardly enthusiastic: 'It is stated that although the competition did not attract any entry which is likely to make history in the art of writing radio plays and sketches, the general standard was good' (*IP*, 7/4/36). Directed by Séamus Ó hAodha, the play was broadcast by Radio Athlone in April 1936. It was published by An Gúm in 1937 and had its first stage production in September of that year when Éamonn de Barra directed it for An Comhar Drámaíochta at the Peacock. A few months later, students at Rathmines Technical Institute performed it (*SI*, 29/5/38). After that the play was revived infrequently, although there were productions by a drama group on Inis Mór on the Aran Islands in 1942 (*Glór*, 9/5/42); by students of the Nobber Technical School at the County Meath Drama Festival in 1959 (*MC*, 28/2/59); by the Craobh Mhuire Drama Group of Silvermines, Co. Tipperary in 1959 (*NG*, 20/6/59); by the Ring, Co. Waterford branch of the Irish Countrywomen's Association in 1963 (*ME*, 19/4/63); and by Ballyvourney's Club na nÓg at the 1975 Oireachtas in Dublin (*SI*, 29/5/75).

While virtually all other Gaelic playwrights would have been as startled as they were pleased had their works had such an extended afterlife, for Ní Ghráda *An Grádh agus an Gárda* was one of her least successful plays. Actually, the play's relative lack of popularity is rather hard to understand, as it is an amusing enough light entertainment in its own right and certainly better than most of the comedies being written in Irish at this time. The action takes place in a small town in Co. Clare to which a newly conferred doctor who has been arrested for kicking a policeman on a drunken night on the town in Dublin sends another young man to impersonate him on a visit to a friend of his aunt. His concern is that the aunt, a strict teetotaller, will disinherit him if she learns he has been jailed for public intoxication. Further complications ensue when the impersonator falls in love with the daughter of the aunt's friend, and things only get worse when the aunt herself arrives unexpectedly in Clare. On her way, she has run afoul of the law for reckless driving and has been forced by a guard to pay restitution for a chicken she killed with her car. Infuriated by her treatment at the hands of the police, she is delighted when she learns her nephew has attacked a policeman in Dublin, and when the culprit himself arrives, she rewards him by buying him 'the biggest and most spacious house in Merrion Square' (an tigh is mó agus is fairsinge i gCearnóg Mhuirbhthean).[35] The play ends with the now well-off nephew set to marry his fiancée, his friend engaged to the woman with whom he has fallen in love, and the local policeman who has so infuriated the aunt presumably on his way to the altar with the maidservant in the house.

Reviewing An Comhar Drámaíochta's 1937 production of *An Grádh agus an Gárda* for *Ar Aghaidh*, an anonymous critic (possibly An tAthair P. Eric Mac Fhinn) wrote: 'We hope that she will continue writing plays – we will be expecting a great big one the next time' (*AA*, Dec. 1937, p. 5).[36] He got his wish with Ní Ghráda's next play, *Giolla an tSolais*. Although it was not produced until March 1945, Ní Ghráda had clearly been hard at work in the intervening years because this play represents a real step forward for her as a full-length play produced by the Abbey company at the National Theatre. More important, after her first two quite conventional farces, we get here for the first time an indication of the kind of innovative and adroit playwright Ní Ghráda would become. *Giolla an tSolais*, which had won first prize in an Abbey contest for plays in Irish, was directed by Frank Dermody and featured Siobhán McKenna in her inaugural appearance on the Abbey stage. Writing of the play for *The Irish Press* in the first significant review Ní Ghráda received as a playwright, 'A. Ó M.' (in all probability Tony Molloy) began by stating that 'in the infant Gaelic dramatic movement there has of necessity been little experimenting'. He then went on to praise Ní Ghráda for doing just that, calling her play 'one of the most interesting and competent contributions to Gaelic drama thus far' and noting of the audience that 'some were pleased and some were puzzled, but each one was excited because there was something to discuss . . .' He was particularly struck by the idea that 'the author is so engrossed in her theme that she breaks the bonds of naturalism'. And while he pointed out that as a consequence the entire production risked going down 'the slippery slope that leads to realism, symbolism and functionalism – slippery because with less than the coolest heads the results could be chaotic', he praised Dermody for the sensitivity with which he ensured that 'imagination was not let out of hand and thereby a pleasing effectiveness was achieved'. Indeed, having acknowledged 'a personal preference for naturalism, especially Abbey naturalism which has won fame the world over', he concluded that 'one can safely say that "Giolla an tSolais" is a serious and well-contrived contribution' (*IP*, 19/3/45).

In a very brief review in the *Irish Independent*, the anonymous critic seems also to have been impressed with the play as something genuinely new, writing: 'It is not easy to say where "Giolla an tSolais" should be put in the world of plays in Irish, but it is likely that it deserves a little place to itself. It is a new effort with new subject matter – if the like is left in this world' (*II*, 19/3/45).[37] The anonymous critic for *Inniu* seems also to have been confused by the play, writing: 'The play is not all that good, but it is enjoyable without being silly.'[38] His biggest complaint was that the play did not 'make clear its meaning and its theme – and that is what is important in any play at all' (a bhrígh nó a chuspóir a shoiléiriú – agus sin tábhacht dráma ar bith). Still, he noted that there was 'strong, true talent in it here and there' (talann tréan fírinneach ann annseo agus annsiúd), and, interestingly enough, he thought that had it been written in English it would have run for weeks, 'for the stuff to draw the public was in it' (mar bhí mianach tarraingte an phobail ann) (*Inniu*, Apr. 1945, p. 3). The play was produced again almost immediately at An Taibhdhearc in Galway, where Walter Macken both directed and played the title role.[39] After this impressive start in 1945, *Giolla an tSolais* seems to have been all but forgotten.

Such neglect is difficult to understand, particularly given the incessant complaints of those involved with Gaelic drama that there were so few worthwhile scripts for them to produce. *Giolla an tSolais* was, as 'A. Ó M.' indicated, something new in its engagement with questions of contemporary relevance, its thematic substance, and its stylistic innovation. These qualities must have been even more striking to theatregoers at the time because Ní Ghráda had set her play in an area then and since seen as one of the great strongholds of traditional Gaelic culture, Corca Dhuibhne or the Dingle Peninsula, Co. Kerry. Readers familiar with the autobiographical books of Tomás Ó Criomhthain, Muiris Ó Súileabháin, and Peig Sayers, as well as books like Nóra Ní Shéaghdha's *Thar Bealach Isteach: Leabhar Eile ón mBlascaod Mór* (Across the way in: another book from the Great Blasket) (1940) or *Peats na Baintreabhaighe* (Peats the widow's son) (1945), may have felt they were in a familiar world when the curtain rose on *Giolla an tSolais*. They must, however, have become increasingly aware that Ní Ghráda's West Kerry Gaeltacht was a rather different place.

Here the local marriage patterns create quite literally a devil's playground. But this devil is no conventional horned and hoofed villain, like the one in An tAthair Peadar Ua Laoghaire's novel *Séadna* (1904). In her play, as 'A. Ó M.' pointed out, 'the devil and the dead ride fast, the former exchanging his fiery chariot for a modern roadster' (*IP*, 19/3/45). Her Lucifer arrives as a cosmopolitan, suave, and mysterious stranger,[40] claiming to be a lawyer bringing a $10,000 inheritance to Colum Ó Dálaigh, one of the two sons of the widow Bríd, Bean Uí Dhálaigh. This money will make it possible for Colum to marry and raise a family in his home place, an opportunity that many of the rural young could not share at the time and the lack of which led to the haemorrhagic emigration from the countryside and especially from the Gaeltacht that was a major thematic concern for writers of Irish. As the old sailor Taidhgín Ó Cathasaigh puts it in the play:

> It will be a nine-day wonder in the parish if Colum marries. No one has married in this place for three years except for Micilín Buí from An Cnoc, and he was over fifty and the bride well past forty . . . There will be no one left in this country in fifty years, if they continue in this way. Half the schools around here are closed for lack of students who would go to them, and the teachers idle, not to mention the doctors and the midwives.[41]

Colum's match is not, however, heaven-made, and will nearly destroy his family, for Nóirín Ní Loingsigh, the woman on whom he sets his heart, is the same woman his brother Micheál loves. Ní Ghráda makes clear both Nóirín's ruthless materialism and the hard-headed realism in which it is rooted when Nóirín rejects Micheál for his now financially secure brother.

To Micheál's romantic plea that they can live on love, she responds: 'Do you think that I should be satisfied with a wretched hovel on top of a cliff, with the two of us in it struggling through life until the love has ebbed from our hearts and nothing is left in its place but bitterness and rancour? We pulling the devil by the tail to the end of our lives.'[42]

It is, however, the devil who is pulling the strings in this play: 'I bring good, big gifts with me, and if the human race is so foolish and so perverse that the gifts turn them to evil and to harm to themselves, what is my remedy for them?'[43] Lucifer is here debating Taidhgín, the only character who knows just who this visitor is, and some of the most effective scenes in the play are those in which the two confront each other. Unfortunately, Taidhgín is unable to intervene in the action for fear that Lucifer will reveal his indirect involvement in a murder committed years earlier in Boston. Given a free hand, the devil soon has Colum's new wife plotting, successfully, to banish her mother-in-law from the family home and trying to seduce Micheál, who despite his bitter resentment of his brother, is scandalised by her behaviour: 'Get away from me, you whore. Your husband will be coming to you soon – the man to whom you promised today in the presence of God to be faithful.'[44] Indeed in an accusation that echoes that in the folk song 'Dónall Óg' (Young Dónall),[45] he despairingly tells her: 'You came between me and God. It's you I used to be thinking about when I was saying my prayers morning and evening. It's you I used to be looking at in the chapel on Sunday when I should have been looking at God's blessed altar. I have been abandoned now, abandoned by you and abandoned by God.'[46]

Lucifer also turns his attention to Colum and Micheál's sister Cáitín, who, having listened avidly to Taidhgín's stories over the years, yearns for a more adventurous life than she can ever have at home: 'Alas that I am not a young man! I would go around the world. I would see Rio and Frisco and Yokohama, and all those fine places. I would see yellow men and black men walking the streets in them. But alas! There is nothing allotted for me but to spend my life on this peninsula – the last place God created!'[47] Lucifer later uses this dream to tempt Cáitín away from a match with Muiris Ó Cléirigh and a life with him on the Great Blasket Island, causing the broken-hearted Muiris to break his pledge to abstain from alcohol and then attempt, while intoxicated, to return with his young brother to the island on a stormy night. Predictably enough, their *naomhóg* (little boat) is swamped and the boy is drowned, leaving Muiris conscience-stricken. Indeed his guilt is so great that, in another example of Ní Ghráda's early iconoclasm, he rejects out of hand the traditional explanation of life's tragedies as the 'will of God' (toil Dé),[48] and instead insists on his own responsibility for what happened: 'My going out on the sea in the darkness, my being drunk caused it. I have killed him as surely as if I had thrust a knife through his heart.'[49] Lucifer's apparent triumph is, however, far from complete in this instance, for he has failed to encompass the death of Muiris – 'the man who had sins on his soul, the man who was drunk, the man who was filled with anger and hate' (an fear go raibh peacaí ar a anam, an fear a bhí ar meisce, an fear go raibh éad agus fuath agus fearg air) as Taidhgín says – while causing the death of 'the boy without a stain on his soul' (an garsún ná raibh smál ar a anam).[50]

Pledging that his prey will not escape him next time, Lucifer in the third act turns his malicious attention again to the triangle of Nóirín, Colum and Micheál. The family is gathered on a stormy night for the birth of Colum and Nóirín's baby. Her labour has been difficult and both mother and child are in danger. At the risk of his life Micheál volunteers to bring a doctor. Immediately after his departure, the stranger slips in, but as the stage directions inform us, 'it is clear that none of the people of the house see him'.[51] He and Colum converse, though it is clear that Ní Ghráda wants the audience to think that Colum is talking to himself, or, perhaps better, wrestling with his conscience. Taunting Colum about how Nóirín has kept Micheál around while driving his mother and sister out of the house, Lucifer goes so far as to hint that Micheál might well be the father of the new baby. Colum's response is venomous: 'Love to a woman! Woe to the one who would give it. Nothing comes of it but heart-scald and tormented thoughts.'[52] Learning that Micheál will be unable to cross a flooded stream on his rescue mission, Colum, Muiris, and Cáitín decide they will take a *naomhóg* to bring him help. At this point the devil again intervenes in an attempt to hold the three back, reminding Cáitín of how Nóirín has treated her mother and herself. Strong in her faith, Bríd immediately rejects any such idea, but such a decision is much harder for Cáitín.

Ní Ghráda makes very effective use of a ghostly chorus, 'Voices of the Men' (Glórtha na bhFear) and 'Voices of the Women' (Glórtha na mBan), conjured up by Lucifer to convey and exacerbate the anxiety of those waiting for help to come.[53] The stage directions read: 'The voices are heard outside. At first they are just like the wind keening. The drowned men and the keening women are seen. No one on the stage raises his head to look at them. They are not visible to them. They are just ghosts.'[54] The basic refrain of these voices is 'Woe the one who is drowned ... And woe the one who is left ... woe the father ... And woe the mother ... Woe the woman who is left without a husband. Woe the orphan who is left alone.'[55] When Cáitín continues to waver and blames God for the tragedy she assumes has overtaken Micheál, Colum, and Muiris, her mother, like Muiris before her, rejects this appeal to God's will and insists that what sent the men out onto the sea was 'the love that was in their own hearts' (an charthannacht a bhí ina gcroí féin).[56] And Lucifer can hardly appreciate the response of the doctor who has risked his life to come with the men. Asked by Bríd how the family can thank him for his heroism, he responds simply: 'Isn't that why we were put in the world.'[57] Lucifer is still in the game, however, for Colum cannot bring himself to go see his wife and child and says he intends to leave home forever because of 'fear that I will find out that my wife was unfaithful to me' (eagla go bhfaighim amach go raibh mo bhean mídhílis dom).[58] Only after Bríd tells him that he must reject 'those passions . . . in your own heart' (na hainmhianta sin . . . id chroí féin), does he relent and go to Nóirín.[59] Instead it is Micheál who leaves home. Firmly resisting the stranger's temptation that he give in to his love for Nóirín, his jealousy of his brother, and his desire for vengeance, he remembers how he and Micheál had stood together against the literal and symbolic storm of the previous night: 'I will remember last night – we struggling with the darkness and with the powers of the darkness.'[60] In the final scene, old Taidhgín again confronts the devil, brushing aside his boasts that his eventual success is guaranteed. Speaking for the author and enlightened members of the audience, Taidhgín, having watched simple, communal virtues thwart the unbridled and selfish individualism of Lucifer, declares: 'I finally understand that you are just a braggart and that it is easy to escape you. Your nets have no more substance than the weaving a spider does. The clever insect knows where the stickiness is and avoids it. But the foolish fly does not see it until it is tangled in it.'[61] That lesson is finally learned by the characters in *Giolla an tSolais*, but only through bitter experience and anguish.

Ní Ghráda's next play, the one-act *Lá Buí Bealtaine* (A sunny May Day), had its premiere at the Abbey in November 1953, but in the eight years since *Giolla an tSolais*, some great changes had taken place at the National Theatre, changes that had a major impact on drama in Irish. First of all, the 1951 fire that destroyed the old Abbey forced the company into exile in the Queen's Theatre across the Liffey. The Queen's was a considerably larger building, and as a result Blythe worried that full-length plays in Irish would never even begin to fill the seats available, creating problems for both the theatre's finances and the morale of Gaelic playwrights, actors, and audiences. As a consequence, productions in Irish at the Abbey between 1951 and 1966 were, with the exception of the annual Christmas *geamaireachtaí* or pantomimes, limited to one-act plays, with sets of necessity simple and easily managed so that the show could start quickly after the featured play ended. The decision to have Gaelic plays follow the main English play reflected Blythe's hope that at least some playgoers would choose to remain for the one-acter or would simply not be quick enough to get out before it started. Thus for 15 years Gaelic dramatists at the Abbey were limited to writing short plays for marginally enthusiastic audiences often less than competent in Irish. Ní Ghráda's four plays after *Giolla an tSolais* were all written with these constraints in mind.

Yet if Ní Ghráda and her fellow Abbey dramatists writing in Irish were forced to work in diminished circumstances at the Queen's, they also benefited considerably from Blythe's 1947 appointment of Tomás Mac Anna to take charge of Irish-language plays. Not only did Mac Anna care deeply about theatre in Irish, but he had also done a good deal of thinking about the great challenges it faced and how some of those challenges could be met, even changed into strengths. Moreover, by the time he began to work with Ní Ghráda he had gained practical experience of capturing or creating audiences through his central involvement with the Abbey's *geamaireachtaí*, comic extravaganzas that threw realism out the window and packed the theatre for weeks every Christmas season, bringing in playgoers who may well have been amazed that they were delighting in stage entertainment in Irish.

We will discuss below the whole question of Mac Anna's collaboration with Ní Ghráda to create the 'Brechtian' production of *An Triail* that stunned audiences on its premiere at An Damer in 1964. Mac Anna himself was always uncomfortable with the idea that he had become a disciple of Brecht during a brief stay at the Berliner Ensemble.[62] Instead, he insisted that his often experimental directorial style had very pragmatic origins in the work he did with short Gaelic plays at the Abbey. Speaking of these plays in his autobiography *Fallaing Aonghusa: Saol Amharclainne* (The cloak of Aonghus: a life in the theatre), he writes:

> But the short plays in Irish were succeeding, and I had every chance to go in a different direction when directing them, to turn my back on realism, the usual style of the plays in English, and make use of every method of stagecraft that was in my power, and one or two that weren't yet ... Not relying on furnishings, however light and simple they were, but going with the theories of Ghéon, with the imagination as master of the stagecraft.

In effect, his new approach was based on his insight that the naturalism that had won such fame for the Abbey's work in English was altogether unsuited for plays in Irish: 'I often thought that drama in Irish was too influenced by that realistic style of the Abbey ... I did not see why drama in Irish would not go its own way, with little regard for realism, relying more on storytelling and verse-making and exaggeration.' Thus instead of following the dictates of a Brecht or a Meyerhold, 'I was just following the style I first came up with when I was working on those little plays in Irish by which the audiences were so entertained.'[63]

He found an eager kindred spirit for this approach in Máiréad Ní Ghráda, and hers would be the most successful of those 'little plays in Irish' that he directed, in terms of both their artistic quality and audience reception. *Lá Buí Bealtaine* was the first play they worked on together. Reviewing the opening night for the *Irish Independent*, an anonymous critic saw it as the 'most interesting item on the opening night's bill of three one-act plays' and praised the way Mac Anna 'superimposed the early scenes on the later ones', and used 'phantom figures' to show 'the little tragedy recollected in the minds of the speakers'. On the whole, this critic felt that 'it made quite a good one-act play, though the ending was unconvincing' (*II*, 2/11/53). The play is set in the present in an institution for the elderly. Ní Ghráda skilfully uses flashbacks to show the two protagonists, Nóinín Ní Chathasaigh and Peadar Mac Fhlannchadha, as both their present older and their former younger selves. Of Peadar, the stage directions tell us that 'he is a very old man and his mind is failing with age. It is, however, clear that he was once a powerful man.'[64] Nóinín is not as old as Peadar and her mind is sound, though her sight is failing and she is a bit deaf. It is Peadar's eighty-eight birthday, but he finds little to celebrate, cursing the birds he hears singing and demanding his pipe, apparently his only consolation in life but one kept from him lest he start a fire. Nóinín, on the other hand, is cheerful despite her infirmities: 'It is a beautiful day, praise be to God. Wind and sun. They are sweet together.'[65] Left alone by the nurses – 'there's no danger that they will escape together while we are away from them' (ní baol go n-éalóidh siad lena chéile faid a bheimíd imithe uathu) – the pair initially seem almost oblivious of each other, with Nóinín talking to herself and Peadar only half listening to what she says. He perks up, however, when she mentions the place name Móin a' Lín and adds: 'Young boys and young girls working on the bog. Their fun and happy laughter. Youth is a fine thing.' In fact he responds to this last phrase: 'Youth is a fine thing for the one who spends it well.'[66]

At this point, in a scene that must have delighted Mac Anna, imagination lets the pair transcend the institutional setting: 'As the old woman tells her story in the following speech, the characters she mentions come on stage and they act out the thing she is saying. The audience understands that they are not actually there but that the old woman sees them with the eyes of her mind. Soft, sweet music is played during the speech.'[67] We now see Peadar and Nóinín through her eyes on the sunny May Day they first met and fell in love: 'Never before or since has there come a summer as fine as that summer. A bright sun during the day. A big yellow moon at night. The two of us walking the lane under the light of the moon, or sitting under the whitethorn, hand in hand, mouth to mouth.'[68] However, unlike the audience, whom Ní Ghráda has drawn fully into this scene, Peadar is fixed in his dismal present and resists Nóirín's idyllic vision of the past, repeating again and again 'gibberish' (gibiris cainte), dismissing love as 'an exhausting disease' (galar cloíte), scorning women as mere babblers, and demanding his pipe. We get a good idea of the source of his bitterness when she tells of how she pretended to be interested in Páid Ó Sé to provoke Peadar's jealousy and heighten his interest in her. Another shift in stage lighting now takes us to a crossroads dance where Nóinín's narration continues, but now Ó Sé, the young Peadar, and Nóinín appear on stage. Peadar and Nóinín dance, but when the music stops Peadar fights with Páid and kills him. As the young men carry the corpse away and the young Peadar and Nóinín exit opposite sides of the stage with their backs to each other, the action returns to the present. We now learn from Nóinín that Peadar spent ten years in prison, during which time she married, had a family, and never saw Peadar again, although she did learn that he also had married and raised a family. Through it all he remained the love of her life, so that she can say of her husband: 'He was good to me, but I never loved him as I loved Peadar Mac Fhlannchadha . . . the unfortunate Peadar Mac Fhlannchadha.'[69] It seems that the elderly Peadar has remained oblivious of her profession of lifelong love for him until the nurse returns and he rubs her hand 'lovingly' (go grámhar) and repeats four times 'Nóinín bheag [little] Ní Chathasaigh'. Apparently Nóinín hears him, for as he is wheeled past her she asks the nurse who he is and when told begins to cry. Peadar, meanwhile, is being pushed around the garden, much to his delight. That delight is, however, short-lived as he once again speaks Nóinín's name, and we learn from his nurse that 'when he is sulking, he draws down all the curses on me, and when he is pleased with me he calls me Nóinín Ní Chathasaigh, whoever she is'.[70]

Lá Buí Bealtaine is a fine little play, perhaps even more effective today with Alzheimer's disease a scourge and ever more elderly people spending their final days in institutions. Indeed in 2000 Pádraig Ó Siadhail said that of the works in his anthology it was 'the play in which a contemporary issue is most effectively joined with appropriate stagecraft' (an dráma is éifeachtaí ina nasctar ceist chomhaimseartha le healaín chuí stáitse).[71] Ní Ghráda here lets us see that the elderly have had and still have lives every bit as complex, challenging, and meaningful as those of the young, while simultaneously leaving us to wonder whether in some cases those afflicted with dementia may at times be better off than those blessed or cursed with clearer memories of a past that can be recalled but never relived. It is, then, disappointing that the play seems to have been revived less frequently than one might have expected. Among those revivals have been productions by Co. Cork's Cumann Drámaíochta Bhéal Átha an Ghaorthaidh at a festival in Baile Ghib in the Meath Gaeltacht (*IP*, 3/4/74); by Co. Galway's Cumann Drámaíochta Chorr na Móna at An Féile Náisiúnta Drámaíochta in Taibhdhearc na Gaillimhe (*CT*, 8/5/81); by students from Coláiste Chnoc Mhuire in Spiddal, Co. Galway in Maynooth and at St Patrick's College, Drumcondra (*CT*, 13/4/84; 20/4/84); and by a group of Irish speakers at Oireachtas na Gaeilge i gCeanada in Tamworth, Ontario (*II*, 6/7/11). It was broadcast over Radio Éireann in November 1956 (*II*, 7/11/56).

The next Ní Ghráda-Mac Anna collaboration at the Abbey was the one-act *Úll Glas Oíche Shamhna* (Green apple Samhain night). The play, which shared first prize for one-act plays at the 1955 Oireachtas,[72] featured both dance and music, the latter composed by Seán Ó Riada. Here Ní Ghráda turned to the kind of folk material that had long been a staple of Gaelic theatre, often used clumsily by writers as a way of giving their plays at least a veneer of *Gaelachas* (Gaelicism). Her approach in this play is quite different to that of these less gifted playwrights, as she uses rural folk belief in divinatory practices on Samhain Eve (Halloween) to explore a timeless theme in a contemporary urban setting. In his review for the *Irish Times*, Risteárd Ó Glaisne rightly noted that 'Máiréad Ní Ghráda's light-hearted satirical play' (dráma aerach aorúil Mháiréad Ní Ghráda) was 'a piece of fun' (píosa spóirt), but he also called it 'modern' (nua-aimseartha) and 'clever in a very simple way' (cliste ar shlí an tsimplí) with 'lovely, mad understanding in it' (tuiscint álainn bhuile ann). He also wrote that the play had 'the proper pace' (an luas ceart) and praised the actors: 'All of the actors were very good – under the influence of the wonderful spirit of the play you would think' (*IT*, 11/11/55).[73] 'T. Ó H.' felt the work was 'a bit of pantomime' (mír geamaireachta) or 'a truly funny sketch' (sceits fíor-ghreannmhar) rather than a play proper, but he also wrote that it was 'very well-written' (scríofa go han-mhaith) (*Inniu*, 11/11/55). The play was immediately popular with amateur groups, being staged by, among others, An Cumann Éigse agus Seanchais at University College, Galway at Féile Drámaíochta na nOllscoil in An Taibhdhearc in 1956 (*IP*, 4/2/56); Nenagh, Co. Tipperary's Craobh Mhuire of the Gaelic League at the 1957 Oireachtas in Dublin, where the production was awarded a first prize (*NG*, 2/11/57); the students of Buncrana, Co. Donegal's Convent of Mercy Secondary School at the 1962 Féile Drámaíochta Dhún Geanainn (*DP*, 22/2/62); An Cumann Gaelach of University College, Dublin at Féile Drámaíochta na nOllscoil in An Damer in 1962 (*IP*, 5/3/62); students from Queen's University, Belfast at Féile Drámaíochta Dhún Geanainn in 1964 (*IP*, 5/3/64); An Cumann Éigse agus Seanchais of University College, Galway at the Oireachtas Drama Festival in An Damer in 1966 (*II*, 29/4/66); Crosshaven, Co. Cork's Aisteoirí an Chuain at the Oireachtas Drama Festival in An Damer in 1967 (*II*, 1/5/67); the students of Scoil Iosef in Waterford at the Oireachtas Drama Festival in the Gate Theatre in 1968 (*II*, 29/3/68); Limerick's Buíon Phádraig at the All-Ireland One-Act Drama Festival in Naas, Co. Kildare in 1971 (*II*, 12/4/71); students of Co. Donegal's Pobalscoil Ghaoth Dobhair in 1985 (*DP*, 14/12/85); and Corcóg–Amharclann Chonamara in Furbo, Co. Galway in 1993 (*CT*, 23/7/93).

The play begins at midnight on Samhain Eve as a party is coming to an end in a Dublin flat. As the guests prepare to leave, they joke about traditional superstitions, including the one that gives the play its title – the belief that if a young woman ate a green apple and then looked in a mirror she would see the image of her future husband over her left shoulder. The host/protagonist Nóra dismisses this *piseog* (superstition) to the laughter of her friends: 'The girl who would eat a green apple at the stroke of midnight would be bothered by her stomach, not her left shoulder.'[74] After her guests leave, however, she thinks again about the superstition and ponders whom she would like to see in such a mirror.[75] Her thoughts turn first to Peadar, a civil servant who could give her a 'quiet, placid life' (saol ciúin sochma). At this point, Ní Ghráda shifts the play to the realm of imagination, specifying in the stage directions: 'There should be "stylised" acting in the following four short scenes, so that it is clear to the audience that they are just the girl's imaginings.'[76] In this fantasy scene Nóra puts on an apron and mimes setting a dinner table for when her husband Peadar comes home – and Ní Ghráda has a very specific entrance in mind for him: 'If possible have the mirror placed in such a way that the audience thinks he comes through the mirror.'[77] As the scene develops, we see that Peadar is a cold, rigid man, deeply set in his entirely predictable ways and little interested in Nóra except for her services as a housekeeper. Exasperated by his indifference to her, she exclaims: 'I would prefer a man . . . who . . . would come home to me drunk. I would prefer a man who . . . who . . . would beat me to a man who would sit there reading his paper with no more interest in me than if I were a lump of stone.'[78]

Not surprisingly, she gets her wish, and the next man through the looking-glass will be Micheál, 'a light-hearted boy' (buachaill aerach). As she puts on a robe and waits with a burnt meal in the oven, he arrives two hours late with a bouquet of flowers that are, as the stage directions indicate, 'a little bit withered after the day' (beagáinín feoite tar éis an lae). He is all blather and excuses, but flares into anger when she shows him the bills that have arrived: 'Bills, bills, bills! I never saw the like of the bills you have for me. Do you think money grows on trees as the daisies grow in the meadows in the middle of summer?' Her reference to the money he wastes in pubs sends him out the door in a rage: 'I will go out. I will go back to the office. I will go to the pub. I will go anywhere that I won't have to listen to a woman giving out with a tongue as sharp as the blade of a razor.'[79]

Nóra's next potential mate is Tomás, 'a gifted man who scorns foolish company, a man interested in scholarship and knowledge' (fear éirimiúil gur scorn leis baothchuideachta, fear go bhfuil suim aige i gcúrsaí léinn agus eolais), but she soon concludes that life is not worth living with 'a man with his nose stuck in his books from morning to night and with no interest at all in the little things that are important to a woman' (fear go mbeadh a shrón sáite ina chuid leabhar aige ó mhaidin go hoíche agus gan aon bhlúire suime aige sna nithe beaga gur mór le mnaoi iad).[80] Her final fantasy man is Seán, 'a sporting man . . . a man who would spend the afternoon outside playing golf and would come home to me with the glow of health shining in his cheeks' (fear spórtúil . . . fear a chaithfeadh an tráthnóna amuigh ag imirt goilfe agus a thiocfadh chugam abhaile agus luisne na sláinte ag lonradh ina leicne), but she quickly learns that he will leave her 'a golf widow' (baintreach goilfe), and 'when he comes home there won't be a word out of his mouth but golf, golf, golf'.[81]

On the verge of giving up on marriage after her experience with these figments of her imagination, she is confronted with a man of flesh and blood when Séamas returns to her flat, supposedly to fetch the briefcase he left there. Finding her in tears, he offers comfort and confesses he has in fact come back to the apartment to ask her to marry him. In response to her questions, he reveals that unlike her fantasy suitors he is 'fairly sensible' (cuíosach staidéartha) and certainly not a drunkard, that he looks at the daily papers, including the social pages and the comics, and that he only plays the occasional round of golf and does that badly. Doubtless surprised by all her questions, he declares: 'There is no mortal man free of fault, nor any woman either. You and your husband will have to put up with each other's faults and make the best of life. You will sometimes walk the road of happiness beside him clothed in joy. At other times you will go through the mud clothed in sorrow.'[82] Enchanted, she calls him a poet, but he quickly disabuses her of any such notion: 'Have sense, girl. I am no poet, nor an angel either. Don't be expecting the joy of Heaven if you marry me, or any other man.'[83] Real-world lesson learned, Nóra ends the play with confidence: 'I'll take a chance on it, Séamas.'[84] *Úll Glas Oíche Shamhna* is obviously no profound psychological study of gender differences with regard to marital expectations, but in its use of traditional Gaelic material in a non-traditional context, its clever deviation from conventional Abbey Theatre realism, and its down-to-earth and commonsensical theme, it accomplishes a fair amount in a short span and certainly stands head and shoulders over most of the one-act comedies regularly inflicted on Gaelic audiences at the time.

Súgán Sneachta (A rope made of snow), a prizewinner at the 1957 Oireachtas, had its premiere at the Abbey in September 1959, again directed by Mac Anna and again with music by Seán Ó Riada. The play was virtually ignored by Dublin critics. Arthur Noonan did, however, write in *The Irish Press* that '"Súgán Sneachta" by Máiréad Ní Ghráda, after the main Abbey play, is well worth staying for' (*IP*, 26/10/59), and the anonymous critic for *Inniu* found it much better than *Úll Glas Oíche Shamhna* and wrote: 'There is humour and humanity and wisdom in it, and the characters are living people' (*Inniu*, 2/10/59).[85] When the play was adapted for radio by Seán Mac Réamoinn and broadcast over Radio Éireann the following year, Pádraig Ó Siochfhradha[86] commented that there was 'much said in few words' (a lán

ráite i mbeagán focal) and that it was characterised by 'a comprehensibility . . .
that Eugène Ionesco would take great delight in rendering obscure as he did
with "La cantatrice chauve"' (sothuigtheacht . . . a mbainfeadh Eugène
Ionesco antaithneamh as a chur i ndoiléire mar a dhéan sé leis 'An Prima
Donna Maol') (*Feasta*, Mar. 1960, p. 15). Ó Siochfhradha was quite perceptive
in his recognition of the play's similarities with Ionesco's absurdist classic *La
cantatrice chauve*, but he seems not to have seen how much Ní Ghráda
herself does in the play to skew reality and the words with which humans try
to encompass it. We will return to this subject below. Although critics were
not all that captivated by the play, it became a favourite with amateur actors
and audiences alike. Among productions of *Súgán Sneachta* over the years
were those by Limerick's Buíon Bhréanainn at Féile Drámaíochta na Rinne
in 1963 (*IP*, 23/4/63) and at the North Cork Gaelic Drama Festival and the
Oireachtas in Dublin in 1964 (*CE*, 7/3/64; *IP*, 6/5/64); by the same city's
Buíon Phádraig at the Limerick Drama Festival in 1964 (*CE*, 25/3/64); by
Nenagh's Craobh Mhuire of the Gaelic League in Nenagh and at the 1964
Oireachtas in Dublin (*NG*, 14/3/64; 7/5/64); by students from Newry, Co.
Down's St Louis Convent at the Ballymena Drama Festival in 1964 (*IP*,
11/3/64); by Dromcollogher, Co. Cork's Aisteoirí Dhrom Chollachair at the
1965 Oireachtas in Dublin (*WE*, 8/5/65); by the Mullingar branch of the
Gaelic League at Feis Átha Cliath in 1969 (*II*, 4/3/69); by students from
Navan's Coláiste Naomh Marta at the Leinster Schools Irish Drama Festival
in Mullingar, at another festival in Navan, and at An Fhéile Náisiúnta
Scoildrámaíochta in the Gate Theatre in 1969 (*MC*, 12/4/69; 23/8/69; *IP*,
22/2/69); by the Carrick-on-Suir, Co. Tipperary branch of the Gaelic League
in 1981 (*ME*, 27/3/81); by Aisteoirí Ghaoth Dobhair in 1985 (*DP*, 14/12/85);
and by Corca Dhuibhne's Aisteoirí Bhréanainn at An Fhéile Drámaíochta
Náisiúnta in Feothanach, Co. Kerry in 2004 (*IT*, 28/4/04). It was broadcast
over Radio Éireann in January 1960 (*IP*, 26/1/60).

    Súgán Sneachta eschews realism from the start, with the characters all
generic types: Eisean (He), Ise (She), an Iníon (the Daughter), an Mac (the
Son), an Baitsiléar (the Bachelor), an tSean-Mhaighdean (the Old Maid),
an Lánú Pósta (the Married Couple). Moreover, as Pádraig Ó Siochfhradha
noted in his review of the radio broadcast of the play in 1960, it shows the
clear influence of Eugène Ionesco, and in particular of his one-act *La
cantatrice chauve* (1950), which Ní Ghráda could have read in the original
French or seen when it had its Irish premiere in English at Dublin's Pike
Theatre in September 1956, or when Compántas Amharclainne na Gaeilge
produced it in Eibhlín Ní Mhurchú's Irish translation at Dublin's Dagg Hall
in March 1957.[87] *Súgán Sneachta* opens with the same staccato, near-
nonsensical question and answer repartee as does *La cantatrice chauve*:

She: What is your name?

He: Seán. What is your name?

She: Siún.

He (sigh): Siún.

She: Seán and Siún.

He: Don't they go together nicely.

She: They do.

He: It is God who brought us together.

She: It is.

He: Are you a Corkwoman?

She: What else? A Corkman yourself?

He: What else?

She: Two Cork people go together well.

He: They do.

She: It is God who brought us together.

He: It is.[88]

Ní Ghráda also adds a metatheatrical touch by bringing 'the Stage Manager' (an Bainisteoir Stáitse) into the play. Having done so, however, she seems not to have known what to do with the character, who never speaks and only appears three times to shift furniture.[89]

Right after their first meeting, He and She are planning a wedding, and they are soon married. The play then follows the course of their relationship with regular comments from the Bachelor and the Old Maid, who function as literally choral voices, singing their lines in counterpoint to each other. The Bachelor is wary of marriage from the start: 'I'm a bachelor myself, / A fine Irish bachelor. / I will not marry / Until I am at the age of reason / the age of discretion – / Forty – or fifty.'[90] For him his freedom is all-important: 'I drink wine and I drink beer, / And the day after that I drink brandy. / If I am drunk once in a while / I don't have a wife to scold me.'[91] And his certainty never wavers: 'I would rather be in prison / Than to give love to a woman / For love is just foolishness, / With no result but sorrow.'[92] Responding to each of his songs, the Old Maid makes the case for marriage: 'I would marry / If I were to get my desire. / I would marry / If a man came seeking me. / Marriage, however bad, / Is better than being single.'[93] For her loneliness is the great enemy: ''Tis cold I am lying by myself, / Lonely and alone in my bed. / Alas for the woman who is by herself, / Without a man to charm her.'[94] To the cynicism of the Bachelor, she responds: 'If you had married in time, my lad, / You would not be as you are now – / A cantankerous little wretch / And you getting old.'[95]

Of course what will ultimately decide the winner of their debate is the success or failure of the relationship between He and She as the play develops. Of particular interest here is the way Ní Ghráda introduces intrusions from the real world into the magical realm she creates for the couple at the beginning of the play. Thus when He and She are still going back and forth about the idyllic future they expect to share, he conjures up 'our own little cottage' (ár dtigín beag féinig), to which she replies 'with the help of the Corporation' (le cúnamh an Bhardais), and he then adds 'or the Building Society' (nó an Chumainn Tógála). Their challenge will be to live in a world in which having a snug refuge will always mean dealing with the state or the banks. We next see the couple five years later, living in their badly built and by now too small house and struggling to deal with two children, too many bills, and too much to do. Ominously, when she recalls the poetry of their early love, he retorts: 'The age of poetry is gone. The age of prose has come,' and heads off to the pub.[96]

Fortunately for them, He learns to live in 'the age of prose' (ré an phróis) without too many visits to his local pub, but as their children grow so do their worries. Their son is now riding a motorcycle, espousing political views his father finds radical, thinking of leaving for England, and showing no respect for the national heroes of the past: 'The heroes who died for me! I never asked anyone to die for me. Let the people who are dead be left dead. Don't always be rattling their bones.'[97] He is more troubled than She as their daughter goes through adolescence, 'dancing every night in the week' (í ag rince gach aon oíche sa tseachtain), wearing short skirts and pants, getting involved with boys from Belfast, and attending a foreign game like rugby. Yet somehow the two muddle through 35 years of marriage and are able to remember even the difficult times, like the death of their twins, with equanimity. And if they feel a bit lonesome in their now empty nest, they can feel satisfaction that their surviving children turned out fine and have now made them grandparents. In a neat little twist, the play ends with the now elderly bachelor and spinster sitting and conversing on a park bench as were He and She when it began:

> Bachelor: What is your name?
> Old Maid: Síle Ní Bhriain . . . What is your own name?
> Bachelor: Pádraig Partholán Ó Mathúna.
> Old Maid: Are you a Corkman?
> Bachelor: What else? A Corkwoman yourself?
> Old Maid: What else?
> Bachelor: It is God who brought us together.
> Old Maid: It is. (They kiss each other.)[98]

Like *Úll Glas Oíche Shamhna*, *Súgán Sneachta* is a vindication of marriage, this time in face of the cynicism of the Bachelor. Both plays also celebrate the good sense and quiet courage of ordinary people as they cobble together lives for themselves. In her next play, *Mac Uí Rudaí*, a prizewinner at the 1960 Oireachtas, she once more focuses on this kind of prosaic Everyman, though this one has an active and colourful fantasy life.[99] First produced at the Abbey in April 1961 with Mac Anna directing and Ó Riada again in charge of music, the play was, for some reason, not reviewed in either *The Irish Press* or the *Irish Independent*. Perhaps the critics for those papers were put off by the unusual nature of the play noted by 'C. E.', their colleague at the *Irish Times*: 'Taken as a whole . . . the work was an interesting experiment, and owed more to an understanding of the trends of modern theatre than many of the three-act English plays produced at the Abbey' (*IT*, 21/4/61). With the advantage of a text, Micheál Ó hUanacháin could be more expansive, writing in his review of the published script that in the play Ní Ghráda uses the well-established dream motif with considerable skill: 'Thurber made an effective short story from this *motif*; Máiréad Ní Ghráda made a wonderfully effective play from it.'[100] Furthermore, he gives her credit for drawing freely from 'the latest movements in contemporary drama' (na gluaiseachtaí is déanaí i ndrámaíocht chomhaimsearach) to involve the audience more actively in the world she creates on stage (*Comhar*, Oct. 1963, p. 26).

Whatever the critics said or failed to say, those audiences seem to have embraced *Mac Uí Rudaí* with enthusiasm, for, as we are told in An Gúm's published text of the play, it had no fewer than a hundred performances at the Abbey, making it as close to a hit as a play in Irish can be.[101] Not surprisingly, it quickly entered the Gaelic repertoire for amateur companies, although its popularity seems to have faded considerably after the initial enthusiasm. Among productions of *Mac Uí Rudaí* were those by Limerick's Buíon Phádraig at the Limerick Drama Festival in 1965 (*II*, 22/3/65); by the students of Donaghmore, Co. Tyrone's St Joseph's Convent at Feis Dhún Geanainn the same year (*UH*, 13/3/65); by Mullingar's Craobh Uí Ghramhna of the Gaelic League in the Peacock at the 1968 Oireachtas (*II*, 4/4/68); by UCD's An Cumann Gaelach in An Damer at Feis Átha Cliath in 1969 (*II*, 26/2/69); by a company from Moycullen, Co. Galway at the Limerick Drama Festival in 1975 (*IT*, 18/12/75); and by the Young Oscar Players on tour in Tralee, Galway, Limerick, and Sligo in 1983 (*II*, 2/2/83).[102]

Like 'C. E.', Máirín Bean Uí Chathasaigh invoked James Thurber when she judged the production of the play at the 1969 Feis Átha Cliath, calling it 'Walter Mitty who Came to Ireland' (Walter Mitty a Tháinig go hÉirinn) (*II*, 26/2/69). The basic premise of the play could not be simpler, as the mild-mannered and ineffectual protagonist Liam Ó Rudaí daydreams his way through a series of improbable adventures while his real life is in what must be its usual shambles. In his fantasies he is a great statesman, the commissioner of An Garda Síochána and thus able to punish a guard who has upbraided him for jaywalking, a winner of the Irish Hospitals Sweepstake who can now order around the boss who has previously criticised him constantly (and usually appropriately), the heroic rescuer of a drowning woman, a great symphony conductor with a highly exciting and glamorous life, and a sultan with a harem of dancing girls.[103] All of these scenes are played out under the eyes of 'the Director' (an Léiritheoir), a metatheatrical character whom Ní Ghráda uses far more capably and effectively than she did his counterpart in *Súgán Sneachta*. But again, as in *Súgán Sneachta*, reality trumps fantasy and Liam is suddenly confronted with two young home invaders, 'dressed in "Teddyboy" clothes' (gléasta in éadaí 'Teidíní') and the Director warns him 'This is no dream.'[104] In the real world, Liam is, needless to say, an inept coward who can only watch as the thugs ransack his house. Rescue comes when his wife arrives to drive the robbers away with her umbrella. Of course he tells her he was just about to attack the pair, who had come on him while he was asleep and dreaming. Her response shows that she has a full understanding of the man she married and loves him anyways: 'Aren't you always dreaming, dear. Well now. Come into the kitchen and I will make you a cup of tea.'[105]

The play ends with the Director responding to her words with the rather cryptic comment 'That's how it is' (Mar sin a bhíonn), and then, on a more positive note, singing: 'We live through dreams, / Full of joy, full of magic, / Full of make-believe that is / Free from sorrow and heartbreak.'[106] Éamon Ó Ciosáin has pointed out that a central theme in Ní Ghráda's plays involves how one finds a way to live in the world as it is, a world usually more full of petty frustrations and personal shortcomings than catastrophes and grand tragedies. In such a world, as she shows in this play and in all three of the short plays that preceded it at the Abbey, people need the escape valve of fantasy to maintain their sanity. The challenge that her characters must then face is how to keep that imaginative impulse sufficiently in check to live in a world that is so relentlessly prosaic and disillusioning.

The stage history of Ní Ghráda's plays has so far been quite straight-forward – they were written, entered in competitions where more often than not they won prizes, and then produced in short order in the 1950s and 1960s at the Abbey Theatre. *Stailc Ocrais* is a very different story. Pádraig Ó Siadhail has informed us that there is in the Abbey archives a reference to the projected production in the late 1930s of a play by Máire (*sic*) Ní Ghráda and Frank Gallagher, a play that Ó Siadhail believes is what was later produced as *Stailc Ocrais*.[107] Ní Ghráda probably knew Gallagher at 2RN, where both were simultaneously employed for a short while in the 1930s, and she obviously based the play on Gallagher's account of the hunger strike he and republican prisoners under his command endured in Mountjoy Jail in 1920.[108] However, Tomás Mac Anna, who eventually directed the play, denies that

Stailc Ocrais was a joint effort by Ní Ghráda and Gallagher, stating: 'I am certain that *Stailc Ocrais* came from the hand of Máiréad herself.'[109] Éamon Ó Ciosáin provides further evidence of her sole authorship by noting the similarities between this play and *Giolla an tSolais* from 1945. (Had *Stailc Ocrais* been staged when it was written in the late 1930s it would have been the most recent work she wrote before *Giolla an tSolais*.) Ó Ciosáin refers specifically to her use of a chorus in both plays and to how she personifies Death in *Stailc Ocrais* as she does Evil in *Giolla an tSolais*.[110] At any rate, it is not difficult to imagine why the play was not staged when originally written. Such subject matter would have been very controversial, as the hunger strike remained an important tactic of republican resistance to the Irish state with men even dying on hunger and thirst strikes during the Second World War under the government of de Valera's Fianna Fáil party. While Ní Ghráda was careful not to specifically indicate the time or setting of the play, simply stating it took place 'some time during the war with the English' (uair éigin i gcaitheamh an chogaidh le Galla) in 'a prison cell' (cillín príosúin), few in Ireland in the late 1930s would have failed to see the play's engagement with controversies by no means safely buried in the past. Ernest Blythe could hardly have missed the relevance of the play; nor would he have liked it. And once he began his long career as director of the Abbey in 1941, he could not have been expected to tolerate such a sympathetic, even heroic, treatment of the kind of hunger strikers he had so adamantly opposed as a member of the first government of Saorstát Éireann during the Civil War.

Stailc Ocrais eventually won Duais na Comhairle Ealaíon (the Arts Council prize) at the 1960 Oireachtas,[111] and had its premiere, directed by Mac Anna, at An Damer in April 1962. Reviewing the play in the *Irish Times*, Tomás Ó Floinn ('Flann Mac an tSaoir') wrote: 'She can always turn out a good piece of theatre, and she has done so here, in spite of the unrelieved tragedy of the hunger strike situation she depicts' (*IT*, 10/4/62).[112] 'S. Mac D.', the critic for *The Irish Press*, was also taken with what he called a 'delightful little play' (dráma beag gleóite) in which there was 'great emotion to be felt' (mothú mór le brath). In particular, he noted the depth of characterisation in the protagonist, a quality he felt Domhnall Ó Cuill had brought out powerfully in his playing of the role (*IP*, 12/4/62). Pádraig Ó Siochfhradha found the play 'a fine piece of theatre' (píosa breá amharclannaíochta) that captured the 'mental torment of the commandant' (crá intinne an cheannfoirt) (*Feasta*, May 1962, p. 16). Reviewing the published text from An Gúm in 1967, L. S. Tuathail wrote that it was 'an ambitious attempt . . . to represent a subjective conflict of conscience through an external theatrical method' (iarracht ardaidhmeannach . . . ar choimhlint siobiochtúil coinsiasa a léiriú tré mhodh seachtarach amharclainne), and continued: 'The basic conflict is in the mind of the person himself, something hard to represent on stage, but Máiréad Ní Ghráda overcomes a good part of that difficulty economically' (*Comhar*, July 1967, p. 23).[113]

The play had some popularity with amateur groups, being produced by, for example, An Cumann Gaelach of Queen's University, Belfast at the Inter-University Irish Drama Festival at An Damer and again at the Oireachtas, both in 1963 (*II*, 25/2/63; *IP*, 6/5/63); the students of St Joseph's College, Fairview, Dublin at An Fhéile Náisiúnta na Scoildrámaíochta in the Gate Theatre in 1965 (*II*, 3/4/65); Mullingar's An Club Gaelach in An Damer at Feis Átha Cliath in 1966 (*II*, 24/2/66); and the students from Queen's again at the Inter-University Drama Festival in Dublin in 1969 (*II*, 7/2/69). Two points seem of particular interest here: the appeal of the play to students in Belfast, and the fact that I have found no references to the play being performed after 1969 when the current cycle of the Northern troubles began to erupt into widescale violence. Perhaps the play's subject matter became too inflammatory, although one would have thought an adventurous young company would have staged it during the protracted ordeal of the republican hunger strikes in 1981.[114]

As we noted above, to give the play broader relevance, Ní Ghráda did not assign a specific date or place for the play's action, but its reliance on Gallagher's *Days of Fear: A Diary of Hunger Strike* is obvious throughout. For example, her protagonist, the Commandant (an Ceannfort), is keeping a diary, as did Gallagher. In both Gallagher's book and the play, a young hunger striker near death refuses to allow a doctor to put a mustard plaster on his chest for fear 'that there was nourishment in the mustard and he was afraid the nourishment would go in through his skin' (go raibh cothú sa mhustard agus go raibh eagla air go rachadh an cothú isteach trína chraiceann).[115] Moreover, in both works the Commandant is torn about allowing a man named Brennan, who has a family, to continue his strike to the inevitable end. And of course in both works the Commandant bravely rejects compromise until in the end the prisoners win their release.

The play is by no means, however, a direct adaptation of Gallagher's book. The distinctively theatrical elements that Ní Ghráda introduces into *Stailc Ocrais* will be dealt with below. Here we may note that in *Days of Fear*, Gallagher is visited by his father, the 'suppressed agony' in whose eyes and the 'despair and pride' in whose handshake give him 'happiness and strength and a strange, weird loneliness, all distinct yet indistinguishable'.[116] In *Stailc Ocrais*, Ní Ghráda introduces a female perspective entirely absent from Gallagher's account by having the visitor be the Commandant's mother, who, instead of tempting him to abandon the strike as he assumes the authorities intended, stands with him in his sacrifice:

I will not cry or keen, son. Nor will I ask you to do anything except what your own heart and conscience choose. I am just an old woman from the country, without much understanding of these matters, but I know this much – that there are things stronger than death itself. You will have to act as your heart tells you . . . May God strengthen you, son, and may He strengthen the other lads who are suffering punishment for Ireland.[117]

Despite this reference to God by the Commandant's mother, the deity is far more central in Gallagher's book than he is in Ní Ghráda's play. Finally, while the strikers win in both works, thereby justifying the Commandant's refusal to compromise, in *Stailc Ocrais* the protagonist dies at the end.

More important than these deviations from her source are the elements Ní Ghráda introduces to create a more powerful theatrical experience for her audience. In *Days of Fear*, Gallagher is not only tempted by food and tobacco, but also tormented by fear as well as by his sense of responsibility for the lives of his men and by the guilt he knows will follow if any of them die. Moreover, he is troubled by his own mixed motives in leading the strike:

It began in the wilful intention to fight and defeat a tyranny which touched ourselves personally and the nation for which we are greatly . . . [*sic*] It had personal gains in it also . . . For me there was personal gain hidden in among the things which prompted me to strike . . . But, liberty and justice, the fight for these overshadowed the sordid things . . . That is true.[118]

In one startling section of the diary, he must face a personified Death itself: 'This is the darkest night yet . . . Death alone could find his way in here now . . . Thought I saw him sitting in that corner last night, waiting . . . Yes . . . He is there again to-night . . . I cannot see him . . . But he is breathing softly, and I hear him . . . It is funny to think of Death breathing . . .'[119] The two then engage in an unresolved philosophical-theological debate about the meaning of human life in face of human mortality:

He is gone . . . 'Death!' . . . He does not answer . . . 'Death! . . . There is more I must ask you, Death . . . more . . . What is beyond you? How do you take the body and leave the soul? With what sense am I to fight the battle you will win? . . . Why don't you answer, Death? . . . Even you in the cell are better than darkness that has no beginning and no end . . .'[120]

Ní Ghráda obviously found this passage both deeply moving and potentially of great dramatic impact. She had, of course, already made use of personified archetypes in the Lucifer character of *Giolla an tSolais*; Eisean,

Ise, an Baitsiléar, an tSean-Mhaighdhean, and an Bainisteoir Stáitse of *Súgán Sneachta*, and an Léiritheoir of *Mac Uí Rudaí*.[121] Here she not only uses Gallagher's personified Death but adds the First Tempter (an Chéad Chaithaitheoir), the Second Tempter (an Dara Cathaitheoir), and a chorus of Voices Outside (Glórtha Amuigh), who, building on Gallagher's references to clocks in his diary,[122] underscore the Commandant's sense of passing time and approaching death as they chant in time with the loud ticking of a clock in the background: 'One, two, three, four, five, six, seven, eight, nine, ten, eleven, twelve. Twelve days. Without food. Without a drink. Without food. Without a drink. Twelve days. Twelve days . . . Men exhausted. Men worn down. Men weak. Men tormented.'[123] Later, as the chorus continues its chant, the two tempters enter to debate the Commandant, in the process making explicit some of the self-doubts Gallagher left unspoken in *Days of Fear*:

> The First Tempter: Children in need. Children in distress. Ó Braonáin's family in distress.
> Commandant: I can do nothing for them.
> The First Tempter: You're afraid.
> Commandant: That's a lie. I am not afraid . . .
> The First Tempter: You're afraid to give up. You're afraid that it will be said that you are a coward.
> Voices Outside: A coward. A coward. A coward.[124]

Indeed after the tempters' pointed accusation that the Commandant is motivated by fear of the opinion of others and a Luciferian pride in his own power and heroism, Ní Ghráda's condensed version of Gallagher's debate with Death is almost anticlimactic:

> Commandant: I know now that we are not afraid of you.
> Death: When I stretch my hand towards a person he becomes afraid.
> Commandant: Are you going to stretch your hand now?
> Death: Your time has not yet come.[125]

Stailc Ocrais is both a fine dramatic interpretation of Gallagher's *Days of Fear*, and a powerfully successful play in its own right. Ní Ghráda manages to deal with highly relevant, controversial material – and she could have had no idea how relevant it would remain as republican hunger strikes seized and held the imagination of the nation and even the world as Northern Ireland exploded years after her play was first produced and decades after it was conceived. In *Stailc Ocrais* she brings together in a coherent way all the various innovative techniques we find in her other works, including those expressionist devices we will investigate in more detail below. Moreover, she manages to deal with emotive political issues without ever lapsing into propaganda for any ideology. She is even willing to borrow a trick from Seán O'Casey when she undercuts the apparently inspirational ending of the play as the chorus shouts 'Hurrá!' in triumph and the Commandant dies, by having the prison doctor, echoing Seamus Shields's final comment in *The Shadow of a Gunman*, reply to the warder's question 'Is he?' (Bhfuil sé?) with 'I told him that the cigarettes were hurting his heart.'[126]

We may now discuss, out of chronological order, Ní Ghráda's least successful play, one quite unlike the series of innovative and thematically engaging works she produced in collaboration with Tomás Mac Anna at the Abbey and An Damer in the1950s and 1960s. Having won a prize for manuscript plays at the 1955 Oireachtas, the one-act *Ríté*,[127] directed by Máirtín Ó Díomsaigh and performed by Aisteoirí Chéitinn of the Gaelic League's Keating branch, had its premiere as one of three one-act plays on An Damer's very first opening night in November 1955. The anonymous critic for the *Irish Independent* was quite taken by the play, writing: 'An excellent presentation. It is up to the minute in its topicality with its theme of convent life in Communist China' (*II*, 15/11/55). Less impressed was Pádraig Mac Gabhann, who wrote: 'But the likes of the Commissar and his comrades never existed. They were a mix of the circus and the musical theatre. They seemed ridiculous when they were trotting around the stage.' Even worse, 'Ríte [*sic*] herself lacked force and spirit' (*Feasta*, Dec. 1955, p. 33).[128] 'S. Mac R.' (Seán Mac Réamoinn) felt that Ní Ghráda offered 'a nice illustration of the mind of the nuns' (léiriú deas ar mheon na mban rialta), but felt that the play failed to live up to its initial promise: 'It descends to the level of a pious novelette. It is entirely improbable' (*Inniu*, 18/11/55).[129] Looking back on the performance the following year in a piece on the future prospects for An Club Drámaíochta, the subscribers for An Damer, Risteárd Ó Glaisne wrote that while Ní Ghráda had 'good subject matter' (ábhar maith) for the play, the acting on the whole was just 'mediocre' (measartha maith) and the production was marked throughout by 'the ambitious amateurism of the rural parish hall' (amaitéarachas ard-aidhmeannach halla an pharóiste faoin tuaith) (*IT*, 6/5/56). Actually, it is hard to imagine how even the most professional of productions could make a success of this inert if earnest play. Here Ní Ghráda fails to find a way to make a political theme transcend its own time and place, and as a consequence *Ríté* remains a propagandistic period piece that never rises above the fervent anti-communism of the vast majority of Irish Catholics in the 1950s, a fervour stoked at the time by the arrest, show trial, and imprisonment of Cardinal József Mindszenty by the communist government of Hungary.[130]

The play is set in the present – that is the 1950s – in the parlour of a convent in an unidentified 'country overseas' (tír thar lear). Given that the anonymous critic for the *Irish Independent* explicitly identifies that country as China, perhaps that setting was indicated in the original production. If anything, however, the action seems to take place in the more probable setting of Eastern Europe.[131] The mother superior and her nuns are well aware that they are under constant threat from 'the Soviet Government that is over us now' (an Rialtas Sóibhéideach atá anois orainn), a regime whose taxes are rapidly impoverishing their community. Indeed several nuns have already fled the convent, and we are told that Ríté, who is believed to be a refugee who may have a vocation, is hiding terrified in her room. Worse, the other orphans for whom the nuns have been caring, one of them quite sick, have been taken from them by state forces. Still, the mother superior resolutely refuses the traditional consolation of Gaelic literature: 'It is not God's will, but the will of people, evil people.'[132] And when she draws a metaphorical line in the sand, none of the remaining nuns, not even the novices, opt to leave. Now, however, a commissar is at the door with his men, and the mother superior must come to terms with what this visit might mean. As she ponders, she arrives at her own reading of God's will: 'If God wants us to be martyrs let us accept his holy will. But let us not be striving for martyrdom.'[133] She also recommends getting Ríté away from the convent.

As Pádraig Mac Gabhann indicates in his review of the play, the commissar is a problematic, even confusing character. He enters as 'a personable young man' (ógfhear pearsanta) who addresses the nuns civilly and rebukes one of his men for insulting them. Yet he is soon accusing the mother superior of breaking the law by giving money to nuns who left the country and of neglecting the children formerly in her care, two of whom have died. When the mother superior answers his charges, he is contemptuous, and it is clear that he is not there to inquire into the facts of the situation but rather to inflict unjust punishment on the nuns. The 'personable young man' turns quickly into a monster who contemptuously dismisses one of the dead orphans as 'the child of a travelling woman' (leanbh mná siúil).[134] Having ordered that the nuns be shot at once, he defends his decision with a recitation of the Party line: 'It is not proper for the person who is working for the Party to think. Let us do something for the leaders who are over us and let us leave the thinking to them.' The dead nuns will serve the Party's purpose: 'The plight of these women will frighten the rest of them, so that we have no more trouble with them.'[135] The person to whom he is speaking here is none other than Ríté, who instead of being a terrified refugee in the care of the nuns is actually a secret operative who has betrayed them to the government. As the commissar tells her: 'You will be a female commissar soon if you continue to give useful service to the Party. Some of them wanted to give this work to

Anna to do. But I knew that you would be better at it. Weren't you raised in a place like this. There was no danger that you would give yourself away through lack of knowledge about the customs of these women.' It is, however, her newfound appreciation of the character of the nuns that leads her to turn her back on this glorious future and on the Party itself: 'This place is a little world in itself . . . A little world without hatred, without jealousy, without spite. A little peaceful world in which people have the opportunity to think . . . You would not believe how long and quiet the nights are here . . . I stretched on my narrow, hard bed in my little cell upstairs there, thinking.'[136] When the commissar spouts the Party line, she responds with the Ten Commandments. When she hears the doomed nuns singing 'Veni creator spiritus', she recites the words with them before running out the door to join them in death. The play then ends anticlimactically with the commissar sizing up the convent as 'a holiday camp . . . for the Party's workers' (campa saoire . . . d'oibrithe an Pháirtí).

For once Ní Ghráda seems to have lost her mastery of the one-act play, as she is unable within such a short work to create a credible motivation for the commissar's abrupt shift from civility to conscienceless malice or, even more important, for Rité's conversion from treachery to self-sacrificing sanctity. It is worth noting that Siobhán Ní Bhrádaigh has commented that Ní Ghráda was not primarily interested in character development, that her characters are there 'to express the message that is being dealt with in the play' (chun an teachtaireacht atá á plé sa dráma a chur in iúl).[137] In a play like *Rité*, however, a meaningful understanding of that message should emerge from just such character development, particularly for Rité herself. Its absence here leaves the play almost as emotionally empty as is the commissar's rote ideology.[138] Ní Ghráda would soon develop a far more sophisticated approach to dealing with political subjects on stage.

It should come as no surprise that *Rité* has been the least popular of Ní Ghráda's mature plays, with just a handful of revivals, among them those by the Gaelic League's Inchicore branch at An Damer during Feis Átha Cliath in 1964 (*II*, 5/3/64); by the students of Belfast's St Dominic's School at the Dungannon Drama Feis in 1965 (*UH*, 13/12/65); by UCD's An Cumann Drámaíochta in An Damer at Feis Átha Cliath in 1969 (*II*, 26/2/69); and by the Us and Them Theatre Company from the Sligo Technical College at the All-Ireland Festival of Drama, Art and Music in Bishopstown, Co. Cork in 1982 (*SS*, 6/3/82). It was also broadcast over Radio Éireann in January 1956 (*II*, 31/1/56) and February 1965 (*II*, 6/2/65), with Risteárd Ó Glaisne writing of the 1956 broadcast that the radio version of the play was far better than the stage production of the previous year (*IT*, 6/5/56).

By 1964, Máiréad Ní Ghráda was a major figure in the Gaelic movement as broadcaster, textbook writer, and above all as the most popular playwright

in Irish, with new plays regularly staged in Dublin and amateur productions
of her work performed annually throughout the country. Nothing, however,
could have prepared either herself or her audiences for the excitement inspired
by her next play, *An Triail*. Once again directed by Mac Anna, the play
opened at An Damer on 22 September 1964 as part of that year's Dublin
Theatre Festival and ran until 12 October, a startlingly long run for a play in
Irish. And, as we will see, it has been regularly revived right to the present in
both Irish and in Ní Ghráda's own English translation *On Trial*. Given the
initial enthusiasm about the play and its continuing viability and relevance,
it seems to make most sense to discuss *An Triail* (and *On Trial*) under two
headings – first as a social and cultural phenomenon and second as a work
of dramatic art.

Ní Ghráda's sensitive and controversial subject matter in the play was
already in the mind of at least some of the public when the play opened due
to Michael Viney's controversial 'No birthright', a series of articles in the
Irish Times that dealt with 'illegitimacy' and provoked a lively debate in the
letters column of the paper, a debate still running while the play was on at An
Damer. *An Triail* put these issues centre stage with an electrifying immediacy
(and prescience) that shocked and indeed continues to shock the Irish conscience. Reviews of the play made abundantly clear that critics understood
that something quite remarkable had happened in the little theatre on
Stephen's Green. Thus 'L. Mac G.' wrote his review for the *Irish Times* in
both Irish and English 'because it would be unfair to the author to allow its
theatrical and social impact to bounce only off Irish-speaking heads'. He felt
that 'this play is significant because it has an urgent theme and is entitled to
rank as the most important offering the Theatre Festival makes available.
Just imagine for a moment the sequence of articles written by Michael Viney
in the *Irish Times* recently . . . crystallized into a searing drama that challenges
every aspect of this social problem.' Moreover, he was just as impressed with
the production as with the play: 'A production so good in the little space that
is the stage in the Damer is a miracle' (*IT*, 23/9/64).[139] Writing in the *Irish
Independent*, Earnán P. de Blaghd called *An Triail* 'a powerful and moving
play' and continued: 'Based on the sordid topic of a case of infanticide
followed by the suicide of the mother, it is in essence a plea for compassion
among men in the difficulties which make them dependent on each other'
(*II*, 23/9/64).[140] In *The Irish Press*, Críostóir Mac Aonghusa wrote that of all
the plays presented at the Theatre Festival that year, 'there is not one of them
that provoked more discussion than *An Triail*. Both Irish people and
foreigners were looking at it and noticing it.' He then continued: 'This is a
play that I myself liked a great deal. I liked the theme but more than that I
liked the way the playwright handled it.' He focused on the effect the play
would have on anyone who saw it: 'He has no doubt about who is to blame.

He thinks everyone in the play is, Máire Ní Chathasaigh and everyone with whom she has dealings. And that is the same thing as saying that he himself and all the people of Ireland are guilty' (*IP*, 9/10/64).[141] In a piece entitled 'Mac Anna ard-draoi na drámaíochta' (Mac Anna high-druid of drama), Éadhmonn Mac Suibhne proclaimed: 'If it is possible to call any play we have a native, traditional play, *An Triail* is not it. Of course, that is not a fault, but the opposite. It could be a sign that drama in Irish is coming of age, that it is dealing with questions that concern today's all-embracing world' (*Feasta*, Nov. 1964, p. 10).[142]

Perhaps the most influential reviews at the time were those least expected. In Dublin to cover the Theatre Festival, critics from two major English papers found their way to An Damer. Writing in the Manchester *Guardian*, the Irishman Peter Lennon, having acknowledged that 'my Christian Brothers Irish has long since evaporated', noted that *An Triail* dealt with 'a modern Irish problem' and that judging from 'hearsay', Ní Ghráda 'handles the problem strongly and with a good sense of theatre' (*Guardian*, 26/9/64). Far more effusive was Harold Hobson, perhaps Britain's best-known theatre critic of the day, who, though he lacked even Lennon's 'evaporated' school Irish, could still write:

> As soon as it began, *An Triail* lit in me a candle of inspiration which was never put out ... I cannot naturally tell whether Miss Ní Ghráda writes well, what I do know is that the cry, three times repeated (in Gaelic of course) which she gives to Miss Maude concerning the baby, the cry of 'she is free, she is free, she is free,' touched me more nearly than anything else in this festival, or indeed any other. (*Sunday Times*, 27/9/64)

More than a few in the British stage community must have been dumbfounded when they read that Hobson had declared to an Irish journalist that 'at the moment I feel that I only want to see plays in Gaelic' (*IT*, 2/10/64).

Had he ever wanted to see this particular play in 'Gaelic' again, he would not have had much trouble doing so. An Damer had the play back on stage from 17 to 28 November, after which the company took it to Belfast, Gweedore, and Cork (*IP*, 17/11/64). In 1965, a televised version of *An Triail*, directed by Michael Garvey, was broadcast over Telefís Éireann and selected as the Irish entry in a European competition for television drama (*MN*, 22/10/66).[143] Reviewing the work of Telefís Éireann in 1965, Tom O'Dea, the television critic for *The Irish Press* stated: 'Telefís Éireann's production of Máiréad Ní Ghráda's play, "An Triail", was unquestionably the most distinguished thing that came from its Drama Department last year' (*IP*, 1/1/66).

Among the many other productions of *An Triail* were those by An Chuallacht Ghaelach of University College, Cork in the Peacock at the 1968

Oireachtas (*SS*, 6/4/68); by Taibhdhearc na Gaillimhe to mark the theatre's fortieth anniversary in 1968, a production then taken to the Abbey (*CT*, 16/2/68; *MN*, 23/3/68); by the Relays Drama Group of Ballinasloe, Co. Galway in 1969 (*CT*, 10/1/69); by Dublin's Kevin Street Drama Group in 1971 (*IT*, 9/2/71); by St Patrick's Drama Society of Dalkey, Co. Dublin in 1972 (*IT*, 17/11/72); by The Group of Tralee, Co. Kerry at the Limerick Drama Festival in 1973 (*IT*, 19/3/73); by students from St Patrick's College, Maynooth at an inter-university drama competition in Limerick in 1974 (*CT*, 15/2/74); by the Carrigaline, Co. Cork branch of Macra na Feirme at the Shandon Macra na Feirme Drama Competition in Cork in 1980 (*SS*, 12/1/80); by Aisteoirí na Tríonóide as a feature of Women's Week at Trinity College in 1980 (*IT*, 12/4/80); by Cumann Drámaíochta Choláiste na hOllscoile, Gaillimh at the university in 1984 (*CT*, 30/3/84); by the Kilmeen Drama Group of Clonakilty, Co. Cork at the West Waterford Drama Festival in 1992 (*ME*, 6/3/92); by students at St Joseph's Convent of Mercy School in Navan, Co. Meath at the Slógadh Drama Festival in Dundalk in 1997 (*MC*, 1/2/97); by Aisteoirí an Spidéil at An Taibhdhearc and then on Inis Oírr in the Aran Islands in 1998 (*CT*, 13/3/98); by Amharclann de hÍde in Dublin, Cork, Spiddal, Donegal, Derry, and Belfast in 1999 (*CT*, 9/4/99); and by students at Belvedere College in Dublin in 2002 (*MC*, 22/12/02). Needless to say the later inclusion of *An Trial* on the syllabus for the Leaving Certificate in both the Republic and Northern Ireland has guaranteed frequent productions of the play. Aisteoirí Ghobnatan of Ballyvourney, Co. Cork performed it in Clonakilty, Co. Cork in 2006 (*SS*, 26/6/06); Aisteoirí Mhúscraí put it on at Féile Drámaíochta Chúil Aodha in the West Cork Gaeltacht in 2007 (*SS*, 28/4/07); the Belfast company Aisling Ghéar staged 'this timeless Irish language drama' in the same year (*CT*, 13/12/07) and again on a national tour in subsequent years; and the Killorglin Catholic Young Men's Society Players produced it in 2011 (*K*, 2/11/11). Undoubtedly the most innovative recent production of the play was that toured by Fíbín Teo in 2014, in which, in the words of Helen Cusack, the company 'brings the seemingly outdated plot into the context of modern society, using puppets, masks, and music to appeal particularly to a younger audience, making it current and more accessible'. Calling the production 'a creative and vibrant interpretation' of Máiréad Ní Ghráda's play, Cusack notes 'subtle changes in the language of the text as well as editing and music choices' to 'make the characters engaging and current' (*Irish Theatre Magazine*, 26/11/14).[144]

Capitalising on the publicity surrounding the play's production in An Damer, Ní Ghráda herself immediately translated it into English, thus giving *An Trial* the kind of visibility enjoyed by no other play in Irish other than Brendan Behan's *An Giall*, which, of course, became an international sensation in its English incarnation as *The Hostage*. Unlike *The Hostage*, however, which was totally reshaped and expanded under the influence of its English director Joan Littlewood with non-Irish audiences in mind, Ní Ghráda's *On Trial* adheres closely to the original Irish script. A few characters' names are changed, but the dialogue remains virtually the same, as does the basic theme of hypocritical intolerance, although the latter is made a bit more explicit by greater emphasis on Ireland's failure to live up to its own self-image as an exemplary Christian society. Phyllis Ryan, the independent producer whose Gemini Productions first performed the English version of the play, stated in 1964: 'I consider this play so good, and so timely, that the language barrier, though it is being slowly surmounted by many eager people now, should not prevent all the public from having an opportunity of seeing it. It is a moving play, intensely human, at times heart-rending. It must be seen again' (*IT*, 3/10/64).[145] Ryan's April 1965 production at Dublin's Eblana Theatre, once more directed by Mac Anna and featuring many of the same actors, was again a success with both critics and playgoers. In his review for the *Sunday Independent*, Gus Smith wrote:

> To say that one feels a compelling sense of guilt leaving the Eblana Theatre after the production of *On Trial* by Máiréad Ní Ghráda, is at once a tribute to the dramatic power of this important new drama . . . It is a controversial and savage theme, yet a hackneyed one in Irish drama, but by sheer ingenuity and imaginative perception, Máiréad Ní Ghráda treats the problem in a fiercely realistic manner . . . It jolts audiences – and makes society guilty. (*SI*, 25/4/65)

Audiences with little Irish clearly welcomed, and still do, the chance to see for themselves what all the excitement was about, and *On Trial* has remained quite popular. Among the productions of the play after its premiere by Gemini were those by James Stack's company at the Opera House in Cork in 1966 (*SS*, 12/2/66); by Naas's Moate Theatre Group in Naas in 1966 and then at the All-Ireland Amateur Drama Festival in Athlone the same year (*II*, 27/4/66); by the Roscrea, Co. Tipperary Players in 1967 (*II*, 24/11/67); by the Wexford Parish Drama Group at the County Tipperary Drama Festival in Thurles and then at the All-Ireland Amateur Drama Festival in Athlone in 1969 (*II*, 11/4/69); by the Relays Drama Group of Ballinasloe, Co. Galway at the Galway Drama Festival in 1969 (*CT*, 7/3/69); by Ryan's Gemini Productions at the Festival of Irish Theatre in Limerick in 1970 (*IT*, 12/8/70); by The 33 Players, a group founded by civil servants in An Foras Talúntais, in Dublin in 1970 (*IP*, 4/12/70); by Belfast's Youth Theatre in 1971 (*IT*, 28/6/71); by the Thurles, Co. Tipperary Drama Group in 1972 (*NG*, 4/11/72); by Tralee's Group Theatre in 1972–3 (*K*, 16/12/72; 6/1/73); by the Whitehall, Co. Dublin Musical and Dramatic Society in 1973 (*II*, 7/4/73); by the Waterford Dramatic Society in 1973 (*II*, 27/10/73); by the Kilrush, Co.

Clare Players at the Kilrush Colleen Bawn Festival in 1973 (*II*, 5/5/73); by the Booterstown and York Road Dramatic Societies in Dublin in 1975 (*IT*, 11/7/75); by the Clooneclare, Co. Leitrim Players at the All-Ireland Amateur Drama Festival Rural Finals in Loughrea, Co. Galway in 1977 (*CT*, 29/4/77); by the Beavers Repertory Theatre in Dublin in 1979 (*SI*, 9/9/79); by the Abbeyleix, Co. Laois Drama Group in 1985 (*City Tribune*, 12/4/85);[146] by the Icarus Drama Group of Shannon, Co. Clare at the All-Ireland Amateur Drama Festival in Ballinamore, Co. Donegal in 1986 (*AC*, 8/5/86); by the Corcaghan, Co. Monaghan Players at the Shercock and Kiltyclogher Drama Festivals in Counties Cavan and Leitrim respectively in 1994 (*AC*, 3/2/94; *FH*, 5/4/94); by the Rusk, Co. Dublin Dramatic Society in 1994 (*IT*, 4/3/94); by Tralee's Group Theatre, again, in 2002 (*K*, 5/12/02); by the students of St Flannan's College in Ennis, Co. Clare in 2003 (*LL*, 1/3/03); by North Tipperary Youth Drama in Thurles in 2003 (*NG*, 3/5/03); by the Creggan, Co. Tyrone Drama Circle at the Enniskillen Drama Festival in 2006 (*UH*, 1/3/06); and by the Killorglin, Co. Kerry Catholic Young Men's Society in 2011–2 (*K*, 2/11/11; 18/1/12).[147]

Despite the efforts of Fíbín Teo to make the original Irish-language play 'relevant' and 'more accessible', it does not seem to have needed all that much updating, for if 'illegitimacy' lost much of its stigma in Celtic Tiger Ireland, the cruel scandal involving Ann Lovett in 1984 and the 'Kerry Babies Case' involving Joanna Hayes the same year exposed ongoing national neuroses concerning sex, as did the so-called 'X Case' in 1992 and the abhorrent saga of clerical abuse that has still in all probability not run its course. At any rate, reviews of both the Irish and English versions of the play over the years regularly comment on its continuing and painful relevance. Thus in a piece on 'Power of "The Trial" as a social document', David Nowlan wrote after seeing the Gemini production in 1970 that the play was 'one of the most powerful social documents ever to be seen on the Irish stage . . . and a great evening's theatre besides', and concluded: 'If the tourists who see it in the City Theatre think that, for the 70s, it is an anachronistic melodrama, we Irish can merely pray that, within the decade, it will be out of date for us, too, and meanwhile acknowledge that it is a searing social document which makes compelling theatre' (*IT*, 12/8/70). His prayer was obviously not answered, for as that decade ended, Gladys Sheehan, who directed the play for Dublin's Beavers Repertory Theatre, stated on opening night:

> I thought the play would have dated since it was first produced in the 1960s, because of our changing attitude to the problem of unmarried mothers. But I was wrong. One member of the cast has a boutique in Blackrock and put a poster in her window advertising the play. A woman came in and said she would not help any

unmarried mothers and that they should be thrown to the bottom of the sea. So perhaps the play is not dated at all. (*II*, 19/9/79)

For Alan Titley, the play remains 'the most harrowing, and yet sympathetic examination of the unmarried mother in Ireland and her savage treatment by society and by the Magdalene laundries'.[148]

By the 1990s, the critical focus had shifted somewhat from the issue of unmarried mothers to the play's broader theme of bigoted intolerance, especially with regard to sexual matters, so that a commentator in *The Anglo-Celt* could call *On Trial* 'a most challenging play' and write that it was 'a powerful play about human weakness and betrayal [of] love' (*AC*, 3/2/94). In like manner, a contributor to the *Ulster Herald* felt the play was about 'the pressure faced by Maura Cassidy, who dared to defy convention and paid the price' (*UH*, 12/3/94). Evidently, despite the changing social and moral climate of the country, *An Triail/On Trial* continued to pack a punch, as Bernie Ní Fhlatharta noted of the touring production by Aisteoirí an Spidéil in 1998: 'Written by Máiréad Ní Ghráda and put on stage for the first time in 1964, it elicited talk and controversy at the time. It is striking that in 1998 the subject matter is as timely as it was then' (*CT*, 13/3/98).[149] And as recently as 2012, a contributor to *The Kerryman*, having seen *On Trial* in Killorglin, wrote that it was 'a story of many families in times gone-by', but added: 'If you ever have the chance of seeing this play somewhere, go and see it. It's well worth a viewing' (*K*, 18/1/12).

In all probability, *An Triail* has in its Irish and English incarnations been viewed by more people than any other full-length play in Irish.[150] Moreover, as the comments quoted above should indicate, the play continues to stir discussion if not the same kind of controversy it did in 1964. This popularity and ongoing relevance are accomplishments of considerable significance, as is the fact that *An Triail* is one of the first Irish literary works in either of the country's languages to shed light on how the Irish state elected to deal with unmarried mothers – fathers seem to have always been off-limits – predating by nearly three decades Patricia Burke Brogan's 1992 play *Eclipsed*. There can, then, be no doubt that the play's place in Irish social and theatrical history is assured. Now we may turn to the question of its success as a work of dramatic literature.

If *An Triail* is a powerful and moving play, it is also a very simple one. From the start, we are trapped in a world where an individual's emotional life at the most profound level is everyone's business, as is symbolised by Ní Ghráda's having the great macaronic song of love and desertion 'Siúil, a Ghrá' (Go, My Love) drowned out by the cries of newsboys hawking papers with lurid headlines. Máire Ní Chathasaigh confesses her 'crime', that she killed her infant child, and then the formal trial that will run throughout the play begins, with the audience immediately summoned by the prosecutor to serve as jurors: 'Ladies and gentlemen, I ask this of you – to put anything you have heard, or anything you have read, about this case out of your minds. Listen to the evidence that will be brought before you, and give your judgement according to that evidence alone.'[151] That will be no easy task, as Máire's confession has already given us the same certainty about her guilt as the jurors in the world of the play would probably have had. That certainty is, however, challenged by Máire herself before the first scene ends: 'They think that they will come to know about all these matters. But there are things that will be concealed from them forever. The things that are hidden in my heart.'[152] Yet unlike the characters on stage, the audience will, in a series of flashbacks that are interwoven with the court scenes, get 'knowledge about all these matters' and thus be able to render a far more informed verdict when the play ends.

Máire is a naive young country woman whom we see in the first flashback meeting and eventually being seduced by the cynical but superficially charming teacher and former seminarian Pádraig Mac Cárthaigh. There is no ploy, however hackneyed and despicable, that Pádraig will not use on her, as when he tells her of his miserable life with an invalid wife whose sickness means 'she could never be a proper wife for me'.[153] After insisting that Máire promise never to reveal their relationship or his name, he is able to convince her that by putting his wedding ring – if that is what it is – on her finger he has made her his true wife, whatever the law or the Church might say. Of course he rejects her as soon as he learns of her pregnancy and is protected from any consequences by her fidelity to her promise not to reveal the father's identity. When his wife – who he has told Máire could live for years – dies, he quickly remarries a fellow teacher with whom in all probability he has had an affair. Meanwhile, Máire has fled her home, so that the next time she, and the audience, see Pádraig, he is drunk in the brothel where she is being sheltered by the stereotypical prostitute with a heart of gold. His treatment of her is brutally dismissive as he refuses to even look at their infant daughter and calls Máire a 'whore' (striapach).[154]

If the man she sees as her husband is a contemptible lout, her blood kin are no better. Her brother Liam, who was supposed to keep an eye on her at the fateful dance at which she meets Pádraig, denies any responsibility when he is questioned in court: 'But none of the blame should be put on me. I had company of my own that night. I couldn't always be at her heels. I am not her keeper . . . I don't know what happened that night, and I don't want to know . . .'[155] When her other brother Seán, who is the one who tips their mother off that Máire has stopped going to Mass and is often sick, is asked by the counsellor for the defence whether he ever made any attempt 'to show

the love of God or Christian charity to your sister, or . . . to protect her' (ar
ghrá Dé nó ar charthannacht chríostaí a thaispeáint do do dheirfiúr, nó . . .
ar í a chosaint), he responds angrily: 'What could I do? . . . She brought
shame on us. She brought public shame on us in the presence of the neighbours. She destroyed our life. She sinned . . . She sinned against God . . . It
would be right to treat her harshly.'[156] Seán is particularly bitter that the
scandal has put an end to his own studies for the priesthood.

By far the most despicable character in the play, worse even than Pádraig,
is Máire's mother, a self-pitying hypocrite we first see giving her testimony
in court:

> None of the blame should be put on me. I raised her in a respectable and Christian
> way. It was God's will to take my husband from me . . . I was left a slavey, with no
> one who would lift a hand to help me . . . And what do I have for it in the end? I am
> shamed before the neighbours. They pointing their fingers at me and mocking me
> if I go to a fair or market or even to God's Sunday Mass.[157]

Moreover, she has been more than willing to sacrifice the independence,
marital prospects, and happiness of her children to her own standing in the
eyes of her neighbours, as Liam makes clear in an outburst to his brother:
'All she wants is that her obituary should read: "Such and such a day, such and
such a year, Máiréad, Bean Uí Chathasaigh died. She was the mother of Seán
Ó Cathasaigh, the parish priest of Ballywayback, and to Mother Columbán
with the Virgin Mary, a missionary in Africa."'[158] If she sees her husband's
death and her subsequent difficult widowhood as the result of God's will,
she takes an entirely more active approach to Máire's pregnancy, trying to
abort the fetus: 'A medicinal drink. A strong drink. That will sort you out,
girl, and if it doesn't, you will get another drink of it tomorrow and every
other day until it does the job for you.' To cover all possibilities, she also
orders Máire to marry the baby's father and suggests that she can go to
England to give birth so no one in their own community would be any the
wiser. Her final words to her daughter, who runs away to Dublin after this
confrontation, are cold and cruel: 'A curse on the one who brought this
shame down on us. And a curse on you, you . . . whore.'[159]

If Máire is failed by the family, that bedrock of Irish society according to
the Irish Constitution of 1937, she is treated no better by either the Catholic
Church or the Irish state. When she goes to confession, the priest, who to be
fair could not be expected to say anything else at the time, thrice refuses her
absolution, for 'you must part from the person who is an occasion of sin for
you. You must part from him altogether and never speak to him again.' When
she says that she cannot do so, he can only offer one of the least helpful New
Testament passages for her guidance: 'Remember what our Saviour said: "if

your right hand sins, cut it off. It is better to be without a hand than to commit a sin.'"[160] Her next contact with institutional Christianity is in the shelter for unmarried mothers where she lives and works. In a choral song that anticipates Brogan's *Eclipsed*, the exploited women are given a voice:

> We are all tired and worn out,
> And we working without any pay.
> We are tired and weak
> And we slaving every day.
> But when he himself comes
> The Elvis Presley of the Irish
> It is then the excitement begins![161]

Of course no Elvis of any description is going to enter this building. Nor, as Máire soon learns, do the women get to keep and raise the children they bear, those children instead being put up for adoption and never again seen by their mothers.

Máire also soon finds out that a doctor's examination she has undergone was not intended to benefit her, but rather to gauge the future health of the baby she is expected to surrender to more respectable and well-off parents. This whole adoption process is being managed by a social worker, who represents the state in the play. She explains to Máire how the real world works: 'Have sense, girl. Look. The lawyer will come. All you will have to do will be to put your name to the documents and no more will be asked of you. You will be free to go and able to go anywhere you want.'[162] The social worker is not so much malevolent as she is blind to a world in which institutional solutions are inadequate, but she does offer Máire one piece of information that turns out to be all too true: 'It's no easy matter for a young girl to have an illegitimate child.'[163]

Failed by family, Church, and state, Máire quickly learns that respectable society will show no respect for her. Thus the woman for whom she works as an underpaid domestic servant wants her to leave as soon as she realises that Máire is pregnant: 'What can I do about it. I have daughters. I couldn't risk leaving them in the company of someone like her. What would the neighbours say? What would the other girls at school say? What would the nuns say?'[164] Máire is again exploited, first by the factory manager who hires her to clean toilets for ten hours a week, and then by a landlady who takes a third of her meagre wages for a room in a house that soon collapses.[165] Máire would now be homeless were it not for her fellow disreputable outcast, the tough-talking but soft-hearted prostitute, who along with the delivery man Seáinín an Mhótair, is the only kind soul she encounters in the play. Mailí, who lashes out at 'the "respectable" women of the neighbourhood' (mná 'creidiúnacha' na comharsanachta) for failing to aid the traumatised Máire after the house collapses, arranges for her to live rent-free in her building in exchange for housekeeping work, work she can also do for other lodgers to make a bit of extra money. It is Seáinín who steps in to drive her to Mailí's flat and asks the central thematic question of the play: 'Who says that this is a Christian country?'[166]

It is, of course, at Mailí's flat that Máire has her devastating final meeting with Pádraig and also hears Colm Ó Sé, Pádraig's fellow teacher and acolyte, propose the following toast: 'Here's to the health of Pádraig Mac Cárthaigh. He buried a wife and he married a wife. Here now, let us drink the health of every little country fool that a little flattering word was enough to seduce.'[167] Realising full well that she has been one such little fool, and, more painfully, that her infant daughter might well become another, she takes the only option she sees left to her, gassing herself and her baby: 'I killed my child because she was a girl. Every girl grows up to be a woman. But my daughter is free. She is free. She will not be a soft yielding little fool for any man. She is free. She is free. She is free.'[168] The play ends with an ineffective anticlimax at the cemetery where Máire and her baby are buried in a single coffin. Mother, brothers, social worker, factory manager – all of the principal characters – repeat their denials of any responsibility for what has occurred. From his own hard-won experience Seáinín an Mhótair dispassionately, though perhaps redundantly, explains the way the world works for the powerless: 'She broke the rules. The person who breaks the rules of the game loses.'[169] Mailí offers a prayer for Máire, her child, and even for the man who betrayed her but whose name she never revealed. Then, in an entirely unconvincing final scene, Pádraig, who has not shown the slightest sign of having a conscience, appears at the graveside with 'Siúil, a Ghrá' playing in the background, stands for a moment without saying a word, turns up his collar, and leaves.

An Trial is in many ways a kind of *Pilgrim's Progress* in reverse, as Máire's journey does not lead to salvation through the repudiation of demonic tempters, but rather to a real hell on earth, tormented at all stages by figures convinced of their own unassailable personal and social rectitude. All of the characters are types, deliberately exaggerated versions of what could have been real people. Ní Ghráda's decision to stage the play as a series of discreet scenes suggests the disjointed nature of a criminal trial in which witness follows witness with no necessary continuity, but it also disrupts the audience's sense of the ordinary flow of life. Her emphasis throughout is not on orderly character development but on the almost ritualistic unfolding of a tragedy all but inevitable in a society where appearances are all and hypocrisy all but instinctive. Critical and audience response leaves no doubt that *An Trial* was and remains an effective and moving piece of theatre, but it holds up less well as a work of literature. Indeed Éadhmonn Mac Suibhne, one of the critics who reviewed the original production praised the play as good and original, but added that it was no 'dramatic masterpiece' (sár-dhráma) and pointed out what he felt were its flaws and shortcomings:

> But I thought the play failed at just the point at which it should have been strong and did not succeed in driving the basic idea home effectively, that is the idea of the trial. The author told the story well, she sketched her characters skilfully and artistically, but I did not at any time at all feel that there was any trial going on. It seemed to me that it was just a narrative, a representation of misery. (*IP*, 21/10/64)[170]

Developing these ideas at greater length the following month, Mac Suibhne identified what he saw as the three major problems with the play: 'The Man in the Street is being accused, and at the same time he is being asked to be the jury. Not only that, but he is being accused of something of which he could not be guilty, no matter how negligent he could have been.'[171] According to Mac Suibhne, by focusing on society's role in Máire's tragedy Ní Ghráda had ignored a crucial point: 'Anything the girl did, she did of her own free will . . . It is she herself consented to commit the sin and it is she herself who should be answerable for it, herself and the man. Everything is taken into account as evidence, but nothing is said about the free will everyone has . . .'[172] But what was most important for Mac Suibhne was that *An Trial* grossly oversimplified the complex issues the play itself raised:

> The trial was held, the evidence was given, and somehow the bottom fell out of the play. I found myself thinking about *Murder in the Cathedral*, when the culprits turn and (in that beautiful, simple prose of Eliot's) reveal to us their side of the story, so that we are almost arguing with ourselves about whether they are guilty or not. I had no wish to argue at the end of *An Trial*; it could be that it was less of a trial than a narrative or it could be that the arguments were drowned in a flood of pity. (*Feasta*, Nov. 1964, p. 10)[173]

Mac Suibhne is both wrong and right here. It is highly unlikely that Ní Ghráda would have agreed with the idea that she did not pay sufficient attention to free will in the play. Given her rigidly controlled conservative Catholic upbringing, Máire's 'sin' is far more the result of her naiveté than of any conscious decision to violate a moral code. Moreover, Ní Ghráda would doubtless have been far more interested in how Pádraig managed to escape the consequences of what he did than in what motivated his actions. On the other hand, Mac Suibhne is correct that despite the play's powerful emotional effect on its audience, it leaves that audience with no doubt about what conclusions are to be drawn from what has transpired on stage. The bad characters are very bad indeed, while someone like Mailí is a mere cliché and Máire herself too clueless to be convincing. As the curtain falls, one is left with an amorphous sense of guilt and a feeling of impotence in the face of the enormous social changes that will be required to remove the source of that guilt. Needless to say, that kind of impotent culpability can generate a sense of one's own commendable moral sensitivity to the problem with no corresponding responsibility to act towards its solution. Instead of wondering at the contradictory moral complexities of human behaviour, we may simply ask why bad people do not stop doing bad things.

Much of the difficulty in reading this play appropriately is due to confusion over what kind of a play it is, and here it makes sense to look at last at the question of expressionism in the plays of Ní Ghráda, as that label is regularly applied to her dramatic style. For example, Siobhán Ní Bhrádaigh sees expressionism in her work from her very first play *An Udhacht*, while Éamon Ó Ciosáin has written that expressionism only becomes really important in her work with *Lá Buí Bealtaine* and her other one-act plays performed in the Abbey Theatre 20 years later.[174] We can certainly see expressionist touches in *Giolla an tSolais* in 1945 with the personified evil of the title character and the ritualised choral scenes during the terrible storms. These expressionist tendencies become clearer with time as Ní Ghráda deviates from the traditional realism of the Gaelic stage and increasingly turns to archetypal characters, flashbacks and a disjointed sense of time, and the use of choruses and metatheatrical devices like the prosecuting and defence attorneys in *An Triail*. Still, Ní Ghráda was always a pragmatic playwright who used such techniques when they suited her purpose rather than an expressionist playwright *per se*. Her experiments were not rooted in theory – although she may well have been quite familiar with that theory – but rather inspired by the challenges she faced in putting plays, particularly short ones, on stage for audiences whose command of her linguistic medium varied greatly. Her interest in blending experimentation with a tested practical approach to crafting effective plays was only confirmed by her work with Tomás Mac Anna, another theatrical innovator willing to try anything he knew or thought would work on stage. Ní Ghráda was no more a strict expressionist than Mac Anna was a doctrinaire Brechtian, despite his admiration for many of that master's tricks of the trade.[175] It was this commonsensical commitment to putting on a good show that made soulmates of Ní Ghráda and Mac Anna and kept their collaboration so successful for nearly two decades.[176] Ó Ciosáin makes this point crystal clear:

What are the reasons Máiréad changed to expressionism? She was a playwright who always wrote with the state and circumstances of the theatre in her mind; she moved towards expressionism because Tomás Mac Anna, a director who spent a while with Brecht's theatre in Berlin, was at the Abbey Theatre in her time. Also, expressionism is more suitable for short plays than naturalism because there are not many opportunities in a short play to develop character or plot.[177]

Ní Ghráda was obviously pleased with how these experimental techniques worked for her on stage, as her final play *Breithiúnas* (Judgement) is in form and style almost identical to *An Trial*. With Mac Anna of course directing, *Breithiúnas* opened in the Peacock Theatre in February 1968, the first play ever done in the round (i.e. with the stage in the middle of the audience) at the theatre. Noting that *Breithiúnas* was 'the first play to test the theatre's experimental capacity to the full', Desmond Rushe declared: 'Máiréad Ní Ghráda's new play is particularly relevant . . . The principal character in "Breithiúnas" has thrived on jobbery and he is put on symbolic trial in a theatrical form as excitingly unconventional and sprawling as was society in "An Trial".' But in the final analysis he found this relevance and superficial excitement insufficient to carry the play: 'The author's humanity is the chief virtue of "Breithiúnas", which is, in many ways, too predictable and unoriginal. It has not got the involving warmth of "An Trial", and there is scarcely an incident in the life of Marcas the T. D. which has not been satirized on the stage before' (*II*, 12/2/68). For Eibhlín Ní Mhurchú,

> 'Breithiúnas' is a kind of 'Everyman'. In 'An Triail' a finger was pointed at everyone and everyone was accused of the crime of negligence, but in 'An Breithiúnas' the finger is pointed again and again at one person . . . This is not a grim, heavy play because the author puts variety into every finger that is pointed so that no finger becomes tedious or tiring . . . (*II*, 14/2/28)[178]

Reviewing the play for the *Irish Times*, Dominic O'Riordan had high praise for Ní Ghráda:

> In this two-act play little of Irish public contemporary life escapes Máiréad Ní Ghráda's satiric mind – *gaimbín* [gombeen] politics; the public statement and the private rebuttal; the cravenry of voters, who follow any line provided it is the party line; the sanctity of sport; the establishment morality; and all the cherished institutions. The dialogue sparkles, and the play contains some of the finest writing I have heard on an Irish stage for many a long year – sharp, concise and witty.

He did, however, feel that apart from the main character, 'the other characters are mere ciphers, without personality of their own helping to reveal facet after facet of the abundant personality of Marcas' and that 'some facets are laboured too much and overemphasised', a problem that could be fixed with 'a little judicious cutting' (*IT*, 12/2/68). Like O'Riordan, Liam Ó Lonargáin liked the play, calling it 'interesting' (spéisiúil) and 'enjoyable' (taitneamhach), but also expressing some frustration with the author's flat characterisations, even of her protagonist:

> I think that she tried too hard to create a tycoon and that she neglected the character of Marcas. And this is the great failing I find in the play. Much of this failing would be removed if even a single small virtue were attributed to the tycoon. That would accentuate the darkness of all his vices . . . (*Feasta*, Mar. 1968, p. 17)[179]

Of course the exact same thing could be said of her treatment of Pádraig, Máire's mother, and others in *An Triail*, but had she followed such advice she would in both cases have written very different plays. Donal Kelly had a better idea of the kind of play Ní Ghráda was actually putting on stage. Having commented on Mac Anna's direction of the play, writing that 'the final presentation might well be described as a "happening" with script by Máiréad Ní Ghráda', he added: 'But the thing about Máiréad Ní Ghráda is that she writes in effect what is one play containing two: the play on stage and the play behind it. This is very true of "Breithiúnas"' (*IP*, 2/9/68).

Despite what may seem to be the play's even greater relevance in light of political developments in Ireland since its first production, in particular the revelations about the machinations of An Taoiseach Charles Haughey, the various tribunals of the 1990s and early 2000s, and the financial scandals surrounding the demise of the Celtic Tiger, *Breithiúnas* has not enjoyed the popularity it deserves. Although it was performed at Maynooth almost immediately after its Dublin premiere and in the following year was taken by the Abbey to the Gaeltacht, to Gweedore in Donegal and to Ventry and Ballyferriter in Kerry, as well as to An Taibhdhearc in Galway, subsequent revivals have been sporadic. Among them have been performances of the play by Co. Antrim's Aisteoirí na Glinntí at Féile Náisiúnta na Drámaíochta at the 1971 Oireachtas; and by Aisteoirí Choláiste Éinde at An Taibhsín, An Taibhdhearc's new experimental theatre in Galway, in 1974.

The audience is once again the jury in *Breithiúnas*, although there is no formal courtroom setting as there was in *An Triail*. Instead, the play opens with a nearly bare stage, with nothing on it but a small table and a few chairs that will be the total furniture for the whole play. A gunshot is heard and a crowd of excited people, who will serve as a chorus, enter and begin speaking more or less all at once: 'Is he dead? What happened to him? Did he put the barrel of the gun in his mouth? It happened by accident. No one would attack him. A public man always has enemies. Did the police come?

Is he dead?'[180] Marcas de Grás, TD is indeed dead, the news announced by his fanatically devoted aide Alabhaois Mac Gabhann, who explains the death as due to a hunting accident. As the group uproar continues, the spirits of de Grás and 'the Other Man' (an Fear Eile) enter to listen and comment, although they cannot be seen or heard by the other characters.[181] Meanwhile, members of the crowd shout their appreciation for the services de Grás has provided them: 'It is he who got the pension for me . . . He got a pension for half the county . . . He got a post in the civil service for my daughter . . . There will never be his like again.' And Alabhaois, with 'a touch of bombast in his voice, like someone delivering an oration' (iarraidh de scaothaireacht ina ghlór, amhail duine a bheadh ag déanamh óráide), sings his praises: 'Never in the political life of this country has there been found a man as honest as Marcas de Grás. He was never accused of crookedness or dishonesty. He never wasted a penny of the people's money.'[182]

When the crowd departs, leaving Marcas and the Other Man alone, the latter asks Marcas whether he deserves all the adulation, to which Marcas responds: 'Why wouldn't I have earned it?' Thereupon the Other Man simply states: 'It is you yourself who knows best.'[183] Thus begins what for Marcas is a harrowing involuntary examination of conscience, guided by the questions of the Other Man. As Ní Ghráda makes clear, however, the Other Man is no overbearing inquisitor: 'The Other Man speaks quietly and sympathetically. It is clear he has an understanding of Marcas and pities him.'[184] Still, he forces Marcas – and the audience – to revisit scenes from Marcas's life as they actually happened, rather than as he has chosen to remember them or crafted those memories for the benefit of his career and legend. We will see the major figures in Marcas's life as they are conjured up by the Other Man as he forces Marcas 'to look into the loneliest places in your heart' (féachaint sna háiteanna is uaigní in do chroí).[185] Brought on stage are the father who becomes an alcoholic after Marcas accidentally kills his own sister; the mother he puts into a substandard nursing home against her wishes and then never visits; the daughter whose potential suitors he drives away; the non-athletic son he bullies and calls 'Miss Nancy', only to see him reject his father's plans for his future and go to Africa as a lay missionary; the young woman he callously abandons to marry someone more politically well-connected; and the wife he chooses solely to advance his career and on whom he cheats while she is dying of cancer, fathering a child with the nurse who attends her.

Just as the Other Man forces Marcas to confront the mess he has made of his personal life and the lives of those around him, he also compels him to come to terms with the hypocritical fraudulence of his public facade. Thus we see him deliver what is fundamentally the same speech three times as he moves up the political ladder, a speech full of platitudes and entirely incompatible promises:

I will do my best to advance the aims of the party. Work for everyone in the constituency. Good pay and short hours. Lowering the cost of living without causing trouble for the farmers or the shopkeepers, free health services, free education, lowering rates and taxes – in a word, work for everyone, a house for everyone, a pension for everyone and health for everyone and my vote for the party.[186]

The third time he delivers the speech, in a campaign for a seat in Dáil Éireann, his voters are able to recite it along with him, and later their voices sound in chorus when he repeats the entire litany in the Dáil chamber itself.

Needless to say, his performance in office has little to do with the promises that put him there. With an understanding of politics that never rises above crude clientelism, he goes through the motions expected of him as when, in a scene that must have amused Ní Ghráda herself, he responds to an invitation to attend a school play. He also makes utterly contradictory pledges to competing interest groups and is even willing, in collusion with a parish priest, to allow a man to escape prosecution after he has embezzled money from his employer and seduced two 'girls' (*cailíní*, age unspecified). His solution is to send this criminal to act as an assistant to his son in Africa, commenting, 'That's the game of politics for you.' When asked by the Other Man whether he feels any shame for his actions, he replies in a way that must have left theatre audiences more than a little unsettled: 'Why? People get the public representatives they deserve. I was too good for them. Too good altogether.'[187]

One of the principal sources of Marcas's appeal to such voters is his record of heroic service as a mere 18-year-old during the War of Independence, service that earns him a full military funeral. As Marcas delights in watching the ceremony, the Other Man reminds him that he knows well 'what you have to do' (cad tá le déanamh agat). Here Marcas tries to resist, but the Other Man quickly and pointedly notes that so far Marcas has only had to confront his sins, but now he must relive something far more humiliating, what Marcas himself calls 'the ugly contemptible things' (na nithe gránna suaracha), for 'they are what a person is most ashamed of' (is iad is mó a mbíonn náire ag duine astu).[188] Now Marcas is forced to acknowledge that the act on which his whole political career is based was a sham. Instead of being the War of Independence hero he has always claimed and been believed to be, he is instead exposed as a coward. Wounded, Marcas begs his commanding officer not to leave him, eventually causing the other man's death when the officer stands up to assist him. When Alabhaois and other volunteers come on the scene, Marcas quickly re-writes this scenario for them: 'I was carrying him . . . I was bringing him with me to get help for him . . . a doctor . . . a priest . . . I said the Act of Contrition into his ear.'[189] As he is nursed back to health by the woman he later abandons, he comes close to telling her the truth about what happened: 'Look, love . . . Say I were a coward, a man the sound of the bullets would scare – a man who would lose his manliness under the firing of the guns – would you love me if I were a person of that sort?' Her curt reply ensures he will never make such an admission: 'You would not be you if you were a person of that sort. I could not love someone like that.'[190] And the legend replaces the sort of man he is, a legend summed up by Alabhaois: 'That boy did a great deed that will be remembered forever. He was hurt and wounded, shedding his heart's blood. Losing consciousness, but carrying his comrade to save him from death.'[191]

Perhaps in response to the criticism that her characters in *An Triail* were too one-dimensional, in *Breithiúnas* Ní Ghráda gives us a little insight into Marcas's psyche. For example, we learn that he bears profound psychological scars from being looked down on when he was young. More important, after his wife Eilís reveals to his secretary one of his little secrets, that the firm set of his mouth the secretary admires as a sign of his strength is the result of poor dental care in his youth, she says: 'Leave it to Marcas de Grás to use everything for his own advantage. That firm strong mouth of his is a great benefit to him; it's worth a couple of thousand votes in every election.' But she then adds 'poor Marcas' (Marcas bocht), and to the secretary's question about why she uses the word 'poor' she replies: 'Because of how much he depends on other people to protect him from life. I and you and Bhuísí and the crowd that strokes him and praises him. He needs them to give him courage and to sustain his self-confidence.'[192] This glimpse of Marcas's wounded vulnerability – and an earlier reference to an inferiority complex rooted in class consciousness – flesh out his character a bit.

We get the best sense of the private man hidden beneath the public icon at the very end of the play. Shocked by all he has been forced to confront, Marcas tries again to absolve himself: 'What can a person do about the person he is? He has to act according to his character . . . according to his heart.' The Other Man pitilessly rejects this sophistry: 'Marcas de Grás, the coward who caused the death of a brave Commandant. Your whole life based on a lie . . . with no foundation under you but falsehood. Your name in everyone's mouth and the brave man forgotten. Your whole life an injustice. An injustice to the dead.'[193] Apparently shaken to the core, Marcas admits that he has never been able to let his sons or his constituents see the kind of man he really is and then continues: 'But I never had peace of mind. Never, never, never, for fifty years there has only been a bitter taste in my mouth. I always stretching my two hands up to grasp sweetness and happiness and failing to find them.' Moreover, he now seems to feel that he has been shriven by his recent enforced soul-searching: 'And now when I have brought all that was hidden into the light, perhaps I could have peace of mind. Is that the meaning of the Church's statement when it prays for eternal peace for the souls of the dead? Everything crooked made straight, everything hard softened . . . everything bitter made sweet . . . every path made smooth . . .'[194] Ní Ghráda is attempting something quite tricky here by trying to turn an archetype into a credible human character right as the curtain falls. While such an ending could offer the audience a gratifying study in the power of remorse and repentance, it seems unconvincingly facile. The Marcas de Grás we have come to know throughout the play would be incapable of such a Pauline conversion. Indeed he would be far more likely to be buying time as he assumes one more mask to present to posterity. In de Grás Ní Ghráda has created a memorable study of a type of politician familiar in Ireland and other democracies. *Breithiúnas* would be a more coherent and effective play had she been satisfied with that accomplishment and not tried to make him into the kind of complex human character he was never intended to be.

'What if?' is one of the great questions running through the Gaelic literary revival. It is also a question for which the career of Máiréad Ní Ghráda provides both some new variants and some actual answers. Over the years, many in the Irish-language theatre community, including Ní Ghráda herself, had lamented the many problems they faced: lack of a theatre dedicated to work in Irish; the absence of talented dramatists to provide original new plays; the shortage of skilled theatre professionals, most notably actors and directors; and the apparent non-existence of a reliable audience with sufficient command of Irish to enjoy and appreciate what playwrights and professionals provided them. What if all these problems were to be solved, even partially? Máiréad Ní Ghráda offered an optimistic answer to that question by writing well-crafted and engaging original plays designed to be accessible to audiences with varying levels of command of Irish, plays creatively directed and performed by actors who were at least competent and often better, produced in either the Abbey Theatre or a centrally located Irish-language theatre in the capital. However, neither she nor her colleagues at the time could work miracles, and in many ways theatre in Irish is no better off than it was when she began to write. We are now left with a series of questions: What if the kind of conditions she and her colleagues created do not return? What if the period when plays by Ní Ghráda, directed by Tomás Mac Anna at both the Abbey and An Damer, must be seen as the high point to which drama in Irish can ever aspire? That is, of course, a question for the present and subsequent generations to ponder. What we can be sure of is that whatever future lies in store for Gaelic theatre, the plays of Máiréad Ní Ghráda will hold an honoured place in its repertoire.

TWO

A NORTHERN VOICE

SÉAMUS Ó NÉILL (1910–81)

In February 1946, Séamus Ó Néill, the editor of the new journal *An Iris*, vented his frustrations with his fellow writers of Irish: 'Since the first number was put out, not a single manuscript worth publishing has come to me, and in addition only one or two came at all, and they were puerile . . . It is a great scandal if we cannot keep one magazine like this alive after "dealing" with Irish for half a century' (*Iris*, Feb. 1946, p. 2).[1] What he had hoped to see coming across his editorial desk were 'works in which there is thought and reflection and research and coherence' (aistí a bhfuil smaointeadh is machtnamh is taighdeadh is cruinneas ionnta). His simple directive to potential contributors was 'Have something to say' (Bíodh rud le rádh agat) (*Iris*, Feb. 1946, p. 4).[2] The rapid failure of *An Iris* after only five issues probably did not surprise him much, nor would he have necessarily put all the blame on the writers. In a 1941 letter to *The Leader* he had protested against the editor's condemnation of Irish writers working in English:

> In some recent editorial notes you compare a man who could write Irish, but who writes English, to a castle-hack. The comparison is so unjust as to be ludicrous. It shows no appreciation of the difficulties that beset the would-be Irish writer at present. There is no inducement for any writer worth a pinch of salt to write Irish. Indeed he will be discouraged and hindered by every possible means. (*Leader*, 29/3/41)

In fact, several months after the demise of *An Iris* he was able to be more understanding of the failure of writers of Irish to provide him with the stimulating contributions he had hoped to receive: 'No person worthy of respect will write in Irish for long if he finds out that his books are not read, unless he can make the odd penny on them.'[3] This pessimism turned at least briefly to despair in this same essay. Telling of how he had asked 'a good number' (cuid mhaith) of young people whether they had read any books in

Irish since leaving school and how 'in every case the answer was in the negative',[4] he concluded that 'both the cause of literature in Irish and the cause of Irish itself were lost' (*Indiu*, 20/12/46). It is, then, hardly surprising that in the following year he became a member of the band of Gaelic authors who have threatened to give up writing in Irish.[5]

He did not, of course, much to the benefit of the literature about whose future he was so uncertain. To a great extent this willingness to soldier on was due to his firm belief that something could be done about the situation and that he himself was particularly qualified to do that something. In a 1962 interview Ó Néill drew an interesting distinction between what had inspired him to write and what motivated him to write in Irish. On the first point, he stated that no external stimulus was needed to start him writing, for 'if you have the talent for writing in you, you begin writing' (má bhíonn féith na scríbhneoireachta ionat, tuisíonn tú a scríobh). Entirely conscious, however, was his choice of linguistic medium, as he acknowledged that his motivation there was 'the national zeal that inspired all of us when we were young' (an díograis náisiúnta a spreag muid uilig nuair a bhíomar óg) (*IMN*, 1962, p. 5). But well before 1962 he was painfully aware that the younger writers and readers essential for the survival of literature in Irish would be unlikely to find that kind of patriotic impulse compelling. Indeed in 1946 he had already proclaimed: 'Literature in Irish has no worse enemy than the writer who writes out of the love he has for the language' (*Indiu*, 20/12/46).[6] By 1962 he saw the most threatening foe as simple apathy, for 'the wave of nationalism is rapidly ebbing, and unless those involved with the Irish language provide literature that will get a grip on the mind of the people, it will have a short life as a living language from here on' (*IMN*, 1962, p. 8).[7] What he saw as even more essential in 1962 than it had been in the days of *An Iris* was writing in Irish worth reading and plays worth seeing, literary 'works in which there is thought and reflection and research and coherence'.

In his 1962 interview Ó Néill stressed that the crucial younger generation of readers would never exchange 'Joyce, Greene, Hemingway, etc. for a handful of proverbs' (Joyce, Greene, Hemingway, etc. ar dhornán seanfhocal), and charged that 'the people who pretend anything different' (na daoine a bhíos ag iarraidh a atharach sin a chur i gcéill) were – once again – 'enemies of the language' (náimhde don teanga) (*IMN*, 1962, p. 8). Of course, he had always been willing to take the fight to such enemies – a courageous move for a language learner like himself if his target was one of the venerated native speakers who had turned their hand to writing. In 1945 he wrote witheringly of a book by one such native speaker, Maoghnus Ó Domhnaill's novel *An Táilliúr* (The tailor): 'We do not understand why public money was spent on so poor a book. As a literary effort, if that is what it is, it is childish. Books like this only draw contempt on the small group of writers of Irish who are able

75

to give us something worthwhile' (*Comhar*, May 1945, p. 1).[8] The previous year he had dismissed the native speaker Seaghán Mac Meanman's story collection *Fear Siubhail* (A travelling man) (1929) in similar terms: 'It would not be possible to choose a book less appropriate for young people than *Fear Siubhail*. When a young person compares a book like this with a book in English or a book in French, or a book in German, it is no wonder at all that he has no interest in Irish' (*Comhar*, May 1944, p. 7).[9]

It is safe to say that Ó Néill himself never doubted his own ability 'to give us something worthwhile in Irish'. As Máiréad Ní Shé tactfully writes, he was 'perhaps a little bit too satisfied with his own creations' (b'fhéidir, beagáinín róshásta lena dhéantús féin) (*IMN*, 1987, p. 96). In many ways, however, he had a right to that confidence, for there were few Irish writers of Irish in his lifetime – and few since – who did so much serious thinking about writing, or who wrote on a wide range of topics more knowledgeably, prolifically and pointedly than did he. For example, writing of his poetry in 1944, Piaras Béaslaí stated: 'His poems reflect a world of to-day – not only the world of the Gaeltacht or Ireland, but the great world outside. He is a good European as well as a good Gael' (*Leader*, 19/8/44). In an appreciation of Ó Néill shortly after his death, his friend and fellow writer Seán Mac Réamoinn wrote: 'Controversy he never avoided: he was an argumentative and, indeed, opinionated man, and for one of such slight stature and gentle kindness, he could dominate, not to say terrify a company, with the ferocity of his thunder, especially on questions of history and literature' (*IT*, 20/6/81).[10] For Mac Réamoinn, Ó Néill was always, as he had pronounced him 20 years earlier, 'among the few truly professional writers we have in Irish' (ar an mbeagán scríbhneoirí fíor-phroifisiúnta atá againn sa Ghaeilge) (*Comhar*, July 1960, p. 22).

An honours graduate of Queen's University, Belfast, where he also took an MA in Celtic Studies, Ó Néill went on to earn another MA from University College, Dublin for a thesis on Irish maritime history directed by Eoin Mac Néill. While at Queen's he had already begun writing seriously, and his first play *Buaidh an Ultaigh* (The victory of the Ulsterman) was performed by the university's An Cumann Gaedhealach in 1934. This play would eventually be followed by nine other published plays, three unpublished historical pageants, two radio plays, and, in conjunction with Ciarán Ó Nualláin, a radio magazine show, as well as two ground-breaking novels, two collections of short stories, two volumes of essays, and three books of poetry. He was also a prolific contributor to many periodicals, most notably the weekly *Indiu* and the daily *Irish Press*, writing dozens of articles on a wide range of topics.[11] In addition, he served for various periods of time as editor not only of *An Iris*, but also of *An t-Ultach* and *Comhar*, and as Irish-language editor of the Dundalk *Examiner*. Moreover, he lectured widely on Irish history and literature, including in the United States and Canada. Among the many organisations with which he was involved over the years were the Gaelic League, the Dublin Institute for Advanced Studies, An Cumann Scoildrámaíochta (of which his wife Caitlín was for a time president), An Club Leabhar,[12] An Comhchaidreamh, Gaedhil Uladh, the Irish Historical Society, the Catholic Stage Guild, PEN Ireland, and Cumann na Scríbhneoirí. All this when he was not at his day job teaching history at Carysfort Training College from 1937 to 1974. After his retirement from Carysfort, he held a research fellowship in the Institute of Irish Studies at his alma mater, Queen's University.

Given this rather daunting resume, one might be tempted to see Ó Néill as an inveterate dilettante, leaving himself little time or energy to develop any single one of his diverse interests. However, as his friend Tomás Ó Floinn recalled, 'The strongest memory I myself have of the time I was close to Séamus Ó Néill was how serious he was about everything important.'[13] And there were few things Ó Néill found more important than literature, and in particular theatre. Máiréad Ní Shé has pointed out that he spent more time on drama than on any of the other genres he cultivated (*IMN*, 1987, p. 84).[14] Moreover, he was convinced that, as was true with all kinds of literature, the creation of a vital theatre in Irish was work of national significance. Praising the Abbey Theatre for a recent tour of the Gaeltacht, an initiative that showed the Abbey 'is what it claims to be, the National Theatre of Ireland', Ó Néill wrote in 1969:

> Those Jeremiahs who are always lamenting the death of Irish, and the failure of the revival, might pause to consider that they may be rather hasty with their judgment, when they see a cast of professional actors performing in Irish on the stage . . . Anyone with a sense of proportion must realise when he sees the Abbey players on the stage acting a play in Irish, that all the work for the language has not been in vain. (*IP*, 29/8/69)

Ó Néill must have been particularly gratified by the Abbey's choice of play for this tour. In the absence of one of his own plays, of course, Máiréad Ní Ghráda's *Breithiúnas* was just the sort of play he felt the Gaelic stage most needed. In the first place, it was an original work. Like most people in the language movement who took an interest in theatre, Ó Néill worried that the lack of engaging new plays – indeed of almost any new plays, and the consequent reliance on translations, many of them of plays in English audiences may already have seen – was the most pressing problem facing the Gaelic stage.[15] In 1948 he wrote that the Abbey had been especially remiss in its failure to generate new plays in Irish, writing of the National Theatre's recent production of *Na Cloigíní* (The little bells), Máiréad Nic Mhaicín's translation of Émile Erkmann and Alexandre Chatrian's *Le Juif polonais*: 'It should now be clear to the directors of the Abbey that they must change their policy, if they are not to kill drama in Irish outright. Is there anyone who would believe that an original drama in Irish better than "Na Cloigíní" could not be found?' (*Comhar*, Nov. 1948, p. 25).[16] And not only was Ní Ghráda's play original, it had what Ó Néill felt was needed to make the Irish language a force in Irish theatre. In his 1947 novel *Tonn Tuile* (Tidal wave), Ó Néill's quasi-autobiographical protagonist is Liam de Faoite, a Dublin intellectual and aspiring playwright who shares his creator's belief 'that there was national work that was important in the writing I was doing' (go raibh obair náisiúnta a bhí tairbheach ins an scríbhneoireacht a bhí mé a dhéanamh)[17] and his insistence that contemporary literature in Irish be marked by 'thought and reflection and research and precision'. Reading the negative reviews of his first play, de Faoite pledges to confound the critics: 'I would write a play yet that would amaze them, that would let them know that they understood nothing. How many Irish-language playwrights had any ideas? That is what confused them, that a Gaelic author would be bold enough to have ideas. They were not accustomed to anything like that.'[18]

Of particular interest for our purposes here is that while Ó Néill insisted that literature in Irish should deal with serious and provocative ideas relevant to contemporary Irish audiences, he seems to have seen fiction and drama as quite different and distinct ways of conveying those ideas. Thus his two novels, *Tonn Tuile* (1947) and *Máire Nic Artáin* (1959), are relentlessly prosaic in their humdrum, even drab, modern settings, their unremarkable characters, and – with a few exceptions in each novel – their uneventful narratives.[19] Much the same can also be said of the stories in his two collections, *An Sean-Saighdiúir agus Scéalta Eile* (The old soldier and other stories) (1945) and *Ag Baint Fraochán agus Scéalta Eile* (Picking bilberries and other stories) (1955). His plays, however, are a different case altogether, being quite consciously and conventionally dramatic, with their focus often on the exotic settings, larger than life characters, and heightened reality of history and saga. Even his plays with modern settings share this fascination with what was unusual in Gaelic literature. Thus the otherwise inconsequential comedy *Up the Rebels* (1952) is set in the home of an Anglo-Irish unionist family during the War of Independence; *An tSiúr Pól* (Sister Paul) (1960) takes place in a convent and deals with, among other things, the Catholic Church's *Ne Temere* decree and a test of wills between a mother superior and the local parish priest; and *Rún an Oileáin* (The secret of the island) (1961) involves mysterious doings and apparent murder on a Gaeltacht island. His other plays are considerably grander in conception, if not always in their realisation of that conception. *Buaidh an Ultaigh* (1934) dramatises an episode from the Fenian tale *Cath Finntrágha* (The battle of Ventry), in which Fionn mac Cumhaill and his Fianna take on the invading forces of the king of the world. *Díolta faoi n-a Luach* (Sold for less than he's worth) (1937) revolves around the activities of an eighteenth-century rapparee and includes among its characters the poet Peadar Ó Doirnín. *'Ní Chuireann Siad Síol' nó 'Poll Bocht'* ('They do not sow' or 'poor Poll') (1940) is a slight enough playlet, but its protagonist is Oliver Goldsmith and Samuel Johnson makes, as far as I am aware, his only appearance on the Gaelic stage. *Colm Cille* (1943) recreates events from the life of one of Ireland's greatest saints and missionaries. *Iníon Rí Dhún Sobhairce* (The daughter of the king of Dunseverick) (1953) brings to life characters from the medieval Irish tale *Fingal Rónáin* (Rónán's kin-killing). Adolf Hitler, Martin Bormann, Eva Braun, and the ghost of Hermann Göring all make an appearance in *An Tusa d'Fhoscail an Fhuinneog?* (Is it you who opened the window?), a curious little skit published in *Feasta* in May 1953 but apparently never performed. *Faill ar an bhFeart* (A neglected grave) (1966) tells of the tragic fate of a radical Ulster Presbyterian minister at the time of the 1798 Rising. And *Iníon Rí na Spáinne* (The daughter of the king of Spain) (1976) gives us Ó Néill's perspective on the personal and political consequences of Henry VIII's marriage to and divorce from Catherine of Aragon. It is these plays – all published and all but three also produced – that will now be the focus of our discussion, omitting Ó Néill's unpublished radio plays *Ceart na mBan* (Women's rights) (1938) and *An tSráidbhaile Malluithe* (The cursed village) (1954);[20] his also unpublished pageants dealing with St Patrick, St Colm Cille, and the heroes of Easter Week 1916;[21] and his 'unusual mime' *Labhraí Loinseach*, staged by Waterford schoolchildren as part of the city's An Tóstal festivities in 1953 (*ME*, 30/4/53).[22]

As was mentioned above, *Buaidh an Ultaigh* was first performed by members of An Cumann Gaedhealach at Queen's University in April 1934 and revived at a drama festival in December of that year, winning prizes in the non-religious category for both the play itself and its large cast.[23] It was revived by An Comhar Drámaíochta at the Peacock in December 1936 with Cyril Cusack directing, and was produced at Feis Thír Chonaill in July 1937 (*IP*, 3/7/37). It was broadcast over Radio Éireann on 17 June 1937. The text was originally serialised in *An t-Ultach* from November 1933 through February 1934, and again in the Dundalk *Examiner* between 15 December 1934 and 9 February 1935. An Gúm issued the play in booklet form in 1936.

Ó Néill himself was with time rather embarrassed by this youthful effort, joking that it was 'as bad a play as was ever written' (ar dhráma chomh holc is a scríobhadh ariamh).[24] Contemporary critics seem, however, to have been quite taken with it, with Aodh de Blácam, one of the judges at the 1934 festival where it was performed, improbably calling it a play 'worthy of a classic dramatist in its sparing and forceful writing, its scholarly use of its material, its clear action, its dramatic rise from mere action to spiritual effect' (*IP*, 28/3/35).[25] Cathal Ó Baoighill likewise pronounced *Buaidh an Ultaigh* 'an excellent play' (dráma ar fheabhas), adding in what was either wild hyperbole or a scathing indictment of the way Irish was taught: 'It is my opinion that this play will benefit the cause of the Irish language more than all the classes there ever were' (*Ultach*, June 1934, p. 8).[26] The anonymous critic for the *Irish Independent* praised its 'skilfully developed plot [that] holds the interest to the end' and called it a play in which 'the author has captured the glamour and spirit of the Fenian times, and not a little of the poetry' (*IP*, 20/12/34).[27] In a review of the text published by An Gúm, 'An Babhdán' stated: 'This play will not be too difficult for young people or too insignificant for adults. Its like is badly needed' (*Ultach*, Easter 1937, p. 8).[28] Far more critical – and accurate – was Seán Ó Meadhra, who wrote after seeing An Comhar's 1936 production: 'But the play itself was pitiably poor stuff (no character development, rather clumsy dialogue and narration instead of action), nor had the players any faith in it – their stage sense, after all, was greater than the author's' (*Ireland To-Day*, Jan. 1937, p. 72).

One can suggest several reasons for Ó Néill's choice of subject here. In the first place, as one with a graduate degree in Celtic Studies, he would have been quite familiar with the original Fenian material. Second, he may well have been influenced by the success of Micheál Mac Liammóir's *Diarmaid agus Gráinne*, a work of which he wrote in 1936: 'You will feel the true spirit of antiquity in this play. The author understood properly how intimate was the link between the life of the people and the wonders of creation' (*Ultach*, Feb. 1936, p. 3).[29] And third, he may have already been thinking along lines he developed more than three decades later in comments on audiences with little command of Irish: 'I have seen Festspiele all over Germany which attract tens of thousands of tourists every year who do not understand a word of the dialogue. But those plays are usually costume plays, and spectacular ones, many of them born of the local culture' (*IP*, 14/4/69). Perhaps Ó Néill's own fondness for costume drama was inspired by his belief that audiences could brush up their Irish while enjoying the spectacle.[30] Like several other Irish-language authors – among them 'Myles na gCopaleen' and his brother Ciarán Ó Nualláin – Ó Néill may also have been determined to rescue the ancient literary tales from what he saw as the stultifying control of scholars of Old and Middle Irish. In 1944 he declared that many of those scholars would prefer the Irish language and the culture it enshrined safely dead on the slab for post-mortem analysis: 'They do not want the Gaelic world to survive. They only want the carcass of the nation to examine, like Egyptologists examine the bones of Tutankhamun, and when they have made the examination they will hang the corpse in a museum' (*Comhar*, Aug. 1944, p. 7).[31]

One might, of course, wonder why Ó Néill never drew on the highly spectacular material in the Ulster Cycle, the stories of Cú Chulainn and his comrades which by the 1930s Irish playgoers would have been at least passingly familiar with from the work of writers like Standish O'Grady, Eleanor

Hull, W. B. Yeats, Lady Gregory, *et al.* The reason is as simple as it is surprising. Ó Néill found the heroes of the Ulster Cycle distasteful, writing of Oliver Sheppard's statue of the dying Cú Chulainn in the General Post Office: 'A figure of the dying Cúchulainn complete with daemoniac raven droops over the most historic spot of the modern Ireland. To anyone who has read the original of the Ulster Cycle Saga all this is nauseating ... Cúchulainn is a treacherous, blood-thirsty, magical, half-human freak, and worse.' For Ó Néill in 1941, the Ulster warriors were 'a barbarous, half-savage people who had reached a stage of civilisation similar to that of some of the African tribes of our times' (*IR*, Jan. 1941, pp 29–31).[32]

Obviously finding the exploits of Fionn and his men more congenial, he turned to Kuno Meyer's 1885 edition of *Cath Finntrágha* as inspiration for his first play.[33] Not content with simply staging the heroic determination of the son of the king of Ulster to join Fionn in his fight against the invading forces of the king of the world, Ó Néill introduced a whole new plotline into his play. In *Buaidh an Ultaigh*, Fionn and the wife of the king of Ulster plot to do away with the king so that they can be together. While the queen anguishes over her planned treachery, Fionn, who was, by the way, played in the Comhar Drámaíochta production by Ó Néill's fellow Gaelic playwright Gearóid Ó Lochlainn, takes the scheme a step further, deciding to get the king's beloved only son Goll killed. When word reaches Ulster of the invasion at Ventry, Fionn sets out to join the Fianna, but, as in the original tale, the king imprisons his son and his followers for their own protection. The men escape – in Ó Néill's play with the help of the queen. In a brief moment of decency, Fionn, aware of his mother's love for the young man, tries to keep him from single combat with the redoubtable enemy hero Dursa Dorbha, but the Fianna, fearful the Ulstermen will make the decision to keep the young man from combat as an attempt to shame them, send him to meet Dursa Dorbha, whom he fights and kills, losing his own life in the encounter. Returning to Ulster after the battle, Fionn boasts of a victory for which he deserves little credit and becomes angry when the queen praises Goll as the true champion. The king, on the other hand, brokenheartedly thanks Fionn for allowing his son to win glory. The king's tragic nobility only adds to his wife's remorse, and in a disappointing anticlimax the play ends with her dismissing the ruthless and still guilt-free Fionn.

What is most striking about this play, apart from the addition of the whole subplot involving Fionn's dalliance with the queen, is the unedifying picture it presents of the leader of the Fianna. In his essay on 'Gaelic literature' for the first volume of Robert Hogan's *Dictionary of Irish Literature*, Ó Néill called *Cath Finntrágha* 'perhaps the most impressive of the stories in which the Fianna play the role of protecting their native land', but wrote of Fionn that throughout the Fenian Cycle in general 'he cuts a rather unstable figure'.[34] 'Unstable' would seem charitable in describing his behaviour in *Buaidh an Ultaigh*. Indeed when his single ethical act in the play, his attempt to keep Goll from combat, is overruled by the Fianna, Fionn, Pilate-like, absolves himself of the consequences: 'Good enough. Do what you want. His death will not be my fault at any rate.'[35] Earlier, we see him as a vacillating, even cowardly figure, when he refuses to fight Dursa Dorbha himself, an act of self-preservation that Goll finds contemptible: 'Why doesn't he go to fight Dursa Dorbha. I always believed that there was not a man on the surface of the earth whom Fionn feared.'[36] When the queen defends Fionn by pointing out that as a leader he could not endanger himself since the fall of the leader meant the defeat of his cause, Goll sarcastically replies: 'And it's likely that it is the leaders and the lords who started that custom.'[37] It should also be noted that as a son of Co. Down, Ó Néill makes his Ulstermen in this play a far more impressive group of self-sacrificing warriors than are the southerner Fionn and his Fianna.[38] While Ó Néill tries to cram far too much into such a short play, none of those things represent the kind of provocative thought that he wanted to see in modern Irish literature. Instead we get a straightforward staging of an episode from the early literature spiced up with the possibility of an illicit love affair and overlaid with Ulster bombast. He would do far better with this kind of material when he returned to it 20 years later.

Díolta faoi n-a Luach was published by An Gúm in 1946, but according to Máiréad Ní Shé had been written 13 years earlier. It was serialised in the Dundalk *Examiner* from 19 June to 17 July 1937, although it seems not to have been performed until actors from the Gaelic League's Craobh na gCúig gCúigí produced it at Feis Átha Cliath in 1947, where it won second prize (*II*, 28/4/47). It was broadcast over Radio Éireann twice in February 1947 and again in September 1952. Ó Néill took his inspiration here from history rather than literature, although, as has been noted above, the poet Peadar Ó Doirnín is among his characters. While with time Ó Néill came to see little value in the play,[39] he must have been stung by Niall Ó Domhnaill's review of the published text. Ó Domhnaill gave credit to Ó Néill as a 'proficient writer' (scríbhneoir oilte) who could catch and hold an audience's attention, and declared that there were few plays in Irish 'as suitable as this to put on the stage' (chomh fóirsteanach le cur ar an stáitse leis). He then, however, continued: 'He had scope in the material for the great ideas that lift the mind out of the mundane caves in which our souls are pent up throughout our lives, but he did not put them into the mind of poet or hero.' For Ó Domhnaill, the play was entertaining enough, but when he put it down and 'I asked myself if there were any ideas in it worth the author's bringing Séamus Mac Murchadha and Peadar Ó Doirnín to life to reveal, I cannot say there are' (*Comhar*, Apr. 1947, p. 4).[40] At least one other critic, his future publisher Seán Ó hÉigeartaigh, was more impressed after reading the text:

The piece has its faults of construction and some of its situations are inadequately developed, as though the author tired of them halfway and passed hurriedly on, but it hints within its small compass of that incessant conflict between the demands of the flesh for the comforts of life and the whisper of the spirit for its glories which must have racked our fathers faced with a struggle against terrible deeds. (*Bell*, Mar. 1947, p. 78)

Set in southeast Ulster in the mid eighteenth century, *Díolta faoi n-a Luach* shows that even early in his career Ó Néill could, as Ó hÉigeartaigh suggested (and Ó Domhnaill denied), draw lessons of contemporary relevance from the Irish past to whose study he had devoted so much time and effort. Here he shows how quite different people with quite different motives try to balance the demands of physical and psychic security against the call of a fuller and freer life for themselves and their country. Ó hÉigeartaigh was quite right that the time of the play was a terrible one for the Irish people, but it is important to understand it was also a diminished time, with memories of significant popular resistance to colonial rule fading into the past and the stirring and horrific deeds of the 1798 Rising still in the unforeseeable future. The parallels with the economic depression and wartime uncertainty of Ó Néill's own Ireland in the 1930s and 1940s are at the very least suggestive.

The basic plot of the play is simple enough. Peig, the daughter of the miserly publican Paitsí an tSléibhe, is in love with the local highwayman Séamus Mac Murchadha (a historical figure also known as 'An Beirneach'), but when she becomes convinced that he is courting another woman, she plots with her father to sell him out to the colonial authorities for a reward of 50 guineas. Discovering later that he really does love her, she tries in vain to save him, but he is arrested in her father's tavern and will presumably be executed in the near future. The play ends with Peig, like Pegeen Mike at the end of Synge's *The Playboy of the Western World*, realising her own complicity with the materialistic cowards who have betrayed her lover. When her father says 'Fifty guineas, Peig. You will yet get all that I have,' the stage directions read: 'She raises her head, stares at him for a moment, then she trembles in front of him.'[41]

Political apathy and ultimately collaboration are the responses of Paitsí an tSléibhe to the oppression under which he lives, oppression personified by Seonstanach na gCeann (Johnston of the heads, a historical character known in English as 'Johnston of the Fews'), the fearsome leader of the local militia. Paitsí is cynical about the anti-English activities of Mac Murchadha, telling Peig: 'Isn't it all the same to you and to me who is in power in the country. We will plant in the spring and reap in the fall, and we will earn our share with the sweat of our brows, whether the Irish or the English are in power in Dublin Castle.'[42] When Peig argues that it is a poor thing to be ruled by foreigners, Paitsí responds: 'It is far worse to be under the control of your own people – you can believe that.'[43] And, in a surprising show of backbone, he later tells Mac Murchadha to his face that he is no Robin Hood: 'I have often heard tell of those men who take the money from the big churls and give it to the poor; but you, what you can't take from the big churls you take from the poor. Shouldn't you be ashamed?'[44] Initially content to simply make a living by serving all paying customers – he tells Peig he has nothing against the English for 'any of them who ever came in here paid for what he drank' (fear ar bith acu a tháinig isteach annseo ariamh, d'íoc sé as an méid a d'ól sé) – he is eventually led by his greed to turn informer in the clear belief that submission to the power of the state offers him the greatest security.

Peig is a more complex character. Rejecting her father's cynical views about Mac Murchadha, she praises him as an Irish patriot: 'It is a good thing that not everyone has the same attitude as you. The English would not be in power in Ireland if we had more men like An Beirneach.'[45] But she is also well aware of the daunting odds Mac Murchadha faces in this struggle, responding to his rather cavalier disregard for Seonstanach na gCeann: 'The power of England is behind him: It does not matter how many children he leaves without fathers, the power of England will be behind him.'[46] She is, however, her father's daughter in her own capacity for cynicism, in her case directed at Peadar Ó Doirnín.

Ó Néill admired Ó Doirnín as a poet, calling him 'a superb artist in the Irish language' and stating that 'no Irish poet has ever achieved greater musical effect than has Ó Doirnín in his song "Úr-Chnoc Chéin Mhic Cáinte" [The newly cultivated hill of Cian mac Cáinte].'[47] The Ó Doirnín of this play is, however, a pitiful figure haunted by the loss of an idealised Gaelic past:

> I often become discouraged when I think of the helplessness of the Irish. But now and again visions come to me – visions in which the Gaels appear to be gathering strength again. I see men fully armed hurrying to battle. I see that and dread coming over the English ... Perhaps it is only that my heart's desire is getting relief in that way, but the visions that come into a poet's mind, who will say that there is not in them knowledge gotten on the edge of eternity.[48]

One who will say so and immediately does is Peig, who responds to these fantasies: 'It's not visions you're having at all but fantasies, Peadar Ó Doirnín.'[49] What Peig wants is for Ó Doirnín and his fellow poets to create works of real contemporary relevance, songs to encourage resistance and satires directed against the enemy. She finds Ó Doirnín's impeccably rational reply timid if not downright cowardly: 'It wasn't fear of Johnston of the Heads that was in my heart, no indeed. And I would strike a blow, if I were in the place to strike it. But it would be no use for me and a swarm of redcoat soldiers with him. He would be more than happy to get the chance to put my head up on a spike above Dundalk Prison.'[50] In the end Peig shames him into composing a satire on Seonstanach na gCeann, intending to use it not to rally the Irish but to convince its target that it was actually written by Mac Murchadha and so set him in even hotter pursuit of the rapparee.

The most interesting character in the play is Mac Murchadha himself. Clearly meant to be a powerful and charismatic figure, he is also a highly conflicted one. He is capable of a hard-headed understanding of exactly what English rule has meant for Gaelic Ireland: 'Don't you know well there is no longer noble nor lowborn person? We are all slaves. Lords, earls, we are all in the slough of ruin since the English defeated us.'[51] But he is also tired of leadership and of fighting an enemy against which he has no chance of significant, much less ultimate success: 'It is often when I am out in the depth of the woods on a dark night that that thought comes into my mind, and I want to go into Dundalk Town and make peace with the English.'[52] Better yet, he longs to flee Ireland altogether, taking Peig to Spain, 'somewhere where the sun is always shining, far away from Ireland where the grief and oppression are always with us' (áit éighinteacht i n-a mbíonn an ghrian ag soillsiú i gcomhnuidhe, i bhfad ar shiubhal ó Éireann mar a shiubhlas an léan agus an leathtrom linn de shíor). Indeed he goes so far as to confess to Peig that he is simply tired of being afraid: 'O God, if I did not have to fight any more, not have that awful fear that you have when you are lying in ambush for the English . . . My heart is always trembling in my chest, Peig, although my men think that I am confident.'[53] As the play ends, he has committed himself to leaving Ireland with Peig, only to have his dream – and hers – shattered by the treachery she has helped set in motion and by the cruel realities of the time and place in which they live.

If *Díolta faoi n-a Luach* was a major advance over *Buaidh an Ultaigh* – it even had a flashback scene indicated by pale blue lighting, a surprising technical innovation for the Gaelic stage at that time[54] – his next play *'Ní Chuireann Siad Síol' nó 'Poll Bocht'*, first published in *An t-Ultach* in July 1939[55] and given its premiere as one of three one-acters by An Comhar Drámaíochta at the Peacock in December 1940, is little more than a skit.[56] Set in London in 1761, the play deals with an imagined episode in the life of the expatriate Irish writer Oliver Goldsmith.[57] While the play might have been of real interest had Ó Néill addressed the question of Goldsmith's Irishness, he unfortunately instead took this little one-acter in a different direction. Actually, he seems to have seen little or nothing Irish in the work of Goldsmith and other eighteenth-century Irish-born writers of English, stating in his 1946 essay 'Ba sráidbhaile Sasanach an "Deserted Village"' ('The Deserted Village' was an English village): 'Would I call him [Goldsmith] an Irish writer? I would not, nor even Anglo-Irish, but rather an English writer.' And he took pains to deny that there was anything distinctively Irish about Goldsmith's humour: 'The sense of humour he had was his own; it was neither Gaelic nor English. It was a trait that left a deep mark on his writing; it was a trait that distinguished him from his acquaintances here in Ireland and over in England' (*Indiu*, 24/8/46).[58] For Ó Néill, Goldsmith was in the final analysis a kind of 'classic writer' (scríbhneoir clasíceach [*sic*]).

While Goldsmith's literary genius is confirmed in this play by no less an authority than 'An Dr Somhairle Johnson', it is not primarily as a literary figure that he is presented. Instead, we see him as a hapless debtor besieged by a landlady with romantic intentions, shopkeepers calling in their credit, a bailiff who insists he is just following orders,[59] and the entitled and pompous Dr Johnson. If Ó Néill seems to have had little or no interest in Goldsmith's nationality as a writer, he does depict him as a proud Irishman in his responses to the ignorantly Hibernophobic bailiff and the other English characters. Faced with having his bed repossessed, Goldsmith states: 'Many of the poor people in Ireland lie on scattered straw, and I have to say that it is far cleaner than many of the beds that I have seen throughout England.'[60] More pointed is his view of the English in general: 'It must be that all of the people of England are bailiffs.'[61] When the play was published, Sean O' Boyle wrote dismissively: 'Although it was produced once by An Comhar Drámaíochta it is surely not intended to be taken seriously by adult dramatic groups' (*Irish Bookman*, Dec. 1946, p. 70). That judgement seems unduly harsh; probably the fairest thing to say about the play is that we need not put any more thought into it than did Ó Néill himself.

The situation is quite different with his next play. Initially serialised in *An t-Ultach* from October 1941 through April 1942, *Colm Cille* was first performed over Radio Éireann on the saint's feast day, 9 June, in 1943. It does not seem to have had a stage production. The life and legends of Colm Cille were a major interest of Ó Néill's, and in addition to this play he wrote an unpublished pageant entitled *Naomh Colmcille* to commemorate the one thousand four hundredth anniversary of the saint's departure into self-exile on Iona in 563. The pageant, directed by Tomás Mac Anna, contained 14 scenes and involved some 300 performers drawn from the students of the Carysfort Training College.[62] Among those in the audience on opening night were President Éamon de Valera and his wife Sinéad, who had herself acted in some of the earliest Gaelic League productions in Dublin. After watching the pageant, the anonymous critic for *The Irish Press* wrote of Ó Néill that 'he showed that he had made a close study of the life of Colm Cille' (theaspáin sé go raibh grinn-staidéar déanta aige ar shaol Cholum Cille); of Mac Anna that 'it would be difficult to find fault in his directing' (ba deacair locht d'fháil ar a chuid léiritheoireachta); and of the production as a whole:

'There were few faults in the scenery, the music, the acting, and the direction, and praise is due to the students of the college' (*IP*, 28/4/63).[63] Scenes from the pageant were later performed in 'many parts of the country', an 'English version of the whole' was produced in Northern Ireland, and the entire piece was broadcast over Radio Éireann.[64]

In a 1946 essay on 'An fhírinne fá Cholum Cille' (The truth about Colm Cille) in *An Iris*, Ó Néill began by stating that the real Colm Cille had been 'lost in the fog of legend' (caillte i gceo na finn-scéaluidheachta) for centuries. In an attempt to cut through this fog he offered a scholarly analysis of the biographical sources we have for the saint, discussed Colm's reputation as a poet, examined the reasons he went into exile, and supported Rudolf Thurneysen's opinion that it was under the influence of Colm Cille, with his command of both the native tradition and Latin learning, that the writing of Irish began on Iona.[65] Ó Néill was here working on what was to be a lifelong project to get at the historical facts about Colm Cille. Among the pieces he published or broadcast about the saint over the years were 'The biographers of St Colmcille' (Radio Éireann, 8/6/42), 'The historical Columcille' (Radio Éireann, 16/9/44), 'Columcille's greatness' (*IT*, 14/6/63), and 'Life and death of Colmcille' (*IP*, 25/10/67). Moreover, it was Ó Néill who delivered a lecture under the auspices of the Legion of Mary to open the ceremonies celebrating the one thousand four hundredth anniversary of Colm Cille's voyage to Iona, telling his audience that 'thanks to the biography by Adamnán . . . Columcille stood out as a clear-cut historical figure against a background wherein his contemporaries were as shadows' (*II*, 23/5/63).[66]

Needless to say, his Colm Cille play was a more modest effort than was the pageant. And once again it was an effort that disappointed its author.[67] In this case his meticulous research seems to have stifled his imagination. Debating Aodh de Blácam on the radio in 1936 on the resolution 'that Ireland had left a grand mark in world history and is yet again a force in the world', Ó Néill took the iconoclastic position that 'the mark left by Ireland was vastly exaggerated and that many Irishmen developed a "superiority complex" in regard to the "Ireland of the Saints and Scholars"' (*IP*, 24/7/36). When he published the text of *Colm Cille* in 1946, he included beneath his cast of characters 'a historical note' (nóta staire): 'For long enough after the death of St Patrick there was intense competition going on in Ireland between the old world of paganism and the new world of Christianity.'[68] The kind of thinking we find in these two statements could have produced a far more interesting play than the one we have. (Indeed, as we will see, the issue of post-Patrician paganism plays a significant and effective role in his later play *Iníon Rí Dhún Sobhairce*.) Reviewing a production of Thomas Kilroy's *The Great O'Neill* at the Abbey in 1969, Ó Néill wrote:

It has been said that every attempt at putting O'Connell on the stage has failed because the playwright has always fallen between O'Connell the man, and O'Connell the public figure, and any dramatist writing a play about Hugh O'Neill, who was a much more complex figure than O'Connell, must be confronted with the same difficulty. (*IP*, 6/6/69)

One must wonder if his own attempt to bring Colm Cille alive on stage a quarter of a century earlier was in his mind at all here.

At any rate, *Colm Cille* is a rather wooden and predictable piece of dramatic hagiography. We certainly see the saint's faults, but they are all faults central to his legend. Thus we discover that Colm Cille's pride in his royal Uí Néill blood crosses easily into arrogance,[69] as does his sense of himself as a poet in the native tradition; that he borders on heresy in his defence of the traditional Irish reckoning of the date for Easter; and that his stubborn refusal to admit he was wrong in copying a borrowed manuscript results in many deaths at the battle of Cúl Dreimhne. None of this is new, but Ó Néill does offer a few suggestive insights into the saint's personality and motivations. Explaining his famous defence of the poets threatened with banishment at Druim Cett in 575, Colm Cille not only addresses the charge that the poets are agents of paganism, but questions whether native paganism might actually have had its virtues: 'I admit that the poets had the old pagan learning, I admit that they have some of it still, and that many of them are reluctant to give it up completely, and I say to you, High-King of Ireland, and to you, the high-born and nobles, that something is not evil because it is pagan.'[70] Invoking the example of St Patrick, he declares: 'He never commanded us to put an end to the old pagan learning either; to tell the truth he asked us to save it, to write it down, as you know; so that we would know how educated, how noble, how learned our ancestors were, our pagan ancestors . . .'[71] He also turns the tables on his opponents, impugning the motives behind their own adherence to Christianity: 'I will not allow anyone, however high-up . . . to use the Church as a support for his benefit. I will not allow anyone, however high-up . . . to use the Church for his own worldly purpose . . . I will not allow anyone to distort or falsify the teaching of the Church for his own benefit.'[72]

Later Colm Cille presents himself as a defender of the prerogatives of the Church against the state, in the person of the High-King Diarmuid mac Cearbhaill, who demands he turn over a killer to whom Colm Cille has granted sanctuary.[73] His pious claim that he is only serving the one heavenly high-king he recognises is, however, almost immediately undercut when we see him fly into a very earthly and personal rage after Diarmuid has the refugee killed: 'My curse on you, dishonest king, my thousand curses. You will answer for this deed to the Northern Uí Néill. I will call the hosts of my kinsmen to arms.'[74] Urged by his friend Gemman – a more conventionally saintly character in the play than is his abbot – to apologise to the king for the carnage he has caused, Colm Cille says he is simply incapable of doing so, for 'I would not be doing penance, but shaming my kinsmen, insulting the brave men who fell for my sake at Cúl Dreimhne.'[75] Instead, he will go into exile on Iona, making his great missionary project the result of his pig-headed pride rather than an act of Christian self-sacrifice. Indeed if we were to judge from this play alone, we could see the foundation of the monastery of Iona and all that followed it as an act of escapism rooted in Colm Cille's inability to come to terms with the complexities of a world shared with other people. As he tells Gemman just before he leaves Derry, 'I am not fit for the work that is yet to be done here. I am too quick-tempered. Over in Scotland it will be easier. It will be dangerous, perhaps, but white will be white and black will be black. The person on my side will be on my side, and the person against me will be against me.'[76]

Unfortunately, Ó Néill was too much the historian, too faithful to his sources, to follow the intriguing leads he himself introduced in his play.[77] Instead of an insight into Colm Cille as a self-conscious religious syncretist, a transitional figure straddling pagan and Christian worlds, a man torn between the conflicting demands of ancestral pride and pious self-control, an authoritarian personality unable to accommodate ambiguity, we get a fairly one-dimensional – and to be honest quite unlikeable – figure whom Ó Néill himself may have come to feel he could more effectively honour in the unquestioning mode of a celebratory pageant.

It is difficult to figure what Ó Néill was trying to do with the slight one-act *An Tusa d'Fhoscail an Fhuinneog?* The play opens with a BBC announcer telling us that it is the tenth anniversary of the end of the Second World War. We then see Adolf Hitler, who escaped the bunker in Berlin and is now attempting to once again impose his will on the world, meeting a scientist who has invented a weapon that will let him get vengeance on 'the skulking Jews' (na hIúdaigh bhradacha) by destroying cities around the world as the Allies did Berlin and Dresden.[78] Eva Braun attempts to reason with Hitler, telling him they could be happy as they once had been in Berchtesgaden when he had claimed to be willing to sacrifice politics for her. In her mind, a new war will only lead to greater misery for the German people. Her opinion is later supported by the ghost of Göring, who points out the results of Hitler's previous megalomania and tells him that he will only fail again if he uses his new weapon. As the play ends, Hitler awakens after what seems only a minute or two, only to have Braun enter and tell him – and us – that it is the fifteenth anniversary of the war's end. Other than advancing the hardly contro-versial view of Hitler as a deluded psychopath, this forgettable minor work tells us nothing of interest about either the man or his murderous movement.[79]

Also of little significance is his next play, the one-act farce *Up the Rebels*, his only attempt at comedy. To be fair, we should not expect much from the play, written for his students at Carysfort and first performed there in 1952. The work is set in 1920 in an upper-class Anglo-Irish household in Rathgar; the main characters are two sisters burdened with a pet parrot that repeatedly cries out 'Up the Rebels!' While the sisters are unionists born and bred, one of them, Edith, has a suppressed sympathy for a local rebel. When English soldiers arrive to search the house, they show no understanding of, much less respect for, either the sisters' Anglo-Irish identity or their unionism. When one of the soldiers hears the parrot cry 'Up the Rebels!' he shoots the bird, inspiring Edith herself to shout the republican slogan. The most interesting thing about this trifling play is that it represents the first time Ó Néill puts Irish into the mouths of characters who would never have spoken it in real life.[80] As we have seen, this question of linguistic verisimilitude has been and to some extent continues to be a vexed question for writers of Irish, calling into question the very possibility of a contemporary Gaelic literature not set in the past, in the Gaeltacht, in the rather hothouse atmosphere of Irish-speaking enclaves in Anglophone Ireland, or in exotic or purely internal realms. For example, in his essay 'Drámaíocht Ghaeilge san am atá le teacht' (Irish-language drama in the future), no less an authority on the successful production of plays in Irish than Micheál Mac Liammóir wrote: 'But until Irish is the usual language in the mouths of the Irish people – and no one knows when that day will come – there's no need for us to be dreaming any more about the school of Realism coming to our aid. Nor is there any need for us to be thinking about the Popular Drama.'[81] Despite his own fondness for plays set in the Irish past, Ó Néill rejected this argument. When in 1962 an interviewer asked 'Isn't it difficult to give an account in Irish of events that "happen in English", as you would say?', he responded: 'I cannot say, because it's not in English that things happen. Pádraic Ó Conaire doesn't have a Gaeltacht setting in his best stories, and when I'm reading them, I don't notice what language he is using, and isn't that the best proof that he is a writer.'[82] Ó Néill would confront this challenge much more directly and effectively in his next play.[83]

An tSiúr Pól was first heard over Radio Éireann on 2 January 1960 and first performed on stage at An Damer in November 1963 under the direction of Tomás Mac Anna. Reviewing the play for the *Irish Independent*, Earnán P. de Blaghd was not all that impressed, calling it 'not an altogether convincing play of convent life' (*II*, 18/11/63). Worth noting in de Blaghd's review, however, is that he did not see the play's being less than convincing as a function of its linguistic medium, but rather because it presents 'an image of convent life' that will not be 'familiar to a lay visitor or acceptable to

Reverend Mothers' (*II*, 18/11/63).[84]Yet given that the play is set in a convent in a midlands town and one of the characters is an Irish-American nun (in de Blaghd's view 'an impossibly stage American nun'), it seems safe to assume that Ó Néill is once again putting Irish into the mouths of characters unlikely to have used it regularly if at all. And *pace* de Blaghd, Seán J.White tells us that a reader of the text for An Gúm was so impressed by Ó Néill's presentation of the nuns that he suggested the play had been written by one (*IP*, 18/11/63).[85] It was, at any rate, the most serious literary work in Irish dealing with convent life to that time. It is also a play in which Ó Néill was able to bring his fascination with his favourite saint into the present in the character of the mother superior, An Mháthair Colm Cille.

In effect, the play shows the reverend mother dealing quite competently with the kinds of challenges and crises that would have pushed her namesake over the edge. In the first place, she wants to build a new secondary school and build it in the most modern style, convinced that the boring timidity of Catholic architecture in Ireland is the product of a post-penal laws inferiority complex and a fear of drawing the ire of Protestants. Her ambition here will bring her into conflict with the reactionary priest of the parish in which the convent is located, who wants the new school built in impeccably conventional style and offering vocational training to keep young people at home.When the priest lashes out at contemporary fashions and the desire of the young to emigrate to England and 'go to the devil there' (dul chun an diabhail ansin), the mother superior draws on her own experience in England in her reply: 'Perhaps, Father, if they had more permission here to go to the devil as they want, that it is here and not over in England that they would be getting married.' And when he calls her an 'odd' (ait) nun, she responds pointedly: 'Perhaps I am an odd person, but I am not an odd nun. Being a nun does not mean blinding your mind to the truth of the world.'[86]

One of the hard truths she herself has to face up to is the whole question of mixed marriage and the Church's demand, set forth in the *Ne Temere* decree, that the non-Catholic partner in such a marriage should convert and must consent to raise all children as Catholics.[87]When her niece falls in love with a Protestant, abstract law becomes human tragedy as An Mháthair Colm Cille cannot condone the union. Her discussion with the niece's fiancé shows both her conviction and her humanity as she argues that he should convert out of simple love for her niece rather than for any theological or doctrinal reasons. Moreover, she is entirely sympathetic about his reluctance to abandon the faith and tradition in which he was raised. She argues that the Church itself would not expect him to do so: 'It does not agree with human nature to do that, and that is the reason that the Church is not favourably disposed to marriage between Catholic and Protestant. It knows the result too well.'[88] Obviously, she is no ecumenical liberal, but she does at least show considerable understanding of the very real suffering adherence to even the most sincerely and profoundly held beliefs can cause.

The third issue on her mind – and the one least satisfactorily developed, much less resolved, despite the play's title – is the campaign for the canonisation of An tSiúr Pól, the founder of her order. This subplot does, however, allow Ó Néill to introduce An tSiúr Breandán, an Irish-American nun from San Francisco whose naiveté about Ireland and on occasion tactless curiosity about An tSiúr Pól and her family inspire some interesting and humorous dialogue. For example, at one point she rhapsodises about the ancestral homeland she is seeing for the first time: 'Haven't I always heard that this is the land of peace and tranquillity, the only place in the world that has not surrendered to the hurry and rush of our time?'[89] She later scandalises the parish priest with some of her opinions, prompting the following over-the-top outburst from him: 'That's the kind of talk the Communists have, and the other atheists when they comment on the attempts we are making to keep Irish girls from their devilry.'[90] She does manage to gather some information on An tSiúr Pól, but, as noted above, the venerated founder remains a cipher for the audience, and the whole campaign for her canonisation is pretty much lost in the play's other, more engaging narrative strands.

One purpose the American nun does serve is to introduce the idea of sending the mother superior's niece to San Francisco for a spell so that she can ponder from a distance her marriage plans and her future. She certainly seems to need some time to think more clearly as, frustrated by her aunt's refusal to support her marriage plans, she suddenly decides instead she should enter the convent. Interesting here is her conception of the cloister as a place of perpetual 'quiet' (ciúnas) and 'peace' (síocháin). While her aunt says she would be delighted were her niece to have a genuine vocation, she doubts she does and rejects her notion of convent life as a tranquil refuge from the real world and all its ambiguities: 'But you have to understand, Síle, that it is not just comfort that would be in store for you as a nun.'[91] Convent life certainly is no refuge for herself, as her heart is soon broken by the niece's elopement to the United States with her fiancé, and she shortly thereafter learns that the bishop has sided with the parish priest against her dream of building a modern secondary school. Instead, the bishop wants the order to build a school in Africa, and she has decided to undertake the mission personally.

Ó Néill should have believed in the play more and foregone naming his protagonist An Mháthair Colm Cille and having her explicitly make the connection between herself and the saint.[92] Parallels between the two are everywhere. She struggles with complex religious and personal challenges, finds her fondest dreams thwarted by people, often those in authority, of far less vision and courage than herself, and goes off to missionary work despite her profound love for her home place and her friends. When he learns of her coming departure, the parish priest tells her how much she will be missed, but also says: 'You are a woman with a mind of your own. You would like to have your own way.'[93] But if she is strong-minded and confident, she does not share the arrogance of Colm Cille or his inability to cope with complexity. In a way, she comes to see her exile as a reward for fulfilling the less stirring but still meaningful responsibilities to which she has devoted her life in the convent. More than either An tSiúr Pól or Colm Cille, she is the real saint in the play, a pragmatic, wry, wise, and fully human one.

With his next play, *Iníon Rí Dhún Sobhairce*, Ó Néill returned to the world of early Irish saga literature for the first time since his apprentice effort *Buaidh an Ultaigh*. Directed by Seán Ó hÓráin, this Oireachtas prizewinning play had its premiere at Taibhdhearc na Gaillimhe in 1953.[94] It was produced at the 37 Theatre Club in Dublin later the same year with Barra Casson directing.[95] In 1966 it was performed by students from Queen's University at the Irish Universities Drama Festival in An Taibhdhearc and at the Ulster Gaelic Drama Festival in Armagh, and in 1981 'there was a very polished one-night production' (bhí léiriú aon-oíche an-snasta) of the play at Carysfort (*IP*, 22/1/82). Radio Éireann presented the play in January and December 1954, with Siobhán McKenna in the title role for the December broadcast. Reviewing the premiere, the anonymous critic for *The Connacht Tribune* stated: 'The story is convincing and retains interest all through. The Taibhdhearc cast combined excellently to make this a brilliant production' (*CT*, 3/7/53).[96] Less impressed was 'L.', who stated in his review for *Inniu* that while there were 'beautiful pieces of writing in it, at times poetry' (píosaí álainn scríbhneoireachta ann, ar amannta filíocht), 'the scenes are put together without the coherence that would give them unity and would affect the audience member' (*Inniu*, 10/7/53).[97] Writing in anticipation of the 1953 Dublin production, Niall Carroll called Ó Néill 'about the best of the living Irish dramatists writing in the native tongue' and reported that he had heard 'this is his finest piece to date', adding: 'It is a powerful drama with at least one part of the sort which any young actress would dream about' (*IP*, 2/11/53).

An anonymous critic for the same paper felt the play lived up to its advance publicity, calling it 'a tragedy of considerable power' and declaring that 'it provides a devastating answer to the Jeremiahs who see no future for Irish on the stage' (*IP*, 12/12/53).[98] Reviewing the published text in 1961, Pearse Hutchinson called it 'a good play, an extremely good play – one that clamours for immediate revival'. Hutchinson continued: 'After a gentle opening, the play soon vibrates, with gathering menace, towards what nearly reaches classic tragedy.' Moreover, he wrote that Ó Néill was one of 'remark-ably few' playwrights who was 'possessed luxuriously' of 'one of the best gifts a dramatist can have . . . that of dialogue' and that 'the play abounds in stirring passages between major antagonists, and – here's the point – they're always worthy of each other's mettle' (*IP*, 30/3/61).[99] His fellow playwright Micheál Ó hAodha wrote of the play: 'Séamus Ó Néill has done something extraordinary by providing a proper play in Irish. Given the state of drama in Irish, not only is an accomplishment like that a source of wonder, but it's almost a miracle . . .' (*Comhar*, Mar. 1961, p. 26).[100] The poet Máirtín Ó Direáin felt that not since Micheál Mac Liammóir had there been any Gaelic playwright working with historical or legendary material who had attempted anything 'as interesting and ambitious as had Séamus Ó Néill in this play' (chomh spéisiúil ná chomh ard-aidhmeannach is rinne Séamus Ó Néill san dráma seo) (*Feasta*, Jan. 1954, p. 13).[101] 'T. Ó H.' was even more laudatory in *Inniu*, stating that the play was 'comparable to Yeats's "Countess Cathleen"' (ionchomparáid le 'Countess Cathleen' Yeats): 'The styles are very similar, and there is the same conflict between the old pagan Ireland and the newly arrived Christianity. I think that it is as good, and in some ways better, than Yeats's play' (*Inniu*, 18/12/53).[102]

Ó Néill had clearly thought a good deal about the dramatic potential of early Irish literature since writing *Buaidh an Ultaigh* 20 years earlier. The potential of this particular source, *Fingal Rónáin* from the twelfth-century *Book of Leinster*,[103] was, as Ó Néill later recalled, suggested to him by his friend, the great Irish scholar Michael O'Brien: 'One day he handed me a handwritten copy of an old story in Irish, a copy he had written himself and he said to me, "Make a play from that."'[104] Writing of *Fingal Rónáin* in his essay on 'Gaelic literature' in the first edition of Robert Hogan's *Dictionary of Irish Literature* in 1979, Ó Néill stated that 'the story has come down to us as little more than a synopsis, which was perhaps intended to be filled out by the storyteller'.[105] It seems obvious that Ó Néill felt liberated by both the creative possibilities allowed by such a text and by the fact that, as the tale's editor David Greene has pointed out, 'the historical basis of *Fingal Rónáin* is vague enough'.[106] At any rate, he takes considerable liberties with the text, in the process focusing the play's action while expanding its thematic range. Needless to say, he retains the powerful main plot of the original, the story of a young woman married to the elderly king Rónán but in love with his son Mael Fhothartaigh, whose rejection of her advances turns that love into hatred, driving her to bring about his death and ultimately her own destruction and that of her whole family. However, whereas the woman in the original story is at least initially a rather stereotypical character in the Deirdre and Gráinne mode[107] – she is never even given a name but simply identified as 'ingin Echach' (Eochaid's daughter) – Ó Néill makes his Dáirine a far more complex figure, frustrated by her marriage to an authoritarian old man, homesick for her native place, surrounded by spies, and all but imprisoned in her husband's *dún* or fort. To heighten our sense of her isolation and confinement, Ó Néill adds scenes involving Rónán, who, while he is an ineffectual and self-deluded old man in *Fingal Rónáin*, is a more authoritarian, though considerably less likeable, character in *Iníon Rí Dhún Sobhairce*. The conflict between Rónán and Dáirine is most evident in a scene Ó Néill has added in which the queen disobeys her husband's command that she not leave the *dún* unless in his company. Although she stands up to him when caught out in the open air, there is no mistaking the threat when he tells her 'If you don't have the manners natural to a queen, they will have to be taught to you.'[108] Rónán's expectations of her are underscored by the comments of Congal, in the original tale a foster-brother of Mael Fhothartaigh but here the king's devious advisor and spy,[109] who boasts of how he restricts his own wife's freedom of movement and activity. Moreover, by introducing a clear thematic contrast between the beauty and freedom of nature and the oppressive restrictions of life in the *dún*, Ó Néill provides a credible motive for the early evolution of Dáirine's deadly malice.

In addition, Ó Néill introduces two original characters who enable him to develop a theme of continuing interest to him but absent from his source. As noted earlier, Ó Néill was well aware that paganism had survived, at times quite robustly, in Ireland well after the time of St Patrick. Here he explores the tensions between that recalcitrant paganism and the officially sanctioned Christianity through the characters of the bishop and the *bean feasa* (wise woman). At one point the *bean feasa* boasts of the powers she has inherited from her druidic forebears as stronger than those of her Christian adversaries: 'They are all under the spell of this superstition that was brought from the east, and so they are afraid of me. They would like to banish me, but fear won't let them do it. They are afraid that I would draw misfortune and destruction down on them.'[110] Ó Néill's bishop is an ominous figure. In one scene, in which the playwright has what for him is a rare recourse to expressionism, he presents the bishop appearing 'stealthily out of a corner' (*formhothaithe as cúinne*) and adds: 'It would be better to show him behind a kind of light gauze with light revealing him; and to darken the rest of the stage in such a way that it is not possible to be certain whether he is there or not.' If, however, Ó Néill is here using the bishop as the externalised voice of Dáirine's conscience, it is an imperious and repressive voice, and thus it comes as no surprise that one of its commands to her is 'Return to the house'.[111]

Dáirine is attracted to the *bean feasa* from the outset, not least because of the fear the woman inspires in priest and bishop, and as the play goes on, her own paganism becomes ever more explicit. Thus when she is told by the bishop to accept her unhappy marriage as 'God's will' (Toil Dé) – a very powerful theme in Gaelic literature right into the 1950s – she replies contemptuously:

I will not listen to you. You do not know what God wills. Does God always will the thing that is contemptible and corrupt and disgusting? That is what anyone would understand from you . . . But I do not believe in your god any more. The old gods our ancestors had were better. They were cruel perhaps, but they were great and imposing and terrifying.[112]

By the play's end, even Rónán himself reveals that paganism has retained a grip on his mind as he is terrified by his breaking of a *geis* (a kind of magical injunction) imposed on him by the *bean feasa*.[113]

Ó Néill adds other details to flesh out what he called the 'synopsis' provided by his source. For instance, he introduces the idea that the king of Tara plans to collect by force the *bóramha* tribute from Rónán,[114] thus increasing our sense of both Rónán's endangered position and his love for Mael Fhothartaigh, whom he, like the king of Ulster in *Buaidh an Ultaigh*, wishes to keep out of danger if war comes. While it never materialises, this threatened invasion also provides the Ulsterwoman Dáirine with a chance to question the courage of the Leinstermen, the most explicit example of the Ulster pride evident in the queen and her servant Úna throughout the play. On a more pragmatic level, Ó Néill provides Rónán an apparent physical proof of his son's infidelity with Dáirine, a proof that modern audiences will find more convincing than Dáirine's ability in the original tale to complete a poetic quatrain of which Mael Fhothartaigh recites the first two lines. Also of interest is Ó Néill's ability to use elements from his original in new ways that are still entirely in keeping with the spirit of that original. In *Fingal Rónáin*, when the jester Mac Glas is killed, he dies writhing with his lips twitching, a grotesque spectacle that the observers find amusing. Ó Néill cuts this barbaric scene, but retains the notion of smiling and laughing as grim, aggressive, and foreboding, most notably with regard to Dáirine and the *bean feasa*.[115]

Yet despite his fidelity to the spirit of his sources, Ó Néill's aim in this play was not a strict retelling of *Fingal Rónáin* for Celtic scholars, but a challenging and enjoyable piece of theatre for modern audiences. Realising those audiences might find a traditional tragedy of fate old-fashioned if not downright unconvincing, he has his protagonist explicitly reject the idea of fate as inevitably controlling her life: 'I will snatch the flower of happiness from the grudging fist of fate.'[116] Of course she and the other character in the play fall prey to a force every bit as implacable, but one that modern audiences might find more compelling from their own experience: 'Human desires are as strong as the river's flow that sweeps everything with it in a springtide.'[117] Ó Néill tells us that his friend Michael O'Brien had no use for Shakespeare,[118] so one must wonder whether O'Brien would have noticed the marvellous subversion of the traditional Shakespearean tragic ending Ó Néill created for *Iníon Rí Dhún Sobhairce*, where the last word is not left to any figure of order and authority; rather, in a sure sign that the world has been turned upside-down, the play ends with comments from the malicious and contemptible jester Mac Glas and the chilling laughter of the *bean feasa*.[119]

With its modern setting and detective story plot, Ó Néill's next play was quite a change from his previous works for the theatre.[120] *Rún an Oileáin*, directed byTomás Mac Anna, had its premiere at An Damer in June 1961, to be followed by a revival in November of the same year;[121] a production in English at Dublin's LanternTheatre in August and November 1963; broadcasts over Radio Éireann in March and August 1964; and a revival in Irish by Aisteoirí Ghaoth Dobhair in 1969.[122] The critics were in general impressed by the play regardless of language. An *Irish Press* contributor pronounced the Gaelic version a 'big hit' and 'one of Gael-Linn's most successful productions for a long time' (*IP*, 13/6/61).[123] Reviewing the production for the *IrishTimes*, 'P. Mac A.' wrote that 'one expects the unusual from Séamus Ó Néill . . . one is somewhat surprised, however, to discover him in a new role as the author of a particularly fine and well-written thriller.'This critic found Mac Anna's whole production 'exceptionally fine', his sets 'magnificent', and the acting 'uniformly good', concluding: 'Altogether *Rún an Oileáin* made for one of the best evening's entertainments supplied by the DamerTheatre for some time' (*IT*, 6/6/61). 'R. S.' thought the second act was a bit of a let down after the tension of the first, but he still declared that 'the play represents a valuable addition to the number of original works in Irish, and breaks new ground in its theme and in the manner of its development' (*II*, 5/6/61). More enthusiastic was 'L. Ó S.', who declared: 'This play is well worth seeing and I would not be surprised if it continued during this next week although according to the programme it will be ending tomorrow' (*Inniu*, 9/6/61).[124] After seeing the November 1961 revival, Risteárd Ó Glaisne wrote that while he had been disappointed by some of the actors and their articulation of Irish, he liked the play 'exceptionally well' (thar na bearta), felt that it was marked by 'a fine, measured movement' (gluaiseacht bhreá thomhaiste), and added that it would make a good film (*IT*, 1/11/61). When the play was produced in English, 'R. M. C.' called it 'a clearly written, atmospheric piece of theatre' and noted that Ó Néill was 'singularly well-served by a cast of young actors and actresses' (*IP*, 8/8/63). Gus Smith was likewise impressed, stating in the *Sunday Independent* that 'Mr O'Neill is at home with the people, and the strong characterisation is always convincing' (*SI*, 11/8/63).

In a not particularly helpful comment on the play just before it opened at An Damer, Ó Néill was reported as saying 'it is not a detective story or a thriller, but a mystery play' (*IP*, 1/6/61). While few are likely to see any obvious similarities with the medieval genre (if that is even what Ó Néill had in mind), it is certainly a play with a mystery at the centre of it, as it deals with the disappearance of an American anthropologist who had come to an island off the west coast of Ireland to learn Irish and to study the customs and folklore of the people. When a police inspector and his sergeant arrive on the island to investigate, they find both a wall of resistance and a plethora of suspects, as everyone on the island with the exception of the schoolmistress seems to have disliked the anthropologist – the priest for his agnosticism, the local gombeen man for his refusal to lodge with him, the schoolmaster for his relationship with the schoolmistress on whom he himself has his eye, and the 'king' of the island, a quite mad *seanchaí* (storyteller), for his failure to properly appreciate his lore, much of which by the way concerns Colm Cille. Despite all the whodunnit potential provided by so many and such disparate suspects, Ó Néill's real interest is not in who may have killed the visitor but in why the islanders have such an immediate and visceral distrust of outsiders. In other words, his policemen are soon themselves compelled to become amateur anthropologists.[125] While the islanders are more than willing to slander each other when they get an opportunity, they are determined to share nothing useful with the police, a point made clear by Ó Domhnaill, the king, when he declares 'there are no spies or informers on this island' and we are told in a stage direction that 'the others repeat this sentence'.[126] For the islanders the party line is that the professor accidentally fell off a cliff and his body was carried away by the currents, or, in Ó Domhnaill's more dramatic version, 'it was the wave of death came over him and swept him out to sea'.[127] Even the priest refuses to help the police, instead accusing them of possibly doing harm: 'For whilst you are here, despite your good intentions, you'll only be stirring up angers and animosity amongst the people. They'll hate one another and they'll hate the government, and everything connected with it.'[128] And when at the end the people again, in behaviour anticipatory of that in John B. Keane's *The Field* (1965), close ranks against the police, who after another death may finally have sufficient evidence to establish what actually occurred, the priest is eager to see the two officers leave the island, stating: 'I knew no good would come of all the searching and enquiring.'[129] As the play ends, with the police leaving the island in frustrated defeat, the gombeen man Mac Con Uladh with smirking obsequiousness bids them farewell for all the islanders:

> And is it goin' away from us all yee are now? Isn't that a pity? We'll miss the both of yee greatly. Two nicer gentlemen than yee never darkened the door of me house, or came to the island. That's the truth indeed. And here is a little present for each of you. A fistful of the blessed clay of the island. Ó Domhnaill, the king, raised it himself. It banishes rats, yee know.[130]

This reference to a bit of island folklore suggests Ó Néill's most original contribution in this play, what makes it more than just an entertaining night out. Like Keane's *The Field*, which would not be produced until four years after *Rún an Oileáin*, Ó Néill's play offers a stark portrayal of obsessive and potentially violent xenophobia in Irish rural communities. Unlike Keane's play, however, it deals with Gaeltacht people, thus anticipating, albeit in a far more restrained fashion, the grotesque depictions of Gaeltacht or breac-Ghaeltacht (semi-Gaeltacht) savagery by Martin MacDonagh from the 1990s on. Second, he presents on stage something of which folklorists had long been aware – the idea that not all folklore is a noble and uplifting heritage from the past, but that it can also be a force for perpetuating old bigotries and hatreds. In his guidelines to contributors to *An Iris* in 1946, Ó Néill wrote: 'You will be throwing stamps away if you send me folklore stories' (*Iris*, Feb. 1946, p. 4).[131] In *Rún an Oileáin*, folklore has the potential to cause more damage than a waste of postage.

If Ó Néill saw *Iníon Rí Dhún Sobhairce* as a play dealing with the irresistible forces of individual human emotions, in the Oireachtas prize-winning *Faill ar an bhFeart* he questions whether similarly overwhelming forces drive politics and history. This play, his first and only explicit engagement with the problems of his native province, was initially written for the 1916 Jubilee Year Commemoration Competition, in which it shared the prize for a play in Irish with Pádraig Ó Giollagáin's one-act *An Coineall* (The candle) (*II*, 6/4/66). Directed by Tomás Ó Murchadha, it had its premiere in October 1967 in the Peacock Theatre, where it was the first full-length play in Irish staged in the new building.[132] Also of note here is that the role of the protagonist, the Reverend James Porter, was played by his fellow writer Annraoi Ó Liatháin, and that a direct descendant of Porter was in the audience on opening night (*IP*, 8/10/67). The general reaction to the play may perhaps best be surmised from the odd opening-night review of 'R. Ó C.': 'This is a well-written, conventional historical play, frequently moving, if sometimes uninspired, with a beginning, a middle and an end, and an author who seems to have escaped the compulsion of all too many playwrights in Irish to show that he knows all about sex' (*II*, 9/10/67). On the other hand, 'P. Ó S.' (probably Padraig Ó Siochfhradha) argued that Ó Néill may have been overwhelmed by all that he did know about history: 'But there were so many events to present so that the story would be complete that the necessary conflict . . . did not get a proper chance to be developed. The mixture was a collection of events, but the substance was missing due to lack of opportunity to develop a central dramatic theme' (*Inniu*, 13/10/67).[133] Liam Ó Lonargáin was certainly unimpressed by both the play and the production, writing: 'The play was slow and dull throughout; none of the characters were particularly alive or interesting, and to add to the pedantry the production itself was sluggish and lifeless' (*Feasta*, Nov. 1967, p. 24).[134] When the Peacock offered it again at the Dublin Theatre Festival, it was withdrawn after an eight-day run 'because the production is not attracting sufficiently large audiences' (*II*, 18/10/67).[135]

Ó Néill must have been keenly disappointed, for he had put a great deal of time and research into the play, and, as he stated when it opened, he felt that 'it has something pertinent to say about Ireland at the present time' (*IP*, 8/10/67). Not surprisingly for a Catholic from Co. Down, Ó Néill had always been concerned with events in Northern Ireland, and his ideas on the subject showed considerable evolution over the years. As an obviously naive young nationalist, he offered readers of *The Leader* the following 'Plan to end partition' in 1934: 'The plan is to build our military strength so that in time of war we would prove ourselves a nasty thorn in the side of England. We would build our military strength so and I feel that England would give us the six counties without firing a shot' (*Leader*, 13/11/34).[136] With time, however, he realised that the end to partition would have to come by changing the hearts and minds of unionists, a process he knew would be difficult but for which he felt there was a genuine historical basis.[137] He set out one main reason for his optimism in a 1966 essay in *Studies* on 'The hidden Ulster: Gaelic pioneers of the North', an essay rooted in the same research that produced *Faill ar an bhFeart*, writing that in the late eighteenth century 'the descendants of the planters were beginning to adopt Irish nationality' and pointing out that if 'the new spirit of the Dissenters vanished after '98 . . . an interest in Irish culture survived among many of the Northern Protestants'. Optimism was no longer naiveté, however, as he acknowledged that cultural pastimes were easily trumped by political passions: 'Unfortunately the acceleration of the Home Rule movement caused many Protestants to turn away from the revival of the language, for they feared involvement in the political struggle' (*Studies*, spring 1966, p. 60).

These were by no means new ideas for Ó Néill. He had, for example, lectured in 1958 to members of the Antrim and Down Association in Dublin on 'the part played by "Northerners" in the preservation of the Gaelic tradition' (*IP*, 27/3/58). And in a lecture to members of An Comhchaidreamh in Dublin the same year, he is reported as having said that 'the origins of partition were to be found in the fact that in the early years of the last century, the Presbyterians of the North turned away from the radical principles which had inspired the rising of 1798' (*IP*, 17/4/58).[138] Predictably enough, his interest in this question became far more pressing and personal as the situation in the North deteriorated rapidly in 1969, so that he could write in the fateful August of that year that 'the recent deplorable happenings in the Six Counties have been . . . in a certain sense, a particular tragedy for a number of Northern nationalists, among whom I count myself, who have worked and hoped for the day when a considerable body of Northern

Protestants would declare for Ireland' (*IP*, 25/8/69).[139] In response, he turned with greater conviction than ever to his belief in a tradition of genuine Presbyterian patriotism rooted in a shared and encompassing sense of Irish identity. What he unfortunately never seemed to think through was that in his scheme the Gaelic element would do most of the sharing with and encompassing of a needy and too long ignorantly recalcitrant planter stock, for he never questioned that the basis of any meaningful Irish nationality would be Gaelic.[140] At any rate, among his pieces on Protestant, especially Presbyterian, interest in such Irish nationality were 'Oidhrí gan fáil Mhac Cracken, Neilson, Haslett . . .: tuige a d'éag spiorad '98 sa Tuaisceart?' (The non-existent heirs of MacCracken, Neilson, Haslett . . .: why did the spirit of '98 die in the North?) (*Indiu*, 25/6/48); 'Gaelic worthies of Athens of the North' (*IP*, 16/6/53); 'Sad days of tone' (*IP*, 22/11/67); 'The Brutus of Belfast' (*IP*, 24/3/68); 'Tragedy for all Ireland' (*IP*, 25/8/69); 'When Presbyterians wore green' (*IP*, 3/10/69); 'Orr of '98' (*IP*, 23/6/70); 'The unity of Gaeldom' (*IP*, 23/11/71); and 'Henry Montgomery: Presbyterian patriot and scholar' (*IT*, 16/11/76).

Ó Néill's major statement on the question of Northern Protestant allegiance to the Irish nation was, however, *Faill ar an bhFeart*. Obviously not wanting that statement to be misunderstood, he spelled it out at least twice while the play was still running, telling potential playgoers that 'its message was that people would always follow an ideal' (*II*, 6/10/67) and that 'the play was about man's inhumanity to man . . . it deals with man against tyranny' (*IP*, 8/10/67). Our question here is, of course, how successfully that message was conveyed through the play itself. The protagonist, the Reverend James Porter, is an intellectual, a scholar, and a scientist, who has come to believe that great, indeed irresistible, forces are at work in his own time that will reshape human history. As he tells his wife, 'There is a stirring . . . a stirring throughout the world. People are no longer willing to stay in subjection . . . You cannot stop the greatest change that has come over the world since the time of the Reformation. It is going forward like a flood wave.'[141] He himself clearly has no desire to stem this rising tide, instead writing essays and letters designed to stir the people against the political and economic oppression under which they live. Porter's courage is beyond doubt from the very start of the play when he turns down a secure academic position in Glasgow lest people think he is betraying his principles and abandoning Ireland after inciting other people to perilous enterprises. Among those principles is an enlightened rejection of sectarianism that enables him to receive the local parish priest An tAthair Ó hÍr as a welcome guest and even friend.

But however brave and right-minded, he is also hopelessly naive.[142] When a neighbourhood woman whose son has been killed in the rising blames him for leading the young man astray with his writings, he seems baffled by the notion that political ideas could have real-world consequences.[143] Nor is his apparently *laissez-faire* attitude to his son's radical ideology and eventual participation in the rising particularly compelling in face of his wife's instinctive desire to protect the young man when she says: 'I don't have the learning to argue with you, but my heart tells me how I should help my son.'[144] Most striking, however, is his inability to understand, much less appreciate, the pragmatic political conservatism of An tAthair Ó hÍr, who tells him he knows full well who will suffer most for an unsuccessful rising inspired by intellectuals like Porter: '*Liberté, égalité, fraternité!* We have heard all that before, but we know what came of it in France – *La Terreur* – horror, slaughter, and blasphemy. I would like to protect my poor people from the like of that and the devils who started it. I know well who will pay for it if there is trouble in the country – the poor Gaels.'[145] When Ó hÍr speaks of the judicial murder of the Tipperary priest Nicholas Sheehy on trumped-up charges, Porter responds by invoking the execution of the Presbyterian patriot William Orr, to which the priest laconically replies: 'Orr was guilty according to the law of the land.'[146] For Ó hÍr, Porter is blind to the ferocity with which the rich and powerful will protect their threatened prerogatives: 'You do not realise that you are attacking the livelihood of the nobles when you try to take the power from them, and there is only one way to stop the person who attacks their livelihood.'[147]

Later, using a pass given him by the authorities and certain that the United Irishmen – 'people in Dublin and Belfast with neither sense nor religion' (dream gan chiall gan chreideamh i mBaile Átha agus i mBéal Feirste) – are bringing the Yeomen down on his people, Ó hÍr successfully uses his influence to keep most of the Catholics out of the rising. When he asks Porter to play a similar role among the members of his own congregation, Porter refuses, stating that since they know of his radical writings they will see such behaviour as cowardice. Once again he refers to the inexorable flow of history, telling the priest it would be 'useless' (díomhaoin) for either of them 'to make an attempt to stand before the flood' (iarracht a dhéanamh seasamh i mbéal na tuile). The priest's response to what Porter must feel is an irrefutable argument is terse and dismissive: 'So your mind is made up.'[148] In the wake of the rout that puts an end to the rising locally, Porter seems at sea, blaming first Napoleon for abandoning Ireland for Egypt and then An tAthair Ó hÍr for pacifying the Catholics.[149] He also tries to deny the stories of Catholic atrocities coming from Wexford[150] and defends the local Catholics against his rebel son, who is contemptuous of their inaction: 'The Papists betrayed us, they didn't rise up at all. If they had we would have won. Bad luck to them, the cowards . . . I will never again carry a green flag. Weren't the Papists cowards?'[151]

At his trial Porter is innocent in every sense; apparently amazed that English justice can be reduced to such a travesty as he hears lying witnesses frame him for treason. One would like to believe he is being sarcastic when he says to the court: 'If you want to condemn me to death on perjured testimony, that is easy to do, but I am assuming that you are honourable soldiers.'[152] But in all probability he is dead serious.[153] The one honest witness called at the trial is An tAthair Ó hÍr, who remains proud of his work to stop the rising, but bravely attempts to defend Porter as a man who could do much to restore peace in the area. He is, however, crystal-clear about their different approaches to confronting the oppression under which they live: 'I did not agree with the opinions he had. But it was the love he had for the people, for the poor people, that was driving him. He wanted them to have a better life, and he was impatient. He did not understand that it is not possible to shape the world as you wish with word or with deed.'[154]

In an echo of another Irish patriot who achieved his greatest triumph in apparent failure, Porter accepts his death sentence with courage and self-sacrificing nobility: 'The people have been beaten. The masters have won. You have won. Therefore do not inflict persecution on the people any more. Be merciful. And as for myself, if you intend to put me to death, I offer my life for the people. Take it as retribution, and I will be satisfied.'[155] The problem with the play is, however, that this heroic note sounded at its conclusion seems far too melodramatic. What is most interesting throughout is how unheroic Porter is. Not only does he usually seem too naive to have a true sense of the dangers that will ultimately enable his grand final gesture, but he is also apparently clueless about his own role in inspiring the rising. One can sympathise with the woman who blasts Porter as an out-of-touch egghead whose political theorising has incited others, including her son, to their deaths. The creation of a more self-aware, consciously conflicted protagonist might have provided Ó Néill the basis for an intriguing play on the role of the principled intellectual in popular political and insurrectionary movements.[156] Too fond of his hero by far, Ó Néill instead wrote a straightforward nationalist celebration of Irish resistance to British tyranny at just the time such traditional readings of the past were about to be subjected to intense and rigorous revisionist scrutiny.[157] The thinking that motivated that kind of scrutiny may well be among the reasons that *Faill ar an bhFeart* has never been revived on stage.[158]

Ó Néill stayed with history in his next play, although this time it was the English past that captured his imagination. *Iníon Rí na Spáinne* deals with Henry VIII's attempts to cajole or coerce Catherine of Aragon into agreeing to end their marriage and allow him to marry Anne Boleyn. Despite winning the 1967 Oireachtas prize for a full-length play and appearing in book form in 1978, it had not been produced by 1980. This fact puzzled Proinsias Ní Dhorchaí, who wrote in her review of the published text:

> It is a good script: there is a play in it if it is only produced. A play in which there would be energy and tension, a play in which matters being hotly debated amongst us now would be dealt with – divorce and the question of authority in particular. I hope that that fine script, *Iníon Rí na Spáinne*, is not left in the limbo of non-production too much longer. (*Comhar*, Feb. 1980, p. 9)[159]

But that is precisely where the play has remained; it seems never to have been performed.

Once again Ó Néill put a good deal of historical research into the play, and once again his interest in his subject matter was long-standing. He had written a piece on Catherine entitled 'Ar son na Spáinne' (For Spain) in *Indiu* as far back as 5 October 1945. It seems reasonable, however, to suggest that a major inspiration for this play may have been Robert Bolt's critical and popular success *A Man for All Seasons*, which had its London premiere in 1960, a very successful production at the Olympia Theatre in Dublin in 1963, was made into an Oscar-winning film in 1966, and was translated into Irish by Seán Ó Carra as *Sárfhear Chuile Thrátha* and produced at Taibhdhearc na Gaillimhe in April 1976. In Bolt's play, it is Thomas More who stands on conscience against the temptations, threats, and violence of Henry VIII. Ó Néill's play comes off badly to say the least in any comparison with Bolt's. Moreover, its shortcomings are quite similar to those of *Faill ar an bhFeart*. Bolt's protagonist is a complex character, deeply committed to both his king and his faith, willing to suffer and even die for either one, but far more interested in staying alive for his family and eager to test his wits against the king and his advisors on issues of law and legal process. Ó Néill's Catherine, on the other hand, too often seems a cardboard saint. Ní Dhorchaí points out quite correctly 'that our attention is directed on Catherine's mind throughout this whole play' (gurb ar mheon Chaitríona a dhírítear ár n-aird tríd an dráma seo ar fad). The problem is that while that mind is noble in every sense of the word, it is not all that interesting. And as with James Porter, one wishes she had realised much earlier and much more insightfully the hopelessness of her situation.[160] We are told several times how sharp and incisive Catherine is. Indeed one of Cardinal Wolsey's men states: 'Catherine's problem is not a lack of intelligence, but too much of it.'[161] If so, we never really see this side of her. Instead, she is simply overwhelmed by the relentlessly malevolent machinations of Henry and his henchmen, from the grasping Wolsey to the insidious Thomas Cromwell with his well-thumbed copy of Machiavelli, to the closet-Lutheran Archbishop of Canterbury Thomas Cranmer.

While Bolt's Thomas More seems at times almost to enjoy outsmarting those who attempt to entrap or intimidate him, Catherine for the most part can only shelter behind her Castilian pride and simple goodness, the latter a theologically potent but theatrically pallid strategy. The only point at which she becomes a really interesting character is when she wonders whether there is some way that she can simultaneously satisfy both king and conscience, a balancing act More attempts throughout Bolt's play. Pressed by Cromwell to do 'the sensible thing' (an rud ciallmhar), to divorce Henry and accept him as head of the English Church, she states: 'I would like to be able to yield to these orders, but I cannot violate my conscience.'[162] Offered leadership of a revolt against Henry, she refuses: 'I cannot make war against my King. He is my husband, he is my King and my lord, despite how unjustly he treated me, and I would be breaking God's law if I waged war on him. I have to be submissive to my husband, and to my King, in everything except in the case of my soul.'[163]

Against Catherine's stand on principle are arrayed the forces of *Realpolitik* – or what Ó Néill in 1945 called *Machtpolitik* (*Comhar*, July 1945, p. 2) – and here, unfortunately for the play's dramatic tension, the devils have all the best lines. Thus when early in the play she says she will rely on the judgement of Rome, Cardinal Campeggio replies: 'You have no guarantee that it is not a judgement against you that would be given even in Rome . . . I have learned from experience in these matters, and I can tell you that it is difficult to be certain ahead of time what judgement will be given.'[164] Later, Catherine's friend, the Spanish ambassador Chapuys, confirms that the Pope himself has indeed accepted the need to live and act in a real world whose political landscape has been altered by the spread of Protestantism. Chapuys tells Catherine that her submission to Henry would please all parties involved in the apparent impasse:

> Henry would be pleased. He could marry the lady Anne. The Pope would be pleased. He would not be obliged to pass judgement in the case. He would not be afraid of driving Henry to Lutheranism through refusing him, and on the other hand he would not be afraid of angering the Emperor by giving him permission to divorce you. And if it comes to that, the Emperor would be pleased since he does not want Henry to make an alliance with France, and he does not want to be in a dispute with the Pope.[165]

The most memorable character in the play is Thomas Cromwell, although he risks throughout turning into the stereotypical villain of melodrama. Despite his reading preferences, Ó Néill's Cromwell is more Mephisto-phelian than Machiavellian. Thus in his first conversation with Henry he tells him that he can make him the richest king in Christendom by seizing the wealth of the monasteries. Moreover, he tempts him with the idea that he should not be subordinate to the Pope, all as part of a grand scheme to make England Protestant. When Catherine later confronts Cromwell directly after he tells her she has been exiled from the court, he responds with a defence with which the world has become all too familiar: 'As I told you, Queen, I greatly regret bringing you any message that would distress you, but I am only fulfilling my duty.'[166] Were Ó Néill to have suggested a more active and engaged response to this kind of worldly evil, some idea of how good people can act both ethically and effectively in the real world, he might have written a play with something to say to late twentieth- and twenty-first-century audiences. Instead, *Iníon Rí na Spáinne* is an academic exercise at best, and hagiography in fancy dress at worst. When Catherine dies after forgiving Henry, her king and 'dear husband' (céile ionmhain), one of her servants immediately opens a window to let her soul go free, proclaiming: 'You can stop praying now, for I am certain that the soul of Catherine of Aragon is already high in heaven.'[167] But while Ó Néill's Catherine may be a saint for her time, she is not one for Ó Néill's or ours, and certainly not one for all seasons.

At his best, Séamus Ó Néill the playwright lived up to Ita Mallon's 1973 claim that he created 'flesh-and-blood-and-brain people, caught up in those human problems which are constant in a changing world' (*II*, 27/2/73). On the whole, however, with the exception of *Iníon Rí Dhún Sobhairce* and *An tSiúr Pól*, it is perhaps more fitting to value his plays for their ambition than for their achievement. But of course given the state of drama in Irish in his time (and since), that kind of ambition was in itself no mean achievement. In the earliest years of the Gaelic drama movement, a downright breathtaking ambition, rooted in patriotic fervour and an utter ignorance of stage history and technique, was common, inspiring history plays like the one-act *Aodh Ó Néill* (1902) by 'Conán Maol' (Pádraig Ó Séaghdha) with its seven scenes and more than 20 characters, and the grandest of them all, the anonymously authored *Eoghan Ruadh Ua Néill, nó Ar Son Tíre agus Creidimh*, which ran for more than five hours when performed at Maynooth in 1906. Unlike these artless amateurs, Ó Néill rooted his plays in a sound knowledge of theatre history and an appreciation, if never a mastery, of techniques that might work successfully on the Gaelic stage. Moreover, there were some things he did very well. For example, like Micheál Mac Liammóir, Micheál Ó Siochfhradha, and Seán Ó Tuama,[168] he used material from Irish history and early Irish literature creatively and with real relevance for modern audiences.[169] And, as suggested above, both *Iníon Rí Dhún Sobhairce* and *An tSiúr Pól* should be part of any Gaelic dramatic canon, while *Rún an Oileáin* might still provide an entertaining evening in the theatre. Furthermore, in keeping with his insistence that writing in Irish needed more intellectual substance, virtually all of his plays offer more than just entertainment, challenging audience members and readers to engage with ideas that even in historical dress were relevant to the Ireland of his time. In the best of his work for the stage, he is, simultaneously and successfully, scholar, thinker, and artist.

THREE

A THEATRE OF IDEAS

EOGHAN Ó TUAIRISC (1919–82)

Invited to participate in a 1970 seminar on theatre in Irish at Trinity College, Eoghan Ó Tuairisc declined, stating that he saw little future for Gaelic drama and

> that drama in the artificial language that is called Irish in English-speaking Ireland is an unnatural growth . . . The plays in Irish of this time (including my own plays) are in the same situation as the Latin plays that were written in the Universities in England in the Middle Ages . . . whatever play will come to fruition at the nib of my pen will be devised and written in English.[1]

At this point in his career, Ó Tuairisc had not written a play in Irish in seven years and would not write another in the language until 1974.[2] There were several reasons for this hiatus, and more important, for his despair about the prospects for a vital theatre in Irish. When he wrote the words above, Máirtín Ó Cadhain, the greatest figure of twentieth-century literature in Irish, had just died, and Ó Tuairisc saw his passing as not only the end of an era, but as quite possibly the end of the kind of rich, deeply rooted, and marvellously adaptive native Irish of which Ó Cadhain was a consummate master. With the loss of that kind of Irish, Ó Tuairisc could see writers like himself from English-speaking Ireland as engaged in a futile effort to express the life of the modern nation in 'an artificial language that is called Irish', producing in the process an ersatz, inert, and sterile body of writing utterly irrelevant to the vast majority of Irish people. Given such a belief, it is little wonder that at that point in his literary life he seems to have come close to yielding to a temptation shared by Ó Cadhain himself – the temptation to give up writing in Irish altogether. Indeed, as we will see, Ó Tuairisc's relationship with the Irish language as a literary medium was complex and contradictory, as he wrestled with persistent doubts about both the viability and even survival of Irish and about what he felt was his own inadequate command of it.[3]

Ó Tuairisc took theatre very seriously, with Shakespeare and even more so the Greeks providing the models he aspired to emulate. After attending Féile Drámaíochta na nOllscoileanna (The universities drama festival) in 1964, he wrote:

> The Theatre is just an intellectual pastime for the bourgeois minority unless it is religious (I am not saying 'pious'); and religion means casting aside the mask of the day, putting behind you the stultifying mundane routine, changing clothes or putting on festive attire, and escaping the hive of the twentieth-century city to taste the Mystery in the twilight where god and the devil have been waiting for you from long ago. (*Comhar*, May 1964, p. 10)[4]

But he was no elitist in the theatre, believing that while playwrights should challenge their audiences to confront the great themes of drama and life, they should never lose contact with those audiences and their legitimate desire to be entertained. Thus in a 1974 interview with Dáithí Ó Coileáin, he stated: 'If you can't put on your play in Mullingar, there is something wrong with the play, no matter how artistic and how interesting it is from the point of view of ideas and themes' (*Comhar*, Oct. 1974, p. 4).[5] Language was, of course, a, if not the, challenge facing a Gaelic playwright trying to reach audiences in an English-speaking town like Mullingar, and Ó Tuairisc was willing to try a range of approaches, including bilingualism, that might assist such audiences in their enjoyment and appreciation of a play in Irish: 'Often the Scholars and the Out and Out True Gaels come down on me for this cohabitation of the Two Languages in my work, but I do not write my books and my plays for the University or for Corca Dorcha, but for the ordinary people of today, who still do not have much Irish.'[6] Obviously another solution for this linguistic dilemma would be to write for Gaeltacht audiences for whom the language would be no problem, but that option would have held little appeal for Ó Tuairisc, who, despite his respect for the Gaeltacht and the language of native speakers, was a town and city man throughout his life. Thus while the Gaeltacht was 'the thing that most affected me as a writer' (an rud is mó a chuaigh i gcionn orm mar scríobhnóir) (*Innti* VI (Oct. 1981), p. 43), and he believed as one of 'the two articles in my Creed' (dhá alt i mo Chreideamh) that 'it is only from the Gaeltacht and from the rural areas influenced by the Gaeltacht will come the liveliness of speech, the naturalness, the sympathy between the stage and the audience from which the drama takes root', he was equally committed to the second article of that creed, that 'only from the Capital will come the teaching and the example with regard to production, for what the people of the Gaeltacht (and the people of Ireland in general) lack most is visual imagination'.[7] In other words, while Gaeltacht people were blessed with 'aural imagination' (samhlaíocht na cluaise), theatre people in the Galltacht, and particularly in Dublin, had a superior sense of the staging and spectacle necessary for the successful production of plays. Nowhere was Ó Tuairisc's commitment to bringing theatre in Irish alive for ordinary playgoers with limited Irish more evident than in his work with Tomás Mac Anna (and others) on the *geamaireachtaí* or Gaelic pantomimes staged by the Abbey Theatre around Christmastime every year from the mid 1940s to the early 1970s, a topic to which we shall return below.

Irish/English, Gaeltacht/Galltacht, collaborator on ephemeral entertainments/self-proclaimed disciple of the classical Greek tragedians, Eoghan Ó Tuairisc was throughout his life a man of conflicts and apparent contradictions that as both an artist and a citizen of the Irish Republic he struggled through his writing to maintain in creative tension. Indeed even his name reflects the complexities of his identity. Born in 1919 in Ballinasloe, an English-speaking former garrison town in East Galway, he was christened Eugene Rutherford Watters, only to learn in primary school that he was also Eoghan Ó hUisge, becoming Eoghan Ó Fuaruisge on his first visit to the Gaeltacht, and finally Eoghan Ó Tuairisc as a writer of Irish. It should, perhaps, not be surprising that he was for years unable to settle on just what he should be called. When his first two books of poetry were published in two languages on the same day in 1964, the author of *The Weekend of Dermot and Grace* was given as Eugene Watters, while that of *Lux Aeterna* was Eoghan Ó Tuairisc. When, in deep depression following the death of his first wife and artistic collaborator Úna McDonnell, he considered giving up writing in Irish, he told David Marcus with regard to a review he had written for *The Irish Press*: 'By all means sign the review – "Eugene Watters" – my real name, in fact: many people inured to the synthetic "E Ó T", just don't believe it.'[8] He went even further in a 1972 letter to his publisher Allen Figgis: 'The understanding I have reached is that I never want to hear the name of "Eoghan Ó Tuairisc" again. It's false.'[9] Yet having been an official Irish representative at a literary conference in England in 1975, a conference at which he was 'appalled' to find that 'the decay of English, the flatulence and flippancy, was even more advanced than it was at home', he declared:

> rightly or wrongly I came to the conclusion that from now on I am an Irish writer writing in Irish, that Irish is a vital force in a devitalised society, that my fate is to spend the rest of my creative life as Eoghan Ó Tuairisc, blindly cultivating my own square mile of territory, bringing Irish idiom to bear on all aspects of life in town and country throughout Ireland, allowing the vibration of our English tradition to pass over as it may into the trickle of modern writing in Irish.[10]

Nevertheless, while he did remain 'Eoghan Ó Tuairisc' for the rest of his creative life, that name appeared as the author of work in both Irish and English.

These vacillations were, of course, far in the future when he first trudged off to primary school in Ballinasloe. As is clear from the fictionalised account of his childhood in his 1977 novel *An Lomnachtán* (The naked person), there was no Irish in his family. Nor did he learn the language in the Gaelic League, for unlike the playwrights we have discussed thus far, he was never a member of that organisation despite the fact that he would regularly win prizes at the Oireachtas, where he also served from time to time as an adjudicator, and would edit the League's official journal *Feasta*. It was also during his time in primary school that he made his first trip to the Conamara Gaeltacht, having received a scholarship from Cumann na bPáistí. In secondary school at St Joseph's College in Ballinasloe, he extended his intellectual horizons far beyond East Galway or even Ireland. Despite the fact that the school had a rugby team and staged a Gilbert and Sullivan opera every year, it was no West British institution. Irish was taken very seriously at the school, and Ó Tuairisc made rapid progress in his study of the language and was soon able to publish work in Irish in the school magazine *Gearrbhaile*, his first work to appear being the poem 'Lá Báistighe' (A rainy day) in 1936. But what most captured his interest at St Joseph's was classical Greek literature, in particular the drama, as he told Dáithí Ó Coileáin in a 1974 interview: 'Well, I spent my youth with the drama of Greece. I am a scholar of Greek and I read most of the playwrights in the original Greek before I read plays in Irish or plays in English. And that left a mark on my mind, do you understand, that classical, Greek mark' (*Comhar*, Oct. 1974, pp 6–7).[11] His interests in Irish and Greek converged, however, when he and some of his fellow students translated the classical texts into Irish in preparation for the Leaving Certificate examinations, in which an extra 10 per cent was added to the scores of those who took the tests in Irish.

One thing that disappointed Ó Tuairisc about St Joseph's was the way in which plays were taught solely as literary texts with no attention paid to their primary role as scripts for live performance. He had had experience of live theatre from early childhood on, as his father Tom was an amateur actor and co-founder of Ballinasloe's Watters, Shiels and Hurley Group. Since this company often rehearsed its plays in the family home, the young Ó Tuairisc had plenty of opportunity to see how plays went from page to stage.[12] Moreover, even when his own company was not performing, Tom Watters worked with other local amateurs as actor, make-up man, and set builder, so that, as Máirín Nic Eoin notes of his children, 'they did not find the atmosphere of the theatre alien with its smell of make-up and its strange lights.'[13] His father also introduced him to the plays of Shakespeare by taking him to see Anew McMaster's touring company on its regular visits to Ballinasloe. It is, then, hardly surprising that even before he started school he and his younger sister Linda were creating their own little plays in a shed behind their house, in one of which, playing the circus acrobat Miss Lulu, he fell and broke his arm.

Ó Tuairisc was also exposed to theatre in school, first at his primary school St Greallan's, where students memorised passages from Shakespeare and put on plays by Lady Gregory in which he took part. All of this youthful experience with performance may explain much of his disappointment with the way drama was taught at St Joseph's, but if drama was a purely academic subject in the classroom the school did provide opportunities for students to take to the stage, either with the annual Gilbert and Sullivan production[14] or in the occasional performance of a play in Irish like *Geamaireacht Droichid an Diabhail*, Liam Ó Briain's translation of Henri Ghéon's *La parade du pont du diable*, in which Ó Tuairisc played the lead role. His performance was singled out for praise by the anonymous critic of *Ar Aghaidh* (probably the editor An tAthair P. Eric Mac Fhinn): 'The hermit Kabo [*recte* Kado] had a hard part, and he performed well. He was very steadfast when he defied the Devil. He nicely conveyed his anxiety and his remorse after that' (*AA*, Jan. 1937, p. 1).[15]

From St Joseph's Ó Tuairisc went on to St Patrick's College in Drumcondra, Dublin, to train as a primary school teacher. Since the majority of the students there were native speakers of Irish – among its alumni were noted writers like Máirtín Ó Cadhain, Séamus Ó Grianna, and Seosamh Mac Grianna, and Irish was both the *de jure* and *de facto* official language of the college – Ó Tuairisc was given an extraordinary opportunity to improve his Irish without actually having to live in the Gaeltacht. While at St Patrick's he also joined Reisimint an Phiarsaigh, an officer training regiment of the Irish army. He had already been a member of a student army unit at St Joseph's and would eventually serve briefly as a second lieutenant on active duty in 1940 and in the reserves until 1946. At this time he had also begun his teaching career, almost all of which would be spent in Finglas, Dublin, until his retirement in 1961 to pursue what would prove to be a precarious existence as a full-time bilingual writer.[16] At night he took courses for the BA and MA degrees at University College, Dublin, earning the former in 1943 and the latter in 1947. His MA thesis on 'The little plays of Shakespeare' – the plays within the main play that one finds in *Love's Labour's Lost, A Midsummer Night's Dream, Hamlet*, and *The Tempest* – provides a fascinating foreshadowing of the direction he would take with his own plays in Irish. Of Shakespeare and his Elizabethan contemporaries he wrote: 'In freedom and elasticity of construction, in the pictorial quality of their plays, and in their use of song, dance, and allegory, they were well on their way towards surrealism, and present a sharp contrast to the hard-and-fast realism which has bound the English drama up to fairly recent years.' He felt that 'this freedom of construction' made possible 'drama of composite plot' as well as the introduction of 'visions, spectacles, surprisings, allegorical figures, routs, masquerades', giving their plays 'a highly picturesque quality'.[17] More than a few of these features would later appear in his own plays.

Throughout all of these activities as student, soldier, and teacher, he continued to write in both Irish and English, concentrating at first on poetry but then moving into drama, fiction, and essay writing. Perhaps surprisingly, his greatest successes – both critical and financial – were from the very beginning achieved in Irish, with the annual literary competitions at the Gaelic League's Oireachtas being of particular importance for him. His Oireachtas awards in the drama categories will be noted when the various plays are discussed. The first of his many Oireachtas prizes in other genres came in 1943 for the poem 'Lus an Chromchinn' (The daffodil), and he would receive other prizes for poetry in 1947, 1948, and 1949.[18] He also won a prize in 1947 for his short story 'An Sean-Trumpa' (The old trumpet). In 1961, the Oireachtas honoured his first novel, *L'Attaque* (The attack), dealing with the Rising in Co. Mayo after the arrival of French forces in 1798, with both the £200 Club Leabhar prize for 'a full-length original work suitable for the ordinary reader of Irish', and Gradam an Oireachtais, 'a special recognition of merit' that was only awarded when a literary work was felt to be truly outstanding (*IT*, 26/9/61).[19] His second novel *Dé Luain* (Monday) did not win an Oireachtas prize, but did share second place in the competition for the Irish-American Cultural Institute's Butler Prize in 1967.

These frequent appearances in the lists of Oireachtas prizewinners in several genres as well as the selection of *L'Attaque* by An Club Leabhar, a selection that guaranteed the book a significant audience for a title in Irish, brought Ó Tuairisc to the attention of the Gaelic literary world, and his involvement with the Abbey's *geamaireachtaí* beginning in 1956 made him even better known. In June 1963, he became editor of the Gaelic League's official monthly journal *Feasta*, one of the most influential positions in the language and literary movement, and by December of that year he felt he had made enough of an editorial mark to give *Feasta* a new subtitle: 'Reiviú don Litríocht, don Eolaíocht, do na hEalaíona, don Pholaitíocht is don Smaointeachas Éireannach' (A review of literature, science, the arts, politics and Irish thought). Looking back in 1976 on his decision to add this resplendent subtitle, he wrote: 'I created the word "Reiviú" (instead of "Magazine") to show the European outlook of the paper . . . As models, or distinguishing characteristics, of the thing I wanted, there were *Criterion*, which T. S. Eliot edited; F. R. Leavis's *Scrutiny*; *Le Figaro Littéraire*; the Spanish-language *A. B. C.* etc.'[20] While he may never have realised such lofty ambitions, under his editorship *Feasta* was a lively and engaging magazine, not least because of his own wide-ranging and trenchant editorials, articles, and reviews. When in February 1965 Ó Tuairisc took a brief leave of absence from *Feasta* to do research on the Easter Rising for his novel *Dé Luain*, Aodh Ó Fearghail was appointed 'sub-editor' (fo-eagarthóir), a position he retained after Ó Tuairisc's return in July of that year, and this arrangement continued until Ó Tuairisc left the journal for good in January 1966. At this same time, Ó Tuairisc was also editing *Ardán*, the journal of An Chomhairle Náisiúnta Drámaíochta, which in 1964 a reporter in *The Irish Press* called 'the only magazine in Ireland . . . in either language solely devoted to theatre' (*IP*, 9/3/64).

Needless to say, given his high visibility in the movement as well as his literary versatility, he found himself in demand at movement functions, in particular as a lecturer and adjudicator of literary and dramatic competitions. For example, in the years before the death of his wife Úna in 1966, he spoke to various groups on topics like 'Religio poetae',[21] 'Dilemma an údair' (The author's dilemma),[22] 'Canúnachas' (Dialectism)[23] and 'an aigneolaíocht sa scríbhneoireacht' (psychology in writing) (*II*, 26/10/63) in 1963; 'Ag scríobh don phobal' (Writing for the public) (*IP*, 5/12/64) in 1964; and 'The spirit of 1916' (*CE*, 18/11/65) and 'Filíocht na talún' (The poetry of the land)[24] in 1965. He was particularly busy as a lecturer in 1966, the fiftieth anniversary of the Easter Rising, when he shared his thoughts and the research he had done for *Dé Luain* with audiences throughout the country. For instance, he spoke again on 'The spirit of 1916' or 'The spirit of the Rising' in, among other places, Tullamore, Co. Offaly; Ennis, Co. Clare;[25] his native Ballinasloe, Co. Galway (*CT*, 30/4/66); and Baltyboy, Co. Wicklow (*II*, 7/5/66). He adapted his lecture on 'An Conradh agus an tÉiri Amach' (The League and the Rising) for local audiences, so that he talked about the Tipperaryman Thomas MacDonagh in Cashel,[26] and about Co. Leitrim's Seán Mac Diarmada in Carrick-on-Shannon (*LO*, 18/2/66). Even in 1966, however, not all his lectures were on the Rising, as in July of that year he spoke in Termonfeckin, Co. Louth on 'The Irish style in literature' (*II*, 18/7/66). We can get a sense of his popularity as a lecturer from the comments of a reporter for the *Irish Independent*, who, having in 1963 gone to 'a well-attended meeting of Cumann na Scríbhneoirí' – including many young people – wrote: 'I rather think some of them were attracted by the prospect of a lecture by Eoghan Ó Tuairisc rather than by an interest in the affairs of the association' (*II*, 6/11/63).

As noted above, after the death of his wife Úna, Ó Tuairisc slipped into a deep depression and ceased almost entirely his engagement in Gaelic activities. Indeed, with a few rare exceptions, he stopped giving lectures until 1973, when his life with his second wife Rita Kelly gave him a new sense of possibility and purpose. From 1973 on we find him speaking regularly again on subjects like 'Why poetry?' in 1973,[27] Matthew Arnold in 1974,[28] Domhnall Mac Amhlaigh in a Thomas Davis lecture over Radio Éireann in 1975,[29] Keats in 1976,[30] and Carolan in 1980.[31]

His activity as an adjudicator for literary and dramatic competitions shows this same pattern of considerable involvement until 1966 and then a hiatus until 1974, at which time he again becomes quite active in this role. Among the drama festivals and competitions for which he served as a judge were Feis Muirtheimhne in Dundalk, Co. Louth (*IP*, 26/2/64); Féile Drámaíochta na nOllscoileanna in Galway (*IP*, 19/3/64); Féile Scoildrámaíochta na Gaillimhe in Galway (*CT*, 6/3/65); the 1965 Oireachtas in Dublin;[32] An Féile Náisiúnta Drámaíochta at An Damer (*IP*, 27/4/66); the 1966 Young Irish Play Competition sponsored by *The Irish Press* (*IP*, 27/10/66); the 1974 Féile Drámaíochta Chorr na Móna in Cornamona, Co. Galway;[33] the 1975 Féile Drámaíochta na Mí in Baile Ghib, Co. Meath (*MC*, 5/4/75); the 1975 Féile Drámaíochta Ghleann Cholm Cille in Donegal; a 1975 festival in Tullamore, Co. Offaly;[34] a 1975 drama festival in Ráth Chairn, Co. Meath;[35] the 1979 Slógadh in Dún Laoghaire, Co. Dublin (*SS*, 24/2/79); the 1979 Slógadh Réigiúnach an Oirdheiscirt in Cork;[36] the 1980 Slógadh Réigiúnach an Iarthair in Galway;[37] and the 1980 Slógadh in Salthill, Galway (*CT*, 4/4/80).[38]

Among his other literary activities through the years were his involvement in writing seminars in Galway in 1976 and 1978,[39] and in Kilkenny in 1980 (*II*, 29/11/80). He was also an official Irish representative at international literary festivals in Belgium with John Montague in 1965, in Cambridge, England with Seamus Heaney and Eavan Boland, in 1975, and in Scotland, with Críostóir Ó Floinn and the *sean nós* singer Nioclás Tóibín, in 1976.[40]

Before we move on to his plays we should briefly examine his other book-length works in Irish and English.[41] As noted above, he began his career as a poet, although his first books of poetry were not published until 1964, when on the same day appeared *Lux Aeterna*, a collection in Irish, and in English the complex and intimidating long poem *The Weekend of Dermot and Grace*, his own favourite of all his works in either language. The dropping of the atom bomb on Hiroshima in August 1945 had a profound effect on Ó Tuairisc's view of humanity in the twentieth century and is the central event in both *The Weekend of Dermot and Grace* and 'Aifreann na Marbh' (The mass for the dead), by far the most significant poem in *Lux Aeterna* and one of the great poems of modern literature in Irish. After he emerged from his silence following the death of his first wife, he would publish three more collections of poetry: *New Passages* (1973) and *Sidelines* (1981) in English and *Dialann sa Díseart* (A diary in the wilderness) (1981), a collaborative collection with Rita Kelly in Irish. While there are some fine, sensitive, and keenly observant poems in all three of these collections, they are minor works in comparison with what he had achieved in his two books from 1964.

In addition to uncollected short stories in Irish and English, Ó Tuairisc also wrote five novels, three in Irish and two in English. The first of them was *Murder in Three Moves* (1960), a competent mystery, the plot of which draws on his considerable skill at chess.[42] Far more important is his first Irish-language novel *L'Attaque*, which, as we have seen, won major prizes at the Oireachtas and was made a Club Leabhar selection on its appearance in 1962. Its inclusion on the Leaving Certificate curriculum ensured it a wide audience, making it, from a financial point of view, the most successful of his works in either Irish or English. In the novel Ó Tuairisc follows a Co. Mayo farmer and his fellows as they are caught up and killed in the 1798 Rising, a rebellion they struggle without success to fully understand. Another historical novel, *Dé Luain* (1966), was less successful with both critics and readers. Written to commemorate the fiftieth anniversary of the Easter Rising, the novel was originally intended to deal with the entire event, but after the death of Úna, who had been actively involved in the project, Ó Tuairisc lost both interest and will and ended the book with the first day of the rebellion. While he himself conceded that his inability to put his whole soul into *Dé Luain* left it an unfinished and flawed work, it is a fine novel, superior to *L'Attaque* in its ambition, its evocation of place – Dublin at the outbreak of the rebellion – and its keen insight into the conflicting, and conflicted, motives of those who set the rebellion in motion, in particular Patrick Pearse.[43] His fourth novel, *The Story of a Hedgeschool Master* (1974), is a well-told historical novel for young readers. Far more ambitious is *An Lomnochtán* (1977), a strikingly original work in which he draws on his childhood in Ballinasloe to delve into the psyche of his young protagonist while simultaneously shaping his linguistic medium to express a world quite different from that in which it had evolved. As he wrote to Caoimhín Ó Marcaigh about the novel, 'there is a noticeable share of English running through the Irish in it: the Irish of English-speaking Ireland to sustain the outlook of English-speaking Ireland.'[44]

Other literary works by Ó Tuairisc are *Focus* (with Desmond Egan) (1972), analyses of 50 poems on school curricula; *Rogha an Fhile* (The poet's choice) (1974), a ground-breaking bilingual edition of modern poetry in Irish; *Infinite Variety: Dan Lowrey's Music Hall 1879–1899* (1975), a work of theatre history he wrote drawing on the research and archive of Matthew Murtagh; *The Road to Brightcity* (1981), a book of his translations of stories from Máirtín Ó Cadhain's first two story collections, *Idir Shúgradh is Dáiríre* and *An Braon Broghach*; and the posthumous *Religio Poetae agus Aistí Eile* (Religio poetae and other essays)(1987), a selection of his essays edited by Máirín Nic Eoin.

As we have seen, Ó Tuairisc's interest in the theatre began in childhood and continued through his years as a primary and secondary school student. As a primary school teacher in Finglas he shared this interest with his students, providing them with chances to get on stage in the little variety shows he created for them, shows that could include short skits or even an original play like *The Death of Cuchulain* that he wrote for one such show in 1957.[45] Shortly after his marriage and his move to Cappagh in Dublin in

1945, he became active as both actor and director with the Finagh Players, a local amateur group that performed plays in English. He was again involved with local English-language theatre companies in Knockananna, Co. Wicklow where he lived in the late 1960s and in his native Ballinasloe in the 1970s.[46]

Ó Tuairisc began writing plays in the 1950s. The first of them, *Droichead Átha Luain* (The bridge at Athlone), a verse play for radio dealing with the Irish defence of this bridge against King William's army in 1689, was broadcast over Radio Éireann in 1950. Ó Tuairisc believed that there had always been 'an innate dramatic heritage' (dúchas drámaiteach) in Gaelic literature and that 'the verse play for radio' (an duanchluiche radio) was 'a form . . . that was wonderfully suited to that innate dramatic heritage' (foirm . . . a fheileann go seoidh don dúchas drámaiteach sin).[47] It is, then, surprising that he did not continue to cultivate that medium through Irish, instead switching to English for his next two verse plays for radio, both of which, *The Vision on O'Connell Bridge* (also *Death on O'Connell Bridge*) and *The Rising*, were rejected by Radio Éireann in 1954. Of course, there was nothing surprising about his writing plays in English. Bilingualism was natural to him and his later play *An Hairyfella in Ifreann* (The hairyfella in hell) would begin life as *The Frogs* in English, while his English-language play *Blue Daisies* is a translation of *Lá Fhéile Michíl* (The feast of St Michael).[48] Moreover, he and Sandra Warde co-wrote a play in English entitled *Song of the Nightingale* that was produced by Ballinasloe's Relays Theatre Company in 1972.[49]

His career as a playwright would take an unexpected turn when he entered a script in a contest sponsored by the Abbey. The National Theatre was not looking for a play, but rather a promising script for that year's *geamaireacht*. The Abbey had staged its first *geamaireacht*, *Muireann agus an Prionsa* (Muireann and the prince) in 1945, beginning a Christmastime tradition that would last 30 years and draw the largest audiences ever seen at Gaelic entertainments. In 1955, the Abbey announced a competition for a script for that year's show, and Ó Tuairisc submitted *Ulyssés agus Penelopé*, a show based on a version of the *Odyssey* he had told his students in one of his regular Friday afternoon storytelling sessions at the school. His entry won first prize in the contest, and he was soon at work on the *geamaireacht* with Tomás Mac Anna, who had been in charge of the Abbey's Gaelic pantomimes from the start and would continue to direct them right into the 1970s. In all, Ó Tuairisc was to work with Mac Anna on no fewer than 12 of these shows, the last in 1977.[50] We can get a good idea of how these collaborative shows were put together from Ó Tuairisc's own account of the process in his 1977 essay 'Oiliúint dhrámadóra' (The training of a dramatist):

> Tomás directing the whole thing. He sitting at a table at the side of the stage, his
> secretary beside him taking notes, some scene being rehearsed, people here and

there rehearsing dances, or at the piano with Seán Ó Riada rehearsing songs, a man in one corner learning how to walk on stilts, two in another corner learning Irish . . . myself in a separate nook on the stage writing hurriedly whatever was needed for the scene that was being put together. A call from Tomás: Ó Tuairisc, six lines for the giant Polyphemus. Verse please. And make it funny.[51]

Ó Tuairisc was obviously very good at this kind of work, and in addition to these seasonal *geamaireachtaí* at the Abbey, he also collaborated with Mac Anna and Niall Tóibín on *Damertásibh* at An Damer in 1962;[52] with Mac Anna and John Stewart on the political review *A State of Chassis*, whose satirical take on events in the north of Ireland sparked considerable controversy when it was staged in the Peacock in 1970; and, briefly, with Mac Anna, Críostóir Ó Floinn, and Gabriel Rosenstock on *Táinbócú* at the Peacock in 1978.[53] We can get a sense of *A State of Chassis* from the title of two of the pieces Ó Tuairisc contributed: *Statues of Kukullin* and *The Gynaecology of Santy Claws*. In 1975, he provided Taibhdhearc na Gaillimhe with a similar though far less political entertainment entitled *M'Asal Beag Dubh – à la carte* (My little black ass – à la carte), with Pádraic Ó Conaire, who of course wrote the original story *M'Asal Beag Dubh*, as the protagonist who defeats an Diabhal Béarla (The devil English) to restore Mac Rí na hÉireann (The son of the king of Ireland) to his throne.

Shows like this and the Abbey *geamaireachtaí* were obviously put together quickly as ephemeral entertainments for audiences whose knowledge of Irish ranged from mastery to just 'an cúpla focal' (the couple of words), and they will not be discussed here.[54] Ó Tuairisc's work on them did, however, influence his evolution as a playwright in Irish, as he makes clear in 'Oiliúint dhrámadóra': 'From that hard work on the planks of the stage I learned a good deal. With regard to speech for the stage, I learned how to shove the college and literature out of sight and to put the meaning of the story into the mouth of an actor without much Irish for an audience with very little.' Moreover, he states that while working on the *geamaireachtaí* he came to understand 'how much the personality relies on the sound, on the rhythm, and on the private imagination of the speaker' (chomh mór is a bhraitheann an phearsantacht ar fhuaim, ar rithim, agus ar shamhlaíocht phríobháideach an chainteora) and that the playwright must be sensitive to these nuances if he wishes 'to bestow a personality of his own on every character of the Dramatis Personae' (pearsantacht dá chuid féin a bhronnadh ar gach carachtar den Dramatis Personae). Above all, 'I was made aware that drama does not live on speech alone: the story must be revealed through the medium of the eyes.'[55] As we will see, all of these lessons learned from working on the *geamaireachtaí* would be applied with considerable effect in his own plays, most notably in the comedies.

Ó Tuairisc took more from the *geamaireachtaí* than just practical tricks of the playwright's trade, and he saw these shows as having an importance that transcended mere entertainment in a language that most Irish people had studied, a great number felt positively about, and a far smaller number had actually mastered. In a 1974 essay on 'Teanga is carachtar an náisiúin' (Language and the character of the nation), he wrote:

> The demographic unit that is called 'Éire' or 'Ireland' has, since the 16th century at least, not been a nation but rather a compound nation. A compound of different peoples – . . . With regard to language, and with regard to character, the compound can be crystallised into parts: the Gael, the Saxon. It is not properly speaking a geographic division, nor a class division either: it is a division according to character, a double personality that is woven into every person in the country, even in the most Scottish Presbyterian part of Belfast, the most Gaelic of the true Gaeltachtaí, the most prosperous and go-go part of Dublin.[56]

Returning to the problem in a piece entitled 'Céad chogar na teanga nua' (The first whisper of the new language), he developed the idea that the primary source of this psychic doubling was linguistic: 'Yes, if I only had English the Richness of Irish would not be trying to enliven this thought under my pen, or if I only had Irish the loving memory of English would not be trying to interfere. And I call down sweet misfortune from the devil on the fate that left us with the two languages.'[57]

His use here of the Irish first person plural prepositional pronoun (*againn*) is significant, confirming that he did not see this problem as peculiar to bilingual writers in Ireland, but rather as one shared, often or even usually subconsciously, by all Irish people. Thus in discussing his own personal predicament he was also telling 'the story of every single person in Ireland . . . since that division was to be noticed in all of us of this generation who have the Anglicised Irish and the Gaelicised English for the words we speak and that dualism woven into our thought in our souls'.[58] Nor could this split be healed by a mere act of will, as he made clear in a 1975 essay on the poet Patrick Kavanagh, who, of course, wrote exclusively in English: 'It is no use our denying one of those cultures and giving ourselves up entirely to the other one . . . The two heritages are woven into the weaving of our minds, and they cannot be avoided.'[59] Moreover, he felt that it would take 'a couple of more centuries . . . to cure the schizophrenia (the personal partition that is in us to the marrow) and to mould the Irish person anew' (cúpla céad bliain eile . . . chun an scitsfréin (an chríochdheighilt phearsanta atá de smior ionainn) a leigheas agus an tÉireannach a fhuineadh as an nua). It was his belief that the successful cure for this cultural schizophrenia, a genuine synthesis of the Gaelic and English aspects of the Irish mind, could only emerge through the work of the bilingual artist who provided his personal rationale for the preservation and revival of Irish:

> Meanwhile, I have no solution to the problem except to preserve the heritage that is most neglected, the clay-black skeleton that comes out of my memory, eternally prodding, Irish, the extraordinary richness under the Stony Grey Soil – I have no solution except to preserve it, to develop it, to reawaken it in myself, and to join it with the precision and the mettle of the English of English-speaking Ireland by which the greatest share of my worldview has been shaped.[60]

The special challenge facing writers of Irish was to find a way to convey to their readers the reality of Ireland's conflicted linguistic and cultural identity. Here we see the main reason why Ó Tuairisc put so much time and energy for so many years into the Abbey *geamaireachtaí* – where else could he ever hope to reach more Irish people whose simple attendance at the shows indicated some interest in or affection for the language. Moreover, his acceptance of the challenge of reaching those people helps explain his concerns about the quality of his own learned Irish.[61] As a young man he had come to realise 'that there was a more precise understanding of human devilment in early literature in Irish than had been revealed to the boy in Garbally Court, dark aspects that had not been revealed to O'Grady himself' (go raibh níos mó de chruinn-tuiscint dhiabhlaíocht an duine i seanlitríocht na Gaeilge ná mar a foilsíodh don ghasúr i gCúirt Ghearrbhaile, gnéithe dorcha nár léiríodh do O'Grady féin),[62] but throughout his life he worried that his incomplete mastery of the full range of the language accessible to a native speaker would prevent him from sharing this more profound and challenging understanding of Gaelic culture with his readers. Scattered throughout his writings are expressions of frustration about his inability to express his ideas adequately through Irish. Thus, after finally completing a short poem in Irish in 1971 after 103 drafts, he wrote in exasperation: 'I fail every time because I haven't got the knowledge and the skill in Irish concepts and structures . . . but how can one sing without a resonant and preconscious feeling for the entirety of the tongue.'[63] Responding in 1980 to a letter from Caoimhín Ó Marcaigh urging him to write a new novel in Irish, Ó Tuairisc wrote:

> I was preparing a collection of short stories, ones that had been published here and there over the past twenty years – but it occurred to me that most of them were altogether too simple in comparison with the kind of short story that is prevalent today; and I feel that I do not have enough native Irish to accomplish the kind of short story I prefer.[64]

But perhaps the clearest expression of such doubts concerning his mastery of his medium is to be found in his 1981 interview with *Innti*, where he described writing in Irish as a 'burden' (ualach): 'Or, when a person who was raised with English is writing Irish, the language is a considerable burden for him. He has to be always thinking about how he is saying something as well as about the thing to be said'[65] (*Innti* VI (Oct. 1981), p. 36). Of course these doubts had their origin in that 'double personality that is woven into every person in the country', the national schizophrenia that he believed it was the writer's duty to try to heal. And despite any reservations about his own capabilities, that was not a duty he could shirk and still consider himself worthy to be called an artist.

That title meant a great deal to him, for he believed profoundly that the artist was not merely a craftsman or an entertainer. Indeed he felt that the poet – a term he used for any writer 'if he provides us with a fully developed work of art through the medium of words' (má chuireann sé saothar foirfe ealaíne ar fáil dúinn i modh na bhfocal) had a mission.[66] And, if the Irish writer had a special obligation to address the divisions that language shift had inflicted on the national psyche, he shared with all artists this more universal vocation:

> By means of his art, with no guidance but the guidance of his own craftsmanship, the *Poeta* discovers the fundamental meaning of the universe: that there are two worlds, two aspects of reality, and he comes to understand that the fundamental reason for his art is to reveal those two worlds and they interwoven in the same story, the same stanza, the same word even, and to find the old link between them that is called *religio* and to express it to the people.[67]

This idea of an apparent dualism underlying human life is the central theme of all of his literary work across the genres. It was, however, in scientific terms that he expressed himself most clearly on this point: 'This formula of Einstein's [$E=mc^2$] shows us that the whole world is a Unit, but that that unity is a mystery to us, a mystery that we cannot understand in this life except by looking at it as if it were two things, two aspects, two sides, with an indissoluble, incomprehensible, invisible bond between them.'[68] In his mind *religio* was 'that power that binds the two sides together, a power that is situated in the human mind, a power of imagination that recognises and reveals the two worlds, the conspicuous world and the spiritual world, and they seamlessly interwoven'.[69]

The poet was, then, the priest and prophet of this *religio*, whose duty it was to expose false dualities in whatever form they took, and they took many in Ó Tuairisc's plays and other literary works: body/spirit, concrete/abstract, death/life, materialism/idealism, convention/freedom, individualism/universality, terror/beauty, and more. To get even a glimpse of the ultimate unity underlying the apparent divisions, the poet had to somehow penetrate the obfuscating flux of everyday existence. For Ó Tuairisc, this challenge was compounded by his belief that in the western world at least we live in what he in 1971 called 'a new Dark Age', one in which 'not merely the humanities, but the very central tenet of humanity itself, is shrinking to its finest point, the tiny spark which must be cloistered and kept alive through all the tremendous adventure of these city-centuries to come'.[70] He returned to this idea five years later: 'A Dark Age has descended on the world, far more terrible than any Norse incursion . . . The burning of the schools was a small thing compared to the infestation of the young mind by the virus of sub-anthropoid culture.'[71] And in this new Dark Age, Ireland would not be the cultural beacon it had been in the previous time of barbarism in Europe, for he and his fellow citizens now lived in what he in 1965 called 'the desert . . . of the long, spoiled, small-minded years, 1922–1965 [i.e. the entire span of his own life to that point] . . . The freedom without culture, the country without a language, the Republic without a people' (díseart . . . na blianta fada beadaí beag intinneacha, 1922–1965 . . . An tsaoirse gan saoithiúlacht, an tír gan teanga, an Phoblacht gan pobal).[72]

Wandering in circles through this desert were his contemporaries in Ireland and elsewhere in the west, sleepwalking (an image that recurs in several of his plays) through what they think is life and worshipping 'the gods of the surroundings . . . the gods of the time . . . the gods of the public' (déithe na timpeallachta . . . déithe na linne . . . déithe an phobail), all of them 'false idols, whether they are imperial gods, national gods, gods of language, poetry, the fair, or pleasure' (íola bréige, is cuma cé acu déithe impiriúla, déithe náisiúnta, déithe teanga, éigse, aonaigh nó pléisiúir iad).[73] Only the artist could, in the words of Máirín Nic Eoin, 'break out of the circular enclosure of life' (briseadh amach as cuibhreann ciorcalach an tsaoil) in order to expose these false gods whose existence was rooted in 'illusion' (*seachmall*, another favourite word in the plays) and see the world as it really was. However even the artist could not sustain such a vision, nor could he offer others more than a brief experience of what he intuitively understood. Any objective explanation was impossible, as Ó Tuairisc stressed in a comment on Shakespeare's *The Tempest* in his MA thesis: 'Life in the last resort is a mystery. Poetic imagination can grasp, and poetic power can reveal, the mystery of being; but not even a Shakespeare can solve the insoluble.'[74] It should be no wonder that for him serious theatre was no mere 'intellectual pastime for the bourgeois minority' (caitheamh aimsire intleachtúil don mhionlucht bourgeois), but a spiritual exercise appropriate to a Greek temple, or perhaps better, a zendo.

It must, then, have been painful for Ó Tuairisc to ponder the state of theatre in Irish in his own time, but ponder it he did. Of particular concern to him was the lack of any dramatic tradition in the language. Having discussed some of the philosophical ideas in 'Aifreann na Marbh', he stated in 'Oiliúint dhrámadóra' that he could never have dealt with such concepts in a play in Irish, for

> the dramatist must lose himself under the spell of some external myth, and by means of that myth he lets loose (often unknown to himself) whatever is cooking in the darkness of his mind. And with regard to the stage at the time, with regard to Irish at any rate, there was no dramatic technique to be seen and to be learned that would enable the writer to spin that mythical connection between the personal need and the public need.[75]

Of one thing he was certain – Gaelic theatre had little to learn from what he called 'the hard-and-fast realism which has bound the English drama up to fairly recent years',[76] 'Victorian realism . . . the deadly naturalism of the English language' (an réadúlacht Victeoiriach . . . nádúrthacht mharfach an Bhéarla).[77] Instead, like Micheál Mac Liammóir, Tomás Mac Anna, and Máiréad Ní Ghráda, he insisted that theatre in Irish should evolve in an entirely different direction from that taken by the English theatre (and largely followed by the Abbey as well). Thus in a 1964 piece entitled 'Caitear amach an driosúr' (Throw out the dresser), he wrote:

> Drama relies on the imagination. The director must awaken the imagination of the audience from the moment the curtain is raised. If that stirring of the imagination is not accomplished, the poor play will remain on the floor of the stage and the miracle of the theatre will not be effected in the hearts and heads of the audience.[78]

We saw above that Ó Tuairisc insisted that theatre required 'visual imagination' (samhlaíocht na súl) as well as 'aural imagination' (samhlaíocht na cluaise). In this 1964 essay he developed this idea at greater length: 'Remember, also, that the term *Lucht Éisteachta* [lit. listeners] is not a very accurate term for the people who pay their money at the door; they are *Lucht Féachana* [lit. watchers] as well as *Lucht Éisteachta*. Drama affects them through the eye as well as through the ear.' Since the Victorian period, however, the English (and Irish) theatre had, in his mind, been dominated by what he called 'the Dresser Style' (an Stíl Driosúrach), a convention that filled the stage with 'a fire, every pot, every hook, and every sod of turf in proper order. Pictures, St Patrick, my grandfather, the Sacred Heart, and my aunt Eibhlín from Boston, Mass. And the dresser, and all the plates, the little jugs, the mugs, the dishes in order, every cup on its hook without a single cup out of place' (tine, gach pota, gach crúca agus gach fód móna i gcaoi is i gceart. Pictiúir, Naomh Pádraig, mo sheanathair, an Croí Rónaofa, agus m'aintín Eibhlín ó Bhoston, Mass. Agus an driosúr, na plátaí, na crúiscíní, na mugaí, na miasa go léir in eagar, gach cupán ar a chrúca gan bun cupáin amach nó barr cupáin isteach). As a result, 'instead of awakening the imagination of the people, the director often smothers it from the start through having too many trappings and an excess of realism in the scenery' (in ionad samhlaíocht an phobail sin a mhúscailt, is minic go ndéanann an léiritheoir í a mhúchadh ó thosach tríd an iomarca feistis agus barraíocht réadúlachta sa radharcra).[79] Ó Tuairisc was also, of course, aware that adherence to this style of elaborate set design could cause financial problems for the kind of amateur companies so important to theatre in Irish. More important, by stressing the verisimilitude of the set, this style of design could often only call attention to the improbability that the characters in many plays would actually be speaking Irish in such settings. It is no wonder then that Ó Tuairisc's message was 'simplicity, directors, be simple. For God's sake throw out the dresser!' (an tsimplíocht, a léiritheoirí, bígí simplí. Ar son Dé caitear amach an Driosúr!).[80]

Like Mac Liammóir, Mac Anna, and Ní Ghráda, Ó Tuairisc urged his fellow playwrights to use all the resources available to them to create theatrical experiences that went beyond the conventions of realism that still to a large extent dominated English-language theatre in Ireland.[81] As Martin Nugent has noted, Ó Tuairisc was particularly interested in the way lighting could be used to shape the audience's response to a play and not just to recreate everyday reality. As he writes of Ó Tuairisc's use of lighting in *An Hairyfella in Ifreann* (1974), 'it is clear that there is also importance in the stage directions that deal with lighting changes during the acts – beyond the changes that are used to convey the time of day. It is the *Verfremdungseffekt* [the distancing effect] that is being used by the author on these occasions.'[82] It is also significant that one of the topics Ó Tuairisc recalled discussing with the Belgian playwright Edmund Kinds at an international poetry festival in Belgium was 'the creative power of light'.[83] In addition to simple sets and imaginative lighting, Ó Tuairisc called on playwrights and directors to be aware of the potential of music and dance to enhance the audience's understanding and enjoyment of the play, and by 1978, when he was getting ready to put his pageant play *Carolan* on stage, he urged the director 'to make use of every aspect of stagecraft – Acting, Storytelling, Music, Dance, Scenery – and to combine them all artistically to bring out the central theme of the Play'.[84] Needless to say, all of these elements would not only create a more emotionally charged experience for playgoers; they could also help convey the meaning of the play to those in the audience unable to follow all of what was being said on stage in Irish. Here we see once again the influence of the *geamaireachtaí* on Ó Tuairisc's approach to the theatre, although he had, of course, first encountered some of these techniques on the page in the Greek tragedies he so admired. And it was from the Greeks that he adopted what was from the start one of his most effective theatrical devices – the use of a chorus to comment on what was happening on stage. His goal was to make the chorus in his plays what he insisted it had been for the Greeks – 'part of the warp and weft of the play . . . the most important character of the *dramatis personae*' (de dhlúth is d'inneach sa dráma . . . an charachtar is tábhachtaí de na *dramatis personae*) (*Comhar*, May 1964, p. 11). This melding of Greek tragedy and Gaelic *geamaireacht*, yet another example of Ó Tuairisc's ability to see through to similarities beneath apparent contradictions, would make it possible for him to create ever more ambitious, textured, and challenging plays as his career as a dramatist progressed.

The first of his plays to be produced on stage was the one-act verse tragedy *Na Mairnéalaigh* (The sailors),[85] which won first prize in a competition sponsored by the Arts Council at the 1959 Oireachtas. He also prepared a version of the play for radio, which was broadcast by Radio Éireann in May 1960 and again in February 1984 (*II*, 24/5/60; 11/2/84). The stage premiere of the play took place at An Damer in April 1962 when, directed by Tomás Mac Anna, it was performed on the same bill with Máiréad Ní Ghráda's one-act *Stailc Ocrais*.[86] According to a brief unsigned notice in the *Irish Independent*, Mac Anna also provided the production with 'effective stage and lighting effects' (*II*, 10/4/62), although those effects do not seem to have pleased all the critics. In a review for the *Irish Times*, Tomás Ó Floinn ('Flann Mac an tSaoir') clearly liked much about the play: 'This play has form – a quality the lack of which makes most Irish drama a travesty of art (and I don't mean drama in Irish). It also has irony, the salt of all true drama, tragic or comic, and wit.' Paradoxically, however, given Ó Tuairisc's interest in developing 'visual imagination' (samhlíocht na súl) in Gaelic theatre, Ó Floinn felt that there was 'perhaps too much visual aid' in the production, for 'the play is really competent to speak for itself' (*II*, 10/4/62). 'S. Mac D.' was not all that impressed with the play, stating: 'I felt that the production of this play was mechanical and made too much use of records. The play itself was written in such a way that there could be sorrowful and hopeful feelings in it without making use of music at all' (*IP*, 12/4/62).[87] So much for Ó Tuairisc's attempt to expand the resources of Irish theatre by incorporating more visual and musical elements. The play seems to have had fewer revivals than one might expect, although it was performed by students from Queen's University, Belfast at the Oireachtas Drama Festival in Dublin in 1966 (*II*, 30/4/66) and again the following year at the Dungannon Gaelic Drama Festival, where it won first prize (*DP*, 12/3/67). It was also staged by An Cumann Gaelach at UCD in 1967 (*IP*, 20/12/67), but does not seem to have had any notable productions since.

As *Na Mairnéalaigh* begins, we see the deck of a steamship on which rests the coffin of 'The Liberator', Daniel O'Connell, being brought back to Ireland after his death in Rome. The year is 1847, at the height of the Great Famine, and the ship is now approaching Dublin. Three sailors, an Irishman, a Cockney, and a German – all stereotypes – serve as a kind of clueless chorus, nervous about being on what is quite literally a coffin ship but having no idea who the corpse in the coffin is. At various points throughout the play, most effectively at the beginning and the end, we also hear a real chorus singing the 'Lux Aeterna' requiem from the Catholic funeral Mass. As the ship approaches Ireland, it is suddenly enveloped by a thick fog, what Cocky the Englishman calls 'yellow filth being blown from Ireland' (salachar buí á shéideadh ó Éirinn). Disgusted by this miasma, the German comments on the 'foul smell on this fog from Ireland' (boladh bréan ar an gceo seo ó Éirinn), whereupon the Irish sailor Páidí Ó Conaill comments: 'The smell of death can be noticed on the fog.'[88] Páidí speaks from experience, recalling earlier scenes of famine from his youth:

> At home in Mayo,
> They say there are three things that cannot be satisfied –
> Hunger, the Sea, and Death.
> When I was a boy in County Mayo
> I saw more corpses stretched out in one day
> Than you have seen in your life, Cocky.

Moreover, he puts blame for famine squarely on 'England's Misgovernment' (Mí-Rialtas Shasana).[89] Páidí is, of course, unaware that the man who many felt could save Ireland from such misrule lies in the coffin behind him.[90]

The argument that erupts after he makes this accusation is interrupted by the sound of a baby crying, a sound that the German interprets as the cry of the Valkyrie and Páidí as that of the *bean sí* (banshee). Cocky is the voice of modernity here, dismissing these superstitions matter of factly: 'This is the middle of the nineteenth century, see, / This is today, the year / Eighteen forty – ah – seven!'[91] Ó Tuairisc has, however, through his use of the requiem, the ominous fog, the reference to folk beliefs, and above all the ever-present coffin, created an atmosphere in which the rational laws of the nineteenth century yield to the timeless force of fate. The baby's wail turns out to be coming from a boat that holds an old man, an old woman, and the new-born child of their daughter. They are the sole survivors of an overcrowded ship bringing cattle and Irish peasants away from famine to England, prompting the steamer captain's expression of horrified amazement: 'The time of Victoria, / Who would think that there would be a tragedy like this / Acted out on the Irish Sea.' But he also realises this is no accident: 'Isn't the sea a strange fate / That prepares the meeting of these coffins, / Introducing the dead to each other.'[92]

While Ó Tuairisc's use of the shipwreck here may seem to be too facile a plot device, it works well as a subtle evocation of Dáibhidh Ó Bruadair's great eighteenth-century poem 'An Longbhriseadh' (The shipwreck), which laments the end of the Gaelic order after the 1691 Williamite defeat of the Irish at Limerick and the subsequent 'Flight of the Wild Geese', those Irish aristocrats and soldiers who left the country to take service in the armies of Catholic Europe. Another irony of the play is that the survivors of the ship-wreck in it would probably not see this connection even if they knew of the poem. This old man and his family have suffered greatly under the tyranny of what the German sailor early in the play calls 'the Masters who understand Realpolitik' (an Herrenvolk a thuigeann an Réalpolitik),[93] but remarkably he and his wife have retained hope – a hope conventionally, and uncon-vincingly, symbolised by their drowned daughter's baby – that they and their country will see better days. The source of their hope is, however, Daniel O'Connell, the man after whom they have named the child and of whose death (and presence as a corpse) they are of course ignorant:

He went across the sea to pray for help for us
From the Pope of Rome himself. The Liberator
[...]
But he will come. He will come as surely as the frost.
His voice will be heard again
Sweeping away this scarcity of the black famine
As if it were a morning fog before the wind.[94]

In a powerful passage he remembers once hearing O'Connell speak and feeling that he and his fellows were finding a voice through the words of their leader:

Myself, do you understand, on top of the hill
Bare-headed, speaking through the mouth of the Liberator. It was a liberation.
A liberation for myself and for thousands of my own race
Who live their lives between the two darknesses
In the hungry field of the years. Yes, indeed,
We ourselves spoke that day,
As one person through the mouth of the Liberator.[95]

That voice will never speak again, nor will the old man, his wife, or his granddaughter ever return to Ireland. The play ends with the requiem and the chugging of the steamboat, the symbol of Victorian realpolitik, saving them only for exile in England.

From the time the elderly couple are brought aboard, the play coalesces and comes alive. Prior to their appearance, Ó Tuairisc devotes too much time to the sailors, none of whom, including Páidí, are all that interesting, in the process diluting rather than enhancing the eerie mood he wants in the play. Nevertheless, the use of the baby as a symbol of what could be a more promising future for the Irish, an idea Ó Tuairisc suggests by having the infant named after O'Connell and makes explicit when the German sailor quotes the proverb 'life arises / From the same bed as death' (go n-éiríonn an bheatha / Ón leaba chéanna leis an mbás) is a cliché.[96] While such an idea is very much in keeping with his philosophy concerning the ultimate unity of apparent opposites, it is unconvincing here in face of the cruel irony of the old couple's fate. Still, even if it is not yet the kind of classically cathartic tragedy Ó Tuairisc aspired to create, *Na Mairnéalaigh* is a well-written and even, once it gets started, a gripping play, one worthy of its inclusion in Pádraig Ó Siadhail's *Gearrdhrámaí an Chéid* (The short plays of the century) as well as of consideration for future productions.

Ó Tuairisc turned to modern Ireland in his next play, the three-act *De Réir na Rúibricí*, which had begun life in English as *According to the Rubrics* before being redone in Irish. Máirín Nic Eoin points out one element of Ó Tuairisc's 'process of composition' (próiséas ceapadóireachta) was 'to create a work in one language and then, as part of the process of revision, to translate it into the other language' (saothar a chumadh i dteanga amháin agus ansin, ar chuid den phróiséas athdhréachtaithe, é a thionntú isteach sa teanga eile).[97] We will see other examples of this approach below. Having won a prize at the 1960 Oireachtas, the play had its premiere, directed by Traolach Ó hAonghusa, at Taibhdhearc na Gaillimhe in February 1961, and was then produced again in October of that year at An Damer with Tomás Mac Anna directing. In an unsigned review of the Galway production in *The Connacht Tribune*, the critic wrote: "'D'réir na Rúibricí" is a mixture of seriousness and comedy. The two ingredients are skilfully mixed to provide very digestible fare' (*CT*, 19/2/61).[98] 'P. Ó D.' was equally impressed with the Dublin production: 'Every character that Eoghan Ó Tuairisc created through his writing was drawn with assurance and imagination. They are all living characters . . . Most of the dialogue is excellent . . . It would be well worth paying a visit to this play' (*IT*, 1/11/61).[99] An anonymous critic for *The Irish Press* declared: 'Eoghan Ó Tuairisc has succeeded in writing a drama in Irish which has all the ingredients for a successful play in any language: well-drawn characters, racy dialogue, witty lines spiced by occasional satirical shafts at the familiar things and all welded together by pleasant and homely sentiments' (*IP*, 27/10/61). Even more effusive was Pádraig Ó Siochfhradha, who wrote:

Somerset Maugham says that the principal and sole business of literature and the theatre is to give pleasure and entertainment to the reading and listening public and that is exactly what Eoghan Ó Tuairisc's play 'De Réir na Rúibricí' does, and it does so better and more abundantly than does any original play in Irish I have yet seen. There was humour, great humour, in it and an edge to it. (*Feasta*, Dec. 1961, p. 23)[100]

As he concluded his review, Ó Siochfhradha predicted that the play would be performed again often, but after a few more productions, including another at An Damer in May 1970,[101] as well as that by the Gaelic League's Craobh Éanaigh at the Oireachtas Drama Festival in the Peacock in 1971 (*IT*, 28/4/71) and that by Cumann Drámaíochta Chorr na Móna in Rosmuc in the Conamara Gaeltacht in 1975 (*CT*, 25/4/75), *De Réir na Rúibricí* seems to have dropped from the repertoire. This neglect is in all likelihood a result of the fact that despite its timeless theme, its plot and many of the 'familiar things' it satirises are now irredeemably dated.

There are some good comic scenes in the play, almost all of them due to the character of Picí, who introduces the notion of 'rubrics' (rúibricí) that gives the work its title. Picí is the brother of the retired schoolteacher and widower Maitiú Macsuel, with whom he shares a house belonging to the local school in the town of Lios an Aicéadaigh. Picí is now the bishop's chauffeur, a position he sees as giving him a certain ecclesiastical standing and the consequent 'responsibility' to make sure that things in town are done 'according to the rubrics', in a manner that is 'canonical' (canónach) and has the proper *imprimatur*. All of this is very much tongue-in-cheek as is clear when he describes his ascent of what he calls 'the ecclesiastical ladder' (an dréimire eaglaisiúil):

> I used to go into the woods of the [bishop's] Palace, and up there under the cloistered quiet of the trees I felt for the first time the call to the church . . . My next step was into the Bishop's orchard at the age of thirteen, where I stole the apple of knowledge . . . My next step up the ladder of the church was into the kitchen of the Palace at the age of seventeen to court the Bishop's servant girl.[102]

Picí is a bit of a rogue, but he is also a kind and decent man and one blessed with a good deal of common sense. Unlike most of the people in the play he understands that while rules and rubrics have an important place in human life, there are times when they must be questioned, bent, and even broken.

His brother Maitiú holds a very different view of the world. For him, obedience to rules and regulations, especially those of the Department of Education, is at the very core of his being. Ó Tuairisc makes this rigidity clear in a stage direction on Maitiú's first entrance: 'After spending forty years dealing with the Government, his personality is regular, his speech, his walk, and his outlook on the world rigid and regular . . .'[103] When his son Marcas, who has succeeded him at the school, is late getting up one morning, Maitiú is outraged:

> We must roust him out on the floor here without further delay. It is a dangerous thing to be late to school. If the Inspector were to hear of it his goose would be cooked. 'The Teacher must be present ten minutes before the official time at which teaching begins in the school' – that's one of the strictest of the Rules and Regulations for the Administration of National Schools. Roust him out.[104]

As Maitiú himself tells a neighbour, he and his late wife – although one may well wonder how much say she had in the matter – laid out their sons' lives when they were still just boys: 'We planned it . . . We planned it long ago . . . We planned to give Seán to the Church since he was the most pious and quiet of the two, and that Marcas would go into the school as principal when it would be time for me to retire.'[105] Now those plans are falling apart as both sons are miserable in the professions into which they have been forced. Maitiú is not at all a bad man, but his certainty that his own invariable adherence to a set of preordained rules is the only way to live turns him into a tyrant who comes very close to ruining the lives of his sons.

Speaking with his father about his decision not to return to the seminary at Maynooth, Seán declares:

> I see now that I was never called. Since I was old enough to wear my first pair of trousers, the Church was put out before me, the road was prepared for me; it never occurred to me to think of any other vocation. I worked diligently at school and I pushed my way through all the exams; then I put on the black coat and off I went to Maynooth.[106]

However as the result of what he earlier called a sudden 'new view on life' (léargus nua . . . ar an saol),[107] all of these old certainties have vanished: 'But . . . I don't know . . . I can't explain it properly . . . Lately I have felt a great dissatisfaction inside me. In the evening when the white mist would come streaming across the playing field from the canal, I would look around me at the dim world and I would feel the loneliness of life blowing around my heart.'[108] Needless to say, his father can make no sense of his son's *cri de coeur*.

His other son Marcas's aversion to the classroom in which he himself had spent his life leaves him even more baffled, in part no doubt because Marcas expresses his dissatisfaction so forcefully: 'Two years ago I left the Training

College and I came home to Lios an Aicéadaigh with a firm intention to fulfil the duties of the post as well as I could. I hadn't spent a half-hour in the classroom down there when I realised clearly that I had made a mistake.'[109] In a later conversation with the young woman Neillí, he expresses his dislike of teaching in almost visceral terms: 'O, Neillí, you would never imagine the utter hatred I have for the four walls of that school with their gloomy maps showing the world and it divided into two halves like two halves of a rotten orange.'[110]

Despite his local prominence, the school's manager, An Dr Ró-Oirmhinneach de Búrca d'Arsaí (Burke-d'Arcy), shares none of Maitiú's complacency, although he does wear a mask of formidable authority, one of the dozen he believes are assumed by 'every mother's son of us' (gach mac máthar againn) in the course of a day.[111] What he does not yet understand is the importance of choosing the mask with which one can live comfortably and honestly. The stage directions present Dr de Burke-d'Arcy from his first entrance as a character who is both quite impressive and somewhat absurd: 'There is power in his voice, bitterness, friendship, mockery, petulance and venom; an occasional odd little expression from the American West can be noticed in his speech . . . and it seems to us that a distinctive, hard to control personality is standing before us.'[112] He can be surprisingly liberal at times – as in his apparent acceptance of the courtship of the young – but he will brook no challenge to his authority and tries to overawe others through his reputation for erudition based on a doctorate from the Sorbonne. This reputation has, however, by this time become an ill-fitting mask worn by a badly used and bitter cleric who, convinced his learning has been wasted in the performance of mundane pastoral duties, has entirely given up the intellectual pursuits that once gave meaning to his life, and he now reads nothing but American westerns. When the English scholar Lucy Skelton, whom he has scorned as his intellectual inferior despite her MA from Oxford, challenges him directly by bringing up one of those westerns, he is initially outraged, but finally faces up to the emptiness of his life as 'a cantankerous old man living on lies and pretence' (seanduine cantalach ag maireachtáil ar an mbréag agus ar an gcur i gcéill).[113] Moreover, he can now humbly ask Marcas to help him resume his life as a scholar-priest: 'Come to me tomorrow and we will begin together on the Gospel of St Luke in the original Greek – it's forty years since I opened the Greek Gospel.'[114]

Lucy is the main catalyst in the play, the exciting outsider who inspires others to face their fears and change their lives. She does so most effectively in conversations near the bonfire on St John's Eve, a brief carnivalesque escape from the routine of daily life. She is also, of course, an entirely improbable character, a beautiful young woman and scholar of comparative religions who has come to a rural town – one not even in the Gaeltacht – to spend time with a retired primary schoolmaster with an interest and expertise in local folklore. Even more unlikely is that she almost immediately falls in love with and marries the bishop's chauffeur Picí. But if we put these hard to ignore improbabilities aside, we can focus on how the new view of life she brings to Lios an Aicéadaigh is a liberating force in the play. One of the things that makes it easier for the people in the play to accept her is the fact that she has converted to Catholicism, although as she reveals, her conversion is not so much based on doctrinal conviction, much less a need for rules and rubrics to provide refuge from a troubling world, but rather from a yearning for what she believes to be a more expansive engagement with life: 'You asked me why I became a Catholic? It seemed to me that it was right to belong to a Church whose walls are as broad as the four walls of the universe.'[115]

At the heart of *De Réir na Rúibrící* is the attempt to reconcile another of Ó Tuairisc's false dichotomies by balancing the spiritual and the material, integrating the call to idealism with the demands of the real world, something that both Picí and Lucy seem able to do almost effortlessly at this point in their lives. For the rest, the play is a learning process as they discover that while they must do something with their lives, what they do must be their own decision if they wish to be happy and fulfilled. Obviously, the ending of the play, in addition to being much too drawn-out, is also far too facile and far-fetched. Seán and Marcas switch places, so that Seán is now teaching in the town he realises he loves and Marcas is off to Maynooth to study for the priesthood. With Seán at the school, Maitiú will be able to continue living in the house, sharing it with Seán and his new wife Neillí as well as Picí and Lucy. In fact, Maitiú is even able to show a bit of flexibility about how Dr de Burke-d'Arcy was able 'to gerrymander the Rules' (jearymandaeracht a dhéanamh ar na Rialacha) to make sure Seán would be appointed to the school. Dr de Burke-d'Arcy is also at peace with himself, his renewed engagement with profound scholarship apparently making it possible for him to see a simple truth beyond the unnecessary complexities and conflicts we create for ourselves: 'There is nothing as simple as Christianity when you think about it – a stable, first, and a wedding feast in the middle, and that simple Cross that it is hard for us to understand, and we make it a complicated affair with our Rules and Regulations.'[116] As we will see, however, simple lessons are for Ó Tuairisc often the hardest to learn, not to mention put into practice, and he returned to many of the ideas in *De Réir na Rúibrící* in his later plays.

Like *De Réir na Rúibrící*, Ó Tuairisc's next play, *Cúirt an Mheán Oíche* (The midnight court) – the title was later changed to *Cúirt na Gealaí* (The court of the moon) so that it would not be mistaken for a straight dramatisation of Brian Merriman's eighteenth-century poem *Cúirt an Mheán Oíche* – had its origin in a play in English. Ó Tuairisc wrote *The Midnight Court* in 1957, after having worked on two of the Abbey's *geamaireachtaí*. He sent the script to the Abbey the following year, but it was rejected despite some quite positive comments and suggestions from the readers, who remarked on its 'vivid and racy' dialogue and 'imagination, exuberance, humour and some command of language – more than many of our dramatists' and found it 'fantastic and delightful up to a point' and 'clever and well-written'. However, all of the readers felt the play was too long, and some expressed concern about Ó Tuairisc's 'violent crudity of thought and language' and thought the play was a propaganda piece motivated by 'the need to educate the frustrated, inhibited Irish out of their mortal fear of sex'. Indeed, as one of these readers wrote: 'I am afraid, however, that all Mr. Watters' adjuration to us Not To Be Embarrassed by Sex would not suffice to prevent a normal Irish audience to be weefully [*sic*] embarrassed by this play, quite moral though it is.' Ó Tuairisc must have been particularly rankled by the attitude of another reader who declared: 'At first I thought that this was something which certainly must be accepted even though it was obviously written for the English market and in that way resembled the work of Honor Tracy.' For this reader, the play was also 'too heavy-handed throughout its whole length' and 'might be less boring if judiciously cut to half its present length'.[117] Ó Tuairisc also sent the play to Longford Productions and Godfrey Quigley's Globe Theatre Company, both of which rejected it.

Obviously not discouraged, Ó Tuairisc put the play aside for a while, and when he returned to it in 1961 he took advantage of some of the Abbey readers' comments, shortened the script, and, most important, did the work in Irish.[118] This version of the play as *Cúirt an Mheán Oíche* won Duais na Taibhdheirce at the 1961 Oireachtas and was first produced at An Damer for the 1962 Dublin Theatre Festival with Tomás Mac Anna again directing. Critical reception was mixed. In the *Irish Times*, 'J. G.' wrote that 'last night's audience obviously enjoyed the many barbed sallies which enliven the dialogue. As an evening's entertainment, it can be recommended strongly, even to those with a moderate knowledge of the Irish language.' 'J. G.' was particularly taken with the 'symbolic trial scene of great ingenuity and con-siderable depth of argument' (*IT*, 27/9/62). The anonymous critic for *The Irish Press* saw it as 'an extravagant, humorous fantasy, which has only a very tenuous link with Merriman's poem', continuing: 'If the plot seemed some-what loose, its stagecraft and construction were extremely efficient and impressive – and had an obvious effect on the audience' (*IP*, 27/9/62). On the other hand, an anonymous critic for the *Sunday Independent*, having acknowledged that 'the audience liked the production' (thaithin an léiriú leis an lucht éisteachta), added 'it would be better for being cut here and there. At any rate it goes on too long throughout, and it becomes tedious in places' (*SI*, 30/9/62).[119] Earnán P. de Blaghd wrote that 'the play suffers from the author's inability to get away from irascible clerics, stage Englishwomen, and courting couples who change partners during the play, all of which were features of its predecessor "De Réir na Rúibricí"'. De Blaghd was also critical of the 'recognisable if sometimes very distorted, caricatures of contemporary Irish types' and 'a rather lifeless first act'. Still, he indicated that after that slow start 'the tempo of the play heightened and the last two acts provided many moments of hilarity and some uncomfortable reflections' (*II*, 27/9/62). The anonymous critic for *The Cork Examiner* saw little of value in the play, declaring that while it took its title from Merriman's poem,

> the work produced . . . is hardly worthy of the celebrated name. Ignoring the dramatic potential of the splendid rhythms, Eoghan Ó Tuairisc has abandoned the great poem – which must surely have been shaped into a sweeping lyric drama similar to 'Milk Wood' – and instead written a straightforward humdrum play which pivots on Brian Merriman's theme, but spends two largely needless acts in preparation for the trial scene of the third. The joke targets are well-tried and trusty . . . The play would have been moderately entertaining if Eoghan Ó Tuairisc had been content to use the theme, but not the title of Brian Merriman's poem. (*CE*, 5/10/62)[120]

Desmond Fennell obviously hated the play, acknowledging that it did provide the audience with 'innocent entertainment', but 'it is the entertainment of the variety show, not of the comic theatre. As satire it is parody on the real thing, for when would-be satire speaks in clichés it induces complacency.' For Fennell, 'The Censorship, the attitudes to sex, and the Celtic phantasy which Mr. Ó Tuairisc jibes at are so obviously remote from anything that really exists in Ireland that he ought to confine himself to jokes' (*Hibernia*, Oct. 1962, p. 15).

Audiences seem to have enjoyed the play, so much so that in a brief note *The Irish Press* reported of the first production at An Damer: 'The followers of drama in Irish are growing in number. As proof, we had to turn people away every night during the Dublin Theatre Festival when "Cuairt [*sic*] an Mheán Oíche" by Eoghan Ó Tuairisc was being produced by Tomás Mac Anna in the Damer.' (*IP*, 24/10/62).[121] The play remained fairly popular over the next 15 years. Among revivals were those by the Gaelic Society of the Christian Brothers' Past Pupils in Dublin's Dagg Hall at the 1964 Oireachtas (*CE*, 8/5/64); by Dublin's Craobh Liam Bulfin of the Gaelic League at Feis Átha Cliath and at the Oireachtas in 1969 (*II*, 7/3/69; *IP*, 2/4/69);[122] by students from Trinity College at Féile an Chomhchaidrimh in An Taibhdhearc in Galway in 1972 (*IP*, 2/2/72); by Taibhdhearc na Gaillimhe, with Pádraig Ó hÉanaí directing, in 1975 (*CT*, 4/4/75); and by Craobh Liam Bulfin again, with Seán P. Ó Ceallaigh as director, at An Damer during An tOireachtas

Drámaíochta in 1976 (*IP*, 20/5/76).[123] Writing bilingually of this 1976 production, Dominic O'Riordan offered a perceptive and balanced view of
Cúirt an Mheán Oíche. Acknowledging that he had not seen the play in years,
he continued: 'And I think, as I thought at that performance, that while it is
innocent and rich in thought, it is rather scattered in many scenes. There are
so many diversions of argument, it is hard to establish the play. Tediousness
is the result. It would seem as if someone had added interpolations in what
was originally a brilliant script.' Most notable was O'Riordan's insightful
appreciation of the 'great point of the play . . . that people try and must live
in what is called the real world, but that to exist, the world of fantasy, creeping
always over the shoulder, is also essential' (*IT*, 14/5/76).[124] O'Riordan also
called attention to the fact that there were only 'around twenty people'
(timpeall is scór daoine) at the performance he saw in 1976, a far cry from
the full houses of 1962 and, in all probability, an indication that while, as
with *De Réir na Rúibricí*, the main theme remains entirely relevant, the play's
plot and characters aged badly after the many changes in Irish life and
attitudes in the 1960s and 1970s.

Merriman's poem begins with the speaker setting out for a walk along the
banks of Lough Graney in Co. Clare and lying down for a brief rest, only to
find himself in the court of the divine Aoibheall, where the men of Ireland,
and in particular the priests, are tried and convicted for their lack of sexual
interest in women, who are consequently left frustrated and childless.[125] In Ó
Tuairisc's play, however, this solitary stroller is replaced by a group of people,
male and female, who will eventually appear in the court of Áine, 'The
Queen of the Moon' (Banríon na Gealaí), a figure who in Irish mythology is
another local divinity, a Co. Limerick counterpart of Aoibheall. Moreover,
with the play set in modern Ireland, Ó Tuairisc's characters are not nature-
loving folk out for a walk in the country, but harried would-be passengers
waiting for a train in a run-down station somewhere in the middle of nowhere
between Dublin and Athlone. It is also, as we soon find out, in the middle of
nowhen, as the stage directions suggest: 'The old bog and the old gods are
taking over the station at Slí an Ghruagaigh.'[126] As night falls on this Eve of
May, we meet the ragged old couple of Aonghus, the station's porter, and his
wife Áine. Áine, who will play the imposing central role as the judge in the
Midnight Court, is considerably less impressive on her first appearance: 'A
bold, lanky woman of forty, indications on her that she was once pretty, but
she is a ragged and slovenly person now, untidy clothes on her, her black
gypsy woman's hair in a bun at the back of her head, mocking eyes sparkling,
a hole in her stockings and a sharp tongue in her head.'[127] She brings Aonghus
the news that passengers are coming to the station, to which he responds in
astonishment: 'Passengers, do you say? In the name of Crom, what would

bring passengers to this graveyard? Don't the gods know that not a single train has stopped in Slí an Ghruagaigh since the time of the war when they used to stop to put a bit of turf in the engine?' The more spiritually attuned Áine quickly wonders whether even greater marvels lie in store: 'There is something strange spreading out there tonight – May Eve with a Full Moon. Do you think, Aonghus, that there is any chance that that ancient time of ours would be returning to the world? The time of the great gods, the time of love?'[128] Aonghus's response to her question is, at this point in the play, that of an earthbound and obtuse civil servant rather than that of one of the 'great gods' (déithe móra): 'You and your love! Shouldn't you be satisfied that there is a roof over your head and that you are married to a respectable man with a good, pensionable post, instead of going to England as a nurse as all the other fair ladies do these days since love was banned in this country?'[129] The clash between these opposing views of life will be at the heart of the play as it develops.

First, however, we must meet the other characters as they gradually come onto the platform. An Canónach Mac Mórna, D. D., D. ès Lit., is head of Ireland's Censorship Board, which watches for, bans, and seizes immoral books and periodicals. As was, however, the case with that other scholar priest de Burke-d'Arcy, he is not, despite his official position, an altogether unsympathetic character, as the stage directions indicate: 'He is a prim man, a perceptive, intellectual person who has a sense of humour, a scholar and a great after-dinner speaker.'[130] Aonghus's welcome to him is not that of the complacent civil servant of moments earlier: 'It's many a place we met each other, Canon. Anywhere there was the great traffic of the universe under the eye of the sun. In Rome, perhaps, when you were a student, or Salamanca; or perhaps you knew me in Egypt long ago, in the valley of the Nile when you were a high priest of Amon-Ra and the pyramids were being built!'[131] The canon is willing to humour him a bit, but he does want to know when the train will come, and he is not at all satisfied with Áine's response to his question: 'It is to come – but will it come?' And he is even more nonplussed when after he checks the schedule posted by Córas Iompair Éireann, the Irish transport service at that time, Áine tells him: 'Ah, may the great gods help Córas Iompair Éireann. They do their best, the loafers, but . . . the Good People have bewitched this station.'[132] As Rod Serling would say, 'we have entered the Twilight Zone'.

The next characters to arrive are the expatriate Irish poet Diarmaid Páircéir, who speaks with 'an educated English accent' (blas oilte Sasanach), and his English girlfriend Gráinne Wycherly, who works in a lingerie shop in London. Gráinne is a little uneasy about what she calls the 'ghostliness' (taibhsiúlacht) of rural Ireland, but Diarmaid rejects any notion of Celtic Twilight mysticism:

You came ashore today on the most unromantic island in the world. This country is under the control of a coalition of farmers, village publicans, and parish priests. They have cleaned romanticism out of the country; they sent the fairies and the leprechauns to America to earn dollars; they banished the poets – and myself among them – to the B. B. C.; and they wiped out the difference between male and female.[133]

Diarmaid is capable of ringing speeches about truth, love, and freedom: 'The great gods never die – imagination, beauty, truth, and love; they live on; although they have been banished by the Government, excommunicated by the Church, and damned by the Censorship Board, they live on – truth and love, like the sun and the moon.'[134] His behaviour does not, however, match his bombast. He has brought Gráinne to Ireland for what he calls 'a platonic weekend' (deireadh seachtaine phlatónach) – using the word 'platonic' in a very different sense than that with which we are familiar, for their weekend is obviously intended to be far more physical than philosophical. He has also provided her with a cheap ring from Woolworth's and explains why: 'You must wear the ring until we are safe and sound on the far side of Athlone. The Fir Bolg of this country do not understand Plato's philosophy. If they were to see a girl not wearing a ring going off in the night with a young man, what they would be thinking would not be the nicest thing!'[135] This little trick is dismissed as 'a foolish plan' (plean seafóideach) by the canon when he learns of it, much to the surprise and probably disappointment of Diarmaid, who expects from him 'an anathema'. Instead, the canon says that were he a young man like Diarmaid he would not take a young woman like Gráinne into the wilderness, but rather into the anonymity of a city where they could be 'passionately in love with each other' (go paiseanta i ngrá lena chéile). Indeed the priest is obviously sick of 'the young bucks of the *intelligentsia*' (boic óga an *intelligentsia*) like Diarmaid: 'Not only must I teach you your moral duties, but I must teach you your immoral duties as well!'[136]

It is precisely Diarmaid's puerile pseudo-intellectualism that led the canon to ban his book *Cúirt an Mheán Oíche*, based of course on Merriman's poem and written, as Gráinne says, 'in the filthy way that is fashionable' (sa mhodh gáirsiúil atá faiseanta).[137] As he makes clear in his argument with the poet, the canon does not fear the book as a forthright celebration of sexual freedom, but rather finds it 'too simple and too childish' (ró-shimplí, ró-leanbaí): 'It isn't passionate enough. There is nothing in it but clever obscenity and intellectual tinkering with love. That is a dangerous thing. Mental pablum that keeps the adult a child. That's not how it was with the poets and the great authors when they were describing love and courtship in the ditch.' These writers – he mentions King Solomon, St Paul, St Augustine, Chaucer, Dante, Shakespeare, and James Joyce – are 'adults. Men in whom passion and the intellect were interwoven' (daoine fásta. Fir a raibh paisean agus an intleacht fíte fuaite ina chéile iontu).[138] Lacking this kind of emotional integrity – the sort of synthesis of apparent opposites central in all of Ó Tuairisc's work – writers like Diarmaid can, in the canon's opinion, only produce 'obscenity' (an gháirsiúlacht) for 'you have no experience at all of love' (níl taithí ar bith agaibh ar an ngrá). When in a metaphorical gesture Diarmaid calls on the audience to serve as the jury in their dispute, the canon dismisses him as 'you who know nothing at all about life except what you learned out of books – you who never had the manliness to marry a girl . . .' (tusa nach bhfuil eolas ar bith agat ar an saol ach an méid a d'fhoghlaim tú as na leabhra – tusa nach raibh d'fhearúlacht ionat riamh cailín a phósadh . . .).[139]

The other characters in the play are all types: Diarmaid's brother Learaí is a farmer who is more interested in his cows than in courting Éadaoin, the lovely woman he is apparently expected to marry. When she flirts with him in the moonlight, asking what is on his mind, he answers: 'The cow, what else – don't you know that her time is up . . . and she is about to birth a calf. That whore of a moon will finish her off for sure and I far from home in this diabolic place.'[140] When she wonders whether there might be some spark of romance in him, 'any little spark of foolishness in your heart' (splaincín ar bith den amaidí i do chroí), his response can leave her in no doubt: 'You wouldn't know. If I had a couple of drinks under my belt, there's a chance I would marry you tomorrow morning!'[141] Diní Mac Cumhaill is a gombeen man and county councillor who feels that courtship is 'the greatest curse on this country' (an mhallacht is mó ar an tír seo):

> Here we have the age of Christian economics; the Church, the Government, and the County Council are of one mind that it is high time for us to banish those old-fashioned pagan customs – to put a stop to the courting in the meadow and the giggling in the ditch at dusk . . . It is not passing time, but losing time. It is not healthy. It is not Gaelic.[142]

He himself has been keeping company with the local schoolmistress for 20 years in an absurd relationship she realises will never lead to marriage:

> It is true that you never gave me a promise . . . unless it is a promise to keep me walking up and down the bank of the river every Sunday afternoon for twenty years. It is true that you never gave me a promise, unless it is a promise to send me a box of biscuits and a bottle of sherry every Christmas. It is true that you never gave me a promise, unless it is a promise that the school children write my name and the name of Diní Mac Cumhaill with chalk on the blackboard any time I leave the room –

Now, as she herself admits, she has become an embittered old maid: 'I came to hate the spring. April put bitterness in my heart. God knows that I was not bitter when I was a young girl –'[143] Unable to continue, she begins to cry. We also have 'the Woman of the House' (Bean a' Tí), the widowed mother of Diarmaid and Learaí, a woman who both dotes on and dictates to the sons whose lives she still wants to control.

Before moving to the climactic scene in the court, we should briefly take note of the names Ó Tuairisc has chosen for his characters. He would have already used names from classical and Irish mythology and literature for comic purposes in the *geamaireachtaí*, but in *Cúirt an Mheán Oíche*, such names are of more than comic interest. The place name Slí an Ghruagaigh immediately evokes images of the hairy and uncouth churls of early Irish literature and folklore, and we have already seen that Áine was the name of a local goddess corresponding to Aoibheall in Merriman's poem. The old porter Aonghus bears the ironic name of the pagan Irish deity Óengus, or Mac ind Óic, the god associated with love, whose residence was in Brú na Bóinne (Newgrange), which in the play is the name of a mysterious disappearing public house that serves drink that acts as a love potion. His surname 'Mac Gréine', means literally 'son of the sun', and this is the name of one of the kings of the divine Tuatha Dé Danann in Irish mythology. Diarmaid and Gráinne are, of course, the names of the lovers who elope to save Gráinne from marriage to the much older Fionn mac Cumhaill in *Tóruigheacht Dhiarmada agus Ghráinne* (The pursuit of Diarmaid and Gráinne), the great love story of the Fenian Cycle.[144] In the play, Ó Tuairisc uses 'mac Cumhaill' as the surname of the gombeen politician, adding the richly inappropriate forename Diníosas (Dionysius). 'Learaí' could be a reference to Labraid, the ass-eared king we will encounter again in Seán Ó Tuama's *Ar Aghaidh linn, a Longadáin* (Onward, Longadáin). At any rate, such an affliction would suit a man so obsessed with farm animals. Éadaoin is the name of the ill-fated peerless beauty in the medieval tales *Tochmarc Étaíne* (The wooing of Étaín) and *Togail Bruidne Dá Derga* (The destruction of Da Derga's hostel). Finally, the canon's surname links him with Goll Mac Mórna, the one-eyed enemy and later comrade of Fionn. While Ó Tuairisc does not use these names systematically, they are all entirely if ironically appropriate for the characters who bear them.

We may now turn to the court scene in Act III to which the whole play has been leading. As previously noted, right from the start we have been given indications that all is not as it should be at this deserted station on this moonlit May eve. Gráinne is dead right when she finds the place and time 'ghostly' (taibhsiúil). The 'Good People' (i.e. fairies) cast a spell on the telephone, which seems able to contact the dead; an announcement posted on the wall of the station was issued by a long defunct railroad company; the weird old pub, which is 'more like a mortuary' (cosúlacha le teach na marbh), at one point simply vanishes from the landscape; and just before the transformed Áine steps on stage in her full magnificence, the stars and moon disappear from the sky. In a comic twist that reflects Ó Tuairisc's belief that to adapt to change traditional values need a regular injection of new influences from the modern world – the role played by Lucy in *De Réir na Rúibricí* – the catalyst for Áine's transformation is her trying on of a sexy nightgown Gráinne has brought with her from the shop where she works in London. As Éadaoin explains, 'she put on the nightgown, trying it on, and at once a sort of change came over her.'[145] The stage directions, which call for a quick switch to darkness and the use of 'a slender thread of music' (téidín caol ceoil) for her entrance, make clear the nature and extent of Áine's metamorphosis: 'Áine walks in a stately manner onto the stage, taller, younger, with a brighter complexion, a nightgown of the "Dreamy" [a brand name] nylon glistening around her, her hair loose in beautiful flowing masses over her shoulders with little stars sparkling through it, her fair limbs bare, the moonlight sparkling out from her figure.' As judge, she will first deal with the case against Diní Mac Cumhaill, who on seeing her thinks he must be dreaming. Her response makes clear that we have left the illusory realm of the mundane for a more challengingly real place: 'You are fully awake for the first time in your life . . .'[146]

She wastes no time getting to work as judge and jury, telling Mac Cumhaill: 'It is not what you have done but what you have not done that is being questioned here tonight. It is not to sell porter and Indian meal or to export pigs, or to spout nonsense at the County Council, that the great gods put blood in your veins –' Her verdict is definitive: 'You are the godly, political, tight-fisted, verbose, useless, provincial man . . . You are the public idler, the gombeen fool, the parish pump statesman, the big mouth with little sense and the two-faced Tadhg –'[147] The funniest line in the play is Áine's response when Mac Cumhaill boasts that he is 'a member of the Gaelic League and Cú Chonnacht himself conferred the golden ring on me' (i mo bhall de Chonradh na Gaeilge, agus bhronn Cú Chonnacht féin an fáinne óir orm): 'O exactly! There you have the difference between the Gael and the Irish enthusiast: long ago the Gael would fall in love with a nice girl and give her the golden ring; but now the Irish enthusiast falls in love with a language and gives himself the ring!'[148]

Learaí the farmer does not come off much better: 'Look at the sensible man, girls! The Young Farmer. The backbone of the country. And isn't he a nice backbone for any country at all when it's up to his mother to do the courting for him!'[149] Nor is Áine impressed with Diarmaid the poet, the self-appointed authority on sex in Ireland: 'You are nothing but a first-class babbler. What good have you ever done in your life for any girl except to deafen her with nonsensical rigamarole that would make a boar sick to its stomach.'[150] To Áine, he is just 'an Irish babbler who puts on corduroy trousers, picks a couple of dirty words out of Dinneen's Dictionary and takes himself off to London as a poet or a daring playwright': 'Have sense, you babbler, your sort lives in literary trousers. You don't understand life's rough love.'[151] And even though she shares the canon's opinion of Diarmaid, she is not about to let the state's censor escape her condemnation: 'I care little about your taboos, Censor. You will impose taboos on the moon that raises the passionate tides in the blood of humans. If there are to be taboos imposed, it's I who will impose them.'[152] While Áine finds all the men guilty of neglecting women and thus causing emigration and the depopulation of the country, the Englishwoman Gráinne offers her own idiosyncratic interpretation of what has gone wrong with love and sex in Ireland: 'And I tell you, if the men are vanishing, the fault is not with the climate, or the shopkeeping, or the farming, or the censorship: all the fault is with the girls. From beginning to end, this national trouble of yours comes down to a question of lingerie manufacture.'[153]

At the sound of the ringing telephone – apparently the Good People calling to warn of the approaching dawn – the court scene comes to an end with Áine bestowing 'my curse on the men forever' (mo mhallacht go deo ar na fir) and leaving the darkened stage as the moon and stars return to the sky. She has, however, had a startling effect on those who appeared before her. In a conclusion that recalls that of *De Réir na Rúibricí*, Learaí and Gráinne realise they have been paired with the wrong people and choose each other instead,[154] and Diarmaid and Éadaoin reach the same conclusion. Even Diní Mac Cumhaill and his long-suffering fiancée are affected. She kisses him 'fervently' (go dúthrachtach) and they walk off 'with their arms around each other's waists . . . singing "Eibhlín a Rún" in harmony' (a lámha thar choim a chéile . . . comhcheol ar siúl acu: 'Eíbhlín a Rún').[155] To top things off, a train actually arrives to carry them all out of the limbo in which they have been trapped at 'the last station before marriage' (an stáisiún deiridh roimh an bpósadh). Just before the curtain falls, we see Áine back on stage offering sartorial proof that the old gods can adapt with the times: 'She is dressed strikingly: a resplendent pair of jeans, a little boating blouse, a stylish sunhat.' Moreover, as she tells Aonghus, Gráinne has left her case full of lingerie behind, 'full of the most beautiful clothes I ever saw' (lán de na héadaí is áille dá bhfaca mé riamh). Aonghus's response is entirely fitting given his mythological connections: 'Well, my darling, you spark up the youth in me.'[156]

As both Máirín Nic Eoin and Martin Nugent have written, the influence of his work with the Abbey *geamaireachtaí* is obvious in this play – in the entirely improbable happy ending (less problematic in a comedy of this kind than in the more realistic *De Réir na Rúibricí*), in the episodic structure, in the many implausible events throughout, in the type characters, in the grandilo-quent names from mythology and literature given those characters, and in the satirical sallies and jokes. On occasion these elements do seem to be at cross-purposes, and the play is quite a bit more repetitive than this simple summary may suggest. Moreover, as noted above, some of the once sharp social commentary has become badly dated. Still, *Cúirt an Mheán Oíche* must have been a breath of fresh air for many theatregoers in its own time, and it could probably still, like the comedies of John B. Keane, amuse a modern audience able to allow its imagination to take it back to a very different but not all that distant Ireland.

With *Lá Fhéile Míchíl* (The feast of St Michael), Ó Tuairisc returned to history and tragedy in what is his finest play.[157] A prizewinner at the 1962 Oireachtas, it was first produced by An Cumann Gaelach of Queen's University, Belfast at the Lyric Theatre in that city in February 1963. Following the performances in Belfast, the Queen's group took the play to Ballymena, Co. Antrim, Dundalk, Co. Louth, Ring, Co. Waterford, and then to the Oireachtas in Dublin, where, with Lionard Ó Coigligh directing, the production was awarded first prize at Féile Náisiúnta na Drámaíochta. On the recommendation of one of the Oireachtas judges, An Damer invited the Queen's students to perform the play there in June 1963; it had also been produced by Taibhdhearc na Gaillimhe, with Traolach Ó hAonghusa directing, in April of that year. Moreover, An Damer mounted its own production of the play in March 1964 with Niall Tóibín as director. Cork and Limerick would also get to see a production of the play by Limerick's Aisteoirí Bhréanainn, directed by Éamon Draper. The Cork performances were at the Little Theatre in that city (*CE*, 23/4/64), while those in Limerick were at a Gaelic drama festival in Shanagolden (*IP*, 7/3/64).

Given all these productions in so short a time, it should be no surprise that the critical response to the play was unanimously positive. The anonymous critic for Belfast's *The Irish News* called the first production at the Lyric Theatre the 'highlight of the evening' (*IN*, 21/2/63), while having seen the play at An Damer in 1963, 'P. Mac A.' pronounced it 'in many ways . . . Ó Tuairisc's most mature play' (ar go leor bealaí . . . an dráma is foirfe ag Ó Tuairisc) (*EH*, 22/6/63). Writing of An Taibhdhearc's production, 'Lugh' proclaimed: 'As long as this author and others like him continue working, Gaelic Drama is in no danger . . . Having a play like this on the boards is a sign of hope for drama in Irish' (*Inniu*, 29/3/63).[158] In a 1963 piece on Ó Tuairisc, Risteárd Ó Glaisne had high praise for the play:

This play moves along very quickly. It is a confident and well-crafted piece. The author deals effectively with the emotions of his audience, now holding something back from them; now thrusting something at them; suddenly throwing new light on something, with humour and irony behind the dialogue or the action much of the time. The characters are people you could believe in. The play keeps the people watching it fully involved. (*IT*, 3/7/63)[159]

In a lengthy review of An Damer's 1964 production in *Feasta*, Brian Ó Baoill devoted most of his attention to the actual performance on the night he attended, but he did neatly isolate one of the central themes of the play – 'love and hate tearing each other apart' (grá agus fuath ag tarraingt as a chéile) – and stated: 'The play was interesting throughout and it kept us on the edge of our seats to the end.' He went on to urge his readers to attend the play, stating that 'It would be worth it for us to go see this play; it was interesting and controversial, and it was another step forward for Eoghan Ó Tuairisc as a playwright' (*Feasta*, June 1964, p. 19 and 21).[160] Writing in the *Irish Times*, 'T. T.' declared: 'This is more than a play about the Civil War. It *is* the Civil War – the Romantic one, with hardly an echo of the aborted social revolution . . . The last scene is pure Hamlet . . .' (*IT*, 14/3/64). Of this same production directed by Niall Tóibín, 'P. Mac G.' wrote: 'The play is a well thought-out piece about the civil war of 1922–23 with good construction and characterization and a well-sustained momentum' (*EH*, 12/3/64). Five years later, the anonymous critic for *The Cork Examiner* described the play as dramatising 'one poignantly stirring episode' set against the background of the Civil War (*CE*, 22/4/69).[161]

Despite the demands it imposes on amateur drama groups in terms of the size of its cast, the subtlety of its characterisation, and the depth of its themes, *Lá Fhéile Míchíl* continued to have some appeal for such groups. Among productions were those by An Cumann Drámaíochta of University College, Galway at Féile Drámaíochta an Chomhchaidrimh in An Taibhdhearc in 1967 (*IP*, 1/2/67); by Co. Antrim's Aisteoirí na nGleanntaí at the Oireachtas Drama Festival in the Peacock in 1970 (*IT*, 20/4/70);[162] and again by UCG's An Cumann Drámaíochta in 1982 (*CS*, 8/3/83). It is indicative of the state of theatre in Irish for the past 30 years that I have found no other major productions of one of the finest plays in the Gaelic repertoire.

Lá Fhéile Míchíl is set in the postulants' garden of a convent some 20 miles south of Dublin in September 1922,[163] three months into the Irish Civil War between the 'Free Staters' who had accepted the 1921 Anglo-Irish Treaty and formed a native government, and the 'Irregulars', the republicans who rejected that treaty and government.[164] From the beginning of the war in late June 1922, the republicans suffered a series of defeats, and even as early as the time in which the play is set, the forces of the Free State were obviously on their way to victory. Ó Tuairisc begins the play with a brief 'preview' (réamhradharc) in which we hear the nuns' chanting of matins interrupted by the fire of machine guns and see a shadowy figure climbing over the garden wall and seeking shelter in a shed. Soon two postulants enter the garden. Although they were good friends on the outside, they have taken different stands with regard to the war, and their conversation quickly grows heated when they turn to that subject. Nuala has a brother who is an officer in the Free State army, while Maeisí was once interested in a young man who fought together with Nuala's brother against the British but is now a republican guerrilla. For Nuala, this man, Pacaí Armstrong, is now 'a murderer from behind walls' (murdróir ó chúl claí), while Maeisí regards Nuala's brother Emmet as 'one of the Free State's arrogant dictators' (deachtóir dalba de chuid an tSaorstáit).[165] Their argument is stopped by the mistress of postulants, but she then finds herself in a similar debate with the convent's gardener Murtagh, who has no use for either side and indeed regards both Emmet and Pacaí as 'bloody murderers . . . slipping around here trying to set fire to the police barracks or to steal the chanies [china] from the Big House' (murdróirí fuilteacha . . . ag sleamhnú thart anseo ag féachaint le tine a chur le beairic na bpóilíní nó na chanies a ghoid as an Teach Mór).[166] Murtagh also tells the nun – and the audience – that during the previous night Free State troops had engaged a group of Irregulars, only one of whom escaped.

Almost immediately, 'the Big Priest' (an Sagart Mór) and 'the Young Priest' (an Sagart Óg) enter. Before long they are engaging in the same political debate, with the Big Priest echoing a nineteenth-century bishop of Kerry's opinion of the Fenians by stating that hell is not hot enough for 'the ruffians' (na rifínigh) who oppose the legitimate government, and the Young Priest defending as an idealist Pacaí Armstrong, whom his clerical colleague calls 'a wild animal' (ainmhí allta) and 'an enemy of the people' (namhaid don phobal). Indeed the Big Priest regards the very idea of a republic as 'a pagan dream' (aisling phágánach) imported from 'republican, non-Christian, democratic, revolutionary, atheistic, red France' (an Fhrainc phoblachtach, neamh-Chríostaí, dhaonlathach, réabhlóideach, ainchreidmheach, dhearg).[167]

Nuala's brother arrives at the convent to search for Pacaí, and the stage directions make clear that he has an impressive military presence: 'A powerful, well-built, zealous, practical young man, the kind who sustains his own vision in his heart without saying much about it. A share of military colour enters with him – the new green uniform, the leather and the brass glistening, the Webley revolver in its holster.'[168] More important, he brings to the convent the authority of the new native state and the reality of the Civil War, a reality of which he has a profound personal understanding: 'There are no rules at all involved in this game of ours. It isn't war but rather personal spite. It is self-destruction – self-destruction on a national scale.' His men are no longer fighting for any abstract ideals: 'There is no longer right or wrong. All that remains with them now is personal vengeance; one death deserves another; it's as if our two sides are bewitched by gunplay, and the slaughter will continue to the bitter end.'[169]

Emmet is soon face to face with Pacaí, 'a slender, powerfully built man . . . who looks wretched, his coat in tatters, his tie missing, his shirt open at the throat . . . the leather of his old Sam Browne belt is unpolished as is the holster holding his pistol' (fear slim téagartha . . . cuma ainnis air, a chasóg ina giobal, a charabhat ar iarraidh, a léine scaoilte ag an scornach . . . níl snas ar leathar a sheanchreasa Sam Browne, ná ar an gcumhdach ina bhfuil a phiostal sáite).[170] Moreover, Ó Tuairisc informs us in a stage direction that while Pacaí is 'a man of spirit with a quick mind and eloquence . . . he is not a realist in the usual sense of the word, for he lives in a dream.'[171] In other words, the divide between the Free State realist Emmet and the republican idealist Pacaí runs far deeper than even their disagreement over the Treaty and the Republic; they view all of life from opposing, perhaps irreconcilable viewpoints. In a 1964 television interview in Belfast, Ó Tuairisc stated: 'My play is quite deliberately set on the Feast of St. Michael. I see Michael the Archangel as the first Free State officer and the other fellow – the eternal rebel, the prince of light – was the first Republican' (*IP*, 9/3/64). And lest we think that as a Catholic and former officer in the Irish army he would find it easy to take sides here, Máirín Nic Eoin has drawn our attention to a note he wrote in his copy of T. S. Eliot's *On Poetry and Poets* in response to Eliot's comment that the civil war of the seventeenth century had never been concluded and that 'I question whether any civil war ever does end'. Ó Tuairisc wrote:

> Curiously true: here in Ireland, at Galbally College, we loved Raftúraí and we loved Milton. Felt Satan the Republican par excellence – the real Son of God – 'Heaven' appeared like the British Government – Adam and Eve like 'Shoneens' – converted with some reluctance, to the Republican State – 'Paradise Won.' Every man, not dead to generous feeling, must sympathise with Satan against the Omnipotent.[172]

The question for Ó Tuairisc in this play is whether those 'not dead to generous feeling' could sympathise with 'the Republican par excellence' while still doing their duty to the Free State in which their actual daily lives would have to be lived.

One character in the play who believes such a synthesis of the ideal and real is possible is the formidable mother superior Mère Michèle de Lattre-Tassigny, whose feast day is about to be celebrated as the play begins. Before we meet her we have been given a clear idea of her character through the joking references of the Big Priest. He calls her 'a female Napoleon' (Napoleon baininscneach) and 'the Church Militant in a black skirt' (an

Eaglais Mhíleatach faoi sciorta dubh) and tells the Young Priest that she is a member of 'the *crème de la crème*' (an craem de la craem) of the French aristocracy and has herself fought against Germans in Paris, 'Indians' in Canada, and, for good measure, cardinals in Rome.[173] On her entrance the stage directions state: 'She is a strong, quick-minded woman, an actor at heart, dignity, understanding and a sense of humour interwoven in her personality. She always has her emotions under the control of her mind . . . and that penetrating mind and unbending spirit underlie everything in her.' Moreover, 'she understands both sides – the need for war, the need for peace, the need for government, the need for revolt. Like all mystics, she is practical . . .'[174]

She has now been drawn into two conflicts, one of which she sees as of minor significance compared to the other. That less important conflict is the political and military one between the Free State and the Republic, a war in which it is obvious that she favours the government side: 'It is easy enough to fight and die for a vision, but it is not easy to fight and die for a physical, practical, imperfect thing called a Free State!'[175] And despite her French origins, she can say 'I am an Irish person . . . And I say firmly that I am proud to finally be welcoming this lad as a member of the National Army of Ireland'.[176] Still, while she respects Emmet's sense of duty to his uniform and country, her own loyalty is to a higher power – 'the international and supranational Church' (an Eaglais idirnáisiúnta agus osnáisiúnta). As she tells the Young Priest, 'I need your help in this civil war, the only civil war worthy of mention: the old war: the Church on one side, and the State on the other side . . . That State out there whose machine guns you are looking at. The new State, the *de facto* Government.'[177] Although, as we have seen, she can feel some human pride in the existence of that state, she has no illusions about its ultimate value: 'A liberal, parliamentary government based on democracy. A dim-witted, decent government of the pious middle class, without history, without imagination, without a gifted aristocracy, without mystique, without spiritual resilience: the sort that changes its sails as every new economic wind blows.' Even the most doctrinaire republican ideologue would find little fault with her dismissal of the new state here: 'The vision of the faith of Easter lost, and the bourgeois gombeenism putting on the crown . . .'[178] Her plan is to somehow 'cooperate with those people outside; but . . . first to let them know that there is a limit to their power and to their authority at those walls' (comhoibriú leis an muintir sin amuigh; ach . . . tabhairt le fios dóibh, ó thosach, go bhfuil teorainn lena gcumhacht agus lena gceart ag na ballaí sin).[179] It is, however, difficult to imagine how the Free State forces will see anything cooperative about her decision to grant Pacaí asylum in the convent. Moreover, the Young Priest has already warned her that she is playing 'a dangerous game' (cluiche contúirteach), for 'you are not playing with abstractions – the policy of the Church or the policy of the State – but with people and with human passion. Fiery people . . . Irishmen; young people . . . who have not yet left their hearts behind on the fields of the years.' Indicating her crucifix, she replies: 'This Young Man was not careful.'[180] One could, however, easily get the impression that she is trusting far more in her own strength of will than in Christ – she states 'These days I am nothing but will and a skeleton' – to impose a solution on this crisis.[181]

In the meantime, she encounters two of those 'fiery' young Irish people, the postulants Nuala and Maeisí, who, in a twist that should by now be familiar from Ó Tuairisc, are finding their initial attractions misplaced. The flighty Maeisí is now infatuated with Emmet – in large part, it seems, due to his uniform – and has turned away from Pacaí, who had once, before she entered the convent, made a sexual advance on her that she says revealed to her 'the ugliness of life . . . the filthiness attached to you and to a man's love on this earth . . . the physical lewdness of the human being' (gránnacht an tsaoil . . . an ghairsiúlacht a bhaineas leat agus le grá fir ar an talamh seo . . . graostacht chollaí an duine dhaonna).[182] Unfortunately, Ó Tuairisc does not do anything with this idea, one far too important to be raised and then left undeveloped. At the same time, Nuala has fallen in love with Pacaí. Needless to say, these very human complications create more problems for Mère Michèle. Nuala, for example, tries to convince her brother to simply allow Pacaí to escape, an action that would, of course, be a total dereliction from his duty, as he makes clear by drawing on a classic trope of civil war litera-ture: 'And I swear to you, girl – if this Armstrong were my own brother – I swear to you that the bond of the womb would not come between me and my duty.'[183] However, as he thinks of his sister's plea and remembers again that Pacaí saved his life during the War of Independence, Emmet is willing to leave the convent and tell his men he did not find Pacaí. At this moment, the republican emerges from hiding with his gun pointed at him. Pacaí's plan is to use Emmet as a hostage for his escape, even though Emmet scornfully dismisses the idea as more of Pacaí's 'ceaseless romanticism' (rómánsaíocht an t-am go léir) and tells him to accept the fact that he and his fellow Irregulars have reached 'the end of the fables' (deireadh na bhfinscéalta).[184] At this point of high tension, the mother superior enters and manages to convince both men to surrender their weapons and join her 'to eat a little meal in the guest house – the two of you: the realist and the dreamer. *Enfants de la patrie*' (chun béile beag a chaitheamh sa teach aíochta – an bheirt agaibh: an réalaí agus fear na haislinge. *Enfants de la patrie*).[185]

When the mistress of postulants warns her superior about what she sees as 'playing both sides' (dá thaobhachas), the attempt 'to have it both ways – to hunt the prey and prevent the hunt' (an dá thaobh a bhreith leat – an chreach a sheilg agus an tóir a chosc), Mère Michèle dismisses her concerns with a characteristic statement of high principle: 'There is only one side, and one cause. A Republic or a Free State, they don't matter in the end, they are just temporary forms for those of us in the army and uniform for the cause of the Cross.'[186] She is, however, rapidly moving from confidence to *hubris*, as is obvious in her denial of the Young Priest's premonition of 'an evil fate being augured for this place' (droch-chinniúint á thuar don láthair seo): 'Celtic visions! The same for the Mistress. Do all of you in this country live in the shadow of a vision?'[187] Her confidence/*hubris* will be challenged most cogently by a mysterious messenger from the Free State government who comes to speak with Emmet but also engages in a very civil debate with the mother superior.[188] In effect, he serves as a tempter, playing on her understanding of the demands the real world makes on those in authority. Identifying himself as a 'Dubliner from the streets' (jackeen sráide) with a great respect for the French, who, he says, may be 'fiery' (teasaí), but are also 'reasonable' (réasúnta). She replies that she has a great respect for 'the National Government' (an Rialtas Náisiúnta), but that its ministers are young and lack experience of statecraft, and could therefore inadvertently make serious mistakes. When the messenger replies that anyone can make mistakes, even a bishop or a nun from France, this particular French nun is unfazed: 'It happens now and again that a new Government tries to do more than it can. They forget that there are forces other than the State, forces more important and rooted in history, perhaps, than the State itself.' To his jab that some people are more familiar with prayer than with the provision of 'the daily bread of the country' (arán laethúil na tíre), she parries with the next line of the Lord's Prayer about forgiving those who trespass againt us.[189] The stalemate is thus unbroken, and the messenger, stymied, can only say: 'We have made a mess of this world without any doubt.' Then, glancing at the prayer on the base of the statue, he adds: 'Yes, indeed, Michael – ora pro nobis!'[190]

He is right, and soon whatever scheme has been concocted by the mother superior is unravelling in face of the kind of human raw material she finds hard to comprehend or sympathise with, as we have been reminded by the mistress of postulants and as we have already been told in the stage directions on her first entrance:

> The greatest fault in her character is that she is a bit blind to the ordinary passions of the ordinary person. Planning great ecclesiastical policy and carrying it out, there is a danger that she will drive people beyond their limits – people who do not have as strong a will and the passion of whose hearts is not under the same firm control that she has.[191]

Moreover, we soon find that she does not understand all of the passions in the heart of lesser mortals. Thus, when speaking of Nuala and Pacaí, she tells the mistress of postulants she realises the depth and power of sexual attraction, but is then utterly baffled by what love drives Nuala to do.[192] Nor, despite her unyielding commitment to her Church, does she understand the similarly resolute republicanism of Pacaí any more than as the pragmatist she prides herself on being can she imagine the lengths to which Emmet will go to fulfil what he believes to be his duty to the state. Indeed Emmet and Pacaí have a far better understanding of each other's motives, as Pacaí makes plain when speaking to his enemy: 'The Split is between the two of us. Between the mental mould of the two of us, between our hearts and our memories, our blood, our veins, our ancestry, and the breastmilk the two of us sucked.'[193] Moreover, Pacaí knows that their personal conflict has far greater repercussions, that they are both archetypes locked in an eternal struggle: 'We are just the two historical shadows. The two kinds have always existed and the two kinds always will: the Free Stater and the Republican. Even if a Republic is established, there will be people to rise up against the Republic, and people rising up against the uprising. Forever.' Among those listening to this tense conversation, the Big Priest understands that what Pacaí is talking about here is the inescapable 'Sin of the Garden' (Peaca an Gháirdín), while the mistress of postulants rejects the republican's ideas out of hand, insisting 'it is not history that shapes the person but the person, with God's grace, who shapes and bends history'.[194] The only character in this play who might have that power is, of course, the mother superior, and it is her personal tragedy and the tragedy that Ó Tuairisc sees us all sharing that even with God's grace she is helpless to stop the inevitable disaster that is approaching.

Emmet finally decides he cannot arrest the man who had saved his life and for whom he still has great respect. Pacaí, however, refuses to accept what he feels is his enemy's pity and challenges Emmet to do his duty. Nuala rushes forward, but Emmet pushes her away. As Emmet then orders Pacaí to open the door to the outside, Nuala snatches a pistol from the base of the statue where the mother superior had put the guns she took from Emmet and Pacaí,[195] and shoots her brother in the back. She is immediately shocked into madness by what she has done.[196] Stunned, but still capable of understanding why Nuala has committed the act, Pacaí prays for God's mercy on her and 'on all of us who are guilty in the bloody tragedy of this feast day' (orainne go léir atá ciontach i ngoldráma fuilteach na féile seo).[197] The mother superior, on the other hand, is dumbfounded in her incomprehension: 'This disaster comes on me out of the clear sky. I was trying to go between them – *enfants de la patrie*. I was not expecting this ugly and extreme passion –'[198]

In a 1963 lecture on 'Catairsis' (Catharsis) to Cumann na Scríbhneoirí, Ó Tuairisc, with reference to the theories of Freud, spoke of 'the great work of the art of tragedy' (mórshaothar na healaíne tragóidí) as a work 'that bewitches us by the excellence of its craftsmanship, that puts us as it were into a hypnotic sleep and makes it possible for us to know the reality of life, without concealing any part of its privacies or any bit of its ugliness' (a chuireann faoi gheasa sinn ag foirfeacht a ceardúlachta, a chuireann sinn mar a bheadh faoi chodladh hipneoiseach, agus a chuireann ar ár gcumas réalachas na beatha a aithint, gan páirt dá phríomháidí ná gan pioc dá ghránnacht a cheilt), so that we are cleansed by 'the Understanding . . . the Terror and . . . the Pity' (an Tuiscint . . . an tUafás agus . . . an Trua) of 'the burden of sin and . . . the pretence of the false conscience of hypocrisy' (ualach an pheaca agus . . . cur-i-gcéill bhréagchoinsias na fuarchráifeachta).[199] In *Lá Fhéile Míchíl* Ó Tuairisc created a work that gives rise to just such a catharsis for modern audiences, and the play is likely to remain among the finest tragedies ever written in Irish.[200]

Audiences would not see Ó Tuairisc's next play in Irish, *An Hairyfella in Ifreann*, until 1974. Once again, the work had its origins in a play in English, *The Frogs*, inspired by the comedy of the same title by Aristophanes. This play in English was completed in 1971, and he prepared the Irish version for entry in the 1973 Oireachtas competitions, where it won a, for him, disappointing second prize.[201] *An Hairyfella in Ifreann* had its premiere at Taibhdhearc na Gaillimhe in 1974, directed by Seán Ó Briain and with music by Tom Cullivan. The first Dublin production was by Maynooth's Aisteoirí na Cuallachta (The actors of the sodality) in An Damer at Féile Náisiúnta na Drámaíochta in 1975. Éamonn Ó Conghaile was the director. Obviously concerned about what audiences would make of the play, Seán Ó Briain discussed it with a reporter from *The Connacht Tribune* before it opened: 'It's extremely complex, highly individualistic, a milestone in drámaíocht na Gaeilge. It makes use of many theatrical, poetical and highly idiosyncratic techniques' (*CT*, 31/5/74).[202] At the first performance in Dublin the following year, the Oireachtas adjudicator Dónall Farmer told the audience that he himself did not understand the play 'in its entirety', explaining that 'this is a very unusual, very clever – possibly too clever – [play] depicting the mores of the present day in Ireland' (*II*, 29/4/75). It is, then, probably not all that surprising that most critics shied away from the play, with the only significant review – a positive one by the way – appearing in the *Galway Advertiser*.[203] The play has also never had a stage revival, although Radio Éireann broadcast it in six parts on six successive Saturdays from 25 January to 29 February 1992, a strategy that could hardly have helped make the play more comprehensible for listeners.

In fact, the play is not all that difficult to follow. It is, however, a bit of a mess – too long, too repetitious, and with too many characters, the presence of one of which, the young black man Djinbawn, remains an unexplained mystery. Perhaps, given his occasional spouting of Irish nationalist shibboleths and his involvement with guerilla activities in Northern Ireland, he is meant to suggest Irish affinities with post-colonial peoples worldwide. If so, this idea is never properly developed. The play opens on 23 April (the Easter Rising of 1916 began on 24 April), in the sleepy town of Baile na gCloch on the Royal Canal in 'the Great Plain of Ireland' (Machaire Mór na hÉireann). The canal port in Baile na gCloch is being closed down and the last barge that will dock there has just arrived. Against a realistic set and a chorus of 'Uch, Uch, Uch' from the frogs, the crew discuss the end of their way of life. The old bargeman Jójó tells Djinbawn: 'We're done for, Djinbawn. Myself and you and the likes of us who live on the path of the water. We're used up now, heaped like old shoes on the dry ground, with the old Royal Canal rotting in the mud –'204 Right from the start, Ó Tuairisc makes clear in the words of Jójó that the moribund state of Baile na gCloch – and in particular the disgusting condition of the canal – are symbolic of what 'búrjúis' (bourgeois) Ireland has become: 'The Gates are allowed to rot in the mire, the water just green dregs with weeds and dead dogs floating in it and the foul rubbish of the Ha'penny Republic, and all of it taken over by the Kingdom of the Frogs.'205 Throughout the play, the croaking of the frogs will underscore the idea that whatever process of evolution produced Baile na gCloch and its inhabitants has reversed direction, leaving these people stuck in the metaphorical mud of their native place. Once again, it is Jójó who best gives expression to this sense of stagnation: 'Time has stopped, and one more grey day is no more concern to me than any other grey day at all.'206 It is no wonder that the old harbourmaster now feels 'I am nothing but a ghost' (nach bhfuil ionam ach taibhse).207

To make things worse, no one expects things to ever get better while the town – and the entire nation – are under the thumb of gombeen men like Jaxy Pat, another version of Diní Mac Cumhaill from *Cúirt na Gealaí*. Jaxy Pat regards himself as 'a man who sees visions' (fear a fheiceann aislingí) and disingenuously claims that 'somehow money sticks to me' (bealach éigin, greamaíonn an t-airgead díom), but there is nothing idealistic or passive about his accumulation of riches, and when he hears that the railroad may come to town, he is eager about the prospects: 'But now, for the Business Man, in this age of the European Markets, there are no small benefits involved with the –' Knowing that the ordinary people will share none of those benefits, the *bean feasa* (wise woman) Nanó cuts him off: 'What good is the Railroad for us except to ship your bullocks and lamb and the poor children of this town to Livverypool in England?'208 Pondering what has made Jaxy Pat rich and will make him richer, the harbourmaster despairingly concedes: 'It's the System. Progress, progress, organising, re-organising, unre-organising. Efficiency. Speed. Economics. The big wheel rolling faster and faster still, paying no attention to and not recognising the human soul –'209

To this stultifying and frog-infested place returns the dramatist Lughaí, born and raised in the poorest section of the town, institutionalised as a juvenile for planting a bomb in a pawnshop there, and now, after emigrating to England, a successful playwright in London. The townspeople, most notably the snobbish mother of Dorotaí, to whom he is about to be married, look down on Lughaí as 'Mac Bucaí na Scuaibe' (The son of Bucky the Brush) because his father made his living cleaning manure from the streets of the town. (He himself recalls the days of his youth as 'the Frog-Story of my life' (Frog-scéal mo Bheatha).)[210] Predictably enough, the locals also find the artist alien, nicknaming him 'Chekovsky' and mocking the play of his that has been produced in the town. Indeed Nanó, who was the midwife at his birth, makes clear that he has been strange from the start: 'A little mist of hair covering him from the top of his head to the stump of his how-do-you-do. Sweet Christ, I said, here comes the Hairyfella!'[211] For Jaxy Pat, Lughaí is 'the strangest little goat I ever saw!' (an pocán is aistí dá bhfaca mé riamh!)[212] There is also an element of envy mixed with their contempt, for now that he is 'a maker of Plays for the Tillyfish' (déantóir Drámaí don Tillyfish), he is able to afford the best hotel in town 'where there is mahogany under the beds, and blue tishy paper in the fare-ye-well' (mar a bhfuil mahagaine faoi na leapacha agus tishy paper gorm sa slán-a-bhéas-tú).[213] Needless to say, rumours abound: that he is a communist, that he lived in London with a 'Japansy' to whom he was not married, that this woman was found mysteriously dead, that the extent of his own involvement in that death is unclear.

The local man with most reason to dislike Lughaí is Dáiví Stein, a young truck driver and IRA man who has had a passionate sexual relationship with Dorotaí 'in the barn, in the backstreets, among the thorn bushes on the night of the barbeque – anywhere at all the Republican Soldier had an hour or two to spare from his attempts to shape the history of Ireland –' (sa scioból, sna cúlsráideanna, i measc na sceach oíche barbeque – áit ar bith a bhí uair nó dhó le spáráil ag an Saighdiúr Poblachtach ó na chuid iarrachtaí ar stair na hÉireann a chumadh –).[214] While they do have one more fling before her scheduled wedding with Lughaí, Dáiví is a changed man since his attempt to write a chapter of Irish history resulted in the death of his cousin, killed by the premature explosion of a bomb. As the lights dim as they do whenever characters express their deepest thoughts and emotions, Dáiví recalls the traumatic experience of watching the horribly injured man die before his eyes: 'The rhythm of the rain on the roof above us, poor Stiofán, whimpering like an injured animal, his blood running onto the paving stones of the floor, my arm stiff where his head was lying on it . . . the broken shanks of the bones poking out through the bloody clothes –'[215] No longer able to face the consequences of his involvement in the guerilla campaign, Dáiví has decided

to go to England. As he relates this tragedy in the liminal space created by
the stage lighting, Dorotaí simultaneously tells of the first time she made
love with Lughaí, a startling juxtaposition of emotions even for Ó Tuairisc:

> Richness in the wet breasts; they were mine and not mine . . . He took hold of them –
> o Christ! The paws of his two hands grasping them, my guts were knifed, a scream
> of joy burst from my throat, I attacked him with my nails, my teeth, a craving in my
> mouth, a hard bone under my teeth, he thrust into me up to my Adam's apple –[216]

If the townspeople are wary of Lughaí, he sees right through them. He
does not, for instance, share their despair over the closure of the canal:
'Sentimentality. The day of the Transport Boats is over. The hell with the
long ago, long ago. It is high time for us to create something new . . . Bugger
our memories! We are a Nation of Memories. A person has to smother his
memories if he wants to live.'[217] When Nanó shares some folk wisdom about
how married people should sleep with their feet towards the rising of the
moon, he is angrily dismissive: 'O God, O God – three million years of
evolution gone by, and we lie with our feet stretched out towards the rising
of the Moon!'[218] He returns to this idea of an evolution gone wrong in a later
conversation with Dorotaí's father the harbourmaster: 'The protoplasm
of the mud under the heat of the sun swelling and coming to life out of the
dirt . . . The miracle of life . . . The second miracle. The hind legs. And the
throngs come limping out onto the dry land, a voyage of discovery.'[219] Soon,
they are 'jumping, fighting, courting, coupling, grunting, babbling, and
playing out their religious and political rituals froggishly from ditch to ditch'
(ag pocléimneach, ag troid, ag suirí, ag cúpláil, ag gnúsachtach, ag cabair-
eacht, ag imirt a gcuid deasghnátha creidimh agus polaitíochta go froguíl ó
chlaí go claí). And these frogs have created 'the most perfect form of the
Economic Republic' (an fhoirm is foirfe den Phoblacht Eacnamaíoch), an
eternally self-replicating and utterly pointless cycle of mere existence: 'In the
end, they slide back into the water. The female blobs open their tailpipes and
they squirt out the ooze of life, and the old story begins again. Again and yet
again. For ages and ages. They are imprisoned by the System.' Surprisingly,
the harbourmaster knows just what Lughaí means: 'Aye. The System. We are
all imprisoned by it.'[220]

The real source of Lughaí's anger is that he actually loves his native place,
a love he tries to awaken in Dorotaí's sister Iffi by getting her to see the stone
from which it is built as he does: 'Now look at it, how magical the colour of
it is . . . The limestone of Baile na gCloch. Look at it! . . . Take off those dark
houri's lamps and look at it!'[221] Not only will the townspeople, led by men
like Jaxy Pat, never understand this love, but they will also willingly destroy
the beauty that has been passed on to them: 'I am talking about the stones of

the Town. An ancient richness, being crushed out of the way under the bulldozers of the idlers of the Ha'penny Republic . . . The Barren System. They clear the living stone out of the way and they fill the country with the rubbish of gravel and coloured concrete, bullshit pretending to be stone!'[222] Listening to the men boast of how the Irish overthrew the old regime in the country and put a bullet in 'that crowd' (an dream sin), Lughaí interjects: 'It seems you didn't put the bullet in the right crowd' (Chosúlacht nach sa dream ceart chuir sibh an píléar) and then offers his opinion of those who make up the town's contemporary 'republican democracy' (deamacrasaí poblachtach) with Jaxy Pat as 'the principal billy goat' (an ardphocán gabhair): 'You will hear them at every rowdy ballad session from here to Loganna an Chaoil, the People, young and old, male and female, bellowing *Awfta Dublin in de Green!* Christ. Fifty Years late.'[223] For him, the townspeople and their like throughout Ireland are 'just like the People have always been, a helpless flock without a Leader. With no pride at all in their own Town. Puppets on a string. Made to dance by the Masters of Money out in the Gombeen Civilisation.'[224]

Lughaí is, of course, responsible for the most significant event in the play, one that occurs offstage. The performance of his play based on the myth of Orpheus and Eurydice is the talk of the town, with everyone having apparently seen it. In his version of the ancient story, a modern street musician descends into hell to rescue the woman he has lost in the Lethe (lit. 'The Water of Sleep' (Uisce an tSuain)). On one level, the play was inspired by the great tragedy of Lughaí's own life in London, the drowning of his drug-addicted Polynesian lover, an artist who 'taught me what art is . . . taught me to speak in the old tongue, by means of images' (mhúin fios m'ealaíne dom, mhúin . . . dom labhairt sa sean-teanga, trí mheán na samhlaídí).[225] But it is increasingly clear, even to himself, that the play is also about his journey to the hell that is Baile na gCloch, where he encounters people quite like the shadowy masked figures his street musician meets in the otherworld: 'The queen of Hell . . . a tongue like a nettle in her mouth . . . and every rigamarole of a blessing and every rural superstition from here to Loganna an Chaoil at the tip of her tongue' (Bainríon Ifrinn . . . teanga ina béal mar neantóg . . . agus gach deilín beannachta agus gach piseog tíre uaidh seo go Loganna an Chaoil go paiteanta chuici ina béal) (Nanó); 'the Old Lad himself, fat-arsed Pluto, with his two sacks of money hanging between his legs, and gathering to himself everything valuable and every bit of beauty that ever shone on the world' (an Sean-Lead féin, Plúton Tóineach, agus a dhá mhála airgid ar sileadh idir na cosa aige, agus gach saibhreas agus gach giota den áilleacht dar lonraigh riamh ar an saol á bhailiú aige chuige féin) (Jaxy Pat); 'the old Boatman, Sleepy Charon, carrying the souls of the dead across the Lethe in his rotten old tub' (an sean-diúlach Bádóra, Caeron

Codaltach, agus é ag iompar anamaí na marbh ina shean-tubán lofa thar Uisce an tSuain) (Jójó).[226]

Dáiví Stein dismisses the play with disdain as 'playacting for children' (playaictéireacht do pháistí).[227] Indeed he will later go further, accusing Lughaí of one of the greatest sins an Irish artist can commit: 'The Paddy-writer, bringing a sarcastic smile to the lips of the fops in cities abroad by presenting exaggerated versions of his own people on stage, mocking their speech, their Religion, their national heritage.' Shaken much more by his own experiences in the town than by Dáiví's insults, Lughaí replies: 'Perhaps you're right. I'm sick of all my craft. I cannot discover the nature of these people. "A clatter without substance." You're right.'[228] But if he has lost confidence in his craft, he has retained faith in the imagination that makes the artist, a faith he shares with Ó Tuairisc 'that it was from that region that the voices rise up to the playwright and that he creates a Mouth for every one of them. That the Characters in his play are far more substantial than anything in his own little personality. That those Characters have an effect on him, that they make use of him, that they speak through his mouth . . .'[229] Lughaí expresses this same idea more concisely when he tells Dáiví that however flawed his art, he must follow 'the call of my craft . . . My own damnable craft. Put some verbal substance into the shade of these shadows, trying to find some glimmer of understanding through the mist of this argument –'[230]

In an earlier talk with the harbourmaster, Lughaí stated that humans have 'one virtue the Frogs don't have' (bua amháin nach bhfuil ag na Froganna) and that virtue is hope. The play and his later assertion of commitment to his art are Lughaí's own expressions of that hope, and to some extent at least he can feel justification for it. While various people in the town who have seen the play have been given fleeting insights into their condition, Dorotaí, who played Eurydice, and her artistic younger sister Iffi have been more deeply moved. Dorotaí tells Lughaí: 'It is wonderful the insight into life I have had since that night . . . a visionary shape on everything – as if I were still acting the part, Eurydice, in the Play . . . I am alive in a way that I was never alive – a restlessness in my bones . . .'[231] Having obviously thought a good deal about the play, she now sees its hell metaphorically as 'the Twilight of the Soul in which we live' (Clapsholas an Anama ina mairimid). She also believes, as she tells Dáiví, that this is a state from which she has been saved through her experience with the play: 'It makes no sense for me to take an interest in these things any more. My youth. The House. The Town. And the sulky little boys. I am Liberated.'[232] It is, however, of interest that she finds Lughaí a mystery: 'I don't know him. No one knows him . . . He has no respect at all for anything in which we take an interest.' And the one thing she thinks she does know about him is wrong: 'Sometimes I get the idea that he is not interested in anything in the world – except me.'[233]

In his play, the street musician is confused by the masks the characters wear and unable to identify the woman he is seeking. Of course we have already seen the idea of a person choosing the wrong person to love in three of Ó Tuairisc's first four plays. Here he adds a bit of authority to such confusion by giving it a mythological context. Dorotaí, despite her beauty and sex appeal, is not the woman Lughaí is seeking after the tragic death of his lover in London. Instead, he discovers that woman in Dorotaí's younger sister Iffi, a novice painter who is truly interested in him as both a man and an artist.[234] It is to Iffi that he tells the story of what happened to him in London. She is not just a passive listener, however, and when he barely glances at the picture she shows him, she stands up for herself and her art, accusing him of condescension: 'Critics! Critics! Critics! All of you are the same. A big mouth and little sense. Puffing yourselves up like male frogs, bewitched by the clatter of your own voices . . . Telling me how to draw my picture and your own stumpy fingers unable to draw the smallest trace of a living line. Huh, Critics!' After a flash of anger, he is impressed by this assertion of her personal and artistic independence and integrity, and apologises, declaring that he is 'like any other bastard envious of the simplicity he himself cannot cultivate' (nós bastaird ar bith eile in éad leis an tsimplíocht nach tiocfadh leis féin a shaothrú).[235] Moreover, she has taught, or reminded him of, an important lesson: 'The danger is shown and shown and shown to him [a person] – but he does not see.'[236] Not surprisingly, he begins to take her seriously as a fellow artist, discussing the painting entitled *Aingeal an Bháis* (The angel of death) with which she is struggling to find a way to present her vision: 'Time at a standstill, a bad taste in my mouth as if the world around me were mud, a tune from your Play in Hell like an echo in my head – Back, back up from the grave, beyond . . .'[237]

Indeed he tells her that like a real artist she has succeeded in seeing and expressing a truth too often ignored: 'Truth is always mixed with terror. That is why we don't like to look at it.'[238] In a later conversation with her sister, Iffi proves that she knows Lughaí far better than does his fiancée: 'That is just a mask he wears. Hardness. But behind the mask he is just a boy, a helpless boy, no small emptiness in his soul.' Nor is she lapsing into conventionality with this reference to his soul: 'I don't want to say "soul" – in the customary way at any rate – I want to say that he is alive in a way, alive and lively, and that in another way he is lost.' Moreover, the relationship she sees possible with him is a collaborative and creative one: 'A girl could give him something – create something with him, share something with him –'[239] Emboldened by her new confidence in her own vision and ability, Iffi responds forcefully to her father's drowsy complaint about 'the System' (an Siostam): 'I would break the System. I would make an attempt to create something new from the skeleton of what is old . . . A play, perhaps – create and paint the scenes and the Masks –'[240] At the end of the play we are left wondering whether she will ever thus cooperate with Lughaí in the creation of a work of art – he writing the script, she working on the sets and costumes – but we do know that each has given the other new hope for a fuller and frog-free life.

The play is, however, at its weakest when Lughaí attempts to give practical expression to that hope. Indeed his idea for the rejuvenation of Baile na gCloch as a tourist destination is reminiscent of Broadbent's plan for Roscullen in Shaw's *John Bull's Other Island* (1904). Of course Lughaí has no intention of involving himself in the realisation of these plans, instead leaving the job as he leaves Dorotaí, to Dáiví, a man he respects as an idealist and a republican, albeit a misguided one: 'Pick the rotten dogs out of your own Canal before you look to pick the orange peel out of your brother's Harbour.'[241] It should, however, be remembered that Dáiví's activities in the North involved blowing up rather than sweeping streets, and that when leaving the IRA he was careful to securely stash his weaponry for future use by his successor.

An Hairyfella in Ifreann is not so much confusing as confused. Once again we see an Ó Tuairisc protagonist struggling to live by his ideals in the real world, and once again that attempt seems possible only if he is able to make the considerable leap of faith he makes at the end of the play. We are obviously meant to see Lughaí's smashing of the ship-in-a-bottle given to himself and Dorotaí as a wedding present as an assertion of freedom from the stifling routine of the town. Still, the final sound we hear is the muted croaking of the frogs.

Ó Tuairisc's next play, *Aisling Mhic Artáin* (The vision of Mac Artáin) is his most experimental. In 1974 he showed an outline of the play, then titled *Na Leaca Dorcha* (The dark slabs), to Roibeárd Mac Góráin of Gael-Linn, who agreed that that organisation, which ran An Damer, would commission the play. When the production was delayed by problems at Gael-Linn, Ó Tuairisc submitted the play as *Aisling Mhic Artáin* to the competition for Duais na Taibhdheirce at the 1975 Oireachtas, where it took first prize. Since the winner of this prize was logically enough expected to have the play's premiere in Galway and Mac Góráin and Gael-Linn were working towards a production at An Damer, Ó Tuairisc found himself in a position not at all common for Gaelic dramatists: having to choose between two major Gaelic companies interested in staging a new play in Irish. The resultant confusion further delayed the opening of *Aisling Mhic Artáin* until October 1977, when it was presented by neither of those two companies, but rather by the Abbey in the Peacock at the Dublin Theatre Festival. Directed by Éamonn Ó Guaillí (Edward Golden) with original music by Tom Cullivan, the play had only two performances at the festival.[242] Perhaps to atone for how they had ignored *An Hairyfella in Ifreann*, the critics paid proper attention to this work by a writer who was by now one of the most prolific and accomplished dramatists to ever work in Irish. Their reception of the play was, however, mixed. In the *Irish Independent*, 'R. O'C.' and Mary Mac Goris were frankly baffled by it. 'R. O'C.' declared:

> Audience reaction to Eoghan Ó Tuairisc's Oireachtas prizewinning play 'Aisling Mhic Artáin' which opened in the Peacock Theatre, Dublin, last night was that it was wonderful. What 'wonderful' meant varied with the spectators: some used the phrase in token of genuine appreciation; others in the sense of 'What the (Expletive Deleted) was the (Epithet) play about?' My own view is nearer to the latter school of thought.

'R. O'C.' particularly disliked what he called 'its exaggerated and stylized characters', which made it virtually impossible for any spectator to identify himself or herself with any of the characters' (*II*, 5/10/77). Mac Goris wrote that while Ó Tuairisc claimed to have been 'dazzled' by the production, 'representatives of the Peacock stood around looking stoically inscrutable' and then added: 'For the comfort of that critic who had written that he couldn't understand the play, let me tell you that the author announced himself as so bemused by the wonder of the performance that he'd have to go again the second night to find out what it was all about' (*II*, 7/10/77).

Proinsias Mac an Bheatha had some reservations about the play, writing that it was on occasion wordy and obscure, that it focused too much on sex, and that it raised questions it did not and could not answer, but added: 'I hope that it is clear from what I have said that this is no insignificant play that I am discussing. It is full of action, there is plenty of laugh-provoking material in it, and as I have said, it asks questions of us to give our own answers to' (*Inniu*, 14/10/77).[243] The most insightful review of the play was by Ó Tuairisc's fellow Gaelic playwright Críostóir Ó Floinn in *The Irish Press*: 'Ó Tuairisc is an author whose work shares the same trait as that of Brian Friel in English-language drama, a bounty of poetry. It is not possible to engage with anything Ó Tuairisc creates without feeling that you are in the presence of art. That is true of this new play of his . . .' For Ó Floinn, 'this play is worth seeing without regard to the question or the cause of the Irish language. Without doubt it is rather scattered and uncertain, but from start to finish it is an attempt to do something modern (*IP*, 5/10/77).[244] The play's only major revival was by Compántas Chorcaí, whose production, directed by Lionard Mac Curtáin, won the Micheál Mac Liammóir award at the All-Ireland Drama Festival at Taibhdhearc na Gaillimhe in March 1979 before being brought to the Everyman Theatre in Cork in May of that year (*CE*, 13/3/79; 14/5/79).

Having seen the play in Galway, an anonymous critic for the *Galway Advertiser* wrote: 'We have not here . . . Eoghan Ó Tuairisc at his best but there are hints of potential greatness.' This critic found the language of the play 'beautifully poetic', but noted that 'there are times when the play has some awful and unnecessary undertones' (*GA*, 22/3/79). Reviewing the Cork production, Donal Buckley declared: 'While many Irish dramatists have in the past been accused, with justification, of failing to experiment, both the author, the producer, and indeed, Compántas, are to be congratulated on their sense of adventure in this production' (*CE*, 15/5/79). Writing in the same paper the following day, Evelyn King called *Aisling Mhic Artáin* a 'delightful flight of fancy into the unknown, undiscovered and unbelievable world of dreams – where all is possible' and concluded: 'Although the play takes many hazardous and unpredictable turns it certainly speaks for itself that the Irish language is very much alive in the theatre' (*CE*, 16/5/79).

King is entirely right here, and if audience members are willing to forget the conventions of realistic drama and think in terms of new forms of theatrical expression, most notably those of the theatre of the absurd, *Aisling Mhic Artáin* is not at all as intimidating a play as 'R. O'C.' and Mary Mac Goris suggested. Nevertheless, when the play was published in 1978, Ó Tuairisc provided some background information in an introductory 'Éirim an Scéil' (The tenor of the plot), in which we are told that the entire play takes place in the mind of the monk Mac Artáin after he falls into 'a deep sleep' (toirchim suain). Ó Tuairisc's choice of title for this play is an inspired one, as the *aisling* can be found as a genre in both medieval Irish prose and later Irish poetry. In both the medieval and more modern forms it is associated with wonders and transformations, as in the prose tales *Aislinge Óengusa* (The vision of Óengus) from the eight century (in which humans turn into swans) and the satirical *Aislinge Meic Con Glinne* (The vision of Mac Conglinne) from the twelfth centuary (in which a 'demon of gluttony' has a central role). In the poems classified as *aislingí* from the seventeenth and eighteenth centuries (and later), the poet encounters a beautiful young woman who turns out to be the personification of oppressed Ireland. Mac Artáin's vision in the play is a grim one in which he sees himself as a political prisoner in exile following a revolution that has created a pagan, collectivist dictatorship in 'Poblacht an Ghaimbín' (The Gombeen Republic, i.e. Ireland) with 'Blah' (i.e. Baile Átha Cliath (Dublin)) as its capital. The prison is situated in Na Leaca Dorcha (The Dark Slabs), a frigid and remote area above the Arctic Circle presided over by one of the indigenous inhabitants of the area, Súil Amháin (One Eye), who is described in the *dramatis personae* as 'a dour, surly person related to the Neanderthal Ape' (duine dúr dorrga, gaol aige leis an Ápa Neandartal).[245] The prisoners there have been found guilty of various 'crimes' for which they have been sentenced to slave labour.

Mac Artáin is a monk, Lispín a lesbian, and Lú and Lúlú circus performers (they also write and sing satirical songs). Not much better off are the civil servants who work at the camp, of whom we meet two, Dr Wilhelm Beerbohm, a botanist in charge of forestry, and his new wife and fellow botanist Saileog. In keeping with the official paganism imposed by the state, the only deity worshipped at the camp is a giant Bulldozer (Buldósar), Christmas has been abolished, and everyone – prisoners, civil servants, even Súil Amháin – must take part in a ritual called An Mhalartú (The Exchange), in which men and women spend the night with someone other than their usual partners. Because he is believed to have no interest in sex, Mac Artáin is given the job of arranging these temporary pairings.

Obviously the play deals with the familiar Ó Tuairisc theme of conflict between freedom and authority, and as in *Cúirt an Mheán Oíche* and *An Hairyfella in Ifreann*, that conflict is often expressed in terms of sexuality. Here, however, sex is both an expression of freedom and a brutal means of control. Nowhere is the repressive use of sex seen more clearly than in the treatment of his wife Kraó by Súil Amháin, as is evident from the stage directions on her first appearance: 'Kraó, his Wife, is trotting at his heels; she is bent, shawled, with a yashmak [Muslim veil] hiding the bottom of her face. He whistles to her as you would to a dog, and gestures with a quick move of his thumb for her to sit. She sits on her haunches in the corner.'[246] As far as the other characters know, she cannot speak. For Súil Amháin, sex is merely one more way to assert his authority, as he makes plain to Lispín when she is critical of his treatment of Kraó: 'Remember that I have your dossier – a filthy little lesbian from the dregs of the city . . . and unless you keep a rein on your tongue, I guarantee that what I will do to your buttocks won't be altogether homosexual.'[247] Moreover, whichever woman is paired with Súil Amháin that night will be killed, for, as he says, 'I can do nothing about it, you can do nothing about it: we are under the spell of fate, and everything happens as the Eternal Bulldozer wants.'[248]

He is, of course, wrong. As the chorus sings, physical pleasures are to some extent allowed in the camp as a means of maintaining control over the prisoners in more important ways:

Prepare, you devils –
you have permission to have a short period of debauchery now,
drug yourselves with the glass, or with the habits of a badger
fumbling around on the dance floor doing the twist,
courting, or playing bingo, what does it matter
in the Slabs, the Slabs, the Slabs, the Slabs,
the black, black dark Slabs![249]

But sex, at least, is a volatile opiate, too powerful and potentially trans-gressive a force to be manipulated at will by the authorities. Thus the newly married Saileog's first response to the Exchange is, as she makes clear to her husband, shock and disgust with a custom she finds 'lewd, filthy, and coarse' (gairsiúil, graosta, garbh): 'You should have told me about it six months ago when we got married. I assure you, Bill Beerbohm, that I would never have come with you to this wretched Leaca Dorcha had I known about it –'[250] Before long, however, she is challenging Mac Artáin about his celibacy: 'O, take the blindfold from your innocent eyes, you little child! Grow up. Look at life. We men and women are not plastic dolls, but wild forces from ancient times acting through the boldness of evolution . . . That is how that God of yours created the situation. One must be realistic and accept it.'[251] She sees the monk as 'a pagan eunuch. A conceited Manichean archangel, a ghost of a man who was not properly incarnated in flesh and blood' (coillteachán págánach, Manichee aircaingeal postúil, taibhse d'fhear nár ionchollaíodh i gceart i bhfuil agus i bhfeoil).[252] As one can imagine, the accusation of Manichaeism is a very serious one for a writer like Ó Tuairisc so concerned with attempting to find a unity underlying apparent contradictions. Mac Artáin must also be stung by her charge that he is obsessed with 'abstraction . . . the fantasies of the middle ages' (teibíocht . . . speabhraídí na meánaoiseanna), and thus unable to experience 'reality' (réalaíocht) as well as by her assertion that 'that Heaven of yours' (an Neamh sin agat) is 'nothing unless it is founded on an under-standing of the blood and the flesh' (neamhní mura bhfuil sé bunaithe ar thuiscint na fola agus na feola).[253] Later, she goes so far as to tell him, 'You are the shadow who does not recognise that you are a man of earthy substance – you are the Devil in the Play, the One Eye! . . . An Intellectual? – Ah, the Celtic mind masturbating the penis of your own imagination.'[254]

Lispín, who has been sent to Na Leaca Dorcha because of her suppos-edly deviant sexuality, also finds the Exchange a deeply troubling experience. Early in the play we see her lamenting the fact that her relationships with women are now just a memory:

> I found lovely once
> a gentle girl cheerful before me,
> with smooth skin like tan silk,
> her breasts round, her voice gentle –
> I kissed my darling, o, I kissed my darling.

Now, as the chorus accompanies her with the refrain 'Fortunate is she who does not kiss a man, / she lives happily' (Méanar di nach bpógann fear, / maireann go súgach), all she has to share her bed with is her doll Brídín. She is, however, having disturbing thoughts: 'Strange is the thought that is growing in my heart. Yes, Brídín, a man. For the first time in my life.'[255] These new urges grow stronger, and her interest turns to Mac Artáin. The monk is entirely accepting of her sexual orientation, telling her, 'It is not a sickness; it happens often according to nature.' But he is startled when she informs him that she is now thinking of seeking a male partner for the Exchange and that he is that male. This scene obviously introduced ideas new to the Gaelic stage, and therefore it is unfortunate that Ó Tuairisc has Lispín base some of her appeal to Mac Artáin on the utterly discredited idea that he can 'cure' her of her lesbianism: 'Think, this is perhaps the last chance for me to grow up and give up the lesbianism that is hurting my life. I will not meet another of your kind –'[256] Far more interesting than her obsolete psychology here is the question of just what kind of man she considers Mac Artáin to be. She does not want anything to do with 'a virile forceful young man' (slataire fearúil fuinneamhail), preferring the monk because of an androgynous quality in him: 'I feel the same attraction in your presence as I felt with my female lover at the University. There is sincerity in you. Sympathy. A fertile mind – a girl's mind – you are alive in a way that the rest of them are not.'[257] When he rejects her, she reproaches him in terms similar to those used by Saileog: 'Give up the Celtic fantasies and observe the world. How is it possible for a man to love an unknown God when he does not love the creature who is standing right in front of him . . . An enemy to life –'[258] Lispín later tells Saileog, 'I have no interest in a man unless he is a full person . . . The two sexes in him, as the two sexes are in us women.'[259]

There is such a figure in the play, or rather two such figures never seen on stage together and clearly meant to represent two sides of the same personality. The newly arrived Lú (who obviously has affinities with the Irish deity Lugh, known as In Samaildánach)[260] has been sent to the prison camp because he is, in his own words, 'a professional fool' (amadán gairmiúil), a singer of satirical songs, and the co-owner with his alter ego Lúlú of a small circus. Back home in Poblacht an Ghaimbín, they had offered audiences a spell of anarchic escape from the strictly regimented and compartmentalised life they were forced to endure. As Lú says, 'they took delight in our tricks. Haha, they were never able to make out which of us was Lú and which of us was Lúlú. Haha, you would see Lú one minute and the next minute he would have cleared off out of sight and the sky woman Lúlú would be magically in his place – do you understand? They would never see Lú and Lúlú together.'[261] Lú/Lúlú is, of course, the artist figure in this play, having the power to comfortably reconcile within his/her psyche apparently contradictory elements. Lispín, looking for a purely rational explanation of the Lú/Lúlú phenomenon, asks 'Is it possible – but it isn't possible – do you mean to say that you are sometimes Lú and other times Lúlú?' Lú's weary response is 'Something like that.' Lispín persists: 'But how – that is to say, are you really Lú or Lúlú?' For Lú/Lúlú this is a meaningless question, but he/she answers nonetheless: 'I am a man with regard to the basic trappings. But I am a woman with regard to art.' To Lispín's next question about what art he/she has in mind, he/she responds with a definition of the role of the artist in society and in particular in a society characterised by Mac Artáin as 'a nocturnal nightmare we are all caught up in' (tromluí oícheadúil a bhfuil muid go léir gafa ann): 'To reveal the queerness and the marvelousness of the night to hearts imprisoned in the day. To make them jump, and laugh.'[262] All artists are, of course, anathema in Poblacht an Ghaimbín, not to mention the camp, as Lú had earlier reminded Mac Artáin: 'Indeed, you know the ha'penny mentality that came in with the Revolution; they find disgusting poetry, art, music in the old style, humour, madness, pantomime. Because they cannot control those things and put a proper price on them.'[263] The opposition between Súil Amháin and Lú/Lúlú comes to a head when they meet in the forest on the night of the Exchange. With 'dizziness in his head' (meadhrán ina cheann), Súil Amháin asks whom he has encountered, to which Lú/Lúlú replies: 'Your opposite, Súil Amháin. Your shadow in Truth' (Do chontrárthacht, a Shúil Amháin. Do scáil san Fhírinne). Needless to say, Súil Amháin can make no sense of this reply, so Lú/Lúlú explains that 'you look at the world through your one eye only. Now you see the truth' (trí do shúil amháin a dhearcann tú ar an saol. Dearcann tú anois an fhírinne). When the jailer remains confused, Lú/Lúlú tells him that the truth is 'the androgynous person. The living person' (an duine déghnéasach. An duine beo). To Súil Amháin, this can only mean that he himself must be 'Death' (an Bás), but he is again wrong as Lú/Lúlú declares: 'You are not, dear. I am Death' (Ní tú, a chroí. Mise . . . an Bás). Lú/Lúlú is, of course, right – and in two senses. First of all, as we soon learn from Lú/Lúlú, Súil Amháin is indeed dead, having fallen through the ice in the dark, 'he going off like Suibhne Menn in the night' (é ag imeacht ina Shuibhne Menn san oíche).[264] In effect, Súil Amháin, the man of rigid categories and certainties, dies of confusion after his encounter with the protean figure in the dark woods, his death a metaphorical expression of Ó Tuairisc's belief that art and mindless orthodoxy cannot co-exist and that art will ultimately triumph. But Lú/Lúlú is also an embodiment of death as part of another of Ó Tuairisc's entangled dualities, that of life and death, a synthesis beyond the understanding of Súil Amháin, who thinks of death merely as another means to control and diminish the lives of others.

Like many provocative works of art, *Aisling Mhic Artáin* raises more questions than it answers. The most important of them in terms of the plot is surely what the death of Súil Amháin will mean for those in the camp. Lispín points out that another Súil Amháin, 'the Dour Aborigine' (an

Dúchasach Dúr), will be sent to rule them. Knowing full well that that rigid primitive being is a part of all of us, keeping us from realising our more polymorphous potential, Lú/Lúlú agrees: 'The Aborigine is always with us –' (Bíonn an Dúchasach i gcónaí againn –). But when Lispín then laments that without Lú/Lúlú to help them against this lower nature they will be helpless, Lú/Lúlú says he/she may well be with them still and suggests that the Dour Aborigine is not the only eternal force in play in our lives: 'Sometimes in the loneliness of my caravan, it seems to me that I have always existed, the Eternal Trickster . . .'[265] Meanwhile, in the short term, Lú/Lúlú, who says he/she is 'a poor example of a man' (bocht an sampla d'fhear), accepts the invitation of Lispín – 'a poor example of a woman' (bocht an sampla de bhean) – to go live with her. Things no doubt go on unchanged in Poblacht an Ghaimbín and a new warder may soon appear in Na Leaca Dorcha, but the seeds of a future and far more expansive revolution are being sown.

What about Mac Artáin, however? Obviously he has found the Exchange a challenging if not yet transformational experience, as he tells Saileog, who is leaving him to resume her ordinary life with Beerbohm: 'The life I had before you came was bleak enough: it will be bleaker still for me after you go.'[266] Right after her departure, Súil Amháin's wife Kraó enters, bundled up and gagged. He receives her kindly and allows her to stay in his hut, not suspecting what is about to happen: 'Life's Fate, of course – beauty is promised us in the Vision, and we get – Kraó!' (Dán an tSaoil ar ndóigh – gealltar an áilleacht dúinn san Aisling, agus faighimid – Kraó!). Nor does he notice what is happening behind his back as he continues to complain: 'H'm such a mess. Kraó!' (H'm a leithéid de chiseach. Kraó!). Of course he might have had a premonition if he remembered the sovereignty figure in early Irish literature, the hideous hag who becomes a luminous beauty when she sleeps with a man worthy of kingship. While he mumbles on 'in the back, unknown to him Kraó thrusts her head out through a slit in the curtain, her young face exposed, her shining hair loose, a merry look on her face . . . A bright light flashing in the hut . . . A merry laugh from the wild girl . . . Kraó appears from the corner as a half-nude sky woman'. However, we still see Mac Artáin 'at the fire, not seeing her' (ag an tine gan í a fheiceáil).[267]

But of course he does. This is, after all, his dream and while the character in the dream may miss this revelation, the dreamer certainly does not. The question then remains, what will he make of it when he awakens? Throughout the dream, Mac Artáin has been keenly aware of his situation, as he struggles 'to recognise a shadow from the living being in this lonely place' (scáil a aithint ón neach beo ar an uaigneas seo), 'lost in a fog of dream . . . for ages and ages' (caillte i gceo aislinge . . . leis na cianta cairbreacha), unable to distinguish 'what is reality and what is a dream' (cé acu an réalaíocht is cé acu an bhrionglóid), longing for the appearance of 'anyone at all from the Light outside to cut these spells from our minds' (duine nó deoraí ón Solas amuigh chun geasróga seo na Dorchachta a scianadh dár n-aigne).[268] Now at least some of the 'spells' have been sliced away, and Ó Tuairisc leaves Mac Artáin – and playgoers – to wonder what the next step should be in his evolution to liberation and full humanity.

Ó Tuairisc's next dramatic work, *Carolan*, was first produced in 1979 at An Damer, which was reopening after renovations as the home of Dublin's first full-time professional theatre company working in the Irish language (*II*, 30/8/79). The director was Áine Uí Dhrisceoil, who was also the new company's artistic director. In general reviews were not good. Writing in the *Sunday Independent*, John Honohan stated that given the interest in Irish traditional music, and in particular in the music of Carolan, 'a play on his life and times would seem a sure winner for a vibrant drama', but then continued: 'Unfortunately it did not work out in such a way as to give complete satisfaction.' Honohan felt that 'the material was too thin', the result being 'an episodic hotch-potch of music, dance, and over narrated story' (*SI*, 9/9/79). For the anonymous critic for *The Irish Press*, *Carolan* was not 'a real play . . . but rather a dramatic telling of the life of Carolan' (dráma dáiríre . . . ach insint drámatúil ar shaol Charolan). His biggest problem, however, was with 'the piece of literature that was the script – grand to read but crammed full from the theatrical point of view. It would have been worthwhile for her [Áine Uí Dhrisceoil] to have signed a scissors contract with the author' (an píosa litríochta a bhí mar scriopt – galánta le léamh ach lán pacála ó thaobh na hamharclainne de. B'fhiú di [d'Áine Uí Dhrisceoil] conradh siosúir a shíneadh leis an údar) (*IP*, 8/9/79). *The Irish Press* also published an anonymous review of the play in English that seems to be the work of the same critic who wrote the piece in Irish. At any rate, the author of the English review certainly agreed that 'a bit of pruning – more than a wee bit – was very much in order'. Still, this writer obviously liked some things about *Carolan*, stating that 'with a snip snip here and a snip snip there it will be even more enjoyable' and urging readers to 'never mind your "droch-Ghaeilge" [bad Irish] – out you go and enjoy the story and the music of "Carolan" – you'll love your experience' (*IP*, 7/9/79). Maeve Kennedy of the *Irish Times* also liked some aspects of the show but was ultimately disappointed, writing that 'for their first presentation in Dublin he [Ó Tuairisc] and the new company have come up with good entertainment, but not yet good theatre' (*IT*, 7/9/79). *Carolan* has not been revived.[269]

Ó Tuairisc was assisted in the writing of the play by a £2,500 bursary from the Arts Council. From the very beginning it is clear that he wanted to offer a new perspective on this well-known icon of Gaelic Ireland, seeing him as an artist able to bridge the cultural divide in his own time and as a model for a similar hybridity in ours. Writing in 1977 to the musicologist Caleb Crowell and his wife Sheila, an authority on Carolan, Ó Tuairisc stated:

> I myself, possibly, can take a somewhat independent view for I am not sold on the 'Folk' mystique. For most of my life I have been engaged in poetry and creative writing, and have no compunction about enriching my Irish with the insights of the English, European and Classical tongues. Therefore, I welcome the possibility of an Italianate influence on Carolan – as I would welcome any living spark of an outside culture into the choking claustrophobia of modern Irish life. Provided only that the Gaelic, or Celtic, substratum is not completely eroded . . . The Blind Music-maker wandering indiscriminately between the House of Lord Inchiquin and the House of the Prince of Coolavin is a myth to be stamped on the soul.[270]

To recreate the reality of the linguistic situation in eighteenth-century Ireland and to underscore Carolan's cultural ecumenism, Ó Tuairisc originally planned to make the play fully bilingual. As he wrote to Áine Uí Dhrisceoil: 'Bilingualism is central to the Period and the Subject Matter . . . Bilingualism is a prominent aspect of the Theme of the Play – the Culture of the Irish language and the Culture of the English language (and a bit of the Culture of Europe) always being in Carolan's character and music.' As usual, he combined artistic vision with a pragmatic awareness of the needs and shortcomings of potential audiences: 'From my experience of the Stage in the Abbey and in the Peacock, it is clear to me that it would be a great help to the ordinary public that there be a good thread of English running through the piece, to make comprehensible to them the substance of the Scene – especially when it is a complicated Scene.' He also added that if the director disagreed, 'it would not be difficult for me to Gaelicise the whole play'.[271] Since the policy of the new company was to produce only works in Irish, the final script of the play as performed had very little dialogue in English.

Carolan is actually more of a pageant than a play proper. It tells the story of the life of Carolan (Toirdhealbhach Ó Cearbhalláin, 1670–1738) in a series of discrete scenes in which we see him as, for example, a young man raging at the blindness that has deprived him of the ability to read and write music; as a rakish frequenter of public houses and the young women who work in them; as an eager young musician hearing Verdi for the first time as sung by Italian plasterers in an Anglo-Irish big house; as a successful contestant in a 'Poetic Insult Contest' (Sciollaireacht Fhileata), besting his sometime friend and rival Cathaoir Mac Cába; as an artist capable of both arrogance and abject humility when he feels he is at the end of a dying tradition; and as the colleague and intellectual equal of Jonathan Swift. Of course at best a staged biography can only give a glimpse of the playwright's own idiosyncratic view of his subject as he tries to fit a life into two hours or so of entertainment for an audience that may or may not have any interest in or knowledge of his subject. Such is certainly the case here, although Ó Tuairisc does create some lively and engaging scenes, perhaps most notably the pub scene against which Carolan's poetic contest with Mac Cába takes place; the scene in which he argues with his wife about his wandering life; and the scene in which he visits Swift, meets members of his circle, and provides inspiration for the Lilliput section of *Gulliver's Travels*.

Strictly as an entertainment, there is no reason why Carolan could not still be successfully performed for appropriate audiences. It is, however, Ó Tuairisc's development of some of his major themes that gives the play its greatest interest and ultimate importance. He takes pains to show that Carolan, whatever his physical disability or the limitations imposed on him by his background and lifestyle, was a serious artist. Thus he curses the fact that he has gone blind and is unable 'to read the music of the great masters . . . to write down my own music properly and accurately' (ceol na máistrí móra a léamh . . . mo chuid ceoil féin a bhreacadh síos i gceart is i gcruinneas).[272] For those who transcribe his music carelessly, he has nothing but contempt, even telling one of the remaining Gaelic aristocrats, 'Damn your transposing! Do not transpose, or dispose or counter suppose anything at all! Or do you want to make a mess of my music like the fiddlers and pipers of the country, hacking and screeching at a piece of princely music, to suit it to the hobnailed boots of rural yahoos prancing on the floor of the randyboo [rendezvous, i.e. get-together].'[273] Not even his son escapes his wrath when the young man tries to alter 'Mábla Shéimh Uí Cheallaigh' (Gentle Mabel Kelly) with the excuse, 'But I prefer it Alegretto. That is faster, more spirited, more modern – you have to put a kick in the tune.' When the young man invokes the authority of 'the great masters' (na máistrí móra) of the newer style, men who call Carolan 'Wooden Fingers', the composer explodes: 'They all have the "virtuosity", the cleverness in their fingers. But which of them can create new melodies? Do you understand? – the arrangement, the rhythmic figures, the melody. Melody first . . .'[274] Ó Tuairisc takes note of the legend that Carolan got his music from the *sí* (otherworld), but the emphasis in the play is on a man who worked hard at his craft and was entirely open to influences from a world far wider than Gaelic Ireland.

He is also a man tormented by his inability to gain full access to the music of Europe and by his awareness that he is one of the last survivors of a Gaelic musical tradition rapidly dying out in a changing Ireland. Like Ó Tuairisc's other artist characters, he is a liminal figure who lives with constant uncertainty about his place in the world, and, every bit as important, his command of his medium. As he tells Mac Cába after they visit the ruins of his ancestral home and Mac Cába exposes the falsity of Carolan's claim to a noble and patriotic lineage:

> I am just a halfwit, without a country, without a home, without ancestry . . . Without ancestry in music either. With nothing but the echo, echo-music, echo-thoughts, echo-verse, that was blown to me by the beggars on the road. I will never have access to the ancient old music of Ireland. Yes, indeed, that musical treasure is gone for good.[275]

After his argument with his son, he again feels lost: 'I am nothing but a dunce. A ghost of a person going fumbling through the darkness . . . With no ability in poetry, not having the art of words, in English or in Irish, to express my vision . . . a liar, a false person, a two-faced person.' At this point he seems to be certain that his art will die with him: 'Whatever music I manage to lure from the darkness, it will be lost, it will be corrupted, a tedious street trinket available to anyone.'[276]

That, of course, did not happen, and Ó Tuairisc attributes the survival of his music to the fact that Carolan's vision and ambition transcended the narrow worldview in which his contemporaries were trapped. In the climactic scene in the play, Carolan is invited to participate in what is called 'a great international occasion' (ócáid mhór idirnáisiúnta), a feast celebrating the return of the O'Connors to Belanagare, from which they had been forced to flee after the Irish defeat at Aughrim in 1691. As part of the festivities, the Bishop of Killala will come out of hiding to say Mass, and in attendance will be 'all of our aristocracy. Princes and Princesses of the line of Ír and Éibhir . . . clergy and monks . . . musicians, poets, and antiquarians, along with Captains and Officers from every Army in Europe.'[277] It is seen as only fitting then that 'the prime master of the music of Ireland' (príomhmháistir Cheol na hÉireann) should be present. And it is indeed Carolan whom the bishop singles out for special praise – in both Irish and English. More important is the fact that the bishop does not laud Carolan as a voice from the past urging futile resistance to what is now inevitable political and cultural change, but rather as an artist endeavouring to come to terms with change and to provide a durable Gaelic substratum for whatever new Irish identity emerges:

> And more than anyone else at all, I praise Carolan. I praise his good Christian example. He bestows his music on everyone – Gael, Englishman, Anglo-Irishman, Scots Gael, Scots Presbyterian – more than any one of us at all he transcends the boundary of the religions, the boundary of blood, the boundary of the languages, and unites the various divisions in Ireland in the vision of his music.[278]

From the other side of the divide, no less an ascendancy figure than Swift sees Carolan – and himself – in a similar light: 'You and I, Carolan, together, we have battles to fight. These are the battles of the future, battles of the mind and spirit. Our two races combined, our two arts, our two languages.'[279] The play ends fittingly with the singing of Carolan's 'Pléaráca na Ruairceach' (The revelry of the O'Rourkes), a tune for which the Gaelic poet Aodh Mac Gabhráin wrote the lyrics that Swift 'translated almost literally out of the original Irish' as 'The Description of an Irish Feast'.[280] These two passages from the play – particularly the latter – are explicitly didactic, but the lesson was one Ó Tuairisc had been trying to teach from the beginning of his career as a bilingual writer, and given the state of affairs in the North in 1979 he obviously felt the need to try again. From the time of his apprenticeship with the *geamaireachtaí*, Ó Tuairisc knew how to entertain audiences, but as *Carolan* shows again, that did not mean that he was not willing to challenge them at the same time.

Many of the ideas in *Carolan* were still on his mind when he wrote *Fornocht do Chonac* (Naked I saw),[281] which in 1979, the centenary of Pearse's birth, won Duais Chuimhneacháin an Phiarsaigh (the Pearse memorial prize), a £1,000 prize funded jointly by Taibhdhearc na Gaillimhe and An Comhlachas Náisiúnta Drámaíochta, and shared first prize for a full-length play at that year's Oireachtas with Micheál Mac Cárthaigh's *Mac Scaidín agus an Pota Draíochta* (Mac Scaidín and the magic pot). The play was published by An Gúm in 1981 and was a Club Leabhar selection for that year. *Fornocht do Chonac* had its premiere at An Taibhdhearc in 1979, with Patricia Kelly directing. As Máirín Nic Eoin has indicated, the play is his most political work for the theatre as well as 'a play that is like a table of contents, or a collection of the major themes of his own work to that time' (dráma ar geall le clár cáipéise é, nó bailiúchán de mhórthéamaí a shaothair féin go dtí sin). Among those themes she lists 'the problems of the artist and he dealing with the economic, anti-artistic outlook of contemporary Ireland . . . the wide-spread lack of interest in Pearse's values and ideals . . . the dilemma of the lack of responsibility and guilt felt by the person who does a brutal and violent deed for a political ideal'.[282] To which list could be added at least two other themes central in his work: the need to reconcile apparent contradictions in an aesthetically if not intellectually satisfying synthesis, and the significance of the linguistic divide in what in the play he calls 'the Irish mind' (an aigne Éireannach). In a prefatory note to the published text entitled 'Úsáid an Bhéarla' (The use of English), Ó Tuairisc states that he could easily have translated into Irish any English in the play, for example that in Pearse's works or in Yeats's 'Easter 1916', but he left them in English because that is how playgoers would know those works, and, in the case of Pearse's writings, putting such selections into Irish would distort 'Pearse's "sculptural style"' ('stíl dealbhóireachta' an Phiarsaigh) and obscure the fact that bilingualism was an important aspect of 'the trace of schizophrenia or the split personality' (iarracht den scitsifréine nó an deighilt pearsantachta) in the man.[283]

In a piece written in advance of An Taibhdhearc's production, an anonymous contributor to *The Connacht Tribune* discussed the central challenge facing Ó Tuairisc in the play:

> At first sight, the author Eoghan Ó Tuairisc appears to have taken an oblique approach to his subject, Pádraig Mac Piarais. But the question is how can such a figure of legend be portrayed as flesh and blood? How can it be made immediate and relevant to an audience which can call upon more than sixty years of hindsight for its answer? What is the relevance of Pearse in 1979? (*CT*, 23/11/79)

As we will see, Ó Tuairisc utilised several quite different ways to find his answers to these questions.

The play opens on a stylised set depicting a stone yard near a cemetery and the ruins of an old monastery. We also see what remains of a medieval Irish high cross. There is a hovel to one side, and loose stones and a stone carver's tools are strewn around the stage. Weeds grow everywhere. Bairbre, an art teacher in a girl's school in the nearby town of Baile an Locha (a version of Ó Tuairisc's native Ballinasloe), enters in search of the sculptor Piaras Mac Aimhirgín,[284] who lives in the hovel and carves headstones for a living. We learn immediately that Piaras is full of self-loathing, seeing himself, as he knows the locals see him, as less than human, as 'a Wild Man . . . the Madman among the stones at the edge of the graveyard living on drink and drugs' (Fear Fiáin . . . an Gealtán Fir i measc na gcloch ar imeall na reilige ag maireachtáil ar an deoch agus ar na druganna). When Bairbre calls him 'an artist' (ealaíontóir), he rejects the title with 'a rough laugh' (gáire garbh), pointing out the sort of work he is doing: 'Look at the sculpture! – a jumble, a mess, "mass-production", gravestones in the Celtic style. God's destruction on the Celtic style!'[285] As Bairbre well knows, however, he was once a serious sculptor who had in the 1960s won an international prize, il Premio d'Italia, for his statue commemorating those who died at Hiroshima. His life falls apart when a competition is held in Ireland for a statue in honour of Robert Emmet and the prize is won by a Jewish-American who creates a work of art from 'scores of pieces of wire, the kind the people of Dublin call "barbedy woire", stuck together as if it were a basket or a rook's nest' (na scórtha de ghiotaí sreangáin, an saghas ar a dtugann muintir Bhaile Átha Cliath 'barbedy woire,' agus iad greamaithe le chéile mar a bheadh ciseach ann nó nead préacháin).[286] Disgusted by the triumph of a work he sees directed at the

'Massmediocracy' – as well as by the near-blasphemy of ignoring Emmet's explicit command that no one write his epitaph until Ireland be totally free – he blows up the statue. Unfortunately, the explosion accidentally kills a five-year-old girl in a passing car, causing her several serious injuries, the fatal one being a fractured skull. Sentenced to seven years hard labour, he spends his time in prison breaking stones, and finds himself unable to practise his art when he is released.

This is the state of profound depression in which Bairbre finds him on her first visit. She has come to tell him that a delegation from the town's chamber of commerce is going to offer him a commission for a statue in honour of Pearse. She explains the statue is to be the centrepiece of a fine new park by the lake, part of a local development plan to attract more tourists to the town. Not surprisingly, Piaras receives the news with contempt: 'Well, as the Father sees us! – Fine Irish Puckfairery altogether. A little bitch of a schoolteacher an artistic adviser –' She, however, will not back down, responding to his crude cynicism with a declaration of her own idealism, an idealism unafraid to face facts:

> Pearse means a great deal to me. Baile an Locha means a great deal to me – although the imagination that some of the people in it have is contemptible. It is one of our small Irish towns. And I would not want to have a contemptible mess of a sculpture standing at the Head of the Loch as a laughing stock for tourists from Europe and farther away.[287]

For Piaras at this point, however, Pearse and his vision are 'as dead as a dodo in these times' (chomh marbh leis an dodo ar na saolta seo).[288]

His cynicism is only confirmed when he meets the members of the delegation: a hotel owner, 'a determined woman wearing expensive looking clothes' (bean storrúil a bhfuil cuma an rachmais ar a héadaí); her daughter, who uses the initials 'TD' after her name because both her father and her grandfather had been in the Irish parliament; the garage owner, a typical Ó Tuairisc gombeen man; and the German manager of the souvenir manufacturer Panseltik Plastiks, or, as Piaras calls it, 'the Leprechaun Factory' (an Mhonarcha Leipreachán), a man entirely ignorant about Irish history and culture. Apart from Bairbre, no one in the delegation knows anything about art or even about what they want Piaras to do, but they are very definite about what they do not want. Responding to a wisecrack by Piaras at the German's expense, the hotelier's daughter snaps at him: 'You are just a recidivist. Your old-fashioned national romanticism is worn out. Ireland is in Europe, and there is a new day in the world. Our economic affairs are on the march.'[289] Piaras's sarcastic 'Heil Hitler!' makes plain that while, like Ó Tuairisc, he is proud of Ireland's place in Europe, he is unwilling to see national identity erased by the trans-national culture of more economically powerful states, a danger implicit in the German's boast that the new company set up to manage the local development will import 'deep-freeze refrigerators from Germany, trained cooks from France, bacon from Denmark, frozen vegetables from the Netherlands, wine from Italy, Medieval clothes from England'.[290] They will not, however, accept anything controversial from an Irish artist – no 'green politics . . . the Shan Van Vocht and I am Ireland, that sort of mental parochialism' (polaitíocht ghlas . . . an tSean-Bhean Bhocht agus Mise Éire, an sort sin paróisteachais aigne); no religion, apart from 'perhaps' (b'fhéidir), RIP or IHS, 'but without going beyond that' (ach gan dul thar sin); and certainly no reference to 'a fight, a battle, violence, brutality – verboten! It frightens the Tourists' (troid, cath, violence, brúidiúlacht – verboten! Cuireann sé scanradh ar na Turasóirí).[291] When Piaras asks what is left, the German answers smugly: 'In one word for you. Kultur. Something Seltik.' Surprisingly, Piaras says he is willing to do the work for free, although he does add a very significant condition: 'You must accept anything at all I will make.'[292] Despite a slight objection from one member, the delegation finds this an offer they cannot refuse.

The rest of the play follows Piaras's attempts to summon the faith, will, and vision he will need to meet this new challenge, in all of which he will be helped by the very real flesh-and-blood Bairbre; by the spirit of his beloved grandfather, a stone mason and veteran of the GPO in Easter Week 1916; and by the spirit of Pearse himself, here presented as a female figure. He interacts with these two spirits through flashbacks, dreams, and visions throughout the play. It is also in this way that Ó Tuairisc incorporates various pieces of Pearse's writings in both Irish and English into the script, allowing the audience to experience passages that influenced Piaras's development as man and artist. Moreover, Ó Tuairisc makes Piaras's identification with Pearse more obvious by showing him reciting some of these passages at various ages and in various contexts – as a primary school student acting in a scene from Pearse's play *Íosagán* (Little Jesus); as a competitor reciting the poem 'Bean Sléibhe ag Caoineadh a Mic' (A mountain woman keening her son) at a *feis* in Rosmuc, where Pearse had a cottage; and as a 17-year-old secondary school student dressed as Pearse and speaking the words of his 1915 funeral oration at the grave of Jeremiah O'Donovan Rossa.

Flashbacks involving his grandfather stress the old man's unyielding idealism and commitment to Pearse's vision of the new Ireland the 1916 Rising was meant to create. Piaras and the old man share a contempt for the 'Buggerwuzzies' (Bourgeoisie), people 'with no imagination but that of the huckster' (gan de shamhlaíocht acu ach samhlaíocht an ocastóra), and for whom 'the base and high point of their religion and politics' (buntús agus barr buaice a gcuid reiligiúin agus a gcuid polaitíochta) is 'to make money, to put money to work to make money, to wear the mask of money before the world' (airgead a sholáthar, airgead a chur ag saothrú airgid, aghaidh fidil an airgid a chaitheamh os comhair an tsaoil).[293] An Ireland run by such people is not what his grandfather – or Pearse – fought for in 1916, as the old man makes clear in one of the flashbacks: 'If there is any sense at all to the bloody drama we acted out in the twilight of the GPO, it was that we would have "Freedom". Freedom of mind. Freedom for the individual, from the state, from authority, from his own family, freedom to carve out his own path and to realise his own vision.'[294] What resulted instead after 1916 was what Piaras calls 'a State without a heart, without imagination, a Republic in which the purse was King' (Stát gan chroí gan samhlaíocht, Poblacht ina raibh an sparán ina Rí), a state that declares 'Death to craftsmanship, death to vision, death to everything that sustains the human spirit and the character of a people'.[295] The key word here is 'imagination' (samhlaíocht), a mental and spiritual capacity his grandfather explains to the schoolboy Piaras in another flashback: 'The person who has the gift of imagination sees something – something relating to the otherworld . . . A kind of "Ide-a". A thought or some strange picture that arises from the soul inside.'[296] This belief that the artist is able to get the occasional glimpse behind the veil of mundane reality was, of course, profoundly important to Ó Tuairisc, as is another of the grandfather's convictions: 'It is no good for a person to see the vision unless he is able to make it clear to other people . . . in a song, or in music, or in a bit of painting, or going out on a voyage of discovery and finding a world, or drawing up a political vision and explaining it to the world.'[297]

For the grandfather, and eventually for his grandson, it is Pearse who best exemplifies the artist's ability to see and share, to use his imagination to allow others to experience his vision.[298] As the grandfather tells Piaras, it was through the vision shared by Pearse with his men in the GPO that 'we all felt that we were not in the old post office on the old street, but as if we were somewhere else, on some stage, taking part in a play – some visionary play that we did not properly understand'.[299] And through the GPO strode Pearse, 'like a ghost – the ghost of the playwright who was creating the whole thing' (mar a bheadh taibhse ann – taibhse an drámadóra a raibh an t-iomlán á chruthú aige). Under the influence of Pearse's vision – 'Ireland, perhaps. Imagination. The flowering of the spirit. Something that had never existed. Something still to be created' (Éire, b'fhéidir. Samhlaíocht. Bláthú an spioraid. Rud éigin nach raibh riamh ann. Rud atá le cruthú go fóill) – the men in the GPO felt that what they were engaged in was not war 'as we understood warfare' (mar a thuigeamar cogaíocht), that they were fighting not the British military and the police, but rather a far more ominous opponent, 'the immense power of the world, the daily tedium, the reason and the common conscience – an immense power that was trying its very hardest to smother the vision in us.

A vision that was growing in our souls, flowering, pushing towards the light' (cumhacht ollmhór an tsaoil, an leadrán laethúil, an réasún agus an coinsias comónta – ollchumhacht a bhí ar a míle dícheall ag dréim leis an aisling a mhúchadh ionainn, aisling a bhí ag borradh, ag bláthú, ag brú chun solais inár n-anam istigh). But of course they are shooting at men, not abstractions, with 'the City in flames around us' (an Chathair trí thine inár dtimpeall).[300]

Ó Tuairisc follows this scene immediately with a flashback in which Piaras and one of the nuns in his primary school act out a scene from Pearse's *Íosagán*, a flashback obviously intended to give us a sense of the gentler side of Pearse after we have heard about the rebel hero. However, after the questions raised by the grandfather's memories of the fight in the GPO, the scene from *Íosagán*, already sentimental, borders on the maudlin. This innocent and artistic side of Pearse is not what Piaras must confront if he wants to create a work of art that genuinely expresses the man's legacy in modern Ireland. And he knows from the most painful personal experience – his own rash attempt to strike a blow for artistic integrity by destroying what he saw as a meretricious statue supposedly in honour of a genuine Irish patriot and hero – that actions of impeccable motive can have murderous consequences, like the death of an innocent five-year-old girl. Tormented by what he has done and haunted by the image of the child's fractured skull, he comes to see Pearse and his at times facile acceptance of violence as the cause of both his own act of folly and a symbol of the bloodshed of centuries of Irish history:

> Eternal damnation on Pearse. I would like to rip his name and everything relating to him out of the nerves of my memory. Pearse, the myth of Pearse, is the foundation stone and primary cause of my torment . . . Living in the twilight of his own imagination, which never saw the little skeleton of a girl, five years old, lying tonight under the clay and the little decomposed brain dust as a result of his drama.[301]

With this dark new understanding of Pearse, he is disgusted by what he now sees as the gospel of Irish warriors, poets, and sages for a thousand years: 'Strike! Shatter, blow up, destroy, kill!' (Strike! Réab, pléasc, scrios, maraigh!), a message that has resulted in nothing but 'human blood, brains, and guts blown out on the street, the red stain on our conscience from generation to generation' (fuil, inchinn, putóga an duine séidte ar an tsráid amach, an smál dearg ar an gcoinsias againn ó ghlúin go glúin). Pearse's poem 'Mise Éire' is now for him just material for parody:

> I am Ireland . . .
> The Butcher's slaughter-house . . .
> Great is my glory . . .
> I gave birth to Mac Aimhirgín the Murderer . . .[302]

Before he reaches this point of despair, he has actually, with Bairbre's help, been making some progress, feeling 'Pearse . . . out of the abyss of the years . . . being aroused again in my memory' (An Piarsach . . . as duibheagán na mblianta – á spreagadh i gcuimhne dom athuair –). In this more positive mood he seems unaware of the problematic juxtaposition of terror and beauty in Yeats's 'Easter 1916' recited by 'The Chorus of the Old' (Cór na Sean).[303] His initial inspiration is the broken high cross near his hut, a work of art he sees characterised by 'intellect' (intleacht) that elevates it above 'the mess that is called "Celtic work" today' (an prácás ar a tugtar 'saothar Ceilteach' sa lá inniu). Explaining this idea to Bairbre, he speaks for Ó Tuairisc in saying that the person who created the cross had 'An *Idea* to make clear . . . an image or a thought from the otherworld that is interwoven with this world of ours' (*Idea* le léiriú . . . samhail nó smaoineamh ón saol eile atá fite fuaite tríd an saol seo againn). Likening that idea to T. S. Eliot's 'still center of the spinning world', he sees the central concept of the cross as 'God's Will' (Toil Dé) and reads the pictorial panels on the cross for Bairbre in that light. Moreover, he regards the worldview expressed by the cross as the product of 'the Irish mind. That mind that sees the two things at the same time, reality and the mystery . . . The Absurdity of life and the Vision of life inextricably woven together' (an aigne Éireannach. An aigne úd a fheiceann an dá rud ag an am céanna, an réalaíocht agus an rúndiamhair . . . Áiféis an tsaoil agus Aisling an tsaoil fite fuaite ina chéile).[304] This insight concerning the Irish mind originally came to him while he was working in Italy with other sculptors, European and American, and gave him his first real sense of being Irish. At that time, however, he saw 'the Irish mind' in comfortingly uncomplicated terms as 'a kind of simplicity in art, a kind of purity, an ironic outlook' (saghas simplíochta san ealaín, saghas geanmnaíochta, dearcadh íorónta). He will have to go through a great deal of suffering and soul-searching before he expands this view of Irish creativity to include contradictions far more terrible than what Bairbre in joking reference to the cross calls 'The Ass and God's Will' (An t-Asal agus Toil Dé).[305]

After he wrestles with his own memories in other flashbacks and visions in which he plays Mac Dara, the protagonist in *The Singer*, Pearse's 1915 play about the redemptive power of blood sacrifice, and listens to the voice of Pearse's mother reciting her lament for her executed sons morphing into the voice of his own young victim's mother, he seems ready to give up on the Pearse statue, calling it 'a waste of time' (cailliúint ama) and 'childishness' (páistiúlacht). Here Bairbre takes charge, blasting his cynicism and snobbery, pointing out that whatever his opinion of the intellectual capabilities of the local children, 'they must be cherished, protected, provided with the richness of our own art'. Bairbre believes that those who look down on such children – and their parents – are in a very real sense traitors:

O, you are fine villains and revolutionaries, the 'avant garde', all of you Stephen Dedaluses running to France and Italy – 'to forge the uncreated conscience of my race!'– But look, down there you have Baile an Locha, there you have the people who are in bondage, there you have the 'real world'– and if there is a conscience to be forged and a battle to be fought, there you have the base and the crust for your efforts.

She knows well what unpromising material many of these people seem to provide: 'They trotting after the asses. Without a protective shield, but the ear and the eye and the poor mouth open for any kind of garbage that is thrown to us from the four corners of the world.'[306] Nor is there native sustenance easily available for, as she tells Piaras, she has searched the town and county libraries and found plenty on Pepys, Padre Pio, Paderewski and Lester Piggott, but nothing on Pearse.

Impressed by her passion, he has a sudden moment of inspiration in which he sees the concept for his statue: 'One figure up there so. And near it, to the right, lower, far lower, the round Figure . . . The contrast . . . the conflict' (Figiúr amháin in airde thuas mar sin. Agus in aice leis, ar deis, níos ísle, i bhfad níos ísle, an Figiúr cruinn . . . An chontrárthacht . . . an choinbhliocht). But he still does not know what these figures represent. In a dream in which he is back in his prison cell, 'the Spirit of Pearse' (Sprid an Phiarsaigh) appears to him in the guise of the 'gentle young woman' (ainnir shéimh) of the seventeenth- and eighteenth-century *aisling* poems. The spirit tells him that he has called to her as he always has 'every time you took hold of a chisel to sculpt' (gach uair do rug tú ar shiséal chun dealbhóireachta) and that she represents far more than the spirit of Pearse alone. She is 'the eternal Spirit. Inspiration . . . There are many names for me, and many a mask I wear, and many a drama I act out through the deep sleep of this night of yours in the world' (an Sprid shíoraí. An Inspioráid . . . Is iomaí ainm atá orm, is iomaí aghaidh fidil a chaithim, is iomaí dráma a ghníomhaím trí thromshuan na hoíche seo agaibh ar an saol).[307] When he was alive she was embodied in Pearse, but now she is 'A Spirit. A Myth. An Inspiration to Action' (Sprid. Miotas. Spreagadh chun gnímh). And when he adds '*Idea?*' she responds with her challenge to the artist: 'To be created by you and to be personified by you, again and again, every one of you according to his own ability, under the masks of the day.'[308] But she is also Ireland, although she quickly adds:

It is not only a country that is in question, or a specific people. It is broader than a country, more ancient than the people who incarnate it. It is a Country, and it is a Language. It is a Language and a Language's understanding of life. It is insight, insight to be defended and cherished against the ordinary great power of the day. A Vision. A Word. A Prophecy. The Irish mind.

Publicity photo of Máiréad Ní Ghráda at the height of her playwriting career. Courtesy of Dublin City Libraries and Archive © Irish Photo Archive.

Notice for the premiere of *Rité*, by Máiréad Ní Ghráda, which was performed along with two other one-act plays at the opening night of An Damer in November 1955. Courtesy of Dublin City Libraries and Archive.

CAD CHUIGE CLUB DRÁMAÍOCHTA?

Ní gá a rá nach féidir le hamharclainn maireachtáil gan lucht féachana agus dúrathas go minic nach mbeadh aon rath ar amharclann Ghaeilge i mBaile Átha Cliath mar nach mbeadh aon tinnreamh sásúil air.

Iarraimíd ortsa a chruthú nach bhfuil san ceart. Iarraimíd ort tacaíocht a thabhairt don iarracht seo chun ceann des na gnéithe is laige den athbheochaint a fhorbairt agus a chur ar a bhonnaibh i gceart.

Tig leat san a dhéanamh tré clárú san gClub Drámaíochta ar 10/-, agus beidh de cheart agat freastal saor in aisce ar na léirithe ar fad.

AN CHÉAD LÉIRIÚ   Samhain 14—19

AISTEOIRÍ CRAOBH AN CHÉITINNIGH
ag léiriú

RÍTA le Máiréad Ní Ghráda

OLC MAITH aistriúchán le Máirtín Ó Díomsaigh

AN CAIDÉAL SA CHLÓS le M. Ó Díomsaigh agus Gearóid
Ó Tighearnaigh

CLÁRAIGH SAN gCLUB le

SEOSAMH Ó hÓGARTAIGH,
10 Br. na Daraighe, Páirc Wyckham, Dúndroma.
Tel. 901772

nó

MUIRIS DE PHRIONNBHÍOL,
34 Bóthar Neifin, Bóthar na hUaimhe, Áth Cliath.

Scene from *Stailc Ocrais*, by Máiréad Ní Ghráda, at An Damer, 1962, with actors Nuala Ní Dhónaill, Pádraig Ó Catháin, Deirdre Ní Dheasúin, Máiréad Ní Bhriain, Máire Ní Oistín, Brian Ó Baoighill, Seosamh Ó Mongaidh, and Dónal Ó Cuill © Irish Photo Archive.

Scene from *Giolla an tSolais*, by Máiréad Ní Ghráda, at Taibhdhearc na Gaillimhe, 1945, with actor Walter Macken (centre) in the title role. Courtesy of the James Hardiman Library, NUIG.

Photo of Séamus Ó Néill at the premiere of his *Rún an Oileáin* at An Damer, 1961. Courtesy of Dublin City Libraries and Archive © Irish Photo Archive.

Portrait of playwright Eoghan Ó Tuairisc in 1979. Courtesy of the James Hardiman Library, NUIG.

Scene from *Aisling Mhic Artáin*, by Eoghan Ó Tuairisc, at the Peacock Theatre, 1977, with actors Máire Ní Ghráinne and Caoimhín Mac Aoidh. Courtesy of Dublin City Libraries and Archive © Fergus Bourke.

Actors Celine Ní Raghallaigh and Mairtín Ó Cearnaigh as the mother superior and Murtach in *Lá Fhéile Míchíl*, by Eoghan Ó Tuairisc, from *Ardán* (Oireachtas edition 1971). Courtesy of Dublin City Libraries and Archive.

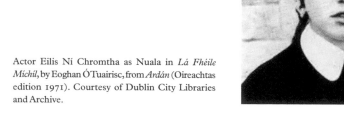

Actor Eilis Ní Chromtha as Nuala in *Lá Fhéile Míchíl*, by Eoghan Ó Tuairisc, from *Ardán* (Oireachtas edition 1971). Courtesy of Dublin City Libraries and Archive.

Scene from *Corp Eoghain Uí Shúilleabháin*, by Seán Ó Tuama, with actors Máirín Dúraic and Séamus Ó Tuama. Courtesy of Dublin City Libraries and Archive.

Publicity photo of playwright Críostóir
Ó Floinn. Courtesy of Dublin City
Libraries and Archive.

Scene from *Cluichí Cleamhnais*, by Críostóir Ó Floinn, at Taibhdhearc na Gaillimhe, 1978, with actors
Loretta Ní Cheallaigh and Antaine Ó Flatharta. Courtesy of the James Hardiman Library, NUIG.

Scene from *Mise Raifteirí an File*, by Críostóir Ó Floinn, at the Peacock Theatre, 1973, with actors Imelda O'Byrne, Terry Donnelly, Peadar Lamb (as Raifteirí), Deirdre Lawless and Áine Ní Mhuirí. Courtesy of Dublin City Libraries and Archive © Fergus Bourke.

A Club Drámaíochta membership card for 1955–6. Courtesy of Dublin City Libraries and Archive.

AN CLUB DRÁMAÍOCHTA

HALLA DAMER

112 Faiche Stiabhna

GEIMHREADH 1955-1956

Sealbhóir Risteárd Ó Glaisne

Gach ticéad díobh seo tabharfaidh sé cead
duit suíochán amháin fháil le linn na seachtaine atá luaite air. Chun bheith deimh-
nitheach go bhfaighidh tú suíochán maith ar
an oíche a oireann duit moltar go gcuirfeá
suíochán ar leith in áirithe roimhré tré
Áisíneacht B.B., 24 Sráid Frederic Theas.
Tel. 65571.

Ticéad Ballraíochta - - - 10/-

LÉIRIÚ 5

AIBREÁN
9-14

203

TICÉAD

Promotional poster by Ryan Long for Fíbín Teo's contemporary production of Máiréad Ní Ghráda's *An Triail*. Courtesy of Fíbín Teo.

Piaras is not, however, intimidated and raises the question that most troubles him: 'And until today, until tonight, as a myth, as an example, you continue the killing, the slaughter, the horror? – Answer, Pearse, are you not guilty?'[309]

When the spirit tersely acknowledges responsibility, Piaras continues his indictment, initially unimpressed by the spirit's assertion that Beauty is nothing but 'a worthless, insubstantial toy unless it is interwoven with Terror' (áilleagán gan tairbhe gan téagar mura mbíonn sí fite fuaite leis an Uafás). At this point, Piaras finds this argument glib and declares: 'It is time for me to tear you out of the nerves of my imagination – it is beyond time for us to pull you and your gospel of blood up out of the clay of our memory as if it were a stinging nettle.'[310] With quiet authority, the spirit tells him that what he wants to do is impossible, for 'I am in the fibre of your being. Long ago they wove me into the warp of your mind. I am the seed from which your imagination flowers.' To tear the spirit out of his memory would be 'to destroy your strength as an artist here and now' (do neart mar ealaíontóir a bhascadh ar an láthair seo). The choice the spirit offers Piaras is, then, to give up his vocation as artist or 'to arise and go forward to the end of the story' (éirí, agus dul ar aghaidh go deireadh an scéil). And she spells out just what that means: 'You must make me whole . . . redeem myself and my work in the Theme of Resurrection.'[311] Moreover, when Piaras says he cannot 'forget the horror, the murder I committed, the little skull' (dearmad a dhéanamh den uafás, an murdar a rinne mé, an cloigeann beag) in order to create his art, the spirit tells him that that is just what he must not do: 'You are obliged to draw the Horror out into the light of day, and stare at it naked.' He must not only face the 'terrible beauty'; he must also face 'the "Terror" and the "Beauty", correlate them and show their relationship in the stone – as you did with your statue in memory of the Dead who Died at Hiroshima' (an 'Terror' agus an 'Beauty' a chomhghaolú agus a fhoilsiú sa chloch – mar a rinne tú le do dhealbh i gcuimhne na Marbh a Fuair Bás ag Hiroshima), an act the guilt for which he, like all members of the human race, shares.[312] In the meantime he must continue, as all artists do, 'wrestling with the truth in your life and in your work' (ag dréim leis an bhfírinne i do shaol agus i do shaothar). In this struggle, 'you will be a blind fool to the end of the story. The whole thing will not be revealed to you until the Great Work of Eternity is revealed to us – in the Resurrection.'[313] With the chorus singing 'Caoineadh na Mná Sléibhe' (Lullaby of woman of the mountain) in the background, Sprid an Phiarsaigh returns and offers Piaras more concrete assistance with his sculpture: 'The Spirit of Pearse appears at the back . . . she is carrying a little Skull out before her in her hands . . . It is a little dark yellow skull.'[314] When Piaras sees the tiny skull he immediately realises both its personal and universal significance: 'Here is where the break happened – in the lamellar bone of the temple. A gapped break – a metal tool, the door handle of the car, a knife, a spear, a bullet, a stone axe – in the long nightmare of the ages. History –' The skull will be one of the two thematic elements in the sculpture of which Piaras now has a clear vision: 'Observe, friends, our history, our ancestry. Here and now, naked. We have no goal, no destination, except for this simple shell on the slab. Staring at the Final Nothing.'[315] Of course this is just one of the two contradictory elements he is trying to meld in the statue; the other now appears to him in another visionary moment in which he sees himself dressed as Íosagán, an image he responds to with astonishment: 'By all that's holy! Pearse himself telling   me . . . "In the beginning was the Word" – the other side, the fulfilment –'[316] As he and Bairbre look at his sketch for the statue, the young Piaras as Íosagán stands up on a stone and stares ahead, with the skull at his feet, seeming to look up at him. Bairbre's response lets Piaras know he has succeeded, has provided catharsis: 'It frightens me. Frightens . . . gives me a kind of joy.' Nothing else need be said, and when she asks him what words he will carve on the statue, he replies 'Nothing' (Dada).[317]

Despite its effective use of theatrical techniques like flashbacks, dreams, dance, and a chorus, *Fornocht do Chonac* is very much a play of ideas, perhaps too many ideas. Since much of the 'action' involves weighty discussions of art, philosophy, and the burden of history, some playgoers might miss the catharsis at the end and instead find the whole thing heavy going, almost an academic exercise, rather than an engaging evening in the theatre. And there are other problems. The flashbacks showing Piaras's youthful engagement with the work of Pearse are often too long and can thus obscure rather than illuminate the development of Piaras's character and Ó Tuairisc's ideas. There is also the question of the statue itself. By showing us what his protagonist has created, Ó Tuairisc deprives his audience of the opportunity to imagine for themselves what he should create. In this way, the success – or failure – of the play depends far too much on how playgoers respond to a very specific work of art as both a metaphor for artistic inspiration and creation in general and a statement about the significance of Pearse in the Irish consciousness. A more open-ended conclusion showing Piaras inspired, but the result of that inspiration not given physical representation, might provide audience members, perhaps wearied by all the abstract theorising, with a greater sense of involvement in the play.[318] Still, *Fornocht do Chonac* is an ambitious, imaginative, and often powerful play that is unafraid to take on, in Irish, questions of major and continuing relevance for Ireland and for Irish artists.

Eoghan Ó Tuairisc's eight plays, six of them full-length, represent a major contribution to theatre in Irish and indeed to theatre in Ireland. Since his premature death in 1982, he has been accorded some of the recognition too often denied him in his own lifetime.[319] For example, in 1982 a Gaelscoil in Carlow was named in his honour and Telefís Éireann broadcast a tribute to him and his fellow poet and dramatist Caitlín Maude, who also died in 1982 (*IT*, 6/11/82). In 1983 Gael-Linn began to offer Trófaí Cuimhneacháin Eoghain Uí Thuairisc (The Eoghan Ó Tuairisc memorial trophy) to the best young poet in Irish at An Slógadh, and in the same year he was honoured by Scoil Merriman (*CT*, 4/12/83). In 1991 his birthplace of Ballinasloe held Éigse Uí Thuairisc (The Ó Tuairisc literary festival) and erected a plaque in his memory (*WP*, 20/11/91). Moreover, his former student, Professor Colbert Kearney of University College, Cork, paid an affectionate tribute to his old teacher in the 'ERW' section of his 1993 novel *The Consequence*, in which he wrote:

> And Eugene was a most unusual man. He was intellectually first-class and could, I believe, have been an outstanding scientist, an outstanding professor of classics, Irish or English . . . He was a distinguished writer of poetry, plays, fiction and critical prose in Irish and English . . . He was the most wonderful teacher I have ever had or heard about.[320]

Yet despite all the praise and all the honours, Ó Tuairisc has been denied what may be the most appropriate tribute to what he accomplished for theatre in Irish: regular and competent, if not professional, productions of his plays in Dublin and throughout Ireland. Sadly, such productions may well never be mounted, a failure for which both the Irish language and the Irish theatre will be the poorer.

FOUR

KNOCKING DOWN OLD WALLS

SEÁN Ó TUAMA (1926–2006)

When Seán Ó Tuama's play *Déan Trócaire ar Shagairt Óga* (Have mercy on young priests) had its premiere at the Catholic Young Men's Society Theatre in Cork in 1970, Uinseann Ó Murchú wrote that Ó Tuama's dramatic work was of 'great importance' (an-tábhacht) for theatre in Irish because he was 'trying to knock down old walls to find a new mould for the drama' (ag iarraidh sean-bhallaí a leagadh chun teacht ar mhúnla nua don drámaíocht) (*IP*, 20/3/70).[1] A superficial glance at those plays might suggest that Ó Murchú was indulging in a bit of hyperbole here, for Ó Tuama's plays seem to fit neatly into just the categories long associated with Gaelic playwrights: history plays, a play based on a tale from the early literature, a work featuring a literary figure from the Gaelic past, a play inspired by subject matter from the Bible, one about the challenges facing a Catholic priest, and one dealing with family tensions arising from the possibility of what is seen as an inappropriate marriage. A closer look at these plays will, however, bear out Ó Murchú's assessment, for Ó Tuama engaged with all of these subjects with a startling originality, in the process creating some of the most important – and popular – plays ever written in Irish.[2]

His accomplishments in this field are even more striking when one considers how brief his career as a playwright was. His first play and in all probability his masterpiece, the history play *Gunna Cam agus Slabhra Óir* (A pistol and a golden chain), had its first performance in 1956, while the last of his plays, *Déan Trócaire ar Shagairt Óga*, was first staged in 1970, so his active engagement with the stage lasted only 15 years or so. Moreover, throughout the time he was writing his plays he was, like most of his fellow Gaelic dramatists, very much a part-time playwright. Indeed his considerable reputation in the Gaelic world and beyond rests largely on those other activities, so that he is in all likelihood far better known today as a scholar, language activist, poet or mentor to the younger poets of the so-called *Innti* group than he is as a playwright. Before attempting to restore him to his rightful place as a major figure in Irish-language theatre, we should, then, briefly examine some of his other activities, for it is clear that his work as scholar, teacher, and activist informed and enriched his achievement in drama.

Born in Cork City in 1926, Ó Tuama was nonetheless raised in an Irish-speaking home, as he boasted of proudly later in life: 'Thus I am a native speaker from Blackpool, Cork' (Cainteoir dúchais is ea mé mar sin ó Bhlackpool, Cork) (*Feasta*, Apr. 1981, p. 14).[3] His primary education was also through Irish, after which he attended the famous North Monastery school and then University College, Cork, where he was taught by Tadhg Ó Donnchadha ('Torna') and Daniel Corkery, the latter of whom would have a powerful and lifelong influence on him, as he acknowledged in 1965: 'I am a disciple of Daniel Corkery. No one likes to admit that he is just a disciple but in this case I cannot avoid it, nor do I want to' (*Comhar*, Feb. 1965, p. 32).[4] He would remain at UCC for the rest of his academic life, becoming an associate professor in 1968 and professor of Irish in 1982 before retiring in 1990. In addition he held visiting professorships at various times at Oxford, Harvard, and Boston College.

The best known of his scholarly works is *An Grá in Amhráin na nDaoine* (Love in the songs of the people) (1960), a book based on his doctoral thesis tracing the love theme in Irish folksong and exploring both native and foreign influences. In 1988 he published the companion volume *An Grá i bhFilíocht na nUasal* (Love in the poetry of the nobles). His *Filí faoi Sceimhle* (Terrified poets) (1978) offers a scholar-poet's insights into the work of Aodhagán Ó Rathaile (*c.* 1670–1729) and Seán Ó Ríordáin (1916–77), the cause of the latter of whom he had championed from the very beginning of Ó Ríordáin's poetic career and whom he had helped to get a position as writer in residence at UCC. His essays, many of them seminal contributions to the study of literature in Irish, were collected in *Cúirt, Tuath agus Bruachbhailte* (Court, country, and suburbs) (1991), *Repossessions: Selected Lectures on the Irish Literary Heritage* (1995), and the posthumous *Aguisíní* (Addenda) (2008). In many ways, his editorial work was nearly as important as his contributions as a literary historian and critic. Of particular note here is his 1961 edition of *Caoineadh Airt Uí Laoghaire* (The lament for Arthur O'Leary), which made the poem easily available to scholars and students. Even better known and more influential in the broader field of Irish Studies is *An Duanaire 1600–1900: Poems of the Dispossessed* (1981), his selection of a range of Irish poems spanning three centuries with accompanying translations by Thomas Kinsella. This work introduced students of Irish culture in Ireland and abroad to significant writers and poems they may have previously known only by name, if at all. He performed a similar service for modern Irish poets, though without translations, in *Coiscéim na hAoise Seo* (The footstep of this century) (1991), co-edited with his former student, the poet and scholar Louis de Paor.

As the son of a father who was a Gaelic League organiser and as a self-professed disciple of Daniel Corkery, Ó Tuama was a lifelong cultural nationalist who never lost his belief in what he called 'the Gaelic League idea'.[5] Indeed his language activism seems to have been as central to his life as was his academic and creative work, which, conversely, could be seen as an expression of his commitment to the cause. Thus commenting on writing in Irish two centuries after 'Cúirt an Mheán Oíche' (The midnight court) and *Caoineadh Airt Uí Laoghaire*, he wrote in 1988:

> Once again poetry in which there is a special value and a special beauty is being composed in Irish. How can any Irish person who would boast of an education – or a love of beauty – be without a knowledge of the most distinctive things said and felt by the people who came before him or by his contemporaries? How can he have that knowledge without Irish?

And responding to what he regarded as the neo-colonial attitude towards Irish internalised by so many of his compatriots, he continued: 'The person who understands . . . the primary place of Irish in his cultural heritage will be very troubled. He will be so troubled that he will learn it and he will speak it' (*II*, 9/1/84).[6]

He certainly did his part to challenge the complacent pessimism of those who saw no future for Irish.[7] Of course he did so most obviously as a charismatic professor of Irish at UCC, a professor of whom his student, the poet, playwright, and novelist Liam Ó Muirthile, has written: 'His teaching left a mark on generations of students . . . He succeeded in making aspects of the literary tradition of Irish keep time with the age.'[8] He was, however, also aware that no matter how important university students were for the preservation and evolution of Irish as a modern scholarly and cultural medium, it was essential that ordinary Irish citizens be given a sound and convincing rationale for the revival and regular use of the language as well as a practical programme to facilitate that revival and use. Thus, to address the questions of the large number of people in all probability more indifferent than hostile to Irish, in 1964 he published *Facts about Irish*, a question and answer style booklet that dealt in lucid detail with the principle concerns about the language and its revival at that time.[9]

To reach those with a deeper interest in the language, the traditions it embodied, and its continuing importance in Irish life, he lectured frequently to groups of all kinds throughout the country. For example, we find him speaking on 'Dónall Ó Corcora, léirmheastóir' (Daniel Corkery, critic) to Cumann na Scríbhneoirí in 1959 (*IP*, 17/10/59); on 'Fáistine na litríochta in Éirinn, 1900–1961' (The prophecy of literature in Ireland, 1900–1961) at the Gaelic League's Oireachtas in Dublin in 1961 (*IP*, 4/11/61); on 'The Irish language: a reappraisal' to An Mhionscoil, a 'workers' educational course' created by trade unionists in Cork in 1962 (*IP*, 5/12/62); on 'An Ghaeilge agus an pholaitíocht' (Irish and politics) to members of An Comhchaidreamh in Dingle, Co. Kerry in 1964 (*IP*, 6/8/64); on 'Dírbheathaisnéis' (Autobiography) to Gaelic Leaguers in Dublin in 1967 (*IP*, 3/3/67); on 'Béaloideas' (Folklore) to a Gaelic League branch in Cashel, Co. Tipperary in 1967 (*IP*, 20/3/67); on 'Dualgas an chéimí i leith an phobail' (The graduate's duty towards the public) to An Comhchaidreamh in 1967 (*II*, 10/7/67); on 'An file agus a mhuintir' (The poet and his people) (on Seán Ó Ríordáin) in Dún Chaoin, Co. Kerry in 1972 (*IP*, 22/2/72); on 'What use is Irish?' at a symposium organised by Glór na nGael in Skibbereen, Co. Cork in 1972 (*SS*, 26/2/72); on recent writing in Irish at the Listowel Writers' Week in 1974 (*IP*, 6/6/74); and on Aodhagán Ó Rathaile to the Tralee, Co. Kerry branch of the Gaelic League in 1983 (*IP*, 11/3/83).

He reached wider audiences through radio and television broadcasts. For instance, on radio he discussed Máirtín Ó Cadhain's *Cré na Cille* and An tAthair Peadar Ua Laoghaire's *Séadna* (*II*, 17/10/53) and 'Lá an dreoilín' (Wren day) in 1953 (*IP*, 22/12/53); modern writing in Irish (*IP*, 12/2/58) and Daniel Corkery in 1958 (and Corkery again in 1965) (*IP*, 19/2/58; 24/4/65); 'Scríbhneoirí agus a noidhreacht ó Yeats i leith' (Writers and their legacy from Yeats on) in 1959 (*TH*, 6/6/59); the poetic schools at Blarney and Carrignavar, Co. Cork in 1961 (*IP*, 9/9/61); *Caoineadh Airt Uí Laoghaire* in 1961 (*IP*, 14/11/61);[10] Irish politics on a panel that included the taoiseach Jack Lynch in 1967 (*IP*, 4/3/67); and the Maigue poets in 1970 (*IP*, 24/4/70). Television viewers could have seen him talk about himself and his work on a programme entitled 'An Fear agus a Scéal' (The man and his story) in 1963 (*IP*, 10/12/63); Daniel Corkery in 1965 and 1969 (*IP*, 23/2/65; 29/8/69); and 'Stability and ambivalence' in 1985 (*IP*, 22/4/85). In addition, he and his fellow scholar and professor David Greene (Dáithí Ó hUaithne) wrote the scripts for two Telefís Éireann series, *Long Ago but Not So Far Away* and *Watch Your Language*, both in 1970 (*IP*, 25/9/70; 23/11/70). The former was described in a press report as 'an examination of various aspects of the life of the Gaels' (scrúdú ar ghnéithe éagsúla de shaol na nGael) (*IP*, 25/9/70). In 2003 Telefís Éireann broadcast a half-hour documentary on his life and work (*WP*, 15/1/03). It must, needless to say, be kept in mind that talks like these were written and delivered in addition to the countless lectures, seminars, and informal discussions with undergraduate and graduate students that were required of him as a university professor.

Of course Ó Tuama knew well that lectures, radio broadcasts, and television appearances would never be enough to change the thinking of a critical mass of the Irish citizenry. An effective public campaign would have to be formulated and implemented, and he would spend his life engaged in various activities and institutions in an attempt to realise his version of the 'Gaelic League idea'. That he was not locked in to outmoded ways of thinking about the language and its revival is clear from his address on 'An Ghaeilge agus an pholaitíocht'. In this speech he is reported as saying that 'many ardent supporters of the language will agree that certain judicious modifications in the revival methods, which have been in operation up to the present, are called for'. But he refused to equivocate concerning what he saw as essential principles: 'But those modifications must be guided by a determination not to compromise basic aims and by a clear demonstration in terms of practical planning that this is not, in fact, being done' (*IP*, 6/8/64). Moreover, he had already in 1963 founded a new 'non-political' party, An Comhar Poiblí (The public partnership), 'to fight harmful propaganda directed against the Irish language' and 'to train young Irish speakers for leadership in public affairs and politics' (*II*, 25/11/63).[11] The following year he stated of this group: 'The main goal of A. C. P. is to find effective ways to influence the public, English-language organisations, and the political parties of Ireland for the benefit of the Irish language, and the benefit of Ireland' (*Feasta*, Apr. 1964, p. 15).[12]

Like several other Gaelic writers, including Máirtín Ó Cadhain and Diarmaid Ó Súilleabháin, Ó Tuama found the Irish state's grand celebration of the fiftieth anniversary of the 1916 Easter Rising deeply troubling in light of what he saw as that state's continuing failure to take any meaningful action to create the free and Gaelic state that was Patrick Pearse's ideal in 1916. Thus in May 1966 he lashed out at the government's lukewarm and ambivalent response to its own 1965 White Paper *The Restoration of the Irish Language*, stating that 'it was nauseating to encounter so much double-thinking and so much inefficiency in translating even the first steps of the 1916 vision into practice' (*IP*, 22/5/66). Nor did he limit his criticism to the government, as he also blasted what had once been called 'West Britons' for their indifference if not downright hostility to the first national language. In March 1966 he was reported as telling a Cork audience that 'the greatest damage done to our nation in recent years had come, not from a rump of anarchists but from a ghetto of bloodless Anglo-Irish reactionaries within the Dublin Pale' (*IP*, 22/3/66).

Of course while such outbursts may have been a satisfying way to vent his frustration with state policy concerning the language, he knew well such state policy would remain a determining factor in the survival and spread of Irish – if such survival and spread were to happen. More typical of Ó Tuama's activism than the anger above was his willingness to work within the system to achieve the incremental implementation of his own ideas. Thus over the years he agreed to serve as a member of several prestigious governmental bodies, among them the Arts Council, the Irish Linguistics Institute, Comhairle na Gaeilge, and Bord na Gaeilge, of which he was eventually the chairperson in the 1980s, playing a key role in the creation of *Plean*

Gníomhaíochta na Gaeilge/Action Plan for Irish, 1983–1986. In addition, he was a member of the Gaelic League, Cumann na Scríbhneoirí, and An Comhchaidreamh, as well as being a shareholder of the AbbeyTheatre and a member of the governing board of UCC.

Ó Tuama's involvement with theatre in Irish developed naturally from his belief in the continuing relevance of the Gaelic tradition and his activism. He clearly understood that no other literary genre available to Irish at that time could create a greater sense of community among Irish speakers or pose a greater challenge to those who believed, or wanted to believe, that, in his words, 'our – or any – national culture should come to be thought of as a mere compendium of different elements or different subconscious [sic] without any underlying unity or common value system' (*IP*, 1/3/74). For Ó Tuama, it was possible for those watching a play in Irish to share the experience of engaging with their own distinctive national culture as it had been expressed for two millennia through a language whose continuing vitality was ensured by their own involvement with it as members of the very real community that was the audience.

Even before the production of his own first play *Gunna Cam agus Slabhra Óir* in 1956, he had been centrally involved with Dan Donovan (Dónall Ó Donnabháin) in the founding of the theatre group Compántas Chorcaí in 1953.[13] In addition to providing Compántas Chorcaí with five of his own plays, the plays that made the theatre's reputation, Ó Tuama seems to have been always willing to try his hand at other aspects of the theatre's work. For example, in 1954 he and Donovan co-produced for the Oireachtas in Dublin *Caimbéal na Coille Móire*, Risteárd Ó Foghludha's translation of J. A. Ferguson's play *Campbell of Kilmhor* (*CE*, 21/2/54). Doubtless the Corkman in Ó Tuama took real and justified pride in Compántas Chorcaí and his own major contribution to the group, but he was also aware that if theatre in Irish were ever to thrive it would have to gain a permanent foothold in the nation's capital. Accordingly, he took an active interest in the work of An Damer, where all of his plays were produced between 1956 and 1972, as was a version of his *geamaireacht* or pantomime play *Scéal ar Phádraig* (A story about Patrick), although as we will see he denied responsibility for that particular production. Moreover, in 1957 he attended a Gaelic League meeting in Dublin where there was discussion of the possibility of founding another Irish-language theatre in the capital, this one in Parnell Square. This theatre was apparently envisioned as a more experimental venue than An Damer, for a report on the meeting states that 'the new theatre sponsors will lay emphasis on the encouragement of young Irish writers to provide plays which could not otherwise obtain public performance' (*IT*, 29/10/57).

While Ó Tuama, perhaps due to all of his other commitments, was never as involved with amateur drama as were many of his fellow Gaelic playwrights, he did on occasion make time to serve the cause in various roles. For example, he made the case for drama in Irish at a symposium on Irish theatre at UCC in 1957 (*IP*, 25/11/57); officially opened drama festivals in Mallow, Co. Cork in 1961 (*IP*, 22/2/61) and Dungarven, Co. Waterford in 1963 (*IP*, 18/4/63); judged plays in Irish for the Irish Life Assurance drama competition in 1966 (*II*, 22/2/66);[14] and took part in a seminar in Galway celebrating the fiftieth anniversary of Taibhdhearc na Gaillimhe in 1978 (*CS*, 24/10/78). He must have had a great deal to say about theatre in discussions with colleagues and students, but he published almost nothing on the subject, and for the most part reports on his many lectures give little indication of whether he said anything about drama in them. Still, while on the whole he seems to have allowed his plays to speak for themselves, we do know that he was well aware of the principal challenges facing playwrights who chose to write in Irish. For instance, as both a playwright eager for an audience and an activist keen to exploit the potential of theatre for the revival, in a 1969 conversation about drama in Irish with Proinsias Mac Aonghusa and Diarmaid Ó Súilleabháin at the Dublin Theatre Festival that was later broadcast on the television show *Féach* (Look), Ó Tuama joined his colleagues in stressing that 'a public must be created for that drama' (nach mór pobal a chruthú don drámaíocht sin) (*IP*, 10/10/69). Of note here, obviously, is his awareness that if English-language playwrights had to attract an audience, Gaelic dramatists faced the more daunting challenge of having to create one in the first place.

Like so many of his colleagues, he also worried about how and even where those audiences would be created. The lack of playing space dedicated exclusively to plays in Irish was, as we have seen repeatedly, a major and ongoing concern for all interested in Gaelic drama. It was doubtless such a concern that inspired Ó Tuama to join Dan Donovan in founding Compántas Chorcaí in 1953, to offer his plays to An Damer in Dublin, and to support the attempt to open another Gaelic theatre in the capital in 1958. Not surprisingly, given his vocation as an educator and his chosen role as a charismatic mentor to his students, Ó Tuama took a particular interest in promoting theatre, and especially theatre in Irish, in the university, an obvious source of future playwrights, directors, actors, theatre professionals, and audiences, whose new ideas and enthusiasm would ensure that that theatre would survive and even, with time, thrive. Thus, when in 1968 he presented the awards at the conclusion of Féile Drámaíochta na nOllscoil at UCC, he is reported as 'deploring' the lack of a theatre at UCC and adding that 'it was incongruous that the Minister for Education should consider that UCC was ready to assume the dignity of a full university, but still did not possess the elementary facility of a theatre, possessed by many secondary schools through-out the country' (*SS*, 17/2/68).[15] It would take time, but since the mid 1980s UCC has had both its own theatre, the Granary, and a full department of theatre arts that supports a wide range of theatrical events, at least some of which are in Irish.

Ó Tuama understood, however, that the kind of theatres and audiences that could make plays in Irish a viable and vital element in the national culture would of necessity be found in the cities, just where, perversely enough, the settings and subjects that would be most immediately appealing to playgoers would be the ones they would find least credible when written about in Irish. In a 1974 piece in *The Southern Star*, Con Ó Drisceoil discussed this problem, stating:

> It is difficult for anyone who writes plays in Irish at the present time to write them in a way that will be credible; that is because Irish is a rural language that is being spoken in a couple of small districts and it is hard for the audience to believe that characters involved in the urban life of the twentieth century are speaking it. Seán Ó Tuama, one of the principal Irish-language playwrights, says that the playwright working in Irish usually has to set his play in the Gaeltacht or set it somewhere in the past, centuries ago if possible, so that we can accept that Irish is being spoken naturally by the characters in the play. (*SS*, 19/1/74)[16]

Ó Drisceoil and Ó Tuama also agreed that while any setting outside of the Gaeltacht or the past would be problematic for a Gaelic playwright to present with linguistic verisimilitude, truly urban settings would create even greater challenges. How, for example, could the language be made to answer in an unself-conscious manner the demands of a modern way of life from which it had long been isolated? Would, for example, the inevitable neologisms required annoy or confuse native speakers of Irish or learners who had taken great pains to master the language as spoken in the Gaeltacht? In a piece on a 1958 radio debate on contemporary poetry in Irish in which Ó Tuama had participated Máirtín Ó Direáin, who spoke from experience as both a writer and an actor, noted that Ó Tuama had focused on 'one great difficulty: the validity of the words themselves' (deacracht mhór amháin: bailíocht na bhfocal féin). Ó Direáin continued:

> Perhaps in this case it would be better for me to say the kinship of the words themselves. The people do not feel a kinship with some of the words that the poet must draw on when he is showing urban life in Irish. This will be better understood when I say – and I am not thinking about technical terms – that a good number of words that are by this time common words in English are still [unusual] terms in Irish. (*IP*, 25/4/58)[17]

What was true for the poet expressing his own ideas and emotions was, of course, even truer for the dramatist attempting to convince an audience that his characters on stage would not only be speaking Irish, but using a lexicon that might sound a bit exotic to many in that audience.

When Ó Tuama sat down to write his first play, he put such challenges aside, choosing instead to set his verse drama *Gunna Cam agus Slabhra Óir* 'somewhere in the past, centuries ago if possible'. Yet in so doing he created his masterpiece, the finest history play ever written in Irish, and one of the best plays on the Irish past in either of the nation's two languages. *Gunna Cam agus Slabhra Óir* won first prize for a full-length play at the 1954 Oireachtas, as well as Gradam an Oireachtais, which 'stamped the play as a work of outstanding merit, for only once previously since 1939 has an Oireachtas competitive work received similar recognition' (*II*, 13/9/54).[18] Commenting on the play that year, Siobhán McKenna declared, 'The play must be staged' (*CE*, 13/9/54). It would, however, be two years before *Gunna Cam agus Slabhra Óir* had its premiere, for one performance only, by the Abbey in the Queen's Theatre at the 1956 Oireachtas. The director, and set designer, was the ubiquitous Tomás Mac Anna, and cast members included Ray McAnally and T. P. McKenna. Critics were unanimously positive. For example, an anonymous reviewer for *The Irish Press* wrote that given the state of Gaelic drama, 'it would probably be welcomed even if it were second rate' (is dócha go bhfáilteochaí roimhe mara mbeadh ann ach an dara scoth féin). But he quickly continued: 'But let us have no doubt about it: if plays in Irish were as common as orations at the Oireachtas, this play of Seán Ó Tuama's would deserve a welcome and praise that is only due to the best.'[19] For this critic the play was 'an excellent work . . . a powerful, substantial work in which there is an understanding of the Gaelic heritage and the human spirit' (saothar ar fónamh . . . saothar neartmhar, téagartha, a bhfuil ciall don dúchas Gaelach ann agus do mheon an duine). Above all, *Gunna Cam agus Slabhra Óir* was no mere costume drama, for

> although it is based on a historical episode you do not ever feel that the human will is under the control of historical fate: public and private affairs are interwoven in a natural way and in the end you feel an equal sympathy for the tragedy of Mánus Mór and the uncertain success of his native place. (*IP*, 22/10/56)[20]

Writing in the *Irish Times*, 'P. Mac A.' also noted that 'in one genre, the drama, the [Gaelic] literary revival has conspicuously failed to produce any work of more than mediocre talent', and then continued: 'Last night's Oireachtas production at the Abbey Theatre of Seán Ó Tuama's "Gunna Cam agus Slabhra Óir" radically changed this situation. It is by far the best piece of dramatic writing seen in Irish yet, and it is more than worthy of the praise given it by the adjudicators of the 1954 Oireachtas.' 'P. Mac A.' was on the whole impressed by Mac Anna's production, the 'artistic and well executed' sets, and the performances of most of the actors. He did, however, think it was a good thing that *Gunna Cam agus Slabhra Óir* was not trying to get by on the glamour of its period dress, since 'the costumes . . . were, apparently, the dregs of the last ten years' Abbey pantomimes, and it is a great credit to the actors that they succeeded in making the audience forget their almost ludicrous appearance . . . The beards and wigs were equally pantomimic, and were in general rather amateurishly put on.'[21] Nevertheless, 'P. Mac A.' pronounced the production 'first-class' and 'one which must have been most encouraging to all those who are interested in Gaelic drama' (*IT*, 22/10/56). The anonymous critic for *The Cork Examiner* wrote that 'the national and personal dilemmas of all the leading characters are splendidly delineated and the conflict and power of the second and third acts made a tremendous impression on the audience'. He pronounced Mac Anna's production 'admirable', but, like 'P. Mac A.', he found a few minor problems: 'Some of the complex changes of set – especially at the end – were not as effective as they might have been, but it must be remembered that these extensive preparations were made for only one performance and there must inevitably be a certain lack of slickness as a result' (*CE*, 24/10/56). Writing in *Comhar*, 'S. Mac R.' (doubtless Seán Mac Réamoinn) called *Gunna Cam agus Slabhra Óir* 'a good play' (dráma fónta), adding 'that it is a long time since I saw from the hand of any Irish person a play in Irish or a play in English that would give me more cause to say: "Here is a man who has something to say, and knows how to say it"' (gur fada ó chonnac ó lámh aon Éireannaigh dráma Gaeilge nó dráma Béarla ba mhó a thiúrfadh orm a rá: 'Seo fear a bhfuil rud le rá aige, agus fios a ráite'). On the other hand, he felt that the production, including the acting, did not always do the play justice, stating: 'On the whole, the production was no more than satisfactory.' For Mac Réamoinn, the main point was that the play should at once enter the Gaelic repertoire: 'I hope that this play will not be forgotten now that it has been produced once. May it not go into that part of Limbo in which too many artistic efforts in Irish are lodged' (*Comhar*, Nov. 1956, p. 19).[22]

Due perhaps to the demands the play makes on drama companies in terms of the large cast, the need for actors able to embody imposing historical characters as well as to speak effectively in verse, and the lavishness of those period costumes, *Gunna Cam agus Slabhra Óir* has not had the popularity with amateur groups one might have expected. Indeed it has not been revived very often even by larger and more established companies, despite having been published by Sáirséal agus Dill in 1964, kept in print almost without interruption since (with seven printings by 1978), and at one point made an optional text on the Irish course for the Leaving Certificate. Its first production after its Dublin premiere was in 1957 by Compántas Chorcaí at the School of Music in the author's native Cork. Reviewing this production, directed by Dan Donovan and attended on the opening night by the President of Ireland

Seán T. Ó Ceallaigh (Sean T. O'Kelly) and his wife, 'S. N.' wrote in the *Irish Independent* that the play was 'beautifully costumed in very good sets' with 'a very well chosen cast', a cast that included Donovan and Niall Tóibín and that 'brought great sincerity to their work'. While 'there was [*sic*] some important incongruities' in the production, 'S. N.' believed that they 'matter little in comparison with the work of the presentation and the merit of the play', which, he declared, 'every Gael in Cork should see' (*II*, 31/5/57). A brief note in *The Southern Star* indicated that many of those Gaels did see the play, for we read that 'local people got so excited about it that the seating accommodation was booked out in advance', showing that 'there is no doubt people in general now have sufficient knowledge of Gaelic to help them to appreciate what is meritorious in a play in the native language' (*SS*, 8/6/57).

The next major production of the play was at An Damer for the Dublin Theatre Festival of 1968. Noel Ó Briain directed, and among cast members were Dónall Farmer and Mae Crowe. Ó Briain staged the play at two ends of the theatre, with the audience sitting in the middle, an arrangement that, according to 'E. M. S.', made those watching the play 'involved in the action, almost' (páirteach sa ghnó, beagnach) (*IP*, 2/10/68). Noting that after the opening performance Ó Tuama called for a professional Gaelic theatre because 'the actors deserved it . . . and also the producer', John Honohan wrote in the *Sunday Independent* that 'in my opinion, the play itself merited it most of all'. For Honohan, the play 'gives a new dimension to Irish history' and 'nothing can detract from the beauty of the language', showing that 'Seán Ó Tuama is both poet and dramatist' (*SI*, 6/10/68). Liam Ó Lonargáin pointed out that *Gunna Cam agus Slabhra Óir* was 'the most expensive play with the biggest cast and the most furnishings that has been put on stage for a long while' (an dráma is mó foirne, is mó feistis agus is costasaí dar cuireadh ar stáitse le fada an lá) and that therefore the mere fact that it was produced at all should be a source of pride for all involved. But Ó Lonargáin believed that the company at An Damer had done far more than merely produce the play, for the inevitable flaws 'were slight beside the dignity and the power of the writing, beside the strength and scope of the production, beside the cleverness and realism of the design, beside the colour and beauty of the costumes, beside the assurance and excellence of the acting. It was a *tour de force* . . .' (*Feasta*, Nov. 1968, p. 13).[23] The play was broadcast over Radio Éireann in August 1958 (*II*, 16/8/58) and again in 1966, as part of a series to commemorate the Easter Rising (*IP*, 5/2/66).[24]

In his rather belated review for *Comhar* in 1968, Micheál Ó hUanacháin stated that it was 'a work in which there is tension and dramatic power. It has a good pace and, something rare in plays nowadays, it is a satisfying script to read' (saothar . . . a bhfuil teannas agus comhacht drámatúil ann. Tá gluaiseacht mhaith faoi agus, rud is annamh le drámaí na laethanta seo, is sásúil mar scriopta é lena léamh). Ó hUanacháin also stated that Ó Tuama had a wonderful 'ability to handle words' (cumas chun focail a láimhseáil), that the verse in the play was 'natural, fluent, and vigorous' (nádúrtha, éasca, fuinniúil), and that the characterisation was developed 'accurately and without any clumsiness' (go cruinn gan aon útamáil). Ó hUanacháin concluded that while the play might initially seem 'old-fashioned' (sean-aimseartha), 'the work done on it was so polished that the most avant garde person would have to admit that it is an excellent play' (*Comhar*, Mar. 1968, p. 25).[25] In his very brief review the following year, the American scholar Charles B. Quinn pronounced Ó Tuama's verse 'natural . . . at times . . . poetic and memorable' and his characters 'well drawn and sharply defined', concluding that 'as a verse drama, this play is a good addition to modern Irish letters' (*Books Abroad*, autumn 1969, p. 642).

Gunna Cam agus Slabhra Óir is set at the castle of the Gaelic chieftain Mánas Ó Domhnaill in Lifford, Co. Donegal in the year leading up to his deposition by his son Calbhach in 1555. In a 1979 article entitled 'Manus "the magnificent" O'Donnell as renaissance prince', the historian Brendan Bradshaw wrote of Ó Domhnaill: 'Machiavelli's hard-headed political entrepreneur, Erasmus's scholarly Christian ruler, Castiglione's prince aesthete, all of these in various degrees was Manus O'Donnell.'[26] This is the man Ó Tuama presents as the protagonist of his play. And his Mánas will need all of those talents in the situation in which he finds himself. Facing ever increasing pressure from the English, whose strategy is to provoke revolt so that the land of the Irish can be seized outright, Mánas realises that the only hope available to him is through negotiation towards a carefully considered compromise with the enemy. His efforts to advance such a compromise with an opponent who may see diplomacy as a mere expedient on the way to unconditional victory will be complicated by his new wife Eileanóir, an embittered Geraldine who has personal experience of English treachery and no interest in compromise; by his spiritual adviser An tAthair Eoghan, who cannot look beyond the Protestantism of the English; and by his son Calbhach, who rejects out of hand his father's carefully formulated statecraft. Here Ó Tuama has neatly reversed traditional expectations by making the older man a committed moderniser, and the younger a hidebound traditionalist blindly bound to a heroic worldview that can now only lead to tragic futility in the chaotically unstable conditions of sixteenth-century Ireland. Neither Eileanóir nor Calbhach can understand Mánas's awareness that their world has changed irrevocably and that survival is entirely dependant on acceptance of that fact and a willingness to act on that acceptance. For Mánas, the only possible salvation for Gaelic civilisation lies in a greater openness to the outside world of both Europe and England. This attitude is given symbolic expression when, in preparation for his wedding feast, he tells his daughter to clear out the dogs that have traditionally settled under the table to get scraps from the diners. Mánas proclaims definitively: 'The age of the dogs is over in this house from now on . . . and the age of the bones.'[27] In the minds of his domestic opponents, the age of rejecting all things English also seems to be over. Thus when Eileanóir's jester mocks the English and states sarcastically, 'An Englishman is – no stranger in this house', Mánas rebukes him in terms of an emerging community of the truly civilised: 'Yes, my friend, no Englishman is a stranger in this house, nor even a black man, if he knows his manners.'[28] For Mánas, the Irish must be willing to give up the moribund elements of their insular culture if they want the more vital and generative aspects of that culture to thrive in the wider European world of which they are now inescapably a part. He tells An tAthair Eoghan:

> But if what you want is for me to take off my jester's clothes before the people, I will do that; and I will reveal the body of my thoughts to all of them. The person who has an eye in his head already knows what I say: the life my father and his father lived as well, is over. The customs and the manners we practise do not make us fit for the new age that is coming. They make us rustics in front of the world, a dour, dull-minded people that do not seek to take any part in the changed world that is today widespread throughout Europe. It is, however, my desire to show that we are willing – and fit – to take part in the newly fashioned world.[29]

Ó Tuama is here anticipating Brian Friel's later treatment of similar ideas in *Translations* (1980), although, unlike Friel, he believed that in both the past and present it would be possible to live a modern European life through the Irish language. Mánas understands full well, however, that to make this major psychic transition he and his people must first survive and retain their autonomy. It is this awareness that motivates his strategy of compromise with the English, violent opposition to whom he sees as suicidal.[30]

As in Friel's play when the Donnelly twins kill Lieutenant Yollande, in *Gunna Cam agus Slabhra Óir* the forces of obdurate extremism eventually overwhelm the voice of reason. And here we should note how often throughout the play Mánas invokes 'reason' (réasún) or 'good sense' (ciall) to explain his actions, as when he tells An tAthair Eoghan that insights based on rational thought cannot be simply ignored when unpalatable: 'Whether you are reasonable or not, Father, the situation the country is in is as clear to you as it is to me.'[31] It is this basic principle that dictates Mánas's decision to do something his son Calbhach and others find shameful, indeed unthinkable. For Mánas, taking the golden chain that will symbolise his submission to the king of England in the colonial hierarchy is the only rational recourse left to him in face of an English aggression he knows he cannot resist. As he tells An tAthair Eoghan:

Will you not see, Father Eoghan, that neither castle nor fort nor remoteness itself is a protection from now on, with all the ordinance, muskets, and countless new guns the English have. And despite the little bit of peace we have had here in the north for the past year or two, it is the end I spoke of that will overtake us as well, if we continue this ridiculous fight.[32]

When the priest asks what he hopes to accomplish by what Mánas calls 'giving up warfare for a while' (ligint don chogaíocht go fóill), Mánas offers a clear and forceful statement of the very real benefits he expects from this policy: 'To secure the land; to make certain that my children and my children's children will not have to head for the damp woods of Lifford or some unknown region overseas.'[33]

This kind of logic has, however, often carried less weight in Irish history than what Yeats called 'MacDonagh's bony thumb', and Mánas's wife, son, and spiritual adviser unite in opposition to his strategy and in support of the traditional Gaelic recourse to armed resistance.[34] Eileanóir, who eventually reveals some of his plans to his Irish opponents, is scornful of his rational and tactical approach to making decisions, one such decision, by the way, being to marry her to protect her son and future Geraldine influence in Irish affairs:

Well, I cannot be submissive to you. I am a Geraldine, and there were once men in my company. And when they were broken, it then fell on me to direct every bit of the dispute, every bit of the conspiracy against Grey and his pack of demons, and it also fell on me to send the last Geraldine of his stock to a safe place. Therefore I understand what fighting is, what suffering is, what hatred for the enemy is – and I find none of it in this place.[35]

And when he, in a rage, calls her 'a whore' (striapach), she responds: 'If I am a whore, I am a whore of this nation.'[36]

An tAthair Eoghan also believes Mánas is betraying both his heritage and his people in his willingness to accept the golden chain. With an appeal to blood over brain, he tells Calbhach:

The ancestral blood in us knows the deeds that are necessary in our situation and the deeds that are wrong altogether; that are harmful. Those of the same blood know one another. You and I know one another . . . but neither of us knows your father any more. He has gone entirely beyond our recognition. The entire project that he has set in motion is not of our blood; it is a fundamental injustice against it.

As a result, according to An tAthair Eoghan, 'At this time and in this place, it is you, his heir and his son, who apparently will have to oppose him – lest the Ó Domhnaills be justly accused that six successive generations of them failed . . . submitted . . . were damned.'[37]

Calbhach needs no convincing to reject his father's course of action. Early in the play he tells his sister, 'Perhaps, Caitríona, the two of us will still be able to say that we saw the man – and it was our own father – and that he was the first of all the Cenél Conaill, who bestowed his patrimony on the King from overseas; and who took in exchange the golden chain.'[38] Mánas may see his son as a 'ghost' (taibhse) trapped in a dead past, but Calbhach remains a very disruptive spirit, returning to his father's wedding feast drunk and unruly from a more traditional Gaelic wedding he has chosen to attend over Mánas's, and insulting Mánas and Eileanóir, after which his father slaps him and has him confined. After this insult there is no turning back for Calbhach, who as a sign of his rejection of his father's policy, takes the *gunna cam*[39] from the fortress wall on which it hangs and accepts that it is his 'clear duty . . . to do the barbarous deed' (dualgas glan . . . an gníomh barbartha a dhéanamh), even if that means 'falling on my knees before my father in submission today but tomorrow, perhaps, hanging him from the highest tree out there on the green!' (titim ar mo ghlúine os comhair m'athar / le humhlaíocht, inniu – is amárach, b'fhéidir, é chrochadh / ar an gcrann is airde amuigh ansan / sa bhfaiche!).[40]

In the year that passes between Acts II and III, Mánas is able to begin putting together an alliance of his subordinate chieftains in support of his strategy of compromise, arguing that the recent English suppression of a revolt in Sligo has made his policy ever more rational and imperative. Still, even his potential allies are wavering, with one asking: 'As soon as you put on the golden chain, the King owns Donegal?' Mánas's answer makes clear that he is perfectly willing to sacrifice a symbolic authority for a very real one that will protect his people and their culture: 'He does according to English law; but in truth it is still yours and mine. We will administer the region for him.'[41] In a fascinating scene that echoes the debate in Dáil Éireann over acceptance of the Anglo-Irish Treaty of 1921, Mánas sets forth the reasons for supporting his compromise with the English: 'But let every man of you remember exactly now that the vote that is presently given is a vote that will determine whether there will be peace ahead of us in this countryside from now on, or disastrous, unendurable war that will wipe us from the face of the earth . . .'[42] Initially An tAthair Eoghan worries about the authority to which he and Mánas's other opponents can appeal to justify their rejection of his compromise and thus bring war on their people, but he quiets his conscience with a startling invocation of just the sort of sanction Yeats symbolised in 'MacDonagh's bony thumb'. When Mánas announces that his policy expresses 'the will of Ó Domhnaill . . . my will – and the will of the majority of my

people' (toil Uí Dhónaill . . . mo thoilse – is toil fhormhór mo mhuintire),
An tAthair Eoghan replies 'the will of the majority of his people is not with
Ó Domhnaill in this submission' (ná fuil / toil fhormhór a mhuintir le hÓ Dónaill
insa ghéilleadh seo) for some are absent. Challenged to identify the missing,
the priest names Mánas's dead father and his unborn grandson. Motivated
by his renaissance sense of 'pure reason' (lomréasún), Mánas can only respond
'Are you out of your mind?'[43]

At this point Mánas still has sufficient influence to press on with the ceremony bestowing on him the golden chain of office. During the ceremony he
gives to the king's representative Sir John Fitzwilliam 'this bit of the fertile
land of Donegal' (an giota so de thalamh méith Thír Chonaill) in return for
the chain that is 'a symbol' (comhartha) of his submission to the English
throne. But if Mánas sees these objects as no more than signs and symbols
of a putative loyalty ceded in exchange for retention of genuine Gaelic
autonomy, for Calbhach and his allies they are very real proofs of surrender
and treason. Calbhach enters the hall with the *gunna cam*, accompanied by
men carrying muskets they took from English soldiers they massacred near
Dundalk. Obviously, Mánas's carefully conceived strategy is now no longer
viable, and his deposition and Calbhach's assumption of the traditional title
of Ó Domhnaill a foregone conclusion.[44] Mocked by one of his erstwhile
subordinates as 'the hero with the golden chain' (gaiscíoch an tslabhra óir),
Mánas is taken away to imprisonment in the tower of his own castle. To the
end, however, he retains the courage of his convictions, telling An tAthair
Eoghan: 'The deed I did, the heart in me sees that it is what my people
wanted, and that it was what was most sensible altogether . . . This conflict
will still be settled in a civilised manner. If I don't do it, someone else will.'[45]
Impressed by Mánas's courage and dignity, An tAthair Eoghan prays for
him and even Calbhach drops to his knees in apparent forgiveness and
respect as the curtain falls.

In addition to being a chieftain, Mánas was also a poet and the author
of *Beatha Cholm Cille* (The life of Colm Cille), a landmark of Irish prose.[46]
Although Ó Tuama does not make much of this fact in the course of the play,
at the end he reminds us of Mánas's literary status. Writing of the five poems
by Ó Domhnaill included in Thomas O'Rahilly's collection *Dánta Grádh*,
([Courtly] love poems), Ó Tuama noted that while three of them were
conventional enough examples of their genre, two of them, one of which,
'Cridhe lán do Smuaintighthibh' (Heart full of thoughts), appears as an
epigraph in the printed text of his play, have 'lyrics that reveal a highly
individual poetic sensibility'.[47] When the deposed Mánas tells his daughter
that she should bring a candle to his cell at night 'so that you could write
down the poetry I have composed in my head during the day' (sa tslí / go

scríofá a mbeadh cumtha d'fhilíocht im cheann agam / i gcúrsa an lae),[48] he is announcing that he will continue his fight for cultural survival on a different and ultimately even more significant battlefield, one on which his insight and integrity will be assets rather than hindrances.

Gunna Cam agus Slabhra Óir offers a powerful and moving picture of a turbulent period that would cast a long and tragic shadow over Irish history. However, as Seán Mac Réamoinn reminds us in his review of the play, Ó Tuama, like all good creative writers who deal with historical topics, was not primarily interested in the past:

> It is not what happened that most interests him but what happens. He thinks that there is still a conflict between the way of the Gun and the way of the Chain: that often reason and honesty back up the Chain, but that, with regard to this nation at any rate, our innate nature backs up the Gun and that is what is strongest in the end. He thinks that neither submission nor compromise are natural for the Gael. (*Comhar*, Nov. 1956, p. 19)[49]

In this play, however, Ó Tuama seems to be asking whether that instinct for rebellion need always dominate. We have already seen how, in the scene in which Mánas and his opponents debate his strategy, there are brief but pointed echoes of the debates that led to the Civil War of 1922–3.[50] But Ó Tuama may also have had in mind the IRA's bloody and futile attacks in England during the Second World War and its equally bloody and futile border campaign that was still going on when *Gunna Cam agus Slabhra Óir* had its first production. Indeed he may also have been pondering what course of action would be most likely to achieve meaningful success as he worked to develop a creative and flexible strategy to adapt the 'Gaelic League idea' to conditions in an Ireland that would be largely unrecognisable to language activists from the early years of the state, not to mention the early years of the Gaelic League.[51] Brian Kennedy, the correspondence secretary of the anti-revivalist Language Freedom Movement, could not have been more wrong when in 1974 he read *Gunna Cam agus Slabhra Óir* as championing what he called 'this extraordinary doctrine' of 'the democracy of the dead', and stated: 'Dr. Seán Ó Tuama of UCC went so far as to write a play – "Gunna Cam agus Slabhra Óir" – to demonstrate the validity of "historical democracy".' Needless to say, he did not make his point' (*II*, 4/1/74). Of course he never tried to make any such point. As we have seen, the protagonist of his play, Mánas Ó Domhnaill, explicitly rejects any such idea as insanity. We get a far clearer idea of what Ó Tuama wanted to say to contemporary audiences from his own comments at a Dublin Theatre Festival press conference in 1968. Present at the event were members of a theatre company from Czechoslovakia who had recently experienced the Soviet suppression of the 'Prague Spring' freedom movement but who reported that Czech artists were still finding means of expression that were 'not perfect but working'. An account of the press conference reported that 'Seán Ó Tuama . . . drew a parallel between the Czech situation and his play in the Damer Hall on the grounds that the latter, set in 15th [*sic*] century Ireland, was about the question of compromise' (*II*, 3/10/68).

Compromise would, however, always be for Ó Tuama a tactic, the main focus remaining on the triumph of basic principles that this tactic might advance in situations otherwise unpropitious if not impossible. The dire result of losing sight of such principles as one negotiated the complexities of such compromises would be the subject of his next play, the one-act verse tragedy *Moloney*. Another Oireachtas prizewinner, the play was first performed by Compántas Chorcaí in the Royal Irish Academy of Music Theatre at the 1956 Oireachtas, only a week after *Gunna Cam agus Slabhra Óir* opened at the Queen's Theatre around the corner. Praising Dan Donovan's production, which won the company first prize at that year's Oireachtas, Frank Dermody called *Moloney* 'a very fine piece of work' that 'deserved to be translated into other languages'. He added that 'Ó Tuama was a playwright of whom we would hear more' (*IP*, 29/10/56). The production was quickly moved to An Damer, where it opened on 31 December 1956 and again received favourable reviews, with an anonymous critic for *The Irish Press* stating in his bilingual notice: 'Last night's play and production undoubtedly excelled the creditable Abbey [*sic*] presentation during Oireachtas week and "Moloney" should attract good houses during its short Dublin run.' This critic felt that Ó Tuama had dealt effectively with what he called 'the priest's terrifying mental plight' and praised Compántas Chorcaí as 'far ahead . . . of most of the companies working with Gaelic drama in Dublin' (fada chun cinn . . . ar an gcuid is mó des na buíonta a bhíonn ag gabháil don drámaíocht Ghaeilge i mBaile Átha Cliath) (*IP*, 1/1/57). For the unnamed reviewer in the *Irish Independent*, *Moloney* was 'a notable contribution to Irish drama': 'The play has not a great deal of action, but there is no monotony either in the flow of Irish dialogue or in the acting of the small cast . . .' (*II*, 1/1/57).[52] Indeed the anonymous critic for *Inniu* found it 'more finished' (níos críochnúla) than *Gunna Cam agus Slabhra Óir* (*Inniu*, 4/11/57).

Moloney has enjoyed some popularity with amateur groups, who doubtless appreciate not only its dramatic quality but its single set, simple props, and small cast. It has, for example, been produced by UCD's An Cumann Drámaíochta at Féile Drámaíochta na nOllscoil in Cork (*SS*, 8/2/69); Feis Átha Cliath (*IP*, 12/3/69); and the Oireachtas in Dublin (*IP*, 2/4/69), all in 1969, and at UCD in 1977 (*II*, 12/2/77). Dublin's Liam Bulfin branch of the Gaelic League put it on at Feis Átha Cliath (*II*, 28/3/73) and Féile Drámaíochta Chorca Dhuibhne (*K*, 31/3/73), both in 1973, and in Rann na Feirste, Co.

Donegal the following year (*DP*, 30/11/74). Aisteoirí na Forbacha from the Galway Gaeltacht brought the play to An Damer for the 1973 Oireachtas (*II*, 6/4/73), and students at Carysfort College performed it at the school during the 1985–6 academic year (*II*, 28/2/86). *Moloney* was also broadcast over Radio Éireann in October 1956 (*II*, 31/10/56), and a version of the play was shown on Teilifís Éireann in December 1972 (*IP*, 22/12/72).

In a review of the published text of *Moloney*, L. S. Tuathail calls it 'the kind of play . . . in which the author withholds information until the end' (dráma den sórt . . . ina gcoimeádann an t-údar eolas siar go deireadh) and adds: 'In this case he does all he can to conceal from us that the prisoner is a priest, and he cannot develop the depth of the character without that information' (*Feasta*, July 1967, p. 23).[53] But while knowledge of the protagonist's vocation may be of great interest to other characters in the play – and maybe also to audience members when it was first performed – for those who see or read the play today his priesthood is far less significant. Ó Tuama's Moloney does not interest us primarily as a priest, but as a very ordinary man who has failed in the greatest moral challenge of his life. Imprisoned in Drogheda until he gives testimony against the saintly bishop Oliver Plunkett (1625–81), Moloney is an anonymous non-entity. The name Moloney is given him by a fellow prisoner, the prostitute Moll, and the stage directions refer to him throughout as simply 'the Prisoner' (an Príosúnach), caught up in historic events far beyond his ability to either understand or control. In this play, as indicated by an anonymous critic for *The Irish Press* who drew attention to Moloney's 'Judas-like despair' (éadóchas Iúdásach) in his discussion of the 1972 television production of the play (*IP*, 22/12/72), Ó Tuama first showed his fascination with the character of Judas, a fascination he would develop at greater length in his 1967 play *Iúdás Iscariot agus a Bhean* (Judas Iscariot and his wife). Not surprisingly, however, Moloney lacks the archetypal stature of Judas, in the end remaining a very ordinary man whose limited courage fails him when his principles are put to a sufficiently severe test.

In this regard, Plunkett, imprisoned in the same jail, is an entirely different order of man. When Moloney timidly asks whether Plunkett is being mistreated by his captors, the jailer replies: 'No one with any sense would ever lay a hand on Oliver Plunkett, even if he is a heretic . . . That would be like a sacrament from heaven coming to him to strengthen him.' He then adds pointedly: 'Of course the situation is not the same with regard to other people.'[54] Moloney is, needless to say, one of those other people. Having previously avoided the court when summoned to testify against Plunkett, and not yet sure whether he will do so now, Moloney is disgusted by Moll's cynical willingness to swear that Plunkett was inciting the Irish against the crown. She states: 'I am going to give evidence – you can bet I will! There is a nice cup of pennies in it for me, boy. Ah well . . . I would have to at any rate.

They have their hooks too deeply into me. Do you know what I mean?' Yet despite this willingness to betray him out of pragmatic self-interest, her opinion of Plunkett is actually quite favourable: 'Nevertheless, it is a pity. He is a simple man . . . a quiet man . . .'[55] Moloney, on the other hand, would seem to have a powerful motive to see Plunkett condemned: 'I hate him. I hate him. I hate him with every bone in my body. I hate him with every turn of my soul.' Moreover, he tells Moll he has a 'case' (cúis) against Plunkett. When she says, 'He must have treated you badly?' (Dhein sé an dubh ort, ní foláir?), he replies curtly 'He did' (Dhein).[56]

Still wavering as to whether he will give evidence, Moloney discusses the consequences of his decision with his jailer, who, having mentioned the tortures Moloney could face, states confidently: 'You know in your heart inside that you will submit to us at last like a scared child. Why wouldn't you submit to us now and be done with it.'[57] At this point Moloney realises that only a miracle can save him from having to make the decision that will define once and for all who and what he is. Asked by the jailer why he cannot decide, he responds that he is waiting 'until my hand would wither away from me, or my tongue would simply fall out of my mouth' (chun go seargódh mo lámh anuas díom, nó go dtitfeadh, go simplí, mo theanga as mo bhéal).[58] From long experience of human weakness, the jailer knows better: 'I am telling you now that there isn't the least basis for your hope. I know your mind; and it has gone completely out of control, has fallen apart completely. It will not endure against us.' Moloney still insists that he will find the faith, hope, and courage to resist the authorities, but when Plunkett himself is led on stage and blesses him, 'the Prisoner half turns away from him' (leathiompaíonn an Príosúnach uaidh).[59] We next see Moloney talking to Moll again, confessing to her his all-encompassing fear – 'Fear. Fear of silence. Fear of noise. Fear of hearing my heart beating. Fear of not hearing it. Fear of everything.' When she tells him of a rumour that Plunkett will be killed while supposedly trying to escape, Moloney seizes on it as a way out of his predicament, an attitude that Moll finds contemptible: 'O you are an unchristian brute. You wouldn't care if he were to die a dreadful death every day of the week – as long as you could say you had no hand in it.'[60]

In an apparent attempt to restore his self-respect, Moloney brags to the jailer that he joined 'a band of young men in my own native place to take what was ours back from the Englishman' (buíon óigfhear dem' dhúthaigh féin chun ár gcuid a bhaint amach arís ón Sasanach). Moreover, he claims that Plunkett's condemnation of those rapparees as 'robbers or tories' (róbálaithe nó tóraithe) was a result of the bishop's friendships with 'the Ascendancy people in Dublin and Drogheda' (lucht an chinsil i mBaile Átha Cliath is i nDroichead Átha). When the jailer states that both he and Moloney understand full well he will testify against Plunkett, Moloney claims that he will not and continues: 'My strength will return to me in the time of need. It will have to. Whatever my sin, however I corrupt myself, I still have possession of an immortal soul and of the faith that moves mountains. If I just make the effort I can endure a thousand deaths.' The jailer knows better: 'Talk. Talk. Talk. You are only blinding yourself now with great foolish bursts of talk, just as over the years you blinded your conscience, and your whole human nature, with great foolish bursts of drunkenness.'[61] With a practiced eye, the jailer sees before him a hollow man:

> And I will tell you now exactly what you yourself already know: that you awoke one morning in the middle of the bright day, and that the whole world exploded from its foundation to the firmament in one soft, half-rotten atom of your brain . . . You no longer belonged to yourself – and a mantle of sweat spread over your body, and fear smothered your heart. And that fear, and the fear of that fear, have been smothering you ever since.

Moloney can only reply 'weakly and confusedly' (go lag, mearbhallach): 'How do you understand all this?'[62]

After agreeing to testify, Moloney briefly reconsiders when he hears that Plunkett has expressed pride in him for his refusal to speak against him. This moment of integrity is, of course, brief, and he signs the statement containing his perjured evidence. Yet he also continues trying to justify himself, claiming that Plunkett expelled him from the priesthood because 'I was fighting . . . I thought . . . for my country'.[63] It is difficult to accept such an excuse for the act of treachery he commits even if we know that he continues to hope that his perjury will not bring about Plunkett's conviction and execution. That last hope is, however, taken away when he learns that Plunkett will be tried before a hostile jury in London rather than by an Irish jury in Dundalk, and he realises he cannot escape his own complicity in the death of a man of principle. The play ends with Moll reciting a prayer taught to her by Plunkett while we hear 'one of the loneliest sounds in the world, a man without hope crying' (ceann de na fuaimeanna is uaigní ar domhan, fear gan dóchas ag gol).[64]

In *Gunna Cam agus Slabhra Óir*, Ó Tuama posits a well-reasoned compromise on extraneous issues as a legitimate means to advance essential principles in a world full of ethical ambiguities. In *Moloney*, he shows the danger of making compromise a way of life, of an inability to keep the essential distinct from the merely important. In the end, Moloney's failure extends far beyond his betrayal of his vocation to a denial of his very existential humanity. It may just be that Moloney, an Príosúnach, has more in common with the *cimí* (prisoners) of Máirtín Ó Direáin's 1959 poem 'Ár Ré Dhearóil' (Our wretched age) than he does with Judas Iscariot.[65]

In his first two plays, Ó Tuama broke the outdated mould for history plays in Irish, virtually all of which up to his time had dealt with what their authors seem to have seen as the two major lessons to be learned from the Irish past: the extraordinary nobility, courage, and integrity of the Gaelic Irish and the dire consequences of the disunity by which they are regularly plagued in their struggle for independence.[66] Both *Gunna Cam agus Slabhra Óir* and *Moloney* are far more interested in individual human beings, in the forces that have shaped them and the beliefs, principles, and failings that motivate them, than they are in propaganda for a cause, however noble. Ó Tuama was a true pioneer in this regard, and his example would be followed by later playwrights like Éilís Ní Dhuibhne, Seán Mac Mathúna, and Gearóid Mac Unfraidh, all of whom have brought a more nuanced and challenging interpretation of the nation's past to Gaelic audiences.

In his next play, *Ar Aghaidh linn, a Longadáin* (Onward, Longadán), Ó Tuama would perform a similar service for plays in Irish involving characters and episodes from early Irish literature. *Ar Aghaidh linn, a Longadáin* had its premiere by Compántas Chorcaí at the Little Theatre of the Catholic Young Men's Society in Cork in April 1959, with Dan Donovan directing and playing the principal role of Suibhne.[67] It was then almost immediately produced in An Damer in June of that year, directed by Frank Dermody. Reviewing the play in *The Irish Press*, 'S. F.' called it 'the funniest play in Irish ever seen and one of the most interesting plays (in Irish or in English) that has been produced for a good many years now' (an dráma is greannúra a chonacthas riamh i nGaeilge agus ceann de na drámaí (Gaeilge nó Béarla) is suimiúla a léiríodh le roinnt mhaith blian anois) (*IP*, 10/6/59). The critic for the *Evening Press* praised Ó Tuama's mastery of the native Irish material, but also called attention to what he felt he had learned during the nine months he spent in France on a travelling scholarship from the Cultural Relations Committee of the Department of External Affairs in 1955–6:

> Not only is this an original new play but it is a play with thoughts and techniques new to the experience of plays in Irish. The author made use of traditional stage techniques, the new stage techniques of the French, the old Gaelic stories, the ideas of science, all interwoven with today's overly civilised life; it is a kind of surrealistic extravaganza he set before us. (*EP*, 9/6/59)[68]

'R. S.' was a bit less impressed by the continental influence on the play, writing: 'The audience could be forgiven if they were slightly baffled at times by the development of the theme of the play. Nevertheless a full house gave the production an enthusiastic reception, enjoying the comedy and not worrying unduly about the deeper philosophical implications – if any' (*II*, 9/6/59).

The play has had several revivals, the first by Compántas Chorcaí in May 1969, with Seán Ó Briain directing. Of this production a critic for *The Southern Star* declared: 'This is sheer nonsense from start to finish and a beautiful social message thrown in with tinsel-delicate seriousness and an odd steely thrust of the Ó Tuama rapier that stimulates, teases, rattles and draws a drop of socially smug self-righteous blood here and there' (*SS*, 31/5/69).[69] In 1975, An Chuallacht, the Irish-language drama group at UCC, performed the play at Féile Drámaíochta na nOllscoil in Cork (*SS*, 22/2/75). The following year Dónall Farmer directed the play at An Damer, a production the critic for the *Irish Independent* found 'a diverting romp through Irish legend – as adapted by the author' (*II*, 18/2/76). Three years later, Taibhdhearc na Gaillimhe staged the play, with Seán Ó Briain again directing.[70] In addition to these stage productions, *Ar Aghaidh linn, a Longadáin*, adapted for radio by Seán Mac Réamoinn, was broadcast over Radio Éireann in April 1960 (*IP*, 6/8/60) and May 1983 (*II*, 7/5/83). The play is now long overdue for another revival.

Ar Aghaidh linn, a Longadáin, set 'around B. C. (or A. D.)' (timpeall ar B. C. (nó A. D.)) is no reverent recreation of one of the nation's cultural treasures. Instead, it is, as Ó Tuama himself called it, an 'extravaganza', a boundary-breaking romp that, like Eimar O'Duffy's *King Goshawk and the Birds* (1926) or Flann O'Brien's *At Swim-Two-Birds* (1939), injects a riotous new life into a traditional literary corpus, a corpus that writers of Irish had all too often treated with an exaggerated and humourless reverence.[71] First of all, Ó Tuama brings together two major characters from different periods in the legendary past, characters who never met – never could meet – in the original texts. His Labhra Ó Loingsigh is based on Labraid Loingseach, the remote ancestor of the Laigin or Leinstermen and the protagonist of the medieval tale *Orgain Denna Ríg* (The destruction of Dind Ríg), while Suibhne is, of course, the mad king and poet of *Buile Shuibhne* (The frenzy of Sweeney), who plays such a central role in O'Brien's *At Swim-Two-Birds*. Of course Ó Tuama takes considerable liberties with both characters, so that while Labhra retains his exemplar's concern that he has the ears of an ass as well as his determination to hide the fact from the world, he becomes in Ó Tuama's play a fanatical botanist, interested in little except his plants. Ó Tuama's Suibhne retains the extraordinary imagination and poetic gift of the character on whom he is based, but he has now become a philosopher and a healer as well. Moreover, drawing on elements from the theatre of the absurd with which he had become familiar in Paris, Ó Tuama sets the play in a world at several removes from normalcy.[72] Even in daylight, Labhra's study is weird, with the light itself 'very dark, very strange, with rays of sun through it suddenly from time to time' (an-dorcha, an-aisteach, is gathanna gréine tríd go hobann ó am go ham).[73] The initial stage direction underscores this point: 'The beginning

of the play is done at dizzying speed and under an unnatural light.
Everything that happens from start to finish smacks of phantasmagoria.' We
are also told that 'most of the characters – the ones who are not mad – speak
as drily and as seriously as bank clerks', and that at least one of the servants
moves 'as if she were a robot' (mar a bheadh robot).[74]

Labhra obsessively monitors all aspects of the growth of his plants. The
only other topic that interests him is his need of a haircut and the difficulty of
finding a barber – no surprise, because as his wife Helen points out, 'you will
have to admit that every one of them whoever cut your hair, disappeared . . .
suddenly.'[75] Labhra's obsession with science has blighted the lives of Helen
and their daughter Bláthnaid, although the latter is herself initially immersed
in the study of snails. Helen, who is confined to a wheelchair, tries to explain
to Labhra what she means when she says she is living 'in the middle of a
desert' (i lár fásaigh):

> You do not understand. You do not understand what I sense. I sense the qualities
> of a desert. A desert that would be waiting, lost, isolated, for thousands of years; far
> from foliage, from fertility, and that every grain of sand in it would begin trembling,
> ready, for – for the explosion that it senses is coming: a great supernatural
> explosion that will tear the whole desert apart. Indeed that is what it was created
> for the first day – so that that explosion would happen in it.

When she asks him 'Do you, love, think that is why deserts were created?' he
misses the metaphor altogether, answering with a quiet laugh: 'I would not
want to say for certain, Helen, I would not. But according to the evidence we
have, that is not what deserts were created for.'[76] Bláthnaid is at first as blind
to the variety and zest of life as are her father and mother. When she asks
Helen why the virile, athletic, and unintellectual Feardorcha never courts
her, Helen ponders whether her daughter is behaving properly around him,
to which Bláthnaid replies that she must be, for 'I have a book about it. In
French.'[77] It is, then, little wonder that Helen suspects there is something
very wrong with her world:

> Sometimes . . . I don't know . . . when I think about Labhra in there under his cap
> and his mop of hair, dirtying his fingers in his little clay dishes – and Bláthnaid out
> here, having twisted the curls of her hair snake-like on top of her head and she
> wondering so passionately about the slippery belly of a snail . . . I don't know . . . I
> don't think I am in any normal and natural house.[78]

Into this world in a blast of thunder steps the flamboyant Suibhne,
identifying himself as 'a poet, a philosopher, and once King of Dál nAraidi'
(file, fealsamh is Rí tráth ar Dhál nAraí), come 'to cut the royal hair' (chun

an folt ríoga a bhearradh). He is accompanied by the mysterious and androgynous Dílleachtaí (Orphan). In a remark that echoes Gulliver's amazement
at the havoc wrought on the natural world by the Laputan scientists in
Gulliver's Travels, Suibhne passes judgement on Labhra's husbandry of the
resources of his realm: 'But it is easy to recognise a great scientist from the
desert he leaves everywhere around him. I saw your idle fields and your
dolorous district on my way here, Loingseach. And now I see your wife.'[79]
When it is clear that Helen responds to Suibhne's magical bee, a symbol of
light, life, and imagination, Suibhne realises there is still hope for her, telling
her husband: 'She's alive! This is a woman who is alive. It is a great disgrace
for you to have her bound there on a bier.' Dismissing Labhra's claim that she
suffers from 'an unknown disease that cannot be cured' (galar do-aitheanta
nach féidir a leigheas), Suibhne replies that 'she has a very well-known disease'
(galar ana-sho-aitheanta atá uirthi), one that he can cure.[80] He will soon take
on Bláthnaid as another patient.

First of all, however, he must deal with Labhra. He arranges to cut the
king's hair in return for a fortnight's lodging for himself and An Dílleachtaí,
neither of whom, as he points out, has even been properly welcomed to
Labhra's home. When Labhra subsequently boasts of his accomplishments
as a scientist-king, Suibhne engages him in a debate that raises issues at the
play's thematic core. For Labhra, 'I am a king who does not believe at all in
tyranny or in the pomp that other kings practise.' He has done away with
feasts and court dress, crowns and wars and barbaric punishments. His
soldiers are now 'assistants in the agricultural work' (cúntóirí in obair na
talmhaíochta) and his realm 'a quiet place of learning and thought. An Institute
as I often say' (ionad ciúin léinn is machnaimh. Institúid mar adeirim go
minic). All are allowed free speech and the right to debate, but 'if someone
comes in here threateningly and idly and breaks the rules relating to sense
and good manners, and does not submit to any sensible order that I, the
king, give –'[81] While Labhra's appeal to sense and reason may recall Mánas
Ó Domhnaill's dedication to these qualities in *Gunna Cam agus Slabhra Óir*,
rationality for Labhra is something entirely different – coldly abstract, devoid
of the flexibility that can make allowances for human beings as they actually
are. Suibhne immediately points out what rational behaviour means for
Labhra in practical terms when he finishes Labhra's incomplete sentence for
him: 'There, Loingseach, you will reveal your scientist's heart – a heart far
more tyrannical than the heart of a tyrant: and a hundred armed men will
stand in front of me. Yes!'[82] Later, Labhra expresses surprise that Suibhne,
despite all the time he has spent in the woods, has so little scientific knowledge of trees. Suibhne's answer once again recalls Swift's praise of common
sense in *Gulliver's Travels*: 'It is a much greater wonder, if you don't mind my
saying so, Loingseach, that you are an expert on trees and yet I have not on

my way here seen in your entire kingdom one tree worth mentioning – or anything else either.'[83]

Whatever can be said about the trees, the women in Labhra's household come to life under Suibhne's influence.[84] When Helen admits that she is fond of Labhra but has never felt with him what Suibhne refers to as 'the speed of rapid running, the marvellous freedom of a foolish leap and the mad foamy spray of the breaking wave' (luas na reatha mire, saoirse mhíorúilteach na baoth-léime, is cáitheadh sobalbhuile na toinne briste), Suibhne tells her that she will never be happy until she experiences such 'sweeping high-spirited love' (grá scóipiúil móraigeanta) and that she is unlikely to find such with Labhra.[85] Needless to say, she soon falls in love with her therapist, Suibhne, as does Bláthnaid, who tells him: 'But tonight I feel freedom in myself. I will let my hair down over my shoulders – and I will make smithereens of these glasses. Don't you sense the freedom growing in me, swelling, lifting me into the air as if I were a light, multi-coloured, easily punctured balloon.'[86] She and Suibhne announce they are to be married, and the effect of that announcement on Labhra's world becomes even more radically disruptive when Suibhne's 'little impaired friends, my fellow citizens from Madmen's Glen' (cairde beaga máchaileacha, mo chomhchathránaigh ó Ghleann na nGealt) appear. Both Helen and Bláthnaid respond joyfully to their arrival, while Labhra can only comment 'drily' (go tur): 'I hope, Suibhne, that . . . these are not very close friends of yours.' To which Suibhne responds with pride that they are, that they welcomed him when he fled his own realm in the north 'seeking freedom for my tormented mind' (ag lorg saoirse dom intinn chráite), and that he is now their king in Gleann na nGealt near Killarney, 'where it is always summer, where lawyers are not trying to get me to put the laws of the country in order, where grammarians are not correcting my poems'.[87]

Two months pass between the second and third acts, during which Helen and Bláthnaid have become prettier and happier, and the latter has given up her snails. Labhra himself is also showing some signs of humanity, noticing his wife's beauty, for example. He is also, however, concerned that Suibhne has still not gotten around to cutting his hair. Suibhne tells him he must first cure Helen and that he will do so by doing 'the right thing . . . the artistic thing' (an ní ceart . . . an ní ealaíonta). His rather extraordinary medical device is a hot iron that he says symbolises 'the heat of love' (teas an ghrá) and that he touches to Helen's shoulder, causing her to leap from her wheelchair.[88] By now Suibhne has obviously shattered the sterile rationality on which Labhra's world rests, and it is nearing time for him to go.

As the fourth and final act of the play opens a week later, we learn that Labhra's prized beech tree has been uprooted and that Bláthnaid and Suibhne are not going to be married after all. In a statement that underscores the central theme of the play Suibhne explains why such a marriage could never work:

Because I have grown tired of this life. The life of the court is pleasant and comfortable – for a while. But it soon grows dull, straitened; a musty smell rises from the chairs, the couches, the people. I miss the woods, the insects, the spaciousness, the fragrance. And I must leave this court at once, just as I once left my own court.

When Bláthnaid pleads to go with him, he, unlike the tramp in Synge's *In the Shadow of the Glen*, is honest enough to tell her that while she might enjoy sunny days in the woods, she would also have to take a walk on the wild side and deal with 'the misery, the wild rainstorms, and the black frost that leaves the courage like a dead bird in your chest' (an ainnise, na stoirmeacha fiáine fearthainne, is an sioc dubh a fhágann an misneach mar a bheadh éan marbh id chliabh).[89] She will be better off with 'the natural thing, the familiar thing' (an rud nádúrtha, an rud muinteartha), and a husband like Feardorcha. Actually, however, Feardorcha has begun to talk like a poet, claiming that 'poetic talk is an infectious disease in this house' (galar tógálach an chaint fhileata sa tigh seo).[90] Indeed according to Helen, even Labhra is 'turning out as he was when we first married . . . cheerful, open, talkative' (ag iompáil amach mar a bhí sé nuair a phósamar ar dtús . . . croíúil, oscailteach, cainteach). All that remains for Suibhne to do is cut 'the most storied mop of hair in Western Europe' (an mothall gruaige is stairiúla in Iarthar Eorpa).[91]

Labhra enters, downcast over the loss of his tree and worried that he will soon be disgraced and deposed when his ass's ears are revealed. Suibhne is having none of this self-pity and tells Labhra he has brought all his woes on himself by his monomaniacal attachment to a narrowly defined scientific view of life, an obsession that demoralised his wife and daughter, emasculated his soldiers, and blighted his land. Moreover, he tells Labhra that it was he who cut down the beech tree because

> I am tired of being agreeable. I am tired of watching the Scientist. I am tired of listening to the Scientist. In this house and everywhere I go. Creating laws, correcting poems, expressing opinions, laying out policies. I wouldn't mind if he stayed out of the way quietly doing his work – but it is the end of the world when someone whose heart is only truly fond of one thing on earth is allowed – to have opinions.

For Suibhne, it is people like Labhra 'who make the women sick and the daughters ugly . . . who make the young men bald and the old people too submissive' (a dheineann breoite na mná is a dheineann gránna na hiníonacha . . . a dheineann maol na fir óga, is na sean-daoine ró-ghéilliúil).[92]

All is anticlimax when Suibhne does cut Labhra's hair, for we learn that once again theory has trumped fact and that Labhra's ears are not those of an ass, just unusually large ones for a man. The play then quickly winds up as An Dílleachtaí appears in rightful form as a young woman and Suibhne's lover, and we hear the voices of the mad calling for Suibhne. Thereupon his fellow madman Longadán arrives to marry Suibhne and An Dílleachtaí as well as Bláthnaid and Feardorcha. Earlier, Bláthnaid had commented of Suibhne that 'when you are not with me, I cannot keep any hold on you. I cannot even imagine you. You are too big for me.'[93] Her inchoate awareness that Suibhne is much more a force than a person is confirmed by Suibhne himself as the play ends:

> You will all be very lonely for a while, perhaps . . . and after that you will only be a little lonely – just as a person would be after a pleasant dream. But there is not one of you who has not benefited from my visit among you, and there is not one of you who will not take more pleasure out of associating with one another from now on.[94]

The only character about whom he still has doubts is Labhra, but not enough to keep him from ending the play with a paean to the wild and creative: 'For this world is still full of beauties and wonders. And I summon to us in the road that is before us bees[95] and white doves, larks and magpies and long-eared owls and butterflies . . . songs from the south and from the north, songs from the East and from the West, – and songs never yet heard in the sky or on earth!'[96]

In his first two plays, Ó Tuama dealt with how people in situations over which they have little or no control succeed or fail in making decisions that define their lives. In *Ar Aghaidh linn, a Longadáin,* he widened his scope considerably, introducing the celebration of freedom that Pádraig Ó Siadhail has identified as one of the central themes of his work after *Moloney*. As Ó Siadhail also points out, *Ar Aghaidh linn, a Longadáin* is by no means an entirely successful work, as it is marked by 'too much talk and a lack of action in places' (an iomarca cainte is an easpa gníomhaithe in áiteanna) as well as by an absurdly false depiction of scientists as unimaginative drudges when compared to literary types. But Ó Siadhail also stresses that Ó Tuama skilfully blends 'satire, absurd comedy, social criticism and fantasy' (an aoir, an greann áiféiseach, an criticeas sóisialta is an fhantaisíocht) in the play in service of an eternally relevant message. The Pacific Northwest poet and environmentalist Gary Snyder has convincingly shown that a proper engagement with external wilderness and internal wildness is essential to human sanity and survival.[97] Ó Tuama's Suibhne is here an exuberant Irish pioneer of this kind of environmental and psychic vision.

Ó Tuama's next work for the stage was not a drama, but rather a mix of pantomime and pageant based on the life of St Patrick, the one thousand five hundredth anniversary of one of whose death dates was being commemorated in 1961.[98] *Scéal ar Phádraig* had its first performance, directed byTomás Mac Anna and Tadhg Ó Muirithe at An Damer in September 1961 during the Dublin Theatre Festival. The music for the show was by Seán Ó Riada. According to an unsigned review in *The Irish Press*, 'this pleasant show is quite an extraordinary mixture of revue, pantomime, music grave and gay, dancing – and morality' (*IP*, 20/9/61).[99] We can get an idea of what the show was like from a review of the production by L. S. Tuathail in *Comhar*:

> Patrick is up in Paradise, and all the saints are sick of listening to his constant storytelling about his coming to Ireland and the work he did there. At the same time, despair and dissatisfaction are growing in the saint because the Irish people are neglecting their native saint, they do not pray to him anymore, and they have more respect now for Colm Cille and this new man Martin de Porres. Therefore, Patrick decides to return to Ireland just in time for the feast day commemorating his death. (*Comhar*, Oct. 1961, p. 29)[100]

Needless to say, as 'R. S.' pointed out in the *Irish Independent*, 'his reaction to much that he finds there provides ample scope for comedy' (*II*, 19/9/61).

However, despite all of this comic potential, the critics who wrote of the play were unanimous in finding it disappointing, most notably for its lack of any underlying unity or direction. The most positive review was that of Tomás Ó Floinn ('F. Mac an tS.', i.e. 'Flann Mac an tSaoir'), who wrote in the *Irish Times* that *Scéal ar Phádraig* was 'a very pleasant entertainment ... Its chief merit lies in the many opportunities presented for shrewd, topical and mildly caustic comment, and the points are well taken and well made.' On the other hand, he indicated that 'a good deal of the first half is wasted on rather arid material' and that the production needed to be 'speeded up considerably' (*IT*, 19/9/61). 'R. S.' stated:

> Generally speaking ... the idea is not a very successful one. The play vacillates between the solemn and the frivolous. When treating his subject seriously, Seán Ó Tuama does enough to show that he might well have created a gripping, dramatic presentation of St. Patrick. When he shifts to comedy it is hard to avoid feeling that the subject is not suitable material for farce. (*II*, 19/9/61)

The anonymous critic for *The Irish Press* wrote that 'the rapid juxtaposition of morality and farce does not come off – indeed, is somewhat embarrassing at times', but added 'there is ample compensation by many good moments throughout' and praised the 'pungent' satire that 'excuses much of the contrived humour' (*IP*, 20/9/61). He also found the production on the whole 'a tour de force' for Mac Anna and Ó Muirithe. Writing in *Inniu*, 'T. Ó H.' stated that it was unlikely that everyone would like the whole show, but added: 'There is something in it for everybody and the basic idea is good'

(Tá rud éigin ann do gach duine agus tá an bunsmaoineamh go maith). Nevertheless, he felt 'that the script would not stand up as a play without the support of the music and the dance' (nach seasfadh an script mar dhráma gan taca an cheoil is an rince), but that there was too much of both for his taste. Moreover, despite the presence of 'an occasional truly dramatic moment' (corrnóiméad fíor-dhrámata), the show was sometimes 'quite tiresome' (tuirsiúil go maith) (*Inniu*, 22/9/61).[101]

L. S. Tuathail was sharply critical of the work of the two directors, stating that the show was 'more like a school entertainment than a new develop-ment in playwriting' (níos cosúla le siamsa scoile ná le fionnachtan úr drámadóireachta) and continued:

> It seems to me that the effort went wrong somewhere between the script and the directing . . . I don't know when the split between the author and the director [*sic*] happened, but it is all too clear from this show that they were not on the same page in the production. At some point it seems to me that the director [*sic*] decided to make a pageant instead of a satire and as a result one senses that there are two styles in the production, two styles that are in conflict the whole night. (*Comhar*, Oct. 1961, p. 29)[102]

Pádraig Ó Siochfhradha agreed:

> But I am afraid that a slip of some kind happened between Ó Tuama's original script . . . and what was presented to us. The entertainment as a whole lacked weight or substance and I sensed in it more of the flavour of an Abbey Pantomime (something that is entirely all right in its own place – in the Abbey). Worse, I could not avoid the opinion that there was not proper cooperation between the writer and the director [*sic*]. (*Feasta*, Nov. 1963, pp 17–18)[103]

Most disappointed of all with the show was the author himself, who in a brief letter to *Comhar* thanked Tuathail for his 'kind (too kind)' (cineálta (ró-chineálta)) review of *Scéal ar Phádraig* and then in effect disowned the work:

> I would like to explain, however, that there was little connection between the script I sent in and the thing that was on the stage of An Damer. A large amount of it was left out; another large amount was changed, new scenes and new characters were put in so that the original meaning of the script was spoiled. And all this without my permission or my advice.

Moreover, he stated that he had never intended to write either 'a play' (dráma) or a revue, but rather, as Gael-Linn, the owners of An Damer had requested, 'an entertainment . . . in which there would be music, storytelling, poetry, etc., dealing with St Patrick . . . "A Night of Storytelling", that is all that was in question' (siamsa . . . ina mbeadh ceol, seanchas, filíocht, etc., a bhainfeadh le Naobh [*sic*] Pádraig . . . 'Oíche Sheanchais', ní mó ná san a bhí i gceist). His final comment was terse: 'But alas!' (Ach mo léir!) (*Comhar*, Nov. 1961, p. 25).[104]

Leaving *Scéal ar Phádraig* in the limbo to which Ó Tuama himself consigned it, we may now return to the plays for which he did take full and deserved credit. After the flamboyant fantasy of *Ar Aghaidh linn, a Longadáin*, Ó Tuama's next drama, *Is É Seo M'Oileán* (This is my island), with its middle-class, urban setting may seem a rather timid retreat into conventional realism. But of course there is really no such thing as conventional realism for urban plays in Irish, and *Is É Seo M'Oileán* is his first attempt to engage with that ongoing bugbear of Gaelic playwrights: how to write credibly in Irish about Irish people who would be highly unlikely to speak that language in their everyday lives. In this way, it suggested how Ó Tuama might have dealt with this whole question had he continued to write plays rather than abandoning the genre in 1970.[105]

Is É Seo M'Oileán, having won second prize for a full-length play at the 1960 Oireachtas, had its premiere at An Damer in January 1963, with Séamas Páircéir directing. It was an immediate success with the Gaelic public, with the *Sunday Independent* reporting that 'because of its great box-office appeal, the Gael-Linn production of "Isé Seo m'Oileán" in the Damer will run for a third week . . .' (*SI*, 10/2/63). The critics seem to have been just as taken with the play. For example, L. S. Tuathail declared: 'With this play . . . Drama in Irish becomes fully mature, or as you would say in English, it is an "adult" play' (*Comhar*, Mar. 1963, p. 25).[106] Pádraig Ó Siochfhradha pronounced the play 'the most important (the best?) that has come from him yet . . . the most important of the "message" plays (an ugly term) that has come from any playwright in Irish or in English' (an dráma is tábhachtaí (is fearr?) dár tháinig fós uaidh . . . an dráma is tábhachtaí de na drámaí 'teachtaireachtúla' (gránna an téarma) dár tháinig ó aon drámadóir i nGaeilge nó i mBéarla). In a flight of hyperbole, he then compared *Is É Seo M'Oileán* favourably with two modern classics, one American, one Irish: 'I do not remember any play since *Death of a Salesman* that would stir one to think or think again as this drama did (except perhaps [Tom Murphy's] *A Whistle in the Dark*)' (*Feasta*, Mar. 1963, p. 21).[107] Reviewing the play for *The Irish Press*, 'M. Ó C.' wrote: 'It is a long time since a play in Irish was written as interesting and as controversial as "Sé Seo M'Oileán" by Seán Ó Tuama . . . This is a human drama, and the author does his very best to make the story truthful. He succeeds in doing so honestly' (*IP*, 29/1/63).[108] For 'T. T.' in the *Irish Times*, it was 'a gripping play' (*IT*, 29/1/63). A dissenting note was sounded by Earnán P. de Blaghd, who wrote that 'the character-drawing in the play varies from the perceptive to the virtual caricature' (*II*, 3/4/68).

Despite its initial popularity and critical success the play has had few revivals, among them productions by Dublin's Liam Bulfin branch of the Gaelic League at the Meath Drama Festival in March 1968 (*II*, 21/3/68) and the Oireachtas the following month (*II*, 3/4/68);[109] and by Compántas Chorcaí, which, after performing the play in Cork in December 1977, took it on tour to the West Kerry Gaeltacht in January 1978 (*K*, 13/1/78), to Féile Náisiúnta na hÉireann in Ráth Chairn in the Meath Gaeltacht in April 1978, where the production won the Micheál Mac Liammóir Prize sponsored by Taibhdhearc na Gaillimhe, and then to An Taibhdhearc itself for a single performance in May (*CT*, 5/5/78). It was broadcast over Radio Éireann in September 1965 (*II*, 23/9/65). Time has not been kind to this play, and its apparently once striking contemporaneity is, as we will see, now badly if predictably dated.

As published, the play is set in 'a city in the south of Ireland' (cathair i ndeisceart na hÉireann) in 1960, but Pádraig Ó Siadhail has pointed out that in the production at An Damer, the geographic setting was the same but the date of the action was changed to 'around 1970' (timpeall 1970).[110] Fifty years on those dates may no longer seem to make much difference, but it should be noted that Ireland, like all western societies, experienced a good deal of change in the tumultuous 1960s, so that the 1970 date makes more sense. Little touches establishing the play's connection with this particular time and its trends include the use throughout of an Irish translation of a Harry Belafonte song (actually more appropriate for the 1960 date), and an insistence 'that Áine is interested in the most avant-garde things in women's fashion' (gurb é an ní is *avant-garde* i gcúrsaí faisean na mban is suim le hÁine).[111] Virtually all of the action takes place in the comfortable middle-class home of the widower Máirtín Ó hAnnracháin, who shares the house with his four daughters and a female servant. As in so many Irish plays in both languages, the question of an appropriate marriage is at the heart of the plot. Áine and Caitlín are both seeing clueless and selfish young men, but those relationships are obviously going nowhere. Áine's suitor is far more interested in his career than in her, and Caitlín's, an admirer of St Thomas Aquinas, is doubtless on his way to permanent bachelorhood. The usual reading of the play from its first performance is that Ó hAnnracháin is, in the words of Earnán P. de Blaghd, 'a harsh employer and domestic tyrant who has broken the spirit of three of his four daughters and impaired their chances of marriage in the process' (*II*, 31/1/63). Yet, as written, Máirtín seems as blustery and ineffectual as he is tyrannical, nor does the spirit of those three daughters seem all that hard to break. The exception, of course, is Áine, who knows all too well what kind of a world she lives in, stating at

one point in an echo of Patrick Kavanagh's 1942 poem 'The Great Hunger':
'I almost feel on occasions like this that some Great Hunger is still going on
in this country – out there somewhere.'[112]

It is, however, Áine's sister Máire that takes the first step that leads to a
crisis by introducing her family to Breandán Jennings, a dissolute Irish
journalist working for a London newspaper.[113] She rather inexplicably
brings the tipsy Breandán home where he immediately attacks her father as
'a slave dealer . . . a big white lout . . . who wields your lash on the little black
slaves . . . a company manager . . . who doesn't pay your workers half what
they have a right to' (ceannaí sclábhaithe . . . bodach mór bán . . . a imríonn
do lasc ar na sclábhaithe beaga dubha . . . bainisteoir comhlachta . . . ní
dhíolann leath a gceart le do chuid oibrithe).[114] He also accuses Máirtín,
whom of course he has just met, of making 'slaves' (sclábhaithe) of his own
daughters. When he then asks Máire and the servant Síle to go with him to a
dance, both quickly refuse, at which point Áine steps forward and says she
will accompany him, for 'we all have too much sense. If it weren't for that we
would have accomplished something.'[115] Moreover, she tells her suitor
Colm to his face that she can see 'the difference between you . . . and him.
This Breandán Jennings is a man' (an difir idir tusa . . . agus eisean. Is fear é
an Breandán Jennings seo).[116] Although a poor substitute for Suibhne, it is
Breandán who will represent the spirit of rebellion and autonomy in *Is É Seo
M'Oileán*.

Three months pass before the next act begins. Áine is now seeing
Breandán regularly, a development that concerns her pietistic and hypocritical sister Fionnuala, who, even more than Máirtín, is the real voice of
convention and authority in the play. Disturbed by the fact that Breandán is
not a practicing Catholic, Fionnuala tells her sister Caitlín: 'It is no good to
be trying to be "broad-minded" – as it were – in a situation like this. The
truth of the matter is that no marriage in which only one of the couple is a
Catholic is successful or tranquil . . .'[117] To underscore how different Áine is
from her sisters, particularly Fionnuala, Ó Tuama now has Áine appear
'well-dressed and trim, very done up' (gléasta piocaithe, an-déanta suas) with
'her hair a different colour – wine-coloured' (athrú datha ar a cuid gruaige.
Í fionnachorcra).[118] Fionnuala is thoroughly scandalised, but there is much
worse to come for her.

Breandán invites Áine to accompany him on a business trip to Tunis,
adding that after a week or so there they can go on to a holiday on Corsica on
their way home. Such a trip would, of course, have been glamorous jet-
setting in 1970 (not to mention 1960), particularly since Áine's original plan
was for a far more traditional holiday on the Aran Islands. Predictably taken
aback by the thought of spending a fortnight abroad with a man to whom
she is neither married nor even engaged, Áine initially declines the invitation.

Even after changing her mind and agreeing to go, she almost misses the opportunity when Fionnuala intervenes by sending Breandán a false message supposedly from Áine. Áine's decision to go with Breandán would clearly have been a radical step for a young woman to take in the Ireland of 1970 and even more so in the Ireland of 1960 – but Ó Tuama tempers that radicalism by having Breandán ask Máirtín's permission to marry Áine, and Máirtín, worried about his self-image as an enlightened and progressive parent, agrees.[119]

Now engaged, Áine and Breandán head off to Tunis and Corsica where she manages to remain a virgin despite spending two weeks in an exotic location with a man she believes has taught her the meaning of freedom and whom she calls 'wild – wild altogether' (fiáin – agus lán-fhiáin). When Caitlín asks whether she was ever afraid of Breandán, Áine responds: 'Yes, I probably should have been . . . And it is even likely that I am . . . But he is in his own way an entirely honest man. I have to say that I never felt so light, so safe, so separated from sermonisers as I felt in the six days of sunshine we spent on the island of Corsica.'[120] Áine's hope of marrying Breandán seems to come to an end when in a moment of genuine intimacy and honesty he reveals to her that he already has a wife who has been committed to a psychiatric hospital for life. Still, if she thinks she cannot have Breandán, she is absolutely certain that she will not have the likes of Colm, who is once again with her father's approval showing an interest in her. By now Áine can no longer control her despair and rage at the situation in which she finds herself as both an Irishwoman and Máirtín's daughter: 'But women have that gift, suffering. To bear everything: children, trouble. I still remember my mother, sitting by a bed in a hospital, cleaning blood from your brother's mouth as he was dying. That is what we were made for.'[121] It is at this point in the play that Ó Tuama finally lets us see the Máirtín Ó hAnnracháin that so far we have only heard about, something he should have done much earlier so that we could better understand the psychic damage he has inflicted on his family. As Máirtín continues to warn her against Breandán, saying Breandán will cause her trouble and disappointment, she responds sarcastically:

Disappointment! It's fine for you to be talking about disappointment! Who always put a cloud over everything in this house? Who put this restraint and that restraint on my own mother, so that all the life and the vitality went out of her? Trying to stop my marriage as you stopped Caitlín's marriage long ago. Trying to break my spirit as you broke her spirit . . .[122]

And she now sees that marriage to Breandán, or perhaps living with him outside of marriage, will not just be an escape from her family, but also an assertion of her own individual integrity and dignity.

Before we see how the play ends, we must, however, turn to a major subplot whose outcome will have a determinative effect on all of the characters. Just when Áine is deciding whether to go to Tunis with Breandán, their young servant Síle reveals that she gave birth to a child out of wedlock.[123] Here Ó Tuama is, of course, anticipating by a year and a half Máiréad Ní Ghráda's more famous stage treatment of this then controversial subject. Disowned by her family, Síle put the infant in an orphanage while she tried to support herself, but she has now been informed that she must either take the child or have it put up for adoption.[124] When Máirtín learns of the situation, his response is immediate and categoric: Síle, no longer 'a respectable girl' (cailín creidiúnach), must be sent away, preferably to England. With a hypocritical show of piety he states: 'Perhaps I am an old-fashioned person. I still believe in sins. And any woman who gives in to lust is not a respectable woman.' But he also lets slip that 'if she stays here it is certain it will cause some harm to the house, to all of us, not to mention to my business affairs'.[125]

It is Áine who takes the lead in arguing Síle's case. When she returns from her trip with Breandán, she immediately tries to put together a plan to help Síle by getting her sisters and their various male friends to set aside money every week so that Síle's child can be put in a temporary foster home and then sent to a private school where Síle can visit. Áine is convinced that with the child thus kept out of sight her father will let Síle stay, but Máirtín remains committed to his decision to get her a job in England, an idea with which his parish priest agrees. Nor will he yield even when Máire and Caitlín belatedly develop some backbone and join Áine in support of Síle. This, then, is the background to Áine's climactic showdown with Máirtín, to whom she suddenly offers a deal that he cannot refuse: 'One more word. One more little word. Listen to it. Carefully. If you keep Síle here . . . on the conditions I mentioned . . . I will not marry Breandán Jennings.' Her father's reply is chillingly rational: 'Good enough. I am a businessman. I think that is a good bargain. Good enough, Áine – I accept your offer.' And now that he has won the battle that mattered most to him, he can be condescendingly gracious: 'But to express the extent of my satisfaction, I am prepared, personally, to look after whatever costs will be involved in raising the child.'[126] Áine's reaction to the success of this bargain is, to say the least, confusing. On the one hand, she acknowledges that it was not really to save Síle that she rejected Breandán but rather because

> my strength gave out. I came to realise clearly . . . whatever I believe in my heart is right for me to do . . . that I would be troubled to the day of my death if I did it. As much as my mother would be about it if she were still alive . . . It would take me long years now . . . by myself . . . before I would be able to even begin to understand the situation I am in.[127]

That situation would seem to have much in common with those in which Mánas Ó Domhnaill and Moloney found themselves in Ó Tuama's first two plays – situations in which a character makes or fails to make the correct ethical choice from a limited set of options. At any rate, unlike *Ar Aghaidh linn, a Longadáin*, with its celebration of the power of freedom to remake the world, *Is É Seo M'Oileán* deals with a repressed world that desperately needs remaking. Áine may try to convince herself that all will be well: 'This coming week even . . . perhaps I would go dancing. I will begin . . . searching again. But I won't have it easy from now on. And if I do not succeed, perhaps we would still be very happy . . . during the Summer holidays . . . Síle's illegitimate child being in our house.' But she knows better, and as she leaves the stage 'she is almost weeping again with bitterness and disappointment'. Nor can it be any real comfort to her that 'for the first time Máirtín Ó hAnnracháin looks like an old man'.[128]

Is É Seo M'Oileán was, in its time, a brave attempt to show that all was not right, particularly for women, in their insular patriarchal homes or on the island of Ireland itself. Indeed Ó Tuama's depiction of the constricted lives they are forced to live renders the sensual calypso rhythms of the Harry Belafonte tune we hear throughout mordantly ironic. Unfortunately, however, the play's awkward and exaggerated attempts to be up-to-date if not avant garde, the inadequate development of all of the characters except Áine, and the play's inconclusive ending will in all probability mean it is unlikely to be revived.

With his next play Ó Tuama once again gave full scope to his imagination while drawing on what he had learned while studying the theatre in France. *Corp Eoghain Uí Shúilleabháin* (The corpse of Eoghan Ó Súilleabháin) was first performed by Compántas Chorcaí at the Little Theatre of the Catholic Young Men's Society in Cork in December 1963. The director was once again Dan Donovan. Here we return to the exuberantly experimental world of *Ar Aghaidh linn, a Longadáin*, but in this play the influence of his time in France is even more obvious. Most notable is his extensive use of techniques he learned from the playwrights of the theatre of the absurd, writers like his own countryman Samuel Beckett, about whose work Ó Tuama would write in 'Samuel Beckett, Éireannach' (Samuel Beckett, Irishman);[129] the Frenchman Jean Genet; and the Romanian Eugène Ionesco, the influence of whose 1954 play *Amédée, ou comment se débarrasser* on *Corp Eoghain Uí Shúilleabháin* is obvious.[130]

The play was still seen as a bit problematic, for when Dublin's Liam Bulfin branch of the Gaelic League, with Seán Ó Ceallaigh as director, performed it twice in March 1974, first at An Damer (*IP*, 6/3/74) and then in Baile Ghib in the Meath Gaeltacht (*NG*, 23/3/74), Pádraig Ó Siochrú (Ó Siochfhradha), the critic for *The Irish Press*, wrote that he had been told by a

member of the branch 'that Seán Ó Ceallaigh has a very interesting understanding of how to go about the play when directing the plays of Seán Ó
Tuama. "The Corpse of Eoghan Ó Súilleabháin" is not a play that many
groups take on. I don't know whether it is Ó Tuama's Becketian direction
that drives off or intimidates directors' (*IP*, 6/3/74).[131] The directors of Cork's
Everyman Theatre, which had to some extent evolved from Compántas
Chorcaí, were obviously not at all intimidated, producing the play the following year, with Dónall Farmer coming from Dublin to direct (*SS*,
25/1/75). Galwegians got their chance to see the play when it was produced
at An Taibhdhearc in 1977 (*CT*, 25/3/77) with Pádraig Ó hÉanaí directing, as
he did again when An Taibhdhearc revived the play in 1990 (*CS*, 23/1/90). By
1977, the play was no longer seen as a baffling experiment, but rather as 'a
breakthrough in Irish language theatre . . . a humorously philosophical play
about our relationship with other people' that would provide 'a good night's
entertainment' (*CT*, 25/3/77).[132] And by 1990 it could be promoted as 'an
hilarious farce, a "whodunnit" and love story all rolled into one' (*CS*, 23/1/90).

Actually, the play was never as challenging as its early critics thought nor
as anodyne as some of these later comments suggest. Ó Tuama makes clear
from the opening stage directions that he has a very specific kind of play in
mind, one with which Gaelic audiences were highly unlikely to be familiar
or immediately comfortable. We are told that the play is 'a pathetic farce in
which there are three different movements: (a) an easy-going *Allegro* (b) a
mad *Scherzo* (c) a lonely *Andante*' (scigdhráma truamhéileach a bhfuil trí
cinn de ghluaiseachtaí difriúla ann: (a) *Allegro* neamhchúiseach (b) *Scherzo*
buile (c) *Andante* uaigneach), adding: 'It is recommended that the three
principal parts of the play be produced accordingly.' The set is to be 'as if it
were by Salvador Dali' (mar a bheadh ag Salvador Dali).[133] As noted above,
the play shows the clear influence of Eugène Ionesco's *Amédée, ou comment
se débarrasser*, in which a couple in a small apartment try to figure out what
to do with a corpse that keeps getting ever larger. Finally, after a long discussion of who the corpse might be, the husband drags it to a river, where in an
attempt to dispose of it he becomes entangled with it so that both are carried
off by the current. In Ó Tuama's play we know the corpse is that of a writer,
Eoghan Ó Súilleabháin, a name that, of course, immediately brings to mind
the eighteenth-century Kerry poet Eoghan Ruadh Ó Súilleabháin (1748–
84). That Ó Tuama wants us to make this connection is obvious from the
parallels he provides between the life of his modern Ó Súilleabháin and that
of Eoghan Ruadh, parallels like their shared occupation as teachers, time as
sailors, sexual escapades, and mysterious, violent deaths. Moreover, Ó Tuama
underscores the connection by making his protagonist a poet like Eoghan
Ruadh and by having Eoghan Ruadh's song 'Im Aonar Seal' (By myself awhile)
'being played on the French horn through the play, and at the beginning of

each scene' (á sheinm ar an gcorn francach tríd an dráma, agus ag tús gach mire).[134]

The key to the play is given to us in a note with the list of characters before the play even begins: 'There is only one living person in this play: the poet Eoghan Ó Súilleabháin.'[135] But which one? The play opens in a modern hospital ward where Eoghan Ó Súilleabháin has just died, his body then being taken to the hospital morgue. In this opening scene he is mourned by a Bean Uí Ghormáin, who believes he was a genius, and by a fellow teacher, who is at best ambivalent about him and who states that he was a terrible teacher and proud of that fact. Soon the corpse of Eoghan, 'white clothes, a sculpted face like the one on Marcel Marceau' (éadaí bána, aghaidh shnoite air mar a bheadh ar Marcel Marceau), is returned to the ward.[136] The lighting now changes to bathe the stage in 'macabre colours' (dathana macabre) and to create 'a dream atmosphere' (atmasféar taibhrimh). The corpse, who functions in this play as did Suibhne in *Ar Aghaidh linn, a Longadáin*, sits up and addresses the characters on stage and, of course, the audience, laughing off his debts, speaking of his visions, and referring to other artists like Homer, Villon, Aodhagán Ó Rathaile, Chekhov, and Lorca, whose bodies were not treated with proper respect after their deaths. He also reveals that he was murdered, but will not reveal the killer's name, for 'the less we know about him, the better' (dá laghad eolas a bhíonn againne air sea is fearr).[137]

Needless to say, this accusation is a source of great excitement and curiosity, and the efforts to track down the culprit give a certain structure to the play as what one critic called a 'whodunnit'. Predictably enough then, we soon have a detective on stage, and he is almost immediately – and appropriately – astounded that those he questions got their information from the corpse of the victim himself. In a little insider's joke, Ó Tuama gives the suspects – professors and an editor – the names of some of the leading Gaelic intellectuals of his time: Ó Cróinín, Ó Céileachair, and Ó hAodha.[138] The detective quickly feels that his investigation is getting out of hand before it even starts: 'Corpses up and down the stairs, corpses talking. Stockings, scapulars. Anyone would think we were in a madhouse.'[139] But things only get worse when Eoghan's corpse goes missing as the first act ends.

The first of the play's two 'interludes' follows, set in the hospital morgue where the detective and the other characters have gone to inspect the empty coffin. Once again, Ó Tuama has a very specific idea of how he wants the scene to look and be played: 'A strange bright white light, and white bright colours everywhere . . . Every speech and every movement like an imitation of the old "silent" films, every action rapid, exaggerated, jerky, stacatto.'[140] As a priest races through his prayers so that he can make his tee-time at the golf course, the academic types debate the quality of the modern Eoghan's poetry and the chances that it will survive him. His 'patron' (patrún) sees him as a major talent born before his time: 'The pity is that the conditions of the country today did not suit someone like him. If he had come in another hundred years, say, he would have been talked about all over the world.'[141] The academics are not convinced, with one conceding that he had 'a natural talent for writing' (bua nádúrtha scríbhneoireachta), while another sniffs: 'It doesn't actually take much intelligence to write poetry.'[142] As this discussion continues, with Eoghan's drinking mates praising him and the priest rushing through his prayers, the detective intervenes to announce that he has to arrest someone for the crime. When, however, a logical suspect is pointed out the scene dissolves into farcical chaos: 'The Mates get up again and run after him around the coffin, around the room, around the priest. A scene out of the Marx Brothers.'[143]

In the second interlude, which immediately follows the first, the debate about the quality of Eoghan's poetry continues. The patron has tempered his praise somewhat, acknowledging that Ó Súilleabháin may not have been 'a wonderful poet' (file iontach), but that he had 'great potential' (mianach mór) and with 'the right chance and the right encouragement' (an seans ceart agus an spreagadh ceart) could have achieved 'a glorious place for himself' (ionad glórmhar . . . dó féin).[144] The editor states that the major problem was that he was not willing 'to do the groundwork' (an bun-obair a dhéanamh) and that 'he thought he was a sort of Mozart to whom everything beautiful would come without any trouble'.[145] To add to the general confusion, Eoghan has a brother who is a far better poet than he is, but who has become a priest, for, as one of the characters states in a line worthy of 'Myles na gCopaleen': 'There was never anyone in this country who achieved fame in anything who did not have a brother who was better than himself except that he became a priest.'[146] By now the detective has had more than enough of this case and its cast of characters and decides that the editor Risteard Ó Cróinín makes as good a culprit as any, his motive a failed poet's envy of his more successful colleague.

Act II is set in Eoghan's house under 'macabre multi-coloured lights' (soilse macabre dathannacha). We see his corpse slouched in a chair, 'looking very shrivelled and very rotten' (cuma an-chraptha an-thruaillithe air).[147] During a surprisingly lucid conversation between himself and his wife Íosult, she expresses her love for him and her regret that their two sons are dead.[148] This touching moment is, however, immediately truncated when she leans over to kiss him and is overwhelmed by the stench of his decomposing flesh. The mood broken, Íosult complains of the frustrations of life with a poet, telling Eoghan: 'If my boys had lived . . . I would never allow a book or a pen in their hands. I would make . . . I think . . . yes, I would make them cooks . . . chefs in a first-rate hotel.'[149] The couple then have a daft talk about what she should do with the corpse when the smell becomes truly unbearable. At this point they hear the detective at the door, and the corpse slithers like a worm across the floor to hide in the oven. For the first time, the detective indicates he knew Eoghan, having often played the pipes with him on a Sunday, and that in fact he considered Eoghan as 'one of his very best friends' (cara thar cairde): 'You could spend a year in his company, day after day, minute after minute, and your mind would be . . . growing lighter.' His spirits now, however, are anything but buoyant as he fears he will never solve the case and 'that this whole business is an insult to my profession. None of it makes sense. You would think everything was happening on another planet' (gur masla dom' ghairm an gnó seo ar fad. Ní féidir aon chuid de a thuiscint. Ba dhóigh leat gur ar phlainéid eile a bhí gach rud ag titim amach). As he and Íosult discuss Eoghan's obscure and irregular biography, his frustration only grows: 'I understand nothing. Nothing. Nothing. A friend of mine, the most faithful friend I ever had . . . Where was he born, where was he raised, where did he go to school, when did he get married . . . no one knows. No one knows exactly. Was he killed? No one knows. Mrs. Ó Súilleabháin, how do I know he died at all?'[150] The detective is also revealed as exactly the same kind of person Labhra was in *Ar Aghaidh linn, a Longadáin*, and he has the very same problems coming to terms with the complexities of life: 'Look, Mrs. Ó Súilleabháin, if someone who does not lead a quiet, moderately steady life, about whom there is no exact knowledge of where he was born, where he was raised, what jobs he had – if such a person is murdered, he cannot expect that someone like me could solve the case.'[151] As we will see, however, what he can do is try to impose a solution on the facts, just as Labhra inflicts his theories on his plants, and with the same unfortunate result.

When the detective leaves, Eoghan reappears, and after a brief conversation in which Íosult claims to want nothing more than respectability, they realise they are two of a kind and end up in a weird dance to the melody of 'Im Aonar Seal': 'The two move around in a circle as if they were performing a ballet; slowly at first, then they speed up. They set up certain "fake" props, as in simple Chinese plays – a bush, a wall, a sign, etc.'[152] They also discuss the kind of life their neighbours live, a life that is in some ways as absurd as that of Eoghan and Íosult. She asks why people drive 30 miles outside of the city for a holiday, to which he responds: 'Because the most beautiful places are only three miles away. It is planted in the bank clerk's mind, dear, that the body and the mind must be exhausted to arrive at beauty and peace.' Seeing his point, Íosult adds: 'And then, of course, every one of them has a car. And they must use them so that they can talk about the great increase that has come in the cost of living.' As Eoghan rather unnecessarily tells her, they themselves are not the sort of people who worry unduly about inflation.[153]

This bizarrely idyllic scene is brief and Eoghan soon recites a poem in which he celebrates 'the animal inside me' (an t'ainmhí istigh ionam) and sees Íosult as a 'stranger' (strainséar). When she asks – almost begs – him to explain what he means, he replies that while at times she is 'a stranger . . . who will never lose your novelty' (strainséar . . . ná caillfidh do nuaíocht go bráth), at other times she is, in the familiar misogynistic stereotype, a hindrance to his freedom and creativity: 'As soon as you have made the whole world poetry, you trample on it. As soon as you have the thing as large as life, you kill it.'[154]

With a quick shift of scene, we are next in a courtroom where Íosult is being tried for the murder of Eoghan. The corpse's testimony leaves the judge and court clerk baffled and frustrated, a situation the clerk remedies by editing that testimony, leaving out of his summary a good deal of what Eoghan has said. Confronted by the judge with this corrupted evidence, Íosult maintains her innocence, claiming Eoghan committed suicide. In a reaction that could only make sense in the world of this play, the judge at once accepts her claim, states that she was never actually even a suspect, and that Eoghan's corpse committed perjury, since 'it is a long time since I heard any talk so nonsensical or so foolish or so prejudicial'.[155] The judge then reveals the real crime of which the corpse is guilty: 'You thought, conceitedly, Eoghan Ó Súilleabháin, that you could create special rules for yourself. You wanted to have pleasure, but without taking any responsibility. You wanted love, but you were not willing to take the trouble, as everyone else does, to earn it and to control it.'[156] In other words, any one of this 'everyone else' would have a good motive for wanting someone like Eoghan dead.

The judge is cutting close to the bone here when he tells Eoghan that he is 'a second-rate revolutionary' (réabhlóidí den tarna grad) and 'there was nothing in your behaviour but lustful adventures, rowdy adventures' (ná raibh id' imeachtaí ar fad ach eachtraí drúise, eachtraí ragairne). In this light, Eoghan's supposed suicide is an act of cowardice and defeat, and the judge's sentence entirely appropriate when he proclaims: 'Speaking for the people, I impose this penalty on you: that you melt away from our sight – imme-diately – that you vanish, and that neither you nor your like be seen again on the surface of the earth.' When the corpse tries to make his case, the judge rejects his argument out of hand: 'Whatever defence you would make for yourself, everyone knows that no population of people could endure as they are if the likes of you were given free rein.' In his response, the corpse, however second-rate as rebel or artist, proves himself more fully human – and alive – than judge, jury, and 'everyone else' by making one of the central thematic statements of the entire play: 'But perhaps they should not endure as they are.'[157]

The courtroom scene ends, and we are back in the 'real' world of the play with the return of the detective to report that the police have arrested

Eoghan's murderer, the editor Risteard Ó Cróinín. For the detective, this arrest neatly ties up all the many loose ends of the case. His satisfaction is, however, short-lived when he and Íosult smell smoke, run to the kitchen, and find that the corpse has been burned beyond recognition. Having thus escaped the kind of soulless and inadequate examination of his life and motives we saw in the courtroom scene, Eoghan is eulogised by his wife, who provides a convincing if entirely illogical explanation of why she stole his corpse: 'I knew that I would have more solace with Eoghan's corpse before it rotted than I would have with all the living people I know.' While the detective is still baffled by what has happened he agrees to help her bury what is left of Eoghan in the garden and even pays him a final tribute, a tribute marked by the kind of 'logic' previously available only to Eoghan and his ilk: 'Íosult, I never saw anyone as good as Eoghan Ó Súilleabháin at making a mad mess of the whole world. His poetry must live forever.'[158]

One could argue that in this play Ó Tuama himself has managed 'to make a mad mess of the whole world', but one might also have to concede that he did so the easy way – by throwing in everything he could think of, piling up zany situations and tricks he had learned from both high and popular culture, to make the play his objective correlative for the madhouse most 'normal' people consider the 'real' world. The problem is, of course, that there is too much going on in the play and that the ideas he wishes to explore and express get lost in all the extraneous nonsense. That lack of discipline is what distinguishes *Corp Eoghain Uí Shúilleabháin* from the far more carefully constructed, cogent, and as a result more troubling and indeed more convincing plays of writers like Beckett and Ionesco whom Ó Tuama was so obviously influenced by. One should, however, remember that the influence of the absurdists on Ó Tuama was always superficial, more a question of his borrowing from them interesting stage tricks, jokes, and striking visual images, than of his having any sympathy for their worldview or philosophy. Thus, despite its grotesque plot twists and often bizarre dialogue, in the end *Corp Eoghain Uí Shúilleabháin* champions the traditional humanist values of freedom, integrity, and the liberating power of the imagination, a power that makes it possible for the shadowy presence of Eoghan Ruadh Ó Súilleabháin to haunt the play and remind us that, in the words of T. S. Eliot, 'the communication of the dead is tongued with fire beyond the language of the living.'[159]

What, then, are some of the ideas under all the madcap motion of *Corp Eoghain Uí Shúilleabháin*? One is certainly the question of identity, of whether a stable personal identity is even possible in the modern world. Ó Tuama neatly introduces this question through his choice of Eoghan Ó Súilleabháin for the name of his protagonist. On our first encounter with the title we in all probability take his bait and expect a play about an eighteenth-century Kerry poet – the sort of protagonist a more traditional Gaelic playwright might have found appealing. And, as noted above, Ó Tuama's many, often subtle references to the eighteenth-century poet only add to an audience member's confusion, even after he has met the modern Eoghan Ó Súilleabháin. Moreover, the modern Eoghan of the play is himself confused about who he is, having told another patient during a stint in a psychiatric hospital 'that he was seeking himself. That he had lost himself. "Everybody nowadays is losing his identity" he used to tell us' (gur á lorg féin a bhí sé. Go raibh sé féin caillte aige féin. 'Everybody nowadays is losing his identity' adeireadh sé linn). In fact he writes a song in English about the problem: 'Everybody nowadays is losing his identity, / I indeed have lost mine too, / And to recover what is now a complete improbability / I'll rest awhile my guiltless friends with you.' By the way, the detective's response when he hears this song is both logical and altogether wrongheaded: 'He had too much to drink.'[160]

Ó Súilleabháin also has a view of love far more expansive than that of most people, as An tSiúr Bonaventura, who talked with him on the night he died, tells the detective: 'He said that a human being is a contemptible thing; after his education and his training for thousands of years he cannot give love, in even one little way, except to one or two people' (Dúirt sé gur suarach an rud é an duine, tar éis a chuid oideachais agus a chuid oiliúna leis na mílte blian anuas, nach féidir leis grá a thabhairt in aon tslí beag féin . . . ach do dhuine nó beirt). Furthermore, he states that married couples are the worst offenders in this regard, for 'what they think of as love is to learn by degrees how to put up with each other and how to despise everyone outside of their own little world' (gurb é is grá acusin ná foghlaim de réir a chéile ar conas cur suas lena chéile agus conas drochmheas a bheith acu ar gach éinne lasmuigh dá ndomhan beag féin).[161] Of course his wife seems to have come to appreciate this view only after Eoghan's death. Surprisingly more perceptive is the plodding detective, who realises at the end of the play that the ongoing influence of at least some of the dead, most notably artists, on the thoughts and beliefs of the living is rooted in their ability 'to make a mad mess of the whole world' (tranglam buile a dhéanamh den saol ar fad), to present alternatives to the received wisdom of their own time and place. It is that mad creativity that has ensured the survival of Eoghan Ruadh's poetry for more than 200 years and that will also allow the play's modern Eoghan a kind of immortality even if, as he fears, 'there is no hell – or heaven' (ná fuil aon ifreann ann – ná neamh).[162]

Corp Eoghain Uí Shúilleabháin may not be an unmitigated success, but it must be seen as a landmark play in any Gaelic dramatic canon, the best of the tiny handful of plays in Irish that show the influence of the theatre of the absurd, one of the most important movements in modern European drama, as well as one in which the Irishman Samuel Beckett played such a major role. After this experiment, Ó Tuama returned to the realistic treatment of subjects from modern Irish life for his last two plays, both of which are of considerable interest, but neither of which matches the creative energy and accomplishment of *Ar Aghaidh linn, a Longadáin* or *Corp Eoghain Uí Shúilleabháin*.

Iúdás Iscariot agus a Bhean is the more intriguing of the two final plays in both its ambition and achievement. Its first production, directed by Noel Ó Briain, took place at An Damer in 1967 during the Dublin Theatre Festival, for which it had been commissioned by Gael-Linn.[163] It seems to have had a real and immediate appeal for the public, with Éadhmonn Mac Suibhne informing us that playgoers, particularly younger ones, attended 'in great numbers' (ina slóite) and adding: 'Even if the hall was packed with them there must have been a good number more of them who were not able to get in at all' (*IP*, 11/10/67).[164] Indeed Earnán P. de Blaghd confessed that he had to pull rank to get a seat: 'For the first time in many years, I crashed a queue at the entrance to the Damer Hall, Dublin, where Seán Ó Tuama's "Iúdás Iscariot agus a Bhean" opened. I had to; otherwise I had no guarantee of getting into the theatre, and less than none of getting a seat' (*II*, 4/10/67).

Once in, however, de Blaghd had mixed feelings about what he saw, a response shared by his fellow critics in Dublin. For him, 'this play fails quite to live up to the potentialities of its theme', although it was 'an interesting experience . . . strictly for adult playgoers only' (*II*, 4/10/67). In his review, Éadhmonn Mac Suibhne stated: 'It is difficult for me to believe fully in the characters that Ó Tuama traces in this play. I sense something missing in them and some emptiness that causes me to think that they are not entirely true' (*IP*, 5/10/67).[165] Dominic O'Riordan clearly admired Ó Tuama's ambition, but was uncertain as to whether the playwright's reach exceeded his grasp:

> *Iúdás Iscariot agus a Bhean* is a great night's entertainment but perhaps the writer, Seán Ó Tuama, has provided too many kinds of entertainment in the one night. His fertile, experimental mind tries to mix themes from the death wish to the bitchiness of theatrical women with too many modes of representation from masque to impressionistic. (*IT*, 4/10/67)

The most positive reviews were those by 'N. Ó G.' (perhaps Nollaig Ó Gadhra). Writing in *Inniu*, 'N. Ó G.' declared that the play was one of the finest at that year's Dublin Theatre Festival and continued: 'If it were in English there would certainly be far more talk about it – it would be "controversial" and a topic of talk for the people on the "Late Late Show" and in the evening papers.'[166] He did think that Ó Tuama failed to focus sufficiently on 'any one at all of the basic themes' (ceann ar bith de na buntéamaí) and that as a result none of those themes were fully developed, but also noted that he used 'almost every theatrical trick there is to inspire the audience to take part in the dramatic experience' (gach cleas amharclainne dá bhfuil ann, nach mór, leis an bpobal éisteachta a spreagadh le páirt a ghlacadh san eachtra dhrámatúil). His final word was that this was a play 'that will live long after we have forgotten the Dublin Theatre Festival of 1967' (a mhairfidh i bhfad i ndiaidh dearmad a bheith déanta againn ar Fhéile Amharclainne Bhaile Átha Cliath, 1967) (*Inniu*, 13/10/67). In *The Times* of London, Ulick O'Connor called it a 'beautifully organised' production and 'a clever blend of ritual drama provided by the masked actors in the play within a play, of realism in the actual play and *commedia del arte* from some delightful harlequins who act as commentators in between the scenes' (*Times*, 18/10/67).

After its premiere at An Damer, the play was produced three times in 1969 by Limerick's Buíon Phádraig, with Seán Ó Morónaigh directing: at the Waterford Drama Festival (*ME*, 14/2/69) where both the production and its director won first prizes (*LL*, 8/3/69); at the Nenagh Drama Festival (*NG*, 1/3/69); and at Féile Luimní (The Limerick festival), where it again won first prize for both the production and the director (*IP*, 17/3/69). In 1972, An Cumann Drámaíochta of UCD performed the play at Féile an Chomhchaid-reamh in Taibhdhearc na Gaillimhe (*IP*, 22/11/72); at Féile Drámaíochta Chonnachta (The Connacht drama festival) in Tourmakeady, Co. Mayo (*Connaught Telegraph*, 30/3/72); and at the Oireachtas in Dublin (*IP*, 17/4/72).

In 1969 Taibhdhearc na Gaillimhe staged *Iúdás Iscariot agus a Bhean*, with Tomás Ó Murchadha from the Abbey Theatre directing.[167] In an anonymous review of the production, the critic for *The Connacht Tribune* pronounced the play 'Ó Tuama's best yet' and challenged potential theatre-goers: 'If you think that this is simply a biblical play, your [*sic*] in for a surprise. Should you go? By all means, it may shock you, but go' (*CT*, 14/11/69). Before the play opened, a critic for the same paper – actually in all probability the same critic – expressed a similar concern that would-be audience members would be put off by the play's apparent subject matter, pointing out that despite 'a somewhat misleading title', *Iúdás Iscariot agus a Bhean* is a 'very modern play ... dealing with some of the problems of present-day society – there is nothing biblical about it' (*CT*, 7/11/69).

He was, however, quite wrong here as the success or failure of the play rests almost entirely on the ability of the audience to draw a parallel between the play's protagonist and the biblical Judas. Ó Tuama sidesteps the perennial issue of verisimilitude – whether it is possible to write credible plays in Irish about people unlikely to speak that language – by having all of the characters in the play members of a (presumably) Irish-language theatre group. Indeed the play begins in the theatre itself during the last performance of a play about Judas. The actors have reached the final scene, and we hear Tony as Judas speaking to Colette, the actress playing Mary Magdalen, in a lament for his lost idealism: 'I always made too much of a habit of big dreams ...

dreams of eternal love . . . so that it would be worth being alive. It is too late . . . now . . .'[168] When the actors go backstage after the final curtain, they find that Tony has hanged himself. The rest of the play follows the events leading to his suicide.

The scene ending in Tony's death is followed by the first of 12 'interludes' in which two guitarists, identified in the list of characters as 'commentators' (tráchtairí), serve as a chorus to shed light on the action. From them we learn that only three months earlier 'you would think he [Tony] had been created for happiness' (ba dhóigh leat gur le haghaidh an tsonais ceapadh é [Tony]', but 'that was the night he met Colette' (b'sin an oíche a bhuail sé le Colette).[169] We soon meet Colette and all the others who will be involved with the production. For the most part, they are an unlikeable bunch. Colette shows herself to be a thoroughly modern young urban sophisticate who, when told the next play in the theatre will be about Judas, responds that Judas never existed and that while Christ did, 'he died. And he never rose again. That is just a fable you would not these days hear anywhere but in Ireland.'[170] Denise, the manager of the theatre, considers herself above all as a 'business woman' (bean gnótha) and intends to make the theatre a fully professional enterprise. Nor does she have any compunction about using others to reach that goal as quickly as possible. Louis, a clerk by profession and the director of the Judas play, hopes to be the theatre's new full-time artistic director, a position that Tony also wants, but only, as he makes plain to Denise, on his own uncompromising terms: 'Look, Denise, it is true that I very much want this job. But despite that I will have to tell you this straight out. If I am chosen as director here, I am not going to put any bad plays on stage here. Nor even mediocre plays, if I may say so – no matter what the Board of Directors says.'[171] Both Tony and Denise know that Louis, in addition to having more experience than Tony, will be far more flexible in his standards and that, moreover, he will always be able, in Tony's words, 'to make a good theatrical show out of any kind of rotten play' (taispeántas maith amharclainne a dhéanamh ar aon tsaghas glugair de dhráma).[172] When Denise tells him that he is 'a person . . . who will never be willing to take the world as it is' (duine . . . ná beidh sásta go deo glacadh leis an saol mar atá), Tony agrees: 'If I were a person of that sort, I would not find living worthwhile.' Tony's chance at the job comes to a definitive end when he tells her flatly: 'And as for your job as director, you can shove it up your arse now.'[173] Denise quickly offers the position to Louis, but tells him that they will have to postpone any announcement of his appointment lest Tony withdraw from the upcoming production.

The job is not, however, the only thing on Tony's mind, as he has met and fallen in love with the considerably younger Colette. Initially, Colette is impressed by Tony, not least because of what she has heard about his independent spirit and idealism. She has been told 'that you aren't a very good actor. That you are too intelligent to ever be a superb actor' (nach aisteoir ró-iontach tú. Go bhfuileann tú ró-éirimiúil chun bheith id aisteoir sár-mhaith go deo) and 'that you would not thrust yourself forward as everyone else in this business does' (ná sáithfeá tú féin chun cinn mar a dheineann gach éinne eile sa gnó seo). She herself believes that Tony will remain 'a beautiful person to the end of your life . . . But you will never get ahead in the theatre!' (id dhuine álainn go deireadh do shaoil . . . Ach ní rachaidh tú chun cinn san amharclann!).[174] Their courtship is brief and blasé:

> Tony: Would you come home with me?
> Colette (Without the least hesitation): I will.
> Tony: You'll sleep with me?
> Colette: I will . . . Let's go. Quickly. Before I get a chance to change my mind.
>   (Stops) O . . . look. Will everything be all right if I go with you?
> Tony: It will be.[175]

Their engagement is every bit as casual, as the very next morning Tony asks her to marry him and she responds: 'I will. On one condition . . . That you will put to death the spiders you have in the shower' (Pósfad. Ar aon choinníoll amháin . . . Go gcuirfidh tú chun báis na duáin alla atá sa bhfolcadán agat). She does, however, have another condition – 'a serious one this time' (dáiríribh an uair seo). She is still engaged to Dónal, a young man her own age, and although she regards the relationship as over, she has promised to see him again and feels she owes it to him to end the engagement in person. Tony accepts this condition without hesitation for he is totally in love – a very traditional romantic kind of love – with Colette: 'Colette, when I watched you singing last night . . . the blood inside me started boiling. For the first time ever in my life, the blood in me recognised the blood in some other person . . .' She finds this declaration embarrassing, even annoying: 'Have a little bit of sense, Tony. I am no angel (She is, you would think a little bit angry).'[176]

Tony clearly feels that he has found a soulmate in Colette, failing altogether to see that she shares none of his idealism. She tells him, for example, that he should have behaved differently with Denise, should even have been willing to use sex to become the artistic director: 'It was right of you to accept the invitation from her to her flat! To stay there a week if necessary. Anything to get the job.' He answers this cynicism by sharing with her his life's ambitions and regrets, telling her that he is a recovering alcoholic and that he has wasted his life 'pottering away at the theatre in this city. Amateur plays, amateur ideas, amateur applause. I am not skilled at anything. Worse still, I am half-skilled at everything' (ag útamáil timpeall ar an amharclann sa chathair seo. Drámaí amaitéaracha, léiriúcháin amaitéaracha, smaointe amaitéaracha, bualadh bas amaitéarach. Nílim oilte ar aon ní. Níos measa fós, táim leath-oilte ar gach rud). At this point, he tells her that he is ready to summon the courage he has so far lacked and try to make a career in London: 'But I will have to get a chance to do something . . . that will bring me lasting satisfaction.' And she is central in this plan: 'Colette, if I could be sure that the two of us would be . . . lasting, I would be satisfied. That would be enough.' Indeed he says that with her support he could even admit failure in the theatre and be content with life as a teacher of French. Her reply is predictably flippant: 'O Tony, Tony, you are so simple. But you are beautiful. I have never met anyone else like you.'[177]

We next see the couple on a passionate 'honeymoon' in Paris. Tony now wants them to marry each other in an informal ceremony of their own creation in their hotel room. This little idyll is, however, interrupted almost immediately by the arrival of a telegram from her old fiancé Dónal. Despite Tony's opposition, she says she will have to go to Dublin to see Dónal but will then return to Paris: 'Tony, Tony, dear, believe me, believe me. I am not abandoning you. I will be back to you again within a fortnight for certain.' Of concern, however, is her belated realisation of how great is the difference in their ages – 'Lord, when I think of it you are almost twice as old as I am.' In response to his admittedly manipulative statement that she is his 'last chance' (seans deireannach), 'she is slightly frightened' (scanradh beag uirthi) and states: 'Don't say that. Everyone has a thousand chances.' Even more ominous for him as a recovering alcoholic is her suggestion that 'we could go on a tear tonight . . . O Tony, you will have to drink with me tonight.'[178]

When she eventually returns to Paris she tells Tony that she and Dónal are back together,[179] and his life goes into a downward spiral, fuelled by the alcohol to which he has returned after their night's drinking. His desperation is revealed to us in a series of letters he writes to her, in one of which he tells her rather melodramatically that he is drinking heavily again, 'for I know well and so do you, that everyone is alone, that no one understands anyone else, that no one is in love with anyone else, that I am not in love with you, nor you with me. That we are all just pretending.'[180] The problem is that he does not believe his own words here, a point Colette stresses when they meet and she accuses him of being 'old-fashioned' (seanaimseartha): 'You are still hoping for the great romantic love – for God – for a faith that will live forever . . . Your standards are too high.'[181] She and Dónal, on the other hand, are 'satisfied to just take everything as it comes for a little while' (sásta gan ach tamall gairid a bhaint as gach rud) and are not expecting 'that things will continue, as you do. The kind of thing you want does not exist in life' (go leanfaidh rudaí mar a bhíonn tusa. An saghas ruda atá uaitse, níl sé sa saol). To his question 'What is life?' (Cad tá sa saol?), she replies with a specious optimism:

'What is life? To get through it, most likely. To get through it unscathed to the extent that that is possible. You also will get through it, Tony. People put things a thousand times worse than this behind them.' Angered, scandalised even, he rejects her facile dismissal of his despair: 'That's life as the aborigines of the world understood it. That is not a life I am willing to live. If that's the life you want, you can have it. But go to hell and live it, and leave me be!'[182] The tragic consequences of his attitude are then immediately underscored by the two commentators, who in alternating lines sing: 'It is a great relief we are not God. / We would go out of our minds / With too much truth and honesty.' These commentators know that it is his own version of this truth that Tony, unlike his colleagues Denise and the playwright Seán, must now face: 'They will keep the show going. / Even if every actor / In the city falls / Dead.'[183]

Now usually drunk, drugged, or both, Tony frequently forgets his lines when rehearsals for the Judas play begin. More troubling to his colleagues, however, is the fact that he now wants to embody rather than merely play Judas, whom he sees as 'a first-rate prophet' (fáidh den chéad scoth) as well as 'a person of the kind you would meet out on the street. A truly human person' (duine . . . den tsaghas a bhuailfeadh leat ar an sráid amuigh. Duine daonna).[184] Denise has come to see Tony as not only changed, but 'far more dangerous' (i bhfad níos dainséaraí). He constantly takes over the rehearsals, re-writing the ending of the play so that it now concludes 'triumphantly instead of despairingly' (go buach in ionad go héadóchasach) as 'a hymn in honour of Judas' (iomann . . . in onóir do Iúdás).[185] Of Tony's changes to the play, Louis states: 'I have to admit that when I read what he had written, I said to myself: "This is so close to my truth. It could be true." That's the difference between Tony and the others.'[186] In fact Louis expresses his envy of Tony's ability 'to find a difficulty and to solve the problem while the rest of us are dealing with theories and opinions' (chun deacracht a aimsiú agus an fhadhb a réiteach, fhaid is atá an chuid eile againn ag plé le teoiricí agus tuairimí). A bit nonplussed, Denise responds characteristically that she too admires people who are 'gifted' (éirimiúil), but only if they are also 'well-mannered' (dea-bhéasach). Denise also mentions that Colette wants to leave the production because she is no longer comfortable on stage with Tony and because she finds 'some of the lines he put in rather personal' (roinnt de na línte a chuir sé isteach beagán pearsanta).[187] For Tony it is, of course, the whole play that is personal, and his identification with Judas is only strengthened when he becomes aware of how Denise has deceived him about the artistic directorship – though truth be told it is difficult to see how he could have thought he was still in the running for the position after his earlier blow-up with her.

At the rehearsals, Tony continues to create problems, refusing to put on the mask he is supposed to wear as Judas and insisting that the hanging scene at the end be made as realistic and convincing as possible, without 'all the screeching and the Grand Guignol' (an scréacháil is an Grand Guignol ar fad).[188] Louis is even more exasperated by Tony's constant suggestions and questions, among the latter 'Do you think, Louis, that Judas was a brave man?' Finally, Louis exclaims in frustration: 'Remember that in the end it is just a play. A play that is, perhaps, not even very good.' There is, of course, no way that Tony can take the play so lightly, any more than he can take Colette's facile suggestion that he simply quit the production: 'Take a break for a couple of months and everything will be all right again. Nothing will look half as important as it looks now.'[189] Nor can he accept when she tells him she will sleep with him again, for he knows full well it will mean nothing.

In the performance itself, Tony has become Judas. Bound before St Peter, being played by Louis, Judas/Tony blasts him as a mediocrity who has risen to a position beyond his capabilities: 'If I had gotten that job, it is I who would be wearing this fake outfit, and who would be talking like a Lord Mayor. In God's name, Peter, throw off those clothes and don't be making a circus clown of yourself altogether.'[190] His bitterness is fuelled by his memories of what Christ had meant to him: 'I could fill a book with the beautiful things he said and did . . . Being with Christ was like being on honeymoon in eternity.' But he is in no way ashamed of what he has done, and when Peter offers to tell the other disciples that Judas feels 'true remorse' (cathú fírinneach), he retorts: 'Tell them anything you want. But don't tell them I am remorseful . . . For I feel no remorse that I denied Christ. The man who would play so damnable a trick . . .'[191] The 'trick' to which he refers here, one apparently invented by the author of the Judas play (and of course by Ó Tuama himself), is that despite Judas's plea, Christ refused to raise the wife of Judas from the dead as he had Lazarus.

Magdalen/Colette enters and tells him of Christ's resurrection and of his willingness to forgive Judas, a willingness he expressed to her in person. At first, Judas is astounded: 'And you tell me that it was the Messiah himself who told you this . . . O Lord of the Universe. If that is true –' But his scepticism wins out as he recalls what Christ told him when he asked that his wife be brought back to life: 'I will think about it' (Déanfaidh mé mo mhachnamh air) and 'Wait and see, man of doubt' (Fan go bhfeictear, a fhir an amhrais). But 'I waited and I did not see. I do not in the end see anything but a person like myself who felt thirst and hunger, a man whose feet the thorns would wound.' Then, in a particularly startling insight, he says to Magdalen: 'I do seriously believe, Magdalen, that he himself did not know and that his heart split on the cross. He was hoping to the end that perhaps he himself was the Messiah . . .'[192] Obviously unable to face the chilling thought that Christ was betrayed by one far greater than himself, he turns to Magdalen, who urges him to repent. While willing to admit that he never thought his actions would lead to Christ's execution, he still insists: 'Someone must tell the truth.' To his obduracy she can only reply: 'And you are a hard, immovable criminal, Judas Iscariot.'[193] The play ends with the corpse of Judas being carried around the stage by the other actors as they sing 'a hymn to Judas' (iomann do Iúdás), remembering him as 'a man who was never understood, nor the good in his heart' (fear nár tuigeadh ariamh, ná an mhaith a bhí ina chroí) and as a man 'who believed in the incredible' (a chreid san ní dochreidte), a faith the audience is told they share.

Not surprisingly, Tony is disgusted by this simplistic reading of the character he has come to embody, and when called back on stage to share in the audience's applause he cannot control his anger:

> There is no need for the applause. There is no need for the applause . . . You think it a fine thing that a person puts himself to death. Oh, you do. You are so satisfied with yourselves. So damned satisfied. But none of you yourselves would ever do it . . . But still you always want to have some Judas putting himself to death for your sake. It is fitting and just that someone should die for the people. Christ![194]

He sees the ordinary person's conviction 'that you must – that you must – live for the things in which you believe' (go gcaithfidh – go gcaithifidh tú – maireachtaint ar son na rudaí go gcreideann tú iontu) as 'Bullshit . . . Absolute bullshit' (Cacamas . . . Dearg-chacamas). The challenge he presents to the audience is either 'to believe completely in one thing' (creideamh go hiomlán in aon rud) or 'put yourselves to death completely' (sibh féin a chur chun báis go hiomlán). Tony sees Judas as having accepted that challenge, but when asked by one of the commentators whether he himself has the courage to do so, he can only answer 'No. But I admit it. I admit it. But I wish I did. I wish –'[195] The play then ends with Tony suddenly vomiting in the single spotlight still on. However, unlike the audience for this opening night performance, we know he will find the necessary courage on the closing night, with tragic consequences.[196]

Ó Tuama presents Judas as both a scapegoat and a redeemer, one who takes on himself the doubts and fears the vast majority of people cannot face, one who faces truths they will not recognise and does what they cannot do. The problem, however, is that the play is not about Judas, but rather about Tony, and Tony quite simply lacks the archetypal stature necessary to give his tragedy the depth and resonance of that of the character he plays. As Earnán P. de Blaghd perceptively noted in his review of the first production, 'Unfortunately the theme is presented to us through a paranoiac actor who feels himself betrayed by all his associates . . . Breandán Ó Dúill, as the actor, struggles valiantly with a massively unsympathetic part . . .' (*II*, 4/10/67).[197] Worse, the two events that shake Tony and finally destroy his idealism do not really seem all that significant. Having worked with Denise and the others in the theatre he should hardly be surprised by the way they treat him, nor does the pettiness of one group of amateur theatre people seem good reason to give up for good the theatre itself. And as for his affair with Colette, it is difficult to imagine how he could feel so deeply about such a flighty and self-absorbed young woman half his age. In effect, Tony is an ageing part-time actor with unrealistic expectations, hoping to reinvigorate himself through an affair with a much younger and sexually available woman who then leaves him.[198] Judas, on the other hand, betrayed someone he believed might be the Son of God, and in the process may have indirectly played a role in the redemption of humankind. It is not hard to see why Ó Tuama was unable to establish a meaningful equivalence between their lives and deaths.[199]

Ó Tuama's final play, *Déan Trócaire ar Shagairt Óga*, is a short and simple, even simplistic, problem play in which a basic predicament is presented and the steps to its (fairly obvious) resolution make up the plot. It is also Ó Tuama's only play with a Gaeltacht setting, one that allows him to avoid the question of linguistic verisimilitude, but at the same time demands of him some courage in suggesting that such horrific behaviour could take place in an Irish-speaking community.

The play had its first performance by Compántas Chorcaí in 1970 at the Little Theatre of the Catholic Young Men's Society in Cork, with Tomás Ó Murchadha directing. Once again, a play by Ó Tuama seems to have had real audience appeal. A critic for *The Southern Star* declared that it was 'so popular that many failed to gain admission to the theatre' (*SS*, 27/3/71). Reviewing the play in *The Irish Press*, Uinseann Ó Murchú called it 'a timely play . . . since there is so much dispute in the Church today' (dráma tráthúil . . . os rud é go bhfuil an oiread san clampair san Eaglais inniu), but he added that it was a pity 'that the author did not develop more fully the personal problems of the priest' (nár dhein an t-údar forbairt níos mó ar fhadhbanna pearsanta an tsagairt) (*IP*, 20/3/70). Séamus Ó Coigligh also drew attention to the play's contemporary relevance: 'A play by Seán Ó Tuama is always an event; a play in Irish about a homosexual priest is a very special event. Indeed when one first heard rumours about the theme of this play, "Déan Trócaire ar na [*sic*] Sagairt Óga", one felt: "O, God no, haven't they enough to contend with already.' But he then went on to stress that 'by its applause, cheers and cries of "Údar, Údar" [Author, Author], the capacity audience – which included a fair percentage of religious – showed that it was not disconcerted in the least on the opening night'. Ó Coigligh also noted that in a curtain speech after the first performance Ó Tuama stated 'that it was not himself who conceived and created the play, that this play actually happened in Germany a while ago' (nárbh é féin a chum nó a cheap an dráma, gur tharla an dráma so dáiríribh sa Ghearmáin tamall ó shoin), making it 'the first of my plays that happened before it was written' (an chéad dráma de mo chuidse a tharla sar ar scríobhadh é) (*IT*, 21/3/70). He does, of course, shift the scene of the play to an unspecified community in the Corca Dhuibhne Gaeltacht, which he here presents as a moribund place, with the young, especially the women, eager to emigrate, the older men without work, and neither sex thinking about marriage.[200]

To judge by Uinseann Ó Murchú's review, there are major differences between the script as we have it and the play as it was originally performed in Cork in 1970. According to Ó Murchú, 'the author uses the technique that Brian Friel had in "Philadelphia Here I Come". The priest is presented as a doubled character through two characters, Dermot Crowley [the actor who played the priest] and his conscience' (*IP*, 20/3/70).[201] This division of the priest into two separate characters is entirely absent from the script we now have, although we do get insight into the priest's character through flashbacks in which he appears as an adolescent. Actually, the entire drama is a flashback narrated by the priest, An tAthair Gearóid, who begins the play by telling us:

> I had only been returned home for six weeks at this time. After my time in Swansea, I little thought that it would be in a little confessional box in the Gaeltacht that I would suffer my worst setback. Something like this probably had to happen to me at some time during my life . . . but when I look back on it now, it all seems rather unbelievable . . . something that would happen in a faraway country . . .[202]

What he has heard in that confessional box is a local man's admission that he sexually assaulted a nine-year-old boy, his explanation for the act being that he experienced 'an impulse' (spreang) and that 'that's the sort I am' (sin é an sórt mé). Needless to say, An tAthair Gearóid does not find the explanation exculpatory, and he tells the man, 'Micheál a' Taxi', that it is his duty to report the crime to the local police. Micheál flatly refuses to do so: 'I will not, Father. Everything will be fine now. I have told it to you . . . and to God as well.'[203] Deeply troubled by Micheál's refusal to talk to the police, An tAthair Gearóid leaves the confessional – provoking intense curiosity from the penitents waiting outside the box – returns to his room, and vomits. The rest of the play will follow his attempts to deal with the crisis of conscience Micheál's confession has created for him.

As he begins his own investigation of what Micheál did, he learns that the other local men seem aware of Micheál's 'impulses', as they tell him that he can often be found staring at young male tourists on a local beach, for 'he is totally infatuated with young children'.[204] In face of this evidence, An tAthair Gearóid cannot avoid the conclusion 'that he could commit the same crime again' (go bhféadfadh sé an choir chéanna a dhéanamh arís). As he prays for guidance one night, 'without any effort, there floated up from the bottom of my mind a tiny little picture of myself as an altar boy' (gan aon iarraidh shnáimh aníos chugham as íochtar m'aigne pictiúir beag bídeach díom féin im bhuachaill altórach). In this first flashback, we see the early stirrings of his own homosexuality in his attraction to his fellow altar boy Brian. It seems that here, for the first time, he realises – or, perhaps better, acknowledges – what his feelings at the time really meant, and he is shocked: 'When I saw myself again laying a hand so affectionately on Brian's shoulder, I have to say that I was startled . . . I decided that I would have to engage seriously in my social work: found the club, fill the day.'[205] This club is his proposed youth organisation for the parish, a co-educational project that his experience in this dying Gaeltacht community has convinced him is an absolute necessity.

When his old-fashioned superior, An tAthair Tomás, tells him that the kind of club he has in mind will mean 'that girls with short skirts on them would be prancing all over the hall, having the run of the place, going out with the boys to Connor's pub and drinking gins –'[206] An tAthair Gearóid angers the older priest with his terse reply: 'Something I would say is no harm' (Rud nach miste adéarfainn féin). But he also provides a far more reasoned response when An tAthair Éamonn, a visiting Jesuit, agrees with An tAthair Tomás and says that the main cause of emigration from the area is the lack of work, not the lack of a social club. Countering this argument, An tAthair Gearóid asks: 'Yes, but what causes those of them who stay here to have turned into unnatural half-wits?'[207] Interestingly, An tAthair Tomás does not reject this argument, but instead insists 'that it is not necessary to go the other road immediately to remedy the situation. Take the middle road' (nach gá dul an bóthar eile láithreach bonn chun an scéal a leigheas. Gabh an bóthar idir-eatarthu). An tAthair Gearóid responds firmly: 'It is too late for the middle road, father.'[208]

That is, however, precisely the road he is seeking to travel in his own crisis of conscience concerning the most dangerous of the local half-wits, Micheál a'Taxi. Hoping to somehow convince the child molester to do the right thing, he visits Micheál in the house he shares with his elderly mother and urges him to think of getting married, to which Micheál responds quite rationally that there is little possibility of that happening even if he wanted it to: 'I would not say that the girl exists who would be satisfied with me, and I with her, and on top of that that she would be satisfied to take my mother as a burden on herself.'[209] An tAthair Gearóid also tries, unsuccessfully, to get Micheál to give up the taxi that both brings him what little cash he has and allows him to travel and attack boys outside of his home area. As he looks back on these failures, the Gearóid who is presenting this whole play to us as a flashback ponders his dilemma:

I was so confused that I thought for a while that he was making it up when he told me the story in confession. But when I went back over in my mind everything he told me at that time I knew that that could not be ... Sunday morning when I saw the taxi leaving again my heart almost fell out of my chest.[210]

Knowing full well what Micheál will be up to after driving his friends to a GAA match in Tralee – the men have already told him that Micheál himself has no interest whatsoever in sports – An tAthair Gearóid goes to seek counsel from the visiting Jesuit, telling him he is thinking of breaking the seal of the confessional, the solemn obligation that prevents him from telling anyone, even the police, what Micheál has confessed to doing. An tAthair Éamonn's response is categorical: 'Well, Gearóid, you know the law yourself ... Under pain of mortal sin, it is not possible for any reason in the world to break the seal of confession.'[211] But he leaves An tAthair Gearóid in even greater spiritual anguish when he tells him

that I think there is something more fundamental than any law or any authority ... Your own conscience ... So that if the time ever comes that his conscience tells a priest that he should reveal the secret of a confession, then I believe not only that it is allowed to him, but that he is bound according to the law of God, to reveal that secret.

When, however, An tAthair Gearóid immediately asks whether there would be any theologian in Ireland who would agree with him, the Jesuit replies: 'I doubt there is' (Tá dabht orm a' bhfuil).[212]

As the days pass after Micheál's trip to Tralee and no news comes of any sexual assaults in the area, An tAthair Gearóid begins once again to nourish the hope that somehow everything will turn out well. This fantasy is abruptly demolished when he hears over the radio that a young boy was attacked the previous night near Tralee. He goes to the police station, where he ineffectually attempts to warn the authorities about Micheál, using the man's well-known cruelty to his horse as a pretext. The attempt is, of course, an utter failure. Tormented once again by his conscience, he has another flashback to his youth, his friendship with Brian, and his first awareness of a priestly vocation. All of these memories are evoked when he thinks about himself and Brian looking at pictures of naked Africans in a geography book at school.

Having convinced himself there must be a way to get Micheál to talk to the police without breaking the seal of the confessional, he next goes to speak with Micheál's mother, with whom he again raises the question of her son's marrying, even offering to help him find a wife – an idea that provides a disturbing insight into his views on women and their role in life. Micheál's mother sees no point in such an effort, pointing out that Micheál is 'the only son of this house . . . and he's a bit odd I fear' (aonmhac an tí seo . . . agus duine ann féin is baolach). An tAthair Gearóid replies that he also is an only son, to which the mother comments: 'But you never married either, Father.'[213] This remark both startles and angers the priest, another indication that no small part of his psychic turmoil is due to his fear that he and Micheál share a sexual fixation.

An tAthair Gearóid the narrator confesses 'that I actually went out of my mind' (gur imíos as mo mheabhair dáiríribh), spending whole nights in prayer, spying on Micheál, and finally writing and then tearing up an anonymous letter to the police. Another direct confrontation with Micheál accomplishes nothing, leaving the priest physically ill and, according to his doctors, in need of a long period of rest. His recovery is set back when he learns over the radio of a fatal sexual assault on a boy near Ennis. No longer able to bear the guilt he feels, he goes to the station and tells the sergeant all he knows. Ironically, it turns out that Micheál's taxi was observed leaving the scene of the crime so that he might well have been arrested even without An tAthair Gearóid's evidence. That evidence will, however, be crucial at the trial if Micheál is to be convicted, and thus the priest will still have to testify in public about what he had been told in the confessional box. Needless to say, An tAthair Tomás, backed by the local bishop, exerts pressure to convince him not to testify, with An tAthair Tomás telling him he will have to leave the parish if he gives evidence in court.[214]

In a nightmare enacted on stage, An tAthair Gearóid finds himself in a courtroom in which he is the defendant, An tAthair Tomás is the judge, and one of the local men is the defence lawyer. This man badgers him about, among other things, his imperfect command of Gaeltacht Irish, a deficiency that may have caused him to misunderstand Micheál's confession and may now be allowing him to avoid answering uncomfortable questions. He also questions whether An tAthair Gearóid may have a bias against homosexuals and, when he responds in the negative, immediately asks: 'Is it true that you have a liking for people like that?'[215] Indeed he even raises the possibility that something questionable may have occurred in the youth club the priest ran in Swansea.[216] After the rapid-fire hostility in this nightmare scene, An tAthair Gearóid has another flashback, this one to a tender moment between himself and Brian that ends with a kiss, a memory that concludes with his 'tormented cry' (liú cráite).[217]

When the real trial is held, it is in many ways an anticlimax. An tAthair Gearóid gives his testimony and Micheál is convicted and sent to a psychiatric hospital. After all the excitement is over, An tAthair Gearóid goes to see An tAthair Éamonn. Once again the Jesuit is of little help, suggesting that An tAthair Gearóid transfer to a new parish and put an end to his guilt over breaking the confessional seal by confessing this sin.[218] This obvious solution is, however, no longer available to An tAthair Gearóid, who, when told all he needs to clear his conscience is a good confession with appropriate repentance, responds:

> Ah yes. But do I feel remorse? I said that I did . . . But if I were to be honest with myself, I would admit that I would do it again tomorrow, if necessary. Actually the only regret I have now is that I did not tell the story to the police the first night I heard it in confession . . . then I would have saved one little boy from death . . . and another boy –

He does, however, have something else to confess to the Jesuit, telling him that when he left Swansea, in an apparent reference to the youth club there, 'I swore to myself . . . I even promised in confession . . . that I would never undertake something like that again.' When the Jesuit responds with melodramatic shock, An tAthair Gearóid continues every bit as melodramatically in a 'weak, despairing' (leamh éadóchasach) voice: 'What I am saying, Father, is that in the end the same disposition is in me as is in Micheál a'Taxi. (In a whisper) I also am a homosexual.'[219] Despite the Jesuit's assurance that he should remain a priest – a celibate one of course – An tAthair Gearóid is unable to reconcile his vocation and his sexual identity, no longer believing in the authority of the Church or in his own ability 'to return to those days long ago when the duties of the priest, the whole faith, were so simple' (filleadh ar na laethanta úd fadó go mbíodh dualgaisí an tsagairt, go mbíodh an creideamh ar fad, chomh simplí sin).[220] The penultimate scene shows him trying to say Mass in his Gaeltacht parish. Unable to complete the consecration of the wine, he turns to his congregation to tell them 'that I will have to stop here today . . . I am not . . . I am not well . . . Please ask God to have mercy . . .' (go gcaithfidh mé stop anseo inniu . . . Níl . . . nílim ar fónamh . . . Iarr ar Dhia len bhur dtoil trócaire a dhéanamh . . .). Unable to go on, he walks off the altar. The play then ends, as it began, with him in a rest home for the clergy, surrounded by old priests unable to understand, much less alleviate, his doubts. His final words in the play are shockingly anticlimactic, as he returns to a kind of hope he must know is altogether illusory: 'But I will stay here . . . for some while more, to see if things get any better.'[221]

Déan Trócaire ar Shagairt Óga was a provocative as well as a brave play in its own time and place. However, even more than Ó Tuama's other realistic plays with modern settings, it has aged rather badly. Ireland has simply changed too much. Given all the revelations about the sexual abuse of children – particularly by Catholic clergymen – few in any audience would have much sympathy for An tAthair Gearóid for allowing his personal moral scruples to make possible the molestation of two boys and the murder of one of them. The treatment of homosexuality in the play is also problematic, as one cannot be sure whether Ó Tuama wants us to see An tAthair Gearóid's tragedy as the result of his being gay or as the result of his having internalised society's homophobic prejudices. Even more disturbing is the priest's own apparent identification of homosexuality with paedophilia when he tells An tAthair Éamonn 'that the same disposition is in me as is in Micheál a'Taxi. I also am a homosexual.' He is wrong here, of course. He, as a gay man, does not have 'the same disposition' as Micheál, who is a paedophile. One would like to see the play as an early call for the right to free expression of sexual identity among consenting adults, but it might just as well be seen as a well-meaning lament for those like An tAthair Gearóid cursed with a dreadful affliction that will leave them suffering from enough emotional and psychic damage to kill any possibility of a full and fulfilling life. On the whole, then, *Déan Trócaire ar Shagairt Óga* is likely to remain of interest mostly as a landmark production for its time rather than as a work that could be revived successfully in ours.

With *Déan Trócaire ar Shagairt Óga*, Seán Ó Tuama's relatively brief career as a playwright came to an end.[222] As he himself never explained in print his decision to stop writing for the theatre, we are left with a few plausible theories as to why he turned away from the stage after 1970. The most obvious is that he simply decided he needed more time for his work as a scholar and academic at University College, Cork as well as for his activities as a leading figure in the politics of language revival. Nor is it all that improbable that as a playwright accustomed to having his plays given high-quality productions, he was concerned about the state of the Gaelic theatre itself.[223] For example, he would certainly have noticed that the work of Compántas Chorcaí was being overshadowed by the plays produced in English by its sister company in Cork, the Everyman Theatre.[224] If he looked to Dublin and An Damer, where all of his plays had been produced, two of them as well as *Scéal ar Phádraig* having their premieres there, he would have seen that theatre experiencing what Máiréad Ní Chinnéide has called 'the time of need' (am an ghátair) in 1970–1, when financial problems compelled the theatre to make serious cuts in both its staff and in its production schedule.[225] Whatever the reason, or more probably combination of reasons, that Ó Tuama stopped writing plays, his departure from the theatre was an enormous loss for Gaelic drama. We can be certain that without him plays of real and lasting merit were never written and that walls that badly needed battering remained – and remain – standing.

FIVE

QUESTIONS OF CONSCIENCE

CRÍOSTÓIR Ó FLOINN (B. 1927)

In May 1968, Críostóir Ó Floinn scored what he called an 'artistic hat trick', a feat never before – or since – achieved by a playwright working in Irish. That month three of his full-length plays were running simultaneously in the three most important venues for Gaelic drama at that time. Dubliners could see premieres of *Aggiornamento* at An Damer and *Is É a Dúirt Polonius* (What Polonius said) at the Peacock, while playgoers in Galway were being offered a revival of *Cóta Bán Chríost* (The white coat of Christ) at An Taibhdhearc. One might conclude that Ó Floinn was a particularly favoured Gaelic playwright, as even in the 1960s, a time he himself regarded as 'the most productive in the century so far as drama in Irish was concerned . . . the golden age of Irish language drama', most of his colleagues were still struggling to get a play, much less three, produced anywhere – much less in comparatively well-appointed theatres with experienced directors and skilled actors.[1] Such a conclusion would, however, be badly mistaken, for the concatenation of circumstances that coalesced to enable Ó Floinn's 1968 'hat trick' was a one-off event, and for most of his career, Ó Floinn has faced challenges every bit as daunting as those confronting his fellow playwrights in Irish. He has certainly never received the recognition due him for the range and quality of his literary work – and in particular his plays – over a career that has lasted more than 60 years.

In many ways, he has been the victim of his own extraordinary versatility, as both he and his work have always escaped the easy categorisation that makes life so much easier for the critic and scholar. For example, is he a writer of Irish or a writer of English – Críostóir Ó Floinn or Criostoir O'Flynn? In a 1969 letter to *The Irish Press*, he wrote that he was 'born in Limerick of Limerick English-speaking parents, learned Irish at school, and so I write in both languages – and am not fully accepted by either camp' (*IP*, 3/1/69). Recalling those early days as a writer in his native Limerick, he states in the autobiographical volume *Consplawkus: A Writer's Life* (1999): 'I made no choice of linguistic medium but seem to have drifted into being a bilingual writer, writing in English or Irish as the theme or the market dictated.' Still, one of those languages exerted a more powerful emotional influence than did the other: 'I had begun to write in English, my home language, but, added to the basic impetus towards artistic creativity, I felt a very strong spiritual urge to write in Irish also, an urge obviously atavistic and patriotic,' to which he added with a wry humour rooted in experience, 'but which commercial sense, if I had been possessed of any, would have advised me strongly to suppress'.[2] That 'spiritual urge' and that accepting awareness of the real-world linguistic situation in which he would have to work have remained central elements throughout his creative life. His views on the question of a writer's linguistic allegiance have, however, fluctuated over the years. Thus in a 1969 column in the *Irish Times* in which he lamented the lack of readership for books in Irish, he also declared: 'We have so much experience in this country of people being divided into two opposing camps with regard to any question at all that we still cannot accept that we have two languages and that there is no need for a writer to stick to one of them over the other if he has literary ability in both' (*IT*, 4/12/69).[3] Indeed earlier that year he had pronounced 'a plague on the unilingual fanatics of both camps' with their 'feckology about linguistic theories' (*IP*, 3/1/69).

It is, then, startling to find him stating in a piece on 'The Irish writer and the two tongues' in July 1973 that

> anyone who talks about Anglo-Irish literature is inventing an original sweet called jelly-custard (or custard-jelly; *de gustibus*, etc). Let learned academics waffle as they will, Irish writers who write in Irish are contributing to Irish literature; Irish writers who write in English, whatever their themes, style, or diction, are adding their jewels, synthetic though they may be, to the great treasure-house of English literature. (*IT*, 17/7/73)[4]

This idea was not, however, a new one for him, as in 1968 he had written in *Feasta*: 'The Irish person who writes in English looks to the great market of the English language, looks to London and New York, to the British Arts Council and the Guggenheim Foundation, hoping to get financial reward and patronage that will make it possible for him to direct all of his ability to literary work.' The writer of Irish could never expect such rewards, 'but he can satisfy his own soul deeply with the knot that binds his own creative work with the full heritage of his people' (*Feasta*, May 1968, p. 9).[5]

As Ó Floinn well knew, however, that satisfaction was not always sufficient considering the struggles writers of Irish had to confront. As a result, we find him twice joining the company of those who at some point in their careers gave up writing in Irish. Indeed, he nearly did so a third time. In 1958, the publication of *Cuas an Óir* (The cove of gold), his Oireachtas prizewinning book for young readers, was greeted with a scathingly negative review by Niall Ó Dónaill in the weekly paper *Inniu* under what Ó Floinn called the banner headline 'Earráidí Gaeilge gan cheartú' (Uncorrected errors in Irish). While Ó Dónaill, a native speaker from the Donegal Gaeltacht, did devote a bit of his review to what he saw as the book's literary shortcomings, he spent most of his time picking apart Ó Floinn's 'learner's' Irish. Ó Floinn had strong feelings about what he saw as the tyranny native speakers and their allies had long attempted to impose on those writers of Irish who had learned the language, referring to it as 'this bigoted attitude' that had done 'untold harm to the revival of Irish because it discouraged many earnest learners of Irish who, despite achieving fluency in the language, were still regarded as inferior simply because they spoke Irish with their own accent'.[6] Fortunately, after what he later called 'a suitable cooling off period of a few years', he returned to Irish.[7] Then, in 1969 An Gúm refused to publish his poetry collection *Ó Fhás go hAois* (From growth to age) unless he agreed to cut two poems, the satirical 'Eoin an Dá Thaobh' (The double-dealing John), which was felt to be disrespectful of, among others, Dublin's Archbishop John Charles McQuaid, and 'Maraíodh Seán Sabhat Aréir' (Seán South was killed last night), a poem that was both a tribute to the young IRA man and old school friend of Ó Floinn's killed in a raid in Northern Ireland on New Year's Day 1957 and a scathing blast at what he saw as the hypocrisy of the Irish state's attitude to partition. Ó Floinn's anger over this act of censorship was exacerbated when minister for education Pádraig Faulkner, speaking in the Dáil, suggested that the poems in question were in some way 'morally objectionable and thus could not be published'.[8] Standing on principle, Ó Floinn announced that he would cease to write creative work in Irish until the minister withdrew his allegations, an action that would not occur until 1972.[9] *Ó Fhás go hAois*, with the offending poems, was published by Sáirséal agus Dill in 1969 (*IP*, 24–26/12/69).[10] In 1975, Ó Floinn once again threatened to stop writing in Irish unless he and his fellow Gaelic authors were paid royalties due them from both An Gúm and independent publishers. In this case, the situation seems to have been addressed if not resolved without his having to give up the language for a third time.[11]

As Ó Floinn himself is well aware, he would have had a much easier life had he stuck with one language or the other, especially if that language had been English. Of course it could also be argued that while he would certainly have suffered financially had he written exclusively in Irish and identified himself more closely with the language movement, he might well have enjoyed a more informed and less ambivalent critical reception than that accorded a writer as determinedly bilingual as is he. As we saw above, however, he finds working in both languages an entirely natural decision for one raised

English-speaking but who learned and loves Irish. And, despite his pro-
nouncements about the alien quality of Irish writing in English, he could in
a more expansive mood accept that he himself and his fellow Irish writers are
producing Irish literature no matter which of the country's two languages
they use: 'Well, then, I am a bilingual writer now. And as a writer I give
recognition to literature, whatever language it is composed in. I am proud of
the literature of Ireland, of the writing Irish people do in Irish or in English . . .'
(*Feasta*, May 1968, p. 10).[12]

Ó Floinn's commitment to the two languages of Ireland has been
matched by his devotion to the full range of literary genres and subgenres.
Looking back on his career in *Consplawkus*, he recalled that 'just as I never
decided to be a writer when I began to write, first at the age of ten and again
a decade later, I never decided what kind of writer I would be, poet, playwright or a writer of fiction. The topics, themes and ideas seemed themselves
to make the technical choice of the particular genre that suited them.'[13] Nor
has his writing been limited to the genres listed above, as he has also produced
essays, biographies and autobiographies, translations, and editions of poetry
in Irish and English. And he has written for all age groups – children, young
readers, and adults. Moreover, it is worth noting that although he has focused
more on biographical and autobiographical writing and on poetry over the
past 20 years or so, his career cannot be neatly divided into periods defined
by a particular genre. He has always been able to switch from drama to
poetry to fiction, with regular forays into other kinds of writing.

Leaving aside the plays for a moment, we find in his bibliography books
for children like *Caisleán na nÉan* (The castle of the birds) (1954), *An Pálas
Marmair* (The marble palace) (1960), and *An Ceannaí Mór ó Chaireo* (The
big merchant from Cairo) (1968); works for young readers like *An Claíomh
Geal* (The bright sword) (1953), *Fé Bhrat na Fraince* (Under the flag of France)
(1955), and *An tIolar Dubh* (The black eagle) (1956); two novels for adults,
Lá Dá bhFaca Thú (The day I saw you) (1955) and *Learairí Lios an Phúca*
(The loafers of Lios an Phúca) (1968); the story collections *Oineachlann*
(Retribution) (1968), *Sanctuary Island* (1971),[14] and *The Heart Has Its Reasons*
(2004); poetry collections like *Éirí Amach na Cásca* (The Easter Rising)
(1967), *Ó Fhás go hAois* (1969), *Aisling Dhá Abhainn* (A dream of two rivers)
(1977) and *Seacláidí Van Gogh* (1996) – he also produced an English version
of this collection as *Van Gogh's Chocolates* in 2000. Moreover, it should be
noted that in *A Writer's Life*, the third volume of his autobiography, Ó Floinn
makes clear that he never simply translates his own work from one language
to the other, explaining:

> Although from the early years of my career as a bilingual writer I had been in the
> habit of writing two versions of a play, a poem or a story, one in Irish . . . the other

in English . . . I never translated my own work directly from one language to the other but wrote each version separately with an awareness of the different linguistic contexts of each medium, a literary dualism similar to that practiced in French and English by Samuel Beckett.[15]

We will return to this 'literary dualism' in our discussion of his plays. Among his other books of poetry in English are *Banana* (1979), *Hunger Strike* (1984), *A Poet in Rome* (1992), *The Obelisk Year* (1993) and *The Easter Rising: A Poem Sequence* (2004), a substantially expanded version of *Éirí Amach na Cásca*. Some of his essays have been collected in *Cead Cainte!* (Permission to speak!) (1971) and *An Poc ar Buile* (The mad buck goat) (1993), while *Remember Limerick* (2014) is a collection of essays dealing with the history of his native city. As a biographer, he has written on Nano Nagle in *Lóchrann Dóchais* (A lantern of hope) (2005), on Joan of Arc in *The One Who Led an Army* (2009), Thérèse of Lisieux in *The One Who Hid Away* (2010), and Bernadette Soubirous in *The One Who Saw Visions* (2010). His autobiography appeared in three volumes: *There Is an Isle: A Limerick Boyhood* (1998), *Consplawkus: A Writer's Life* (1999), and *A Writer's Life* (2001). Editions and translations include Michael Hogan's *Drunken Thady and the Bishop's Lady* (1977, 2nd edn 2014), *Trí Gheata na Síoraíochta* (Through the gate of eternity, i.e. the first three cantos of Dante's *Divina Commedia*) (1988), *The Maigue Poets* (1995),[16] *Irish Comic Poems* (1995), and *Blind Raftery* (1995).

In none of these genres was Ó Floinn a dilettante, as is attested by the many literary awards he has won. Thus, again leaving the plays aside for now, he has been awarded prizes at the Oireachtas for an adventure story for young readers in 1953, short stories in 1955 and 1956, a long poem in 1968, a poetry collection in 1976, and a translation in 1988. In addition, he was awarded the Club Leabhar prize in 1955, the National Short Story 1916 Award in 1966, and the Abbey Theatre's Playwright's Bursary in 1973. In 2004 the library at the University of Limerick organised a special exhibition of his work. He is a member of Aosdána.

Somehow he managed to find time to train as a national teacher at St Patrick's College, Drumcondra, take an honours degree in English at University College, Dublin, and earn a H. Dip. in Education at Trinity College, all while supporting a family on his teacher's salary and whatever royalties and prizes came his way. His financial challenges were considerably augmented when, having taken a job with the Irish Tourist Board in 1961, he felt he had to resign to protest the underhanded way he was denied a promotion he had every right to expect, a situation that inspired his play *Is É a Dúirt Polonius*. Even worse, in 1963 he had to emigrate to find work after losing his teaching position in Co. Limerick as the result of his parish priest's puritanical objection on moral grounds to his play *Romance of an Idiot* when it was produced in Limerick.[17]

Ó Floinn learned his Irish at school in Limerick with the Sisters of Mercy and the Christian Brothers. Surprisingly, however, he never joined the Gaelic League, although he did 'frequent the League premises', enjoyed the music and dances there, and held an apparently *sui generis* position as a 'cultural officer', a position for which he was recruited by his schoolmate Jack South (i.e. Seán Sabhat or South). Moreover, in 1936 he was awarded a Gaelic League scholarship that enabled him to spend a month in the West Cork Gaeltacht, where, he says, 'apart from learning some songs I had acquired more knowledge of rabbits and birds than of Irish'. More successful would be his six-month stay in Corca Dhuibhne in 1953 on a scholarship from Comhdháil Náisiúnta na Gaeilge. Of course, as he notes in *Consplawkus*, the Gaelic League in the Limerick of his youth was, like the Gaelic League everywhere else in the Irish Free State at the time, 'only a poor shadow of itself' as a result of 'the internecine bitterness caused by the . . . tragic Civil War'.[18] However, as he looked back on his own lack of involvement with the League and the institutional language movement in general, he saw a deeper motivation at work: 'Perhaps the writer I had become was instinctively aware the artist *qua* artist must not only be a loner but must also be wary of expending time and energy on activities, however worthwhile in themselves, which are a distraction from the purpose of the artist in life, which is simply to create art in one form or another.'[19]

Of course his lack of engagement with the Gaelic League in no way diminished his commitment to the Irish language or his belief in the need for its preservation and cultivation as a modern literary medium, and he had characteristically strong opinions on the place of the language in contemporary Irish culture. As we have noted, he once gave up writing in Irish when his competence in the language was questioned by the writer, lexicographer, and native speaker Niall Ó Dónaill. His angry response to what he saw as Ó Dónaill's sterile pedantry was rooted in what he called 'my antipathy to dialect and colloquial speech as the medium for literature'.[20] From the very beginning of the language revival there had been tension between learners of the language and those native speakers active in the revival and their disciples who tried to sound, and often think, as much like native speakers as they could.[21] This linguistic civil war became even more intense after the establishment of the Irish Free State in 1922, when a perceived mastery of Irish could open doors to permanent and pensionable employment in the bureaucracy of the new state. By no means was this contention a thing of the past when Ó Floinn began publishing in Irish, and there was no way that someone with his pugnacious sense of fair play was going to back down, even in the face of an opponent as respected and established as Ó Dónaill. Nor would he have wanted to, as he believed that an exaggerated deference to the language – and even at times to the life experiences – of native speakers posed a dire threat to the possibility of making Irish a fully modern language of literature and culture. In a 1989 piece in the *Irish Times* in which he argued for 'creative freedom for the author when he is involved with the art of literature in any language at all' (saoirse cheapadóireachta an údair agus é i mbun ealaín na litríochta i dteanga ar bith), he recalled hearing a native speaker on the radio, 'a writer of Irish, a man who was born in the Gaeltacht' (scríbhneoir Gaeilge, fear a rugadh sa Ghaeltacht), assert 'that no one could write a play in Irish except for the author who was born and raised in the Gaeltacht' (nach bhféadfadh aon duine dráma a scríobh i nGaeilge ach an túdar a rugadh agus a tógadh sa Ghaeltacht). Rather than argue this absurd proposition, Ó Floinn simply stated: 'Despite my coming into the world in the fair city of Limerick by the Shannon . . . your man's literary principles caused me no uneasiness as an author; three plays of mine in Irish were being produced that same year . . . ' (*IT*, 27/2/89).[22]

For him it has always been the drama itself, not its linguistic medium, that is the primary concern of the dramatist. Of necessity a part-time writer for much of his career, Ó Floinn has for the most part let his plays illustrate his dramatic principles. Nevertheless, he has from time to time expressed his thoughts on drama in general and drama in Irish in particular. For example, he has written that while theatre in Irish has the potential to contribute significantly to the cultural life of the nation in the future, its survival in the present is far from certain. Thus in remarks opening the Oireachtas Drama Festival in the new Peacock Theatre in 1967, he stated:

> It is altogether appropriate that the place in which we are gathering for this Festival is this underground catacomb. The word 'catacomb' sets us thinking about matters of faith and religion, about oppression, and about resurrection. That reminds us that drama began in antiquity as an aspect of religion, that it was the Church that revived drama as a means of illustrating the gospel and the doctrine of salvation to the people. (*Feasta*, May 1968, p. 5)[23]

As was appropriate on such an occasion, he also declared:

> But as the Faith strengthened proudly in the catacombs until it rose again to triumphant glory in the city of Rome and in the whole world, the Irish language and the art of the dramatist will survive. They are strengthening each other in events like this Drama Festival. They concern the heritage of the nation and the human spirit, and the nation and the spirit are more lasting than the empire or the organisation, or the desire for money. (*Feasta*, May 1968, pp 5–6)[24]

Away from a congregation of the faithful at a Gaelic drama festival, he has been considerably more sceptical, focusing on the way the empire of the English language and the desire for money have endangered the very viability of theatre in Irish. What is essential for him is that worthwhile new work in the language be put on stage: 'From the point of view of drama, the play that was never produced but is just a bundle of pages turning yellow and rotting in a trunk of which the key has gone missing is not much benefit to the artistic treasure of the human race' (*Comhar*, Dec. 1971, p. 8).[25] Most of the obstacles he has seen keeping new plays from being written and produced are, of course, long familiar to those in the Gaelic theatre community. For example, in 1972 Ó Floinn humorously but pointedly criticised speakers of Irish for their failure to attend plays in the language. Noting that he might soon have a play on stage at the Peacock, he wrote: 'The majority of you, loyal supporters of Irish, who do not go to plays in Irish at all, be careful to make arrangements to go to the priest's bingo or to a meeting of some Gaelic Organisation the night the play will be on' (*IP*, 5/12/72).[26] Of course as he had made plain earlier that year, one reason for this lack of interest in the theatre among Irish speakers was the fact that since so few new plays were being published or produced, too often potential theatregoers were only being offered translations of plays they had already seen in English. Once again he drew on his own experiences to make his point: 'In the year 1968 An Gúm accepted three of my plays. They have still not been published – and the drama groups looking for new plays, Taibhdhearc na Gaillimhe staging translations of *Moll* and *Big Maggie*' (*IP*, 18/7/72).[27] He put some of the blame here on the fact that there were influential people in Irish theatre circles who did not know or care much about Irish, commenting bitterly: 'But what does that matter nowadays, darling? That all went out with old Blythe and De Valera, didn't it?' (*IP*, 15/2/79). There were also other factors that he felt virtually guaranteed the failure of plays in Irish when they were staged. Writing of the 1968 production of his own *Is É a Dúirt Polonius*, he stated in 1970: 'I know, dear, I know that you did not get a chance to see it. A play in Irish is left on for five nights in the Peacock so that it is being taken off the stage by the time the public knows it is going on (it is thought that there is no need for advance publicity for the true-Gaels) (*IP*, 24/11/70).[28]

At least as important as publicity before a play was criticism after it was performed, and Ó Floinn offered his thoughts on this question in 'Ceird na léirmheastóireachta' (The craft of criticism) in 1971. On the one hand, he seems to have felt in this essay that critics have little real influence in the modern world, declaring: 'And from the point of view of the art of writing, I think that it is a waste of time and space when reviews of new works of literature are published; still it is a good thing that they exist, for they give publicity to new-born works and they help the critic to earn his living.' On the other hand, he saw a not insignificant role for 'the critic who continues to practise this craft long enough' (léirmheastóir a leanann fada go leor de chleachtadh na ceirde seo), for, 'provided that he has the humility and the power of reflection for it, he comes to see that there is mystery in the work of art'. However, while neither praise nor blame could affect 'whatever merit there is in the literary work' (pé fiúntas atá sa saothar litríochta), he wrote that it is possible for 'discerning people to come and find out and elucidate its merit' (daoine tuisceanacha teacht agus a fhiúntas a fháil amach agus a léiriú). Unfortunately, it is also possible for an incompetent or malicious critic to do real harm: 'The way the critic does harm is, in my opinion, that it has come about that it is the craft and not the art that is respected in the market place, the place where the artist has to sell his work to earn his living' (*Comhar*, Dec. 1971, p. 5 and 7).[29]

It is also of interest that Ó Floinn feels that universities have a role to play in the development of Gaelic drama and that departments of modern Irish in those universities have failed to meet their obligations in this regard, an accusation as true today as it was in 1972, when he wrote of his anger 'when I look at a booklist that some commission or committee of scholars put together for the Irish course in the Leaving Certificate, a list on which there is only one play . . .' (*IP*, 26/9/72).[30]

Perhaps his most interesting comments on the Irish theatre scene – particularly in light of the controversy that arose in 2015 over the Abbey Theatre's failure to include more than one play by a woman in its schedule commemorating the centennial year of the 1916 Easter Rising – are to be found in his 1972 piece 'No women playwrights'. Some of this article is taken up with what were at the time ubiquitous sexist jibes about 'the shriekings of Women's Lib movements' and 'les Dames aux burning bras', but Ó Floinn also raised the still pertinent question of why there have not been more Irish women writing for the stage. He also pondered whether women were submitting work to the Abbey Theatre that was being 'sniffily rejected by those expert judges of a paper play, the Abbey's paid readers'. He did, however, point out with some pride that of the four female dramatists who came to his mind – Máiréad Ní Ghráda, Christine Longford, Siobhán Ní Shúilleabháin, and Caitlín Maude – three of them wrote their plays in Irish (*IP*, 2/3/72).[31] Ó Floinn would never claim to be a feminist in the movement sense, but this brief piece remains one of the earliest contributions to a debate that continues to this day.

The mention of Ernest Blythe earlier and the dig at the 'expert judges of a paper play, the Abbey's paid readers' raises the question of Ó Floinn's own troubled relationship with the National Theatre. As we will see later, he began his career as a dramatist writing for the radio, with his first radio play, *Na Cimí* (The prisoners), broadcast over Radio Éireann in February 1952 (*IP*,

18/2/52).[32] This play was also given a single performance, directed by Ray McAnally, as part of the St Patrick's Day celebrations at the seminary at Maynooth that same year, and then later, according to Ó Floinn, by 'some amateur companies in Irish drama festivals and in some schools and colleges'.[33] Encouraged by this Maynooth production, Ó Floinn submitted the play to the Abbey, where it was rejected, with, as he tells us, 'no reason given'.[34] This rejection would set the pattern for his dealings with the Abbey from then on.

He did, however, get to see some of his work on the Abbey stage in this same year of 1952 when he collaborated with Tomás Mac Anna and others on that year's *geamaireacht*, *Setanta agus an Cú*, work for which he was paid £1 for each set of song lyrics he provided. By no means was he dismissive of the *geamaireachtaí*, recalling in *Consplawkus* that the Abbey's Gaelic pantomime was 'a regular outing for many families. Many parents were glad to find their rusty school Irish being revived and the children discovered that Irish could be a means of fun and entertainment instead of a mere school subject.' Furthermore, 'unlike those in other Dublin theatres, the Abbey pantomimes were based on Irish legends instead of being imitations of the British product based on English folktales'.[35] Unfortunately, however, when he realised he had been grossly underpaid for his work on *Setanta agus an Cú*, he rejected an offer to write the entire script for the next year's show, costing himself £100 or more rather than overlook the way he had been mistreated by Blythe.[36]

In 1962, Blythe and the Abbey rejected his play *Romance of an Idiot* (later renamed *Land of the Living*), explaining to Ó Floinn that the readers thought 'that this play would disgust the audience' (go gcuirfeadh an dráma seo déistean ar an lucht féachana).[37] Blythe also in 1966 rejected the one-act *Is Fada Anocht* (Tonight is long) despite the play having won an Oireachtas prize. Worst of all in Ó Floinn's mind was Blythe's unwillingness to have the Abbey produce *The Order of Melchizedek*, the English-language version of *Cóta Bán Chríost* and the play he regards as his most important literary work.[38] Nor can Ó Floinn have been pleased when, having entered three plays – *Is É a Dúirt Polonius*, *Cóta Bán Chríost*, and *Cad d'Imigh ar Fheidhlimidh?* (What happened to Feilimidh?) – in a competition to celebrate the opening of the new Peacock Theatre, he learned that none of his plays were regarded as worthy of the award, although *Is É a Dúirt Polonius* was given a 'consolation prize'.[39] Blythe did, however, accept one of Ó Floinn's plays, and in 1959 the Abbey produced *In Dublin's Fair City*, although to the author's considerable annoyance it was only given a two-week run before making way for that year's *geamaireacht*, and then returning for an additional week in February 1960.[40] It should, therefore, come as no surprise that Ó Floinn's final verdict on Blythe as expressed in *Consplawkus* is that 'whatever God intended this zealous and forthright man to be, it certainly was not anything to do with the arts, and especially with the theatre'. Indeed he once suggested that Blythe 'would have made an excellent manager of a yard producing concrete blocks'.[41]

If anything, he had worse professional relations with Tomás Mac Anna, who despite having directed his radio plays and worked with him on the 1952 Abbey *geamaireacht* would as artistic director of the Abbey reject several of his plays – *Solas an tSaoil* (an abbreviated Irish version of *The Light of the World*); the English versions of *Aggiornamento*, *Is É a Dúirt Polonius*, and *Homo Sapiens*; *The Creators*; and *A Man Called Pearse*. Ó Floinn addressed this situation in a 1970 piece in *The Irish Press* provocatively titled 'Dún Amharclann na Mainistreach!' (Close the Abbey Theatre!), in which he wrote: 'Therefore I would like to assert publicly, as a citizen and as a writer, that it is time . . . to close the Abbey Theatre. Anyone of you who does not understand by this time what I am driving at, is someone who is not even suitable for the job of theatre critic' (*IP*, 2/6/70).[42] Five years later, he returned to the subject, questioning the National Theatre's right to its title:

> But I am not speaking on my own behalf when I say that the Abbey has gone far from the goal that was laid down for the National Theatre. And I understand why it would displease the Directors of the Abbey when I tell the public that certain plays of my own that Mac Anna and his friends refused insultingly are succeeding very well. (*IP*, 18/2/75)[43]

Mac Anna remains a *bête noir* for Ó Floinn, who writes of him in *A Writer's Life* that 'whenever he had been in a position to do so Mac Anna had rejected the stage plays in Irish and English I submitted to the Abbey; also, as an adjudicator in the Oireachtas literary competitions, he had consistently deemed my entries unworthy of any reward'.[44] It is one of the great missed opportunities for Gaelic theatre that these two major figures never worked together except on the radio plays by Ó Floinn that Mac Anna directed in the early 1950s and their collaboration on the Abbey's *geamaireacht*. One can only wonder what Mac Anna would have done with a comedy like *Aggiornamento*, not to mention imaginative scripts like *Cad d'Imigh ar Fheidhlimidh?* or *Homo Sapiens*, had he been able to appreciate what Ó Floinn was creating.

We may now turn our attention to the plays themselves. Once again we will only be discussing Ó Floinn's plays in Irish, leaving aside the plays in English as well as the radio plays with which he began his career as a dramatist and his award-winning 1969 television play *Oileán Tearmainn* (Sanctuary Island). Of course some of those radio plays were also presented on stage and therefore will be considered here. As we have seen, *Na Cimí* was given a single performance at Maynooth in 1952, with Ray McAnally directing, and thereafter, according to Ó Floinn, 'by some amateur companies in Irish drama festivals and in some schools and colleges'.[45]The play has never been published, but the author offers the following succinct summary of its plot: '*Na Cimí* . . . was about the death of an Irish priest in the Korean war – several missionary priests had been murdered by the North Koreans.'[46] Given the considerable contemporary relevance of this play in 1952 when it was broadcast over Radio Éireann and staged at Maynooth, it is unfortunate that it was never produced by one of the major Gaelic companies in Dublin, Cork, or Galway. Another of his one-act radio plays, *Is Fada Anocht*, won a prize from the Arts Council, was first broadcast over Radio Éireann in March 1946 (*CE*, 14/3/56), and was published by An Gúm in 1968. Since the published text was clearly intended to make the play available for performance, and since it has been performed at least twice, by UCD's An Cumann Gaelach in 1968 (*II*, 26/2/68) and by Limerick's Buíon Phádraig at a festival in New Ross, Co. Wexford in 1971 (*ME*, 12/3/71), we will begin our discussion of the plays with *Is Fada Anocht*.

Set during 'the time of the Penal Laws' (aimsir na bPéindlíthe), the play takes place in Co. Limerick in the wretched hovel of Micheál Ó Conchubhair and his wife Máire, to which has come 'a poor wanderer' (siúlóir bocht). Micheál and Máire have no food, as the potato crop has failed throughout Munster. The tramp, however, arrives well fed after a stop at the house of the neighbouring Ó Mórdha family, who have converted to Protestantism to avoid starvation. Micheál is bitterly resentful of the converts, but Máire understands their motives and forgives them. Micheál takes great pride in the fact that he has been able to keep his name on at least some of his land, and he expects his son Piaras to do the same: 'He must keep hold of this place, keep the Ó Conchubhairs' possession safe until we get our rights.'[47]To prove his resolve, Micheál shows the tramp an old pistol he took from a dead enemy at the siege of Limerick in 1691.

That hope will soon be gone. Father and son have in the past argued over Piaras's love for the Protestant convert Síle Ní Mhórdha. Suddenly Síle herself enters and tells Micheál that she and Piaras have married 'in the presence of God, without a priest or a minister' (i láthair Dé, gan sagart, gan mhinister). Enraged, Micheál disowns his son and is unwilling to relent even when he learns he is to have a grandchild. When she says that she will now be able to help her husband's parents, Micheál rejects her offer, saying that God will provide for them and that she is 'a messenger of the devil' (teachtaire ag an diabhal). To make matters yet worse for Micheál, Síle tells him that Piaras is converting to Protestantism and will thus be legally entitled to take control of his father's land and so keep it in the family's name. Realising the painful pragmatism of Piaras's decision, the tramp urges Micheál and Máire to leave the farm to Piaras and join him on the road. Micheál's response is immediate and violent as he rejects the idea, grabs the pistol, and shoots Síle dead. At this point Piaras arrives, and Micheál drops the pistol, hangs his head, and says bitterly: 'Let him come now, and let him take his share in life.'[48]

Obviously Ó Floinn has packed a good deal of drama (and melodrama) into this little play, but there are also some ideas that must have set both radio listeners and those who saw the play thinking. First of all, in Micheál Ó Conchubhair, Ó Floinn created a character who, in the frightening intensity of his attachment to the land, anticipates the Bull McCabe in John B. Keane's 1965 play *The Field*. Second, it is significant that Síle, despite what orthodox Irish Catholic consensus would have regarded at the time as her apostasy, is a thoroughly decent and generous young woman as well as one who understands just why her family, herself, and Piaras have converted and would do it again in the circumstances facing her. Replying to the tramp's question why she will not return to Piaras's Catholic faith to marry him and presumably placate Micheál, she asks in return: 'Would you prefer four corpses on the hearth to three? And to find yourself by the ditch when you come again to this district, since there would be no one alive before you to offer you alms?'[49] Third and most provocative is Ó Floinn's suggestion that there are situations in which despair can be a more successful adaptive strategy than a hope beyond chance of realisation, an idea given explicit expression by Máire with regard to Micheál: 'It is a pity for so fine a man to be tormented by hope.'[50]

Is Fada Anocht is a competent one-act play, with a clear focus and characters quickly drawn but entirely credible. However it gives no indication of what was to come in Ó Floinn's next play, *Cóta Bán Chríost*, a full-length drama in what the author calls three 'movements' (gluaiseachtaí). The work apparently began as a novel before being begun again as a play in Irish that turned into a play in English with the title *The Order of Melchizedek*.[51] Ó Floinn then returned to and finished the Irish version as *Cóta Bán Chríost*.[52] As noted above, Ernest Blythe rejected *The Order of Melchizedek*, declaring that 'nobody likes the play here'. One of the Abbey's readers went further, calling it 'blasphemous and disgusting', while another said that it was 'vulgar and obscene'. A third added that 'the author is like a schoolboy who sets out to shock his elders; but the play succeeds only in being incredible and unacceptable in all senses'.[53] This English version of the play finally had its premiere at the Gate Theatre during the 1967 Dublin Theatre Festival. Critical reception was mixed. Writing in *The Irish Press*, 'J. J. E.' stated that 'I stayed after the first act only because it was my professional duty to do so . . . But I was glad that I remained,' adding that 'it is to the credit of playwright, producer and actors that the present play not only kept every seat filled, but provoked the most animated conversation between acts that I have ever heard'. Still, his final word on the evening was that Ó Floinn had written 'what I predict will be the most successful play of the festival – and one of the worst to appear in any festival to date. But it is a play that could not have been written by an inferior talent – only an exceptional skill with dialogue, situation and construction could have made this weird fable survive for three hours.' His hope was that Ó Floinn would go on 'to exploit his virtues as a creative writer and leave religious melodrama to the devil' (*IP*, 4/10/67). Desmond Rushe of the *Irish Independent* wrote that 'there is a good central idea and strong elements of surprise and conflict in Críostóir Ó Floinn's "The Order of Melchizedek" . . . but all its promising qualities are, unfortunately, completely crushed by an overpowering unreality. This play is a sincere and ambitious effort, but it is totally unconvincing' (*II*, 5/10/67).

Ó Floinn himself was enraged by what he saw on stage at the Gate, telling a Theatre Festival press conference that his work had been 'mutilated', that he had not written the opening or closing scenes, and that while the play held audiences in its altered form, it would 'do better when his version was staged' (*IP*, 5/10/67).[54] Commenting on the controversy in *The Mayo News* the following January, Risteárd Ó Glaisne wrote of the play that it was 'very interesting, but you could find many faults with it' (an-suimiúil, ach is iomaí locht a gheofá air) and then added rather prophetically given Ó Floinn's occasional later run-ins with theatre managements: 'The worst thing about all this controversy is that a theatre will be reluctant to take plays by Críostóir Ó Floinn at all if they think that he is difficult to deal with' (*MN*, 6/1/68).[55] Apparently Ó Floinn and the play's producer, Phyllis Ryan's Gemini Productions, came to an agreement by the end of its run, as we read in the *Irish Independent* that

> Mr. Criostoir O'Flynn . . . is now satisfied with the present staging of the prize-winning play 'The Order of Melchizedek' by Gemini Productions . . . Mr. O'Flynn had threatened to seek a Court injunction restraining production of the play in its Theatre Festival stage form . . . After seeing last night's production in the Gate Theatre, he said that the play had now reverted nearer to his script. (*II*, 31/10/67)[56]

The Irish version of the play, *Cóta Bán Chríost*, winner of a £200 prize for a full-length play at the 1966 Oireachtas as well as the prestigious Duais an Chraoibhín (The Douglas Hyde prize), had its premiere at An Damer in April 1969 with Noel Ó Briain directing. Judging the play for the Oireachtas competition, Walter Macken, the playwright, novelist, and former artistic director of Taibhdhearc na Gaillimhe, wrote: 'This play is very skillfully constructed and it has a powerful and original theme, but since there are only two characters, great care will be needed in casting and producing the play if the full impact of its unusual theme is not to be harmed.'[57] Judging from the reviews, critics seem to have felt the care that was taken was not altogether sufficient. Dominic O'Riordan declared: 'Not even the genius of

Noel Ó Briain, who produced the play, could redeem it from its basic obscurity. Dialogue is long and repetitive. *Taedium vitae* should not be tedious on stage' (*IT*, 9/4/69). 'É. Mac S.' (Éadhmonn Mac Suibhne) of *The Irish Press* compared the production to that of *The Order of Melchizedek* at the Gate, assuming the English version was translated from the Irish: 'I say at once that I think that the translation would be a better play than the original in this particular case . . . The production in the Damer does not reach the same depth: it does not reach, you could say, the hell of tragedy. It is drawn-out, wordy, especially in the first act . . .' (*IP*, 10/4/69).[58] On the other hand, the anonymous critic for the *Sunday Independent* wrote: 'When does an incredible and highly improbable drama become credible and even plausible? Answer – when it is produced in Irish! . . . The author has much to thank the cast for in achieving the transformation from the English version . . . while producer Noel Ó Briain works wonders on the small stage' (*SI*, 13/4/69). Most positive of all was the anonymous critic for *The Cork Examiner*, who in a very brief notice stated: 'It is . . . a very difficult play, with the balance very finely poised between drama and melodrama. In this fine production Noel Ó Briain manages to keep the balance; the result is very rewarding' (*CE*, 9/4/69).

A common feature in many of the reviews of both the English and Irish versions of the play was their insistence that *The Order of Melchizedek/Cóta Bán Chríost* was meant to be a realistic play and could therefore be judged on the plausibility of its depiction of the actions of real people in the real world. One could, however, argue that such a reading does the play an injustice. In fact, Ó Floinn wrote a play for which the criteria of conventional stage realism are largely irrelevant. In a 1961 piece entitled 'An púca san amharclann' (The pooka [hobgoblin] in the theatre), prompted by a recent Dublin production of Harold Pinter's *The Birthday Party*, Ó Floinn began: 'The pooka I see in the theatre is the author of the mystery play, this modern play in which it is not clear to anybody what is the top, what is the bottom or what is the middle except – I hope – the pooka who wrote it.' But he saw nothing new in this modern movement for 'life is the most mysterious mystery of all, and mystery and miracle were midwives when the Church brought the modern drama into the world in its medieval cradle.' The problem, he felt, was that twentieth-century writers and audiences were obsessed with the mundane 'mysteries' of the natural world and ignored those of the spiritual, and here is where he saw a special opportunity – and duty – for the Christian playwright: 'If it is true the mystery is in fashion in today's theatre, that should be a source of joy for the Christian writer. His bag or book is overflowing with mystery.' Moreover, he was guardedly optimistic about the possibility of a renaissance of genuine mystery plays: 'We will, perhaps, see the theatre again rising from the cradle from which it grew, mystery and faith' (*IP*, 23/5/61).[59]

Given his own strong lifelong allegiance to the Catholic Church – despite his serious disagreements with individual priests and bishops – it seems no stretch to read *Cóta Bán Chríost* (and, of course, *The Order of Melchizedek*) as modern mystery plays, a reading that makes a traditional realistic interpretation absurdly reductive.[60] In *Consplawkus*, Ó Floinn recalls one of the epiphanies that inspired the play. Seeing a priest reading on a train,

> I began to think about the unique place and function of the priest in human society. The priest claims to be a middleman between God and the rest of us. If there is a God, therefore, and if we are destined to go from this world to eternity, the priest is the most important person in the tribe; if there is no God and if we are merely rational animals, the priest is either a fool or a knave.[61]

In *Cóta Bán Chríost*, An tAthair Iúd Ó Conaire is certainly in human terms so foolish as to be all but incredible; the question Ó Floinn raises, however, is whether human reason can cope with what he sees as the deeper mysteries in life.

Cóta Bán Chríost is a difficult and challenging work. There are only two characters, both of whom are on stage for almost the entire three hours the play runs.[62] Moreover, the emotional level remains at a very high pitch from start to finish, giving the audience no relief, much less a welcome return to normalcy. But then Ó Floinn clearly does not want these characters, their situation, or the questions tormenting them to ever seem normal. We are far from the world of middle-class domestic drama here. Instead, we have been taken deep into the realm of enigmatic archetypes. Still, the opening of the play is mundane enough, as a young priest, An tAthair Iúd, is resting after having entertained his colleagues on Christmas Eve. Ó Floinn makes clear that Iúd is a decent, but hardly extraordinary man. Indeed he may even be a bit smug in his enjoyment of his clerical status and modest comforts:

> His satisfaction is in his grey eyes, and although he shows no trace of dissipation, it is certain that he could not have let this great day pass without tasting a drop at the Canon's urging. There is a greater than usual reason for his satisfaction tonight – the first Christmas for him as a parish priest, and he had the honour of being host and provider for the senior clergy of the neighbourhood.[63]

His comfortable world is, however, about to be shattered. Before his own entrance on stage, a young woman, 'looking cold and hungry . . . looking ghostly and moving in a dreamy, slow, almost angelic manner' (cuma fhuar ocrach uirthi . . . cuma thaibhsiúil agus imeacht bhrionglóideach fúithi, mall, ainglí nach mór), has snuck into the room. When he sees her he at first thinks she has come to bring him on a sick call or to beg for money, but when he comments that she does not look well, she responds: 'I look the same way that the Virgin did when she was turned away from the door of the inn. And I am in the same condition.'[64] Startled, he again tries to view the situation rationally, telling her that he is going to call the police to clear things up. Her response leaves him even more confused and troubled, as she says he is calling the police 'to protect you from the will of God' (chun tú a chosaint ar thoil Dé). The fact that she is able to quote from the gospels in answer to his scepticism only makes him more unsure of himself: 'It is a great pity that you were not sent to some level-headed man, a qualified man, the Canon, say. He would have had you out on the road before you would have had the chance to open your mouth at all.'[65] Her challenge to him is to be more of a man of God than is his superior: 'So be a priest now fully, and let your trust and your faith be constantly in the most high Lord who sent me to you to say . . . "My soul magnifies the Lord / And my spirit rejoices in God my Saviour".'[66] He is to be the Joseph to her Mary, 'pregnant without knowledge of a man' (torrach gan aithne fir). When he tells her he cannot believe her story, she responds with another challenge to his vocation: 'You ask the human race to believe the like every day. It should be easier for you to understand the will of God.'[67] Still unable to accept her story, but also unwilling to refuse her 'for fear that I refused his divine will' (le heagla gur dhiúltaíos dá thoil naofa), he lets her stay in the rectory for the night and suddenly feels 'as if a wave of peace were filling my soul' (mar a bheadh tonn suaimhnis ag líonadh isteach i m'anam).[68]

The next scene in the first act, or first 'movement' (gluaiseacht) as Ó Floinn calls it, occurs two months later. The young woman (who of course gives her name as Máire or Mary) is still living in the rectory, and An tAthair Iúd is as perplexed as ever, praying 'O Sacred Heart of Jesus, what am I to do? What is in store for me? I, your priest, wanting only to be a priest, to do your will. Is that what I am doing, or am I a laughing stock for the host of hell?'[69] Not surprisingly, his parishioners are beginning to see his arrangement with Máire as a source of scandal, but she continues to insist that what he is doing is according to God's plan, however incomprehensible that plan may be. His startling response is that he now sometimes envies atheists who are 'without any doubt at all, as calm and easy as your mind would be if your conscience were not being vexed from submitting to this Omnipotent God who knows everything and loves everyone and everything'.[70] By the third scene of this movement, his parishioners are insulting him and throwing rocks at Máire, and the bishop has ordered him to send her away. Rejected by all who had respected him, he believes that it is God's will that he leave the parish and take Máire with him.

As the second movement, 'Páis' (Passion), begins, we see An tAthair Iúd and Máire in a shabby urban flat in England.[71] She has dropped any pretence

to saintly humility, lashing out at the priest with, as she boasts, 'hatred –
black, devilish hatred' (fuath – fuath dubh diabhlaí): 'Die, *die*, I say, now, at
once! And if there were a hell it would be heaven to me to see you being
roasted there for all eternity, you and every other dirty deceiver of a priest
who is polluting this world for the human race!'[72] Seeing Iúd's anguish, she
revels in her deceit: 'I tricked you. I tricked the pious little priest of God. And
you will have to admit that I did so beautifully.'[73] Yet despite her contempt for
him and his faith, he continues to believe 'that God chose me for something'
(gur roghnaigh Dia mé do rud éigin).[74] In a stunning revelation, she tells him
there has been nothing personal in her malevolence towards him; rather,
'you were just a priest' (ní raibh ionatsa ach sagart).[75] She does, however,
admit that his treatment of her has surprised her, for she had expected him
to throw her out or to leave after her *volte-face*. Still, she insists that as long as
he stays she will do all in her power to torment and humiliate him.

In Máire, Ó Floinn created one of the handful of major roles for women
in Gaelic theatre, a role to test the capacity of anyone taking it on. And while
from what we have seen so far, she might seem entirely despicable, a one-
dimensional if intimidating villain, Ó Floinn now for the first time in the play
lets us see her deeply wounded humanity as, initially reluctant, she explains
to Iúd the reasons for her hatred of the Church and its priests. Her father was
an alcoholic actor who deserted her saintly mother, whose death she blames
on the Church. Moreover, she believes the Church inflicted what she calls
'yet more barbaric abuse on my brother' (íde níos barbartha fós ar mo
dheartháir), leaving him 'a dissipated, imbecilic fool' (amadán drabhlásach
éigiallda).[76] While the brother was home on holidays from the seminary, a
local woman attempted unsuccessfully to seduce him, and when she became
pregnant by another man, claimed Máire's brother as the father. Máire
relates how 'that bollix of a parish priest believed every word that foolish
whore told him; my brother was expelled with the curse of Rome, without a
chance to defend himself against the lying stories the celibate spies and their
little Mary Magdalenes created'.[77] The parish priest dismisses Máire's
mother from her teaching job in the local school, and the three head for life
in a city where they soon sink into alcoholic despair, with Máire herself
turning to prostitution and eventually seducing her brother, whom she
describes as having 'the body and the needs of a man . . . and the mind of a
child' (colainn agus riachtanas fir . . . agus aigne linbh). The child she is now
carrying is thus a product of incest. Yet in the midst of all this sordidness, she
still sees her brother and mother in terms of the religion in which she was
raised: 'I thought – I thought he was a priest, I say . . . A priest – the priest of
the sacrifice, the one suffering, gentle lamb of God whom the human race
would respect if they understood; and my mother was the Mother of Sorrow –
my mother – and never mind that Jewish banshee in your medieval

picture.'[78] The vengeance she is now inflicting on him as the present priest of the parish from which her mother was banished is thus ultimately rooted in the suffering of her family and her love for them.

When, however, she mocks him as 'the priest I put an end to' (an sagart ar chuir mise deireadh leis), he points out that what she claims to have done is impossible, for

> the priest's vocation is deeper than the round collar and the building where the sacrifice is made. To reveal the truth to you, girl, one cannot put an end to a priest. A priest for one day, a priest forever. Or perhaps you came upon this statement while you were cramming the Scriptures: 'You are a priest forever, according to the order of Melchizedek.'

His unearthly equanimity only further infuriates her, and she tells him that having lost the chance to abort her fetus when her plan took too long to play out, she now intends to kill the baby when it is born. In response, he offers to marry her to make the child 'legitimate' and tells her that by no means will he allow her to kill the child for 'it is the God of glory who is the source of every life, no matter how it is conceived. Every new child who comes into the world is Emanuel – "God in our midst".' Finally she does manage to shatter his self-restraint by saying that if his bishop offered him a chance to resume his parochial duties he would abandon her, go home, and grovel for forgiveness. Enraged, he strikes her, but she just says she prefers his anger to 'your sermonising' (do chuid seanmóireachta). She then challenges him to join her now in the six other deadly sins. After attempting unsuccessfully to seduce him, she says she will not harm the child if he will consummate their proposed marriage. As the second movement ends with her mocking laughter, An tAthair Iúd, overwhelmed 'under the burden of passion' (faoi ualach na páise), looks up 'in torment . . . as if he were seeking God' (go céasta . . . faoi mar a bheadh Dia á lorg aige) and echoing the crucified Christ, cries out 'God – God – why have you forsaken me?'[79]

The third movement, 'Aiséirí' (Resurrection), begins two months later. The flat has been made considerably brighter and more homely, a change that the weak and exhausted Máire notices on her return from giving birth to a daughter in hospital. Throughout this scene we see a different Máire emerging, able to laugh with Iúd about a neighbour's seeing a resemblance between Iúd and the baby, telling Iúd he will have a respite from her tongue while she recovers, and even beginning to feel love for the child. Moreover, she now seems to take an interest in Iúd as a person, and they are able to talk seriously about their lives. Indeed when he acknowledges to her that having agreed not to take the baby to church he has baptised her in secret, she replies jokingly: 'I am a woman who understands her man.'[80] However, though tacitly accepting that he says Mass every day, she continues to insist that she is an atheist. Nevertheless, she is now willing to recognise his priesthood, even admitting: 'Do you know, Iúd, I imagine that my brother would have been like you if – if he had been –'[81]

At this point, this very unorthodox play would appear to be moving towards a very orthodox and even sentimental conclusion, an ending Máire herself is obviously beginning to see as possible when she says to Iúd, 'If – if you succeed in getting another job, we could buy a little bed for this room. That ugly couch – Iúd, are you – are you cross with me.'[82] Such an ending would, of course, turn the play into an unlikely love story rather than the exploration of the priestly vocation that Ó Floinn set out to write. Instead, despite Máire confessing her love for him, An tAthair Iúd tells her he plans to leave her 'as soon as you are able to do for yourself' (chomh luath is a bhíonn tú ábalta ar dhéanamh duit féin).[83] In the final scene a fortnight later, he is sadly preparing to depart the next day and promising to support her and the child 'as long as you need it' (fad atá gá agaibh leis). As he goes to work on their final night as a couple, she for the first time calls him her 'love' (grá). Then, alone with the baby, she hangs the picture of the Virgin Mary she has never let him put up, seals the windows and door, and turns on the gas, killing herself and her child. The play ends with a voice-over reading the note she leaves for him, a note in which she sets him free, while An tAthair Iúd, having asked God to impose on him any guilt for her actions, begins to say his daily Mass. For many today, this conclusion may seem cold, almost smug, with the priest shirking his real-world human obligations to satisfy the demands of the vocation that gives meaning to his own life. But for Ó Floinn and other believers, Iúd's actions are clearly a heroic affirmation of his commitment to God and his priesthood in face of the most profound challenges imaginable. Certainly any audience will leave this play with more than enough to ponder. Unfortunately, however, few audiences have had that opportunity, for given the play's controversial subject matter, the demands it makes on its two actors, and its considerable length, it has had, as far as I can determine, just one revival, by the company Na Fánaithe at Dublin's Focus Theatre in August 1989.[84]

In order to devote a unified discussion to the issues raised by both the English and Irish versions of this play, I have left aside until now Ó Floinn's full-length comedy *Aggiornamento*,[85] which had its premiere between the productions of *The Order of Melchizedek* in October 1967 and *Cóta Bán Chríost* in April 1969. *Aggiornamento* was first performed at An Damer in May 1968 with Noel Ó Briain directing. The play would be quite popular, with major revivals at An Taibhdhearc in 1970, An Damer in 1971, the Everyman Theatre in Cork in 1972, and, on tour by the group Na Stocairí, at 20 venues around Ireland, also in 1972.[86] Ó Floinn submitted an English-language version of the play to the Abbey, where it was rejected (*IP*, 18/7/72). This English version of the play, with the title *Legion of the Rearguard*, was eventually shown on Telefís Éireann in November 1975.[87] It was broadcast over Radio Éireann in 1980 (*II*, 4 and 11/10/80).

The critics liked *Aggiornamento*. Writing of the premiere at An Damer in the *Irish Times*, Dominic O'Riordan declared: 'In this new play by Críostóir Ó Floinn sophistication joins naiveté in a mad, splendid riot of argument . . . It is one of the wittiest plays I have seen for a long time.' O'Riordan was particularly impressed by the success of Noel Ó Briain's decision to stage the play in the round: 'This is in every sense theatre in the round and Noel Ó Briain, who produces it without a whit of the facilities available to other theatres, creates in the Damer a sense of drama and movement, which underlines every word of the play. Never was a playwright better served, seldom a play in Irish better to be served' (*IT*, 22/5/68). 'Seán Mac C.' wrote: 'There is a strong vein of compassion in the play and a timely understanding of the (eternal?) problem of communication between the generations.' He also declared that 'the whole audience was caught in the author's clever trap', and he urged his readers to see 'this very enjoyable show before it is translated into English (French, Japanese) on the television for the masses or turned into a big, "tender", technicolour film and lost its great good heart' (an tseó rí-thaitneamhach seo sul a mbíonn sé aistrithe go Béarla (Fraincis, Seapáinis) ar an teilifís don daoscarshlua, nó ina scannán mór 'bog' ildaite a mbeidh a chroí maith mór caillte aige!' (*Indiu*, 31/5/68).[88] Liam Ó Lonargáin praised Ó Floinn for 'a fine flow in the writing (very witty and clever dialogue)' (an-sruth sa scríbhneoireacht (agallamh thar a bheith deisbhéalach agus aibí)), adding: 'Ó Floinn artistically bound the tragedy and the irony with the wittiness. Indeed, I could make a very long list of the things I liked about the play, not to mention the production and the acting' (*Feasta*, June 1968, p. 27).[89]

Ó Lonargáin was, however, disappointed by An Damer's revival of the play three years later with Noel Ó Briain again directing: 'The main fault I found, however, was how similar this production was to the one we saw in 1968. They were almost identical, act for act and scene for scene. The cast was the same, part for part . . .' Still, he could add:

> And as I give that judgement I understand well that the play gave pleasure to many who were present . . . I myself enjoyed it as well. People will say that *Aggiornamento* fell short this time not as a play but by comparison. I would not say but that there could well be a good deal of truth in that. (*Feasta*, Feb. 1971, p. 20)[90]

The anonymous critic for *The Irish Press* also noted that the 1971 production was little changed from that of 1968, but seems to have been less troubled by this lack of innovation than was Ó Lonargáin, writing: 'Three years ago, Noel Ó Briain directed "Aggiornamento" in the Damer and he created a sensation. It is a bold person who would say that he did not create another sensation when he directed the same play there last night' (*IP*, 7/1/71).[91] In his review of the 1971 production, 'E. de B.' (doubtless Earnán P. de Blaghd, the son of Ó Floinn's nemesis at the Abbey) called *Aggiornamento* 'this most entertaining play', adding: 'If you missed its first performance in 1968, you might well do worse with your time than come to its "Aggiornamento"' (*II*, 6/1/71).

It is easy to see why *Aggiornamento* was popular with both audiences and critics at the time. Ó Floinn shows a real gift for comedy in this play, and that comedy is directed at what was a centrally important issue in Irish society in the 1960s and 1970s. Dublin's formidable Archbishop John Charles McQuaid had notoriously returned from the Second Vatican Council in 1965 to tell Ireland's Catholics: 'You may have been worried by much talk of changes to come. Allow me to reassure you. No change will worry the tranquillity of your Christian lives.'[92] He was, of course, wrong, and the changes set in motion by Pope John XXIII's call for *aggiornamento* (bringing up to date) in the Catholic Church were to reshape Irish Catholicism as well as many other aspects of Irish life in the decades that followed Vatican II. Ó Floinn's *Aggiornamento* is by no means an in-depth analysis of this religious and cultural transformation, but it does offer a witty, warm, and generous look at what movements of world significance could mean to the ordinary people eventually affected by them.

The central characters in the play are Seán Ó Murchú and his sidekick Máirtín Mac Áis, two ageing veterans of the War of Independence and the Civil War. They are also long-time and now sole members of the board of St Patrick's Temperance Society in their parish in a provincial town.[93] Their lives are turned upside-down when a new curate is made chairman of the board and decides to change the way the two old men have done – or largely failed to do – things in the past. Left alone by their former clerical chairman, the two friends limited the society's activities to running a billiard room and providing themselves with a place to go and a certain status in their own minds if not in the local community. The new chairman, An tAthair Ó hAicín, arrives with all sorts of terrifying new ideas. He is going to enlarge the board to 12 members, create a development plan, update the hall's reading room, begin keeping minutes for the first time in many years, and, most shockingly, organise dances – and not traditional Irish ones – in the hall. In effect, as he tells Seán and Máirtín: 'I am going to recommend to the bishop that this place be fully renovated.'[94] *Aggiornamento* has come with a vengeance to St Patrick's Temperance Society.

Seán and Máirtín try to temper An tAthair Ó hAicín's zeal for change by agreeing that the hall could use a few renovations – 'a little bit of paint here and there, I'd say that's what you had in mind, chairman?' (blúirín péinte anseo is ansiúd, is dócha, b'in a raibh ar intinn agat, déarfainnse, a chathaoirligh?).[95] Of course the priest has much bigger plans: 'I have decided to start a club in this building, a club for the young people of the parish, yes and for the young people of the whole town.' Naturally, the old men have no intention of surrendering to him: 'Good enough so, Father, if you intend to provide those young people with this Club. Go ahead, yourself and those young people, and make that place for yourselves as we had to do when we were young in this town and needed a place . . .'[96]

In the second act, set a week later, we again see the old men's place in a changing Ireland called into question. Peadar Óg Ó Cionna is the fiancé of Seán's daughter Siobhán and also the temperance society's solicitor, a job he inherited from his own father. Peadar is very much a man on his way up, one for whom the patriotic actions of Seán and Máirtín were a form of madness. He is particularly distressed that during the War of Independence the flying column Seán commanded burned a big house in the area, a house Peadar thinks might have made a fitting home for himself and his new bride. An tAthair Ó hAicín is also ambivalent about their service in the national cause, and when the custodian of the temperance hall tells him that Seán's brother was killed by the Black and Tans, we are told of the priest's reaction in a sly stage direction: 'Perhaps he thinks it a pity that Seán hadn't died for Ireland instead of his brother.'[97] The old men briefly think they have defeated another invader in the person of An tAthair Ó hAicín, but they are soon disabused of this idea when the priest informs them that the temperance society is now defunct, replaced by what will become 'Club N. Doiminic Savio'. Seeing themselves as latter-day Fenians again facing repudiation by the Church, Seán and Máirtín declare war – 'the trumpet sounded, the flag on high!' (an stoc séidte, an bhratach in airde!).[98] Their first plan is to sue the bishop, but they can get neither Peadar Óg Ó Cionna nor even a local Protestant lawyer to take the case. Among the results of this failed attempt is that Siobhán sides with her father and breaks off her engagement with Peadar.

When the old men go to take a look at the renovated hall, they are greeted by a sign announcing a dance featuring the music of 'Binky and the Bongos'. Scandalised, they beat a quick retreat to a pub to devise a new plan of campaign. Máirtín has even brought his old revolver from his active service days, but Seán reminds him that they tried that strategy without success in the Civil War. Instead, he says that they will advance their cause with cash – the more than £300 that they have tucked away out of the billiard fees and that will now get them to Rome to appeal to the Pope himself. Covering their tracks by telling everyone that they are making a pilgrimage, they head off confidently to the Eternal City.

At this point, Ó Floinn cleverly divides the stage into three separate 'little scenes' (mionradhairc) to be lit one after the other, although he also adds a note that the director could 'break them or mix them to get a heightened effect from the whole thing' (iad a bhriseadh nó a mheascadh chun barr éifeachta a bhaint as an iomlán).[99] The first of these scenes shows An tAthair Ó hAicín smugly presiding at a meeting of his new board. Another has Seán and Máirtín drinking wine in a café in Rome, 'trying to make conversation with a pair of Italians, young women who are not members of any club or society at all under the influence of Dominic Savio' (ag iarraidh comhrá a dhéanamh le beirt Iodáileach, mná óga nach bhfuil ina mbaill de chlub ná le cumann ar bith atá faoi thionchar Dhoiminic Savio).[100] In the third, Peadar and Siobhán, now reconciled, are sitting in the moonlight looking at the site of the burned big house where they will soon be building their own good-sized residence and puzzling over the photographs Seán has sent from Rome, photos in which the two old friends most certainly do not look like pilgrims. As the play ends, all three scenes are illuminated simultaneously. Intentional and thematic anticlimax is a regular feature of Irish drama in both Irish and English, and here we see it again, neatly underscoring the point that even as these two old Irishmen think they are fighting change, they are being swept along with it.[101] But then again, this genial and entertaining play suggests that that need not be a bad thing after all.

There is nothing amusing or genial in Ó Floinn's next play, *Is É a Dúirt Polonius*, which, as *Beatha Duine a Thoil* (To each his own), won a 'special prize of recognition' at the 1965 Oireachtas (*II*, 27/9/65) and was first produced, with Frank Bailey directing, at the Peacock in May 1968. Ó Floinn hated the production, and the reviews were strikingly mixed. Liam Ó Lonargáin wrote: 'Ó Floinn handles his theme straightforwardly and simply. He creates a good number of his characters convincingly . . . The author presented his theme straightforwardly throughout the play, restraining himself within the boundaries of the theme' (*Feasta*, June 1968, p. 25).[102] Writing in *Inniu*, 'D. P. F.' found Ó Floinn's theme both relevant and 'very interesting' (an-spéisiúil) and praised him for his ability 'to convey some of his thoughts effectively' (roinnt dá chuid smaointe a chur in iúl go héifeachtach). On the other hand, he thought the play was 'too neat' (ró-néata): 'It is almost a sermon. It is too obvious throughout the play that the scenes are just examples to prove the author's thesis.' As a result, 'I missed the conflict that is necessary in a play of this sort – the conflict between good, half-good, and evil.' His conclusion was 'that Críostóir Ó Floinn has the ability to write a better play – on the same theme' (go bhfuil sé ar chumas Chríostóir Uí Fhloinn dráma níos fearr a scríobh – ar an téama céanna) (*Inniu*, 17/5/68).[103] Dominic O'Riordan was more enthusiastic in the *Irish Times*: 'The matter of this play is very important – the uselessness of a man facing a paper society, the stupidity of men with irrevocable documents, provided there is a signature on them, and the H. P. Kathleen Mavourneen system of modern Ireland where men can live on the air, future and promise crammed.' For O'Riordan, 'this is a delicate and sensitively thin play about the dilemma of a man, spreadeagled by the current jargon of our innate [*sic*] and inbred society' (*IT*, 13/5/68). O'Riordan's use of the word 'thin' in such a positive review is odd. There is, however, no confusion in the way Éadhmonn Mac Suibhne uses the Irish equivalent *tanaí* in a brief note on the play in *The Irish Press*: 'I must say that "Is é Dúirt Polonius" disappointed me more than a little. The play itself was thin, but the production did not help at all' (*IP*, 22/5/68).[104] 'R. Ó C.' of the *Irish Independent* was also unimpressed: 'Audiences who were electrified – or simply shocked – by Críostóir Ó Floinn's "The Order of Melchizedek" will find the theme of his play "Sé a Dúirt Polonius" . . . rather disappointingly dull' (*II*, 13/5/68).

Reviewing the published text in 1975, Ó Floinn's fellow playwright Eoghan Ó Tuairisc was utterly dismissive. Having rather formulaically acknowledged that it is difficult to judge how well a play will work on stage by simply reading the dialogue, he went on to make just such a judgement: 'No matter what power of imagination the reader would have, it would be difficult for him to have a visionary reading experience with this dialogue. There is not as much as a single statement that would lure him to provide the author with the "unwilling [*sic*] suspension of disbelief".'[105] Ó Tuairisc found 'the same mechanical speech in the mouth of every speaker, a neutral speech, neither English nor Irish, not the living speech of a woman nor the blather of a man, nor any example at all of the living dialects of the human race'.[106] Indeed he saw all the characters in the play as 'ghosts' (taibhsí), their sole individuality 'the name that is given them in the script' (an t-ainm a chuirtear leo sa script). And he was not done: 'They are all thin "typicalities", imposters, without the least little breath of deviltry or angelic quality or humanity to be noticed in their speech.' Nor did he feel the play was redeemed by either its plot or theme, 'the dramatic web in which these types are caught' (an líonra drámata ina gcastar na típeanna seo): 'When the characters are not clear from the speech so that they make an impression on the imagination I do not care in the least about the story that the author is trying to tell about them' (*Comhar*, Apr. 1975, pp 10–11).[107]

Of course *Is É a Dúirt Polonius* is neither as important as O'Riordan claimed nor as dull and inert as it seemed to 'R. Ó C.' and Ó Tuairisc. Once again, the problem might well be that those who dismissed it were judging it by inappropriate standards. In effect *Is É a Dúirt Polonius* is not a realistic play of modern life, but rather a contemporary morality play with exaggerated, semi-allegorical characters and stark moral choices.[108] The question of the play's success may thus be rephrased as: was this a morality play relevant to the Ireland of 1968 (and after)? As noted above, Ó Floinn himself has made clear that the play was based on his own experiences fighting the bureaucracy of the Irish Tourist Board, but it also has considerably greater ambition as a critique of the soulless regimentation of modern Irish, indeed modern global, social organisation. Thus while all of his characters are based on real people – the protagonist an easily recognisable representation of himself – they are also, and quite intentionally, presented as the types or 'typicalities' of which Ó Tuairisc was so critical. As a personal story of institutional injustice, *Is É a Dúirt Polonius* is both interesting and moving; as a depiction of how modern society uses people and tries to break those who resist, it becomes an indictment of a way of life to which we have often without reflection become accustomed. Here Ó Floinn's idealistic – and, to be fair, on more than one occasion self-righteous – protagonist becomes Everyman, 'The Lone Person' (An Duine Aonar). Diarmaid Ó Rodaí – and, as we saw in Ní Ghráda's *Mac Uí Rudaí*, 'Ó Rodaí' is the Gaelic name for just such an Everyman – wants only to make an honest living according to the terms on which he was hired into the state bureaucracy. Instead, he finds himself entangled in the machinations of characters who, without ever losing credibility altogether, have become allegorical figures: the ruthlessly ambitious middle manager, the unabashedly treacherous co-worker, the hypocritically self-serving union offical, the maliciously envious neighbour – but also the genuinely Christian Dr Mac Cofaigh and Bráthair Mac an Rí.

The play begins with the over-qualified Diarmaid expecting, as he had been promised, to be made permanent in his post after a trial period, with a pay increase of £30 a year. Among his co-workers at the office is the noisome Jimmy Ó Sí, a lazy and crudely sexist hypocrite who flatters Diarmaid when Diarmaid thinks he might be promoted: 'If there were justice to be gotten, it is you who would be a Manager, you who have degrees and qualifications that the schemer above doesn't have a whiff of.'[109] Diarmaid soon learns that instead of being made permanent he will be kept on for a further trial period at the same pay. With debts piling up at home and his children needing a doctor, he decides to take a stand against what he calls 'The Declaration of Bondage' (Forógra na Daoirse), telling his wife: 'That's management for you, little woman! They leave me alone for a year, and then twenty-four hours to make a choice between the will of the Directors and my own will, between the fat lie and the thin truth.' And he knows full well the odds facing him: 'I know, Eibhlín, dear, that if I do not agree to it we will be without a job. But – they also say, to each his own.'[110]

That sliver of hope leads him to fight the bureaucracy for what he believes is his due. First, he goes to speak with an official of his union, a man who, as Ó Floinn makes clear in a stage direction, is the mirror image of

Diarmaid's boss: 'The Official is sitting at his desk, talking on the telephone, just like the section manager when Diarmaid went to talk with him . . . The position of this Official is on the same level of power and salary as the position of that manager in the other organisation.'[111] Moreover, despite the union man's bluster about the oppression of workers in Ireland's 'Christian Democracy' (Daonlathas Críostaí), he offers Diarmaid no practical assistance whatsoever. Indeed he is far more interested in having Diarmaid help him by recruiting more members for the union from among his office mates. One of those office mates, Jimmy Ó Sí, is even less helpful, hypocritically sympathising with Diarmaid, denouncing their superiors, and urging him to get a copy of 'Staff Regulations' (Rialacha Foirne), a document that, as Diarmaid learns, applies only to permanent staff. After commiserating with and 'advising' Diarmaid, Jimmy immediately phones one of the bosses to report on what Diarmaid is doing to challenge management's decision.[112]

Despite his wife's concern about what his stand will mean for himself and his family, Diarmaid is still unwilling to surrender his principles: 'But if I submit now – Eibhlín, my love, I cannot submit to them. I am not going to put my name to a slander on myself and accept a punishment that I have not deserved.'[113] Unable to find another job, Diarmaid turns to the law for protection, only to be again disabused of his idealism by the solicitor he consults: 'Think about that also, Mr. Ó Rodaí. Whatever other benefit there is in this profession of ours, it teaches us that there are great, wicked criminals who are esteemed and honoured, while there are decent people suffering injustice and torment . . .' Indeed the solicitor warns Diarmaid that taking the matter to court could result in his being charged for initiating 'a false case against honest people out of malice and a desire to slander them' (cúis bhréagach in aghaidh daoine macánta le neart mailíse agus d'fhonn clúmhilleadh a dhéanamh orthu).[114] His advice to Diarmaid is to emigrate to England, get work, and then bring his family to join him.

By now desperately in need of spiritual as well as material sustenance, Diarmaid goes to see his old teacher An Bráthair Mac an Rí. As they converse in the monastery, the brother offers strong support for Diarmaid's decision not to submit to his superiors and asks innocently, 'Isn't it like the stories we used to hear about the Communist countries?' An Bráthair Mac an Rí insists that his friend take his protest to the highest levels of government, for 'It is no petty matter, Diarmaid; it is a question of human rights and integrity. It doesn't just concern you, but also every person in the country, the generations to come, the human race.'[115] Inspired by the brother's words, Diarmaid shares a secret with him: 'I will tell you the strange thought that came to me – that it is likely that the men who went out to fight in the 1916 Rising were suspected like that . . .'[116] When he apologetically adds 'not that I am comparing myself with those heroes' (ní hé go bhfuil mé do mo chur i gcomparáid leis na gaiscígh sin), An Bráthair Mac an Rí interjects: 'And why wouldn't you?' (Agus cad ina thaobh nach gcuirfeá?). For Mac an Rí, Diarmaid's duty is clear. Having invoked the example of religious suffering in anonymity in communist prisons or that of those communists who dared to speak out against their governments, he continues: 'If you make a sacrifice for the cause of justice, your hardship – and I consider the hardship of your dependants as part of what you will have to suffer – that is like the torment the servants of the devil inflicted on the human body of the Son of God, may He be forever praised.'[117] On a less exalted note, he then adds that he will write on Diarmaid's behalf to a government minister he once taught.[118]

When he finally gets to present his case to a board made up of precisely those people whose decision is now under review, Diarmaid is presented as a martyr in a just but lost cause.[119] A stage direction here compares him to 'Joan of Arc on her stool before the committee of the inquisition' (Jeanne d'Arc ar a stóilín i láthair choiste na cúistiúnachta).[120] Yet despite his full awareness that his appeal is doomed, Diarmaid feels 'joy in his spirit' (lúchair ar a sprid), a sense 'that this appeal is a fulfillment of the sacrifice that shapes a person's integrity' (gur comhlíonadh an t-achomharc seo ar an íobairt a mhúnlaíonn ionracas an duine).[121] But when he attempts to turn the discussion to the moral issues at stake, his judges dismiss such concerns as altogether irrelevant. Nor is he any more successful when he argues that they are 'trying to save money and leave me with no respect for myself . . . trying to keep from me what I have earned and my rights, something that is against the law of God and the law of the country' (ag iarraidh airgead a shábháil agus mise a fhágáil gan meas orm féin . . . ag iarraidh mo luach saothair agus mo cheart a choimeád uaim, rud atá in aghaidh dhlí Dé agus dhlí na tíre).[122] He is, of course, right, but as he knows well by now, that will make no difference at all.[123]

In the final scene of the play, we see Diarmaid boarding the ship that will take him to England and exile. Here, for the first time, Ó Floinn allows his protagonist to surrender to the kind of doubts he must have fought to suppress throughout the play: 'Was it worth it –? Perhaps I am just a pompous fool, a stubborn brat, a beetle under the feet of fate. O moon and stars, what is in store for me, for myself, for my wife and for the children we brought into the world? And what is in store for our descendants?'[124] The play ends with a chorus of voices, the voices of all who have had to emigrate, the voices with which he will soon join his own as another lost Irish soul.[125]

The very power of this ending may help explain what some of the critics found disappointing about the play. Our final, wrenching view of Diarmaid Ó Rodaí as a conflicted and questioning human being is at cross-purposes with his consistent depiction as a rather one-dimensional allegorical figure in the contemporary morality play that is *Is É a Dúirt Polonius*. As a result, the other characters can seem in retrospect even more flat and unrealistic, as indeed they are and, in terms of the play's subgenre, should be. Every character but Diarmaid is meant to be seen as one of T. S. Eliot's 'hollow men . . . stuffed men' or, perhaps better, as the rootless bureaucrats of many of Máirtín Ó Direáin's poems or a paper-pushing nonentity like 'J' in Máirtín Ó Cadhain's story 'An Eochair' (The key). Unfortunately, our brief encounter with the more fully rounded Diarmaid of the play's conclusion can make us remember those other characters as, to use the critics' word, 'dull'. On the other hand, it may just be that with rare exceptions morality plays no longer have the power to move modern audiences more interested in psychological complexity than moral clarity. At any rate, apart from a revival directed by Seán Stafford and featuring Mick Lally at Taibhdhearc na Gaillimhe in 1972 (*IP*, 7/10/72), *Is É a Dúirt Polonius* seems to have been largely forgotten by Irish theatre companies.[126]

Cóta Bán Chríost and *Is É a Dúirt Polonius* were two of the three plays Ó Floinn submitted to the Abbey's competition to celebrate the opening of the new Peacock Theatre in 1967. Unlike the other two works, the third play he submitted, *Cad d'Imigh ar Fheidhlimidh?* has never been produced, a remarkable fact, given the play's quality, originality, and the chronic shortage of stageworthy scripts in Irish.[127] In *A Writer's Life*, Ó Floinn refers to this work as 'a very complicated Irish play based on *Táin Bó Cuailnge* [The cattle raid of Cooley]' and 'my play on *Táin Bó Cuailnge*'. The *Táin*, as it is commonly known, is the great Irish epic tale, some of which dates to as early as the eight century, although the oldest – and quite different – manuscript versions of it we have are from the twelfth century. The *Táin* is the story of a great cattle raid into Ulster by 'the men of Ireland' assembled and led by queen Medb ('Maeve') of Connacht and her consort Ailill, assisted by a band of Ulster exiles under the former king of Ulster Fergus mac Róich. Because the Ulster king Conchobar, who had once been Medb's husband, and his warriors have been laid low by a mysterious affliction that incapacitates Ulstermen when they are in greatest danger, the province is defended single-handedly for months by the teenaged hero Cú Chulainn, who is not a full-blooded Ulsterman and is thus exempt from the affliction. The tale recounts the extraordinary feats of the young Cú Chulainn, leading up to the recovery of the Ulstermen and their victory over Medb, Ailill, and Fergus in a great battle.[128] Associated with this central text is a collection of so-called *remscéla* or introductory stories that provide information about the events leading up to the great raid itself. By far the most famous of these *remscéla* is *Longes Mac nUislenn* (or its later variant *Oidheadh Mac nUisnigh*), far more commonly known as the Deirdre story.

In the original scheme, this story is primarily intended to explain why Fergus and the other Ulstermen have gone into exile to assist the

Connachtmen against their own king. The story tells of how Conchobar and his entourage go to a feast at the house of the storyteller Feidhlimidh. There the fetus in the womb of the storyteller's wife screeches and the druid Cathbad predicts the child will be a girl and will bring destruction on the kingdom. The Ulstermen want to have the fetus destroyed, but they are over-ruled by Conchobar, who plans to have the child raised to be his wife. The girl is kept in isolation until she is a young woman, but one day she sees and falls in love with the youthful warrior Noísiu and compels him, and his two brothers, to carry her away to Scotland. There Deirdre and Noísiu live happily as man and wife, although the brothers miss Ireland and their warrior com-rades. Meanwhile, Conchobar decides – to take advantage of the desire of his men to recall the brothers – to send Fergus with promise of safe conduct home. The gullible Fergus accepts the responsibility of guaranteeing their safety, but is then tricked by Conchobar into sending them on while he himself stays behind at a feast. Shortly after their arrival at the court of Conchobar, the brothers are killed on Conchobar's orders, causing Fergus to fly into a rage, slaughter many of Conchobar's men, and leave for Connacht with his own followers. Grief-stricken, Deirdre commits suicide.[129] Not surprisingly, it is this passionate love story with its familiar triangle of beautiful young woman, powerful older suitor, and young, handsome lover, that has inspired generations of Irish writers, among them Yeats, Synge, George Russell ('AE'), Eva Gore-Booth, James Stephens, and most recently Vincent Woods. It also provides the inspiration for Ó Floinn's 'very complicated Irish play based on *Táin Bó Cuailnge*'.

In a preface to the published play, Ó Floinn explains that unlike most writers who have adapted this story – James Stephens would be an exception here – he wanted to keep 'that great drama that happened between Meadhbh and Conchúr' (an dráma mór sin a tharla idir Meadhbh agus Conchúr) as part of his play. He also notes that since in Gaelic Ireland 'the theatre of the imagination in the mind of the storyteller and the audience' (amharclann na samhlaíochta in aigne an scéalaí agus an lucht éisteachta) had taken the place of 'the formal theatre' (an amharclann fhoirmiúil), 'I took the director in the theatre as a storyteller who is presenting stories to his audience as entertainingly and as artistically as he can'.[130] Moreover, he specifically linked Conchobar's storyteller in the play, Feidhlimidh, with the director 'by means of the art of the theatre' (trí mheán ealaín na hamharclainne). Significantly, he makes clear in this preface that while 'certain people' (daoine áirithe) who had read the play told him 'that there should be some particular play being rehearsed by the actors, and that that play should have a connection with the story of Deirdre etc.' (gur chóir go mbeadh dráma éigin faoi leith á chleachtadh ag na haisteoirí, agus baint a bheith ag an dráma sin le scéal Dheirdre srl.), he regarded that as 'an inartistic point of view . . . something . . . that would ruin altogether this attempt of mine to make a match between this classic of the Irish language and the living art of the theatre in terms of our time' (dearcadh neamhealaíonta . . . rud . . . a mhillfeadh ar fad an iarracht seo agam ar chleamhnas a dhéanamh idir chlasaic seo na Gaeilge agus ealaín bheo na hamharclainne i dtéarmaí ár linne).[131]

Obviously there was a reason Ó Floinn called this 'a very complicated Irish play'. Like Seán Ó Tuama's *Iúdás Iscariot agus a Bhean*, it is a meta-theatrical piece in which the characters' lives on the stage and their real lives are interwoven. Unlike Ó Tuama, however, Ó Floinn limits his set to 'a theatre stage' (stáitse amharclainne) while expanding his time frame to 'now and long ago' (anois agus fadó).[132] As the play opens, the director and his cast are taking a break from rehearsing a play the director finds 'as tepid as urine . . . old manner, old style, old, old and worn-out' (chomh leamh le fual . . . sean-nós, seanstíl, sean, sean seanchaite).[133] Still, he is resigned to directing it, for 'It is probably a good thing that, however bad, it exists; plays in Irish are so scarce.'[134] Pondering what a genuine Gaelic drama would have become 'if the English had left us alone' (dá ligfeadh na Sasanaigh dúinn), he asks 'Where is the Irish-language Yeats, who would give us a stirring, poetic version of the beautiful ancient stories?' In response, 'Actor A' points out 'that we have long dealt mockingly with those ancient heroic stories in the Christmas *geamaireachtaí*. Wouldn't it be difficult for the audience to accept them as serious now?' (go bhfuil na seanscéalta gaisce sin seanphléite againn go scigiúil sna geamaireachtaí Nollag. Nár dheacair don lucht féachana glacadh leo anois i ndáiríre?).[135]

For the director, however, this problem is a challenge to their artistry: 'Isn't it the essence of our craft that the audience will accept anything if we present it to them artistically?'[136] A glance at a lovely young actress brings to his mind 'Deirdre . . . Deirdre of the sorrows. The beauty . . . the youth . . . the innocence . . . and . . . the loneliness, the lust, the love . . . Death . . . Deirdre . . . she . . . would make . . . ah, if we had the script!'[137] The actor who dismissed the ancient tales as now appropriate only as source material for *geamaireachtaí* finds the director's enthusiasm absurd: 'Yerra, forget about Deirdre! Isn't that theme the most worn-out theme of them all – Yeats, Synge, AE, Samuel Ferguson – yes, and Donagh Mac Donagh, the son of Thomas who died for Ireland.'[138] For the director, however, the work of these writers has been a poor attempt at cultural appropriation: 'Didn't some of those boys nicely and easily earn plenty of money putting English-language rags on an Irish-language body!'[139] He then begins to set a very different scene in the imaginations of those around him: 'If we had a magic lamp, or a time machine, that would turn us back . . . back . . . back . . . how would the story strike us? Does anyone of you at all have the beginning of the story, or have your memories been destroyed altogether by this contemporary popular culture of ours?'[140] As 'Actor B' recites the opening of *Longes Mac nUislenn,* a young woman, apparently called forth from the collective Irish unconscious, steps onto the stage. She is, of course, Deirdre, and the director and actors immediately assume roles in her story, with 'Actor B', for example, declaring: 'I am Feidhlimidh, Conchobar's storyteller. I tell appropriate stories for pay.'[141] As this story unfolds, the other characters from the ancient tale – Conchúr, Cathbhadh, Fearghas, Meadhbh *et al.* – appear on stage and act out the speaker's narrative 'in the back, in mime' (ar chúl i modh aithrise).[142] For the rest of the play the action shifts back and forth between the stage of the modern theatre and the world of the Deirdre tale.

Obviously the key question raised by the play involves the potential appeal of this kind of ancient subject matter for modern audiences, and this is an issue the director and his cast confront head-on. In their first return from the imaginary world they have briefly inhabited, the director is ambivalent: 'Do you know, it would be a bit difficult for the audience to follow something like that when they are used to – well, silence is golden and the walls have ears.'[143] Now it is 'Actor A' who is enthusiastic about such source material: 'It would be a good thing for us and for everyone to make an attempt. It is no easy thing to get to know a person's heart or soul, and the higher his state, the more complicated his mind and his desires.'[144] And when the director again laments the lack of a script for a Deirdre play, the actors have a startling reply:

> Actor A: What need is a script? Don't you know all there is to be known about
> *Stanislavsky* and the *Actors' Studio?*
> Actor B: About *Ionesco,* the *Commedia dell'Arte, Pirandello?*
> Actor A: Let us awaken it out of our own souls.
> Actor B: Out of the primeval memory of our people.[145]

One thing they all agree on, however, is that they should not consult any scholars: 'They would begin competing with each other, every cockerel of them calling from his own mound. It wouldn't be long until there would be proof available for you . . . that there had been three or four Deirdres . . .'[146] Before long, the director and actors are immersing themselves in the Deirdre story, blurring the lines between their modern selves and the characters they are embodying. Increasingly the director finds enacting the ancient tale an intimidating experience and is actually relieved to return to the trivial modern play they are rehearsing: 'O Virgin Mary, but in a way it was a great relief to us to be back on that farm expecting the young son from San Francisco!' For 'Actor A', this sense of uneasiness is entirely compre-hensible: 'O without a doubt it is easier to cook a sausage than the salmon of knowledge.'[147] By now, the director, like Ó Floinn in his 'Réamhrádh' (Preface), realises that what is needed is 'a new outlook' (dearcadh úr) on the source text.

Ó Floinn has for the most part followed *Longes Mac nUislenn* quite faithfully up to this point, but from here on he begins to introduce some of his own innovations into the play. For example, he gives an important role to Bricriu, the trickster and troublemaker in the so-called Ulster Cycle tales of early Irish literature. He also introduces a *geis*, a supernatural injunction guiding a character's behaviour,[148] that is not in the original when he has Deirdre say that it is *geis* for her to sleep with a man who does not have raven-black hair, snow-white skin, and blood-red cheeks. In the original tale she simply desires to have such a mate after seeing a raven feeding on a flayed calf on snowy ground. More importantly, in a total deviation from the original, Ó Floinn has Deirdre tell Leabharcham that when she next sees Conchúr she will tell him that Leabharcham had brought Naoise and his brothers to her and that they had raped her. Then she will kill herself. The first act ends with 'Actor A' jokingly asking whether an audience would return to such a play after the interval.

The second act takes place the next day, again on the rehearsal stage. The director tells the actors he has had 'a nightmare' (tromluí) in which he wrote a Deirdre play and submitted it to the manager of the theatre in which they will be performing the trifling play they all hate. Their own improvised version of the Deirdre story has left them even more dissatisfied with this modern play, and they begin to imagine how a play on Deirdre should be done. They reject a traditional interpretation, lament that a modern audience would not appreciate the terse, stark style of the original tale, and realise they would probably have to make regrettable accommodations to their own time and place: 'To be sure, if your work were to be shown in the West End or on Broadway, you would have to examine enthusiastically every aspect of the sex and of the perverse sex.'[149] For the most part, however, their play as they imagine it here follows the tragic course of the original, with Naoise and his brothers recalled to Ireland and treacherously killed by order of Conchúr. Ó Floinn does, however, make one major change from the conclusion in *Longes Mac nUislenn*. In the original, Conchobar, having decided to turn Deirdre over to the man who actually killed Naoise, parades her in front of his people and makes a cruel sexual joke at her expense, whereupon she commits suicide by jumping from his chariot and smashing her head to pieces against a rock. Perhaps to simplify the staging, Ó Floinn has his heroine die, as Deirdre does in some later versions of the story, by stabbing herself immediately after Naoise's death.

As the play moves into the third act, Ó Floinn also introduces material from the *Táin* itself as it appears in the *Book of Leinster* version from the mid twelfth century. This part of the play is considerably less successful, as the narrative of the *Táin* is far too long to fit into a full play, much less part of one. As a result, the ancient characters pretty much disappear, and we are left with thematic statements about their significance and that of the *Táin* itself. Thus, a petty squabble between two of the actors prompts the director to see the Irish epic as yet another expression of the inescapable violence in human nature: 'Tonight I understand. It is fundamentally a question of art. Tonight I understand Julius Caesar, Alexander the Great, Napoleon, Hitler . . . Let us understand the atomic war that is approaching, the war between the celestial bodies when this Universe is blown up; let us understand Cain shedding the blood of his brother.'[150] More specifically, he has come to see the *Táin* as emblematic of a very Irish and entirely contemporary neurosis: 'I never went to school but I met the students in the market place. Every Ulsterman who binds himself with the sash to the standing stone of memory, who knows that he is not the heir of Cú Chulainn?'[151] He could, of course, have said the same thing of every Ulsterman in the IRA who bound himself to that same stone with the strap of an armalite.

It is interesting that one of the characters in the play, 'Actor A', also seems to see the play as ultimately unsuccessful, telling the director: 'You were making very fine progress there a while ago richly in the style of tomorrow, and here you are now with a thud back to the Annals of the Four Masters.'[152] In the final analysis, the director is simply unable to come to terms with the ancient material. Indeed, when one of the actors asks him about the epic single combat between Cú Chulainn and his beloved foster brother Fer Diad, the director dismisses the idea of staging it successfully, saying that he is thinking instead of 'the next *geamaireacht* . . . that I could bring the two bulls onto this stage dancing' (an chéad gheamaireacht eile . . . go dtabharfainn an dá tharbh ag damhsa ar an stáitse seo).[153] And as *Cad d'Imigh ar Fheidhlimidh?* ends, he is back in the real world, off to get a pint and think about the following day's rehearsal, accepting the fact that while as a director he may be Feidhlimidh, as a worker in the modern business of theatre, he is 'a man presenting stories, for pay' (fear scéalta a chur i láthair, ar tuarastal).[154]

Cad d'Imigh ar Fheidhlimidh? is not an entirely successful play. There are too many loose ends, the connections between the modern actors and the characters in the ancient story are not fully developed, and the plot begins to unravel after the Deirdre tale has been told. It is, however, a strikingly original and admirably ambitious work, certainly one of the most interesting plays written in Irish over the past half-century. That an audience has never gotten to see it and that Ó Floinn has never been given the opportunity to rethink it in light of that audience's response, are among the inexplicable mysteries of the Gaelic stage.

In 1968, An Gúm published Ó Floinn's one-act *Éalú ó Chill Mhaighneann* (Escape from Kilmainham).[155] With its sketch of the set and elaborate stage directions it was obviously meant to be performed, although I have found no record of such a production. The play is based on, and follows closely, the first-person account of a 1921 prison break by IRA volunteers in Ernie O'Malley's *On Another Man's Wound* (1936). Ó Floinn does add one character, a young woman in Cumann na mBan who is a spy for Michael Collins, passing along information she gets from an English warder she pretends to be courting. In one scene she meets Collins and discusses a possible escape; in another she brings the warder to meet Collins; in a third she tries to brace the man up after a first botched escape attempt; in a fourth she waits with Collins for news of the escape; and in a final silent scene she appears with Collins and the successful escapees, listening to the prison bells announcing the execution of the volunteer who refused to accompany them. In both O'Malley's account and Ó Floinn's play, the central focus is on whether that volunteer, Paddy Moran (Pádraig Ó Móráin), who is facing trial for a capital offence, will escape with his fellow prisoners or remain in prison, believing witnesses will gain him an acquittal and unwilling to put those witnesses at risk of a perjury charge should he run. Ó Floinn adds two nice dramatic touches to O'Malley's account. In the play, O'Malley (Earnán Ó Máille) says he could order Ó Móráin to join the others, to which Ó Móráin replies simply: 'You could, Commandant O'Malley' (D'fhéadfá, a Cheannasaí Uí Mháille), after which we are told that they look at each other 'in torment' (go cráite) and Earnán salutes his friend, who returns the salute. Then, as Ó Máille departs, Ó Floinn has Ó Móráin, as if still torn, take a step and quietly call his name.

As well as introducing these moving little scenes into his source narrative, Ó Floinn also raises interesting thematic questions in the play. In *On Another Man's Wound*, we are told nothing about the sympathetic warder, whereas in *Éalú ó Chill Mhaighneann*, he is given a personality and a conscience. As a former soldier and one-time prisoner of the IRA who was treated well by his captors, he is disgusted by the idea of hanging enemies who have proved their courage in battle. He hates both the guerilla tactics of the IRA and the conduct of the Black and Tans, but he worries that by helping the men in Kilmainham to escape he is betraying his own country. Nor does he seem entirely convinced by the justification provided him by Michael Collins: 'If you help to get these lads of ours safe from the gallows, you will also save the soldiers who would be killed to avenge them ... Tommy, if you were where Lloyd George is, peace and friendship would long ago have been established between these two countries of ours.'[156]

In 1972, Ó Floinn, to his great astonishment, was awarded the Abbey Theatre's Playwright's Bursary. Without his knowledge he had been nominated for the award by An Chomhairle Náisiúnta Drámaíochta and chosen by a panel of judges made up of Lelia Doolin, then artistic director of the Abbey, the playwright Micheál Ó hAodha, then chairman of the Abbey's board, and the playwright Brian Friel. The bursary gave him a year away from his teaching duties, time he used to write *Mise Raifteirí an File* (I am Raftery the poet), which had its premiere at the Peacock in October 1973, directed by Colm Ó Briain and with a cast that included Éamonn Kelly, Micheál Ó Briain, and Macdara Ó Fatharta.[157] The play has enjoyed some popularity. It was produced in 1976 by Compántas Chorcaí in Cork with Pádraig Ó Cearúil directing (*CE*, 8/12/76); by Taibhdhearc na Gaillimhe in 1974 and again in 1989 (directed by Seán Stafford and Seán Ó Briain, respectively);[158] by the Claremorris, Co. Mayo branch of the Gaelic League in 1975 at Féile Drámaíochta Chluain an Iarainn and at that year's Oireachtas (*Connaught Telegraph*, 27/2/75; *IP*, 7/5/75);[159] and by the Claremorris group again in 1993, with Séamus Ó Maoilearca and Colmán Ó Raghallaigh directing (*WP*, 7/4/93). Reviewing the Peacock production for the *Sunday Independent*, Gus Smith, having confessed 'my own limited knowledge of the language', was pleased that 'I had little difficulty in involving myself in the story of the blind poet' and commended Ó Floinn for his use of 'not a few English lines' in the play. He added: 'Perhaps all language lovers will not agree with Ó Floinn's approach, but if Gaelic drama is ever to win a wider appeal, one imagines this dramatist's work is more geared to a bigger audience and one not necessarily fluent in the native tongue.' On the whole, Smith declared, the play provided 'a thoroughly entertaining evening's theatre' (*SI*, 11/11/73). Considerably less taken with the play was Dominic O'Riordan, who wrote in the *Irish Times* that *Mise Raifteirí an File* was 'a mixum-gatherum of a play', whose first act was 'a turgid repetitivity of verse, quotation, argument and song . . . quotation follows quotation in such lack of creativity that the mind boggles at the research'. Still, having wondered whether it was Ó Floinn's intention 'to write a book on the subject or devise a radio play', he continued: 'Yet Críostóir Ó Floinn has made a brave attempt at an impossible effort.' That effort was the writing of 'a successful historical play about Ireland', something O'Riordan felt had never been done because 'every Irish writer lives too close to history – he lives today, yesterday and tomorrow with the result that the objective view dies and the past does not come to life on stage. Present social comment cannot change what is gone. It can only lecture and a seminar cannot make a play' (*IT*, 25/10/73). Leaving aside the fact that O'Riordan's dictum on the impossibility of Irish historical drama simply identifies a challenge facing writers anywhere in the world who would turn to history for their inspiration, it seems odd that he says nothing in his brief review about anything except the first act. More illuminating is the equally brief review of the play by 'D. Ó M. B.' in *Feasta*: 'He probably tried too much with it . . . It is, perhaps, too polemical for all the aspects to coalesce as a single unit. But there were bits that were excellent . . .' (*Feasta*,

Dec. 1973, p. 13).[160] 'L. Mac R.' concentrated on what he saw as the playwright's greatest success in the piece, 'that Ó Floinn grasped the mind of the dead poet and that he put flesh on the skeleton' (go bhfuair Ó Floinn greim ar aigne an fhile mhairbh agus gur chuir sé feoil ar an chnámharlach) (*Inniu*, 5/11/73).

As noted above, Gus Smith called attention in his review to how much English there is in the play, entirely missing the point that it was consciously written as a bilingual play, a subgenre that one might think would by now have taken root in Ireland. It is certainly a form whose potential has long fascinated Ó Floinn, one of whose radio plays from the beginning of his career was a bilingual work based on the eighteenth-century poem *Caoineadh Airt Uí Laoghaire* (The lament for Arthur O'Leary). The play was rejected by the novelist Francis MacManus, then director of features at Radio Éireann, who told Ó Floinn he should write in one language or the other. Ó Floinn remembers his reaction in *Consplawkus*: 'I can still recall my total astonishment at this negative verdict and blunt directive, which I considered to be totally mistaken, if not actually nonsense.'[161] There is nothing gimmicky or unnatural about the bilingualism in *Mise Raifteirí an File* – characters who would have spoken Irish speak Irish, characters who would have spoken English speak English; characters who were or are bilingual may speak in either language. That is, of course, the way it works in real life and would seem an entirely normal way to write a play in a bilingual society, as well as being an approach that could, if regularly practised, create an entirely new kind of Irish drama.

In *Cad d'Imigh ar Fheidhlimidh?* Ó Floinn introduced the question of cultural appropriation when his director character speaks of how early Irish literature has been adapted by writers of English like Yeats and Stephens. The issue is never really developed in that play, but it lies at the very heart of *Mise Raifteirí an File*. In one sense Dominic O'Riordan was right about this play. It is very much a 'mixum-gatherum'.[162] It does not, however, lack unity, although that unity is certainly not a unity of time or place, for the play covers nearly two centuries, moving from the Connacht of the late eighteenth century to Lady Gregory's house at Coole, to Dublin and Galway in the early years of the Gaelic League, and on to the Abbey Theatre in 1973. Nor is there any possible unity of style given all the quotations from different authors and periods. Instead, Ó Floinn tries to impose a thematic coherence on a play nearly as wayward and undisciplined as its protagonist. And his unifying theme is cultural oppression and subsequent appropriation, whether in the form of attempts to suppress the Irish language and its culture in Raifteirí's time, the campaign to stop the language revival in the early twentieth century, or the effort since to marginalise Gaelic culture by arguing that the best of that culture could be preserved and transmitted through English.[163]

Ó Floinn's time-travelling Raifteirí takes his idiosyncratic, poetic, and often solitary stand against all such attacks.

Antoine Ó Reachtabhra or Raifteirí (1779–1835) was, of course, a real person, as were most of the other characters in the play: Douglas Hyde ('An Craoibhín Aoibhinn'), Lady Gregory, John Pentland Mahaffy, Archbishop Richard Whately, Marcas Ó Callanáin, Antaine Ó Dálaigh, James Hardiman, Frank O'Connor. However, while Ó Floinn does draw abundantly – some, like Dominic O'Riordan, would say excessively – on direct quotations from historical sources, most of the dialogue in the play is of his own creation. In addition, while he is to some extent restricted in his characterisation by what we know about these people, he does throughout shape his characters according to their thematic role in the play.

The play is a collection of discrete scenes in which we are shown episodes in Raifteirí's life, like his meeting with one of his muses, the beautiful Máire Ní Eidhin (Mary Hynes), his poetic contest with Marcas Ó Callanáin, or his trial for being a member of the agrarian resistance movement known as the Whiteboys. Interspersed with these biographical scenes are others in which he interacts with characters from later times or in which those characters discuss him or debate the quality of his work and the broader question of the place of the Irish language in the cultural life of modern Ireland. Thus we see the young Douglas Hyde learning of the existence of the poet and his poems; Lady Gregory making a similar discovery in the poorhouse near her estate in Gort, Co. Galway; Hyde confronting the Trinity professor and provost John Pentland Mahaffy before a government commission inquiring into the advisability of including Irish on the curriculum of intermediate schools; a member of the 1960s anti-revivalist Language Freedom Movement rising from the audience at the Abbey Theatre to protest the production of a play in Irish by the National Theatre; and Frank O'Connor condescendingly discussing the significance of the Gaelic revival in a broadcast over 'European Television' (Telefís na hEorpa).

The characters in the play divide starkly into three groups: Raifteirí and the people of his time; figures from an Anglo-Irish cultural background sympathetic to him in varying degrees; and those who question or oppose the idea that Irish has a place, indeed a central place, in the cultural life of the nation.[164] By far the most human characters in the play are Raifteirí and those who actually knew him. Ó Floinn does idealise the poet to a certain extent, for example by making him a fervent Irish nationalist who can discuss the significance of Catholic emancipation and hopes to see an alliance between Daniel O'Connell and the Whiteboys, who are presented as committed republicans rather than as rural activists and agitators.[165] On the other hand, his Raifteirí seems incapable of realising that O'Connell will never renounce parliamentarianism for armed revolt. Moreover, while

Ó Floinn does, as one might expect in a play using Raifteirí as a symbol of cultural resistance at a time when the Gaelic tradition was most threatened, exaggerates the quality of his work and the extent of his influence, he also shows us some of the poet's flaws, like his cantankerous arrogance, most notably evident when he is humiliatingly bested in a poetic contest by Marcas Ó Callanáin.

The good guys and the bad guys have virtually nothing in common in the play, functioning mostly, and quite intentionally, as one-dimensional embodiments of principles to be honoured and emulated or prejudices to be ridiculed and rejected. The villains are especially cartoonish. Ó Floinn allows Professor Mahaffy to caricature himself by simply lifting much of what he said during his 1899 testimony before the Commission on Intermediate Education that was investigating the proper place of Irish (or 'Celtic') in the post-primary curriculum for Irish schools.[166] For example, like the real Mahaffy in 1899, his namesake in the play pontificates: 'The experts are agreed that it is impossible to find any text in Irish that is not either silly or religious or indecent. It is impossible that a nation which was uncivilized up to the sixteenth century should have produced any worthwhile literature in its undeveloped and primitive dialects.'[167] As the real Hyde did before the Commission, Ó Floinn's Hyde demolishes all of Mahaffy's arguments. Ó Floinn deals with the nineteenth-century Archbishop Richard Whately, one of the most forceful proponents of the aggressively Anglicising national school system of Irish education, by linking him with a member of the modern Language Freedom Movement and a woman representing the privileged membership of the Foxrock Residents' Literary, Cultural and Debating Society.[168] His sharpest attack is, however, reserved for the short story writer, playwright, translator, and cultural commentator 'Frank O'Connor' (Michael O'Donovan), doubtless because he saw O'Connor as betraying his own earlier idealism and commitment to the language.[169] O'Connor is depicted in *Mise Raifteirí an File* as a comic figure, an irascible apostate who dismisses Raifteirí's poetry as 'poor doggerel', calls 'poor old Hyde' a 'naïve idealist', and regards Lady Gregory as 'the other half of the '*à la recherche du poète perdu* team'. Hyde and Gregory interrupt O'Connor as he is broadcasting his programme 'Literary Viewpoints' over 'Radio-diffusion Télévision de l'Europe' and easily defeat him in debate, with Lady Gregory in the end chasing him off the stage with her umbrella.

There is never any doubt about whose side Ó Floinn is on. Still, while his heroes are as one-dimensional as his villains, they are considerably more interesting. The first character we see on stage is the young Douglas Hyde, who sets forth the rationale for remembering and celebrating a figure like Raifteirí:

The poet falls from heaven into the world; when his time is come, death sweeps him from us, but the disturbance, the cultural movement that he put together, remains like a wave on the water of life, a wave that flows out far from the poet's native place. In my own case, the cultural wave I was hit by was raised by a poor blind poet in County Galway, a poet who died more than forty years before I heard mention of him.[170]

His close ally in this project of cultural reclamation is his fellow Protestant Lady Gregory, who shares his commitment to work 'so that the honour of Ireland would be saved and magnified' (le go mbeadh oineach na hÉireann dá shlánú agus dá mhéadú).[171] In a comic scene early in the play, Ó Floinn suggests both Lady Gregory's initial naiveté and the psychic and cultural distance she will have to traverse to realise her new mission. In this scene Lady Gregory expresses regret that she and Hyde were not contemporaries of Raifteirí 'so that we could welcome him to this house, so that we could write down every word of the poems straight from his mouth, so that we could hear his noble, poetic speech with our own ears . . .' Immediately there is a shift in lighting – the technique Ó Floinn uses to take us across the years – and we see and hear Raifteirí reciting a verse that begins 'I shit on Coole House . . .' (mo chac anuas ar Theach an Chúil . . .).[172]

Ó Floinn makes clear that Raifteirí could never have imagined that he would one day find posthumous allies in the likes of Hyde and Gregory. Of his own time and place, he states: 'I realise that there are two peoples everywhere in this country, those in power, the English Protestants from over yonder, the thieves who violently dispossessed us, and ourselves, the Catholics, the Irish, the servile class in their own country.'[173] Indeed we get a notion of how deep was that divide when we are introduced to a man who tried tentatively to reach across it. Ó Floinn sets one scene in the Galway home of the scholar and early Gaelic enthusiast James Hardiman, in which a social gathering is taking place to the accompaniment of songs by Thomas Moore. Hardiman seems to take an interest in Raifteirí, but he consistently treats him with condescension and is concerned that the poet might offend his guests by expressing his opinions on political and social issues. For example, when in a conversation that takes place in the kitchen Raifteirí curses a tyrannical judge 'and every other English serpent that is driving Gaels out of their own country' (agus gach péist Ghallda eile atá ag díbirt Gael as a dtír féin), Hardiman chides him: 'Raftery, dear friend, have sense. I cannot welcome you to this house unless you keep control of your tongue.'[174] Hardiman goes so far as to say that he is glad 'that the nobles of Galway are turning away from Irish' (go bhfuil uaisle na Gaillimhe ag tabhairt cúl leis an nGaeilge), for otherwise they would understand what Raifteirí says about them. Moreover, he claims that among the cultured guests in his house, national identities are irrelevant: 'In this house tonight we are not Englishmen or Irishmen, Catholics or Protestants, but people who love song and music and poetry.'[175] Symbolic of this cultural erasure are the poetry and music of Thomas Moore, in which Gaelic subjects and themes have been domesticated in English. A later offhand comment by Raifteirí makes clear that he is well aware of the real basis of Moore's popularity: 'I have already heard that song if I am not mistaken. Is this Thomas Moore claiming that the entire composition is his own?'[176]

Both Hyde and Lady Gregory have a far deeper appreciation than does Hardiman of what the Irish language and Gaelic culture mean for Ireland – and for themselves.[177] Speaking on the stage of the Peacock in 1973, when the real Lady Gregory was 40 years dead and Coole House long demolished to provide building materials, Ó Floinn's Lady Gregory expresses her mature understanding of Raifteirí's significance when she says of the barn (scioból) in which the poet died: 'If that barn were still standing, people would be coming to it, and not to Coole House, to pay homage to Raifteirí . . .'[178] Ó Floinn does not, however, allow his audience to bask in the glow of such bicultural harmony. Instead, he shows us Hyde meeting again with Peatsaí an Bhrosna, who had introduced him to the work of Raifteirí. This time their meeting is in modern Ireland, of which Peatsaí is a thoroughly acculturated citizen: 'I have National School English from the children, and I have American English from the television. And I have Birmingham English from going on a visit every summer to the family of my son, who is grown up and married in that fine city.'[179] Peatsaí's interest in Raifteirí is now due to the fact that he is mentioned in the advertising for 'the Culchee Festival at – eh – Kil-ti-magh . . .wid leadin' Dublin and Cross-Channel pop groups' and the selection of 'Miss Kil-ti-magh'.[180] In this new Ireland, there is obviously no place for Raifteirí or idealists like Hyde and Gregory who understand what he could mean in a genuine national culture. The play ends with Raifteirí, Hyde, and Gregory standing in the meagre shelter of the thorn bush featured in one of the poet's most famous works, 'Seanchas na Sceiche' (The lore of the thorn bush).

As we have seen above, Ó Floinn's plays have on more than one occasion been judged by critical standards inappropriate to them, and one can make the case that *Mise Raifteirí an File* has suffered the same mistreatment. Actually, it may well be that Gus Smith's otherwise superficial review of the play as 'a thoroughly entertaining evening's theatre' is more perceptive than Dominic O'Riordan's more considered view that it was a dramatic lecture rather than a play. It is hard to think that anyone could consider *Mise Raifteirí an File* as an attempt at a traditional play. Rather, it is very much a show, an extravaganza, or, in the author's own words, 'a theatrical entertainment' (siamsa amharclainne). Ó Floinn underscores this point in his 'Preface' (Réamhrádh): 'If it is a concern among the learned how fluent Lady Gregory becomes in speaking Irish early in the play, the philosophers will understand that it is not a diary or a history that I am writing, but a play.' Moreover, he insists that it was essential to use any theatrical tricks that might work to enhance the show: 'It is clear that the effect of the play as a theatrical entertainment will depend to a large extent on the use that is made of design, music, lighting, and the coordination of the scenes.'[181] *Mise Raifteirí an File* is very much a thesis play and its thesis is an important one, but it is hard to see how anyone could mistake it for a lecture.

Ó Floinn's next play, *Homo Sapiens*, opened at An Damer in 1975 with Áine Uí Dhrisceoil directing.[182] It does not seem to have had a major revival, although it was broadcast over Radio Éireann in January 1987 (*IT*, 24/1/87). In a 1977 letter to the *Irish Times*, Ó Floinn provides the background to An Damer's production, telling us that the Abbey had been 'vying with Gael-Linn [which managed the Damer] for the production rights of the Irish version of my most recent play "Homo Sapiens"', which, apparently, Tomás Mac Anna found 'a very interesting play which they would be glad to do at the Peacock'. When, however, he submitted 'an identical version in English' for the Peacock, he claims that Mac Anna rejected it as 'a poor piece not worth putting on there' (*IT*, 1/3/77).[183] Ó Floinn's disappointment about Mac Anna's rejection was exacerbated by the fact that despite what he felt were excellent performances by the actors, An Damer's production was a commercial failure.[184]

Reviews were mixed, but more were negative than positive. While he did not think it was 'the best play Ó Floinn has written' (an dráma is fearr atá scríofa ag Ó Floinn) and thought the script 'wordy in places' (foclach in áiteanna), 'M. R.' still enjoyed the play, calling it 'a philosophic play' (dráma fealsúnach) and pronouncing Uí Dhrisceoil's production 'polished' (snasta) (*IP*, 9/10/75). Considerably less impressed was the anonymous reviewer for the *Irish Independent*, who called the play's theme 'rather depressing' and stated that 'the play signally failed to grip me', largely because he found it 'completely impossible to identify with the characters'. The problem, he wrote, was not with the actors, who 'struggled valiantly – if not altogether successfully with virtually impossible parts'. Indeed he declared that 'the setting of the play was more convincing than the play itself' (*II*, 9/10/75). In what was essentially a five-sentence review in *The Cork Examiner*, Risteárd Ó Glaisne wrote: 'One person outside the railings, a mentally impaired person inside. A conversation begins between them. A very interesting main idea, but it is not effectively developed. Witty speech is not enough' (*CE*, 20/11/75).[185] Dominic O'Riordan of the *Irish Times* wrote: 'But I could not follow the continuity of the endless conversation of Jekyll becoming Hyde and Billie physicking Jack.' And while he enjoyed some of the comedy, on the whole he felt 'there are so many points in the play that one misses the point' and that 'because there is so much concentration on so many themes, the play lacks the essentials of intelligible drama – humour and movement. It could have finished at any moment and I for one would not have been any less [*sic*] wiser.' Still, he could conclude his review by calling the production 'a fascinating night of theatre because it makes you wonder what might be wrong with your own mind' (*IT*, 8/10/75).

O'Riordan is quite correct when he states the 'shades of Pinter and Beckett haunt the play, for *Homo Sapiens* is Ó Floinn's only experiment with the theatre of the absurd.[186] He is, however, quite wrong when he states that the play has 'so many points . . . that one misses the point'. As is true in more than a few absurdist plays – one thinks, for example, of Ionesco's *La cantatrice chauve* or *Rhinocéros* – an irrational surface obscures a fairly straightforward and even conventional central theme. Such is certainly the case with *Homo Sapiens*. The play is set 'on the two sides of the bars that are a boundary between the grounds of a hospital for the mentally ill and the highway to the city' (ar dhá thaobh na mbarraí atá ina dteorainn idir fearann ospidéil mheabhairghalar agus mórbhealach na cathrach), and Ó Floinn makes clear that he wants the audience to have the impression that the wall in which these bars are set extends on beyond the limits of the stage.[187] There are only two characters, Jaic and Billí. Jaic is the working-class Everyman, 'a middle-aged man . . . of medium height and medium build' (fear meánaosta . . . ar mheánairde agus ar mheántéagar), a painter who drags himself to work every day 'reluctantly, with heavy feet . . . looking as if constant worry and bitterness are coming between him and his peace of mind' (go drogallach tromchosach . . . cosúlacht air go bhfuil síorimní agus searbhas ag teacht idir é agus a shástacht aigne). He has 'a habit . . . of talking to himself, and this talk is an incomprehensible complaint about everything, his work, the place where he is working, life in general' (nós . . . labhairt leis féin, agus an chaint seo ina chasaoid dothuigthe faoi gach ní, a chuid oibre, an ball ina bhfuil sé ag obair, an saol ar fad).[188] His current job is to scrape, prime, and paint the apparently endless line of bars around the asylum. Billí is one of the inmates of that asylum. In 'age, height, and build' (aois, airde, agus déanamh) as well as in clothing, he is virtually identical to Jaic, but 'where Jaic is dolorous and suspicious, Billí is alive and active, overflowing with joy and a big smile for everyone and everything' (an áit a bhfuil Jaic dólásach amhrasach, tá Billí beo bíogúil, ag cur thar maoil le gliondar is le dea-aoibh do chách agus do chuile shórt).[189] Society regards Jaic as sane, while Billí, in Jaic's phrase, is seen as 'a crazy blackbird – what else is in there' (lon dubh craiceáilte – cad eile istigh ansin). The play will, of course, call into question that simplistic dichotomy between sanity and madness.

At first, however, Ó Floinn stresses how different the two men are. Indeed each man finds the other 'strange' (aisteach), and Jaic is a bit afraid of Billí. Where Jaic regards rain as a source of 'dirt, mud, muck, and mire' (salachar, puiteach, draoib, láib), Billí sees it as 'baptism for the flower, greenness for the grass' (baiste don bhláth, glaise don fhéar), leaving 'the highway a skyway, every car a star travelling, every colour, every shape, all of them a rainbow rushing past throughout the universe' (an bóthar mór ina bhealach spéire, gach carr ina réalta ag taisteal, gach dath, gach cruth, iad uile ina mbogha báistí ag scinncadh thart ar fud na cruinne).[190] Where Jaic sees bars, Billí sees a gate. While the supposedly free Jaic is described in a stage direction as 'like a wretched animal in the zoo' (ar nós ainmhí dearóil sa zú), the confined Billí sees the asylum as 'the Garden of Eden, the Land of the Living' ('Gairdín Éidin, Tír na mBeo).[191] Jaic works on a footpath just a few feet from city traffic, while Billí has the run of the asylum grounds with their flowers, shrubs, and bird calls. Above all, Jaic's spirit has been broken by his stultifying job, a domineering mother with whom he lives, his sexual frustration, and most painfully, his own inability to envision anything different, much less better: 'Millions, billions of bars, iron bars, wooden bars, the brush pulling me ceaselessly, bars, bars eternally moving ahead of me, bars stretching before me, around the world . . .'[192]

Their differences are actually, however, quite superficial, as Ó Floinn makes clear, not only through their words, but also, as has been noted, through their appearance, as well as through their behaviour. Thus in a scene that recalls both Samuel Beckett and the Marx Brothers, Jaic and Billí perform some comic stage business, including a series of perfectly synchronised movements.[193] In another scene, the distinction between the two is blurred so that we see a ladder being carried across the stage but cannot tell who is carrying it.[194] This device is used again later in the play when we see a man painting the bars, but cannot immediately tell whether it is Jaic or Billí.[195]

A more profound similarity between the two is seen when they switch places. Having listened to Billí's praise of life in the asylum, where Jaic will have 'company you never imagined to be in this world' (comhluadar nár shamhlaigh tú a bheith ar an saol seo),[196] Jaic after an initial reluctance accepts the idea to change places with Billí. Almost immediately, Billí is miserable outside the wall and is soon sitting dejectedly against it 'as is the custom with Jaic himself' (mar is nós le Jaic féin).[197] Meanwhile, when we see Jaic, the stage directions state: 'He now looks carefree and moves in a lively manner.'[198] He is also, as was Billí earlier, leaping playfully from shrub to shrub and whistling bird calls. Ó Floinn further underscores the idea that it is external circumstances rather than mental illness that create the differences between them when he has the two, with their positions reversed, repeat the opening dialogue of the play word for word. It is now Jaic who speaks of the delights inside the walls, while Billí slaves away in fear of his boss.[199]

It is somewhat of a commonplace in literature dealing with the insane to suggest that mental illness is a social construct imposed by the 'normal' on those found to be subversive, difficult, or merely embarrassing. One thinks here of Ken Kesey's novel *One Flew over the Cuckoo's Nest* (1962), the film version of which came out in 1975, or Liam Ó Muirthile's play *Fear an Tae* (The tea man) (1995). There is a bit of that in Ó Floinn's play, but his real theme is that life cannot be neatly dichotomised, that there is a continuum between madness and sanity, and that what is essential for a *homo sapiens* capable of enjoying the world as it is is an integrated balance between utilitarian logic and a more anarchic creativity, a balance different for each individual. In *Homo Sapiens* we ultimately see Billí not as the insane victim of an oppressive, homogenising social structure – though he may well be such a victim – but as a sane man who views life holistically. In the first scene of Act II, Billí, still inside the walls, decides to pick up Jaic's brush and help him with the painting. Singing as he paints, Billí sees the job as just one of life's activities, not as the way he defines himself. For him the meaning of work – any work – is simple:

> Help for Jaic, help for the bars. Because Jaic can only see clearly his own side of the bars, he has left rust like measles on a backbone and on lovely calves here and there. Here you are getting to work in the morning, retreating and in no hurry, announcing that your brush is weaving painfully [between the bars] to put the final coat like a shroud around them. But the undercoat has not been applied properly on their smooth bodies. I, Billí, demand justice for the bars.[200]

Jaic, of course, finds this attitude absurd: 'Yerra, a spot here and there on your side. The Boss wouldn't see those.'[201] From his broader perspective and more subtle understanding of who the boss might be, Billí replies: 'The bushes see them, and the blackbird.'[202] Of course Billí is also sane because he understands the way the world works and knows that one cannot always have things the way one wants them. At the end of the play we see him, now on the outside, painting away, worried about the boss but still able to pity Jaic more than himself: 'Three more days without pay, without a cigarette, without company except the . . . the . . . ah, well, may the God of mercy watch over you, Jack my man.'[203]

Jaic, on the other hand, is indeed mad as the play ends, not because society has so labelled him, but because he can no longer see life through anything but the narrowest selfish focus. Soon after he switches places with Billí and enters the asylum grounds, we see him, still ranting about his job and carrying a bloody knife with which he has apparently killed one of the nurses, thinking she was his mother. He is soon slashing at the shrubs and jabbering meaninglessly. When he tells Billí he will not return to his old life, he also claims to be Billí. That of course means that Billí must now become Jaic. But to Jaic's comment 'We agree' (Táimid ar aon fhocal), Billí responds 'If it weren't for the bars' (Mura mbeadh na barraí).[204] He is, of course, right, but he is not referring to the same bars that have so unhinged Jaic. Billí's bars are altogether real and to a sane *homo sapiens* make perfect sense. There are certainly more than a few loose ends in the play – far more than have been noted in this brief discussion. *Homo Sapiens* is not, however, either a 'depressing' play or an inadequately developed one. Ó Floinn's experimental venture into the theatre of the absurd is a humorous, thought-provoking, at times profound dramatic study of what it is that makes humans *sapiens* and what happens when we forget that.

In 1978, Taibhdhearc na Gaillimhe celebrated the reopening of its refurbished theatre with Ó Floinn's comedy *Cluichí Cleamhnais* (Matchmaking games), which had its premiere at An Taibhdhearc in February, with Seán Stafford directing and a cast that included Máire and Maelíosa Stafford. Surprisingly, while the Galway papers gave the event considerable advance publicity and covered the festivities afterwards, they did not provide reviews of the play. We are, then, fortunate that the veteran Taibhdhearc director Aodh Mac Dhubháin shared his thoughts on *Cluichí Cleamhnais* in *Comhar*, where he praised Ó Floinn for 'the wonderful gift of imagination he has' (an bua iontach samhlaíochta atá aige), but suggested that despite 'a strong effort to tie up the threads tightly' (sár-iarracht na snaithí éagsúla a cheangal go dlúth), he had taken on too much in the play: 'I think that he chose too complex a web and I think that he attempted to weave together too many strands "of the life of our people today".'[205] In general, Mac Dhubháin felt 'that the polish and the finish that are notable in other plays by Ó Floinn were missing. I think that the basic idea is excellent but it is a pity that the author did not shorten the work and that he did not tighten up the action.' The result was 'that the play is a bit tedious and it isn't as engaging as one expects it to be' (*Comhar*, Apr. 1978, p. 23).[206]

The only other significant engagement with the play was Dónall Mac Amhlaigh's review of the text, which had been published by Foilseacháin Náisiúnta Teoranta almost simultaneously with the play's premiere in 1978. Mac Amhlaigh acknowledged that he had not been able to see the play at An Taibhdhearc, but wrote that he enjoyed reading it. In particular, he was impressed by how Ó Floinn managed to work serious themes into what could have been a simple farce: 'As I said, this is a comic play, but there is much more than drollery and humour in it for there are mature opinions about the state and the course of the rural areas and of the entire country . . . in it; I believe that any audience at all would enjoy it' (*IP*, 11/4/78).[207]

Ó Floinn shares some of these 'mature opinions' with us in his preface to the published text, calling *Cluichí Cleamhnais* 'a comic entertainment in which there would be some insight presented into the life of our people today' (siamsa grinn a mbeadh léargas á dhéanamh ann ar shaol ár muintire sa lá atá inniu ann) and adding that if anyone finds 'a breath of bitterness blowing through the humour . . . I hope that there is not a grain of the poison of malice in that breeze, and that it will be tasted as salt on the meat' (anáil an tsearbhais ag séideadh tríd an ngreann . . . tá súil agam nach bhfuil aon ghráinne de nimh na mioscaise ar an ngaoith sin, agus gur ina shalann ar an bhfeoil a bhlaisfear é). Yet he could not resist a dig at 'this age in which the arts, like the life on which they are based, are going astray, without finish, without order, without rule' ([an] ré seo ina bhfuil na healaíona, ar nós an tsaoil a bhfuil siad bunaithe air, ag imeacht ar seachrán gan slacht gan reacht gan riail).[208]

If, however, the world is going to hell in a handbasket in *Cluichí Cleamhnais*, it is doing so in a way more likely to inspire laughter than despair. The play is set in Baile na Lachan, a parish Ó Floinn describes as being 'in a remote district in the west between a hill and the coast' (i ndúiche iargúlta thiar idir cnoc agus trá). It is, however, close enough to Galway to enable doings in the city to have ramifications in the village. The first members of the large cast we meet are An tAthair Pól Ó Brúiligh, the parish priest, Donncha Ó Confhaola, the head teacher, and Sinéad Ní Chonfhaola, his sister. All three are celibates, with Donncha and Sinéad sharing a house. The priest has come in with the bad news that the local school is to be shut down by 'that crowd up in Dublin' (an dream sin thuas i mBaile Átha Cliath) because enrolment is so low. There are simply too few marriages and thus children in Baile na Lachan. It is now Shrove Tuesday, the traditional time for making matches, but there has only been one wedding in the parish in the last five years, and that couple emigrated. We soon meet two more of the local people, Dainí de Brún, the local shopkeeper and publican, who is totally under the thumb of his mother, with whom he lives; and the local police sergeant, whose barracks in the parish has already been closed. Desperate, this group decides they must 'bring new children into the world, and do that as quickly as possible' (leanaí nua a chur ar an saol, agus é sin chomh gasta agus is féidir).[209] They appoint themselves a committee for that purpose and are soon making matches for the young people in the parish, with their 'first Eve' (céad Éabha) the young teacher Miranda, who appears on stage to be instantly surrounded and inspected by the committee as if she were a heifer at an auction. Miranda hates her job and longs to be an actress in London, though she will settle for Dublin in the meantime. For now, she performs as a dancer in the summer show for tourists at An Taibhdhearc, where, she says, 'they understand nothing about the art of the theatre'.[210]

Seeing no chance of meeting a mate in Baile na Lachan, she rushes off to Galway at the end of every school day, even though she finds it 'a crazy maze of crooked lanes' (meascán mearaí de bhóithríní cama) unworthy to be called a city. The elders' proposed match for Miranda is Tomás Seosamh Ó Maolruáin, BA, H. Dip., who sees a seat in Dáil Éireann in his future and who, although he spends most of his time in Galway, is willing to live in the parish to advance his career.

The next match planned is to be between Caitlín Shéamais Rua, a farmer's daughter who is 'as knowledgeable about agricultural affairs as any man at all' (chomh heolach le fear ar bith i gcúrsaí talmhaíochta), but of whom the sergeant says, 'You wouldn't know that that one is a woman at all unless you took all of her father's old rags off her.'[211] The elders see a logical mate for her in Maidhc Ó Flatharta, who owns the farm bordering her father's, but whose main love in life is at present his prizewinning sow. The final couple the committee plans to bring together is the snobbish Jacqueline d'Arcy-Blake and Paidí Tom Ó Gallchobhair, 'dressed like a Hollywood director's idea of an Aran fisherman' (gléasta ar nós iascaire Árann dar le stiúrthóir i Hollywood). Jacqueline is 'a poultry teacher' (teagascóir éanlaith clóis), and although the 'natives' (dúchasaigh) think she is wealthy, she declares 'Actually the only wealth I have is my name and my soul, and my noble ancestors, and my noble desires.'[212] While Paidí Tom has neither a venerable name nor noble qualities, he does have a bit of money, and that is enough to pique Jacqueline's initial interest. That interest is then considerably heightened by the fact that she sees him in exactly the kind of absurdly romantic light in which he sees himself: 'It seemed to me that this beautiful young man arose before me right out of *Riders to the Sea* and Jack B. Yeats.'[213] Paidí's motives are more primal, as he uses his 'traditional' fisherman's costume to attract the notice of female tourists in the summertime. One of those tourists, a German, has read to him from *The Playboy of the Western World*, and he has memorised some of 'this speech that the tourists like' (an chaint seo a thaitníos leis na turasóirí). As a result he spends more time seducing women than he does fishing.

With couples matched, the elders now get to work bringing them together, keeping them in the parish, and encouraging them to reproduce. Needless to say, their misdirected and consistently thwarted attempts to carry out these plans provide most of the humour in the play. At first, however, they actually get a lucky break that promises to make their work a great deal easier. The local solicitor, Labhrás Ó Lorgadáin, introduces them to Mitsuko Matsaki, a Japanese businessman interested in building a factory in the parish. Matsaki has learned Irish by listening to tapes of Irish politicians speaking on special occasions, with the result that everything he says sounds like a political oration:

O gentry and nobility of Ireland, it is a great honour for me to be here in your presence today . . . I would now like, on behalf of the Government and the people of Japan, to declare to you how great is our respect for the people of this country, an ancient, delightful, beautiful country that the countries of the world respect –[214]

The local people find it both confusing and amusing that Matsaki would feel the need to learn Irish to do business in Ireland, and indeed while he was in Dublin before coming to Baile na Lachan he was held for a week in Mountjoy Jail on the suspicion 'that he was one of the "Gaelic-speaking fanatics" about whom the Dublin newspapers speak . . .' (gurb é a bhí ann duine de na 'Gaelic-speaking fanatics' seo a mbíonn nuachtáin Bhaile Átha Cliath ag insint fútha . . .).[215] Matsaki's factory would certainly be a great help in keeping local newlyweds and their families in Baile na Lachan, but the elders are finding it ever more difficult to create those married couples in the first place.

Miranda, for example, is now singing at the newly opened parish disco with a rock group from Galway whose lead singer is her lover. Instead of objecting, her would-be fiancé, the aspiring TD Tomás Ó Maolruáin, is encouraging her relationship with the singer, whose uncle is an influential politician. We also find that Caitlín Shéamais Rua is coming out of her shell under the influence of Matsaki, who takes pictures of her in a bikini for a 'Country Girl Competition' sponsored by a magazine. She has no interest at all in Maidhc as a potential husband, for she sees Matsaki as 'my only playboy of the Eastern World'.[216] Things are going even worse for Jacqueline, who at one point runs naked around the stage in flight from Paidí Tom, who has predictably enough assaulted her.[217] Obviously, all of the committee's plans are falling apart, with none of their planned matches working out. Instead, Caitlín Shéamais Rua marries Matsaki; Miranda has been abandoned by both her rocker boyfriend and Tomás Ó Maolruáin; Ó Maolruáin, his political prospects in Ireland finished, emigrates to Africa to try his luck there; and Jacqueline becomes a nun. On the other hand, four members of the committee itself have decided to marry, although all are too old to have children.[218] As the play ends, the factory will be built, as will a supermarket, and the police barracks will be reopened. The school, however, cannot be saved – though workers at the factory may one day provide it with a new crop of students.

Ó Floinn also has a lot of fun in the play with An Taibhdhearc itself. At one point a drama group is founded in Baile na Lachan and immediately faces the question of what its first production should be. The rock 'n' roller from Galway joins, hoping the group will perform his play *Faoistiní Bhean Tí Lóistín Ollscoile i gCathair na Gaillimhe* (The confessions of a woman who keeps a lodging house for university students in the city of Galway). The parish priest, on the other hand, prefers *Diarmaid agus Gráinne*, the play with which An Taibhdhearc opened in 1928. His puritanical young curate, An tAthair Macdara Mac Shíoradáin, whose disagreements with the more liberal parish priest run throughout the play, objects to *Diarmaid agus Gráinne* on the grounds that it is 'a thoroughly pagan story, a story in which lust and sexuality are powerful and shameless' (scéal págánach é tríd is tríd, scéal a bhfuil an drúis agus an chollaíocht ann go tréan mínáireach).[219] He would prefer something along the lines of *Céasadh agus Bás Naomh Sebastian* (The torture and death of St Sebastain) or *Físeanna Fatima* (The visions at Fatima), 'or even the Irish-language version that fine actress Siobhán McKenna made of *Saint Joan* by George Bernard Shaw' (nó fiú amháin an leagan Gaeilge a rinne an t-aisteoir breá mná sin, Siobhán Nic Chionnaith, de *Saint Joan* le George Bernard Shaw), this last play one of An Taibhdhearc's greatest successes when it was produced in Galway and Dublin in 1951. Forced to accept the committee's decision in favour of *Diarmaid agus Gráinne*, An tAthair Macdara is determined 'to make the script suitable' (an scríbhinn a chur in oiriúint) by cutting 'those pieces that would give scandal to the public or arouse lust in young people –' (na píosaí sin a thabharfadh scannal don phobal, nó a mhúsclódh macnas i ndaoine óga –). Warily, the parish priest accepts the idea, but insists that his curate be watched closely 'lest he drown the art with a bucket of his holy water' (le faitíos go mbáifeadh sé an ealaí le buicéid dá chuid uisce coisricthe).[220]

The summary above can give only a hint of the copious and complicated comic misadventures of the characters in *Cluichí Cleamhnais*. As Dónall Mac Amhlaigh stressed, however, the play also raises some quite serious issues. Obviously the threats of emigration and rural depopulation hang over a stagnant Baile na Lachan as the play begins, with the young leaving for Irish cities and towns and beyond to find work and excitement. Of interest in this context is the obvious suspicion the rural people have of Dublin and its highly centralised state bureaucracy. But Ó Floinn also raises – sometimes just in passing – other important questions. For example, in their initial discussion of Tomás Ó Maolruáin, the members of the committee take note of his alcoholic father and bring up a rumour that his daughters went to America because he was 'trying to get his daughters into bed with him' (ag iarraidh na hiníonacha a thabhairt chun na leapa leis).[221] Family planning – or at least an incipient awareness of it – has come to Baile na Lachan as part and parcel of what is perceived as a selfish new lifestyle:

> Yerra, wouldn't they now sooner have a fine house, a carpet on every floor, a car and a television and holidays in Spain, than the job for which the God of glory created men and women. Sinéad will tell you about all the pills and devices that the scientists have created so that people can have their cake and eat it too, you could say.[222]

And that is not the only moral challenge on the horizon. One member of the committee states: 'And still worse, they are killing children in the womb over there in England and in America, and in other countries.' To which comment another character replies: 'If so, it is here in Ireland that many of those children that are smothered over in Britain are conceived.'²²³ There is also reference to euthanasia of the elderly. And, of course, we see Jacqueline fleeing a sexual assault by Paidí Tom Ó Gallchobhair. When one adds in a now highly ironic reference to Bishop Éamonn Casey's attitude to sexually explicit magazines, we can appreciate how presciently Ó Floinn in 1978 foresaw many of the controversies that were to roil Ireland in the years to come.

In the final analysis, Ó Floinn once again tries to do too much in *Cluichí Cleamhnais*. The play works best when he gives free rein to his talent for comedy and satire. While the overarching themes of emigration, rural depopulation, and social change work well as an ominous background to the frivolity of the plot, other issues like incest, abortion, and sexual abuse are discordant and would better have been explored in another and much darker play. In a review of the published text, 'R. Mac G.' (probably Riobard Mac Góráin) wrote that he was certain 'the amateurs will have a great welcome for it' (go gcuirfidh na haimitéirigh an-fháilte go deo roimhe) and that he hoped 'that we would be given a chance to see it in An Damer, in the Peacock or elsewhere' (go dtabharfaí seans dúinn é fheiceáil sa Damer, sa Phéacóg nó eile) (*II*, 1/4/78). Neither those major venues nor amateur companies responded, and the play has not been revived.²²⁴

That same year of 1978 also saw publication by An Gúm of Ó Floinn's one-act comedy *cum* detective play *Lámh Dheas: Lámh Chlé* (Right hand: left hand). It does not seem to have ever been produced, although it is hard to imagine some amateur company somewhere in Ireland has not put it on. The play is set in an upper-class suburb of Dublin where the wife of a wealthy businessman is working on arrangements for a charity gala. A priest comes to her house soliciting funds for the poor children of the city, telling her his order does its charity work in obscurity, unlike the rich people who will support her event: 'You undoubtedly do great good for those orphans, but you benefit yourselves as well . . . and you can get publicity and great praise for every ha'penny you spend on charity.'²²⁵ Moreover, he reminds her that Christ was not impressed by her kind of almsgiving, adding 'Charity isn't so easy the way that our Lord laid down it should be done.'²²⁶ When she offers him a cheque, he replies that he cannot accept 'anything that would earn recognition for the person who gives it' (rud ar bith a thuillfeadh aitheantas don té a thugann é).²²⁷ Naturally she is a bit suspicious until he sadly tells her that many share her suspicions and that only two of the eight people he has approached have been willing to donate on his terms. Moved by his appeal and the fact that 'you did good for my soul and it is too seldom that I remember that I have a soul', she agrees to give him the quite exorbitant donation he seeks – the equivalent of the total amount she will spend on the gala for her tickets, clothes, dinner, etc.[228]

In the second scene of the play, a detective comes to the house. He tells the woman that it is likely an international criminal gang has entered Ireland to steal the money raised by the gala. He then informs her of a scam the gang used in England, sending around one of its members disguised as an old woman to solicit donations. In addition, he urges her not to become paranoid and relates how one woman had actually beaten up a priest who came to her house on behalf of a legitimate charity. Not surprisingly, he tells her to keep their conversation secret. As he goes on talking, she notices that the detective uses some unusual phrases the priest used earlier and even gives her the same phone number the priest did. The woman, now aware that she has been tricked, sees the detective out and then collapses in her chair, exclaiming: 'O! Why didn't I marry the son of a tailor or a milkman!'[229] In a final scene the 'priest' and the 'detective' meet up in the street and prepare to visit their next victim.

In 1980, An Gúm published two more of Ó Floinn's one-act plays, *Solas an tSaoil* and *Mair, a Chapaill!* (Live, horse!). Again, neither of these works seem to have been produced, although *St Hubert's Day*, the English-language version of *Mair, a Chapaill!* had been broadcast over Radio Éireann as early as December 1968 (*II*, 5/12/68)[230] and *Solas an tSaoil*, which was a shortened version of Ó Floinn's English-language play *The Light of the World*, won an Oireachtas prize in 1978 and was broadcast over Radio Éireann in April of that year (*II*, 1/4/78).[231]

Inspired by an incident in the Gospel of John, *Solas an tSaoil* is set in Jerusalem near the end of the life of Jesus. Nicodemus is worried that his daughter Miriam has become a follower of Christ. Moreover, her fiancé's father is thinking of breaking the engagement for the same reason. Predictably, that fiancé, a temple guard who is gathering information for the high priest Cáiafas, also warns her against Christ. Maois, a once blind man who has been cured by Jesus, is brought before Cáiafas, who questions him contemptuously, referring to the miracle as 'this devilish trickery' (an chleasaíocht dhiabhlaí seo).[232] Cáiafas is concerned that Christ will cause trouble in Jerusalem and wants to silence Maois, but Nicodemus says they should hear his story. After they do so, Nicodemus defends the actions of Christ, angering the high priest. When Maois expresses his belief that Christ has been sent by God, Cáiafas has him expelled from the temple, a judgement questioned immediately by Nicodemus. In the next scene, Maois is being sheltered in the home of Nicodemus, having been brought there by Miriam's fiancé, who has met Christ near the temple and has been converted: 'When he looked at me, I remembered the words Maois said to the High Priest in the court today. "I am the light of the world." I understand him now.'[233] The play ends with Nicodemus announcing that Maois's story should be written down, for 'None of us knows what is in store for us, or why these things are happening. Only the God of Glory knows everything.' The important thing is 'that there would be a report after us about these wonderful things we have seen in our time' (go mbeadh tuairisc in ár ndiaidh ar na nithe iontacha seo atá feicthe againn lenár linn).[234] Ó Floinn's little play provides us with a dignified and respectful dramatisation of those 'wonderful things'.

Mair, a Chapaill! is an entirely different kind of play. A convent school has lost a good deal of much-needed money after running a lottery based on a horse race. Unable to even pay off all the winners in their lottery, a young nun and two laywomen involved with the contest decide, without consulting the mother superior, to bet the £60 the lottery brought in on a long-shot in a steeplechase. A teacher at the convent school is dispatched to place the bet on 'Yellow Jack' at 100–1 odds, but when the women listen to the race on a transistor radio they learn that 'Yellow Jack' has fallen at the penultimate jump and thus lost to 'Red Biddy'. The women are as surprised as they are disappointed, for their confidence was high after the mother superior told them just before the race that it was St Hubert's Day and that Hubert was the patron saint of hunters, and thus in all probability of horsemen as well. At this low point the young teacher returns from the betting shop where she was utterly flummoxed by 'that foul place, the smell, the cloud of smoke, all the men standing around scratching themselves and spitting' (an áit bhréan sin, an boladh, an scamall toite, na fir go léir ina seasamh thart á dtochas féin is ag caitheamh seile). Thinking that she is about to tell them she could not place their bet, her friends are delighted that at least they still have their £60. Instead, they find out that in her confusion she mixed up her colours and put their money on 'Red Biddy' instead of 'Yellow Jack', and thus her mistake has saved the day. To celebrate, the missionary nun in support of whose work the lottery was originally held and who will now get a substantial sum, decides to order a statue of St Hubert from Dublin. When told by the sculptor that he has none and has never even heard of Hubert, she tells him to make one for her to take back to Peru, 'where the faith is alive' (mar a bhfuil an creideamh beo), adding 'And listen, my good man, don't think that you can trick me with an old statue of St Patrick!'[235]

In 1987, Taibhdhearc na Gaillimhe again commissioned Ó Floinn to write a play, this time to commemorate its sixtieth anniversary, which coincided with the sixtieth anniversary of the death of the Galway writer Pádraic Ó Conaire (1882–1928). This was not the first play by Ó Floinn in which Ó Conaire appeared. In 1978, Aisteoirí an Damer, a new, professional company, toured Ireland with the one-act *M'Asal Beag Dubh* (My little black ass), which had been commissioned by the company's patrons the Arts Council and Bord na Gaeilge to commemorate the fiftieth anniversary of Ó Conaire's death.[236] Directed by Áine Uí Dhrisceoil, the play had its premiere at Éigse Uí Chonaire (The Ó Conaire literary festival) in Rosmuc in the Conamara Gaeltacht and was also performed in Cork City and in Cúil Aodha in the West Cork Gaeltacht (*IT*, 13/11/78; *CE*, 12/2/79).

It was this work that in 1988 became *Taibhsí na Faiche Móire* (The ghosts of Eyre Square). Much of the action of the play is based on Ó Conaire's most famous short story 'M'Asal Beag Dubh', a story familiar to several generations of Irish schoolchildren. In the story the narrator buys an old donkey from a sharp-dealing traveller ('An Tincéir Rua'). In the play, however, it is not Ó Conaire the man who appears, but Ó Conaire in the form of the statue commemorating him in Galway's Eyre Square. He – or it – begins by reciting the opening lines of the story verbatim, at which point An Tincéir Rua rushes on to dispute his account, for 'I was the one who owned that little black ass about which you have been telling your black lies for long years now.'[237] Their argument and the attempt of a policeman to resolve it will run throughout the play. We also hear the voice of another of the 'ghosts' of Eyre Square, that of John F. Kennedy, who visited Galway in June 1963, was made a freeman of the city, and delivered a famous speech.[238] Eyre Square was later renamed the John F. Kennedy Memorial Park – although no one in Galway speaking either Irish or English would call it that – and a bas-relief of the assassinated president was put there. In the play we hear the voice of J. F. K. from time to time reciting excerpts from his rather sentimental speech as 'a ghostly blue light' (solas gorm taibhsiúil) plays around his monument.

Soon an old Conamara woman and a young man enter. She is 'Brighid na nAmhrán' (Brighid of the songs), the title character of one of Patrick Pearse's stories, and the young man is Pearse himself, who of course had a cottage in Rosmuc.[239] Ó Conaire offers the pair the use of his ass and cart for free, while An Tincéir Rua wants to charge them. As Ó Conaire and the traveller bicker again, the policeman returns, angry that they have taken advantage of his trip to the nearby toilets to renew their squabbling. Exasperated, he decides he will have to get the testimony of the ass if he is to settle the dispute. As the three men go to get the donkey, we hear again the voice of J. F. K.: 'In the years since independence, you have undergone a new and peaceful revolution, an economic and industrial revolution, transforming the face of this land while still holding to the old spiritual and cultural values.'[240] It now becomes clear that Ó Floinn is using the albeit florid and overblown Irish-American idealism of Kennedy's view of the new Ireland to set up a comic contrast with the pettiness and obsession with the past we see in the scenes with Ó Conaire, An Tincéir Rua, and the policeman.[241]

Some of those values are subjected to Ó Floinn's gift for irony, as when the ass, a philosophical beast, asserts his independence of both men claiming ownership and announces that since nobody has fed him for a good while he is going to die right then and there. An Tincéir Rua seizes on the animal's death to call for 'a wake in the old Gaelic style' (tórramh ar an sean-nós Gaelach) and brings in a couple of bottles of *poitín*. But Ó Conaire points out that first the ass must be buried in Eyre Square 'or perhaps the residents would be complaining and saying that there was a mouldy smell in the delightful fresh air of Eyre Square' (nó b'fhéidir go mbeadh na *residents* ag gearán agus a rá go bhfuil seanbhlas tagtha ar aer úr aoibhinn na Faiche Móire).[242] While they set to work, J. F. K.'s voice intones that 'Ireland has excellent relations with both the old and the new, the confidence of both sides, and an opportunity to act where the actions of greater powers might be looked upon with suspicion'.[243] As the play nears its end, we see little confidence or ability to act but a great deal of suspicion, as An Tincéir Rua, his cart, and his *poitín* are taken off to the police station. For the last time J. F. K. praises Ireland as 'a very special place . . . the mother of a great many people, a great many millions of people, and in a sense, a great many nations'.[244] To balance this grandiloquence, the play concludes with the statue of Ó Conaire again sitting on his rock and reciting the opening of 'M'Asal Beag Dubh'. *Taibhsí na Faiche Móire* must have been an entertaining play, easy to follow for the many who knew the story 'M'Asal Beag Dubh'. However, even with Ó Floinn's introduction of the voice of J. F. K. and the ironic if not always immediately clear light it sheds on the Ireland of 1978, the play has been largely forgotten and would probably be difficult to revive for audiences in an Ireland so different from that of 1978, not to mention that of 1963.[245]

Ó Floinn's more substantial play on Ó Conaire, the full-length *An Spailpín Fánach* (The wandering farm labourer), was first performed at Taibhdhearc na Gaillimhe in November 1988, with Seán Ó Murchú directing and Diarmuid Mac an Adhastair in the title role. Reviewing the play for Galway's *City Tribune*, an anonymous critic felt that it would be helped by a few cuts, but praised Ó Floinn for the research he had done and stated: 'But I will wager that there was not anyone in the audience of "An Spailpín Fánach" during this week who did not add to his understanding of one of the principal writers of Irish . . . After seeing this play, there will be no one at all who will not understand this poor man better' (*City Tribune*, 18/11/88).[246] The play has never been revived or published.[247]

Like *Mise Raifteirí an File*, *An Spailpín Fánach* is a bilingual play, but unlike the earlier work, it follows the life of its protagonist pretty much in chronological order apart from an occasional flashback. A major exception is that the play begins with Ó Conaire's death in the charity ward of Dublin's Richmond Hospital, where he is seen as 'number fifteen in ward seven . . . the old tramp with the walking-stick and the long coat' whose cause of death

is 'too much booze and too little food'.[248] The play then shifts to the otherworld, where Ó Conaire meets an officious 'Functionary' (Feidhmeannach)
with 'a big account book' (leabhar mór cuntais).[249] As the Functionary, acting
as *advocatus diaboli*, brings up some of his many roguish misdeeds and Ó
Conaire responds, the play moves back in time to show the young Pádraic
learning his catechism. We then follow the orphaned and Anglophone boy as
he goes to live with his wealthy uncle in Rosmuc, studies Irish in school, is
sent off to study for the priesthood although he has no vocation, emigrates
to London to work in the imperial civil service, becomes involved with the
Gaelic League there, begins to write, and marries and then abandons his
wife and three children.

Act II again opens in the present with An tOllamh Leadrán Mac Leimhe
(Professor Tedium McInanity) of UCG lecturing on Ó Conaire. The action
quickly shifts back to the past, and we see Ó Conaire's Canadian friend
Kathleen Hughes attempting to create a fellowship at UCG that would enable
the writer to devote most of his time to literature. At this point, Ó Floinn
incorporates into the play at some length a debate that took place when An
tAthair Peadar Ua Laoghaire agitated to have Ó Conaire's novel *Deoraíocht*
(Exile)(1910) removed from the list of required readings for matriculation and
First Arts examinations in the National University of Ireland. In the play,
unlike in real life, Ó Conaire himself participates in the discussion.[250]
The play then moves on to show Ó Conaire being tried for refusing to use
English when speaking with a member of the Royal Irish Constabulary and
drunkenly disrupting the opening night of *Diarmaid agus Gráinne* at An
Taibhdhearc. We also see the doctor and nurse of the opening scene in
Richmond Hospital discovering to their surprise that 'that old tramp of ours'
was 'apparently' a writer, although the doctor thinks the pencil stub and
folded piece of paper in his pocket were for jotting down the names of horses he
planned to back. The play ends with Ó Conaire's abandoned English daughter
looking out a hotel window at the statue of the writer in Eyre Square and
wanting to drop a coat over its shoulders, because 'I felt sorry for him, out
there, because he felt – to me – real again, and alone, sitting on the stone, in
the cold. And he had been like that sometimes, wet through, alone, homeless.
And there he was, this man, the back of this man, all sad-looking . . .'[251]

Ó Floinn does a fine job of bringing Ó Conaire alive at pivotal moments
in his life, and the play is thus not only a worthy tribute to the writer, but an
engaging and painfully honest picture of the man. Most interesting are the
imagined conversations in which Ó Conaire discusses his vocation as a writer.
For example, when his soon-to-be-deserted wife questions his writing in Irish
and argues that he should remain in London and write in English as does
Shaw, he tells her that he writes in Irish because of 'something in my blood'
and goes on to say that it would be 'cultural treason to my own nation to

write in the language of the nation that conquered us and tried to destroy our culture'. Echoing Stephen Dedalus, he proclaims: 'I have a sacred duty to use my talent as a writer in trying to create a new literature in Irish for the Irish race.'[252] These ideas are developed at greater length in several conversations with Liam O'Flaherty, conversations based on O'Flaherty's recorded memories of his friendship with Ó Conaire.[253] Here Ó Conaire expresses both his high ideals and his deepest misgivings about his life as a writer of Irish. Believing his friend has 'a poet concealed inside your heart' (file faoi cheilt i do anam istigh), O'Flaherty wants 'to banish you to an island in the sea far from the company of people and from that bottle that is killing you. I would supply you with enough food and plenty of paper and pens, and I wouldn't allow you to come home to Ireland until you had written this great novel I'm sick of listening to you talk about.'[254] In response, Ó Conaire notes that James Joyce and himself were born in the same year, but while Joyce had won international fame with *Ulysses*, 'I am not allowed to write anything except books for schoolchildren, or to be a Fearfeasa Mac Feasa making jokes for the readers of the "Connacht Sentinel".'[255] Worse, he has come to believe it is now too late for him: 'My soul is as withered, as empty, as the shell of that horse chestnut that fell from the tree in the middle of the woods. I have nothing left to say . . .' O'Flaherty also says that his friend could be 'the Dostoevsky of Ireland' (i do Dostoevsky na hÉireann) if he would only write in English. Again, Ó Conaire refuses to do so, but he is obviously troubled when O'Flaherty asks what he has gained from his pledge 'not to write or speak English' (gan Béarla a scríobh ná a labhairt).[256] Later, O'Flaherty tempts him by saying that his ever-growing 'despair' (éadóchas) could be cured were he to write in English, but Ó Conaire is adamant in his refusal: 'But you are wrong, you and any other Irish person who turns his back on the heritage and culture of his own people for the sake of money or fame.'[257] Moreover, replying to O'Flaherty's jibe 'Faithful until death, to land and language, is that how it is?' Ó Conaire asserts:

> That is the lesson I learned from my ancestors, that is the heritage that I have as an inheritance from Flaithrí Ó Maolchonaire and the rest of them who suffered torture or exile for the sake of the Gaelic people. I have hope for the Gaelic people. The vision remains with me that Ireland will be free and Gaelic some day in the future.[258]

He also predicts that Irish will be 'alive again throughout the country' (beo arís ar fud na tíre) in 'two generations, fifty years or so' (dhá ghlúin, leath-chéad bliain nó mar sin).[259] This is stirring stuff, but the play was, of course, written 50 years after Ó Conaire made the prophecy and Ó Floinn himself had to come to terms with the possibility that O'Flaherty's counter prediction might be closer to the truth than was Ó Conaire's optimistic assessment: 'I say that Irish will be dead altogether by that time. There will be no Gaeltacht left at all. There will most likely be university scholars dealing with Irish as Latin is dealt with now, as a dead language.'[260]

Críostóir Ó Floinn's lengthy literary career has, of course, been a refutation of such pessimism. At the same time he has always been a realist about the linguistic situation in Ireland. One wonders, then, what to make of the fact that most of what he has written over the past two decades and more has been in English. Perhaps even more troubling from the point of view of this study is that he has not had a new play in Irish or English produced or published since 1988. The reason may not be far to seek. Ó Floinn has always written his plays to be seen and enjoyed by audiences, but as time has gone on it has become ever more difficult – and it was never easy – to get new plays produced. In a 1968 piece on 'An scríbhneoir in Éirinn' (A writer in Ireland), he stressed the significance of An Damer for the survival of drama in Irish: 'For long years now it was left to Gael-Linn and An Damer to provide consistent support for drama in Irish' (*Feasta*, May 1968, p. 9).[261] By 1988, An Damer was only a memory. Nor did he believe that the Peacock had lived up to the expectations of those who hoped to see plays in Irish performed there regularly and well. Furthermore, he felt the situation with amateur groups and Gaelic League companies was no more promising, as he makes clear in *Consplawkus*: 'While it was true that English plays by writers like John B. Keane, Brian Friel and Hugh Leonard, all contemporaries of mine, were frequently performed by amateur groups, the performance of plays in Irish by any groups associated with the Gaelic League or other Irish organisations was likely to occur as often as a blue moon . . .' And while he is realistic, and experienced, enough to know that a writer of Irish will never get rich from his work, he cannot disregard altogether the sorry truth that 'while I gained the fulfillment of literary creation and that inexplicable feeling of ethnic cultural inheritance from writing those plays in Irish, my total financial reward from performances and publication was probably not much more than a competent busker in Dublin's Grafton Street would earn in a few weeks'.[262] His latest two plays to be premiered, after *Homo Sapiens* was on at An Damer in 1975 and *Taibhsí na Faiche Móire* toured in 1978, were commissioned by Taibhdhearc na Gaillimhe, a theatre with which his relations have not, as we have seen, always been untroubled. In a 7 June 2015 email to me, Ó Floinn wrote of how 'around six years ago' (timpeall sé bliana ó shoin) he submitted to An Taibhdhearc the script for *Taibhsí na Faiche Móire* along with a copy of *Homo Sapiens*, and 'I asked that they be considered to be produced together, I got a letter back from someone from the Board saying that the plays would be put before the Artistic Director and referring kindly to the other plays of mine that filled An Taibhdhearc in years past. I haven't heard another word since.'[263]

Críostóir Ó Floinn long ago earned the right to have his plays produced and revived regularly in Dublin, Galway, and wherever else plays in Irish might be staged. He also deserves to see his work reviewed and discussed with considerably greater insight and knowledge of theatrical genres and techniques than has often been the case. Indeed, it almost seems at times that critics have gone out of their way to judge his work by standards irrelevant or inapplicable to it. The superficial and ill-informed treatment his work for the Gaelic stage has as often as not received must be considered yet another factor in his apparent decision that he can gain 'the fulfillment of literary creation and that inexpressible feeling of ethnic and cultural inheritance' by cultivating other genres in which he has also gained recognition. One can only hope that he has not come to believe that he can adequately give voice to that inheritance exclusively through English.

Whatever the reason, Críostóir Ó Floinn's absence from the underground world of theatre in Irish – a world if anything even more subterranean today than it was when he first used the metaphor in 1967 – has been a loss for both Irish and for the Irish theatre. Over more than three decades he provided audiences on radio, television, and in the theatre with a diverse body of engaging, provocative, and strikingly contemporary plays, plays worth seeing in any language. We can perhaps leave the last word to another versatile and accomplished Gaelic man of letters, the playwright, novelist, translator, fabulist, critic, and controversialist Alan Titley, who in 1981 called Ó Floinn 'an impeccable craftsman and a caustic wordsmith' who 'has never been too popular with the literary establishment because of the independence of his views and the refreshing lack of modesty with which he wields them'. It was, of course, that creative independence and assertive confidence that helped Ó Floinn leave such a profound mark on theatre in Irish with what Titley quite correctly called 'the overall excellence and versatility of a large corpus'.[264]

AFTERWORD

Had one of the founders of An Comhar Drámaíochta returned to Dublin in the 1980s or 1990s – or since – he or she would have been amazed by how little had changed on the Gaelic theatre scene. Indeed he or she might well have been shocked by the fact that in some ways the situation had gotten worse. After all, in the 1920s and 1930s An Comhar Drámaíochta itself had put and kept Irish on stage at the Abbey and Peacock, guaranteeing the language a regular place in the National Theatre. After 1980, Irish vanished altogether from the Abbey[1] and was relegated to ever more infrequent appearances in the Peacock, although, to be fair, some of the productions in Irish the Peacock either mounted or hosted were memorable and significant events. Thus it was at the Peacock that playgoers first got to see Antaine Ó Flatharta's *Gaeilgeoirí* (Learners of Irish) (1982), *Imeachtaí na Saoirse* (The events of freedom) (1983), *Ag Ealaín in Éirinn* (Arting around in Ireland) (1986) and *An Solas Dearg* (The red light) (1995), the last produced at the Peacock by the independent professional company Amharclann de hÍde (The Hyde theatre). Other major works first staged at the Peacock were Alan Titley's *Tagann Godot* (Godot turns up) (1990), directed by Tomás Mac Anna, and Seán Mac Mathúna's *Gadaí Géar na Geamh Oíche* (The bitter thief of a winter's night) (1992), directed by David Byrne. These were fine plays, but they were far outnumbered by productions in English at the Peacock. Thus, with the language largely excluded or side-lined in the National Theatre complex and An Damer defunct, Gaelic theatre companies in the Dublin of the new millennium, like those in the Dublin of the 1920s and 1930s, were in effect wandering homeless players.

As was also true in those previous decades, however, Gaelic companies did emerge to provide what audiences they could find with plays in the first official language. Perhaps the most important of these since 1980 was Amharclann de hÍde, founded as a professional company in 1992 with Clíodhna Ní Anluain as its first artistic director. She was eventually succeeded in 1998 by Bríd

Ní Ghallchóir, who has since become one of the most creative forces in Gaelic theatre. Amharclann de hÍde ceased operations in 2001. Yet despite its short life and the fact that it never had its own stage, the group premiered some of the finest plays in Irish ever seen, works like Éilís Ní Dhuibhne's *Dún na mBan trí Thine* (The fort of the women on fire) at the Peacock in 1994 and her *Milseog an tSamhraidh* (The summer pudding) at the Samuel Beckett Centre at Trinity College in 1997; Antaine Ó Flatharta's *An Solas Dearg* at the Peacock in 1995; Liam Ó Muirthile's *Fear an Tae* (The tea man) at the Andrew's Lane Theatre in 1995 and his *Liodán na hAbhann* (The litany of the river) at the Crypt Arts Centre in 1999; Alan Titley's *An Ghráin agus an Ghruaim* (Hate and gloom) at the Samuel Beckett Centre in 1999; and Celia de Fréine's *Nára Turas é in Aistear* (May it not be a wasted journey) at the New Theatre in 2000. The first two of these plays were directed by Kathy McArdle, the third by Deirdre Friel, all the others by Bríd Ní Ghallchóir.

Amharclann de hÍde was not the only (unsuccessful) attempt to create a professional Gaelic company in Dublin. It was preceded by Deilt (Delta), founded by Ray Yeates in 1983. Despite the involvement of an impressive group of writers, among them Nuala Ní Dhomhnaill, Liam Ó Muirthile, and Gabriel Rosenstock, the company lasted less than a decade. Perhaps its most interesting productions were Seán Ó Broin's *Daoine ar an DART* (People on the DART), a series of short plays directed by Yeates for the 1987 Dublin Theatre Festival and actually performed on DART (Dublin Area Rapid Transit) trains, and Antaine Ó Flatharta's *An Fear Bréige* (The scarecrow), directed by Yeates at the Project Arts Centre in 1991.

As always, however, it has been amateur companies that have been the mainstays of the Gaelic theatre movement, with the most active in Dublin being Aisteoirí Bulfin (The Bulfin actors), a group that emerged in 1967 from the Gaelic League's Liam Bulfin branch, which had long been involved with Gaelic drama. Over the past half-century Aisteoirí Bulfin have remained a force in the capital, regularly producing new work, most notably by Aodh Ó Domhnaill, who has provided the company with no fewer than nine plays to date. Aisteoirí Bulfin also produced Gearóid Mac Unfraidh's *Geasa* (Taboos), directed by Roy Yeates at the Axis Arts Centre in Ballymun, Dublin, in 2004.[2]

In Galway, Taibhdhearc na Gaillimhe remains the most important venue for plays in Irish, although the last four decades have in many ways been the worst of times and the best of times for the theatre. On the negative side, much overdue renovations in the 1970s and a serious fire in 2007 kept the theatre dark for extended periods of time. More troubling, however, have been the periods when An Taibhdhearc was simply idle, or, as has frequently been the case, hired out to companies performing in English. On two recent stays in Galway totalling over a year, I found it just as likely to see a play in English there by Lady Gregory or even David Mamet as to see something in

Irish. Moreover, when the play was in Irish the quality of the production was not always all that could be desired. It should also be noted that problems at An Taibhdhearc have been exacerbated by occasionally bitter internal disputes about the theatre's management and direction.

On the other hand, during these same decades An Taibhdhearc, like the Peacock, has produced some of the best work it has ever done. In particular, it has introduced first-rate new plays by native speakers from the neighbouring Conamara Gaeltacht, a development that would certainly have delighted the theatre's original founders and funders. Among such plays that had their premieres at An Taibhdhearc were Joe Steve Ó Neachtain's *Níor Mhaith Liom Do Thrioblóid* (I'm sorry for your trouble) (2000), directed by Maidhc P. Ó Conaola,[3] *In Ainm an Athar* (In the name of the father) (2006), also directed by Ó Conaola, and *Faoi Dheireadh Thiar* (At long last) (2008), directed by Josie Ó Cualáin; Micheál Ó Conghaile's *Cúigear Chonamara* (Five Conamara people) (2003), directed by Darach Mac Con Iomaire, *Jude* (2007), directed by Seán Ó Tarpaigh, and *Go dTaga Do Ríocht* (Thy kingdom come) (2008), directed by Brendan Murray and performed at Áras na Gaeilge at NUIG during the Galway Arts Festival;[4] and Breandán Ó hEaghra's *Gaeilgeoir Deireannach Charna* (The last Irish speaker in Carna) (2005), directed by Darach Ó Dubháin.

Nor has An Taibhdhearc been alone in staging work in Irish in Galway. In 1987, Diarmaid de Faoite, Marina Ní Dhubháin, Aodh Ó Coileáin, and Trevor Ó Clochartaigh founded Na Fánaithe (The wanderers), who, in addition to touring nationwide and running drama classes in Conamara, also performed in Galway. This venture lasted until the mid 1990s, producing several plays by Ó Clochartaigh. Companies currently working in Irish in Galway are the bilingual group Moonfish, founded in 2006 by the sisters Máiréad and Ionia Ní Chróinín, and the explosively inventive Fíbín Teo[5] founded by Darach Ó Tuairisg and Micheál Ó Domhnaill in 2003 and using music, puppets, masks, videos and whatever else it thinks will work to create vibrant theatre in Irish, particularly for young audiences. In addition to performing throughout Ireland as well as in the United Kingdom, the United States, and Europe, Fíbín was invited by the Abbey to produce Paul Mercier's *Setanta* at the Peacock in 2006. Other productions of note include *Stair na hÉireann* (The history of Ireland) (2004), *Stair na gCeilteach* (The history of the Celts) (2013), and *Dracula: An Chéad Gaeilgeóir* (Dracula: the first Irish enthusiast) and Mercier's *Réiltín* (both 2014), as well as a strikingly original revival of Ní Ghráda's *An Triail* (The trial), first performed in 2006 and toured regularly since. Based like Fíbín in Conamara, the Salamander Theatre Company was founded in 2006 by the playwright, novelist, and publisher Darach Ó Scolaí, whose own plays *Craos* (Gluttony) and *An tSeanbhróg* (The old shoe) were given their first productions by the group in Dublin, the former directed by the author himself at the New Theatre, the latter directed by Darach Mac Con Iomaire at the Project Arts Centre.[6]

While theatre in Irish has remained in the shadows in cities like the post-Compántas Cork, Limerick, and Waterford,[7] it has found a home in West Belfast, where one of the most heartening developments since 1980 has been the success of Aisling Ghéar (A bitter vision).[8] Founded in 1997, it is now the resident theatre company at Cultúrlann McAdam Ó Fiaich (The MacAdam Ó Fiaich cultural centre). Aisling Ghéar does not, however, limit its efforts to its Belfast base, but also tours throughout Ireland. The company performs both original work and translations, often from unexpected sources like Niccolò Machiavelli, Eugène Ionesco, Samuel Beckett, or Dario Fo.[9] Perhaps its most significant original productions to date have been Biddy Jenkinson's *Ó Rajerum* in 1999 and *Mise Subhó agus Maccó* (Myself, Subhó and Maccó), both at the Cultúrlann, the former in 1999, the latter in 2001; Celia de Fréine's *Anraith Neantóige* (Nettle soup) at the Dublin Theatre Festival in 2004; and Dan Duggan's sci-fi play *Makaronik* at the Lyric Theatre in Belfast in 2014. To reach audiences with little Irish, the company regularly provides simultaneous translation of its performances. With Máiréad Ní Ghráda's *An Triail* on both the Northern Irish A-Level and the Republic's Leaving Certificate examinations, Aisling Ghéar has also taken this play on the road annually since 2004. All of these plays were directed by Bríd Ní Ghallchóir, the company's artistic director. In 20 years, Aisling Ghéar has established itself as one of the most prolific and creative forces in contemporary Gaelic theatre.

If that theatre has remained almost entirely a part-time amateur venture with no home to call its own except in Galway and Belfast and just a small and never predictable audience, those hard facts have not discouraged a fair number of accomplished playwrights, writers who could make a name for themselves with similar work in English. We have met more than a few of them in passing so far. Here we can say a bit more about their work. As previously noted, a gratifying development in the years since 1980 has been the emergence of excellent playwrights from the Gaeltacht. Conamara has definitely taken the lead here. The first of these Conamara dramatists to appear was Antaine Ó Flatharta, who has, in plays like *Gaeilgeoirí*, *Imeachtaí na Saoirse*, *An Fear Bréige*, and *An Solas Dearg*, shown a gift for treating issues dealing with language revival and the survival of Irish in the Gaeltacht – issues that could have been seen as already written to death – in ways that are new, provocative, and able to generate fresh thinking. At the same time, he always takes for granted that the Gaeltacht is inhabited as it always has been by actual human beings with lives, aspirations, and problems as complex as those of people anywhere. Indeed he underscores this point in his play *Grásta i Meiriceá* (Grace in America) (1990), in which two undocumented young Irishmen from Conamara wrestle with their mid-Atlantic identity on a trip to Memphis to see Elvis Presley's mansion and grave. Like Ó Flatharta, Breandán Ó hEaghra and Darach Ó Scolaí, the latter not a native speaker but now resident in Conamara, have made the language movement itself a theme in their work. The difference, however, is that they have treated issues of language survival and revival through comedy, as in Ó hEaghra's *Gaeilgeoir Deireannach Charna* or Ó Scolaí's hilarious *Coinneáil Orainn* (Carry on), first performed at An Taibhdhearc in 2005, in which the government tries to track down the last living native speakers of Irish, or *An Braon Aníos* (The drop down), which premiered at Galway's Áras na nGael in 2006 and in which the search for housing for language students in the Gaeltacht and the search for Osama Bin Laden intersect against a background of rising seas due to global warming. We have already mentioned the plays of Joe Steve Ó Neachtain and Micheál Ó Conghaile, who have brought a similar insider's incisive eye to life in contemporary Conamara, capturing the ethos and customs that make the place special while showing their characters wrestling with the same universal issues that confront people elsewhere in modern Ireland and throughout the western world.

The Donegal and Munster Gaeltachtaí have been considerably less prolific in playwrights. The poet Cathal Ó Searcaigh from Gort a' Choirce, Co. Donegal has tried his hand at plays, mostly one-acters, but also the full-length *Oíche Dhrochghealaí* (Night of an evil moon), his reworking of the story of Salome. This play had its premiere at the Grianán Theatre in Letterkenny, Co. Donegal in 2001, with Páraic Breathnach directing. At the other end of the country, Corca Dhuibhne's Breandán M. Mac Gearailt has written of Gaelic footballers in *Scaoil leis an gCaid* (Let the ball go) and of university students in shared housing in *An Saol Eile* (The other world). The former was first performed at Féile Drámaíochta na gColáistí (The colleges' drama festival) in Dublin in 1997, the latter at the same festival in Cork the following year.[10] An Lab in Dingle has provided a home for both the youth group AnnÓg and the Ar Aghaidh (Onwards) company, which have produced recent work by local playwrights Maria Ní Mhurchú and Ceaití Ní Bheildiúin (originally from Co. Dublin), with AnnÓg performing the former's *An Préachán Bán* (The white crow) in a Centra supermarket in Dingle in 2006. Ní Mhurchú's *Tomás na bPúcaí* (Thomas of the ghosts) was performed in 1999 by another important Corca Dhuibhne company, Aisteoirí Bhréanainn.

Native speakers have not, of course, had the stage to themselves. Alan Titley has brought his anarchic and mordant wit to bear on a modern classic in *Tagann Godot*, in which the title character is the one who most regrets an arrival he does not survive. In *An Ghráin agus an Ghruaim*, Titley sends up virtually every cliché associated with rural stage-Irish characters, with special attention to Martin MacDonagh's version of the species. Rather unexpectedly, Titley has also written a play based on Irish folklore about the otherworld people or 'fairies' in his *Méar na Sióige Aerai Áille* (The finger of the merry, beautiful fairy), first produced by Aisteoirí Ráth Chairn at Dublin's THEatre SPACE in 2004, with Beairtle Ó Curraoin directing.[11] Such creative use of folklore is a speciality of the bilingual writer Éilís Ní Dhuibhne, as is evident in her haunting play *Dún na mBan trí Thine*, where a suburban Dublin wife and mother believes the traditional otherworld and its denizens exist in eerie proximity to her home and family. Ní Dhuibhne has also shown a talent for bringing together folklore and history in new and intriguing ways in *Milseog an tSamhraidh*, a play that follows two young Irishwomen who come to Wales to escape the Great Famine and end up in the home of the famous early Anglo-Irish feminists Eleanor Charlotte Butler and Sarah Ponsonby, the 'Ladies of Llangollen'. History is also a central concern for Gearóid Mac Unfraidh, whose *Geasa* offers a rare Gaelic look at the lives of those Irishmen who fought in the British army in the trenches of the First World War. More immediately political are his *Éiric* (Retribution) (2001) and *Séanadh* (Denial) (2015). The former, set in Israeli-occupied Lebanon and drawing on the author's own experience as an Irish soldier on peace-keeping duties with the United Nations, was given its first production at An Taibhdhearc in 2001. The latter, which had its premiere at the Pearse Centre in Dublin in 2015 and then went on to that year's Oireachtas, offers a republican perspective on the Irish state's plans for the centennial commemoration of the 1916 Easter Rising. Political issues are also at the forefront of Celia de Fréine's *Anraith Neantóige*, which involves its audience in the absurdity of life in a country plagued with endemic and pointless warfare. Her *Tearmann* (Sanctuary) is a more realistic engagement with another of the major social issues of the twenty-first century, the plight of refugees and asylum seekers in Ireland and throughout the developed world. Here, as does Donal O'Kelly in *Asylum! Asylum!* de Fréine shows us how the asylum seekers themselves can be psychologically warped by what they have suffered and the need to manipulate those who control their destinies. Startlingly, this play does not seem to have been performed yet. Her *Nara Turas é in Aistear* (May it not be a wasted journey), a joint 2000 production by Amharclann de hÍde and Aisling Ghéar, was directed by Bríd Ní Ghallchóir and first performed at Dublin's New Theatre before being taken on tour. It is set during the 1979 visit of Pope John Paul II to Ireland, a visit of little relevance to the lives of the young Irish people we see on stage. *Cóirín na dTonn* (Cóirín of the waves), which also does not seem to have been produced, is set in Conamara and deals movingly with middle-aged lovers in the shadow of sickness, incapacity, and death.

These are all fine and challenging plays, and there are others that could have been mentioned. All of them deserve to be seen and not just for a few performances (much less a single one) when first produced. Too many of them may, however, sink into the oblivion that has always threatened the work of Gaelic playwrights. Yet still those playwrights soldier on in a theatre that is still very much a subterranean movement, and it is such dedication, as well as their sheer talent, that should ensure drama in Irish will survive, however precariously, into the new millennium, making necessary other books like this one in the future.

Notes

Foreword

1   An authoritative overview of developments since 1980 is provided in Máirín Nic Eoin, 'Contemporary prose and drama in Irish 1940–2000', in *The Cambridge History of Irish Literature*, vol. 2, ed. Margaret Kelleher and Philip O'Leary (Cambridge: Cambridge University Press, 2006), pp 270–316.

Introduction

1   Is oiriúnach an mhaise é gurb é áit ina bhfuilimid ag cruinniú chun na Féile seo ná an catacóm seo faoi thalamh. It is worth noting that another of the most important venues for Gaelic drama in Dublin, the Damer Hall, was also in a basement.

2   See Philip O'Leary, *The Prose Literature of the Gaelic Revival, 1881–1921: Ideology and Innovation* (State College: Pennsylvania State University Press, 1994), p. 296; and Ciarán Ó Coigligh, 'An teispéireas drámata: stracfhéachaint ar dhrámaíocht Chríostóra Uí Fhloinn' (The dramatic experience: a quick look at the drama of Críostóir Ó Floinn), in *Mangarae: Aistí Litríochta agus Teanga* (Miscellany: essays on literature and language) (Cathair na Mart: Foilseacháin Náisiúnta Teoranta, 1987), p. 19.

3   Is mór an t-adhbhar aithbhéile dhúinne gan scríobhnóireacht dhúthchais i gcomhair an árdáin a bheith mar shompladh fé n-ár gcúram anois.

4   The programme can be found in the collection of the Pearse Museum (in what was Scoil Éanna) in Rathfarnham, Dublin.

5   The Irish name for this organisation is Conradh na Gaeilge, but since the English form of the name is far better known among general readers it is the form that will be used throughout this book.

6   Pádraig Ó Siochfhradha, quoted by Seán Ó Morónaigh, 'Drámaíocht ó dhúchas: ábhar ar leith ón dtraidisiún' (Drama from the native tradition: remarkable material from the tradition), in *Drámaíocht ó Dhúchas ó Bhéalaithris Thaidhg Uí Chonchubhair* (Drama from the native tradition from the oral narration of Tadhg Ó Conchubhair) (Camas: An Comhlachas Náisiúnta Drámaíochta, 2005), p. 19. Níl na rudaí céanna i gceann aon duine eile in Éirinn . . . Saghas deilbhe leo féin sa litríocht is ea na h-eachtraithe filíochta atá ag Tadhg. Cia h-é do dhein ar dtúis iad?

7   Ó Morónaigh, 'Drámaíocht ó dhúchas', in *Drámaíocht ó Dhúchas ó Bhéalaithris Thaidhg Uí Chonchubhair*, p. 21.

8   While these three *drámaí* have a good deal in common with the *agallaimh* (dialogues) Mac Coluim also collected from Ó Conchubhair, there are enough significant differences to justify Ó Siochfhradha's seeing them as a separate form. At any rate, these three little skits were not to have their first modern performance until Corca Dhuibhne's Aisteoirí Bhréanainn, with Seán Ó Morónaigh directing, performed them in Corca Dhuibhne in 2004 (*An Dá Dhrúncaer*) and 2005 (*Caismirt na gCearc* and *Cleamhnas an Bhacaigh*). The texts, photos of the casts, and examples of Ó Conchubhair's *agallaimh* can be found in *Drámaíocht ó Dhúchas ó Bhéalaithris Thaidhg Uí Chonchubhair*.

9   This information was provided by the late Professor Kenneth Nilsen of St Francis Xavier University in Antigonish, Nova Scotia to Professor Nollaig Mac Congáil of the National University of Ireland, Galway, who shared it with me.

10   Lady Gregory, *Poets and Dreamers: Studies and Translations from the Irish* (Teddington: The Echo Library, 2006 [1903]), p. 101. I discuss Lady Gregory's involvement with theatre in Irish in '"What would Willie say?": Lady Gregory and popular theatre in Irish', *Journal of the Galway Archaeological and Historical Society* LXIII (2011), pp 158–80.

11   Tabhairfimíd an chéad leabhar de *Bhanba* arís do'n té 'neosfaidh dúinn cionnus a chuirfidhe tonn ar bogadh ar an árdán, cionnus a chruinneochadh móir-sheisear fear timcheall poill phludaigh ann, agus bó do tharrac amach as le téadaibh agus le málaibh, cionnus fhéadfaidhe an bhó do choimeád 'na leidhpín ar an árdán agus uisce is pluda ag scéitheadh ó na slineánaibh, cionnus thiomáinfidhe as san go dtí an cró í, cionnus, – cionnus, – cionnus a chuirfear an *dráma* ar an árdán, sin é tá uainn.

12   It is worth noting that it has always been the case that plays that win Oireachtas prizes are by no means guaranteed production, and many have never been performed.

13   Is mór an díoghbháil i n-aghaidh dráma na Gaedhilge, daoine do chur ar an árdán agus ná feadair siad ó thalamh an domhain cad é an bhrigh atá leis an méid cainte a deirid.

14   He was referring here to plays in Irish produced on the Abbey stage by An Comhar Drámaíochta. Acht an chéad dráma a sgríobhfas duine aca, dá mba i ndán nach mbeadh ann acht rud sgaoilte gan chuma gan déanamh – agus nach mbeadh áit ar bith aca le n-a léiriughadh acht i mbóitheach ag tóin na bó, agus coinneal i mbuidéal pórtair mar sholus aca – beidh buadh aige nach rabh ag na drámaí a bhí i n-Amharclainn na Mainistreach. Tús nádúrtha a bhéas ann agus tiocfaidh as le linn na h-aimsire.

15   See Proinsias Mac Aonghusa, *Ar Son na Gaeilge: Conradh na Gaeilge 1893–1993: Stair Sheanchais* (For the Irish: the Gaelic League 1893–1993: a history) (Baile Átha Cliath: Conradh na Gaeilge, 1993), pp 131–5. In some ways, this feud paralleled a split between the League in Cork and the Central branch in Dublin. See Traolach Ó Ríordáin, *Conradh na Gaeilge i gCorcaigh, 1894–1910* (The Gaelic League in Cork, 1894–1910) (Baile Átha Cliath: Cois Life, 2000).

16   See Pádraig Ó Siadhail, *Stair Dhrámaíocht na Gaeilge 1900–1970* (A history of theatre in Irish 1900–1970) (Indreabhán: Cló Iar-Chonnachta, 1993), p. 51.

17   Béaslaí himself fought during Easter Week and was interned afterwards. He spent much of the War of Independence on the run. During the Civil War he was an officer in the Free State army as well as being the state censor. Bhíomair ag treabhadh chun cinn go maith nuair a tháinig Seachtain na Cásca, agus d'imthigh scaipeadh ar na hAisteoirí, mar ní raibh éan bhuachaill ortha ná go raibh baint aige le hobair na Seachtaine sin.

18   An saoghal buadhartha fé ndeara é, is dócha, ach pé nidh é ba chúis leis, ba mhór an chéim síos agus ba mhór an cheataighe d'obair na Gaedhilge é.

19   The Oireachtas returned in diminished form in 1924 and was then suspended until 1939. The loss of this annual festival, which had sponsored competitions for the writing of plays since 1901 and was the major venue for the performance of plays in Irish, was a major setback for playwrights and performers.

20   Its original name seems to have been An Comhar um Drámaí Gaedhilge (The society dealing with plays in Irish). See 'Plays in Gaelic: a notable movement', *II*, 8/10/23. It was Risteárd Ó Foghludha ('Fiachra Éilgeach') who came up with the name An Comhar Drámaíochta. See Donncha Ó Súilleabháin, 'Tús agus fás na drámaíochta i nGaeilge' (The beginning and growth of drama in Irish), *Ardán*, spring 1972, p. 17.

21   De réir mar a chloisim tá buidhean bheag ann fé láthair gurb é a gcuspóir bun-chloch an stáitse Ghaedhilge a leagan agus ná stadfaidh den obair go dtí go mbeidh a háit dlisteanach cheart ag an nGaedhilg i ndrámaidheacht na tíre.

22   The reference to 'Liverpool Irish' was a dig at Béaslaí, who had been born and raised in that English city. Déarfar liom ar ndóighe nach bhfuil eolas na ceirde sin ag muintir na Gaedhealtachta. Aidhmhighim. Acht dá olcas iad tá siad chomh maith leis an dream a bhí i n-Amharclainn na Mainistreach le cúig bliadhna. Ins an chéad chás de níl siad i muinghin Ghaedhilg Liverpool.

23   Tá sé dona go leor againn an Ghaedhealtacht a bheith ag imtheacht, agus gan sgaifte de yahoos mhacánta gan béal gan teangaidh a bheith a' snagarsaigh ar ardán agus ag iarraidh a chur i gcéill dúinn gur teanga ár sinnsear atá aca.

24   The plan is spelled out in 'Amharclann Ghaedhealach: gádh na huaire' (A Gaelic theatre: the need at this time), *IP*, 11/10/37.

25   Ernest Blythe, 'Gaelic drama', in *The Irish Theatre: Lectures Delivered during the Abbey Theatre Festival Held in Dublin in August 1938*, ed. Lennox Robinson (London: Macmillan and Co., 1939), p. 186. The job would still not be easy: 'And even if we had everything we could desire in the way of players and producer, it would be by no means easy to do consistently good work in a Gaelic Theatre in Dublin.'

26   See Philip O'Leary, *Writing beyond the Revival: Facing the Future in Gaelic Prose 1940–1951* (Dublin: University College Dublin Press, 2011), p. 284.

27   For a more positive view of the potential of Blythe's plan, see the comments of the anonymous reviewer of Máiréad Ní Ghráda's 1945 play *Giolla an tSolais* (Lucifer) at the Abbey: 'Some night Blythe's plan will come to fruition and it will be hard for us to get seats for a play worth standing to see' (Oidhche éigin tiocfaidh bláth ar rún an Bhlaghdaigh agus beidh sé doiligh againn suidheacháin a fháil fá choinne dráma ar bhfiú seasamh le h-amharc air) (*Inniu*, Apr. 1945, p. 3).

28   For a discussion of the Abbey's takeover of An Comhar, see Donncha Ó Súilleabháin, 'Tús agus fás na drámaíochta i nGaeilge', *Ardán*, summer 1972, pp 9–11.

29   See the listings of theatre productions in the Dublin daily papers during the Christmas pantomime season for these years.

30   The Civil War and the bitterness that accompanied and survived it had a disastrous effect on the League's membership figures and thus its finances. See Aindrias Ó Muimhneacháin, *Dóchas agus Duainéis: Scéal Chonradh na Gaeilge 1922–1932* (Hope and difficulty: the story of the Gaelic League 1922–1932) (Corcaigh: Cló Mercier, n.d.); and Donncha Ó Súilleabháin, *Scéal an Oireachtais 1897–1924* (The story of the Oireachtas 1897–1924) (Baile Átha Cliath: An Clóchomhar, 1984).

31   The whimsical names of these shows do not translate well, but the meanings should be fairly obvious nonetheless.

32   The schools became particularly active in drama after the foundation of An Cumann Scoildrámaíochta (The schools drama society). See Donncha Ó Súilleabháin, *An Cumann Scoildrámaíochta 1934–1984* (Baile Átha Cliath: An Clóchomhar, 1986).

33   See Liam Ó Lonargáin's interview with Pilib Ó Ceallaigh, the manager of the Peacock, in *Feasta*, Sept. 1968, pp 14–16.

34   For Gael-Linn, see Máiréad Ní Chinnéide, *Scéal Ghael-Linn* (The story of Gael-Linn) (Indreabhán: Cló Iar-Chonnachta, 2013), esp. pp 163–6. See also Máiréad Ní Chinnéide, *An Damer: Stair Amharclainne* (The Damer: history of a theatre) (Baile Átha Cliath: Gael-Linn, 2008), esp. pp 13–14.

35   Níos mó airgid, níos mó scríbhneoirí, níos mó daoine ag freastal ar na drámaí. An rud is tábhachtaí thar aon rud eile ná scríbhneoirí a spreagadh agus a chothú. Dá mbeadh na scríbhneoirí go flúirseach againn thiocfadh na rudaí eile.

36   See Michael Sheridan's perceptive thoughts on this new venture in 'Cultural script', *IP*, 18/12/79; and 'An complacht nua drámaíochta Gaeilge' (The new Irish-language drama company), *Inniu*, 7/9/79.

37   This show took its inspiration from the seventeenth-century prose work *Pairlement Chloinne Tomáis* (The parliament of Clan Thomas), a satirical attack on social climbers in the new class system that emerged in Ireland after the Cromwellian wars.

38   Blythe, 'Gaelic drama', in *The Irish Theatre*, ed. Robinson, p. 188.

39   Minutes of the meeting of 12 May 1930, Taibhdhearc Papers, NUIG.

40   A rá's de gur thug tú fá thuairim 1,500 daoine le chéile le n-a bheith ag éisteacht le Gaeilge ar feadh thrí n-uair a' chluig oíche gheimhridh agus an flú ar dhuine as gach ceathrair ins an phríomh-chathair! Táim ag déanamh iontais de do éacht ó shoin agus ní stadfad de, óir ní thig liom deire iontais a dhéanamh de.

41   Shaothraigh Aisteoirí na Gaillimhe cáil dóibh féin de bharr na ndrámaí a léirigheadar in Amharclainn an Gheata . . . Is breágh an bhuidhean aisteoirí atá anois ag an Taibhdhearc; tá a gcéird foghlumtha aca chomh fada a théigheas geáitsí agus gothaí an stáitse dhe; tá chuile eolas aca a théigheas le soillsiú agus feistiú stáitse.

42   Amateur companies received assistance from An Chomhairle Náisiúnta Drámaíochta, established by the Gaelic League in Dublin in 1959. Among the activities of this group was the publication of the journal *Ardán*, which provided material of all kinds relating to theatre in Irish, including practical suggestions with regard to acting, staging, etc. An Comhlachas Náisiúnta Drámaíochta, based in Camus in the Conamara Gaeltacht, was created by people who felt that the Comhairle, which had its offices in the Gaelic League headquarters, was too Dublin-centric and too closely linked to the institutional language movement. An Comhlachas replaced the Comhairle as the major clearing-house for Gaelic theatre activities. In 1999, An Comhlachas began publishing *Stáitse: Iris na Drámaíochta Gaeilge*, its own journal along the lines of *Ardán*.

43   Among its early patrons was Daniel Corkery.

44   According to Pádraig Ó Siadhail, the reason that Compántas Chorcaí did not do the premiere of this play was because 'it is likely that it was believed that the little group could not do a production worthy of it' (is dealraitheach gur creideadh nach bhféadfadh an bhuíon bheag léiriú fiúntach a dhéanamh air). See Ó Siadhail, *Stair Dhrámaíocht na Gaeilge*, p. 157.

45   These three plays were all originally produced at An Damer.

46   Introducing this quote in *Stair Dhrámaíocht na Gaeilge*, Ó Siadhail writes: 'Working under the auspices of Everyman, Compántas Chorcaí maintained the high standard that was to be found in the productions in English' (Agus Compántas Chorcaí ag obair faoi choimirce Everyman, cloíodh leis an chaighdeán ard a bhí le fáil sna léirithe Béarla) (p. 159).

47   Vera Ryan, *Dan Donovan: An Everyman's Life* (Cork: The Collins Press, 2008), pp 99–100.

48   Máirín Breathnach Uí Choileáin, *Aisteoirí an Spidéil* (The Spiddal actors) (Indreabhán: Cló Iar-Chonnachta, 2015).

49   Ibid., p. 72. At a February 2016 Dublin conference on theatre in Irish, a long-time member of the company, the actor and playwright Joe Steve Ó Neachtain, recalled how warmly the Spiddal players were welcomed at these festivals.

50   By this year of 1937 the group had already taken the stage 87 times. See 'I nGaedhealtacht Thír Chonaill: léiriú drámaí i nGaoth Dobhair' (In the Donegal Gaeltacht: performance of plays in Gaoth Dobhair), *IP*, 1/9/37.

51   Ócáid í í gcónaí í nuair a thagann Aisteoirí Ghaoth Dobhair go dtí an Damer – togha Gaeilge sa tuin ar leith gur annamh a chloistear ar stáitse na cathrach . . . Tá sé mar a bheadh gaoth ghlan ón dtaobh ó thuaidh ag séideadh trí Fhaiche Stiabhna . . . Is breá liom go raibh an teach lán go doras.

52   See Áine Nic Giolla Bhríde, 'Drámaíocht i nDún na nGall' (Drama in Donegal), in *Scríbhneoireacht na gConallach* (Writing by Donegal people), ed. Nollaig Mac Congáil (Baile Átha Cliath: Coiscéim, 1990), p. 203.

53   I have relied heavily in this introduction on Pádraig Ó Siadhail's *Stair Dhrámaíocht na Gaeilge 1900–1970*; Donncha Ó Súilleabháin's 'Tús agus fás na drámaíochta i nGaeilge', *Ardán*, Oireachtas 1971, spring and summer 1972; Diarmaid Ó Coileáin's five-part series 'Drámaíocht na Gaeilge' (Drama in Irish), *Inniu*, 31/8, 7/9, 14/9, 21/9 and 28/9/79; Caoimhe Ní Bhaoighill's 'An drámaíocht Ghaeilge 1954–89' (Drama in Irish 1954–89), *IMN*, 1991, pp 131–61; Alan Titley's '"Neither the boghole nor Berlin": drama in the Irish language from then until now', in *Nailing Theses: Selected Essays* (Belfast: Lagan Press, 2011), pp 267–77; Brian Ó

Conchubhair's '"Twisting in the wind": Irish-language stage theatre 1884–2014', in *The Oxford Handbook of Modern Irish Theatre*, ed. Nicholas Grene and Christopher Morash (Oxford: Oxford University Press, 2016), pp 251–68; *Taibhdhearc na Gaillimhe 1928–2003*, the booklet compiled by Fiona Bateman, Kieran Hoare, and Lionel Pilkington for the exhibit '75 Years of Taibhdhearc na Gaillimhe', which ran from 14 July to 8 August 2003 at the James Hardiman Library, National University of Ireland, Galway; Máiréad Ní Chinnéide's *An Damer: Stair Amharclainne*; Máirín Breathnach Uí Choileáin's *Aisteoirí an Spidéil*; Áine Nic Giolla Bhríde's 'Drámaíocht i nDún na nGall'; and Pádraig Ó Baoighill's 'Aisteoirí Ghaoth Dobhair', *Comhar*, Nov. 1955, pp 3–5 and 23. I discuss the history of the theatre in Irish in *The Prose Literature of the Gaelic Revival, 1881–1921*, pp 294–315; *Gaelic Prose in the Irish Free State 1922–1939* (Dublin: University College Dublin Press, 2004), pp 458–503; and *Writing beyond the Revival*, pp 281–386.

CHAPTER ONE
Unlikely Iconoclast

1 Diarmuid Breathnach and Máire Ní Mhurchú, *1882–1982: Beathaisnéis a hAon* (Biography one) (Baile Átha Cliath: An Clóchomhar, 1986), p. 75.
2 Siobhán Ní Bhrádaigh, *Máiréad Ní Ghráda: Ceannródaí Drámaíochta* (A pioneer of drama) (Indreabhán: Cló Iar-Chonnachta, 1996), p. 17. She seems to have joined the Gaelic League as soon as she came to Dublin.
3 Ibid., p. 20. For a detailed discussion of her full-time career in radio, see Eileen Morgan, '"Unbroken service": Máiréad Ní Ghráda's career at 2RN, Ireland's first broadcasting station', *Éire-Ireland*, fall-winter 2002, pp 53–78.
4 Quoted in Ní Bhrádaigh, *Máiréad Ní Ghráda*, p. 20.
5 See Pádraic Ó hEithir, 'Máiréad Ní Ghráda', in *Comóradh Mháiréad Ní Ghráda: Drámadóir – Craoltóir – Gearrscéalaí, Cill Mháille, Co. an Chláir, 14–15 Meitheamh, 1997. Leabhrán Cuimhneacháin* (A commemoration of Máiréad Ní Ghráda: dramatist – broadcaster – short story writer. Kilmaley, Co. Clare, 14–15 June, 1997. Commemorative booklet), p. 16.
6 The subjects of these 'pictures' are not always identified, but we do know, for example, that the one for 28 and 30 June 1947 was John Mitchell and that for 14 June 1947 was the composer Schumann (from the radio listings in the *Irish Independent*).
7 See the list in Ní Bhrádaigh, *Máiréad Ní Ghráda*, pp 78–9.
8 Ursula Ní Dhálaigh, 'Máiréad Ní Ghráda oideachasóir' (Educator), in *Comóradh Mháiréad Ní Ghráda . . . Leabhrán Cuimhneacháin*, p. 4. Is beag Éireannach os cionn 40 bliain d'aois nach raibh ceann éigin de leabhair Mháiréad aici/aige ar scoil. See also Domhnaill Ó Loingsigh, 'Mo chéad leabhar scoile!: na seoda litríochta a d'fhág Máiréad Ní Ghráda againn' (My first school book!: the literary gems Máiréad Ní Ghráda left us), in *Comóradh Mháiréad Ní Ghráda . . . Leabhrán Cuimhneacháin*, p. 19.
9 For a list of the textbooks she wrote, see Ní Bhrádaigh, *Máiréad Ní Ghráda*, pp 82–4.
10 Pádraig Ó Siadhail, *Stair Dhrámaíocht na Gaeilge 1900–1970* (A history of theatre in Irish 1900–1970) (Indreabhán: Cló Iar-Chonnachta, 1993), p. 58.
11 See Sheila Walsh, 'The play that shocked', *IP*, 27/1/65.
12 Ní Bhrádaigh, *Máiréad Ní Ghráda*, p. 11.
13 Máiréad Ní Chinnéide, *An Damer: Stair Amharclainne* (The Damer: history of a theatre) (Baile Átha Cliath: Gael-Linn, 2008), p. 11.
14 See Ní Bhrádaigh, *Máiréad Ní Ghráda*, p. 33.
15 She became one of the Abbey's shareholders in 1965 (*IP*, 17/2/65).
16 See, for example, 'An Fhéile Náisiúnta Drámaíochta' (The national drama festival), *II*, 18/3/55.

17 See, for example, 'An drámadóir ar fhoireann amharclainne' (The dramatist on the staff of a theatre), the text of her talk to open the National Drama Festival at the Oireachtas in 1967, *Feasta*, June 1967, pp 19–20.
18 Quoted in Ní Bhrádaigh, *Máiréad Ní Ghráda*, p. 30. I gcúrsaí drámaidheachta na Gaedhilge, caithfimíd a adhmháil go bhfuil an bhearna is mó gan líonadh fós. Níl aon Amharclann Gaedhealach ann. Agus nuair a deirim é sin, ní hé an tigh nó an halla léirighthe atá i gceist agam. Ní hé i n-aon chor. Sé rud atá i gceist agam ná comh-cheangal na dtrí nidhthe atá riachtanach i nAmharclann, mar atá na drámaí, na h-aisteoirí, agus an lucht éisteachta. Ní Bhrádaigh dates 'An drámaíocht sa chathair' (Drama in the city), the unpublished piece from which this excerpt is taken, to 1933–4. It can be found in the RTÉ radio archives.
19 Éamon Ó Ciosáin, 'Tábhacht Mháiréad Ní Ghráda' (The importance of Máiréad Ní Ghráda), in *Comóradh Mháiréad Ní Ghráda . . . Leabhrán Cuimhneacháin*, p. 27. Más aisteoirí amaitéaracha ba mhó a bhí ag gabháil den drámaíocht Ghaeilge, scríobh sí drámaí dóibh, mar a rinne Dúghlás de hIde roimpi.
20 The play was an adaptation of an 1885 story by Tolstoy with the same title (though in Russian of course).
21 Ba mhaith agus ba thairbheach an ní dúinn aistriúcháin a bheith againn de shaothar mórscríbhneoirí na Mór-Roinne. Tá a lán-lán le foghlaim againn uathu agus ba chóir gur shuim linn a saothar . . . Ach ná bíodh oiread sin plandaí againn ón iasacht is go múchfar an lag-ghas lúbach dúchasach . . . Tá seo, leis, le tabhairt faoi deara i dtaobh na n-aistriúchán: ní suim le pobal Bhaile Átha Cliath iad; níl a fhios agam i dtaobh na muintire lasmuigh den phríomhchathair. Ach b'fhearr le muintir Bhaile Átha Cliath bundráma dá laige ná aistriúchán dá fheabhas . . . Má chothaítear na haistriúcháin an iomad is eagal liom go ndéanfar dhá rud a bheidh díobhálach, dhá rud nach fearrde drámaíocht na Gaeilge iad: cuirfear an pobal ó bheith ag freastal ar an amharclann agus cuirfear cosc le fás na drámaíochta dúchasaí. She did, however, feel that there was a place for translations – 'a few, chosen thoughtfully and translated artistically' (beagán agus iad a thoghadh go tuisceanach agus a aistriú go healaíonta).
22 Is é rud ba mhian liomsa a fheiceáil á dhéanamh . . . ná an drámadóir a bheith mar dhuine d'fhoireann na hamharclainne mar a bhí Shakespeare san Globe Theatre fadó – an drámadóir agus na haisteoirí ag obair as lámha a chéile – an drámadóir i gcónaí ag foghlaim a cheirde tríd an gceird a chleachtadh . . . Amharclann do scríbhneoirí ba ea Amharclann na Mainstreach i dtosach a ré, nuair a bhí Yeats agus Synge agus Lady Gregory i mbun na hoibre ann.

23 See, for example, Declan Kiberd, *Inventing Ireland:The Literature of the Modern Nation* (London: Jonathan Cape, 1995), pp 520–2. She incorrectly calls the English version *Borstal Boy*, which was the title of the Frank McDonald-Tomás Mac Anna adaptation of Behan's prose work of that name.

24 De bharr comórtas is ea a d'fhás agus a bhláthaigh an drámaíocht ab fhearr dá raibh riamh ar an saol, drámaíocht na Gréige fadó. I gcomhar na gcomórtas drámaíochta i gCathair na hAithne is ea a scríobh Aeschylus, Euripides agus Sophocles a gcuid traigéidí agus Aristophanes a chuid coiméidí.

25 Ach dar ndóigh, má bhíonn an duine sásta leis féin tá deireadh leis mar ealaíontóir. An iarracht chun foirfeachta, an síor-chuardach ag lorg an ní is airde – an ní nach bhfaigheann sé riamh – an tsástacht agus an mhíshástacht trí chéile a ghabhann leis an iarracht, sin é luach saothair an ealaíontóra.

26 Ní ceart an drámaíocht a chúngú.

27 The Language Freedom Movement (LFM) was a pressure group founded in 1966 to oppose the Irish state's efforts to revive Irish through what the LFM regarded as the undemocratic 'compulsion' of Irish citizens, most notably in the educational system. See the propaganda sheet the group used during the 1969 general election in Seán Ó Riain, *Pleanáil Teanga in Éirinn 1919–1985* (Language planning in Ireland) (Baile Átha Cliath: Carbad, 1994), p. 4.

28 Éamon Ó Ciosáin, 'Máiréad Ní Ghráda agus a saothar liteartha' (Máiréad Ní Ghráda and her literary work), in Máiréad Ní Ghráda, *An Triail/ Breithiúnas: Dhá Dhráma* (The trial/judgement: two plays) (Baile Átha Cliath: Oifig an tSoláthair, 1978), p. 176. Bhíodh beagán éadóchais uirthi maidir leis an nGaeilge. Dúirt sí uair amháin go raibh áthas uirthi nár bhain sí leis an nglúin a chaillfeadh an Ghaeilge go deo – chuir smaoineamh ar Éire gan Ghaeilge gruaim uirthi.

29 Ó Ciosáin, 'Tábhacht Mháiréad Ní Ghráda', in *Comóradh Mháiréad Ní Ghráda . . . Leabhrán Cuimhneacháin*, p. 27. D'oibrigh sí taobh istigh de shrianta an chomhthéacs a fuair sí roimpi, ach ba mhian léi an saol a fheabhsú.

30 Tá an chaint ann fírinneach beo, agus ní lúbtar smaointe ar mhaithe le chorrchaint, seanfhocal nó le fiodóireacht focal de Bhaldraithe a tharraingt isteach.

31 Quoted in Ó Ciosáin, 'Tábhacht Mháiréad Ní Ghráda', in *Comóradh Máiréad Ní Ghráda . . . Leabhrán Cuimhneacháin*, p. 27.

32 Ní Bhrádaigh, *Máiréad Ní Ghráda*, p. 36.

33 They performed the play under the title *An Tiomna* (The will).

34 Ní Bhrádaigh, *Máiréad Ní Ghráda*, p. 38. Is í an stíl atá le feiceáil in *An Uacht* an stíl a d'úsáid Máiréad níos deireannaí sna gearrdhrámaí. Is cosúil gur shíl sí gurbh é seo an stíl ab fhearr agus ab fheiliúnaí do lucht féachana nach mbeadh an Ghaeilge acu. Níor léiríodh *An Grá agus an Gárda* mórán nuair a bhí na gearrdhrámaí i mbarr a réime ach léiriodh *An Uacht* agus drámaí eile Mháiréad atá scríofa sa stíl chéanna go minic.

35 Máiréad Ní Ghráda, *An Grádh agus an Gárda: Dráma Grinn Aon-Mhíre* (Love and the policeman: a comedy in one act) (Baile Átha Cliath: Oifig Díolta Foillseacháin Rialtais, 1937), p. 37.

36 Tá súil againn go leanfa sí den drámaidheacht – beidh muid ag 'súil le ceann maith mór an chéad uair eile.

37 Ní furusta a rádh cia'n áit i saol na ndrámaí Gaedhilge ar chóir 'Giolla an tSolais' a chur, ach is cosúil go bhfuil ionad beag dó féin ag dul dó. Iarracht nua é le hadhbhar nua – má tá a leithéid fágtha ar an saol so.

38 Ní dráma ró-fhiúntach é ach bhí sé taitneamhach gan a bheith sgigeamhail.

39 There is a picture from the production in Ní Bhrádaigh, *Máiréad Ní Ghráda*, p. 29. The reviewer for *The Connacht Tribune* wrote: 'It is not a great play but it is developed along interesting lines and does not lag' (*CT*, 29/9/45).

40 He plays Beethoven on his violin at a local dance.

41 Máiréad Ní Ghráda, *Giolla an tSolais: Duais-Dráma Trí Mír* (Lucifer: a play in three acts) (Baile Átha Cliath: Oifig an tSoláthair, 1954), p. 9. Beidh iontas naoi lá sa pharóiste má phósann Colum. Níor phós éinne san áit seo le trí bliana ach amháin Micilín Buí ón gCnoc, agus bhí seisean os cionn leathchéad agus an bhrídeach go maith thar an dachad . . . Ní bheidh duine fágtha sa tír i gceann leathchéad blian, má leanaid den bhfuadar atá fúthu. Tá leath na scoileanna sa cheantar dúnta, cheal scoláirí a raghadh orthu, agus na múinteoirí díomhaoin, gan trácht ar na dochtúirí agus na mná cabhartha.

42 Ibid., pp 16–17. An dóigh leat gur ceart dom bheith sásta le botháinín dealamh ar bharr na haille agus an bheirt againn ag stracadh leis an saol ann go dtí go dtráfadh an grá dár gcroí agus ná beadh fágtha ina ionad ach searús agus cancar?

43 Ibid., p. 25. Tugaim tabhartaisí maithe móra liom, agus má bhíonn an chine dhaonna chomh baoth agus chomh claon san go n-iompaíd na tabhartaisí chun oilc agus chun díobhála dhóibh féin, cad é mo leigheas orthu.

44 Ibid., p. 37. Bog díom, a mhéirdreach. Beidh t'fhear céile ag teacht chugat láithreach – an fear gur gheallais i láthair Dé inniu go mbeifeá dílis dó.

45 See 'Dónall Óg', in *Nua-Dhuanaire Cuid 1* (A new poem book part 1), ed. Pádraig de Brún, Breandán Ó Buachalla, and Tomás Ó Concheanainn (Baile Átha Cliath: Institiúid Ardléinn Bhaile Átha Cliath, 1971), pp 73–4.

46 Ní Ghráda, *Giolla an tSolais*, p. 36. Thángais idir mé agus Dia. Ortsa a bhínn ag cuimhneamh nuair a bhíodh mo phaidreacha á rá agam maidin is

tráthnóna. Ortsa a bhínn ag féachaint sa tséipéal Dé Domhnaigh nuair ba chóir dom bheith ag féachaint ar altóir bheannaithe Dé. Táim tréigthe anois, tréigthe agatsa agus tréigthe ag Dia.

47 Ibid., p. 8. Mairg nach buachaill mé! Raghainn timpeall na cruinne. Chífinn Rio agus Frisco agus Yokohama, agus na háiteanna breátha san go léir. Chífinn fir bhuí agus fir dhubha ag siubhal na sráideanna iontu. Ach foiríor géar! Níl d'áirithe romham ach mo shaol a chaitheamh ar an leithinis seo – an áit is deireannaí dár chruthuigh Dia!

48 For a discussion of this theme in Irish-language literature, see Philip O'Leary, *Gaelic Prose in the Irish Free State 1922–1939* (Dublin: University College Dublin Press, 2004), pp 159–62; and O'Leary, *Irish Interior: Keeping Faith with the Past in Gaelic Prose 1940–1951* (Dublin: University College Dublin Press, 2010), pp 116–18.

49 Ní Ghráda, *Giolla an tSolais*, p. 64. Mé do dhul ar an bhfarraige sa doircheacht, mé bheith ar meisce fé ndeara é. Tá sé marbh agam chomh maith céanna agus dá sáifinn scian trína chroí.

50 Ibid., p. 46.

51 Ibid., p. 48. Is léir ná feiceann éinne de mhuintir an tí é.

52 Ibid., p. 50. Grá do mhnaoi. Mairg a thabharfadh! Ní thagann as ach scóladh croí agus smaointe cráite.

53 The anonymous critic for *Inniu* felt the play would have been better and 'truer' (níos firinnighe) had Ní Ghráda left out the devil, whose presence, he felt, turned and characters into 'Puppets' (Puipéidí). Of the chorus, he wrote: 'And the keening chorus was a big mistake. That added to the unnatural atmosphere that the author should have tried to do away with when she first took on the devil as a character' (Agus ba bhotún mór an cór caointe. Chuir sin leis an atmoisféar mí-nádúrtha ar chóir do'n ughdar bheith ag iarraidh é a chur ar ceal ó ghlac sí leis an diabhal mar charactéir ar dtús) (*Inniu*, Apr. 1945, p. 3).

54 Ní Ghráda, *Giolla an tSolais*, p. 59. Cloistear na glórtha amuigh. Níl iontu i dtosach ach mar a bheadh an ghaoth ag caoineadh. Chítear na fir bháite agus na mná caointe. Ní thógann éinne ar an stáitse a cheann chun féachaint orthu. Ní léir dóibh iad. Níl iontu ach taibhsí.

55 Ibid., p. 60. Mairg a báitear . . . Is mairg a fágtar . . . mairg don athair . . . Is mairg don mháthair . . . Mairg don mhnaoi a fágtar gan chéile . . . Mairg do dílleacht a fágtar in' aonar.

56 Ibid., p. 61.

57 Ibid., p. 64. Nach chuige sin a cuireadh ar an saol sinn.

58 Ibid., p. 65.

59 Ibid., p. 66.

60 Ibid., p. 67. Cuimhneod ar an oíche aréir – sinn ag coimheascar leis an ndoircheacht agus le cumhachtaí na doircheachta.

61 Ibid., p. 68. Tuigtear dom tar éis an tsaoil, ná fuil ionat ach scaothaire agus gur fuiriste dul uait. Níl de théagar id líonta ach oiread leis an bhfiochán a dheineann an duán alla. Tuigeann an fheithide chliste cá bhfuil an greamúchán agus seachnaíonn sé é féin air. Ach ní fheiceann an chuileog bhaoth é go dtéann sí in achrann ann.

62 See Karen Carleton's interview with Mac Anna in *Theatre Talk: Voices of Irish Theatre Practitioners*, ed. Lilian Chambers, Ger Fitzgibbon, Eamonn Jordan, Dan Farrelly, and Cathy Leeney (Dublin: Carysfort Press, 2001), p. 281. It was his highly successful production of Brecht's *The Life of Galileo* at the Abbey in 1965 that convinced many that he was a disciple of Brecht.

63 Tomás Mac Anna, *Fallaing Aonghusa: Saol Amharclainne* (The cloak of Aonghus: a life in the theatre) (Baile Átha Cliath: An Clóchomhar, 2000), pp 125–6. Ach bhí ag éirí leis na cluichí gearra Gaeilge, agus gach uile sheans agam dul ar bhealach eile ar fad á léiriú, cúl a thabhairt leis an réadaíocht, stíl choitianta na ndrámaí i mBéarla, agus úsáid a bhaint as gach uile ghléas stáitsíochta a bhí ar mo chumas agus ceann nó dó nach raibh go fóill . . . Gan bheith ag brath ar fhearas, cuma chomh héadrom agus chomh simplí a bhí siad, ach dul le teoiricí Ghéon, agus an tsamhlaíocht a bheith mar mháistir ar an stáitsíocht . . . Ba mhinic mé ag ceapadh go raibh an drámaíocht Ghaeilge rómhór faoi stíl réadúil sin an Abbey . . . Ní fhaca mé cad ina thaobh nach mbeadh an drámaíocht Ghaeilge ag dul a bealach féin, beag beann ar an réadaíocht, ag brath níos mó ar an scéalaíocht agus an rannaireacht agus ar an áiféis . . . Ní raibh mé ach ag leanúint den stíl a cheapas i dtosach báire agus mé ag gabháil do na cluichí beaga sin i nGaeilge agus an lucht éisteachta ag baint sult go leor astu. See also Micheál Mac Liammóir, 'Drámaíocht Ghaeilge san am atá le teacht' (Drama in Irish in the future), in *Ceo Meala, Lá Seaca* (A honey mist, a frosty day) (Baile Átha Cliath: Sáirséal agus Dill, 1952), pp 227–40. This essay originally appeared in *Éire: Bliainiris Ghaedheal: Rogha Saothair Ghaedheal mBeo* (Ireland: an annual for Gaels: a selection of the work of living Gaels) (1940), pp 38–45.

64 Máiréad Ní Ghráda, *Lá Buí Bealtaine: Dráma Aonmhíre* (A sunny May Day: a one-act play) (Baile Átha Cliath: Oifig an tSoláthair, 1954), p. 5. Fear an-chríonna atá ann agus tá ag dul dá mheabhair ag an aois. Is léir, áfach, go raibh sé ina fhear cumasach, tráth.

65 Ibid., p. 8. Is aoibhinn an lá, moladh le Dia. Gaoth agus grian ann. Is milis iad in éineacht.

66 Ibid., pp 9–10. Buachaillí óga agus cailíní óga ag obair ar an bportach. Spórt agus gáirí geala acu. Is breá an ní an óige . . . Is breá an ní an óige an té a chaitheann ar fónamh í.

67 Ibid., p. 10. De réir mar a inseann an tseanbhean a scéal sa chaint seo leanas, tagann na

pearsain a luann sí ar an ardán agus déanann siad geáitsí aithrise ar an rud a bhíonn aici á rá. Tuigtear don lucht féachana ná fuilid ann dáiríre ach gurb amhlaidh a chíonn an tseanbhean le súile a meabhrach iad. Seinntear ceol bog binn i gcaitheamh na cainte.

68 Ibid., p. 11. Níor tháinig riamh ná ó shoin samhradh chomh breá leis an samhradh san. Grian gheal ann sa ló. Gealach mhór bhuí ann san oíche. An bheirt againn ag siúl an bhóithrín fé sholas na gealaí, nó inár suí fén sceach gheal, lámh ar láimh, agus béal le béal.

69 Ibid., p. 15. Bhí sé féin ina cheann maith dom, ach níor thugas grá dó mar a thugas grá do Pheadar Mac Fhlannchadha . . . Peadar Mac Fhlannchadha an mhí-áidh.

70 Ibid., p. 17. Nuair a bhíonn staincín air bíonn gach aon mhallacht aige anuas orm, agus nuair a bhíonn sé buíoch liom tugann sé Nóinín Ní Chathasaigh orm, pé hí féin.

71 Pádraig Ó Siadhail, 'An phrológ' (The prologue), in *Gearrdhrámaí an Chéid* (Short plays of the century), ed. Pádraig Ó Siadhail (Indreabhán: Cló Iar-Chonnachta, 2000), p. 9.

72 The other play was Risteárd de Paor's *Saoirse* (Freedom).

73 Bhí na haisteoirí go léir go han-mhaith – iad faoi anáil spioraid sheoigh an dráma, dar leat. In a letter to the *Irish Times*, H. Nelson wrote that 'the attendance from Dublin's Irish-speaking population was *lamentably* small' (*IT*, 19/11/55).

74 Máiréad Ní Ghráda, *Úll Glas Oíche Shamhna: Dráma Aonmhíre* (Green apple Samhain night: a one-act play) (Baile Átha Cliath: Oifig an tSoláthair, 1960), p. 7. An cailín d'íosfadh úll glas ar uair an mheán oíche, ní hí a guala chlé a bheadh ag déanamh tinnis di, ach a goile.

75 She seems to just finger the apple, not eat it. We are not told what colour it is.

76 Ní Ghráda, *Úll Glas Oíche Shamhna*, p. 7. Ba chóir aisteoireacht 'stílithe' a bheith sna ceithre gearr-radharcanna seo leanas, ionas gur léir don lucht féachana ná fuil iontu ach samhluithe an chailín.

77 Ibid., p. 8. Más féidir é socraítear an scathán sa tslí is gur dóigh leis an lucht féachana gur tríd an scathán a thagann sé.

78 Ibid., p. 10. B'fhearr liom fear . . . a . . . thiocfadh abhaile chugam agus é ar meisce. B'fhearr liom fear a . . . a . . . bhuailfeadh mé ná fear a bheadh suite ansan ag léamh a pháipéir agus gan aon bhlúire suime aige ionam ach oiread is gur stúmpa cloiche a bheadh ionam.

79 Ibid., p. 11. Billí, billí, billí! Níl aon tseó ach a mbíonn de bhillí agat dom. An amhlaidh is dóigh leat go bhfásann an t-airgead ar crainn fé mar a fhásann na nóiníní ar na bánta i lár an tsamhraidh? . . . Raghad amach. Raghad thar n-ais chun na hoifige.

Raghad go dtigh an óil. Raghad áit ar bith ná beidh orm bheith ag éisteacht le bean ag cur aisti agus a teanga chomh géar le lann rásúir.

80 Ibid., pp 12–13.

81 Ibid., pp 13–14. Nuair a thiocfaidh sé abhaile ní bheidh focal as a bhéal aige ach golf, golf, golf.

82 Ibid., p. 16. Níl aon fhear saolta saor ó locht ná aon bhean ach oiread leis. Caithfidh tú féin agus t'fhear céile cur suas le lochta a chéile agus an chuid is fearr a dhéanamh den saol. Siúlfaidh tú bóthar an aoibhnis lena chois uaireannta in éadaí an áthais. Uaireannta eile geobhaidh tú tríd an lathaigh in éadaí an bhróin.

83 Ibid. Bíodh ciall agat, a chailín. Ní file mé, ná aingeal ach oiread. Ná bí ag súil le haoibhneas na bhFlaitheas má phósann tú mé, nó aon fhear eile.

84 Ibid. Raghad sa tseans leis, a Shéamais.

85 Tá greann agus daonnacht agus tuigse ann, agus is daoine beo iad na carachtair.

86 Unless otherwise indicated, the Pádraig Ó Siochfhradha (Ó Siochrú) referred to here and elsewhere in this book is An Capt. Pádraig Ó Siochfhradha (Ó Siochrú), one-time chairman of Comhairle Náisiúnta na Drámaíochta (The national drama council), and not the writer who used the pen-name 'An Seabhac'.

87 See Ó Siadhail, *Stair Dhrámaíocht na Gaeilge*, p. 132; and 'Ag teastáil: lucht éisteachta' (Wanted: an audience), *IP*, 19/3/57. In 1957 the Pike also produced the Irish premieres of Ionesco's *Victims of Duty* (*Victimes du devoir*) (1953) and *The Shepherd's Chameleon* (*L'Impromptu de l'Alma*) (1956) (*IP*, 3/10/57).

88 Máiréad Ní Ghráda, *Súgán Sneachta: Geandráma Aon-mhíre* (A rope made of snow: a comedy in one act) (Baile Átha Cliath: Oifig an tSoláthair, 1962), p. 5. Ise: Cad is ainm duit? / Eisean: Seán. Cad is ainm duitse? / Ise: Siún. / Eisean (osna): Siún. / Ise: Seán agus Siún. / Eisean: Nach deas a ghabhann siad le chéile. / Ise: Is deas. / Eisean: 'Se Dia a thug le chéile sinn. / Ise: Is É. / Eisean: Corcaíoch tú? / Ise: Cad eile? Corcaíoch tú féin? / Eisean: Cad eile? / Ise: Is deas a ghabhann beirt Chorcaíoch le chéile. / Eisean: Is deas. / Ise: 'Sé Dia a thug le chéile sinn. / Eisean: Is É.

89 He does, however, age as the play goes on.

90 Ní Ghráda, *Súgán Sneachta*, p. 9. Baitsiléar mé féinig, / Baitsiléar breá Gaelach. / Pósadh ní dhéanfad / Go mbead in aois na céille, / I mblianta discréide / Dhá scór – nó leathchéad.

91 Ibid., p. 14. Ólaim fion is ólaim lionn, / 'S an lá 'na dhiaidh san ólaim branda. / Má bhím ar meisce uair nó dhó / Níl bean agam chun mé a scalladh.

92 Ibid., p. 17. B'fhearr liom bheith i bpríosún / Ná grá a thúirt do mhnaoi / Mar níl sa ghrá ach amaidí, / Gan toradh ann ach brón.

93 Ibid., p. 10. Pósadh do dhéanfainn / Dá bhfaighinnse mo mhian. / Pósadh do dhéanfainn / Ach fear a theacht im iarraidh. / Pósadh dá olcas / Is fearr ná bheith díomhaoin.

94 Ibid., p. 14. Is fuar a bhím im luí liom féin, / Go huaigneach aon'rach ar mo leaba. / Mo bhrón an bhean a bhíonn léi féin, / Gan fear aici chum í a mhealladh.

95 Ibid., p. 18. Dá bpósfá i dtráth, a mhic, / Ní bheifeá 'nois mar taoi – / Id chráiteacháinín cancarach / Is tú ag dul in aois.

96 Ibid., p. 13. Tá ré na filíochta imithe. Tá ré an phróis tagtha.

97 Ibid., p. 20. Na laochra a fuair bás ar mo shon! Níor iarras ar éinne bás d'fháil ar mo shon. Na daoine atá marbh fágtar marbh iad. Ná bítear i gcónaí ag claiscirt a gcuid cnámh.

98 Ibid., p. 23. Baitsiléar: Cad is ainm duit? / Sean-Mhaighdean: Síle Ní Bhriain . . . Cad is ainm duit féin? / Baitsiléar: Pádraig Partholán Ó Mathúna. / Sean-Mhaighdean: Corcaíoch tú? / Baitsiléar: Cad eile? Corcaíoch tú féin? / Sean-Mhaighdean: Cad eile? / Baitsiléar: 'Sé Dia a thug dá chéile sinn. / Sean-Mhaighdean: Is É. (Pógann siad a chéile.).

99 Dinneen's *Foclóir Gaedhilge agus Béarla/An Irish–English Dictionary* defines *Rudaidhe* (i.e. *Rudaí*) as a form used 'in bogus surname . . . e.g., Tadhg Ó R., Tadhg Such-a-one'. See Patrick S. Dinneen, *Foclóir Gaedhilge agus Béarla/An Irish–English Dictionary* (Dublin: Irish Texts Society, 1927), p. 922.

100 Gearrscéal éifeachtach a rinne Thurber den *motif* seo, dráma sár-éifeachtach a rinne Máiréad Ní Ghráda de.

101 See Máiréad Ní Ghráda, *Mac Uí Rudaí: Duaisdráma Oireachtais na Bliana 1960* (Oireachtas prize play for the year 1960) (Baile Átha Cliath: Oifig an tSoláthair, 1962), p. 3.

102 Apparently the National Touring Agency promoted the play as a work for children. Ní Ghráda prepared what she called an 'unpolished' translation of the play into German for possible production on German television. I do not know whether the broadcast ever occurred (*II*, 31/10/61). According to a brief note in *Inniu*, a German version of the play was performed in Munich (*Inniu*, 16/10/64).

103 One is reminded here of Piaras Béaslaí's 1925 short story 'Tram an Taidhrimh' (The dream tram) in which an unassuming Dublin clerk boards a tram to Rathmines and travels to his dream Teheran.

104 Ní Ghráda, *Mac Uí Rudaí*, p. 14. Ní haon bhríonglóid í seo.

105 Ibid., p. 16. Nach ag bríonglóid a bhíonn tú i gcónaí, a stór. Sea anois. Tar isteach sa chistin agus déanfaidh mé cupán tae duit.

106 Ibid. Mairimid trí bhríonglóidí, / Lán den aoibhneas, lán den draíocht, / Lán de chur-i-gcéill a bhíonn / Saor ó bhrón agus briseadh croí.

107 See Ní Bhrádaigh, *Máiréad Ní Ghráda*, p. 50.

108 See also Gallagher's account of the hunger strike in 'David Hogan' (i.e. Gallagher), *The Four Glorious Years* (Dublin: Irish Press Ltd, 1953), pp 160–93.

109 Quoted in Ní Bhrádaigh, *Máiréad Ní Ghráda*, p. 51. Tá mé cinnte gur ó lámh Mháiréad fhéin a tháinig *Stailc Ocrais*.

110 Ó Ciosáin, 'Máiréad Ní Ghráda', in Ní Ghráda, *An Triail/Breithiúnas*, p. 184.

111 It shared the prize with Máirtín Ó Corrbuí's *Mo Chara Peatsaí* (My friend Patsy) (*IT*, 27/9/60).

112 Ó Floinn devoted most of his attention to the other play on the bill, Eoghan Ó Tuairisc's *Na Mairnéalaigh* (The sailors).

113 Istigh in aigne an duine féin atá an bhunchoimhlint, rud an-deacair a léiriú ar stáitse, ach sáraíonn Máiréad Ní Ghráda cuid mhaith den deacracht go tíosach.

114 Perhaps one did, but I have found no record of such a production in the press.

115 Máiréad Ní Ghráda, *Stailc Ocrais: Tragóid Stairiúil: Dráma Aonghnímh* (Hunger strike: a historical tragedy in one act) (Baile Átha Cliath: Oifig an tSoláthair, 1966), pp 8–9.

116 Frank Gallagher, *Days of Fear: A Diary of Hunger Strike* (Cork: Mercier Press, 1967 [1928]), p. 45.

117 Ní Ghráda, *Stailc Ocrais*, p. 13. Ní dhéanfad gol ná caoineadh, a mhic. Ná ní iarrfad ort aon ní a dhéanamh ach an ní is rogha le do chroí agus le do choinsias féin. Níl ionam ach seanbhean tuaithe, gan mórán tuisceana agam sna cúrsaí seo, ach tá fhios agam an méid seo – go bhfuil nithe ann is treise ná an bás féin. Caithfidh tú déanamh mar déarfaidh do chroí leat . . . Go neartaí Dia thú, a mhic, agus go neartaí Sé na buachaillí eile atá ag fulaingt pionóis ar son na hÉireann.

118 Gallagher, *Days of Fear*, p. 77.

119 Ibid., p. 63.

120 Ibid., p. 67.

121 Since we do not know if or when *Stailc Ocrais* was revised, we cannot know whether this personification predated these other characters.

122 See Gallagher, *Days of Fear*, p. 25 and 39.

123 Ní Ghráda, *Stailc Ocrais*, p. 7. A haon, a dó, a trí, a cheathair, a cúig, a sé, a seacht, a hocht, a naoi, a deich, a haon déag, a dó dhéag. Dhá lá dhéag. Gan bia. Gan deoch. Gan bia. Gan deoch. Dhá lá dhéag. Dhá lá dhéag . . . Fir go tréithlag. Fir go tnáite. Fir go cloíte. Fir go cráite.

124 Ibid., pp 17–18. An Chéad Chaithaitheoir: Leanaí faoi ghátar. Leanaí faoi angar. Tá clann an Bhraonánaigh faoi angar. / Ceannfort: Níl aon leigheas agam orthu. / An Chéad Chaithaitheoir: Eagla atá ort. / Ceannfort: Thugais t'éitheach. Níl aon eagla orm . . . / An Chéad Chaithaitheoir: Tá eagla ort géilleadh. Tá eagla ort go ndéarfar gur meatachán tú. / Glórtha Amuigh: Meatachán. Meatachán. Meatachán.

125 Ibid., p. 21. Ceannfort: Tá a fhios agat anois nach bhfuil eagla orainn romhat. / Bás: Nuair a shínim mo lámh chun duine, tagann eagla air. / Ceannfort: Bhfuilir chun do lámh a shíneadh anois? / Bás: Níl d'uainse tagtha fós.

126 Ibid., p. 23. Dúirt mé leis go raibh na toitíní ag goilliúint ar a chroí.

127 I am using here a copy of the typescript of the play from An Chomhairle Náisiúnta Drámaíochta, which was graciously provided to me by Éamon Ó Ciosáin. The use (or lack) of length marks in the play's title varies in various sources. 'Ríté' is the spelling used in the typescript.

128 Ach an Commissar agus a comrádaithe ní raibh a leithéid riamh ann. Ba mheascán iad den siorcas agus den cheoldráma. Bhí cuma na háiféise orthu agus iad ag sodar ar fud na stáitse . . . Ríte [*sic*] féin, bhí sí gan gus agus gan spreagadh.

129 Íslíonn an scéal go leibhéal novelette chráifigh. Níl dealramh ar bith leis.

130 See Brian Fallon, *An Age of Innocence: Irish Culture 1930–1960* (Dublin: Gill and Macmillan, 1999), p. 178.

131 In his review, Earnán P. de Blaghd wrote that the play was set 'somewhere behind the Iron Curtain' (*II*, 5/3/64). An anonymous reviewer of a 1969 production of the play by UCD's An Cumann Drámaíochta also wrote that the play was set 'somewhere across the Iron Curtain' (*II*, 26/2/69).

132 Máiréad Ní Ghráda, *Ríté: Dráma Aonmhíre* (A one-act play), p. 4. Ní hé toil Dé é, ach toil daoine, droch-dhaoine.

133 Ibid., p. 5. Más áil le Dia sinn a bheith inár mairtírigh glacaimís lena thoil naofa. Ach ná bímís ag cur dúil sa mhairtíreacht.

134 Ibid., p. 9.

135 Ibid., p. 10. An té a bhíonn ag obair don Pháirtí, ní healaí dhó machnamh a dhéanamh. Deinimís rud ar na taoisigh atá orainn agus leigimís fúthu-san machnamh a dhéanamh . . . Cuirfidh íde na mban so scanradh ar an gcuid eile acu, ionas ná beidh a thuilleadh trioblóide againn leo.

136 Ibid., p. 11. Ban-chommissar a bheadh [*sic*] ionat ar ball má leanann tú de bheith ag tabhairt seirbhíse fónta don Pháirtí. Theastaigh ó chuid acu an obair seo a thabhairt le déanamh d'Anna. Ach bhí fhios agamsa gur tusa ab fhearr chuige. Nach in áit mar seo a tógadh tú. Ní raibh aon bhaol go scéithfeá ort féin cheal eolais ar nósanna na mban so . . . Domhan beag ann féin is ea an áit seo. Domhan beag gan fuath, gan éad, gan mioscais ann. Domhan beag síochánta agus uain chun machnaimh ag daoine ann . . . Ní chreidfeá ach a fhaid agus a chiúine atá na hoícheanta anso . . . Mé sínte ar mo leaba chaol chruaidh im chillín beag in airde staighre ansan agus mé ag machnamh.

137 Ní Bhrádaigh, *Máiréad Ní Ghráda*, p. 46.

138 One recalls Pádraig Mac Gabhann's comments about the hollow unreality of the characters (*Feasta*, Dec. 1955, p. 33).

139 Míorbhúilt cheart é léiriú comh maith sin ins an spás beag atá mar ardán [ins] an Damer.

140 He stressed that the play was for adults only.

141 Níl ceann acu is mó bhain caint amach ná *An Triail*. Bhí idir Ghael agus Ghall á dhearcadh is á thabhairt faoi deara . . . Is dráma é seo a thaithnigh go mór liom féin. Thaithnigh an téama liom ach is fearr ná sin a thaithnigh an iomghabháil a thug an drámadóir air . . . Níl amhras air sin cé air a bhfuil an milleán. Dar leis tá sin ar gach duine sa dráma, ar Mháire Ní Chathasaigh agus ar gach duine lena raibh a caidreamh. Agus is ionann sin agus a rá go bhfuil sé féin ciontach agus muintir na hÉireann fré chéile.

142 Más féidir dráma dúchasach traidisiúnta a thabhairt ar aon dráma atá againn, ní hé *An Triail* é. Ar ndóigh, ní locht é ach a mhalairt. D'fhéadfadh gur comhartha é go bhfuil drámaíocht na Gaeilge ag teacht in aois, go bhfuil sí ag plé le ceisteanna a bhaineann le domhan uilegabhálach an lae inniu.

143 It was in Irish with translations provided and was rebroadcast in 1966 (*IT*, 3/2/66). Fionnula Flanagan played Máire.

144 See irishtheatremagazine.ie/Reviews/Current/An-Triail. The play was translated into Flemish by Staf Gebruers of Cork and performed in Antwerp in February 1967 (*MN*, 22/10/66). There were also plans to produce the play in Rome, but they fell through for financial reasons (*SI*, 11/10/64; *MN*, 22/10/66).

145 She added that she had gone to see the play at An Damer and found that 'the theme transcended the language of which I know too little' and then added: 'Do you know that that play has set me learning Irish.'

146 For some reason, the contributor who listed coming events for the *City Tribune* referred to *On Trial* as 'very little known' (*City Tribune*, 12/4/85).

147 A brief note in the *Sunday Independent* in 1966 reported that '"On Trial" by Máiréad Ní Ghráda is to be presented in Belgium and Mexico' (*SI*, 23/10/66). As we have seen, a translation of the Irish version was produced in Antwerp, but I do not know if the play was ever translated and performed in Mexico.

148 Alan Titley, '"Neither the boghole nor Berlin": drama in the Irish language from then until now', in *Nailing Theses: Selected Essays* (Belfast: Lagan Press, 2011), pp 272–3. Of these institutions he writes: 'Máiréad Ní Ghráda could not have known the real and abiding horror of those places of iniquitous punishment and horrific self-righteousness, and yet her imagination invented a fraction of the awfulness of those times, lifting the spotted, spunked, and stained veil on an Ireland which we willingly and wittingly hid from view' (p. 273).

149 Scríofa ag Máiréad Ní Ghráda agus curtha ar stáitse don chéad uair i 1964, tharraing sé caint agus conspóid ag an am. Is ait go bhfuil an tábhar chomh tráthúil céanna i 1998.

150 Doubtless more people have seen Brendan Behan's *An Giall* in its English version *The Hostage*,

but *The Hostage* is a very different play from *An Giall*
so that someone who has seen *The Hostage* has little
sense of what the play in Irish is like.
151 Máiréad Ní Ghráda, *An Triail*, in *An Triail/
Breithiúnas*, p. 19. A uaisle, iarraim é seo oraibh – aon
ní atá cloiste agaibh, nó aon ní atá léite agaibh i
dtaobh na cúise seo, é a chur as bhur n-aigne. Éistigí
leis an bhfianaise a thabharfar os bhur gcomhair,
agus tugaigí bhur mbreith de réir na fianaise sin
amháin.
152 Ibid., p. 20. Is dóigh leo seo go bhfaighidh siad
eolas ar na cúrsaí go léir. Ach tá nithe ann a bheidh
ceilte orthu go brách. Na nithe atá folaithe i mo
chroíse.
153 Ibid., p. 28. Níor fhéad sí riamh a bheith ina
beanchéile cheart dom.
154 Ibid., p. 87.
155 Ibid., pp 24–5. Ach ní ormsa is cóir aon phioc
den mhilleán a chur. Bhí comhluadar de mo chuid
féin agam an oíche sin. Ní fhéadfainn a bheith ag a
sála sin i gcónaí. Ní mise a coimeádaí . . . Níl a fhios
agam cad a tharla an oíche sin, agus ní theastaíonn
uaim a fhios a bheith agam . . .
156 Ibid., pp 40–1. Cad a d'fhéadfainn a dhéanamh?
. . . Tharraing sí siúd náire orainn. Tharraing sí náire
shaolta orainn i láthair na gcomharsan. Loit sí an
saol orainn. Chiontaigh sí . . . Chiontaigh sí in
aghaidh Dé . . . Ba chóir a bheith dian uirthi.
157 Ibid., p. 29. Ní ormsa is cóir aon phioc den
mhilleán a chur. Thóg mise go creidiúnach agus
go críostúil í. Ba é toil Dé m'fhear chéile a thógáil
uaim . . . Fágadh mise im sclábhaí agus gan duine
ann a thógfadh lámh chun cabhrú liom . . . Agus cad
tá agam dá bharr i ndeireadh na dála? Mé náirithe os
comhair na gcomharsan. Iad ag síneadh a méar fúm
agus ag magadh fúm má théim ar aonach nó ar
mhargadh nó fiú chun an Aifrinn Dé Domhnaigh.
158 Ibid., p. 37. Níl uaithi ach go léifí ar fhógra a
báis: 'A leithéid seo de lá, a leithéid seo de bhliain,
cailleadh Máiréad, Bean Uí Chathasaigh. Ise ba
mháthair do Sheán Ó Cathasaigh, sagart paróiste
Bhaile i bhfad síos, agus don Mháthair Columbán le
Muire, misiúnaí san Afraic.' Her mother had
planned for Máire to become a nun and for that
reason kept her from developing a more mature
attitude to the world that might have made her more
appropriately sceptical of Pádraig's intentions.
159 Ibid., pp 41–2. Deoch leighis. Deoch láidir.
Socróidh sé sin thú, a chailín, agus mura socróidh,
gheobhaidh tú steancán eile de amárach agus gach
aon lá eile go dtí go ndéanfadh sé beart duit . . .
Mallacht ar an té a tharraing an náire seo anuas
orainn. Agus mallacht Dé anuas ortsa, a . . . striapach.
160 Ibid., p. 34. Caithfidh tú scaradh leis an té is
ábhar peaca duit. Caithfidh tú scaradh leis glan
amach, gan labhairt leis go deo arís . . . Cuimhnigh
ar an bhfocal a dúirt ár Slánaitheoir: 'má pheacann

do lámh dheas, bain díot anuas í. Is fearr a bheith
gan lámh ná peaca a dhéanamh.'
161 Ibid., p. 55. Táimidne tuirseach tnáite, / Is muid
ag obair gan aon phá. / Táimid tuirseach tréith / Is
muid ag sclábhaíocht gach lá. / Ach nuair a thagann
sé féin / Elvis Presley na nGael / Is ea a thosaíonn an
rí rá! Elvis is also a presence in Brogan's play.
162 Ibid., p. 63. Bíodh ciall agat, a chailín. Féach.
Tiocfaidh an dlíodóir. Ní bheidh le déanamh agat
ach d'ainm a chur leis na cáipéisí agus ní iarrfar a
thuilleadh ort. Beidh cead do chos agat agus neart
duit dul in aon áit is mian leat.
163 Ibid., p. 64. Ní haon dóichín do chailín óg
leanbh tabhartha a bheith aici.
164 Ibid., p. 46. Cén leigheas a bhí agam air. Tá
clann iníon agam. Ní fhéadfainn iad a fhágáil i
mbaol caidrimh lena leithéid. Cad a déarfadh na
comharsana? Cad a déarfadh na cailíní eile ar scoil?
Cad a déarfadh na mná rialta?
165 Several decrepit residential buildings did
collapse with fatal results in Dublin in the 1950s and
1960s.
166 Ní Ghráda, *An Triail*, p. 75. Cé a deir gur tír
chríostaí í seo?
167 Ibid., p. 87. Seo sláinte Phádraig Mhic
Chárthaigh. Chuir sé bean agus phós sé bean. Seo
libh, ólaimis sláinte gach aon óinsín tuaithe ar leor
focal bog bladrach chun í a mhealladh.
168 Ibid., p. 88. Mharaigh mé mo leanbh de bhrí
gur cailín í. Fásann gach cailín suas ina bean. Ach tá
m'iníon saor. Tá sí saor. Ní bheidh sí ina hóinsín
bhog ghéilliúil ag aon fhear. Tá sí saor. Tá sí saor. Tá
sí saor.
169 Ibid., p. 89. Bhris sí na rialacha. An té a
bhriseann rialacha an chluiche cailltear ann í.
170 Ach shíleas gur theip ar an dráma ag an bpointe
áirithe inar cheart dó bheith láidir is nár éirigh leis an
bunsmaoineamh a chur i gcéill go héifeachtach, is é
sin smaoineamh na trialach. D'inis an t-údar an
scéal go maith, rianaigh sí a cuid charachtar go
haclaí ealaíonta, ach níor bhraitheas-sa am ar bith go
raibh aon triail ar siúl. Chonnaicthes dom nach
raibh ann ach insint scéil, léiriú ainnise.
171 Tá Seán na Sráide á chúisiú, agus ag an am
céanna táthar ag iarraidh air bheith ina ghiúiré.
Ní amháin sin, ach tá sé á chúisiú as cor nach
bhféadfadh sé bheith ciontach as, ainneoin de
chomh fallaitheach is a d'fhéadfadh sé a bheith.
172 Aon ní a rinne an cailín, rinne sí dá deoin féin
é . . . í féin a thoiligh an peaca a dhéanamh agus í féin
a chaithfeadh bheith freagrach as, í féin agus an fear.
Cuirtear gach rud san áireamh mar fhianaise, ach ní
thugtar aon ghuth don saorthoil atá ag gach aoinne . . .
173 Cuireadh an triail, tugadh an fhianaise, agus ar
chuma éigin thit an tóin as an dráma. Bhraitheas mé
féin ag smaoineamh ar *Murder in the Cathedral*, nuair
a chasann na coirpigh agus (sa phrós álainn simplí

sin ag Eliot) léiríonn siad dúinn a dtaobh-san den scéal, sa chaoi is go mbímíd beagnach in achrainn linn féin faoi an ciontach atáid nó a mhalairt. Ní raibh aon fhonn argóna orm ag deireadh *An Triail*; d'fhéadfadh gur lú den triail a bhí ann ná den insint scéil, nó d'fhéadfadh gur bádh na hargóintí faoi thuille [*sic*] na trua.

174 See Ní Bhrádaigh, *Máiréad Ní Ghráda*, p. 36; and Ó Ciosáin, 'Máiréad Ní Ghráda', in Ní Ghráda, *An Triail/Breithiúnas*, p. 182.

175 See Mac Anna, *Fallaing Aonghusa*, p. 163 and 168.

176 See Pádraig Ó Siochrú's comments on their collaboration in 'Freagra amháin is féidir thabhairt' (One answer it is possible to give), *IP*, 30/7/75.

177 Ó Ciosáin, 'Máiréad Ní Ghráda', in Ní Ghráda, *An Triail/Breithiúnas*, p.188. Cé na fáthanna a d'athraigh Máiréad go dtí an t-eispriseanachas? Ba dhrámadóir í a scríobh agus staid agus cúrsaí amharclainne ina haigne aici i gcónaí: ghluais sí i dtreo an eispriseanachais toisc go raibh Tomás Mac Anna, léiritheoir a chaith tamall le h-hamharclann Bhrecht i mBeirlín, in Amharclann na Mainistreach lena linn. Chomh maith leis sin, tá an t-eispriseanachas níos oiriúnaí do dhrámaí gearra ná an nádúrachas toisc nach mbíonn mórán deiseanna i ndráma gearr chun forbairt a dhéanamh ar charachtar nó ar phlota. Mac Anna had not yet spent time in East Berlin when their collaboration at the Abbey began.

178 Saghas 'Cách' ann féin is ea 'Breithiúntas' [*sic*]. Sa 'Triail' síneadh méar cách agus cúitíodh gach duine i gcoir na faille ach i 'Breithiúntas' [*sic*] síneadh agus athshíneadh an mhéar chun aon duine amháin . . . Ní dráma dúr trom é seo mar cuireann an t-údar éagsúlacht ins gach méar a síntear ionas ná héiríonn méar ar bith tuirseach ná tuirsiúil . . .

179 Sílim gur chaith sí róstró le *tycoon* a chruthú agus go ndearna sí faille i gcarachtar Mharcais. Agus is é seo an locht mór a fhaighim ar an dráma. Bhainfí cuid mhaith den locht seo dá luafaí oiread agus suáilce bheag amháin leis an *tycoon*. Chuirfeadh sin le duibhe a dhuáilcí uile . . .

180 Máiréad Ní Ghráda, *Breithiúnas*, in *An Triail/Breithiúnas*, p. 97. An bhfuil sé marbh? Cad a tharla dó? An amhlaidh a chuir sé bairille an ghunna ina bhéal? Trí thimpiste a tharla sé. Ní thabharfadh aon duine faoi. Bíonn naimhde ag an bhfear poiblí i gcónaí. Ar tháinig na gardaí? An bhfuil sé marbh?

181 One wonders whether Ní Ghráda was influenced here by Gearóid Ó Lochlainn's one-act play *Ag an Ladhrán* (At the junction) (1941), which had been produced by An Comhar Drámaíochta in the Abbey.

182 Ní Ghráda, *Breithiúnas*, p. 100. Is é a fuair an pinsean domsa . . . Fuair sé pinsean do leath an chontae . . . Fuair sé post sa Státsheirbhís do m'iníon-sa . . . Ní bheidh a leithéid arís ann . . . Fear

chomh hionraic le Marcas de Grás ní raibh le fáil i saol polaitiúil na tíre. Camastaíl ná caimiléireacht níor cuireadh riamh ina leith. Pingin d'airgead an phobail níor chuir sé amú.

183 Ibid., p. 102. Cén fáth nach mbeadh sé tuillte agam? . . . Agat féin is fearr a fhios.

184 Ibid. Labhrann an Fear Eile go ciúin báúil. Is léir tuiscint aige do Mharcas agus trua aige dó.

185 Ibid., p. 110.

186 Ibid., p. 121. Déanfaidh mé mo dhícheall aidhmeanna an pháirtí a chur chun cinn. Obair do gach duine sa dáilcheantar. Pá maith agus uaireannta gearra. An costas maireachtála a ísliú gan cur isteach ar na feirmeoirí ná ar na siopadóirí, seirbhísí sláinte in aisce, oideachas in aisce, rátaí agus cánacha a ísliú – in aon fhocal amháin, obair do gach duine, teach do gach duine, pinsean do gach duine agus sláinte do gach duine agus mo vóta don pháirtí.

187 Ibid., p. 134. Sin é cluiche na polaitíochta duit . . . Cén fáth? Faigheann daoine na hionadaithe poiblí a bhíonn tuillte acu. Rómhaith a bhí mé dóibh. Rómhaith ar fad. Reviewing the play for *Inniu*, 'M. N.' wrote: 'All of us are responsible for Marcas de Grás. We are the electorate who made him a deputy . . . The fault is not on the likes of Marcas, but on ourselves' (Sinne go léir atá freagrach as Marcas de Grás. Sinne an cór vótála a cheap ina theachtaire é . . . Ní ar shaghas Mharcais atá an locht, ach orainn féin) (*Inniu*, 16/2/68).

188 Ní Ghráda, *Breithiúnas*, p. 143.

189 Ibid., p. 163. Bhí mé á iompar . . . Bhí mé á thabhairt liom chun cabhair a fháil dó . . . dochtúir . . . sagart . . . Dúirt mé an Gníomh Croíbhrú isteach ina chluais.

190 Ibid., p. 165. Féach, a stór . . . Cuir i gcás gur meatachán a bheadh ionam, fear a scanródh fuaim na bpiléar mé – fear a chaillfeadh a chuid fearúlachta agus é faoi lámhach na ngunnaí – an dtabharfá grá dom dá mba dhuine den sórt sin mé? . . . Ní tusa a bheadh ann dá mba dhuine den sórt sin tú. Ní fhéadfainn grá a thabhairt do dhuine dá leithéid.

191 Ibid., pp 166–7. Dhein an buachaill sin éacht a mbeidh cuimhne air go deo. É gonta créachtach, fuil a chroí á dhoirteadh aige. É ag titim i laige ach a chomrádaí á iompar aige chun é a shábháil ar an mbás.

192 Ibid., p. 151. Fág faoi Mharcas de Grás gach aon ní a chur chun tairbhe dó féin. Is mór an sochar dó an béal teann daingean sin air, is fiú cúpla míle vóta é i ngach toghchán . . . Ar a mhéid atá sé ag brath ar dhaoine eile chun é a chosaint ar an saol. Mise agus tusa agus Bhuísí agus an dream a bhíonn ag cuimilt boise dó agus á mholadh. Ní mór dó aige iad chun misneach a thabhairt dó agus chun féinmhuinín a chothú ann.

193 Ibid., p. 169. Cén leigheas a bhíonn ag duine air féin? Caithfidh sé déanamh de réir a mheoin . . . de

réir a chroí . . . Marcas de Grás, an meatachán ba
thrúig báis don Cheannaire cróga. Do shaol ar fad
bunaithe ar bhréag . . . gan de bhunchloch fút ach an
t-éitheach. D'ainm i mbéal cách agus an fear calma
dearmadta. Gan i do shaol ach éagóir. Éagóir ar an
marbh.

194 Ibid. Ach ní raibh suaimhneas aigne riamh
agam. Riamh, riamh, riamh, le leithchéad bliain ní
raibh i mo bhéal ach blas géar goirt. Mé ag síneadh
mo dhá lámh in airde i gcónaí ag iarraidh breith ar
mhilseacht agus ar aoibhneas agus é ag teip orm
teacht orthu . . . Ach anois nuair atáim tar éis a raibh
folaithe a thabhairt chun solais, b'fhéidir go mbeadh
suaimhneas aigne agam. An é sin an chiall atá le
ráiteas na hEaglaise nuair a ghuíonn sí suaimhneas
síoraí d'anamnacha na marbh? Gach castacht dírithe,
gach crua bogtha . . . gach seirbhe milsithe . . . gach
casán réitithe . . .

CHAPTER TWO
A Northern Voice

1   Ó cuireadh an chéad uimhir amach, ní tháinig lámhsgríbhinn ar bith chugam ar bhfiú a fhoillsiú, agus le n-a chois sin ní tháinig ach ceann nó dó, agus iad leanbhuidhe . . . Is mór an scannal é, mur tigadh [*sic*] linn iris amháin mar í seo a choinneál beo i ndiaidh a bheith ag 'pléidhe' leis an Ghaeilg ar feadh leith-chéad blian.

2   It is interesting to note that he had waited until the fourth issue to set out his goals, writing that he distrusted those who put their emphasis on extravagant aims and that his original ambition had been 'to found a journal that would be every bit as good as one like it in English' (iris a bhunú a bhéadh lán chómh maith le n-a mhacasamhail i mBéarla) (*Iris*, Feb. 1946, p. 1).

3   Ní scríobhfaidh aon duine fiúntach Gaeilg i bhfad má gheibh sé amach nach léightear a chuid leabhar, mura dtigidh leis corr-phighinn a ghnóthú orthu.

4   This phrase is in English in the original article.

5   See his letter to the *Irish Bookman*, Jan. 1947, p. 84.

6   Níl námhaid is measa ag litríocht na Gaeilge ná é siúd – an scríbhneoir a scríobhann as an ghrá atá aige don teangaidh. John Gerard Cassidy has written: 'Often when he was writing and talking about literary matters he also mentioned the state of the Irish language or the saving of the Irish language. It is at times difficult to separate those two things from each other' (Go minic nuair a bhí sé ag scríobh faoi chúrsaí litríochta luaigh sé fosta staid na Gaeilge nó slánú na Gaeilge. Is deacair, in amanna, an dá rud sin a scaradh óna chéile). See John Gerard Cassidy, 'Séamus Ó Néill: a shaol agus a shaothar' (His life and work), unpublished MA thesis, Queen's University, Belfast, 1983, p. 20. While this statement might well be true of Ó Néill (as it might be true, say, of Máirtín Ó Cadhain) when he was writing or speaking as a critic or literary historian, when he wrote as an artist he (again like Ó Cadhain) tried to take his linguistic medium for granted.

7   Tá tonn an náisiúnachais ag trá go gasta, agus muna dtig le lucht na Gaeilge litríocht a sholáthar a gheobhas greim ar intinn na ndaoine, is gairid a seal feasta mar theanga bheo.

8   Ní thuigimid féin cad chuige ar caitheadh airgead ar leabhar chómh bocht. Mar iarracht liteardha, más sin an rud atá ann, tá sé leanbuidhe. Ní dhéanann a leithéid ach droch-mheas a tharraingt ar an dream bheag de scríbhneoirí na Gaedhilge atá i n-ann rud ínteacht fiúntach a thabhairt dúinn.

9   Níor bhféidir leabhar a ba mhí-fhóirstinighe ná 'Fear Siubhail' a thoghadh do dhaoine óga. Nuair a chuireann an léightheoir óg leabhar mar í seo i gcómh-mheas le leabhar Béarla, nó leabhar Frainncise, nó

leabhar Gearmánaise, ní h-íontas ar bith é gan dúil a bheith aige san Gaedhilg. His emphasis on the need of attracting young readers to literature in Irish was widely shared at the time. It is also worth noting that he regretted that Muiris Ó Droighneáin had not included more literary criticism in his *Taighde i gcomhair Stair Litridheachta na Nua-Gaedhilge ó 1882 anuas* (Research for the history of literature in modern Irish since 1882) (1936). See his review of Ó Droighneáin's work in *An t-Ultach*, May 1937, p. 3.

10   Mac Réamoinn also wrote of Ó Néill and Seamus Kelly, the long-time drama critic for the *Irish Times*, that 'their Ulsterness and their Irishness were all of a piece . . . closely woven with a sharp edge to it' (*IT*, 20/6/81).

11   For biographical material on Ó Néill, I am indebted to Diarmuid Breathnach and Máire Ní Mhurchú, *1882–1982: Beathaisnéis a Trí* (Biography three) (Baile Átha Cliath: An Clóchomhar, 1992), pp 131–3.

12   Writing in 1967, he claimed that in a 1946 article in *Inniu* he had been one of the first to suggest such a scheme (*IP*, 16/10/67).

13   Quoted in Breathnach and Ní Mhurchú, *Beathaisnéis a Trí*, p. 133. Is í an chuimhne is láidre atá agam féin ar mo thréimhse chaidrimh le Séamus Ó Néill ná a dháiríreacht a bhí sé faoi gach ní tábhachtach.

14   It is, however, worth mentioning that in 1951 Tomás Mac Anna, who had worked closely with him on more than one occasion, was critical of Ó Néill for not devoting more time and effort to learning his craft, writing: 'If Séamus Ó Néill has failed – and I say that he has – to give us even one worthwhile play, the fault is his own. He was willing to learn the craft of writing and the very difficult craft of writing a novel, but he does not see that the dramatic craft is another craft altogether' (Má theip ar Shéamus Ó Néill, agus deirim-se gur theip air, fiú dráma fiúntach amháin a thabhairt dúinn is air féin atá an locht. Bhí sé sásta ceard na scríbhneoireachta a fhoghlaim agus ceard rí-dheacair na húrscéalaíochta, ach ní fheiceann sé gur ceard eile ar fad ceard na drámaíochta) (*Comhar*, Feb. 1951, p. 4).

15   When asked in a 1963 interview about the production of a play translated from English at the Dublin Theatre Festival, Ó Néill stated: 'The Damer ought to understand that people would be mocking the Irish-language community if they had nothing to produce during the festival except a translation from English' (Ba chóir go dtuigfeadh an Damer go mbeadh daoine ag fonóid faoi lucht na Gaeilge mura mbeadh le léiriú acu le linn na Féile ach aistriúchán ón mBéarla). He believed that people would attend such a translation 'just for the sake of the Irish language' (mar mhaithe leis an nGaeilge amháin) and that there could never be an authentic Irish-

language drama 'unless the followers come to the theatre to see the play itself' (munar chun an dráma féin a fheiceáil a thagann na leantóirí chun na hamharclainne) (*IP*, 27/9/63).

16 Ba chóir go mbeadh sé soiléar anois ag lucht stiúrtha na Mainistreach go gcaithfidh siad a ndúnghaois a athrú, muna bhfuil siad le drámaíocht na Gaeilge a mharbhadh amach is amach. Bhfuil aoinne a chreidfeadh nár bhféidir bun-dráma Gaeilge ní b'fhearr ná 'Na Cloigíní' a fháil?

17 Séamus Ó Néill, *Tonn Tuile* (Tidal wave) (Baile Átha Cliath: Sáirséal agus Dill, 1947), p. 115.

18 Ibid., p. 146. Ach scríobhfainn dráma go fóill a chuirfeadh íontas orthu, a bhéarfadh le fios dóibh nár thuig siad a dhath. Cá mhéid drámadóirí Gaeilge a rabh aon smaointeadh acu? Ba sin an rud a chuir mire orthu, go mbeadh sé dhánaíocht ag údar Gaeilge smaointeadh a bheith aige. Ní rabh siad cleachtaithe le n-a leithéid. See also pp 142–5.

19 Of course both the middle-class Dublin setting in *Tonn Tuile* and the Northern – and urban – setting in *Máire Nic Artáin* broke new ground in Gaelic fiction, and there were some dramatic events in both novels, most notably the German bombings of Dublin in *Tonn Tuile* and the sectarian riots in Belfast in *Máire Nic Artáin*. One also gets the impression that Ó Néill found his alter ego Liam de Faoite quite remarkable.

20 A brief synopsis of the latter is provided with the radio listings in *IP* for 21/12/54. I regret that I am here perpetuating the ignorance about radio plays about which Ó Néill complained in a 1949 letter to *The Irish Press* (*IP*, 6/9/49).

21 *Glór-réim Naomh Pádraig*, directed by Tomás Mac Anna, was broadcast over Radio Éireann on 20 June 1961. According to Pádraig Ó Méalóid, the show was seen by 'myself and four or five thousand other people' (mise agus ceathair nó cúig de mhílte duine eile) and was 'the most enjoyable and poetic history lesson [Séamus Ó Néill] ever taught' (an ceacht staire is taithneamhaí agus is fileata dár thug [Séamus Ó Néill] ariamh) (*Feasta*, June 1961, p. 14).

22 Ó Néill praised the way Tomás Mac Anna adapted this story for the stage in the 1971 Gaelic *geamaireacht* (pantomime) in the Peacock Theatre. See 'Celtic imagination at the Peaock', *IP*, 13/1/72.

23 See the picture of the cast in costume, *IP*, 2/5/34.

24 Séamus Ó Néill, '"Cath Finntrágha" agus scoláire mór' ('Cath Finntrágha' and a great scholar), in Ó Néill, *Lámh Dearg Abú!* (Red hand forever!) (Baile Átha Cliath: Foilseacháin Náisiúnta Teoranta, 1982), pp 42–3.

25 See also his comments as 'Roddy the Rover' in his regular column 'Seen, heard and noted', *IP*, 9/2/37.

26 Sé mo bharamhail gur mó a rachas an dráma seo chun tairbhe do chúis na Gaedhilge ná a rabh de rangannaibh ariamh ann.

27 An anonymous critic in *An t-Ultach* conceded that Ó Néill was not Shakespeare but felt that he had written a fine play (*Ultach*, Apr. 1934, p. 6). An anonymous critic in *Ar Aghaidh* found *Buaidh an Ultaigh* too static and felt it might have made a better novel (*AA*, Jan. 1937, p. 2). Having seen the production of the play by An Comhar Drámaíochta, an anonymous critic for *An t-Éireannach* wrote that the play was of interest simply because it was an original play in Irish, but then continued: 'It could not really be called a play at all. What it is is four very short scenes' (Ní maith go bhféadfaí dráma a thabhairt air chor ar bith. Séard atá ann ceithre radharcanna agus iad an-ghearr) (*Éireannach*, 12/12/36).

28 Ní bheidh an dráma seo ró-dhoiligh ag daoine óga nó ró-shuarach ag daoine fásta. Tá a leithéid 'e dhíth go cruaidh. He also reviewed the published play in similar terms for the Dundalk *Examiner*, where he stated that it was 'a play in which there was moderate depth' (dráma . . . a bhfuil measardhacht doimhneachta ann) (*Examiner*, 8/5/37).

29 Mothóchaidh tú fíor-anál na sean-aimsire ar an dráma seo. Thuig an t-ughdar i gceart an dlúthcheangal a bhí eadar saoghal na ndaoine i n-allód agus íontaisí na cruinne.

30 Ó Néill was well aware of the difficulties Gaelic playwrights faced in attracting an audience. See, for example, Séamus Ó Néill, 'Amharclann na Mainistreach: dea-léiriú ar dhráma sean-aimseartha' (The Abbey Theatre: a good performance of an old-fashioned play), *Indiu*, 15/10/48; Séamus Ó Néill, 'The spirit of drama', *IP*, 27/10/66; and his comments as quoted by fellow playwright Annraoi Saidléar in a letter to *The Irish Press* (*IP*, 8/12/71).

31 See also Séamus Ó Néill, 'Cuspóir' (Goal), *Iris*, Feb. 1946, p. 3.

32 He compared Cú Chulainn unfavourably to Roland and King Arthur among others. But several years earlier he had referred in a lecture to the 'power' of the Cú Chulainn tales (*IP*, 29/6/37), and in his essay on 'Gaelic literature' in Robert Hogan's *Dictionary of Irish Literature*, he dealt with the Ulster Cycle more dispassionately. See *Dictionary of Irish Literature*, vol. 1, ed. Robert Hogan (Westport, CT: Greenwood Press, 1996 [1979]), pp 21–5. It should be noted that he was far more respectful of African culture in his review of Pádraig Ó Máille's *Dúdhúchas* (Black heritage), *IP*, 23/9/72.

33 He published the excerpt on which he based the play in *An t-Ultach*, Feb. 1934, pp 2–3.

34 Ó Néill, 'Gaelic literature', in *Dictionary*, vol. 1, ed. Hogan, p. 25.

35 Séamus Ó Néill, *Buaidh an Ultaigh: Dráma Nua* (The victory of the Ulsterman: an original play) (Baile Átha Cliath: Oifig Díolta Foillseacháin Rialtais, 1936), p. 42. Maith go leór. Déanaigidh mur gcomhairle féin. Ní orm-sa a bhéas a bhás, cibé ar bith.

36 Ibid., p. 28. Cad chuige nach dtéid seisean chun an comhraic le Dursa Dorbha. Chreid mé ariamh nach rabh an fear ar dhruim an domhain a mbéadh eagla ar Fhionn roimhe.

37 Ibid., p. 29. Is cosamhail gurbh' iad na taoisigh agus na tighearnaí a chuir tús leis an ghnáthas sin.

38 See, for example, ibid., pp 24–8 and 30.

39 See Máiréad Ní Shé, 'Séamus Ó Néill: saol agus saothar' (Life and work), *IMN*, 1987, p. 101.

40 Bhí fairsingeacht san ábhar aige do na smaointe móra sin a thógas an intinn amach as na pluchógaí saolta a mbíonn ár n-anamnacha cuachta ionta eadar dhá fhaoiside ach níor leig sé fá mheanmain an fhile nó an laoich iad . . . Chuir mé ceist orm féin an rabh aon smaoineadh ann ar bhfiú don údar Séamus Mac Murchadha agus Peadar Ó Doirnín a thabhairt chun an tsaoil lena léiriú. Ní thig liom a rá go bhfuil. He did also say that the play was 'very interesting' (an-suimiúil).

41 Séamus Ó Néill, *Díolta faoi n-a Luach: Dráma Cheithre Radharc* (Sold for less than he is worth: a play in four scenes) (Baile Átha Cliath: Oifig an tSoláthair, 1946), p. 50. Leith-chéad giní, a Pheig. Gheobhaidh tusa a bhfuil agam go fóill . . . Tógann sí a ceann, agus stánann sí air bomaite, annsin creathnann sí roimhe.

42 Ibid., p. 7. Nach cuma duit-se agus domh-sa cé tá i dtreis sa tír? Cuirfimid san Earrach agus bainfimid san Fhoghmhar, agus dhéanfaimid ár gcuid a shaothrú as allus ár malacha, bíodh Gaedhil nó Gaill i réim i gCaisleáin Bhaile Átha Cliath.

43 Ibid. Is measa i bhfad a bheith faoi smacht ag do chine féin – féadann tú sin a chreidbheáil.

44 Ibid., p. 35. Is iomaidh sin uair a chuala mé trácht ar na fir údaí a bhaineas an t-airgead de na bodaigh mhóra agus a bheir do na bochta é; ach tusa, an méid nach dtig leat-sa a bhaint de na bodaigh mhóra baineann tú de na bochta é. Tá an tír uilig scriosta agat. Nár chóir go mbéadh náire ort.

45 Ibid., p. 7. Is maith nach ionann manadh do achan duine agus duit-se. Ní bhéadh na Sasanaigh i dtreis i n-Éirinn, dá mbéadh tuilleadh fear againn ion-churtha leis an Bheirneach.

46 Ibid., p. 18. Tá comhacht na Sasana taobh thiar de: Is cuma cá mhéad páiste a fhágas sé gan athaireacha, béidh comhacht na Sasana taobh thiar de.

47 Ó Néill, 'Gaelic literature', in *Dictionary*, vol. 1, ed. Hogan, p. 52.

48 Ó Néill, *Díolta faoi n-a Luach*, pp 24–5. Is minic a thig beag-uchtach orm agus mé ag machtnamh ar dhímbrígh Gaedheal. Ach anois agus arís tig aislingeacha chugam – aislingeacha i n-a samhaltar domh na Gaedhil a bheith ag cruinniú treise ath-uair. Tchím fir fá iomlán arm ag deifriú chun catha. Tchím an spas sgaoll ag dhul ar na Sasanaigh . . . B'fhéidir nach bhfuil ann ach go bhfuil mian mo chléibh ag faghail faoisimh ins an dóigh sin; ach na h-aislingeacha a thig fá mheanmain an fhile, cé

déarfas nach bhfuil sin ionnta fios a gheibhtear ar imeall na síorruidheachta.

49 Ibid. Ní aislingeacha ar chor ar bith a bhíos oraibh ach rámhailleach, a Pheadair Uí Dhoirnín.

50 Ibid., p. 26. Chan eagla a bhí ar mo chroidhe roimh Seonstanach na gCeann – chan eadh, leoga. Agus bhuailfinn buille, dá mbínn i n-áit a bhuailte. Ach ní bhéadh maith dhom ann agus sgaoi shaighdiúir dearg leis. Ba bhuidhe bocht leis an seans a fhagháil mo cheann a chur i n-áirde ar bhior os cionn Phríosúin Dhún Dealgan.

51 Ibid., p. 52. Nach bhfuil fhios agat go maith nach bhfuil uasal ná íseal anois ann? Tá muid uilig 'nár sglábhuidhthe. Flatha, iarlaí, támuid uilig i n-umar na h-aimhléise ó fuair na Gaill an bhuaidh orainn.

52 Ibid., p. 19. Is minic agus mé amuigh i nduibheagán na coilleadh, oidhche dhorcha, a thig an smaoineadh sin i m-intinn, agus ba mhaith liom a dhul isteach go Sráid-Bhaile Dhún Dealgan agus síothcháin a dhéanamh leis na Sasanaigh. He recovers quickly, however, telling Peig: 'I will never yield to Johnston of the Heads or to any child-killer who ever sucked from an English breast. I'd rather die than surrender to him' (Cha ghéillim go h-éag do Sheonstanach na gCeann nó d'aon dúnmharbhthóir páiste a dhíol cíoch Ghallta ariamh. B'fhearr liom an bás ná géillstin dó) (p. 20).

53 Ibid., p. 19. A Dhia, gan agam le troid a dhéanamh níos mó, gan bheith faoi'n eagla mhillteanach sin a bíos ort agus tú ag déanamh luigheacháin roimh na Sasanaigh . . . Bíonn mo chroidhe ar crith in mo chliabh, a Pheig, gidh go measann mo chuid fear go bhfuil mé dána.

54 In the scene a young Paitsí is threatened with a blackthorn stick by his father. In a note Ó Néill wrote that the scene could be omitted if it was 'too difficult for the director' (ró-dheacair ag an léirightheoir) (p. 8).

55 In an editorial note in *An t-Ultach*, we are told that when members of the RUC saw the page proofs of the play being carried by the editor, they were concerned that the work might be seditious (*Ultach*, July 1939, p. 6).

56 The critic for *The Irish Press* dealt with the play in two sentences, concluding that 'the plot was somewhat thin' (*IP*, 10/12/40). The play was revived by students from Kells Vocational School at Féile Drámaíochta na Mí in 1953 (*MC*, 6/3/53).

57 In a note in the published text, Ó Néill wrote: 'If I am told that this play does not agree with the truest accounts we have, the answer I'd give is "Does it matter?"' (Má deirtear liom nach bhfuil an dráma seo ar aon dul leis na cunntaisí is fíre dá bhfuil againn, sé'n freagra a bheirim air sin: 'Nach cuma?'). See Séamus Ó Néill, '*Ní Chuireann Siad Síol' nó 'Poll Bocht*' ('They do not sow' or 'poor Poll') (Baile Átha Cliath: Oifig an tSoláthair, 1952), p. 4.

58 An dtabharfainn scríbhneoir Éireannach air? Ní thabharfainn, ná Anglo-Irish féin ach scríbhneoir Sasanach ... An acfuinn grinn a bhí aige, ba leis féin; ní rabh sí Gaelach ná Gallda. Ba tréith í a d'fhág a lorg go doimhin ar a chuid scríbhneoireachta, ba tréith í a dhealuigh óna lucht aitheantais é, i bhfus i nÉirinn agus thall i Sasana. See also Séamus Ó Néill, 'Oliver and his friends', *IP*, 30/8/74. In general, Ó Néill took a more generous attitude to Irish literature in English than did many of his colleagues. See Philip O'Leary, *Writing beyond the Revival: Facing the Future in Gaelic Prose 1940–1951* (Dublin: University College Dublin Press, 2011), pp 219–20.

59 Ó Néill, *'Ní Chuireann Siad Síol'*, pp 14–15. In his unpublished pageant *Adhaint na Tine Beo* (Kindling the live fire) (1967), performed as *Spiorad na Saoirse* (The spirit of freedom), Ó Néill depicts bailiffs as heartless oppressors. I am here using an unpaginated typescript of the pageant given by Ó Néill to Professor John V. Kelleher, who gave it to me.

60 Ó Néill, *'Ní Chuireann Siad Síol'*, p. 16. Luigheann cuid mhór de na daoine bochta i n-Éirinn ar chocán sgaithte agus caithfidh mé a rádh gur glaine i bhfad é ná cuid mhór de na leabthacha a chonnaic mé ar fud na Sasana.

61 Ibid., p. 14. Caithfidh sé gur báillí atá i muinntir Shasana uilig go léir.

62 The pageant had an all-female cast.

63 Bhí an feisteas stáitse, an ceol, an aisteoireacht agus an léiritheoireacht ar bheagán locht agus tá moladh ag dul do aos léinn an choláiste.

64 See Séamus Ó Néill, 'No drama', *IP*, 31/3/69. Some of the poems from the pageant with Ó Néill's translations were published in the 'Aistriúcháin' (Translations) column in *The Irish Press*. See, for example, *IP*, 3/4, 25/4/69, and 15/2/72. According to a note accompanying these translations, An Gúm was planning to publish the pageant; that plan was not carried out.

65 See Séamus Ó Néill, 'An fhírinne fá Cholum Cille' (The truth about Colm Cille), *Iris*, Jan. 1946, pp 49–56.

66 See his review of another work on Colm Cille, Robert Farren's *The First Exile* (*Standard*, 21/4/44), and his essays 'Adamnán and the holy places', *IP*, 1/11/67; and 'Adamnán and the holy shroud', *IT*, 8/5/79. Ó Néill also wrote on other figures of the early Irish church like St Brendan the Navigator (*Indiu*, 30/11/45); St Colman (*Inniu*, 28/7/50); and Diciúil (*Indiu*, 6/3/51).

67 See 'Séamus Ó Néill ag comhrá le Risteárd Ó Glaisne' (Séamus Ó Néill in conversation with Risteárd Ó Glaisne), *Inniu*, 2/4/71.

68 Séamus Ó Néill, *Colm Cille: Dráma i gCeithre Radharcanna* (A play in four scenes) (Baile Átha Cliath: Oifig an tSoláthair, 1946), p. 4. Ar feadh fada go leor i ndiaidh báis Naomh Pádraig bhí dian-

choimhlint ar siubhal i n-Éirinn eadar sean-saoghal na págántachta agus nua-shaoghal na Críostaidh-eachta.

69 See ibid., p. 20.

70 Ibid., p. 12. Admhuighim go rabh an sean-léigheann págánta ag na filí, admhuighim go bhfuil cuid de acú go fóill, agus gur leisc le n-a lán acú é a thabhairt suas go h-iomlán, agus deirim-se leat, a Áird-Rí Éireann, agus libh-se, a mhaithe agus a mhór-uaisle, nach bhfuil rud olc ar an adhbhar go bhfuil sé págánach.

71 Ibid., p. 13. Níor chros sé orainn deireadh a chur leis an tsean-léigheann phágánach ach oiread; leis an fhírinne a rádh d'iarr sé orainn é shábháil, é scríobhadh síos mar is eol díbh; san dóigh go mbeadh fhios againne comh h-oilte, comh h-uasal, comh léigheannta is bhí ár gcuid sinnsear, ár gcuid sinnsear páganach ... See also p. 16.

72 Ibid., p. 12. Cha leigim d'aoinne, dá aoirde é ... crann-taca a bhaint as an Eaglais 'e mhaithe leis féin. Cha leigim d'aoinne, dá aoirde é ... crann-taca a bhaint as an Eaglais 'e mhaithe le cuspóir saoghalta ... Ní leigfidh mé d'aonduine claon-innsint ná leagan bréagach a chur ar theagasc na h-Eaglaise 'e mhaithe leis féin.

73 See the discussion of Colm Cille's dispute with Diarmuid in Francis John Byrne, *Irish Kings and High-Kings* (London: B.T. Batsford, 1973), pp 94–7.

74 Ó Néill, *Colm Cille*, p. 40. Mo mhallacht ort, a Rí bhradaigh, mo mhíle mallacht. Freagróchaidh tú as an ghníomh seo do Chlann Néill an Tuaiscirt. Cuirfidh mé gairm ar shlóighte mo chineadh.

75 Ibid., p. 49. Ní bheinn ag déanamh aithrighe, ach ag náiriú mo chineadh, ag masladh na bhfear cródha a thuit ar mo shon i gCúl Dreimhne.

76 Ibid., pp 45–6. Níl mise fóirsteanach ag an obair atá le déanamh annseo go fóill. Tá mé ró-thobann. Thall i n-Albain béidh sé níos fusa. Béidh sé contabhairteach, b'fhéidir, ach béidh an bán i n-a bhán agus an dubh i n-a dhubh. An té a bhéas ar mo thaoibh béidh sé ar mo thaoibh, agus an té a bhéas i m'éadan béidh sé in m'éadan.

77 Ó Néill had a good deal to say about historians and their craft. See, for example, 'Must our history be re-written?', *Leader*, 9/5/42; review of *The Great O'Neill* by Sean O'Faolain, *Indiu*, Mar. 1943, p. 3; 'History must be taught with great care', *IP*, 22/6/67; 'National bias in teaching of history', *IP*, 10/7/67; 'History and tradition', *IP*, 8/4/68; 'History is made by historians', *IP*, 17/11/72; and 'The trouble with Irish history', *IP*, 28/8/73.

78 The protagonist of Ó Néill's 1947 novel *Tonn Tuile* is explicitly anti-Semitic. See Ó Néill, *Tonn Tuile*, p. 4 and 106.

79 See *An Tusa d'Fhoscail an Fhuinneog?* (Is it you who opened the window?), *Feasta*, May 1953, pp 7–10. Indeed one could well feel that his favourable

presentation of Eva Braun and Hermann Göring in the play is insensitive if not downright offensive.

80 Oddly enough the parrot's cry is always in English, as, of course, one would expect it to be in Dublin.

81 Micheál Mac Liammóir, 'Drámaíocht Ghaeilge san am atá le teacht' (Drama in Irish in the future), in *Ceo Meala, Lá Seaca* (A honey mist, a frosty day) (Baile Átha Cliath: Sáirséal agus Dill, 1952), p. 239. Ach go dtí go mbeidh an Ghaeilge mar ghnáth-theanga i mbéal mhuintir na hÉireann – agus ní feasach d'éinne cé an uair a thiocfas an lá sin – ní gá dhúinn bheith ag brionglóidigh a thuilleadh faoi scoil an Réaliostachais theacht i gcabhair orainn. Ní gá dhúinn ach oiread bheith ag cuimhneamh ar an *Popular Drama*.

82 'Agallamh le Séamus Ó Néill' (An interview with Séamus Ó Néill), *IMN*, 1962, p. 7. Nach doiligh cuntas a thabhairt i nGaeilge ar eachtraí a 'thiteann amach i mBéarla,' mar adéarfá ... Ní thig liom a rá, mar ni i mBéarla a thiteann rudaí amach. Ní suíomh na Gaeltachta atá ag Pádraic Ó Conaire ins an chuid is fearr dá chuid scéaltach, agus nuair a bhím féin á léamh, ní thugaim fá dear cén teanga atá aige, agus nach sin an cruthú is fearr gur scríbhneoir é.

83 Of course nowhere is his response to this challenge more impressive than in his two novels.

84 In a review of the published text in 1961, Pearse Hutchinson praised Ó Néill as 'a writer ... who has a brilliant and deep understanding of the primary truths of the heart, perhaps a stronger and more precise understanding than anyone else in this modern literature' (scríbhneoir ... a bhfuil tuiscint lonrach dhoimhin aige do phríomhfhírinní an chroí, tuiscint níos láidre b'fhéidir agus níos dírí ná éinne eile sa nualitríocht seo), but added that he was always threatened by 'some devil of distorted naiveté always setting an ambush for him' (diabhal éigin na saobh-shaontachta ag síordhéanamh luíocháin roimhe) (*Comhar*, May 1961, p. 21). Like de Blaghd he was critical of Ó Néill's stage-American nun, to which he added reservations about the niece's stage-Protestant suitor. Not surprisingly, Ó Néill was not about to let this review pass unchallenged, pointing out in the same issue of *Comhar* that Hutchinson had written positively about the broadcast of the play and that anyone caught in such a contradiction should 'stop the pontificating about literature that he goes on with, if there's any shame at all in him' (staid den pontificating fá litríocht a bhíos ar siúl aige, má tá náire ar bith ann) (*Comhar*, May 1961, p. 33). See also Hutchinson's response, which concludes: 'As far as I know, my "pontificating" never bothered Mr. Ó Néill when I was canonising him' (Go bhfios dom, níor ghoill mo chuid 'pontificating' ar an Niallach nuair a bhíos á naomhainmniú) (*Comhar*, July 1961, p. 32).

85 Ó Néill had long experience working with nuns at Carysfort.

86 Séamus Ó Néill, *An tSiúr Pól: Dráma i dTrí Gníomha* (A play in three acts) (Baile Átha Cliath:

Oifig an tSoláthair, 1961), p. 11. B'fhéidir, a Athair, dá mbíodh níos mó ceada acu anseo dul chun an diabhail mar is toil leo, gur anseo agus nach thall i Sasain a bheadh siad dá bpósadh ... B'fhéidir gur ait an duine mé, ach ní hait an bhean rialta mé. Ní hionann a bheith id mhnaoi rialta, agus d'intinn a dhalladh ar fhírinne an tsaoil.

87 While this issue is also raised in *Máire Nic Artáin* (Baile Átha Cliath: Cló Morainn, 1959), p. 94, Pearse Hutchinson, in his otherwise quite favourable review of the novel, wrote that with regard to *Ne Temere* Ó Néill was 'guilty of one of the most singular side-stepping acts in modern fiction' (*IP*, 11/3/60). The same could not be said of how he treats the question in *An tSiúr Pól*.

88 Ó Néill, *An tSiúr Pól*, p. 28. Ní luíonn sé le nádúir an duine sin a dhéanamh, agus sin an fáth nach bhfuil an Eaglais geallmhar ar phósadh idir Caitliceach agus Protastúnach. Tá sí ró-eolach ar an toradh a bíos air.

89 Ibid., p. 17. Nach é a chuala mé i gcónaí go mba í seo tír na síochána, agus an tsuaimhnis, an t-aon áit sa domhan nár ghéill do dheifre agus do mhire na haimsire seo?

90 Ibid., p. 35. Sin an cineál cainte a bíos ag na Comhchumannaigh, agus ag ainchreidmhigh eile nuair a bhíonn siad ag trácht ar na hiarrachtaí a bhíonn muid a dhéanamh le cailíní na hÉireann a shábháil ar a gcuid diabhlaíochta.

91 Ibid., p. 21. Ach caithfidh tú a thuigbheáil, a Shighle, nach só ar fad a bheadh i ndán duit mar mhnaoi rialta.

92 One wonders if this explicit connection between nun and saint is what Earnán P. de Blaghd had in mind when he wrote that 'the last act, where Mother Superior's plans have gone agley, is embarrassing in its sentimentality' (*II*, 18/11/63). For Hutchinson, this ending was 'dénouement ... *parish-pageant*-úil' (*Comhar*, May 1961, p. 22).

93 Ó Néill, *An tSiúr Pól*, p. 63. Bean tú a bhfuil intinn de do chuid féin agat. Ba mhaith leat do dhóigh féin a bheith agat.

94 He was not always happy about the way he was treated by An Taibhdhearc. See Séamus Ó Néill, Letter, *Leader*, 13/9/41. On the other hand, in the Taibhdhearc Papers at NUIG is a letter he wrote dated 28 October [1953], in which he thanked the board of An Taibhdhearc for sending him royalties of 12 guineas and wrote: 'You can be certain that I am fully satisfied with that amount, for it is seldom that an Irish-language author gets anything from his plays' (Féadann tú a bheith cinnte go bhfuil mé lánsásta leis an mhéid sin, mar is annamh a gheibh údar Gaeilge aon rud as a chuid drámaí). Perhaps his dissatisfaction was due to the fact that *Iníon Rí Dhún Sobhairce* was the only play by him produced at An Taibhdhearc during his lifetime – or after.

95 It is also worth noting that what was left of An Comhar Drámaíochta provided a subsidy for this production (*Inniu*, 12/12/53).

96 Apparently attendance on opening night was disappointing as this critic commented that the play 'merits better support from the general public'. Micheál Mac Liammóir and Hilton Edwards were in attendance for the final performance, which was almost sold out (*Inniu*, 10/7/53).

97 Tá na míreanna curtha le chéile gan an comhdhlúthú a chuirfeadh aontacht iontu agus a rachadh abhaile ar an éisteoir. This critic was disgusted with the quality of the Irish spoken by some of the actors.

98 The seemingly intractable issue of poor attendance affected this production as well. Recalling the Dublin production in 1955, Niall Carroll wrote: 'When Mr. O'Neill's fine drama was staged in a major Dublin professional theatre not long ago . . . an average of 26 people per night paid to see it in a ten-night run' (*IP*, 21/2/55).

99 He was not without reservations, writing: 'The failure is only in a handful of rhetorical lapses at just the wrong moments, and (here the "only" can't apply) at the final curtain.'

100 Tá éacht déanta ag Séamus Ó Néill agus dráma fónta i nGaeilge a sholáthair. Agus an bhail atá ar dhrámaíocht na Gaeilge, ní hamháin gur ábhar iontais a leithéid ach is geall le míorúilt é . . .

101 He did feel that some of Ó Néill's characters could have been better developed, and he was sharply critical of the Irish of several of the actors.

102 Tá an stíl an-chosúil leis, agus tá an choimhlint chéanna ann idir an tsean-Éire phágánta agus an Chríostúlacht nua-thagtha. Dar liomsa go bhfuil sé comh maith, agus i slite níos fearr ná drama Yeats. He continued: 'It does not matter what our opinion of Yeats's Romanticism is; it is no small thing that we have a play in Irish that can be compared to the "Countess", when you think that English is hundreds of years ahead of us with regard to the drama' (Is cuma cad é ár mbarúil de Románsaíocht Yeats, ní beag an rud é go bhfuil dráma Gaeilge againn atá ionchurtha leis an 'Countess,' is a rá go raibh Béarla na céadta blian chun tosaigh orainn i gcúrsaí drámaíochta).

103 The tale also appears in the Trinity College manuscript H.3.18, but as its editor David Greene points out, 'the two manuscripts go back to a common archetype and diverge hardly at all.' See *Fingal Rónáin and Other Stories*, Medieval and Modern Irish Series XVI, ed. David Greene (Dublin: Dublin Institute for Advanced Studies, 1955), pp 1–2.

104 Séamus Ó Néill, '"Cath Finntrágha" – agus scoláire mór', in O'Néill, *Lámh Dearg*, p. 44. In 1947 Aodh de Blácam had suggested that *Fingal Rónáin* would provide 'fine material for the stage' (*Irish Bookman*, June 1947, p. 41). Lá amháin shín sé chugam cóip lámhscríofa de sheanscéal Gaeilge, cóip a scríobh sé féin, agus 's é dúirt sé liom, 'Déan dráma de sin.'

105 Ó Néill, 'Gaelic literature', in *Dictionary*, vol. 1, ed. Hogan, p. 29.

106 *Fingal Rónáin*, ed. Greene, p. vii.

107 Dáirine herself mentions Deirdre. See Séamus Ó Néill, *Iníon Rí Dhún Sobhairce: Tragóid Trí Ghníomh* (The daughter of the king of Dunseverick: a tragedy in three acts) (Baile Átha Cliath: Sáirséal agus Dill, 1960), pp 20–1.

108 Ibid., p. 26. Mura bhfuil na béasa agat is dual do bhanríon, caithfear iad a theagasc duit.

109 Ibid., p. 10, 16, and 19.

110 Ibid., p. 43. Tá siad go léir fá gheasa ag an phisreogacht seo a tugadh anoir, ach mar sin féin tá eagla orthu romhamsa. Ba mhaith leo mise a dhíbirt, ach ní ligfidh an eagla dóibh a dhéanamh. Tá eagla orthu . . . go dtarraingeoinn mí-ádh agus scrios anuas orthu.

111 Ibid., p. 49. B'fhearr é thaispeáint faoi chineál de scannán éadrom agus solas á léiriú; agus an chuid eile den ardán a dhorchú sa dóigh nach féidir a bheith cinnte cé acu a tá sé ann ná nach bhfuil . . . Fill chun tí. See also pp 29–30. Máirtín Ó Direáin was less impressed by the bishop, 'a character who lacked substance, authority, presence, or dignity' (caractaer a bhí gan éifeacht, gan údarás, teacht i láthair, ná dígnit) as well as 'the good sense, prudence or shrewdness of the Church' (ciall, stuaim ná gliocas na hEaglaise), resulting in a less equal and dramatically satisfying contest between bishop and *bean feasa* – a character Ó Direáin found far more impressive (*Feasta*, Jan. 1954, p. 14).

112 Ó Néill, *Iníon Rí Dhún Sobhairce*, p. 50. Ní éistfead leat. Níl fhios agat cad is toil le Dia. An toil le Dia i gcónaí an rud a tá suarach truaillithe samhnasach? Sin an rud a thuigfeadh aoinne uait . . . Ach ní chreidimse i do dhia-sa níos mó. B'fhearr na seandéithe a bhí ag ár sinsir. Bhí siad cruálach b'fhéidir, ach bhí siad mór maorga scáfar.

113 For *geis*, see Philip O'Leary, 'Honour bound: the social context of early Irish heroic *geis*', *Celtica* XX (1988), pp 63, 85–107.

114 According to tradition, this was a cattle tribute the Leinstermen were obligated to pay to the Uí Néill kings of Tara. See Byrne, *Irish Kings and High-Kings*, pp 144–6.

115 See Ó Néill, *Iníon Rí Dhún Sobhairce*, pp 46 and 60–1, but see also p. 5, where it is Congal whose smile is threatening. For laughter in early Irish literature, see Philip O'Leary, 'Jeers and judgments: laughter in early Irish literature', *Cambridge Medieval Celtic Studies* XXII (winter 1991), pp 15–29.

116 Ó Néill, *Iníon Rí Dhún Sobhairce*, p. 50. Sciobfaidh mé bláth an tsonais as dorn doicheallach na cinniúna. See also p. 46.

117 Ibid., p. 63. Tá mianta an duine chomh láidir le tuile na habhainne, a chartann gach rud léi ina mhaidhm rabhartais. See also p. 48.

118 Ó Néill, '"Cath Finntrágha" – agus scoláire mór', in Ó Néill, *Lámh Dearg*, p. 43.

119 Pearse Hutchinson was less affected by that laugh, calling it 'the curtain-fall cackle of the gloating witch' (*IP*, 30/3/61).

120 Reviewing the production for *Feasta*, Pádraig Ó Siochfhradha wrote: 'Up until now in Gaelic drama we have been almost entirely reliant on translations from English with regard to thriller plays, but now we have one from the pen of Séamus Ó Néill' (Go dtí seo i ndrámuíocht na Gaeilge bhíomar go hiomlán geall leis i muinín aistriúcháin ón mBéarla i gcás sceondrámaí, ach anois tá ceann againn ó pheann Shéamais Uí Néill). Ó Siochfhradha had some minor reservations about the play – among them that the professor's wife from California somehow knows Irish – but pronounced the production 'an enjoyable night in the theatre' (oíche thaithneamhach san amharclainn) (*Feasta*, July 1961, pp 18–19).

121 In a 1963 interview, Ó Néill stated that An Damer had initially refused the play, as it had an earlier play by him (*IP*, 26/9/63). That earlier play must have been *Iníon Rí Dhún Sobhairce*.

122 The company claimed that this was 'the first play that they have not had to translate into Donegal Irish' (*IT*, 16/5/69).

123 Gael-Linn founded and ran An Damer.

124 Tríd is tríd is fiú an *drama* seo a fheiceáil agus ní bheadh iontas orm dá maireadh sé rith na seachtaine seo chugainn, cé go mbeidh sé ag críochnú amáireach de réir an chláir.

125 In a touch reminiscent of that other amateur anthropologist, Lady Gregory's Resident Magistrate in *Spreading the News* (1904), the inspector turns his binoculars on the island at the beginning of the play.

126 Séamus Ó Néill, *Rún an Oileáin*, p. 21. For quotations from this play I will be using the script provided by An Comhlachas Náisiúnta Drámaíochta with Ó Néill's own translations from *The Secret of the Island*, 'this English version' as he called it (Dublin: Progress House, 1965). Níl spíodóirí ar bith ar an oileáin seo. (Deir an chuid eile an rud céanna.)

127 Ó Néill, *Rún an Oileáin*, p. 21. Tonn an bháis a tháinig air agus a scuab amach chun na farraige é.

128 Ibid., p. 32. Ná, fad is bhéas sibh anseo beidh sibh, bhur n-ainneoin féin, ar ndóigh, ag cothú spíde agus iaróige, agus amhrais i measc na ndaoine. Beidh fuath acu dá chéile agus fuath don Rialtas agus do gach rud a bhaineann leis.

129 Ibid., p. 47. Och, bhí a fhios agam nach dtiocfadh de bharr an fhiosrúcháin ach an mí-ádh agus an tubaiste.

130 Ibid., pp 48–9. Agus an ag imeacht uainn atá sibh? Nach mór an trua? Is mór a chrothnós muid an bheirt agaibh. Is mór go deimhin, ná beirt fhear ba dheise ná sibh ní tháinig ariamh chun an oileáin, nó a sheasaigh ar urlár mo thí. Sin an fhírinne anois, an fhírinne ghlan. Agus tá bronntanas beag agam do gach duine agaibh. Lán deoirn de chréafóg bheannaithe an oileáin – cuireann sí an tóir ar na luchógaí, tá a fhios agaibh.

131 Beidh tú ag cur stampaí amudha má chuireann tú scéalta béaloidis chugam.

132 Ó Néill had high hopes for the new Peacock, writing in July 1967: 'The opening of the new Peacock should mark the beginning of a new era in Gaelic drama. For the first time dramatists who write in Irish will have the chance of a professional production, not merely in a professional theatre, but in what is probably the best-equipped small theatre in the world . . . The chance of seeing their work in such a superb theatre as the Peacock should send scores of writers to their desks or tables' (*IP*, 26/7/67).

133 Ach bhí an oircad sin cachtraí le cur i láthair le go mbeadh iomláine ag baint leis an scéal nach fuair an choinbhlíocht riachtanach . . . aon chaoi cheart forbartha. Cnuasach d'eachtraí a bhí sa chumasc, ach an téagar ar iarraidh ceal caoi forbartha lárthéama dhrámataigh. 'P. Ó S.' also felt that the production suffered because playwright and director lacked a shared vision of the play.

134 Bhí an dráma mall, spadánta tríd síos; ba bheag an bheocht nó an spéis a bhain le carachtar ar bith, agus le cur leis an saoithínteacht bhí an léiriú féin spadach, marbhánta. In the brief unsigned review of the published text of *Faill ar an bhFeart*, the critic regretted that it was brought out in hardback as the higher price would limit sales and make it less likely that amateur groups would produce the play. He also called the play 'a quite welcome addition to our all too inadequate list of original plays in Irish' (*IP*, 5/1/68).

135 There do not seem to have been any radio broadcasts of *Faill ar an bhFeart*. Perhaps the full-length format was problematic for radio.

136 More in line with the policy of the Fianna Fáil government at the time and for many years thereafter, he also wrote: 'The second plan is to organise a campaign against Partition in Ireland and throughout the world.'

137 For examples of his evolving attitude to Partition, see his review of Ernest Blythe's *Briseadh na Teorann* (The breaking of the border), *Feasta*, Apr. 1955, p. 13; 'The unity of Gaeldom', *IP*, 23/11/71; and 'Easter Rising: triumph or blunder?', *IP*, 26/3/78.

138 See also Séamus Ó Néill, 'Cúlra stairiúil na críchdheighilte' (The historical background of partition), *Comhar*, Apr. 1954, pp 6–7.

139 His reference to the 'Six Counties' would have offended 'a considerable body of Northern Protestants'.

140 For example, in 1934, he urged his fellow nationalists to try to Gaelicise Northern Protestants and to educate them in a proper national outlook, for 'they had that before and some of them have it still; why would all of them not have it again?' (Bhí sin acu roimhe agus tá sé ag cuid acu go fóill, cad chuige nach mbeadh sé acu uilig arís?) (*Éireannach*, 23/6/34). In many ways he answered his own question here in

a 1971 piece dealing with a recent debate between Conor Cruise O'Brien and Tomás Mac Giolla of Official Sinn Féin. Ó Néill here rejected Mac Giolla's assertion that 'the Protestants, or the Unionists, or the Orangemen in the North have never claimed to be a different nation'. Ó Néill declared: 'Unfortunately they have done that, time after time . . . Indeed, as one of their own historians records they were wont to describe themselves as "the Scottish nation in the North of Ireland"' (*IP*, 9/11/71). Ó Néill could not avoid emphasising the shared culture of Irish people on both sides of the border because of his belief that there were two great forces shaping a country's 'moral unity' (aondacht mórálta), religion and nationality. Since the Irish people lacked a common religion, nationality and – 'the heart of nationality – the language' (croidhe an náisiúnachais – an teanga) would have to provide 'the one great force for unification' (an t-oll fhórsa amháin chun an aontuighthe) (*Glór*, 14/4/45). He was willing to make some sacrifices, for example accepting the need to repeal Article 44 of the Irish Constitution, which recognised 'the special position' of the Catholic Church in Irish society. See Séamus Ó Néill, 'A matter for whose conscience?', *IP*, 6/12/72.

141 Séamus Ó Néill, *Faill ar an bhFeart: Dráma Trí Ghníomh* (A neglected grave: a play in three acts) (Baile Átha Cliath: Sáirséal agus Dill, 1967), pp 6–7. Tá corraíl ann . . . corraíl ar fud an domhain. Níl daoine sásta fanacht faoi smacht níos mó . . . Ní féidir leatsa stop a chur leis an chlaochlú is mó a tháinig ar an saol ó aimsir an Athrú Creidimh. Tá sé ag dul ar aghaidh mar a bheadh tonn rabharta ann. He deals more subtly and effectively with this idea of the implacable forces of history in *Máire Nic Artáin*: 'There was not a lessening but an increase in the strife that summer, until there was a tale of horror to be told at the end of every day, and everyone would go to sleep in fear. People were being killed, people were being injured, houses were being burned until in the end every mind was blinded by the hatred, and every heart overflowing with anger' (Ní maolú ach méadú a tháinig ar an achrann an samhradh sin, go dtí go raibh scéal uafáis le hinse i ndeireadh gach lae, agus gurbh eaglach a théadh cách fá chónaí. Bhí daoine á marú, daoine á lot, tithe á ndó, go dtí ins an deireadh go raibh gach intinn dallta ag an fhuath, agus gach croí ag cur thar maoil le fíoch). Seeing her Protestant husband in an Orange parade on 12 July, the Catholic protagonist is shocked: 'Seoirse was just like a clump of foam being swept from her atop a flood, or a child being drowned and that she was not able to save' (Ní raibh i Seoirse ach mar bheadh cnapán cúir ann a bhí á chartadh uaithi ar bharr tuile, nó leanbh a bhíthear a bhá agus nach raibh sí in ann a tharrtháil). See Séamus Ó Néill, *Máire Nic Artáin* (Baile Átha Cliath: Cló Morainn, 1959), p 134 and 148.

142 In a brief, highly positive review of the published play, Séamus de Bhilmot saw Porter in purely heroic terms, stating that Ó Néill found his inspiration in 'probably the greatest material for tragedy – the solitary person standing his ground against the mass. *Unus contra mundum*' (an t-ábhar tragóide is mó is dócha – an duine aonair ag seasamh an fhóid i gcoinne an tslua. *Unus contra mundum*) (*Feasta*, Dec. 1968, p. 33).

143 See Ó Néill, *Faill ar an bhFeart*, pp 77 and 109–11.

144 Ibid., p. 9. Níl an léann agam le díospóireacht a dhéanamh leat, ach insíonn mo chroí dom conas a dhéanfainn leas mo mhic.

145 Ibid., p. 21. *Liberté, égalité, fraternité*! Chualamar sin uilig cheana féin, ach tá a fhios againn cad é tháinig as an Fhrainc – *La Terreur* – uafás, ár, slad, agus dia-mhasladh. Ba mhaith liomsa mo phobal bocht a chosaint ar a leithéid sin agus ar na diabhail a chuir tús leis. Is maith atá a fhios agamsa cé íocfas as má bhíonn trioblóid sa tír – na Gaeil bhochta. In his review for *Inniu*, 'P. Ó S.' saw the conflict between An tAthair Ó hÍr and Porter as similar to that between Mánas Ó Dónaill and his son Calbhach in Seán Ó Tuama's 1956 play *Gunna Cam agus Slabhra Óir* (A pistol and a chain of gold), which will be discussed later in this book.

146 Ibid., p. 24. Bhí Orr ciontach de réir dhlí na tíre.

147 Ibid., p. 25. Ní aithníonn sibh gur ag ionsaí beatha na n-uaisle atá sibh nuair atá sibh ag iarraidh an chumhacht a bhaint díobh, agus an té a ionsaíonn a mbeatha níl ach dóigh amháin ann len é a chosc.

148 Ibid., p. 58. Tá d'intinn déanta suas agat, mar sin.

149 It is worth noting that in his review of the published text Séamus de Bhilmot seems to see An tAthair Ó hÍr as a collaborationist 'who had his insurance policy in his pocket in the form of a military pass from General Nugent' (a raibh a pholasaí urrúis i bhfoirm phais mhíleata ón nGinearál Nugent ina phóca aige) (*Feasta*, Dec. 1968, p. 33).

150 Ó Néill himself offers a quite facile dismissal of sectarian outrages committed by the nationalist side, particularly in Wexford, in 'Eagla a spreag iad: an bhréag agus an t-uafás i '98' (Fear drove them: the lie and the terror in '98), *Indiu*, 26/11/48. See also Séamus Ó Néill, 'One as bad as the other?', *IP*, 26/9/69.

151 Ó Néill, *Faill ar an bhFeart*, p. 98. D'fheall na Pápairí orainn, níor éirigh siad amach ar chor ar bith. Dá n-éireodh, bhí an bua againn. Droch-rath orthu mar chladhairí . . . Ní iompród brat glas a choíche arís. Nárbh iad na Pápairí na cladhairí?

152 Ibid., p. 158. Má theastaíonn uaibh mé a thligean chun báis ar fhianaise bhréagach, is furasta sin a dhéanamh, ach tá mé ag glacadh leis gur saighdiúirí onóracha sibh.

153 He does eventually catch on. See ibid., p. 167.

154 Ibid., p. 162. Níor aontaigh mé féin leis na tuairimí a bhí aige. Ach ba é an grá a bhí aige do na daoine, do na daoine bochta, a bhí á ghríosú. Theastaigh uaidh go mbeadh saol níos fearr acu, agus bhí sé mífhoighneach. Níor thuig sé nach féidir an saol a mhúnlú mar is toil leat le briathar ná le gníomh.

155 Ibid., p. 169. Tá briste ar na daoine. Tá buaite ag na máistrí. Tá buaite agaibhse. Dá bhrí sin, ná himrítear géarleanúint ar na daoine níos mó. Bígí trócaireach. Agus i dtaca liom féin de, más amhlaidh atá rún agaibh mé a chur chun báis, tairgim mo bheatha ar son na ndaoine. Bíodh sí ina héiric agaibh, agus beidh mise sásta.

156 In his review Liam Ó Lonargáin wrote: 'I felt sorry for the cast, especially for Annraoi Ó Liatháin in the part of the Minister. He was like a man whose heart had been broken by the lifelessness and who could not rid himself of the fit' (Bhí trua agam don fhoireann – do Annraoi Ó Liatháin i bpáirt an Mhinistir ach go háirithe. Bhí sé mar fhear a mbeadh an croí briste ann ag an mharbhántacht agus nár fhéad sé an taom a chur de) (*Feasta*, Nov. 1967, p. 24).

157 There is one expressionist bit in the play when hoofbeats approaching the frightened Porter family rise to a terrifying din. See Ó Néill, *Faill ar an bhFeart*, p. 90.

158 Ó Néill's ambivalence about traditional physical-force nationalism is evident in his pageant *Adhaint na Tine Beo*, called by 'I. M.' 'this dramatically effective cavalcade of Irish revolutionary history' (*II*, 13/4/67). In the body of the pageant the parliamentarians O'Connell, Parnell, and even John Redmond ('The struggle for freedom was continued by John Redmond') are introduced, treated with respect, and join James Connolly on stage in what seems to have been one possible ending of the pageant. However, in another possible ending included in the typescript, the entire emphasis is on the physical-force tradition: 'Tone and the United Irishmen, the Fenians, the men of Easter Week – They lit the living fire' (Siad a d'adhain an tine bheo). Information here is from the typescript of *Adhaint na Tine Beo* given by Ó Néill to John Kelleher, who gave it to me. It should be noted that Ó Néill offers a more critical view of Redmond in 'Réamonnachas san S. D. L. P.', serialised in the March, April, and May issues of *Comhar* in 1974.

159 Is script mhaith í: tá dráma ann ach é léiriú. Dráma a mbeadh idir fhuinneamh agus theannas ann, dráma a mbeadh plé ann ar chúrsaí atá go mór faoi chaibidil inár measc inniu – cealú pósta agus ceist an údaráis ach go háirithe . . . Tá súil agam nach rófhada eile a fhágfar an script bhreá seo, *Iníon Rí na Spáinne*, i liombó an neamhléirithe.

160 St John Fisher, who is mentioned in the play, might have made a more effective protagonist.

161 Séamus Ó Néill, *Iníon Rí na Spáinne* (The daughter of the king of Spain) (Baile Átha Cliath: Oifig an tSoláthair, 1978), p. 11. Ní easpa éirim aigne atá ag cur ar Chaitríona, ach an iomarca di.

162 Ibid., p. 68. Ba mhaith liom a bheith in ann géilleadh do na horduithe seo, ach ní thig liom mo choinsias a shárú.

163 Ibid., pp 84–5. Ní thig liom cogadh a chur ar an Rí. Is é m'fhear céile é, is é mo Rí agus mo thiarna é, ainneoin a ndearna sé d'éagóir orm agus bheinn ag briseadh dlí Dé dá gcuirfinn cogadh air. Caithfidh mé a bheith umhal do m'fhear céile, agus do mo Rí in achan rud, ach amháin i gcás m'anama. She does, however, express her respect for the rebels and her gratitude for their loyalty to her.

164 Ibid., p. 22. Níl aon bharántas agat nach breith i d'éadan a bhéarfaí sa Róimh féin . . . Tá ciall cheannaithe agamsa sna cúrsaí seo, agus thig liom a rá leat gur doiligh a bheith cinnte roimh ré cén bhreith a bhéarfar.

165 Ibid., pp 50–1. Bheadh Anraí sásta. Thiocfadh leis an bhantiarna Anne a phósadh. Bheadh an Pápa sásta. Ní bheadh fiacha air breith a thabhairt sa chúis. Ní bheadh eagla air Anraí a thiomáint chun Liútarachais tríd an diúltú a thabhairt dó agus ar an láimh eile ní bheadh eagla air fearg a chur ar an Impire trí cead a thabhairt dó tusa a chur uaidh. Agus má théann sé go dtí sin, bheadh an tImpire sásta mar ní theastaíonn uaidh sin go ndéanfadh Anraí comhghuaillíocht leis an Fhrainc, agus ní theastaíonn uaidh a bheith in achrann leis an Phápa.

166 Ibid., p. 55. Mar a dúirt mé leat, a Bhanríon, is mór is aithríoch liom teachtaireacht ar bith a thabhairt chugat a ghoillfeadh ort, ach níl mise ach ag comhlíonadh mo dhualgais.

167 Ibid., p. 88. Féadann sibh stad den ghuíodóireacht anois, nó tá mé cinnte go bhfuil anam Chaitríona na hAragóine go hard sna flaithis cheana féin. As in *Iníon Rí Dhún Sobhairce*, Ó Néill leaves the final word to a servant, although here Catherine's going to a better place diminishes the subversive impact that decision had in the earlier play.

168 I am thinking in particular here of Mac Liammóir's *Diarmaid agus Gráinne* (1928), Ó Siochfhradha's *Aon-Mhac Aoife Alban* (The only son of Aoife of Scotland) (1937), and Ó Tuama's *Gunna Cam agus Slabhra Óir*.

169 It is, therefore, unfortunate that he never wrote a play about Brian Bóroimhe and Gormfhlaith, a subject that in 1949 he called 'material for a great play' (ábhar dhráma mhóir), stating that Gormfhlaith was worthy of comparison with Helen of Troy and that Brian could provide 'a play . . . to compare with *Lear*' (dráma . . . le cur ar aon-iomaire le *Lear*) (*Indiu*, 4/11/49).

CHAPTER THREE
A Theatre of Ideas

1   Quoted in Máirín Nic Eoin, *Eoghan Ó Tuairisc: Beatha agus Saothar* (Life and work) (Baile Átha Cliath: An Clóchomhar, 1988), p. 278. He wrote 'gur fhás mí-nádúrtha í an drámaíocht sa teanga shaorga ar a dtugtar an Ghaeilge i nGalltacht na hÉireann . . . Tá drámaí Gaeilge na linne seo (agus mo dhrámaí féin san áireamh) sa chás céanna leis na drámaí Laidine a scríobhadh sna Coláistí Ollscoile i Sasana sna Meánaoiseanna . . . cibé cén dráma eile a ghéarfar chun toircheasa i ngob pinn liom, is i mBéarla a chumfar is a scríobhfar é.' See also p. 260.

2   Éadhmonn Mac Suibhne was troubled by his absence from the Gaelic theatre scene. See 'In áit na geamaireachta' (In place of the pantomime), *IP*, 29/12/71.

3   After interviewing Ó Tuairisc in 1972, Risteárd Ó Glaisne offered a summary of his curious ideas about the Irish language, writing that Ó Tuairisc believed that no two Indo-European languages were closer than Irish and Latin and that as a result, 'Irish is not human enough. It is too classical, too platonic, too catholic, too Roman, too mathematical, too angelic for the concrete, musically questioning outlook that has been struggling to life in Ireland from 1601 on . . . There is everything in English – except for the special wisdom of Irish. There is wisdom in Irish. We recognise that. If not for that, you would never write in Irish, nor would I' (Níl an Ghaeilge daonna go leor. Tá sí róchlasaiceach, róphlatónach, róchaitliceach, rórómhánach, rómhatamataiciúil, ró-ainglí don dearcadh nithiúil, ceol-cheistiúil, atá ag sracadh chun saoil in Éirinn ó 1601 i leith . . . Tá gach rud sa Bhéarla – ach amháin saintuiscint na Gaeilge. Tá tuiscint sa Ghaeilge. Aithnímid é sin. Murach sin, ní scríobhfása, ná ní scríobhfainnse an Ghaeilge riamh) (*Inniu*, 28/7/72). He must have had fun coming up with that.

4   Quoted by Nic Eoin, *Eoghan Ó Tuairisc*, p. 7. He liked the production of *Oedipus Rí* by students from UCD. Níl sa Téatar ach caitheamh aimsire intleachtúil don mhionlucht *bourgeois* mura bhfuil sé reiligiúnda (ní 'cráifeach' a deirim); agus is ionann an reiligiún agus aghaidh fidil an lae a chaitheamh i leataobh, gnáthchúrsa marfach na seachtaine saolta a chur ar do chúl, athrú éadaí nó feisteas féiltiúil a chur umat agus éalú amach ó chroiceóg chathair an fhichiú aois chun an Mistéir a bhlaiseadh sa chlapsholas, mar a bhfuil an dia agus an diabhal ag feitheamh leat ón anallód. One of his characters refers to the bourgeoisie as 'an búrjúis' in *An Hairyfella in Ifreann*, and in *Fornocht do Chonac*, the artist protagonist uses the term 'Buggerwuzzies', stating: 'They have no imagination but the imagination of the huckster. They give their hearts to nothing but money. Making money, making money make money. Wearing the mask of money before the world. That is the basis

and the high point of their religion and their politics' (Gan de shamhlaíocht acu ach samhlaíocht an ocastóra. Ní thugann siad croí do rud ar bith ach don airgead. Airgead a sholáthar, airgead a chur ag saothrú airgid. Aghaidh fidil an airgid a chaitheamh os comhar an tsaoil – sin buntús agus barr buaice a gcuid reiligiúin agus a gcuid polaitochta). See Eoghan Ó Tuairisc, *Fornocht do Chonac* (Naked I saw) (Baile Átha Cliath: Oifig an tSoláthair, 1981), p. 20.

5   Muna dtig leat do dhráma a chur ar siúl i Muileann Cearr tá locht ar an dráma, cuma cé chomh healaíonta agus cé chomh suimiúil is atá sé ó thaobh na smaointe agus ó thaobh na dtéamaí de.

6   Quoted in Nic Eoin, *Eoghan Ó Tuairisc*, p. 371. Corca Dorcha is the absurd fictional Gaeltacht in *An Béal Bocht* (The poor mouth) by 'Myles na gCopaleen'. Minic a bhíos na Scoláirí agus an Fhíor-Ghaeil Amach is Amach sa mhullach orm as comhluí seo an Dá Theanga i mo shaothar, ach ní don Ollscoil ná do na Corca Dorcha a scríobhaim mo chuid leabhar agus mo chuid drámaí, ach do ghnáthphobal an lae atá go fóill ar bheagán Gaeilge.

7   Eoghan Ó Tuairisc, 'Críochdheighilt na drámaíochta' (The partition of the drama), in *Religio Poetae agus Aistí Eile*, ed. Máirín Nic Eoin (Baile Átha Cliath: An Clóchomhar, 1987), p. 46. There had recently been a split in the Gaelic dramatic movement over the question of whether An Chomhairle Náisiúnta Drámaíochta should, as it did, relocate from Dublin to Conamara. The result was the creation of two competing bodies, one in Dublin, one in Camus in the Conamara Gaeltacht. He believed that 'ón Ghaeltacht amháin, agus ó na ceantair tuaithe atá faoi anáil na Gaeltachta a thiocfaidh an bhíogúlacht chainte, an tiriúlacht, an chomhbhá idir an stáitse agus an lucht éisteachta, as a bpréamhaíonn an drámaíocht' and 'ón Ardchathair amháin a thiocfaidh an teagasc agus an eiseamláir i gcúrsaí léirithe, mar gurb é an rud is mó atá in easnamh ar mhuintir na Gaeltachta (agus ar mhuintir na hÉireann i gcoitinne) ná samhlaíocht na súl.'

8   Quoted in Nic Eoin, *Eoghan Ó Tuairisc*, p. 267. He told Dáithí Ó Coileáin that her death was 'the atom bomb that fell on me personally' (an buama adamhach a thit orm féin go pearsanta) (*Comhar*, Oct. 1974, p. 5).

9   Quoted in Nic Eoin, *Eoghan Ó Tuairisc*, p. 299.

10   Ibid., p. 349.

11   Bhuel, do chaith mé m'óige le drámaíocht na Gréige. Is scoláire Gréigise mé agus do léigh mé an chuid is mó de na drámadóirí sa bhun-Ghréigis sar ar léigh mé drámaí Gaeilge nó drámaí Béarla. Agus d'fhág sin rian ar mo mheon, an dtuigeann tú, an rian claiseacach Gréigeach sin.

12   Lady Gregory's plays were favourites of the company.

13   Nic Eoin, *Eoghan Ó Tuairisc*, p. 29. Níor coimhthíoch leo atmaisféar na hamarclainne lena bholadh péinte agus a shoilse aduaine.

14 See ibid., p. 43.

15 Bhí cuid deacair ag an Dithreabhach Kabo, agus chruthuigh sé go maith. Ba bhreágh seasamhach é agus é a' tabhairt dhubhshlán an Diabhail. Ba mhaith a chuir sé a chuid imnidhe agus a chuid aithmhéala i n-iúil i n-a dhiaidh sin.

16 He disliked the term 'professional' writer, telling Dáithí Ó Coileáin in a 1974 interview: 'I do not like words like "professional". They always remind me of a little bowler hat and a briefcase!' (Ní thaithníonn na focail sin 'gairmiúil' nó 'proifisiúnta' liom. Cuireann siad hata beag babhlaeir agus briefcase i gcuimhne dom i gcónaí!) (*Comhar*, Oct. 1974, p. 5). See also p. 8.

17 Quoted in Nic Eoin, *Eoghan Ó Tuairisc*, p. 96.

18 This is not a complete list of his Oireachtas prizes for poetry.

19 It had only been awarded twice before, to Séamus Ó hAodha's poem 'Speal an Ghorta' (The scythe of the famine) in 1945 and to Seán Ó Tuama's *Gunna Cam agus Slabhra Óir* in 1954.

20 Quoted in Nic Eoin, *Eoghan Ó Tuairisc*, p. 189. Chum mé an focal 'Reiviú' (in ionad 'Iris'), chun dearcadh Eorpach an pháipéir a léiriú . . . Mar mhúnlaí, nó comharthaí sóirt, den rud a theastaigh uaim, bhí *Criterion*, a d'eagair T. S. Eliot; *Scrutiny* ag F. R. Leavis; an *Figaro Littéraire*; A. B. C. na Spáinnise, etc.

21 Ibid., p. 183.

22 Ibid., p. 172.

23 Ibid., p. 177.

24 Ibid., p. 209.

25 Ibid., p. 217.

26 Ibid.

27 Ibid., p. 318.

28 Ibid., p. 339.

29 Ibid., p. 351.

30 Ibid., p. 352.

31 Ibid., p. 380.

32 Ibid., p. 209.

33 Ibid., p. 341.

34 Ibid., p. 356.

35 Ibid.

36 Ibid., p. 458, n. 36.

37 Ibid., p. 37.

38 See ibid., p. 295, 297, 384 and 388. See also 'Oireachtas na Gaeilge', *NG*, 19/9/64; 'Féile na Máighe' (The Maigue festival), *IP*, 25/4/75; and Donnchadh Ó Súilleabháin, 'Cuspóirí an Chonartha i Londain' (The goals of the League in London), *IP*, 5/1/82.

39 See Nic Eoin, *Eoghan Ó Tuairisc*, p 352 and 369.

40 See ibid., pp 358–9.

41 Nic Eoin provides a chronological bibliography of his published work in ibid., pp 463–70.

42 See ibid., pp 111–12.

43 For *Dé Luain*, see ibid., pp 221–3; Alan Titley, *An tÚrscéal Gaeilge* (The novel in Irish) (Baile Átha Cliath: An Clóchomhar, 1991), pp 416–25; and Philip O'Leary, 'Reasoning why after fifty years: the Easter Rising in Eoghan Ó Tuairisc's *Dé Luain* (1966)', *Proceedings of the Harvard Celtic Colloquium* XXXI (2011), pp 253–81.

44 Nic Eoin, *Eoghan Ó Tuairisc*, p. 354. Tá sciar suntasach den Bhéarla tríd an Ghaeilge ann: Gaeilge na Galltachta, chun dearcadh na Galltachta a chothú.

45 See ibid., p. 414.

46 See ibid., pp 264–5, 274, 278–9, 285, and 292.

47 Quoted in ibid., pp 142–3.

48 He made this translation for the Relays Theatre Company in Ballinasloe, which produced it four times in Ballinasloe and once in Loughrea in 1971. It was also broadcast over Radio Éireann that year. Ó Tuairisc felt that the opening night was 'a bloody shambles', but was more satisfied with subsequent performances. See ibid., pp 285–6.

49 He found this production in his home town a bitter experience, writing to Rita Kelly: 'I'll never forget the experience of producing *Song of the Nightingale* last season. People – and people whom you would least expect – went out of their way to make it a failure. I found myself in a nest of vipers.' Quoted in ibid., p. 308.

50 The other *geamaireachtaí* to which he contributed were *Crúiscín Lán* (Full little jug) (1956), *Muireann agus an Prionsa* (Muireann and the prince) (1957), *Oisín i dTír na nÓg* (Oisín in the Land of the Young) (1958), *Gráinne na Long* (Gráinne of the ships) (1959), *Diarmaid agus Balor* (1961), *An Claíomh Solais* (The sword of light) (1962), *Aisling as Tír na nÓg* (A vision from the Land of the Young) (1964), *Emer agus an Laoch* (Emer and the hero) (1965), *Dragan '71* (Dragon '71) (1971), *Mise le Meas* (I am, respectfully) (1975), and *Oisín* (1977). He also wrote lyrics for pop songs in Irish.

51 Eoghan Ó Tuairisc, 'Oiliúint dhrámadóra' (The education of a playwright), in *Religio Poetae*, ed. Nic Eoin, p. 169. Tomás ina Stiúrthóir ar an iomlán. É ina shuí ag bord ar thaobh an ardáin, a rúnaí taobh leis ag breacadh nótaí, radharc éigin á chleachtadh, daoine thall is abhus ag cleachtadh rincí, nó ag an phianó le Seán Ó Riada ag cleachtadh amhrán, fear i gcúinne amháin ag foghlaim conas siúl ar *stilts*, beirt i gcúinne eile ag foghlaim na Gaeilge . . . mé féin i gclúid faoi leith ar an ardán ag scríobh faoi dheifir de réir mar a bheadh ag teastáil ón radharc a bhí le cur le chéile. Glaodh ó Thomás: Ó Tuairisc, líne don fhathach Polyphemus. Véarsaíocht le do thoil. Agus bíodh sé greannmhar.

52 See Máiréad Ní Chinnéide, *An Damer: Stair Amharclainne* (The Damer: history of a theatre) (Baile Átha Cliath: Gael-Linn, 2008), p. 122. The title is a play on the Ulster Irish version of 'How are you?'

53 See Nic Eoin, *Eoghan Ó Tuairisc*, p. 373.

54 These shows often had only the most rudimentary and disorganised scripts. See my discussion

of the *geamaireachtaí* in *Writing beyond the Revival: Facing the Future in Gaelic Prose 1940–1951* (Dublin: University College Dublin Press, 2011), pp 339–48.
55 Ó Tuairisc, 'Oiliúint dhrámadóra', in *Religio Poetae*, ed. Nic Eoin, p. 170. Ón diansaothar sin ar phlainceanna an ardáin d'fhoghlaim mé cuid mhaith. Ó thaobh cainte don ardán, d'fhoghlaim mé conas an coláiste agus an litríocht a bhrú as amharc agus brí an scéil a chur go simplí i mbéal an aisteora gan mórán Gaeilge do lucht éisteachta a bhí ar an ghannchuid . . . Cuireadh i dtuiscint dom nach ar an chaint amháin a mhaireann an drámaíocht: ní mór an scéal a léiriú trí mheán na súl.
56 Eoghan Ó Tuairisc, 'Teanga is carachtar an náisiúin' (Language and the character of the nation), in *Religio Poetae*, ed. Nic Eoin, p. 73. An t-aonad daonghrafaíochta ar a dtugtar 'Éire' nó 'Ireland,' ón 16ú hAois ar a laghad ní náisiún é, ach comhnáisiún. Coimpléasc de chiníocha éagsúla – . . . Ó thaobh teanga, agus ó thaobh carachtair, is féidir an coimpléasc a chriostalú ina dhá chuid: An Gael, an Sasanach. Ní deighilt áitiúlachta ó cheart í, ní deighilt aicme í ach oiread; is deighilt charachtair í, dúbláil phearsantachta atá d'inneach i ngach duine sa tír, fiú an chuid is Albanaí de Bhéal Feirste, an chuid is Gaelaí de na Fíor-Ghaeltachtaí, an chuid is bláfaire agus is gó-gó de Bhaile Átha Cliath. The similarity of his ideas here to those of W. E. B. Du Bois concerning the 'double consciousness' of African Americans is striking. See W. E. B. Du Bois, *The Souls of Black Folk*, ed. David W. Blight and Robert Gooding-Williams (Boston: Bedford/St Martin's, 1997 [1903]), pp 2–3.
57 Eoghan Ó Tuairisc, 'Céad chogar na teanga nua' (The first whisper of the new language), in *Religio Poetae*, ed. Nic Eoin, p. 74. Sea, mura mbeadh ach an Béarla agam ní bheadh Saibhreas na Gaeilge ag iarraidh an smaoineamh seo faoi mo chleite a shoilbhriú, nó mura mbeadh ach an Ghaeilge agam ní bheadh dilchuimhne an Bhéarla ag dréim lena ladar a chur isteach. Agus guím mí-ádh milis ón diabhal aníos faoin chinniúint a d'fhág againn an dá theanga.
58 Ibid. See also 'Gaelachas Goldsmith' (Goldsmith's Gaelicism), in *Religio Poetae*, ed. Nic Eoin, p. 56. He was telling 'scéal gach uile dhuine in Éirinn . . . ó tharla an deighilt chéanna le sonrú orainn go léir den ghlúin seo a bhfuil an Ghall-Ghaeilge nó an Gael-Bhéarla ar ár mbriathra cinn, agus an déachas céanna d'inneach smaoinimh againn san anam istigh'.
59 Eoghan Ó Tuairisc, 'Stony grey soil: dándearcadh ar éigean an dá chultúr' (A poetic look at the conflict of the two cultures), in *Religio Poetae*, ed. Nic Eoin, p. 163. Níl gar againn cultúr amháin acu a shéanadh agus luí go hiomlán leis an chultúr eile . . . Tá an dá oidhreacht fite i bhfíodóireacht ár n-aigne, agus níl dul astu. See also his comments in his 1981 inter-

view in *Innti*: 'Ní thiocfadh leat maireachtáil ar theanga amháin . . . sin mar a d'fhéach mise ar an scéal' (You could not live with only one language – that's how I look at the matter) (*Innti* VI (Oct. 1981), p. 33).
60 Ó Tuairisc, 'Stony grey soil', in *Religio Poetae*, ed. Nic Eoin, p. 163. Idir an dá linn, níl de réiteach agam ar an fhadhb ach an oidhreacht acu is mó a ndéantar faillí inti, an cnámharlach crédhubh a thagann de shíor ag priocadh as mo chuimhne, an Ghaeilge, an saibhreas as cuimse faoin Stony Grey Soil – níl de réiteach agam ar an scéal ach í a chaomhnú, a shaothrú, a athmhúscailt ionam féin, agus a chur i bpáirtíocht le cruinneas agus le miotal Bhéarla na Galltachta as ar fuinneadh an chuid ba mhó de mo shaoldearcadh. Ó Tuairisc had considerable respect for Kavanagh and his work. What he says here is very much in line with Declan Kiberd's idea that virtually all Irish writers can now in some sense be considered 'Anglo-Irish' writers. See Declan Kiberd, 'Seán Ó Ríordáin: file Angla-Éireannach' (An Anglo-Irish poet), in Declan Kiberd, *Idir Dhá Chultúr* (Between two cultures) (Baile Átha Cliath: Coiscéim, 1993), pp 261–87.
61 See Nic Eoin, *Eoghan Ó Tuairisc*, p. 207.
62 Quoted in ibid., p. 94. He is clearly referring here to the scholar Standish Hayes, not the populiser Standish James O'Grady.
63 Quoted in ibid., p. 282.
64 Quoted in ibid., p. 382. Bhí cnuasach gearrscéalta á ullmhú agam, cinn a foilsíodh thall is abhus le fiche bliain anuas – ach rith sé liom gur ró-shimplí ar fad a bhí an cuid is mó acu, i gcomparáid leis an chineál gearrscéil atá chun tosaigh sa lá atá inniu ann; agus braithim nach bhfuil mo dhóthain Gaeilge ó dhúchas agam chun an saghas gearrscéil is rogha liom a chur i gcrích.
65 Nó, nuair atá Gaeilge á scríobh ag duine a tógadh le Béarla, is ualach dó an teanga cuid mhaith. Caitheann sé i gcónaí a bheith ag smaoineamh ar conas atá an rud á rá aige chomh maith leis an rud atá le rá.
66 Eoghan Ó Tuairisc, 'Religio poetae', in *Religio Poetae*, ed. Nic Eoin, p. 13. This essay began life as a lecture to An Comhchaidreamh in November 1962. Alan Titley discusses Ó Tuairisc's thinking about literature's role in human life in 'An léirmheastóir' (The critic), *Comhar*, Oct. 1985, pp 42–4.
67 Ó Tuairisc, 'Religio poetae', in *Religio Poetae*, ed. Nic Eoin, p. 15. Trí mheán a ealaíne, gan treoir ar bith ach treoir a cheardaíochta féin, tagann an *Poetae* ar bhunbhrí na cruinne: go bhfuil an dá shaol ann, an dá ghné den réalachas, agus tagann sé i dtuiscint gurb í is bunchúis dá ealaín ná an dá shaol sin a léiriú agus iad fite ina chéile sa scéal céanna, sa rann céanna, san fhocal céanna fiú, agus an sean-nasc eatarthu ar a dtugtar an *religio* a aimsiú agus a chur i gcéill don phobal.

68 Ibid., p. 11. Léiríonn foirmle seo Einstein [E=mc²] dúinn go bhfuil an domhan uile ina Aonad, ach gur mistéir dúinn an aontacht sin, mistéir nach dtig linn a thuiscint ar an saol seo ach amháin trí bhreathnú uirthi mar a bheadh dhá rud ann, dhá ghné, dhá thaobh, agus ceangal doscaoilte, do thuigthe, do fheicthe eatarthu.

69 Ibid., p. 12. *Religio* was 'an cumas sin a cheanglaíonn an dá thaobh le chéile, cumas atá suite in aigne an duine, cumas samhlaíochta a aithníonn agus a léiríonn an dá shaol, an saol dalba agus an saol spioradálta, agus iad fite gan bun cleite amach ná barr cleite isteach ina chéile'.

70 Quoted in Nic Eoin, *Eoghan Ó Tuairisc*, p. 278.

71 Ibid., p. 346.

72 Quoted in ibid., p. 208.

73 Ó Tuairisc, 'Religio poetae', in *Religio Poetae*, ed. Nic Eoin, p. 25.

74 Quoted in Nic Eoin, *Eoghan Ó Tuairisc*, p. 97.

75 Ó Tuairisc, 'Oiliúint dhrámadóra', in *Religio Poetae*, ed. Nic Eoin, p. 168. Ní mór don drámadóir é féin a chailleadh agus é faoi gheasa ag miotas seachtrach éigin, agus is trí mheán an mhiotais sin a ligeann sé srian (i ngan fhios dó féin go minic) le cibé atá ag bruith i ndorchacht a anama istigh. Agus i gcúrsaí ardáin ag an am, i gcúrsaí Gaeilge ach go háirithe, ní raibh aon teicníc dhrámata le feiceáil agus le foghlaim a chuirfeadh ar chumas an scríbhneora an nasc miotasach úd a shníomh idir an gá pearsanta agus an gá poiblí.

76 Quoted in Nic Eoin, *Eoghan Ó Tuairisc*, p. 96.

77 Quoted in ibid., p. 195.

78 Eoghan Ó Tuairisc, 'Caitear amach an driosúr' (Throw out the dresser), in *Religio Poetae*, ed. Nic Eoin, p. 42. Braitheann an drámaíocht ar an tsamhlaíocht. Ní mór don léiritheoir samhlaíocht an lucht éisteachta a mhúscailt ón nóiméad a ardaítear an brat. Mura ndéantar an bíogadh samhlaíochta sin, fanfaidh an dráma bocht ar urlár an ardáin agus ní chuirfear míorúilt na hamharclainne i bhfeidhm ar chroí agus ar cheann an lucht éisteachta. This essay first appeared in *Ardán*, a short-lived journal published by An Chomhairle Náisiúnta Drámaíochta to provide practical information and advice to those involved with theatre in Irish.

79 Ibid., p. 42. Cuimhnigh, freisin, nach ró chruinn de théarma é *Lucht Éisteachta* ar na daoine a íocann a gcuid airgid ag an doras: is *Lucht Féachana* iad chomh maith le *Lucht Éisteachta*. Téann an drámaíocht i bhfeidhm orthu tríd an tsúil chomh maith leis an chluais.

80 Ó Tuairisc, 'Caitear amach an driosúr', in *Religio Poetae*, ed. Nic Eoin, p. 44.

81 There were, of course, exceptions – the Gate in the 1930s and the Pike in the 1950s, for example.

82 Martin Nugent, *Drámaí Eoghain Uí Thuairisc* (The plays of Eoghan Ó Tuairisc) (Má Nuad: An Sagart, 1984), p. 102. Is léir go bhfuil tábhacht freisin

leis na treoracha stáitse a bhaineann le hathrú solais i rith na ngníomhartha – taobh amuigh de na hathruithe a úsáidtear le ham an lae a chur in iúl. Is é an *Verfremdungseffekt* atá á chothú ag an údar ar na hócáidí seo.

83 See Nic Eoin, *Eoghan Ó Tuairisc*, p. 210.

84 See ibid., p. 370. He wanted the director 'feidhm a bhaint as gach gné den ardánaíocht – an Aisteoireacht, an Scéalaíocht, an Ceol, an Rince, an Radharcra – agus iad go léir a chaomhaontú go healaíonta chun lár-théama an Dráma . . . a léiriú'.

85 He took a great deal of trouble with the verse in this play, writing, for example: 'I have attempted to suit that metre [the epic metre of Irish] to ordinary conversation through refining the system of consonance and giving free reign to the unaccented syllables' (Tá iarracht déanta agam an mheadaracht sin [bhéarsaíocht eipiceach na Gaeilge] a chur in oiriúint don ghnáth-chomhrá trí scéim na gcomhfhuaim do scagadh agus trí chead a gcos a thabhairt dosna siollaí éadroma). Quoted in ibid., p. 149.

86 Also on the bill was a recitation of his poem 'Marche Funebre'.

87 Do bhraitheas an léiriú ar an dráma seo a bheith meacainiúil agus an iomarca tairbhe á bhaint as céirníní. Bhí an dráma féin scríte sa dóigh go bhféadfadh an mothú brónach agus dóchasach a bheith ann gan feidhm a bhaint as ceol chuige in aon chor.

88 Eoghan Ó Tuairisc, *Na Mairnéalaigh* (The sailors), in *Gearrdhrámaí an Chéid* (Short plays of the century), ed. Pádraig Ó Siadhail (Indreabhán: Cló Iar-Chonnachta, 2000), p. 115. Tá boladh an bháis le sonrú ar an gceo.

89 Ibid., p. 116. I Maigh Eo sa mbaile, / Trí rudaí adeir siad nach féidir a shásamh – / An tOcras, an Fharraige, agus an Bás. / Nuair bhí mise i mo ghasúr i gContae Mhaigh Eo / Chonaic mé níos mó corpáin sínte in aon lá amháin / Ná mar a chonaic tusa, a Chocky, led' bheo.

90 Actually, Páidí is not all that impressed with O'Connell.

91 Ó Tuairisc, *Na Mairnéalaigh*, p. 118. Seo é lár na naoú haoise déag, *see*, / Aimsir na Banríona Victoria, *see*, / Seo é an lá atá inniu ann, an bhliain / Míle ocht gcéad daichead – a – seacht!

92 Ibid., p. 123. Aimsir Victoria, / Cé cheapfadh go mbeadh goldráma mar seo / Achtaithe amach ar Mhuir Meann . . . Nach ait mar chinniúint í an fharraige / A ullmhaíonn coinne na gconraí seo, / Ag cur na marbh in aithne dá chéile.

93 Ibid., p. 113.

94 Ibid., p. 129. Chuaigh sé thar lear chun cabhair a ghuí dúinn / Ar Phápa na Róimhe féin. An Liberator . . . / Ach tiocfaidh sé. Tiocfaidh sé chomh siúráilte le sioc. / Cloisfear a ghlór arís / Ag scuabadh roimhe an ghanntanas agus an ghorta dhubh / Mar bheadh ceo maidine roimh an ngaoth.

95 Ibid., pp 129–30. Mé féin, an dtuigeann sibh, ar bharr an chnoic / Ceann-nochtaithe ag labhairt i mbéal an *Liberator*. Fuascailt a bhí ann. / Fuascailt dom féin agus do na mílte dem' chine féin / A chaitheann a saol idir an dá dhorchadas / I ngort ocrach na mbliadhan. Sea, mhaise, / Labhramar an lá sin, sinn féin, / Mar dhuine amháin i mbéal an *Liberator*.

96 Ibid., p. 124.

97 Ibid., p. 151.

98 This critic reported that Ó Tuairisc, speaking from the stage on the first night, told his audience that 'the Irish language and Taibhdhearc na Gaillimhe are a menace and a threat to present-day stage rameis [*sic*] which finds its expression in the term "modern English drama"'. In a brief note in *The Irish Press*, Maurice O'Brien reported that '"De Réir na Rúibricí", by Eoghan Ó Tuairisc, has been so popular at the Damer Hall that its run has been extended to Wednesday, Thursday and Friday nights' (*IP*, 6/11/61).

99 Tá gach cairictéir dar chruthaigh Eoghan Ó Tuairisc ag scrí dhó tarraingte le cinnteacht agus samhailteacht. Cairictéirí beo iad go léir . . . Tá an chuid is mó den agallamh ar fheabhas . . . B'fhiú go maith cuairt a thabhairt ar an dráma so.

100 Deir Somerset Maugham gurb é príomhghnó agus aonghnó na litríochta agus na hamharclainne pléisiúr agus taithneamh a thabhairt don phobal léitheoireachta agus éisteachta agus sin é go díreach a dhéan dráma Eoghain Uí Thuairisc, 'De Réir na Rúibricí,' agus dhéan sé an gnó sin níos fearr agus níos fairsinge ná mar a dhéan aon bhundráma Gaeilge atá feicthe go fóill agam. Bhí greann agus an-ghreann ann agus faobhar air.

101 See Ní Chinnéide, *An Damer*, p. 141.

102 Eoghan Ó Tuairisc, *De Réir na Rúibricí: Coiméide Tríghníomh* (According to the rubrics: a three-act comedy), p. 34. The play has not been published. I am working here with the typescript made available by An Comhlachas Náisiúnta Drámaíochta. See also p. 5 and 8. Isteach i gcoillte an Phaláis a théinn, agus thuas ansin faoi chiúnas clabhastrach na gcrann is ea a bhraitheas den chéad uair an ghairm chun na heaglaise . . . B'é an chéad chéim eile agam ná isteach in úllórd an Easpaig in aois mo thriú bliain déag mar ar ghoid mé úll na haithne . . . B'é an chéad chéim eile agam ar dhréimire an eaglais suas ná isteach i gcistin an Phaláis in aois mo shéú bliain déag ag déanamh suirí le cailín aimsire an Easpaig.

103 Ibid., p. 3. Tar éis dó daichead blian a chaitheamh ag plé leis na Rialacha, tá a phearsantacht rialta, a chaint, a choiscéim agus a dhearcadh ar an saol righin rialta . . .

104 Ibid., p. 7. Ní mór dúinn é a ruaigeadh amach ar an urlár anseo gan a thuilleadh moille. Is contúirteach an rud é bheith déanach sa scoil. Dá gcloisfeadh an Cigire é bheadh a chosa nite. 'Ní mór don

Oide bheith i láthair deich nóiméad roimh an am oifigiúil ar a dtosaíonn teagasc na scoile' – sin ceann de na rialacha is daingne de na Rialacha agus na Riaracháin Do Chum Scoileanna Náisiúnta do Riaradh. Ruaig amach é.

105 Ibid. Bheartaíomar é . . . bheartaíomar fadó é . . . Bheartaíomar Seán a thabhairt don Eaglais mar is é ba chráifí ciúine den bheirt, agus go rachadh Marcas ina Phríomh-Oide isteach san scoil nuair a bheadh sé in am domsa éirí as.

106 Ibid., p. 48. Feicim anois nár glaodh orm ariamh. Ó bhí mé in aois mo chéad bhríste cuireadh an Eaglais romham amach, ullmhaíodh an bóthar dom, níor rith sé liom ariamh smaoineamh ar aon ghairm bheatha eile. D'oibrigh mé go dícheallach ar scoil agus bhrúigh mé mo bhealach tríd na scrúdaithe go léir; ansin chuir mé an cóta dubh orm agus siúd ar aghaidh liom go Mánuat.

107 Ibid., p. 2. It is worth noting that the father and both of his sons are near-sighted and need glasses.

108 Ibid., p. 48. Ach . . . níl fhios agam . . . téann díom é a mhíniú i gceart . . . mhothaigh mé míshásamh mór ionam féin le déanaí. Tráthnóna nuair a thagadh an ceo bán ag sileadh ón gcanáil thar pháirc an imeartha, d'fhéachainn i mo thimpeall ar an domhan doiléir agus mhothainn uaigneas an tsaoil á shéideadh faoi mo chroí.

109 Ibid., p. 17. Dhá bhliain ó shoin d'fhág mé an Coláiste Oiliúna agus tháinig mé abhaile go Lios an Aicéadaigh, agus rún daingean agam dualgaisí an phoist a chomhlíonadh chomh maith is bhí ionam. Leathuair a chloig ní raibh caite agam insan seomra ranga thíos nuair a cuireadh i bhfios dom go soiléir go raibh dul amú orm.

110 Ibid., p. 31. Ó, a Neillí, ní mheasfá go deo an dearg-ghráin atá agam do cheithre bhalla an scoil sin lena léirscáileanna smúiteacha ag taispeáint an domhain agus é roinnte go simplí ina dhá leath amhail is dá mba dhá leath d'oráiste lofa iad.

111 Ibid., p. 16.

112 Ibid., p. 13. Tá cumhacht ina ghuth, tá seirfean, cáirdeas, fonóid, cantail agus binb ina ghlór, tá corr abairtín ait Iar-Mheiriceánach le sonrú ar a chaint . . . agus samhlaítear dúinn go bhfuil pearsantacht shainiúil do-cheannsaithe ar an urlár isteach chugainn.

113 Ibid., p. 41.

114 Ibid., p. 42. Tar chugam amárach agus tosóimid le chéile ar Shoiscéal Naomh Lúcás a léamh insan Ghréigis bhunaidh – tá daichead blian ó shin ann ó d'oscail mé an Soiscéal Gréagach.

115 Ibid., p. 44. Walls are significant symbols throughout the play. See p. 59, for example. D'fhiafraigh tú díom cén fáth gur iompaigh mé i mo Chaitliceach? B'fhacthas dom gur cheart dom cloí le hEaglais a bhfuil a cuid ballaí chomh leathan le ceithre bhalla na cruinne.

116 Ibid., p. 51. Níl rud ar bith chomh simplí leis an gCríostaíocht nuair a smaoineann tú air – stábla, i

dtosach, agus fleá na bainise ina lár, agus an Chrois shimplí sin gur deacair dúinn é a thuiscint, agus déanaimid scéal casta de lenár gcuid Rialacha agus Riaracháin.
117 Quoted in Nic Eoin, *Eoghan Ó Tuairisc*, p. 150.
118 Nic Eoin discusses these changes in ibid., pp 181–2.
119 Dob fhearrde é a ghearradh anso is ansúd. Ar aon nós leanann sé ró-fhada tríd síos, agus téann sé chun leadráin in áiteanna.
120 The reference here is to Dylan Thomas's *Under Milk Wood: A Play for Voices* (1954).
121 Tá lucht leanúna na Drámaíochta Gaeilge ag méadú. A chruthú sin go mb'éigin dúinn daoine a chur ó dhoras chuile oíche le linn Féile Drámaíochta Bhaile Átha Cliath nuair a bhí 'Cuairt [*sic*] an Mheán Oíche' le Eoghan Ó Tuairisc á léiriú ag Tomás Mac Anna sa Damer. To accommodate those turned away, two additional performances were added.
122 Their production won the £50 first prize in the full-length play category.
123 I do not know whether he directed the 1969 Oireachtas production.
124 I do not know what he meant by 'innocent' here. Agus measaim, mar a mheas mé ag an taispeántas sin, cé go bhfuil sé soineannta is saibhir i smaointíocht, go bhfuil sé scaipthe go leor in a lán eachtraí dhe . . . Leanann dá bharr leadránacht.
125 In 1946 the Irish Censorship Board banned Frank O'Connor's English translation of the poem as indecent.
126 Eoghan Ó Tuairisc, *Cúirt na Gealaí: Coiméide Trighníomh* (The court of the moon: a three-act comedy) (Baile Átha Cliath: An Gúm, 1988), p. 2. Tá an seanphortach agus na seandéithe ag breith bua ar stáisiún Shlí Ghruagaigh.
127 Ibid. Bean rábach scaillaigéanta in aois a daichead bliain, iarsmaí le sonrú uirthi go raibh sí dathúil tráth den saol, ach í ina sraoillín gliobach anois, éadaí gan slacht uirthi, gruaig dhubh ghiofógach ceangailte ina cocán ar chúl a cinn, súile magúla ag glinniúint, poll ina stocaí agus teanga ghéar ina cloigeann.
128 Ibid., p. 3. Paisinéirí, a deir tú? In ainm Chroim céard a thabharfadh ar phaisinéirí teacht chun na reilige seo? Nach bhfuil a fhios ag na déithe nár stad traein ar bith i Slí Ghruagaigh ó aimsir an chogaidh nuar a stadaidís chun glaicín móna a chur san inneall? . . . Tá aiteas éigin ag borradh amuigh anocht – Oíche Lánghealach na Bealtaine. Meas tú, a Aonghuis, bhfuil seans ar bith go mbeadh an tseanaimsir úd againn ag filleadh ar an saol? Aimsir na ndéithe móra, uair an ghrá?
129 Ibid. Tú féin agus do chuid grá! Nár cheart go mbeifeá sásta go bhfuil díon os do chionn agus tú pósta le fear fiúntach a bhfuil post maith inphinsin aige, in ionad imeacht go Sasana i do bhanaltra mar a dhéanann na spéirmhná eile go léir na laethanta

seo ó cuireadh an grá faoi chosc sa tír? This reference to emigration, particularly by young women, foreshadows a theme that becomes important later in the play. A *spéirbhean* was a beautiful otherworld woman who, representing Ireland, appeared to poets in *aisling* (vision) poems from the seventeenth through the nineteenth centuries
130 Ibid. Fear bláfar é, duine géarchúiseach intleachtach a bhfuil acmhainn grinn ann, scoláire agus cainteoir mór tar éis proinne.
131 Ibid., p. 4. Is iomaí áit inar casadh ar a chéile sinn, a Chanónaigh. Áit ar bith a raibh trácht mór na cruinne faoi shúil na gréine. Sa Róimh, b'fhéidir, nuair a bhí tú i do mhac léinn ann, nó i Salamanca; nó b'fhéidir gur aithin tú mé san Éigipt fadó, i ngleann na Níle, nuair a bhí tú i do ardsagart ag Amón-Rá agus na piriméidí á dtógáil!
132 Ibid. Tá sí le teacht – ach an dtiocfaidh sí? . . . Och, go bhfóire na déithe móra ar Chóras Iompair Éireann. Déanann siad a ndícheall, na leiciméirí, ach . . . tá an stáisiún seo curtha faoi gheasa ag na Daoine Maithe.
133 Ibid., pp 7–8. Tháinig tú i dtír inniu ar an oileán is neamhrómánsaí ar domhan. Tá an tír seo faoi smacht ag comhrialtas d'fheirmeoirí, de thábhairneoirí sráidbhailteacha, agus de shagairt pharóiste. Tá an rómánsaíocht glanta amach as an tír acu; chuir siad na síóga agus na leipreacháin go Meiriceá chun dollair a thuilleamh; dhíbir siad na filí – agus mé féin orthu – go dtí an B. B. C.; agus scrios siad amach an difríocht idir fireann agus baineann.
134 Ibid., p. 8. Ní fhaigheann na déithe móra bás go deo – an tsamhlaíocht, an áilleacht, an fhírinne, agus an grá: maireann siad, cé go bhfuil siad díbeartha ag an Rialtas, curtha faoi choinnealbhá ag an Eaglais, agus damnaithe ag an mBord Cinnsireachta, maireann siad – an fhírinne agus an grá – mar a bheadh an ghrian agus an ghealach.
135 Ibid. Ní mór duit an fáinne a chaitheamh go dtí go bhfuilimid slán sabháilte ar an taobh thall d'Áth Luain. Ní thuigeann Fir Bolg na tíre seo an platónachas. Dá bhfeicidís cailín ag imeacht san oíche in éineacht le fear agus gan fáinne á chaitheamh aici, ní hé an rud is deise a cheapfaidís! Apparently he believes that once past Athlone they will be out in the country on their way to the caravan and will be safe from prying eyes. In Irish pseudohistory the Fir Bolg were rather primitive mythic beings who inhabited Ireland before the divine Tuatha Dé Danann and the Gaels.
136 Ibid., p. 10. Ní hé amháin go gcaithfidh mé bhur gcuid dualgas morálta a mhúineadh daoibh, ach ní mór dom bhur ndualgais mhímhorálta a mhúineadh daoibh chomh maith!
137 Ibid., p. 12.
138 Ibid. Níl sé paiseanta go leor. Níl ann ach gáirsiúlacht chliste agus tincéireacht intleachtúil leis an ngrá. Is rud contúirteach é sin. Brúitín do aigne a

choimeádann an duine fásta ina leanbh. Ní mar sin do na filí agus do na húdair mhóra ag cur síos dóibh ar an ngrá agus ar an tsuirí cois claí. Some might question his inclusion of Paul and Augustine here.

139 Ó Tuairisc, *Cúirt na Gealaí*, p. 54. It is worth noting that earlier in the play the canon had said to Gráinne, 'We are both discerning artisans, my child, myself in the craft of the soul, you in the craft of the body! The two kinds are needed, you and I, to guide this republic of ours that is called the great world' (Is ceardaithe tuisceanacha sinn araon, a leanbh. Mise i gceird an anama, tusa i gceird an choirp! Tá an dá shórt ag teastáil, mise agus tusa, chun an phoblacht seo againn ar a dtugtar an saol mór a stiúradh) (p. 13).

140 Ibid., p. 17. Ar an mbó, céard eile – nach bhfuil a fhios agat go bhfuil a haimsir istigh . . . agus í ar tí lao a bhreith. Déanfaidh an striapach gealaí sin an gnó di go siúráilte, agus mise i bhfad ó bhaile san áit dhiabhalta seo.

141 Ibid., p. 20. Ní bheadh a fhios agat. Dá mbeadh cúpla deoch faoi mo chrios agam, seans go bpósfainn thú ar maidin amárach!

142 Ibid., p. 25. Seo againn aois na heacnamaíochta Críostaí; tá an Eaglais, an Rialtas, agus an Chomhairle Contae ar aon intinn go bhfuil sé thar am dúinn na nósanna seanaimseartha págánacha sin a dhíbirt – stad a chur leis an tsuirí sa mhóinéar agus leis an sciotaíl cois claí sa chlapsholas . . . Ní caitheamh aimsire, ach cailliúint aimsire, atá inti. Níl sí sláintiúil. Níl sí Gaelach.

143 Ibid., p. 47. Is fíor nár thug tú gealltanas dom . . . mura gealltanas mé a choinneáil ag siúl síos suas ar bhruach na habhann gach tráthnóna Domhnaigh le fiche bliain. Is fíor nár thug tú gealltanas dom, mura gealltanas é bosca brioscaí a chur chugam gach Nollaig agus buidéal seirí. Is fíor nár thug tú gealltanas dom, mura gealltanas é go mbíonn na páistí scoile ag scríobh m'ainm agus ainm Dhiní Mhic Chumhaill le cailc ar an gclár dubh uair ar bith a fhágaim an seomra – . . . D'éirigh fuath ionam don earrach. Chuir an tAibreán seirfean i mo chroí. Tá a fhios ag Dia nach raibh mé searbh nuair a bhí mé i mo chailín óg –

144 Ó Tuairisc's long poem *The Weekend of Dermot and Grace* (1964) was inspired in part by this tale.

145 Ó Tuairisc, *Cúirt na Gealaí*, p. 45. Chuir sí sin an léine oíche uirthi, ag baint trialach aisti, agus ar an bpointe boise tháinig . . . sórt athrú uirthi.

146 Ibid., p. 43. Siúlann Áine go maorga isteach ar an ardán, í níos airde, níos óige, níos gile snua, léine oíche den níolón 'Brionglóideach' ag glioscarnach ina timpeall, a gruaig scaoilte ina slaoda áille thar a guaillí agus réaltóigíní ag glinniúint tríthi, a géaga geala go lomnocht, solas na gealaí ag drithliú óna pearsa amach . . . Tá tú i do lándúiseacht den chéad uair le do bheo . . .

147 Ibid., p. 48. Ní hé an rud atá déanta agat ach an rud nach bhfuil déanta agat, atá i gceist anseo anocht. Ní chun leann dubh agus mín choirce a dhíol ná chun na muca a chur thar sáile, ná chun seafóid a stealladh uait ag an gComhairle Contae a bhronn na déithe móra fuil ar do chuislí – . . . Is tú an fear sráidbhailteach, diaganta, polaitiúil, ceacartha, cabach, beagmhaitheasach . . . Is tú an leiciméir poiblí, glincín an ghaimbín, státaire phumpa an pharóiste, béal mór na céille bige agus Tadhg an dá thaobh.

148 Ibid. Ó, go díreach! Sin agaibh an difríocht idir an Gael agus an Gaeilgeoir: thiteadh an Gael i ngrá fadó le cailín deas agus bhronnadh sé an fáinne óir uirthi; ach titeann an Gaeilgeoir anois i ngrá le teanga agus bronnann sé an fáinne air féin! The *fáinne* is a ring-shaped pin that indicates its wearer is an Irish speaker.

149 Ibid., p. 50. Breathnaígí, a chailíní, ar an bhfear stuama! An Feirmeoir Óg. Cnámh droma na tíre. Agus nach deas mar chnámh droma ag tír ar bith é nuair a bhíonn ar a mháthair an chúirtéireacht a dhéanamh ar a shon!

150 Ibid., p. 55. Níl ionat ach ceolán den chéad scoth. Cén mhaitheas a rinne tú do chailín ar bith le do bheo ach a cluas a bhodhradh le rangalam raiméise a chuirfeadh tinneas boilg ar chollach muice.

151 Ibid., p. 56. He is 'glincín Gaelach a chuireann bríste de chorda-an-rí air féin, agus a phiocann amach cúpla focal gáirsiúil as Foclóir Uí Dhuinnín nó go n-ardaíonn sé na cosa leis go Londain Shasana ina fhile nó ina dhrámadóir dána'. . . Heits, a cheoláin, maireann do shórtsa i mbrístí liteartha. Ní thuigeann sibh grá garbh an tsaoil. See also p. 59.

152 Ibid., p. 56. Tá mé beag bearán ar do gheasa, a Chinsire. Ní chuirfidh tú geasa ar an ngealach agus í a chosc ó bheith ag líonadh na hoíche le haoibhneas. Ní chuirifdh tú geasa ar an ngrian a ardaíonn na taoidí paiseanta i bhfuil an duine. Má tá geasa le cur is mise a chuirfeas iad.

153 Ibid., p. 58. Agus deirimse libh, má tá na fir ag dul as radharc, nach ar an aeráid atá an locht, ná ar an tsiopadóireacht, ná ar an talmhaíocht, ná ar an gcinsireacht: tá an locht ar fad ar na cailíní. Ó thús deireadh, tá an trioblóid náisiúnta seo agaibh ag brath ar cheist na cóirséadaíochta.

154 Ibid., p. 61.

155 Ibid., p. 62.

156 Ibid., p. 63. Tá sí gléasta go feiceálach: péire niamhrach de bhrístí géine ('jeans') uirthi, blúisín bídeach bádóireachta, hata galánta gréine . . . Ambasa, a mhuirnín, bíogann tú an óige ionam.

157 It was also his own favourite among his plays. See Nic Eoin, *Eoghan Ó Tuairisc*, p. 9. For a penetrating discussion of the influence of *Genesis*, *Paradise Lost*, and especially Sophocles's *Antigone* on the play, see Mícheál Mac Craith, 'Geineasas, Antigone agus Lá Fhéile Míchíl', *Comhar*, Oct. 1985, pp 46–52.

158 Chomh fada is a leanfaidh an t-údar seo agus a mhacasamhail ag saothrú ní baol don Drámaíocht Ghaelach . . . Is tuar dóchais do dhrámaíocht na Gaeilge a leithéid seo de dhráma ar chláir.

159 Téann an dráma ar aghaidh go maith gasta. Tá cinnteacht agus ceardaíocht ag roinnt leis. Is éifeachtach mar a phléann an t-údar le mothúcháin a lucht éisteachta, é anois ag coimeád ruda siar uathu; anois é ag raideadh ruda chucu; ag caitheamh solais nua ar rud éigin go tobann, agus an greann agus an íoróin taobh thiar den chaint nó den ghníomh cuid mhaith den am. Daoine iad na caractéirí a gcreidfeá iontu. Coinníonn an dráma na daoine atá ag féachaint air ar bior.

160 Tríd síos bhí an dráma spéisiúil agus choinnigh sé ar chipíní muid go deireadh . . . B'fhiú dúinn dul ag breathnú ar an dráma seo, bhí sé spéisiúil agus conspóideach, agus ba chéim eile chun tosaigh ag Eoghan Ó Tuairisc mar dhrámadóir é.

161 Writing of the 1963 Taibhdhearc production, the critic for *The Connacht Tribune* also referred to the 'tragic and poignant circumstances of the play' and added that 'Mr. Ó Tuairisc, however, is sufficiently adept at the craft of playwriting to make sure that the gloom is appropriately lightened by a humour that is both intelligent and pungent' (*CT*, 16/3/63). With *Lá Fhéile Míchíl* on the syllabus for the Leaving Certificate examinations in 1967, *Inniu* ran a regular column on the play in the spring of that year to prepare students to write about it.

162 Guns – presumably not real ones! – were needed for the production, but the group could not bring the ones they had across the border (*IP*, 13/4/70). The production won second prize in its category at the Oireachtas.

163 The published text of the play gives the date as 1923 as does Martin Nugent in *Drámaí Eoghain Uí Thuairisc*, but the CivilWar was over by September 1923.

164 See Nic Eoin, *Eoghan Ó Tuairisc*, pp 22–6, for the young Ó Tuairisc's experience of the Civil War in his native Ballinasloe. He presents a lightly fictionalised account of those experiences in his novel *An Lomnachtán*.

165 Eoghan Ó Tuairisc, *Lá Fhéile Míchíl* (The feast of St Michael) (Baile Átha Cliath: Clódhanna Teoranta, 1967), p. 8.

166 Ibid.

167 Ibid., pp 11–12.

168 Ibid., pp 14–15. Ógfhear cumasach, deachumtha, dícheallach, praiticiúil, an sórt a chothaíonn a aisling féin ina chroí gan a bheith geabach fúithi. Tagann cuid den dathannacht mhíleata isteach leis, – an ghlaséide nua, an leathair is an prás ag glioscarnach, an gunnán Webley sáite sa chumhdach.

169 Ibid., p.19. Ní bhaineann rialacha ar bith leis an gcluiche seo againn. Ní cogadh é ach faltanas pearsanta, fíoch bhunaidh. Féinídiú atá ann . . . féinídiú ar scála náisiúnta . . . Níl ceart ná mícheart ann a thuilleadh. Ní fhanann anois acu ach an díoltas pearsanta; tuilleann an bás bás eile; tá an dá pháirtí againn mar a bheimís faoi gheasa gunnaíochta, agus leanfar den slad go dtí an deireadh dearg.

170 Ibid.

171 Ibid. Pacaí is 'duine . . . a bhfuil faghairt ann, gastacht intinne agus cumas cainte . . . ní réalaí é i ngnáthchiall an fhocail sin, mar is san aisling a mhaireann sé'.

172 Quoted in Nic Eoin, *Eoghan Ó Tuairisc*, pp 178–9. See his comments concerning 'a civil war that has existed since ancient times and that will always exist' (cogadh cathardha atá ann ó chian aimsir agus a bhéas ann i gcónaí) in his 1974 interview with Dáithí Ó Coileáin (*Comhar*, Oct. 1974, p. 6).

173 Ó Tuairisc, *Lá Fhéile Míchíl*, p. 48 and 50.

174 Ibid., p. 26. Is bean acmhainneach, luathintinneach í, aisteoir ina croí istigh, an dínit, an tuiscint, agus acmhainn an ghrinn insníofa ina pearsantacht. Bíonn an mothú faoi smacht na haigne aici i gcónaí . . . agus fanann an aigne ghrinndearcach agus an sprid do lúbtha aici faoin iomlán . . . Tuigeann sí an dá thaobh, an gá leis an gcogadh, an gá leis an tsíocháin; an gá leis an rialtas, an gá leis an éirí amach. Dála na misteach go léir tá sí praiticiúil . . .

175 Ibid., p. 30. Tá sé éasca go leor troid a dhéanamh agus bás a fháil ar son na haislinge, ach níl sé éasca troid a dhéanamh agus bás a fháil ar son rud chorportha, phraiticiúil, neamh-fhoirfe ar a dtugtar Saorstát!

176 Ibid., p. 31. Is Éireannach mé . . . Agus deirim go diongbháilte go bhfuil bród orm ag deireadh thiar bheith ag fáiltiú roimh an gasúr seo mar bhall d'Arm Náisiúnta na hÉireann.

177 Ibid., p. 36. Tá do chuidiú de dhíth orm sa chogadh cathartha seo, an t-aon chogadh cathartha ar fiú trácht air: an seanchogadh: an Eaglais ar thaobh amháin, agus an Stát ar an taobh eile . . . An Stát sin amuigh a bhfuil tú ag breathnú ar a chuid meaisínghunnaí. An Stát nua, an Rialtas *de facto*.

178 Ibid. Once again we see Ó Tuairisc's contempt for the bourgeoisie here. Rialtas parlaiminteach, liobrálach, bunaithe ar an daonlathas. Rialtas maolaigeanta macánta den mheánaicme chráifeach, gan stair, gan samhlaíocht, gan uasaicme éirimiúil, gan mystique, gan teacht aniar spioradálta: an sort a athraíonn a sheolta de réir mar a shéideann gach nuaghaoth eacnamaíoch . . . Aisling chreideamh na Cásca caillte, agus an gaimbíneachas *bourgeois* ag teacht i gcoróin . . .

179 Earlier, the nun in charge of the convent's novices tells the Big Priest: 'The patch of land belongs to the Great Republic of Charity. In this case, in this place, no one at all has authority except the Reverend Mother, Mère Michèle' (Baineann an paiste talún seo le Poblacht Mhór na Carthanachta.

Sa chúis seo, ar an láthair seo, níl údarás ag duine ar bith ach ag an Máthair Oirmhinneach amháin, an Mère Michèle) (p. 17).

180 Ó Tuairisc, *Lá Fhéile Míchíl*, p. 36. Ní leis an teibíocht atá tú ag plé – polasaí na hEaglaise nó polasaí an Stáit – ach le daoine, agus le paisean an duine. Daoine teasaí . . . Éireannaigh; daoine óga . . . nár fhág an croí ina ndiadh go fóill ar mhachairí na mblianta . . . Ní raibh an Mac seo cúramach.

181 Ibid., p. 35. Níl ionam na laethanta seo ach an toil agus an conablach cnámh.

182 Ibid., p. 21.

183 Ibid., p. 45. Agus mionnaím duit, a ghirseach – dá mba dheartháir dom féin é an Armstrong so – mionnaím duit nach rachadh ceangal na broinne idir mé agus mo dhualgas.

184 Ibid., p. 47.

185 Ibid., p. 49.

186 Ibid. Nic Eoin discusses the importance of the symbol of the cross for Ó Tuairisc in *Eoghan Ó Tuairisc*, p. 145. Níl ach taobh amháin ann, agus an t-aon chúis amháin. Poblacht nó Saorstát, is cuma fúthu i ndeireadh na dála, níl ionta ach foirmeacha sealadacha dúinn atá in arm agus in éide ar son chúis na Croise.

187 Ó Tuairisc, *Lá Fhéile Míchíl*, p. 57. Aislingeacha Ceilteacha! Mar an gcéanna don Mháistreás. An maireann sibh go léir sa tír seo faoi scáth na haislinge?

188 The stage directions would seem to indicate that he is supposed to look quite a bit like Arthur Griffith, the chief executive of the Irish Free State, who died in August 1922.

189 Ó Tuairisc, *Lá Fhéile Míchíl*, pp 62–3. Tárlaíonn sé anois is arís go dtéann Rialtas nua thar a n-acmhainn. Déanann siad dearmad go bhfuil fórsaí eile ann seachas an Stát, fórsaí ar tábhachtaí agus ar stairiúla iad, b'fhéidir, ná an Stát féin.

190 Ibid., p. 63. Tá an phraiseach ar fud na mias ar an saol seo againn gan aon agó . . . Sea mhaise, a Mhíchíl, – ora pro nobis!

191 Ibid., p. 27. Is é an locht is mó ar a carachtar ná go bhfuil sí pas beag dall ar ghnáthphaisean an ghnáth-dhuine. Ag beartú ardpholasaí eaglaisiúil di agus á chur i gcrích, tá contúirt ann go gcuirfidh sí daoine thar a n-acmhainn – daoine nach bhfuil an toil chomh foirfe ionta agus nach bhfuil paisean an chroí faoin diansmacht céanna acu is atá aici féin.

192 See, for example, ibid., p. 55.

193 Ibid., p. 69. Is eadrainn beirt atá an Scoilt. Idir mhúnladh mheanma na beirte againne; idir ár gcroíthe is ár gcuimhní cinn, ár bhfuil, ár gcuislí, ár sinsearacht agus bainne na cíche a dhiúigeamar beirt.

194 Ibid. Níl ionainne beirt ach an dá scáil stairiúla. I gcónaí bhí an dá shórt ann, agus beidh an dá shórt ann i gcónaí: An Státaire, agus an Poblachtach. Fiú amháin má chuirtear Poblacht ar bun, beidh daoine ann chun éirí amach i gcoinne na Poblachta, agus

daoine ag éirí amach i gcoinne an éirí amach. Go deo . . . Ní hí an stair a mhúnlaíonn an duine, ach an duine faoi ghrásta Dé a mhúnlaíonn agus a lúbann an stair.

195 Mícheál Mac Craith finds it incredible that someone as worldly wise as Mère Michèle would ever leave two loaded guns unsecured in wartime, but acknowledges that this act of apparent naiveté is necessary to make possible the climax of the play. See Mac Craith, '*Geineasas, Antigone* agus *La Fhéile Míchíl*', *Comhar*, Oct. 1985, p. 51.

196 She bears more than a little resemblance to Shakespeare's Ophelia here.

197 Ó Tuairisc, *Lá Fhéile Míchíl*, p. 73.

198 Ibid., p. 74. Tagann an tubaiste seo orm as an spéir ghlan. Bhí mé ag iarraidh dul eatarthu – *enfants de la patrie*. Ní raibh mé ag súil leis an bpaisean míofar as cuimse seo –

199 Eoghan Ó Tuairisc, 'Cataírsis' (Catharsis), in *Religio Poetae*, ed. Nic Eoin, p. 42.

200 Martin Nugent writes of the play: 'The perfect Catharsis is created. The author succeeds in accomplishing this through a play that is at once moving, powerful, forceful and enjoyable' (Cruthaítear an Cataírsis foirfe. Éiríonn leis an údar é seo go léir a chur i gcrích trí dhráma atá corraitheach, cumhachtach, fuinniúil agus taitneamhach ag an am céanna). See Nugent, *Drámaí Eoghain Uí Thuairisc*, p. 95.

201 The first prize was won by Éadhmonn Mac Suibhne for *An tAonarán* (The solitary person). See Nic Eoin, *Eoghan Ó Tuairisc*, p. 450, n. 18.

202 The reporter himself referred to Ó Tuairisc as 'one of the most enigmatic writers to emerge on the Irish scene, in Irish or English'.

203 It was not even reviewed in *The Connacht Tribune*.

204 Eoghan Ó Tuairisc, *An Hairyfella in Ifreann* (The hairyfella in hell), p. 2. The play has not been published. I am working here with the typescript made available by An Comhlachas Náisiúnta Drámaíochta. Tá ár gcosa nite, Djinbawn. Mise agus tusa agus ár leithéidí a mhaireann ar bhóithrín an uisce. Muid caite anois, carnaithe mar sheanbhróga ar an talamh tirim, agus an tsean-Chanáil Ríoga á lobhadh sa lathach –

205 Ibid., p. 3. Ligtear do na Geataí lobhadh sa phuiteach, an t-uisce ina scutar glas le fiailí, madraí marbha ar snámh ann agus bruscar bréan Phoblacht na Leithphingine, agus an t-iomlán gafa ag Ríocht na bhFroganna.

206 Ibid., p. 23. Tá an tAm ina stad, is ní cás liom lá liath seachas lá liath ar bith eile.

207 Ibid., p. 17.

208 Ibid., p. 23. Ach anois now [*sic*], don Fhear Gnóthaí, in aois seo na Margaí Eorpacha, tá buntáistí nach beag ag baint leis an – . . . Cén tairbhe dúinn mar Bhóthar Iarainn é ach do chuidse bullán agus caoireola agus leanaí bochta an bhaile a sheoladh go Livverypool Shasana?

209 Ibid., p. 24. Is é an Siostam é. Dul ar aghaidh, dul ar aghaidh, ag eagrú, atheagrú, dí-atheagrú. Éifeacht. Luas. Eacnamaíocht. Rothaí móra a' rolladh níos gasta agus níos gasta fós, gan aird gan aithne acu ar anam an duine –
210 Ibid., p. 10.
211 Ibid., p. 13. Smuitín gruaige á chlúdach ó mhullach a chinn go dtí stumpa a ché-chaoi-bhfuil tú. Chríost mhilis, arsa mise, seo chugainn an Hairyfella!
212 Ibid., p. 22.
213 Ibid., p. 25.
214 Ibid., p. 35.
215 Ibid., p. 39. Rithim na clagarnaí ar an díon ós ár gcinn, Stiofán bocht, é ag giúnaíl nós ainmhí gortaithe, a chuid fola ag sileadh ar chlocha pábhála an urláir, géag liom stalcaithe mar a raibh a cheann ina luí uirthi . . . speireanna briste na gcnámh ag gobadh tríd an éadach fuilteach amach –
216 Ibid., p. 40. Saibhreas sna cíocha fliucha, ba liomsa iad agus níor liomsa . . . Rug sé orthu – a Chríost! Crága a dhá lámh go tobann ag breith orthu, scianadh m'ionathair, scread áthais ag réabadh mo scornaí, ghabh mé de le mo chuid ingne, mo chuid fiacal, cíocras i mo bhéal, cnámh crua faoi m'fhiacail, shá sé ionam chomh fada le húll mo bhráid –
217 Ibid., p. 9. Maoithneachas. Tá lá na mBád Iompair thart. Don diabhal leis an fadó fadó. Thar a bheith in am againn rud nua a chruthú . . . Bugar ár gcuimhní! Táimid inár Náisiún de Chuimhní. Ní mór do dhuine a chuid cuimhní a thachtadh más mian leis maireachtáil.
218 Ibid., p. 12. A Dhia, a Dhia – tríocha milliún bliain den Éabhlóid gafa tharainn, agus luímid lenár gcosa sínte i dtreo éirí na Gealaí!
219 Ibid., p. 50. Protoplasma an phluda faoi theas na gréine ag at agus ag bíogadh chun beatha ón salachar amach . . . Míorúilt na beatha . . . An dara míorúilt. Na cosa deiridh. Agus tagann na sluaite ag bacadaoil amach ar an talamh tirim, turas fionnachtana.
220 Ibid., pp 50–1. Ag deireadh na scribe, sleamhnaíonn siad san uisce ar ais. Osclaíonn na budóga baineann a gcúlphíopaí agus scaírdeann siad púscadh na beatha uathu, agus tosaíonn arís ar an seanscéal. Arís agus arís eile. Leis na cianta cairbreacha. Tá siad faoi ghlas ag an Siostam . . . Aidh. An Siostam. Táimid go léir faoi ghlas aige.
221 Ibid., p. 45. She is wearing sunglasses. Anois dearc uirthi, chomh draíúil is atá an dath uirthi . . . Aolchloch Bhaile na gCloch. Dearc uirthi! . . . Bain díot na lampaí dorcha houri sin agus dearc uirthi!
222 Ibid. The bulldozer will be a central symbol in his next play, *Aisling Mhic Artáin*. Is faoi chlocha an Bhaile atá mé ag labhairt. Seansaibhreas, é á bhascadh as an bhealach faoi na bulldósairs ag leiciméirí Phoblacht na Leathphingine . . . An Siostam Seasc. Cartalann siad an bheochloch as an bhealach nó go

líonann siad an tír le brioscarnach de ghairbhéal agus de choincréid dhaite, cac tairbh ag ligean air go bhfuil sé ina chloch! See also p. 46.
223 Ibid., p. 75. Cloisfidh tú iad, ag gach seisiún ragairneach bailéadach uaidh seo go Loganna an Chaoil, na Daoine, óg agus aosta, fireann agus baineann, ag bomsáil *Awfta Dublin in de Green!* Chríost. Caoga Bliain deireannach. He continues: 'Yes, exactly, Awfta Dublin in de Green – but it's few of them, Dáiví, who will go with you Awfta Belfast in the Black!' (Sea, go díreach. Awfta to Dublin in de Green – ach is beag acu, a Dháiví, a rachas leat Awfta Béal Feirste sa Dubh!).
224 Ibid., p. 76. They are 'dírcach mar a bhí na Daoine gach lá riamh, ina dtréad éitreorach gan Taoiseach . . . Gan mórtas ar bith acu as a mBaile féin. Puipéidí ar shreang. Á gcur ag rince ag Máistrí an Airgid sa Ghaimbín-Sibhialtacht amuigh.'
225 Ibid., p. 56.
226 Ibid., p. 66. These are Jaxy Pat's and Jójó's descriptions of these characters in the play. Needless to say, they do not recognise themselves in those characters. The description of the character who represents Nanó is Jaxy Pat's.
227 Ibid., p. 65.
228 Ibid., p. 73. An Páidín-scríbhneoir, ag cur a mbéal ar leathadh le leamhgháire ar ghaigí na cathrach thar lear, trí leaganacha áiféiseacha dá mhuintir féin a léiriú ar an ardán, é ag magadh faoina gcaint, faoina gCreideamh, faoina n-oighreacht náisiúnta . . . Ceart agat, b'fhéidir. Bréan liom mo cheardaíocht uile. Téann sé díom nádúr na muintire seo a aimsiú. 'Gliogram gan téagar.' Ceart agat.
229 Eoghan Ó Tuairisc, 'An aghaidh fidil sa dráma' (The mask in drama), in *Religio Poetae*, ed. Nic Eoin, p. 87. He believed 'gur ó réigiún úd a éiríonn na guthanna chuig an drámadóir agus go gcumann sé Béal do gach guth acu. Go bhfuil Pearsana an dráma aige i bhfad níos bunúsaí ná rud ar bith ina phearsantacht beag féin. Go dtéann na Pearsana úd i bhfeidhm air, go mbaineann siad úsáid as, seal gearr, go labhraíonn siad trína bhéal . . .'
230 Ó Tuairisc, *An Hairyfella in Ifreann*, p. 79. He must follow 'glaoch mo cheirde . . . Mo cheird dhamanta féin. Cur téagair éigin foclaíochta isteach i scáil na scáileanna seo, ag iarraidh léas tuisceana éigin a aimsiú trí cheo na hargóna seo –'
231 Ibid., p. 10. Is iontach an léargas atá agam ar an saol ón oíche úd . . . Crot aislingeach ar chuile rud – mar a bheinn-se fós ag gníomhú na páirte, Euridiosaí, sa Dráma . . . Tá mé i mo bheo i slí nárbh bheo dom riamh – míshuaimhneas i mo chnámha . . .
232 Ibid., p. 36. Ní ealaín dom suim a chur sna rudaí seo a thuilleadh. M'óige. An Teach. An Baile. Agus na buachaillí beaga stuacánta. Tá mé Liobaráilte.
233 Ibid., p. 37. Níl aithne agam air. Níl aithne ag éinne air . . . Ní meas madra aige ar aon rud a gcuirimidne suim ann . . . Tuigtear dom ar uaire nach suim leis ní ar bith ar an saol – ach mise.

234 See ibid., p. 6 and 8. When the sisters recite lines from Lughaí's play, we see that Dorotaí learned the lines to play her part; Iffi truly understands them.

235 Ibid., p. 54. Criticí! Criticí! Criticí! Sibh go léir den déanamh céanna. Béal mór na céille bige. Ag bhur mbolgú féin suas nós froganna fireann agus sibh faoi gheasa ag gliogram bhur nglóir féin . . . Ag insint dom conas mo phictiúir a dhearadh, agus gan de chumas ar bhur stumpaí méireanna féin an smuitín is lú den line bheo a tharraingt. Huch, Criticí!

236 Ibid., p. 55. Taispeántar agus taispeántar agus taispeántar an chontúirt dó [an duine] – ach ní fheiceann sé.

237 Ibid., p. 58. An t-am ina stad, drochbhlas i mo bhéal, mar a bheadh an saol timpeall ina phuiteach orm, tiún as do Dhráma in Ifreann nós macalla i mo cheann – Ar ais, ar ais, ón uaigh aníos, tar . . . She tells him that doing the painting may have saved her from suicide (p. 57).

238 Ibid., p. 58. Bíonn an t-uafás i gcónaí ag roinnt leis an fhírinne. Sin é an fáth nach toil linn breathnú uirthi.

239 Ibid., p. 69. Níl ansin ach aghaidh fidil a chaitheann sé. An cruas. Ach laistiar den aghaidh fidil níl ann ach gasúr, gasúr éidtreorach, folúntas nach beag ina anam istigh . . . Ní mian liom 'anam' a rá – sa sean-nós ar aon chuma – mian liom a rá go bhfuil sé beo ar bhealach, beo bíogúil, is ar bhealach eile go bhfuil sé caillte . . . Thiocfadh le cailín rud éigin a bhronnadh air – rud éigin a chumadh in a chuideachta, rud éigin a roinnt leis –

240 Ibid., p. 81. Bhrisfinn an Siostam. Dhéanfainnse iarracht an nua a chruthú as creatlach an tsean-rud . . . Dráma, b'fhéidir – na radharcanna agus na hAghaideanna Fidil a chumadh agus a dhathú –

241 Ibid., p. 77. Pioc amach na madraí lofa as do Chanáil féin sula bhféachann tú leis an gcraiceann oráiste a phiocadh amach as Cuan do dhearthár.

242 See the discussion of these problems in Nic Eoin, *Eoghan Ó Tuairisc*, pp 337–8. Both of the performances at the Theatre Festival were, according to Nic Eoin, 'full to the door' (lán go doras). This was the first time a play by Ó Tuairisc had a professional production. See Nic Eoin, *Eoghan Ó Tuairisc*, p. 366.

243 Tá súil agam gur léir óna bhfuil ráite agam nach aon dráma gan tábhacht atá faoi thrácht agam. Tá sé lán gníomhaíochta, tá ábhar gáire go leor ann, agus mar atá ráite agam, cuirtear ceisteanna orainn féin lenár bhfreagraí féin a thabhairt orthu. He pointed out that the play was drawing full houses, and that therefore more performances should have been added.

244 Údar é Ó Tuairisc a bhfuil an tréith chéanna ag baint lena shaothar is atá le saothar Brian Friel i ndrámaíocht an Bhéarla, oineach éigse. Ní féidir dul i ngleic le rud ar bith dá gcumann Ó Tuairisc gan a

mhothú go bhfuil tú i láthair na healaíne. Is amhlaidh don dráma nua seo aige . . . Is fiú an dráma seo a fheiceáil gan trácht ar cheist nó ar chúis na Gaeilge. Tá scaoilteacht agus éiginnteacht ag roinnt leis, gan amhras, ach is iarracht nua-aimseartha é ó thus go deireadh.

245 Eoghan Ó Tuairisc, *Aisling Mhic Artáin* (The vision of Mac Artáin) (Baile Átha Cliath: Clódhanna Teoranta, 1978), p. 10.

246 Ibid. Tá Kraó, a Bhean, ag sodar lena shála, í cromtha, seálaithe, agus yashmak ag folú íochtar a haghaidhe. Ligeann sé fead léi mar a ligfí le madra, agus sméideann de gheit ghonta ordóige di suí. Suíonn sí ar a gogaide sa chúinne.

247 Ibid., p. 57. Cuimhnigh go bhfuil do dhossier agamsa – salachán leisbeach de dhríodarchuid na cathrach . . . agus mura gcoimeádann tú srian ar do theanga mise i mbannaí duit nach hamaighnéasach ar fad an mhaise a imreos mise faoi na másaí ort.

248 Ibid., p. 64. Níl feidhm agam air, níl feidhm agatsa air: táimid faoi gheasa ag an chinniúint, agus titeann gach rud amach mar is áil leis an Bhuldósar Síoraí. See also his 'tuneless recitativo' (recitativo gan tiún) on p. 63.

249 Ibid., pp 11–12. Gléasaigí a dhiabhala – / cead agaibh tamaillín drabhlais a chaitheamh anois, / drugaigí sibh féin leis an ghloine, nó le béasa an bhroic / ag útamáil timpeall ar urlár an rince sa twist / ag suirí, nó ag imirt an bhingo, nach cuma sa chip / sna Leaca, na Leaca, na Leaca, na Leaca, / na Leaca dú-dú-dhor-a-cha!

250 Ibid., p. 20. Ba chóra duit é insint dom sé mhí ó shin nuair a pósadh muid. Dearbhaím duit, Bill Beerbohm, nach dtiocfainn leat go dtí na Leaca Dorcha dóite seo dá mbeadh fhios agam é – Her husband accepts the situation as 'one of the customs of the place . . . the Winter Ceremony . . . An old regional ceremony' (nós de chuid na háite . . . Searmanas an Gheimhreadh. Sean-nós réigiúnda).

251 Ibid., p. 73. Ó bain an dallamullóg de do shúile soineanta, a leanabán! Fás suas. Dearc ar an saol. Ní bábóga plaisteacha atá ionainn fir agus mná, ach fórsaí allta ón ársaíocht ag feidhmiú trí dhalbacht na héabhlóide . . . Sin mar a chruthaigh an Dia sin agat an scéal. Ní mór beith réadúil agus glacadh leis.

252 Ibid., p. 75.

253 Ibid., p. 74.

254 Ibid., pp 90–1. Tusa an scáil, nach n-aithníonn gur fear de shubstaint na talún thú – tusa an Diabhal sa Dráma, an tSúil Amháin! . . . Intleachtach? – ea, an aigne Cheilteach ag tarraingt as bod do shamhlaíochta féin.

255 Ibid., p. 27. B'álainn liom tráth den saol / cailín caoin go suairc i mo chomhair, / mín a cneas mar shíoda bhí, / cruinn a cíocha, séimh a glór – / phóg mé mo rún, ó phóg mé mo rún . . . Ait an smaoineamh atá ag borradh i mo chroí. Sea, a Bhrídín, fear. Den chéad uair le mo bheo.

256 Ibid., p. 44. Ní galar é, tarlaíonn sé go minic de réir nádúir . . . Cuimhnigh, b'fhéidir gurb é seo an seans deireannach agam féin fás suas agus éirí as an leisbeachas atá ag leonadh mo shaoil. Ní chasfar an dara duine de do shórtsa orm –

257 Ibid., pp 42–3. Mothaím an tarraingt chéanna i do láthairse is a mhothaigh mé le mo chomrádaí cailín ar an Ollscoil. Cneastacht ag roinnt leat. Tuiscint. Torthúlacht aigne – aigne chailín – tá tú beo ar bhealach nach beo don chuid eile acu.

258 Ibid., pp 44–5. Éirigh as na speabhraídí Ceilteacha agus breithnigh an saol. Conas is féidir le fear grá a thabhairt don Dia anaithnid nuair nach dtugann sé grá don chréatur atá ina choilgsheasamh os a chomhair amach . . . Namhaid don bheatha –

259 Ibid., p. 55. Ní suim liom fear mura bhfuil sé ina dhuine go hiomlán . . . An dá ghnéas ann, mar atá an dá ghnéas ionainne mná.

260 Lú is the modern spelling of Lugh. 'In Samaildánach' means 'the one who has mastered many skills simultaneously'.

261 Ó Tuairisc, *Aisling Mhic Artáin*, p. 17. Bhain siad spraoi as ár gcuid cleasannaí. Haha, ní raibh siad in ann riamh a dhéanamh amach cé againn Lú agus cé againn Lúlú. Haha, d'fheicfeá Lú bomaite amháin, bomaite eile bheadh sé glanta as amharc agus an spéirbhean Lúlú go taibhsiúil ina ionad – a' dtuigeann tú? Ní fheicfidís choíche Lú agus Lúlú le chéile.

262 Ibid., p. 82. Ar féidir – ach ní féidir – an mian leat a rá gur Lú tú amannta is gur Lúlú tú amanta eile? . . . Rud éigin mar sin . . . Ach conas – is é sin le rá, cé acu Lú nó Lúlú tú ó cheart? . . . Is fear mé sna hearraí bunúsacha. Ach is bean mé san ealaín . . . Aiteas agus aistil na hoíche a léiriú do na croíthe atá i ngéibheann an lae. Geit a bhaint astu, agus gáire. A stage direction at one point states that many of the characters act 'as if they were sleepwalking, caught up in the rhythm and the gaiety of the night' (mar bheidís gafa ag an rithim agus ag aeraíl na hoíche ina suansiúl) (p. 66). See also Ó Tuairisc, *An Hairyfella in Ifreann*, pp 38–9 and 66.

263 Ó Tuairisc, *Aisling Mhic Artáin*, p. 17. Mhuise, tá's agat meon na leathphingine a tháinig i réim leis an Réabhlóid, is bréan leo an fhilíocht, an ealaín, an ceol ar an sean-nós, an greann, an ghealtacht, an gheamaireacht. De bhrí nach dtig leo na rudaí sin a smachtú agus praghas ceart a chur orthu. See also the chorus's hymn of praise to the Bulldozer (p. 65).

264 Ó Tuairisc must have meant Suibhne Geilt, the mad protagonist of the medieval tale *Buile Shuibhne* (The frenzy of Suibhne), rather than the far less interesting king Suibhne Menn.

265 Ó Tuairisc, *Aisling Mhic Artáin*, p. 97. Amanta in uaigneas mo charabháin, samhlaítear dom go raibh mé i gcónaí ann, An Cleasaí Síoraí . . .

266 Ibid., p. 100. Lom go leor a bhí an saol agam sular tháinig tú: níos loime fós a bheas sé agam tar éis d'imtheachta.

267 Ibid., pp 102–3. Ar a chúl, gan fhios dó, sánn Kraó a ceann trí shliota an chuirtín amach, a haghaidh óg nochta, a folt loinnireach ar sileadh, dearadh na meidhréise ina dreach . . . Solas gléineach ag léimneach sa bhothóg . . . Gáire meidhréise ón chailín allta . . . Taibhsítear Kraó ón chlúid amach ina spéirbhean leathnochtaithe. She had previously had this appearance in 'Suantraí na hOiche' (The lullaby of the night) (p. 86).

268 Ibid., p. 12, 16, 65, and 78.

269 In a 1980 letter to Cyril Ó Céirín, Ó Tuairisc wrote: 'And now the BBC is asking me to do the dialogue and dramatisation for them for the programme they are making – *Carolan*' (Agus anois tá an BBC ag iarraidh orm an dialog agus an drámú a dhéanamh dóibh ar an chlár atá á chumadh acu – *Carolan*). Quoted in Nic Eoin, *Eoghan Ó Tuairisc*, p. 383. The project never materialised, although Ó Tuairisc did provide the BBC a script.

270 Quoted in ibid., pp 367–8.

271 Quoted in ibid., p. 371. Ó mo thaithí ar an Ardán sa Mhainistir agus sa Phéacóg, is léir dom gur mór an chabhair don ghnáthphobal go mbeadh snaithe maith den Bhéarla tríd an phíosa, chun bunús an Radhairc – go mórmhór nuair is Radharc casta é – a chur i dtuiscint dóibh . . . Ní bheadh stró orm an Dráma go léir a ghaelú. His experience at the Abbey was, of course, with the *geamaireachtaí*.

272 Eoghan Ó Tuairisc, *Carolan*, p. 6. The play has not been published. I am working here with the type-script made available by An Comhlachas Náisiúnta Drámaíochta.

273 Ibid., p. 12. Breast ar do chuid transposing! Ná transpose ná dispose ná countersuppose rud ar bith! Nó ar mian leat praiseach a dhéanamh de mo chuid ceoil, ar nós fidileoirí agus píobairí na tire, ag sceanairt agus ag scréachaíl ar phíosa de cheol prionsúil, chun é a chur in oiriúint do bhróga tairní yahoos na tuaithe ag pramsáil ar urlár an randyboo?

274 Ibid., pp 29–30. Ach is fearr liom Alegretto é. Tá sé sin níos gaiste, níos spreagúla, níos modern – ní mór cic a chur sa tiún – . . . Tá acu go léir an 'virtuosity,' clisteacht na méar. Ach cé acu atá in ann meileadaí nua a chruthú? An dtuigeann tú? – an tséis, an figiúir, an meileadaí. Meileadaí i dtosach . . .

275 Ibid., p. 26. Níl ionam ach leathdhuine, gan tír, gan treabh, gan sinsireacht . . . Gan sinsireacht agam sa cheol ach an oiread. Gan agam ach an macalla, mac-cheol, macsmaointe, macvéarsaíocht, a séideadh chugam ó bhochtáin an bhóthair. Níl fáil go deo agam ar sheancheol uasal na hÉireann. Sea mhaise, tá an ceolshaibhreas úd imithe le haer an tsaoil.

276 Ibid., p. 30. Gan ionam ach dallarán. Taibhse de dhuine tríd an dorchacht ag útamáil . . . Gan cumas ar fhilíocht agam, gan ealaín na bhfocal agam, i mBéarla ná i nGaeilge, chun m'aisling a rá . . . bréagadóir, fear fallsa, tadhg an dá thaobh . . . Cibé ar bith ceol a éiríonn liom a mhealladh ón dorchacht,

caillfear é, déanfar é a thruailliú ina áilleagán leadránach sráide faoin láimh chomónta.
277 Ibid., p. 32. In attendance will be 'ár gcuid aristocracy uile, Prionsaí agus Banphrionsaí de shliocht Ír agus Éibhir . . . cléir agus manaigh . . . lucht ceoil, lucht éigse agus lucht seandálaíochta, maraon le Captaein agus Oifigigh de gach Arm de chuid na hEorpa'.
278 Ibid., p. 35. Agus thar dhuine ar bith eile, molaim Ó Cearbhalláin. Molaim a dhea-shampla Críostaí. Dáileann sé a chuid ceoil ar chuile dhuine – Gael, Gall, GallGhael, ScotsGhael, SacsAlbannach – thar dhuine ar bith eile againn éiríonn leis teorann na gcreideamh, teorainn na fola, teorainn na dteangacha, a shárú, agus aicmí éagsúla Éireann a aontú in aisling a chuid ceoil.
279 Ibid., p. 44. This passage is in English in the text.
280 See Vivian Mercier, 'Swift and the Gaelic tradition', in *Fair Liberty Was All His Cry: A Tercentenary Tribute to Jonathan Swift 1667–1745*, ed. A. Norman Jeffares (London: Macmillan, 1967), pp 282–5.
281 The title is taken from the first line of Pearse's 1916 poem 'Renunciation'.
282 Nic Eoin, *Eoghan Ó Tuairisc*, p. 375. The themes are 'fadhbhanna ealaíontóra agus é i ngleic le meon cúng agus dearcadh eacnamaíoch frithealaíonta na freacnairce Éireannaí . . . an neamhshuim fhorleathan i luachanna agus in idéil Mhic Phiarais . . . aincheist na freagrachta agus na ciontachta a mhothaíonn an duine a dhéanann gníomh brúidiúil foréigneach ar son idéil pholaitiúil'.
283 Ó Tuairisc, *Fornocht do Chonac*, n.p.
284 His name is doubly significant, with 'Piaras' echoing the Gaelic form of Pearse's name, Pádraig Mac Piarais, and 'Mac Aimhirgin' recalling the name of Amairgin, the poet of the mythological Tuatha Dé Danann and creator of the first poem ever recited in Ireland.
285 Ó Tuairisc, *Fornocht do Chonac*, p. 3. Breathnaigh an dealbhóireacht! – prácás, praiseach, 'mass-production,' leachtanna uaighe sa stíl Cheilteach . . . Scrios Dé uirthi mar stíl Cheilteach!
286 Ibid., p. 55.
287 Ibid., p. 8. One is reminded of Lughaí's pride in his native place in *An Hairyfella in Ifreann*. Bhuel, mar a fheiceann an tAthair sinn! – Pocféaireacht bhreá Ghaelach amach is amach. Pitseoigín de mhúinteoir scoile ina comhairleoir ealaíne – . . . Is mór agamsa an Piarsach. Is mór agamsa Baile an Locha – cé suarach go leor an tsamhlaíocht atá ag cuid de na daoine ann, is ceann dár gcuid bailte beaga Éireannacha é. Agus níor mhaith liom go mbeadh prácás suarach dealbhóireachta ina sheasamh ag Ceann an Locha agus é ina cheapmagaidh ag turasóirí ón Eoraip agus ón imigéin.
288 Ibid., p. 9.

289 Ibid., pp 10–11. Níl ionatsa ach *recidivist*. Do chuid rómánsaíochta náisiúnta ar an seandéanamh, tá sí smolchaite. Tá Éire san Eoraip, agus lá nua ar an saol. Tá ár gcúrsaí eacnamaíochta ag máirseáil.
290 Ibid., p. 12. They will import 'cuisneoirí *deep-freeze* ón nGearmáin, cocairí oilte ón bhFrainc, bágún ón Danmhairg, glasraí reoite ón Ísiltír, fíon ón Iodáil, éadaí na Meánaoiseanna ó Shasana'.
291 Ibid., p. 13.
292 Ibid., p. 14. In aon fhocal amháin duit. Kultur. Rud éigin Seltik . . . Ní mór daoibh glacadh le cibé ar bith a dhéanfaidh mé.
293 Ibid., p. 20.
294 Ibid., p. 45. Piaras's mother utterly rejects this idea. Má bhí ciall ar bith leis an dráma dearg a d'achtaíomar amach i gclapsholas an GPO, ba é go mbeadh 'Saoirse' againn. Saoirse aigne. Saoirse ag an duine, ón Stát, ón údarás, óna chlann féin, saoirse chun a bhealach féin a ghearradh amach, agus a aisling féin a chur i gcrích.
295 Ibid., p. 21. Bás don cheardaíocht, bás don aisling, bás do chuile rud a chothaíonn anam an duine agus carachtar cine.
296 Ibid., p. 24. An duine a bhfuil bua na samhlaíochta aige feiceann sé rud éigin – rud a bhaineann leis an saol eile . . . Sagas 'Ide-a.' Smaoineamh nó pictiúr aisteach éigin a éiríonn óna anam istigh.
297 Ibid., pp 24–5. Ní haon mhaith don duine an aisling a fheiceáil muna bhfuil sé in ann é a léiriú do dhaoine eile . . . in amhrán, nó i gceol, nó i ngiota péintéireachta; nó dul amach ar thuras fionnachtana agus domhan a aimsiú, nó aisling pholaitíochta a dhearadh agus a léiriú don saol.
298 One thinks here of Pearse's poem 'The Fool' in which he wrote: 'O wise men, riddle me this: what if the dream come true / What if the dream come true? and if millions unborn shall dwell / In the house I shaped in my heart, the noble house of my thought?' See Patrick Pearse, 'The Fool', in *Collected Works of Padraic H. Pearse: Plays, Stories, Poems* (Dublin: The Phoenix Publishing Company, n.d.), pp 335–6.
299 Ó Tuairisc, *Fornocht do Chonac*, p. 26. Bhraitheamar go léir nár sa seanofig-an-phoist ar an tseansráid a bhíomar: ach mar a bheimís áit eile, ar ardán éigin, ag glacadh páirte i ndráma – dráma aislingeach éigin nár thuigeamar i gceart. This same image and idea can be found in *Dé Luain*, Ó Tuairisc's novel about Easter Week. See Eoghan Ó Tuairisc, *De Luain* (Monday) (Baile Átha Cliath: Allen Figgis and Co., 1966), pp 18, 72, 79–80, 117, and 119–20. See also O'Leary, 'Reasoning why after fifty years', *Proceedings of the Harvard Celtic Colloquium* XXXI (2011), pp 253–81.
300 Ó Tuairisc, *Fornocht do Chonac*, pp 25–6.
301 Ibid., pp 61–2. Damnú síoraí air mar Phiarsach. Ba mhian liom a ainm agus gach a mbaineann leis a

stróiceadh amach as néaróga mo chuimhne. Is é an Piarsach, miotas an Phiarsaigh, bunchloch agus príomhchúis mo chéasta . . . Ag maireachtáil istigh i gclapsholas a shamhlaíochta féin, nach bhfaca an cnámharlach beag cailín, cúig bliana d'aois, ina luí anocht faoin gcréafóg agus an inchinn bheag lofa ina dusta mar thoradh ar a chuid drámaíochta.

302 *Ibid.*, p. 62. Mise Éire . . . / Seamblas an Bhúistéar . . . / Mó mo ghlóir . . . Mé do rug Mac Aimhirgín an Murdaróir . . .

303 These archetypal figures are wearing 'stone-grey, stylised dress . . . with a painted half-mask over their eyes' (feisteas clochliath stílithe . . . agus leathaghaidh fidil daite thar na súile). They are also provided with appropriate props. Piaras parodies the final stanza of Yeats's poem on p. 22.

304 Ó Tuairisc, *Fornocht do Chonac*, pp 52–3.

305 *Ibid.*, p. 53.

306 *Ibid.*, p. 74. Ní mór iad a chaomhnú, a chosaint, ár gcuid saibhris ealaíne féin a sholáthar dóibh . . . Ó is breá na méirligh sibh agus na réabhlóidithe, an 'avant garde,' sibh go léir in bhur Stephen Dedaluses ag rith go dtí an Fhrainc agus an Iodáil – 'to forge the uncreated conscience of my race!' – Ach féach, sin agat thíos Baile an Locha, sin agat an mhuintir atá i mbraighdeanas, sin agat an 'real world' – agus má tá coinsias le gaibhniú agus cath le cur, sin agat bun agus forscreamh do chuid iarrachtaí . . . Iad ag sodar i ndiaidh na n-asal. Gan scáth againn. Gan sgiath cosanta, ach an chluais agus an tsúil agus an béal bocht oscailte do gach aon saghas truflaise a chaitear chugainn ó cheithre ranna an tsaoil.

307 *Ibid.*, pp 81–2.

308 *Ibid.*, p. 81. Le cruthú agaibh, agus le pearsanú agaibh, arís agus arís eile, gach duine agaibh de réir a chumais féin, faoi aghaideanna fidil an lae.

309 *Ibid.*, pp 82–3. Ní tír amháin atá i gceist, ná pobal áirithe. Tá sí níos leithne ná tír, níos ársa ná an pobal a ionchollaíonn í. Is Tír í, agus is Teanga. Is Teanga í agus saolthuiscint Teanga. Is léargas í, léargas atá le cosaint agus le caomhnú in éadan ollchumhacht chomónta an lae. Fís. Focal. Fáistine. An aigne Éireannach . . . Agus go dtí an lá atá inniu ann, go dtí an oíche atá anocht ann, i do mhiotas, i do theagasc, i d'eiseamláir, leannan tú den mharú, den dúnorgan, agus den uafás? – Freagair, a Phiarsaigh, nach tú atá ciontach?

310 *Ibid.*, p. 83. Tá sé in am agam tú a stróiceadh as néaróga mo shamhlaíochta amach – tá sé thar a bheith in am againn tú féin agus do shoiscéal fola a

stoitheadh mar a bheadh neantóg nimhneach ann as cré ár gcuimhne.

311 *Ibid.*, p. 84. Tá mise de dhlúth ionat. Fadó riamh, rinneadar mise a shníomh isteach i ndeilbhíocht d'aigne. Is mé an síol as a mbláthaíonn do chuid samhlaíochta . . . Ní mór duit mé a iomlánú . . . Mé féin agus mo shaothar a shlánú i dTéama an Aiséirí.

312 *Ibid.*, p. 85. Is geis duit an tUafás a tharraingt amach i solas an lae, agus stánadh air fornocht. This is one of the principal themes of his long poems 'Aifreann na Marbh' (The mass of the dead) and *The Weekend of Dermot and Grace* (both 1964). One is reminded here of Lughaí's comment to Iffi in *An Hairyfella in Ifrinn*: 'Truth is always mixed with terror. That is why we don't like to look at it.'

313 Ó Tuairisc, *Fornocht do Chonac*, p. 86. I do dhallarán a bheas tú, i do dhallarán go deireadh an scéil. Ní léireofar an t-iomlán duit nó go léireofar dúinn Ollsaothar na Síoraíochta – san Aiséirí.

314 *Ibid.*, p. 91. Nochtann Sprid an Phiarsaigh ar cúl . . . tá Cloigeann beag á iompar aici i ngreim a dhá láimh roimpi amach . . . Cloigeann beag cróndorcha atá ann.

315 *Ibid.*, p. 93. Anseo a tharla an bhris – i gcnámh lannach na huisinne. Bris mhantach – uirlis mhiotail, cnapán dhoras an ghluaisteáin, scian, sleá, piléar, tua cloiche – i dtromluí fada na n-aoiseanna. Stair – . . . Breathnaígí, a chairde, ár stair, ár sinsireacht. Ar an láthair seo, lomnocht. Gan de chuspóir againn, gan ceann scribe, ach an sliogán simplí seo ar an leac. Ag stánadh ar an Dada Deireannach.

316 *Ibid.*, p. 94. Dar a bhfuil ag Dia! An Piarsach féin á rá liom . . . 'I dtús ama bhí an Focal' – an taobh eile, an t-iomlánú –

317 *Ibid.*, pp 94–5. Cuireann sé scanradh orm. Scanradh agus . . . saghas áthais. In his 1954 poem 'At the Kavanagh Trial', he writes: 'What is truth? / – A skull in an aftermath.' See Eoghan Ó Tuairisc, 'At the Kavanagh Trial', in *Sidelines: A Diary of Poems 1951–1974* (Dublin: Raven Arts, 1981), p. 25.

318 This is, of course, the same problem Ó Tuairisc created for himself by spelling out Lughaí's plan for the future of Baile na gCloch in *An Hairyfella in Ifrinn*.

319 See the following tributes after his death: 'Death of writer Eoghan Ó Tuairisc', *IP*, 25/8/82; Tomás Mac Anna, 'Eoghan Ó Tuairisc: an appreciation', *IT*, 27/8/82; and Gerald Dawe, 'Eoghan Ó Tuairisc 1919–82', *CT*, 3/9/82.

320 Colbert Kearney, *The Consequence* (Dublin: Blackstaff Press, 1993), p. 169.

CHAPTER FOUR
Knocking down OldWalls

1   Pádraig Ó Siadhail has written: 'Ó Tuama used realism, surrealism, the absurd, and fantasy in his dramatic work, and although he did not always manage to handle those elements in a satisfactory manner, he was an experimental, progressive playwright' (D'úsáid Ó Tuama an réalachas, an t-osréalachas, an áiféis is an fhantaisíocht ina shaothar drámata, is cé nach ndeachaigh aige i gcónaí na gnéithe sin a láimhseáil go sásúil, ba dhrámadóir trialach forchéimnitheach é). See Pádraig Ó Siadhail, 'Drámaí Sheáin Uí Thuama' (The plays of Seán Ó Tuama), *IMN*, 1986, p. 7.

2   In a 1984 interview in *Innti*, Ó Tuama acknowledged that his plays were 'hit-shows' and that there was 'a big attendance' (an-fhreastal) at them because 'it was felt that there was something new in them at the time' (braitheadh go raibh rud éigin nua iontu san am). See '"Slabhraí óir . . .": comhrá le Seán Ó Tuama' ('Chains of gold . . .': a conversation with Seán Ó Tuama), *Innti* IX (1984), p. 40.

3   In his 1984 interview in *Innti*, he stated: 'I was raised mostly with Irish. I didn't know any English until I was six or seven, until I went to school' (Le Gaeilge is mó a tógadh mé. Ní raibh puinn Béarla agam go dtí go rabhas a sé nó a seacht, gur chuas ar scoil). See ibid., p. 28.

4   Deisceabal mé do Dhónall Ó Corcora. Ní maith le haon duine a admháil ná fuil ann ach deisceabal ach sa chás so níl aon dul as agam; ná ní theastaíonn dul as uaim. Ó Tuama took part in a tribute to Corkery on his eightieth birthday broadcast over Radio Éireann in February 1958 (*IP*, 19/2/58) and spoke on him again over the radio in February 1965 and August 1969 (*IP*, 23/10/65; 30/8/69).

5   See his book *The Gaelic League Idea*, a collection he edited containing essays by various writers based on Thomas Davis lectures broadcast over Radio Éireann (Cork: Mercier Press, 1972).

6   Tá filíocht á cumadh aris sa Ghaeilge . . . a bhfuil fiúntas ar leith is áilleacht faoi leith inti. Conas ab fhéidir d'aon Éireannach a mhaífeadh go raibh oideachas air – nó gean don áilleacht aige – gan eolas a bheith aige ar na nithe is suaithinsí a dúirt agus a mhothaigh a mhuintir roimhe nó lena linn? Conas ab fhéidir an t-eolas sin a bheith aige gan Ghaeilge? . . . An té a thuigeann . . . príomhionad na Gaeilge ina oidhreacht chúlturtha, beidh sé an-bhuartha. Beidh sé chomh buartha sin go bhfoghlaimeoidh sé í is go labharfaidh sé í

7   See his praise of Máirtín Ó Cadhain as 'the most remarkable example in modern Ireland of the writer *"engagé "* ', in 'A writer's testament', *IT*, 23/1/73. He was not a bad example of that breed himself.

8   Quoted by Diarmuid Breathnach and Máire Ní Mhurchú, *Beathaisnéis a Naoi: Forlíonadh agus*

Innéacsanna (Biography nine: supplement and indices) (Baile Átha Cliath: An Clóchomhar, 2007), p. 124. D'fhág a chuid teagaisc rian ar na glúnta mac léinn . . . D'éirigh leis gnéithe de thraidisiún liteartha na Gaeilge a chur ag seinm ar chomhbhuille leis an ré.

9   In particular he rejected the term 'compulsory Irish' as used by enemies of the language revival, writing in *Facts about Irish* (Baile Átha Cliath: Comhdháil Náisiúnta na Gaeilge, 1964), p. 6: 'There has been a quite unreasonable "plugging" of the phrase "compulsory Irish", as if Irish were the only compulsory subject in education. English is compulsory in the National schools (even in the Gaeltacht).' See also 'Most dishonest slogan invented is: "compulsory Irish"', *IP*, 20/10/64.

10   In December 1960 and January 1961, he broadcast over Radio Éireann 'Mo Chara Thú Is Mo Thaithneamh' (You are my friend and my delight), 'a new arrangement' (nua-chóiriú) of *Caoineadh Airt Uí Laoghaire* (The lament for Arthur O'Leary) (*K*, 31/12/60; *IP*, 3/1/61).

11   See 'Irish is vital to retain nation's individuality', *IP*, 19/4/63.

12   Is é is príomh-aidhm do A. C. P. ná teacht ar shlite éifeachtúla chun dul i bhfeidhm ar phobal, ar eagraíochtaí Béarla, agus ar pháirtithe polaitíochta na hÉireann ar mhaithe leis an nGaeilge, agus ar mhaithe le leas na hÉireann. See also, 'Gluaiseacht na Gaeilge (The Irish-language movement): the home playing its part', *NG*, 4/12/65; 'Dr. Seán O'Tuama [*sic*] speaks on Irish culture', *ME*, 19/11/65; and 'Origin of F. G. [Fine Gael] Irish policy?', *IP*, 8/8/66.

13   See Vera Ryan, *Dan Donovan: An Everyman's Life* (Cork: The Collins Press, 2008), pp 87–105; and Tom Moore, 'People I meet', *IP*, 24/10/61.

14   His work as an adjudicator was not limited to drama competitions. For example, in 1966 he was named one of the judges of a competition sponsored by the Union of Students in Ireland for a 'thriller' in Irish (*IP*, 17/11/66). In 1984 he was one of the judges for the Seán Ó Ríordáin Memorial Prize for poetry at the Oireachtas (*IT*, 20/10/84). And in 1986 he adjudicated the competition for Duais Bhord na Gaeilge in fiction at the Listowel Writers' Week (*IT*, 2/6/86).

15   See also 'Snob student image draws strong protest: for art's sake', *SI*, 3/3/68.

16   Éinne a scríonn drámaí Gaeilge fé láthair, is deacair dó iad a scríobh ar shlí a chreidfear; sé sin toisc gur teanga tuaithe í an Ghaeilge atá á labhairt i gcúpla ceantar beag, agus is deacair don lucht éisteachta a chreidiúint go bhfuil caractéirí a bhaineann le saol cathrach sa fichiú aois á labhairt. Deir Seán Ó Tuama, duine de phríomh-dhrámadóirí na Gaeilge, go gcaithfidh an drámadóir Gaeilge a dhráma a shuíomh de ghnáth sa Ghaeltacht nó é a shuíomh áit éigin sa stair, na céadta bliain ó shoin más féidir, sa

tslí gur féidir linn a ghlacadh go bhfuil Gaeilge á labhairt go nádúrtha ag na pearsana sa dráma.

17 B'fhéidir gurbh fhearr dom dáimh na bhfocal a rá sa gcás seo. Níl dáimh na muintire le cuid de na focail nár mhór don fhile a tharraingt chuige agus é ag léiriú saol cathartha i nGaeilge. Tuigfear níos fearr é seo nuair adéarfas mé – agus ní focal teicniciúla atá i gceist agam – gur téarmaí i nGaeilge fós cuid mhór focal is focail comónta faoi 'n am seo i mBéarla.

18 The previous winner was Séamus Ó hAodha's poem 'Speal an Ghorta' (The scythe of the famine) in 1945.

19 Ach ná bíodh aon amhras orainn 'na thaobh: dá mbeadh na drámaí Gaeilge chomh flúirseach is a bhíonn óráidí ar an Oireachtas thuillfeadh an saothar seo Sheáin Uí Thuama fáilte agus moladh nach dual ach don scoth. He did feel that the first act was 'a little slow' (buille mall), that there were occasional lapses into 'empty rhetoric' (reiteoiric fholamh) and that the play as a whole was sometimes 'wordy' (foclach).

20 Bíodh gur eachtra stairiúil is bun leis ní bhraitheann tú in am ar bith go bhfuil an toil daonna faoi smacht go hiomlán ag cinniúint na staire: tá cúrsaí poiblí agus príobháideach fite ina chéile mar is dual agus i ndeireadh scribe is comhchás leat oideadh Mhághnuis Mhóir Uí Dhomhnaill agus rath éiginnte a dhúthaí.

21 In his review of the production in *Feasta*, Máirtín Ó Direáin also found the costumes 'shabby' (go suarach), but added: 'The set and the scenery gave us some sense of the "many-doored court of Donegal"' (Thug an suíomhra agus an radharcra léargas éigin dúinn ar 'chúirt dhoirseach Dhún na nGall') (*Feasta*, Dec. 1956, p. 27).

22 Tríd is tríd níor mhó ná sásúil an léiriú é . . . Tá súil agam nach ndéanfar dearmad ar an dráma seo anois ón uair a léiríodh aon uair amháin é. Ná téadh sé isteach sa roinn úd de Liombó ina bhfuil an iomad d'aistí éigse na Gaeilge ar lóistín.

23 Ba bheag iad le hais maorgacht agus cumas na scríbhneoireachta, le hais neart agus scóip an léirithe, le hais clisteacht agus réalachas an deartha, le hais dathúlacht agus áilleacht na gcultacha, le hais cinnteacht agus feabhas na haisteoireachta. *Tour de force* a bhí ann . . .

24 The play was adapted for radio by Proinsias Ó Conluain.

25 Tá an obair a deineadh air chomh foirfe go gcaithfeadh an té is faide *avantgarde* [*sic*] a admháil gur sár-dhráma é.

26 See Brendan Bradshaw, 'Manus "the magnificent": O'Donnell as renaissance prince', in *Studies in Irish History Presented to R. Dudley Edwards*, ed. Art Cosgrave and Donal McCartney (Dublin: University College Dublin, 1979), pp 15–36.

27 Seán Ó Tuama, *Gunna Cam agus Slabhra Óir: Dráma Véarsaíochta Thrí Ghníomh* (A pistol and a

golden chain: a verse play in three acts) (Baile Átha Cliath: Sáirséal agus Dill, 1964), p. 9. Tá ré na ngadhar thart sa tigh seo feasta . . . agus ré na gcnámh.

28 Ibid., p. 18. Ní haon strainséir – Sasanach sa tigh seo . . . Sea, a chroí, ní haon strainséir aon tSasanach sa tigh seo – ná an fear gorm féin, má bhíonn aige fios a bhéasa.

29 Ibid., p. 21. Ach más é atá uait go mbainfinn díom anuas mo chulaith / mhagaidh os comhair na ndaoine, déanfad san; / is nochtfad corp mo smaointe dóibh go léir. An té a bhfuil / aon tsúil 'na cheann is eol dó cheana féin / An ní a deirim: an saol a chaitheadh m'athairse is a athair siúd / arís, tá deireadh leis. Na nósa is / na béasa chleachtaímid, ní chuirid in oiriúint sinn don / ré nua atá ag teacht. Tuathánaigh dheinid dínn / os comhair an domhain, cine dúr spaidaigeanta ná loirgíonn / aon pháirt a bheith acu sa mhalairt / saoil atá forleathan inniu ar fud na hEorpa. / Is é mo mhiansa, áfach, a thaispeáint / go bhfuilimid sásta – is oiriúnach – bheith rannpháirteach insa / tsaol nuamhaisithe.

30 In 'Drámadóir gan traidisiún: staidéar ar thrí dhráma le Seán Ó Tuama' (A playwright without a tradition: a study of three plays by Seán Ó Tuama), Tadhg Ó Dubhshláine offers a very different reading of the play, seeing Mánas as a failed ruler who gets what he deserves and Calbhach as 'a hero of the old kind' (laoch ar an sean nós) who would remind one of Fionn mac Cumhaill (*IMN*, 1971, pp 45–8).

31 Ó Tuama, *Gunna Cam*, p. 47. Pé acu réasúnta tú, a Athair, nó / a mhalairt is follas duitse chomh maith domsa an staid a bhfuil an tír.

32 Ibid., p. 48. Ná feicfir, a Athair Eoghan, nach díon caisleán ná dún ná an iargúlacht / féinig feasta, is a bhfuil d'ordanás / de mhuscaeidí is de ghunnaí nua gan áireamh ag / an Sasanach. 'S ainneoin an tsuaimhnis bhig / atá againne anso ó thuaidh le bliain nó dhó anuas, / gurb é an chríoch a dúrt a bhéarfaidh sinn, / leis, má leanaimid den troid áiféiseach seo.

33 Ibid., pp 48–9. An talamh a ghreamú; deimhin a dhéanamh / nach ar choillte tais Leithbhirr, ná ar réigiúin anaithnide / thar lear a bheidh mo shliochtsa, is sliocht / mo shleachta ag tabhairt a n-aghaidh. Later, in an echo of Michael Collins's stepping stones to freedom defence of the Anglo-Irish Treaty of 1921, Mánas says his compromises will buy his people the time to prepare for war if it becomes necessary (p. 65).

34 His daughter, on the other hand, seems to understand him. See ibid., p. 11.

35 Ibid., p. 57. Bhuel, ní fhéadaim bheith géilliúnach duit. / Is Gearaltach mise, agus bhí fir im chuibhreann tráth. Is nuair / a briseadh iad, is ormsa thit sé ansan / gach pioc den aighneas, den chomhcheilg, a stiúradh i gcoinne Ghrey / is a phaca deamhan; agus is ormsa a thit sé, / leis, an Gearaltach deireannach dá shliocht a chur ar láimh / shábhála. Mar sin, tuigim cad is

troid ann, / cad is fulaing, cad is fuath don namhaid – is ní bhfaighim aon phioc de / ins an áit seo. She has sent her son into the very exile that Mánas hopes to avoid.

36 Ibid. Más striapach mé, is striapach den náisiún seo / mé.

37 Ibid., p. 40. Is eol don bhfuil ionainn le sinsireacht na bearta atá riachtanach dár gcás, is na bearta atá as an tslí ar fad; atá urchóideach. Aithníonn an fhuil a chéile. Aithnírse is aithnímse a chéile . . . ach ní aithníonn ceachtar againn a thuilleadh d'athair. Tá sé imithe as ár n-aithne glan. An beart ar fad atá ar bun aige ní dár gcuidne fola é, is éagóir ó bhonn ina coinne . . . An t-am so, san áit seo, is tusa, a chomharba is a mhac, a chaithfidh, de réir dealraimh, an trasnú a dhéanamh – ar eagla go dtiocfadh sé chun baile dos na Dónallaigh go raibh sé ghlúin acu i ndiaidh a chéile a theip . . . a ghéill . . . a damnaíodh.

38 Ibid., p. 12. B'fhéidir fós, a Chaitríona, / go mbeadh sé le rá againn beirt / go bhfacamar an fear – 's gurb é ár n-athair féin é – is gurb / é ba thúisce de Chinéal Chonaill ar fad / a bhronn a oidhreacht ar an Rí thar lear; is a ghlac mar mhalairt / uirthi slabhra óir.

39 In the original account in the *Annals of the Four Masters*, this weapon seems to have been some kind of artillery piece. See *Annála Rioghachta Éireann/ Annals of the Kingdom of Ireland by the Four Masters, from the Earliest Period to the Year 1616*, vol. 5, ed. and trans. John O'Donovan (Dublin: Hodges, Smith and Co., 1856), p. 1541 (entry for AD 1555).

40 Ibid., p. 31.

41 Ibid., p. 69. An túisce chuireann tusa ort an slabhra / óir, is leis an Rí Tír Chonaill? . . . Is leis de réir dhlí Shasana; ach le fírinne / is leatsa, is liomsa i gcónaí í. Sinne a riarfaidh / dó an dúthaigh.

42 Ibid., p. 77. Ach cuimhníodh gach fear / agaibh go cruinn anois, an guth a thabharfar láithreach, gur guth é / shocróidh an suaimhneas atá romhainn / sa taobh so feasta, nó cogadh tubaisteach dofhulangtha, a scriosfaidh sinn d'uachtar na talún . . . The British prime minister David Lloyd George threatened the Irish delegation at the 1921 Treaty negotiations with 'immediate and terrible war' unless they signed the agreement.

43 Ibid., p. 85. An as do mheabhair atáir?

44 Calbhach himself later accepted the title of Earl of Tír Chonaill under the crown but died before receiving his charter.

45 Ó Tuama, *Gunna Cam*, p. 96. An beart a dheineas, chíonn an croí ionam / gurbh é ab áil lem mhuintir, agus gurbh / é ba chiallmhaire ar fad / . . . Réiteofar go / sibhialta fós an choimhlint seo. Mura ndeinim féin é, / déanfaidh duine éigin eile.

46 It was the first prose work in Irish in which the author's name was given.

47 Seán Ó Tuama, 'Love in the medieval Irish literary lyric', in *Repossessions: Selected Essays on the Irish Literary Heritage* (Cork: Cork University Press, 1995), p. 182.

48 Ó Tuama, *Gunna Cam*, p. 93.

49 Ní sa rud a tharla is mó a spéis, ach sa rud a tharlaíonn. Dar leis go mbíonn ina choimhlint i gcónaí idir bealach an Ghunna agus bealach an tSlabhra: gur minic an réasún agus an chneastacht ina dtacaí ag an Slabhra ach, i gcás an náisiúin seo ach go háirithe, gurb é an dúchas is taca don Ghunna agus, mar sin gurb é is treise faoi dheireadh. Dar leis nach dual géilleadh, ná comh-ghéilleadh féin don Ghael.

50 Alan Titley has called the play 'a palimpsest of our civil war, a subject still touchy enough at the time only to be approached with gingerly caution'. See Alan Titley, '"Neither the boghole nor Berlin": drama in the Irish language from then until now', in *Nailing Theses: Selected Essays* (Belfast: Lagan Press, 2011), p. 269. Ó Tuama was explicit about the parallels between the debates in the play and those about the Civil War and its aftermath that were still being fought out when he was growing up in Cork in the 1930s and 1940s. Speaking of this ongoing argument in his 1984 interview in *Innti*, he stated: 'It was involved with the world of that time, in the thirties and forties. But I had no way to work that out in Irish in a play that would be relevant to the people in the Buildings around me. But when I came on the story of Mánus Ó Domhnaill, how he had to make a compromise and some people did not accept that compromise, I saw that it was the counterpart of what was going on around me' (Bhain sé le saol na linne sin, sna tríochaidí is sna daicheadaí. Ach ní raibh aon tslí agamsa ar é sin a oibriú amach i bhfoirm Ghaeilge i ndráma a bhainfeadh le daoine sna Buildings timpeall orm. Ach nuair a thánag ar scéal Mhánuis Uí Dhomhnaill, conas gur chaith sé féin comhréiteach a dhéanamh is nár ghlac daoine eile leis an gcomhréiteach chonac gurbh é macasamhail an ruda é a bhí ar bun i mo thimpeallacht féin) (*Innti* IX (1984), p. 43).

51 In 1984 he stated that what was essential for the ultimate success of the language revival was 'detailed, patient, thoughtful, political planning within the democratic system' (pleanáil mhion, fhoighneach, thuisceanach, pholaitiúil laistigh den chóras daonlathach) (*Innti* IX (1984), p. 44).

52 It may be worth noting that *The Cork Examiner* reported that 'although Seán Ó Tuama's play "Moloney", presented by the Compántas Chorcaí at the Damer Hall . . . was reviewed with favour by critics, yet it has not succeeded in getting full houses'. Lack of 'adequate advance publicity' was suggested as the reason (*CE*, 4/1/57).

53 Sa chás seo tá sé ar a dhícheall ag ceilt orainn gur sagart é an príosúnach, agus ní féidir leis an

doimhneacht a shaothrú san charachtar in éamais an eolais sin.

54 Seán Ó Tuama, *Moloney: Dráma Aonghnímh* (A one-act play), in *Moloney agus Drámaí Eile* (Moloney and other plays) (Baile Átha Cliath: An Clóchomhar, 1966), p. 5. Ní chuirfeadh éinne a bhfuil aon chiall aige aon lámh go deo ar Oilibhéar Pluincéad, más eiriceach féin é . . . Dob ionann sin agus sacramaint ó neamh chuige á neartú . . . Ar ndóigh níor mhar a chéile an scéal i gcás daoine eile.

55 Ibid., p. 6. Táimse chun fianaise a thabhairt . . . bíodh geall go bhfuilim! Tá corn deas pinginí ann dom, a bhuachaill. Á bhuel . . . do chaithfinn ar aon nós . . . Tá a gcrúcaí ró-cheangailte acu ionam. An dtuigeann tú leat mé? . . . Ina dhiaidh sin, is é an trua é. Is fear simplí é . . . fear ciúin . . .

56 Ibid., pp 7–8. Is fuath liom é. Is fuath liom é. Is fuath le gach cnámh im' cholainn é . . . Is fuath le gach cor dem' anam é . . .

57 Ibid., p. 10. Tá's agat id chroí istigh go ngéillfir dúinn ar deireadh mar dhéanfadh páiste scanraithe. Cad fáth ná géillfeá dhúinn anois agus bheith réidh leis?

58 Ibid., p. 11.

59 Ibid., p. 13. Táimse á rá anois leat ná fuil bun dá laghad agat led' dhóchas. Tá's agam t'aigne; is tá sí imithe ort gan smacht, í titithe ar fad. Ní sheasfaidh sí inár gcoinnibh. Ó Siadhail sees the jailer as symbolising 'the realist part of Moloney's mind' (páirt réadúil d'intinn Moloney) and the whole play as 'an external representation . . . of the conflict in Moloney's mind' (léiriú seachtrach . . . ar an aighneas in aigne Moloney) (*IMN*, 1986, p. 16).

60 Ó Tuama, *Moloney*, pp 14–15. Eagla. Eagla roimh tost. Eagla roimh fothrom. Eagla roimh mo chroí a chloisint ag bualadh. Eagla roimh gan é chloisint. Eagla roimh gach rud . . . Ó is mí-chríostúil an t-ainmhí tú. Cuma leatsa dá bhfaigheadh sé bás gráinniúil gach lá den tseachtain – ach ná beadh sé le rá go raibh aon lámh agatsa ann.

61 Ibid., pp 18–19. Casfaidh chugam mo neart arís in am an ghátair. Ní féidir ná go gcasfaidh. Pé peaca atá orm, pé truailliú a dheinim orm féin, tá seilbh fós agam ar anam atá do-mharfa, is ar an gcreideamh a chorraíonn na sléibhte. Féadaim ach cur chuige míle bás a fhulaingt . . . Caint. Caint. Caint. Nílirse ach id' chaochadh féin anois le ráigí móra baotha cainte, díreach mar do chaochais do choinsias, is do nádúr dhaonna ar fad, i rith na mblian, le ráigí móra baotha meisce.

62 Ibid., p. 19. Ach neosfad duit go cruinn anois an rud is eol duit féinig cheana: gur dhúisís lá amháin, i mbolg geal an lae, is gur phléasc an saol ar fad ó bhonn go firmaimint, in adamh bog leath-lofa amháin ded inchinn . . . Níor leat tú féin a thuilleadh – is do leath brat allais ar do chabhail, is do mhúch an t-eagla do chroí. Is tá an t-eagla sin, is eagla na

heagla sin, id' mhúchadh riamh ó shoin . . . Conas go dtuigeann tusa é seo go léir?

63 Ibid., p. 27. Bhíos ag troid . . . do cheapas . . . ar son mo thíre. The uncertainty here is interesting in comparison with his earlier boasts about his service to Ireland.

64 Ibid., p. 28.

65 In 'Drámadóir gan traidisiún', Tadhg Ó Dubhshláine links Moloney with Judas and Hamlet as tragic victims of despair (*IMN*, 1971, p. 45).

66 See Philip O'Leary, *The Prose Literature of the Gaelic Revival, 1881–1921: Ideology and Innovation* (State College: Pennsylvania State University Press, 1994), pp 216–20; *Gaelic Prose in the Irish Free State 1922–1939* (Dublin: University College Dublin Press, 2004), pp 336–8; and *Irish Interior: Keeping Faith with the Past in Gaelic Prose 1940–1951* (Dublin: University College Dublin Press, 2010), pp 173–4.

67 Donovan regarded this as his favourite of Ó Tuama's plays, telling Vera Ryan that 'I adored playing Sweeney and I adored every moment of the production. It was full of exuberant language and full of colour and has a very important message.' See Ryan, *Dan Donovan*, p. 95.

68 Ní hamháin gur dráma úr nua-cheaptha é seo ach dráma nua-smaointeach nua-theicniúil é i gcleachtadh na ndrámaí i nGaeilge. Do bhain an t-údar feidhm as sean-teicníc stáitse, as nua-theicníc stáitse na bhFrancach, as na sean-scéalta Gaelacha, as smaointe nua na heolaíochta agus iad fite fuaite le saol ró-shibhialta an lae inniu, saghas *surrealistic extravaganza* a chuir sé os ár gcomhair. In a 1975 interview with Gabriel Rosenstock, Seán A. Ó Briain saw Jean Anouilh as the greatest influence on Ó Tuama in this play (*IP*, 19/5/75).

69 Of Donovan in the role of Suibhne, this critic wrote: 'I have never seen him give such a balanced, extravagant, and completely virtuoso performance.' He also felt that 'though even one with little Irish can get the message I feel it's a pity the play isn't translated'.

70 He also played Suibhne (*CS*, 13/2/79). There is a picture of the cast in costume in this same issue of *The Connacht Sentinel*.

71 See O'Leary, *Prose Literature of the Gaelic Revival*, pp 270–3; and *Gaelic Prose in the Irish Free State*, p. 374.

72 Seán Ó Cuimín has drawn attention to parallels between Ionesco's *Rhinocéros* and Ó Tuama's *Ar Aghaidh linn, a Longadáin*. See Seán Ó Cuimín, 'An áiféis agus an teiseachas i ndrámaí Sheáin Uí Thuama' (Absurdity and existentialism in the plays of Seán Ó Tuama), *IMN*, 1988, p. 40.

73 Seán Ó Tuama, *Ar Aghaidh linn, a Longadáin: Extravaganza Cheithre Ghníomh* (Onward, Longadán: an extravaganza in four acts) (Indreabhán: Cló Iar-Chonnachta, 1991), p. 7.

74 Ibid., pp 5 and 7–8. Tosach an dráma á dhéanamh ar luas mearbhaill agus faoi sholas mínádúrtha. Blas phantasmagoria ar gach a dtarlaíonn ó thosach go deireadh . . . labhraíonn formhór na bpearsain – nach geilt iad – chomh tur dáiríre le cléirigh bainc. Such arid and joyless characters also appear in his poems 'Trí Phictiúr dem Namhaid' (Three pictures of my enemy) and 'D'Fhear Aitheantais' (To an acquaintance) in *Saol fó Thoinn* (A world under water) (Baile Átha Cliath: An Clóchomhar, 1978), p. 35.

75 Ó Tuama, *Ar Aghaidh linn, a Longadáin*, p. 12. Caithfidh tú a admháil, gach duine riamh acu a bhearr do chuid gruaige, gur imigh sé ar ceal . . . go hobann.

76 Ibid., pp 10–11. Ní thuigeann tú mé. Ní thuigeann tú cad é a bhraithim. Braithim cáilíocht fásaigh. Fásach a bheadh ag feitheamh go caillte, go hiargúlach, na mílte blian; i bhfad ón bhfás, ón dtórthúlacht. Is go dtosnódh gach gráinne gainimh ann ar crith, ar tinneall, roimis – roimis an bpléasc a bhraitheann sé ag teacht: pléasc mhór ósnádúrtha a réabfaidh an fásach ar fad as a chéile. Go deimhin, gur chuige sin a ceapadh é an chéad lá – chun go ndéanfaí an phléasc san ann . . . An dóigh leat, a chroí, gur chuige sin, a ceapadh fásaigh? . . . Níor mhaith liom a rá go dearfa, a Helen, nárbh ea. Ach de réir na fianaise atá againn, ní chuige sin a ceapadh fásaigh.

77 Ibid., p. 14. Tá leabhar agam 'na thaobh. As Fraincis.

78 Ibid., p. 15. Uaireannta . . . n'fheadar . . . nuair a chuimhním ar Labhra istigh ansan féna chaipín is a mhothall gruaige, ag sailiú a chuid mhéaranna 'na chuid méiseanna beaga cré – is Bláthnaid amuigh anseo, a dualaí gruaige casta go piastúil ar bharr a cinn aici agus í ag déanamh iontais, chomh paisiúnta san, de bholg sleamhain seilmide . . . n'fheadar . . . samhlaím nach in aon tigh ceart nádúrtha atáim.

79 Ibid., p. 18. Ach is fuirist mór-eolaí a aithint ar an bhfásach a fhágann sé gach áit 'na thimpeall. Chonnac do chuid páirceanna díomhaoine is do dhúiche dhólásach ar mo shlí anso, a Loingsigh. Is chím anois do bhean. In Ó Tuama's long poem 'Baoithín a d'Fhill ar Éirinn' (Baoithín who returned to Ireland), Baoithín, a monk from St Colm Cille's famous monastery on the island of Iona, returns to an Ireland strikingly similar to Labhra's blighted realm: 'When I opened my eyes in the glen of my people I saw / men as tall as trees walking. But I did not see / a single tree. The place that used to be so splendid with rich soil, / so green, was now a scree of stones under black sticks of furze . . .' (Nuair d'osclaíos mo shúil i ngleann mo mhuintire chonac uaim / fir chomh hard le crainn ag siúl. Ach ní fhaca / ann aon chrann. An ball a bhíodh chomh binn le méithreas, / chomh glas, 'sé bhí anois ann screalmh cloch / fé dhú-chipíní aitinn . . .). See Seán Ó Tuama,

'Baoithín a d'Fhill ar Éirinn', in *Faoileán na Beatha* (The seagull of life) (Baile Átha Cliath: An Clóchomhar, 1962), p. 42. For a discussion of this poem, see Caoimhín Ó Maoláin, '"Baoithín a d'Fhill": staidéar ar dhán le Seán Ó Tuama' (A study of a poem by Seán Ó Tuama), *IMN*, 1968, pp 71–88.

80 Ó Tuama, *Ar Aghaidh linn, a Longadáin*, p. 20. Tá sí 'na beathaidh! Is bean í seo atá 'na beathaidh. Is mór an náire dhuit í bheith ceangailte ansan agat ar chróchar.

81 Ibid., p. 23. Is rí mé ná creideann puinn sa tíorántacht ná sa taispeántas a chleachtann rithe eile . . . Má thagann duine isteach anso go bagarthach díomhaoin is go mbriseann sé na rialacha a bhaineann le céill is le dea-bhéas, is ná géilleann sé d'aon ordú ciallmhar a thugaimse, an rí, uaim –

82 Ibid. Ansan, a Loingsigh, nochtfaidh tú do chroí eolaí – croí is tíoránaí ar fad ná croí an tíoránaigh: is seasfaidh céad fear armtha ansan os mo chomhair amach. Sea!

83 Ibid., p. 51. Is mó ar fad d'iontas é, munar mhiste leat mé a rá, a Loingsigh, gurb eolaí ar chrainn tusa agus fós ná feaca id ríocht ar fad, ar mo shlí anso dhom, aon chrann amháin gur fiú trácht air – ná puinn eile ach an oiread. Trees are important throughout *Buile Shuibhne* (The frenzy of Suibhne), and Suibhne's poem about the trees of Ireland is one of the literary highlights of the tale.

84 One thinks here of the vivifying effect the heat of the sun has on the speaker in Ó Tuama's poem 'Teas' (Heat) in *Saol fó Thoinn*, p. 36.

85 Ó Tuama, *Ar Aghaidh linn, a Longadáin*, pp 35–6.

86 Ibid., p. 40. Ach anocht braithim saoirse ionam féin. Ligfidh mé anuas mo ghruaig thar gualnaibh orm féin – is déanfaidh mé smidiríní des na gloiní seo. Ná braitheann tú an tsaoirse ag borradh ionam, ag at, am ardú san aer fé mar gur éatroman éadrom dathannach so-phollta mé.

87 Ibid., p. 53. Tá súil agam, a Shuibhne, nach . . . cairde ródhlútha iad seo agat. Gleann na nGealt is 'áit go mbíonn sé ina shamhradh i gcónaí, áit ná bíonn dlíodóirí ag áiteamh orm eagar a chur ar dhlíthe na tíre, áit ná bíonn lucht gramadaí ag ceartú mo chuid dánta'.

88 Ibid., pp 58–67.

89 Ibid., pp 74–5. Mar go bhfuilim éirithe tuirseach den saol anso. Saol na cúirte is aoibhinn é agus is compordach – tamall. Ach gan mhoill éiríonn sé leamh, cúngraithe; éiríonn fuar-bholadh ós na cathaoireacha, na toilg, na daoine. Braithim uaim na coillte, na feithidí, an fhairsingeacht, an chumhracht. Is caithfidh mé an chúirt seo a fhágaint láithreach, díreach mar fhágas mo chúirt féin tráth.

90 Ibid., p. 76.

91 Ibid.

92 Ibid., p. 82. Táim tuirseach de bheith pléisiúrtha. Táim tuirseach de bheith ag féachaint ar an Eolaí. Táim tuirseach de bheith ag éisteacht leis

an Eolaí. Sa tigh seo is gach áit dá dtéim. É ag ceapadh dlíthe, é ag ceartú dánta, é ag nochtadh tuairimí, ag leagadh amach polasaí. Ba chuma liom dá bhfanadh sé ar leataoibh go socair ag déanamh a chuid oibre – ach sé deireadh an tsaoil é nuair a tugtar cead don té nach báidh lena chroí go fírinneach ach rud amháin ar domhan – polasaí a bheith aige.

93 Ibid., p. 72. Nuair ná bíonn tú liom, ní fhéadaim aon ghreim a choimeád ort. Ní fhéadaim tú shamhlú, fiú amháin. Tánn tú ró-mhór dom.

94 Ibid., p. 95. Beidh uaigneas mór oraibh tamall, b'fhéidir . . . is 'na dhiaidh san ní bheidh oraibh ach uaigneas beag – díreach mar a bheadh ar dhuine taréis taibhrimh aoibhinn. Ach níl éinne agaibh nár bhain tairbhe as mo chuairt 'n bhur measc, is níl éinne agaibh ná bainfidh breis suilt feasta as bhur gcaidreamh ar a chéile.

95 His own magical bee vanishes from the play after its initial appearance.

96 Ó Tuama, *Ar Aghaidh linn, a Longadáin*, p. 96. Mar tá an saol so lán fós d'áilleacht is d'iontaisí. Agus gairim chugainn sa ród tá romhainn beacha is colúir bhána, fuiseoga is snaga is ceann cait is peidhleacáin . . . ceólta ón ndeisceart is ón dtuaisceart, ceólta ón Oirthear is ón Iarthar, – is ceólta nár cloiseadh fós sa spéir ná ar thalamh!

97 See Gary Snyder, *The Practice of the Wild: Essays by Gary Snyder* (San Francisco: North Point Press, 1990).

98 In a brief note just before the production, *Inniu* called it 'a kind of pantomime' (cineál geamaireachta) (*Inniu*, 15/9/61).

99 In a piece in the same paper a week earlier, we read that 'a new group of singers are rehearsing songs, ranging from Irish ballads to Negro spirituals and new compositions for a production about St. Patrick to be presented by Gael-Linn at the Damer next week' (*IP*, 13/9/61).

100 Tá Pádraig thuas ins na Flaithis agus tá na naoimh uile bréan de bheith ag éisteacht len a shíorsheanchas fén a theacht go hÉirinn agus an saothar a rinne sé ann. Ag an am chéanna tá éadóchas is míshástacht ag borradh sa naomh féin toisc go bhfuil muintir na hÉireann ag déanamh faillí ina naomh-phátrún, ní ghuíonn siad chuige a thuilleadh agus tá meas níos mó aca anois ar Cholm Cille is ar an bhfear nua so Máirtín de Porres. Mar sin, shocraíonn Pádraig ar filleadh ar Éirinn díreach in am don fhéile ag comóradh a bháis.

101 He did, however, pronounce it 'a very interesting attempt' (iarracht an-suimiúil).

102 Feictear dom gur chuaigh an iarracht in aimréidh áit éigin idir scriopt is stiúrú . . . N'fheadar cathain a tharla an scoilt idir údar agus stiúrthóir, ach is ró-shoiléir é ón seó seo nach raibh siad i gcomhar lena chéile sa léiriú. Ag pointe éigin chítear dom gur dhírigh an stiúrthóir ar pageant a dhéanamh

in áit aoire agus dá bharr sin tá dhá stíl le breathnú sa léiriú, dhá stíl atá i ngleic an oíche go léir.

103 Ach is eagal liom gur tharla sciorradh de shaghas éigin idir bunscript Uí Thuama . . . agus an rud a cuireadh romhainn. Ní raibh téagar ná substaint shásúil ag baint leis an siamsa ina iomláine agus bhraitheas breis de bhlas Gheamaireacht na Mainistreach air (rud atá ceart go leor ina áit féin – sa Mhainistir) . . . Ní fhéadfainn gan teacht ar an tuairim nach raibh comhoibriú ceart idir an scríbhneoir agus an léiritheoir. The reference to the Abbey was obviously a dig at Mac Anna.

104 Ba mhaith liom a mhíniú, áfach, gur beag an bhaint a bhí ag an script a chuireas-sa isteach leis an ní a bhí ar stáitse an Damer. Fágadh mórchuid dí ar lár; athraíodh mórchuid eile; cuireadh isteach míreanna nua, caractéirí nua. Sa tslí gur loiteadh bun-bhrí na scripte. Agus é seo go léir gan mo chead, ná mo chomhairle.

105 Asked in his 1984 interview in *Innti* about his setting several of his plays 'back in time' (siar san am), Ó Tuama responded: 'I felt that things could be set up in a far more natural way back in time than to have them going on in Cork city in the present. That the language would better serve historical events' (Bhraitheas go mb'fhéidir nithe a chur ar bun ar shlí i bhfad níos nádúrtha siar san am ná iad a bheith ar siúl i gcathair Chorcaí i láthair na huaire. Go bhfreastalódh an teanga níos fearr ar eachtraí stairiúla) (*Innti* IX (1984), p. 41).

106 Leis an dráma seo . . . tagann an drámaíocht sa Ghaeilge chun lánaoise nó mar adéarfá as Béarla, dráma 'adult' is ea é.

107 Ní cuimhin liom aon dráma ó *Death of a Salesman* anall a bhíogadh chun machnaimh nó chum athmhachnaimh duine mar bhíog an dráma seo (ach b'fhéidir *A Whistle in the Dark*). Tadhg Ó Muirighthe wrote of the play: 'If I were only to mention "Sé Seo m'Oileán" by Seán Ó Tuama, I would say it would be a good play in any language at all' (Mura luafainn ach 'Sé Seo m'Oileán' le Seán Ó Tuama, déarfainn go mbeadh sé ina dhráma maith i dteanga ar bith) (*IP*, 13/9/63).

108 Is fada é ó sgríobhadh dráma Gaeilge chomh suimiúil agus chomh conspóideach le "Sé Seo M'Oileán" le Seán Ó Tuama . . . Is dráma daonna é seo, agus déanann an túdar a lán-dhícheall le fírinne a chur ar an scéal. Éiríonn leis é sin a dhéanamh go cneasta.

109 Of this production, an anonymous contributor to the *Irish Independent* wrote that Frank Dermody, serving as an Oireachtas adjudicator, had stated that 'the production . . . had failed through being too static, and through lacking the element of mimicry which must form the basis of the portrayal of character on the stage'. Dermody, did, however, praise the work of some of the actors (*II*, 3/4/68).

110 Ó Siadhail, 'Drámaí Sheáin Uí Thuama', *IMN*, 1986, p. 41, n. 65.

111 Seán Ó Tuama, *Is É Seo M'Oileán: Trí Ghníomh* (This is my island: three acts), in *Moloney agus Drámaí Eile*, p. 34.

112 Ibid., p. 44. Níl ann ach go mbraithim ar ócáidí mar seo go bhfuil Gorta Mór éigin ar siúl sa tír seo fós – amuigh ansin in áit éigin.

113 Ó Siadhail argues that Breandán's role as the 'antihero' (frithlaoch) in this play is similar to that of Suibhne in *Ar Aghaidh linn, a Longadáin*, but Breandán has none of Suibhne's rambunctious charm (*IMN*, 1986, p. 24).

114 Ó Tuama, *Is É Seo M'Oileán*, p. 55. See also p. 47.

115 Ibid., p. 57. An iomad céille atá againn go léir. Marach sin bheadh crích éigin orainn.

116 Ibid., p. 58.

117 Ibid., p. 61. Ní haon mhaith a bheith d'iarraidh bheith 'leathan-aigeanta' – mar dhea – i gcás mar seo. Sé fírinne an scéil, aon phósadh nach Caitliceach ach duine amháin den mbeirt, ná bíonn aon rath ná suaimhneas . . .

118 Ibid.

119 We are given very little evidence in the play that there is any basis for this self-image.

120 Ó Tuama, *Is É Seo M'Oileán*, p. 84. Sea is dócha gur chóir go mbeadh . . . Is dócha, fiú amháin, go mbíonn . . . Ach is fear díreach ar fad é ar a shlí féin. Caithfidh mé a rá nár bhraitheas riamh chomh héadrom, chomh sábhálta, chomh scartha le lucht seanmóna, agus a bhraitheas na sé laethanta gréine a thugamar ar oileán na Corsaice. She does not actually know whether she loves him (p. 85).

121 Ibid., p. 95. Ach tá an bua sin ag na mná, fulang. Gach rud iompair: leanaí, trioblóid. Is cuimhin liom fós mo mháthair, suite síos cois leapan in ospidéal, is í ag glanadh fola de bhéal do dhearthár-se, is é ag fáil bháis. Is chuige sin a deineadh sinn.

122 Ibid., p. 96. Díomá! Is breá dhuitse a bheith ag caint ar dhíomá! Cé chuir scamall ar gach rud riamh san tigh seo? Cé chuir an bac seo agus an bac siúd ar mo mháthair féin, gur imigh an t-anam go léir is an spionnadh aisti? Ad' iarraidh mo phósadh a stop mar a stopais pósadh Chaitlín fadó. Ad' iarraidh mo spioraid a bhriseadh mar a bhris a spioraid sin . . .

123 In the script as we have it, Síle's child is now two years old. In the original production, she was apparently pregnant with the child. See Ó Siadhail, 'Drámaí Sheáin Uí Thuama', *IMN*, 1986, p. 27 and 41, n. 65.

124 For some reason Ó Tuama never reveals the baby's gender.

125 Ó Tuama, *Is É Seo M'Oileán*, p. 72. B'fhéidir gur duine den tseana-shaol mé ach creidim fós i bpeacaí. Is aon bhean a dheineann an drúis ní bean chreidiúnach í. Sin a bhfuil . . . Má fhanann sí anseo is cinnte go ndéanfaidh sé dochar don tigh, dúinn go léir, is dá n-abrainn é, dom' chúrsaí gnótha-sa. For Breandán's attitude to this situation, see pp 76–7.

126 Ibid., p. 102. Focal amháin eile. Focal beag amháin eile. Éist leis. Go cúramach. Má choimeádann tusa Síle anseo . . . ar na coinníollacha a luas . . . ní dhéanfadsa Breandán Jennings a phósadh . . . Maith go leor. Is fear gnótha mé. Is margadh maith é sin, dar liom. Maith go leor 'Áine – glacaim led' thairiscint . . . Ach chun méid mo shástachta a chur in iúl, táim ullamh, go pearsanta, ar fhéachaint i ndiaidh pé costaisí a bhainfidh le hoiliúint an linbh.

127 Ibid., p. 103. D'imigh mo neart uaim. Tuigeadh dom go soiléir . . . pé ní a chreidim im' chroí is cóir dom a dhéanamh . . . go mbeadh buairt orm go lá mo bháis, dá ndéanfainn é. Oiread is a bheadh ar mo mháthair féin dá mairfeadh sí . . . Thógfadh sé blianta fada ormsa anois . . . liom féin . . . sara n-éireodh liom tosnú fiú amháin ar an gcás ina bhfuilim a thuiscint.

128 Ibid., p. 104. An tseachtain seo chugainn fiú amháin . . . b'fhéidir go rachainn ag rince. Tosnód . . . ag cuardach arís. Ach ní bheidh sé furasta agam feasta. Agus muna n-éiríonn liom, b'fhéidir go mbeadh ana-áthas orainn fós . . . i rith laethanta saoire an tSamhraidh . . . leanbh tabhartha Shíle a bheith sa tigh seo againn . . . Tá sí nach mór ag gol arís le searbhas agus díomá . . . Feictear don gcéad uair gur seanduine tuirseach é Máirtín Ó hAnnracháin.

129 Seán Ó Tuama, 'Samuel Beckett, Éireannach' (Irishman), *Scríobh* III (1978), pp 37–41. See also his poem 'Godot', in *Saol fó Thoinn*, p. 14.

130 Pádraig Ó Siadhail sees Harold Pinter's *The Birthday Party* (1957) and especially N. F. Simpson's *One Way Pendulum* (1959) as influences on *Corp Eoghain Uí Shúilleabháin* (*IMN*, 1986, p. 29). Seán Ó Cuimín suggests Brecht's *Das Elephantkalb* as another influence (*IMN*, 1988, p. 44). See also his brief discussion of Ó Tuama's use of Brechtian *Verfremdungseffekt* (distancing or alienation effect) in the play (p. 47). Ó Siadhail argues convincingly, however, that Ó Tuama never shared the philosophy of the absurdists and that as a result 'it is difficult not to say that what we have here is just a clever imitation of "l'absurde," although it is an accomplished imitation' (is deacair gan a rá nach bhfuil againn anseo ach aithris chleasach ar 'l'absurde', cé gur aithrios shnasta atá ann) (*IMN*, 1986, p. 32). It is also, of course, a theatrically effective one.

131 He had been told 'go bhfuil cur amach ana-shuimiúil ag Seán Ó Ceallaigh i mbun léirithe dhráma Uí Thuama ar conas ba cheart tabhairt faoin dráma. Ní dráma é "Corp Eoghain Uí Shúilleabháin" go dtugann mórán cumann faoi. N'fheadar an í treoir Bhecketiúil Uí Thuama a chuireann léiritheoirí ó dhoras nó a imeaglaíonn iad.'

132 There is a picture from the production in this same issue of *The Connacht Tribune*.

133 Seán Ó Tuama, *Corp Eoghain Uí Shúilleabháin: Dhá Ghníomh agus Dhá Eadarlúid* (The corpse of Eoghan Ó Súilleabháin: two acts and two interludes),

in *Moloney agus Drámaí Eile*, p. 107. Moltar léiriú dá réir sin a dhéanamh ar thrí phríomh-mhír an dráma.
134 Ibid. See Ó Siadhail, 'Drámaí Sheáin Uí Thuama', *IMN*, 1986, p. 30.
135 Ó Tuama, *Corp Eoghain Uí Shúilleabháin*, p. 107. Níl ach pearsa bheo amháin sa dráma seo: Eoghan Ó Súilleabháin fíle.
136 Ibid., pp 115–16.
137 Ibid., p. 119.
138 Donncha Ó Cróinín, Donncha Ó Céileachair, and Micheál Ó hAodha. The great scholar Osborn Bergin is alluded to in the name of the hospital – Bergin's Hospital.
139 Ó Tuama, *Corp Eoghain Uí Shúilleabháin*, p.127. Corpáin síos is suas an staighre, corpáin ag caint. Stocaí, scapulars. Ba dhóigh le héinne gur istigh i dtigh na ngealt a bhíomar.
140 Ibid., p. 133. Solas geal, geal, aisteach agus dathanna bána i ngach áit . . . Gach caint is gach gluaiseacht a deintear is geall sin le aithris ar na sean-scannáin 'tostacha;' gach gníomh tapaidh, áibhéileach, scinneadach, stacatto. One recalls Beckett's fondness for silent comedies here.
141 Ibid., p. 134. Is é an trua é ná raibh coinníollacha na tire inniu oiriúnach dá leithéid. Dá dtiocfadh sé i gcionn céad bliain eile, abair, chloisfí trácht air ar fuid an domhain.
142 Ibid. Ní gá mórán éirim aigne, dáiríribh, chun filíocht a scríobhadh.
143 Ibid., p. 137. Éiríonn na Páirtithe arís is ritheann ina dhiaidh timpeall an chónra, timpeall an tseomra, timpeall an tsagairt. Radharc as na Marx Brothers.
144 Ibid., p. 140.
145 Ibid., p. 141. Cheap sé gur sórt Mozart é féin go rithfeadh gach ní álainn leis gan aon trioblóid.
146 Ibid. Ní raibh éinne riamh sa tír seo a bhain cáil amach in aon ní, ná raibh dearthair aige a b'fhearr ná é – ach gur imigh sé le sagartóireacht.
147 Ibid., p. 145.
148 As Ó Siadhail points out, however, their marriage has hardly been a success, with Eoghan stating that in effect it had died four years earlier 'and I have not been alive since' (agus ní rabhas feasta im' bheathaidh) (*IMN*, 1986, p. 28). Indeed Ó Siadhail stresses that marriages are almost invariably sterile and constricting relationships in Ó Tuama's plays.
149 Ó Tuama, *Corp Eoghain Uí Shúilleabháin*, p. 146. Dá maireadh mo bhuachaillí . . . ní scaoilfinn leabhar nó peann ina lámhaibh go deo. Dhéanfainn . . . is dóigh liom . . . sea, dhéanfainn cócairí díobh . . . *chefs* i dtigh ósta den chéad ghrád.
150 Ibid., p. 151. D'fhéadfaí bliain a chaitheamh ina theannta, lá i ndiaidh lae, neomat i ndiaidh neomaite, agus is ag . . . éadromú a bheadh t'aigne . . . Ní thuigim faic. Faic. Faic. Cara dhom féin, an cara is dílse a bhí riamh agam . . . Cár rugadh é, cár

tógadh é, cár chuaigh sé ar scoil, cathain a pósadh é. . . ní fios. Ní fios go cruinn. Ar maraíodh é? Ní fios. A Bhean Uí Shúilleabháin, cá bhfios domsa an bhfuair sé bás in aon chor?
151 Ibid. Féach, a Bhean Uí Shúilleabháin, éinne ná caitheann saol socair, cuíosach seasamhach, ná bíonn eolas cruinn ar cár rugadh é, cár tógadh é, cad iad na postanna a bhí aige – má dúnmharaítear an duine sin, ní féidir leis a bheith ag súil go ndéanfadh mo leithéidse an cás a réiteach.
152 Ibid., p. 154. Gluaiseann an bheirt timpeall i bhfáinne mar a bheadh ballet ar siúl acu; go mall ar dtúis, ansin luathaíonn siad. Cuireann siad fearaistí 'bréige' áirithe ina seasamh, mar a bheadh i ndrámaí simplí Síneacha – tor, falla, fógra, etc.
153 Ibid., p. 155. Toisc ná fuil na háiteanna is áille ach trí mhíle ó bhaile. Tá sé sáite in aigne an chléirigh bhainc, a chroí, go gcaithfear an corp agus an aigne a thraochadh chun teacht ar an áilleacht agus ar an suaimhneas . . . Agus ansin, ar ndóigh, tá gluaisteán ag gach duine acu. Agus ní mór dóibh iad d'úsáid chun gurbh fhéidir leo trácht a dhéanamh ar an árdú mór atá tagaithe ar an gcostas maireachtana.
154 Ibid., p. 158. An túisce a bhíonn filíocht déanta agat den saol ar fad, satlaíonn tú uirthi. An túisce a bhíonn rud ina steillebheathaidh agat, maraíonn tú é.
155 Ibid., p. 163. Is fada ó chualamar aon chaint chomh baoth ná chomh hamaideach ná chomh damnaitheach.
156 Ibid. Cheapais-se, le mórchúis, a Eoghain Uí Shúilleabháin, go bhféadfá rialacha faoi leith a cheapadh dhuit féin. Theastaigh uait pléisiúr a bheith agat, ach gan aon fhreagracht a bheith ort. Theastaigh grá uait, ach ní rabhais sásta ar nós gach éinne eile dua a chaitheamh len é a shaothrú agus len é a cheansú.
157 Ibid., p. 164. Ag labhairt ar son an phobail dom cuirim é seo mar phionós ort: go leaghfá – láithreach – as ár radharc, go n-imeófá ar ceal, is ná feicfí arís tú, ná do leithéid ar dhroim an domhain . . . Pé cosaint a dhéanfá ort féin, tá fhios ag cách ná féadfadh aon phobal daoine seasamh mar atáid, dá scaoilfí led' leithéid-se . . . Ach b'fhéidir nár chóir dóibh seasamh mar atáid.
158 Ibid., p. 169. Bhí a fhios agam gur mó an sólás a bheadh agam i dteannta chorp Eoghain sara lobhfadh sé, ná mar a bheadh agam i dteannta a bhfuil agam de dhaoine beo ar m'aithne . . . A Íosult, ní fhaca mé riamh éinne chomh maith le hEoghan Ó Súilleabháin chun tranglam buile a dhéanamh den saol ar fad. Ní foláir ná mairfidh a chuid filíochta go deo.
159 T. S. Eliot, 'Little Gidding', in *Four Quartets* (NewYork: Harcourt, Brace andWorld, 1971 [1943]), p. 51.
160 Ó Tuama, *Corp Eoghain Uí Shúilleabháin*, p. 126. Bhí an iomarca ólta aige.

161 Ibid., p. 130.

162 Ibid., p. 164.

163 There is a picture from the production on the front page of *Inniu*, 13/10/67.

164 Má bhí an halla féin brúite leo ní foláir nó bhí roinnt mhaith eile díobh nár éirigh leo dul isteach ar chor ar bith.

165 Is deacair domsa géilleadh go hiomlán do na caractéirí a rianaíonn an Tuamach sa dráma seo. Braithim easnamh orthu agus folús éigin a thugann le tuiscint dom ná fuilid fíor amach is amach. There is a picture of a scene from the play in *The Irish Press*, 3/10/67.

166 Dá mba dráma Béarla é is cinnte go mbeadh i bhfad níos mó cainte faoi – bheadh sé 'conspóideach' agus ina ábhar cainte ag lucht an 'Late Late Show' agus na páipéir tráthnóna.

167 This production has been inadvertently omitted from the list of Taibhdhearc productions in Pádraig Ó Siadhail's *Stair Dhrámaíocht na Gaeilge 1900–1970* (A history of theatre in Irish 1900–1970) (Indreabhán: Cló Iar-Chonnachta, 1993).

168 Seán Ó Tuama, *Iúdás Iscariot agus a Bhean* (Judas Iscariot and his wife), p. 22. The play has not been published. I am working here with the typescript made available by An Comhlachas Náisiúnta Drámaíochta. Bhí an iomarca taithí agamsa riamh ar aislingí móra . . . aislingí de ghrá síoraí . . . ionnas go mb'fhiú a bheith beo. Tá sé ró-dhéanach . . . anois . . .

169 Ibid., p. 3.

170 Ibid., p. 6. Fuair sé bás. Agus níor éirigh sé arís. Níl ansin ach fabhal-scéal ná cloisfeá in aon áit ach in Éirinn na laethanta seo.

171 Ibid., p. 13. Féach, Denise, is fíor go dteastaíonn an post seo go mór uaim. Ach ina ainneoin sin, caithfidh mé an méid seo a rá leat glan amach. Má toghtar mise mar léiritheoir anseo, nílim chun aon dráma gan mhaith a chur ar an stáitse anseo. Ná drámaí leathchuíosacha féin, dá n-abrainn é – pé rud adeir an Bord Stiúrtha.

172 Ibid., p. 14. Tony says he likes and respects Louis.

173 Ibid., pp 14–15. Dá mba dhuine den tsórt sin mé, níorbh fhiú liom maireachtaint . . . Agus maidir led' phost mar léiritheoir is féidir leat anois é sháthadh suas i bpoll do thóna. Basing his opinion on Tony's thinking in scenes like this, Seán Ó Cuimín regards *Iúdás Iscariot agus a Bhean* as inspired by the existentialists, most notably Albert Camus. See Ó Cuimín, 'An áiféis agus an teiseachas', *IMN*, 1988, p. 51.

174 Ó Tuama, *Iúdás agus a Bhean*, p. 7.

175 Ibid., p. 8. Tony: An dtiocfá abhaile liom anocht? Colette (Gan ach an stad is lú a bhaint aisti): Tiocfad. Tony: Codlóidh tú liom? Colette: Codlód . . . Seo leat. Go tapaidh. Sara bhfaighim seans ar m'aigne athrú. (Stopann) Ó . . . féach. An mbeidh gach rud i gceart, má théim leat? Tony: Beidh.

176 Ibid., pp 10–11. Colette, nuair a fhéachas ort aréir ag amhránaíocht . . . thosnaigh an fhuil istigh ionam ag beiriú. Don chéad uair riamh im shaol, d'aithin an fhuil ionam an fhuil istigh i nduine éigin eile . . . Bíodh léas éigin céille agat, Tony. Ní haon aingeal mé (Beagán an-bheag feirge uirthi ba dhóigh leat).

177 Ibid., p. 18. Bhí sé ceart agat glacadh leis an gcuireadh uaithi go dtína fleait! Fanacht seachtain ann dá mba ghá é. Aon ní ach an job a bhaint amach . . . Ach caithfidh mé seans a fháil ar rud éigin a dhéanamh . . . a thabharfaidh sásamh buan dom . . . Colette, dá bhféadfainn bheith cinnte go mbeadh an bheirt againne . . . buan, bheinn sásta. Ba leor san . . . Ó Tony, Tony, tá tú chomh simplí. Ach tá tú go hálainn. Níor bhuail mé riamh le héinne eile ded shórt.

178 Ibid., pp 25–6. Tony, Tony, a chroí, creid mé, creid mé. Nílimse ad thréigint. Beidh mé arais arís chugat laistigh de choicíos cinnte . . . Thiarna, nuair chuimhním air tánn tú nach mó dhá uair chomh haosta liom . . . Ná habair é sin. Bíonn míle seans ag gach duine . . . D'fhéadfaimís dul ar ragairne istoíche anocht . . . Ó Tony, caithfidh tú ól im theannta anocht.

179 She later tells Tony that one of the things that draws her back to her old lover is that 'Dónal and I belong to the same generation of people. We understand each other' (bainim féin agus Dónal leis an nglúin chéanna daoine. Tuigimíd a chéile) (ibid., p. 30).

180 Ibid., p. 29. Mar tá fhios agamsa go maith agus tá fhios agatsa, go bhfuil gach éinne ina aonar, ná tuigeann éinne éinne eile, ná fuil éinne i ngrá le héinne eile, ná fuilim-se i ngrá leatsa, ná tusa liomsa, ná Dónal leatsa. Ná fuilimid ar fad ach ag ligint orainn.

181 Ibid., p. 31. Bíonn tú ag súil fós leis an ngrá mór rómánsúil, – le Dia, – le creideamh a mhairfidh go deo . . . Tá na caighdeáin ró-ard agat.

182 Ibid. Cad tá sa saol? Teacht slán, is dócha. Teacht slán chomh fada agus is féidir . . . Tiocfaidh tusa slán leis, Tony. Cuireann daoine nithe míle uair níos measa ná é seo díobh . . . Sin é an saol mar a thuig aborigines an domhain é. Sin é an saol mar ná fuilim-se sásta é chaitheamh. Más é sin an saol atá uaitse, bíodh agat. Ach imigh leat sa diail agus caith é, agus lig domhsa!

183 Ibid., p. 32. Is mór an faoiseamh nach ann Dia. / Raghaimís as ár gcéill / Le hiomarca de'n fhírinne is de'n mhacántacht . . . Coimeádfaidh siad an seó ar siúl. / Fiú má thiteann / Gach aisteoir sa chathair / Marbh.

184 Ibid., p. 35.

185 Ibid., p. 38.

186 Ibid. Caithfidh mé a admháil nuair a léas an méid a bhí scríte aige, dúras liom féin 'Tá sé seo chomh gar do'm fhírinne. D'fhéadfadh sé bheith fíor.' Sin an difríocht idir Tony agus an chuid eile.

187 Ibid.

188 Ibid., p. 43.

189 Ibid., p. 46. An dóigh leatsa, Louis, arbh fhear misniúil é Iúdas? . . . Cuimhnigh ná fuil ann ar deireadh [ach] dráma. Dráma b'fhéidir ná fuil ró-mhaith féin . . . Sos cúpla mí a thógaint agus beidh gach rud i gceart arís. Ní fhéachfaidh aon rud leath chomh tábhachtach is a fheiceann sé anois.

190 Ibid., p. 48. Dá mba mise gheobhadh an post sin, mise a bheadh ag caitheamh an fheistis bhréige seo, agus a bheadh ag caint ar nós Ard Mhéara. In ainm Dé, a Pheadair, caith anuas díot na héadaí sin, agus ná bí ag déanamh fear siorcais díot féin ar fad. In the play Judas feels that Peter has cheated him out of leadership of the apostles as Tony feels that Louis cheated him out of the directorship.

191 Ibid. D'fhéadfainn leabhar a líonadh leis na neithe áille a dúirt sé agus a dhein sé . . . Dob ionann bheith i dteannta Chríost is bheith ar mí na meala sa tsíoraíocht . . . Abair leo éinní is maith leat. Ach ná habair leo go bhfuil cathú orm . . . Mar níl aon chathú ormsa gur shéanas Críost. An fear a bhuailfeadh bob chomh damanta sin . . .

192 Ibid., p. 51. Agus deir tú liom gurb É An Messiah féin a d'inis an méid seo duit? . . . A Rí na Cruinne. Más fíor é sin – . . . D'fhanas, is ní fhaca. Ní fhaca ar deireadh ach duine ar mo chuma féin go mbíodh tart air is ocras, fear go ngortaíodh na deilgne a chosa . . . Creidim dáiríribh, Mhagdalen, nárbh eol dó fhéin an fhírinne agus scoilt a chroí ar an gcrois. Bhí sé ag súil go deireadh go mb'fhéidir gurb é féin an Messiah . . .

193 Ibid. Caithfidh duine éigin an fhírinne a insint . . . Agus is coirpeach cruaidh do-chorraithe tusa, Iúdáis Iscariot.

194 Ibid., p. 52. Ní gá an bualadh bas. Ní gá an bualadh bas . . . Is breá libh duine éigin á chur féin chun báis. O is breá. Tánn sibh chomh sásta libh féin. Chomh damanta sásta. Ach ní dhéanfadh éinne agaibh féin go deo é . . . Ach fós is maith libh i gcónaí Iúdás éigin a bheith á chur féin chun báis ar bhur son. Is cuí agus is cóir go bhfaigheadh duine amháin bás ar son an phobail. A Chríost!

195 Ibid., pp 53–4. Níl. Ach admhaím é. Admhaím é. Ach ba mhaith liom go mbeadh. Ba mhaith liom –

196 Ó Cuimín reminds us of Camus's statement 'Il n'ya qu'un problème philosophique vraiment sérieux: c'est le suicide' (There is only one truly serious philosophic question: suicide) (*IMN*, 1988, p. 56).

197 Dominic O'Riordan found the principal characters in the play 'cardboard' (*IT*, 4/10/67). Pádraig Ó Siadhail has written that Ó Tuama's Judas is not 'a developed person' (pearsa fhorbartha) because 'in the final analysis, he is just a device to make clear Judas's crisis' (ar deireadh thiar thall, níl ann ach uirlis chun aincheist Iúdáis a shoiléiriú) (*IMN*, 1986, p. 34).

198 Ó Tuama's use in the play of the song 'Do Bhí Bean Uasal' (There was a noblewoman), also known as 'Carrickfergus', is clearly ironic.

199 Ó Siadhail writes of Ó Tuama, 'he fails to present us with a credible comparison between Tony and Judas, and fails to portray the two in sufficient depth' (téann de comparáid inchreidte idir Tony agus Iúdás a chur os ár gcomhair, is teipeann air an bheirt a tharraingt go sách doimhin). For Ó Siadhail, the main problem with Tony as a character, one 'that ruins the whole work' (a scriosann an saothar iomlán), is 'that we do not see, despite all that Ó Tuama has done, that Judas and Tony are alike, for the two dilemmas are not alike' (nach bhfeicimid, in ainneoin a bhfuil déanta ag Ó Tuama, gurb ionann Iúdás agus Tony, mar ní hionann an dá aincheist) (*IMN*, 1986, pp 35–6). See also Ó Cuimín, 'An áiféis agus an teiseachas', *IMN*, 1988, p. 57.

200 See, for example, Seán Ó Tuama, *Déan Trócaire ar Shagairt Óga* (Have mercy on young priests), pp 5–6 and 22. The play has not been published. I am working here with the typescript made available by An Comhlachas Náisiúnta Drámaíochta.

201 Úsáideann an t-údar an teicníocht a bhí ag Brian Friel i 'Philadelphia Here I Come.' Léirítear an sagart mar phearsain dúbalta trí dhá charactéar, Dermot Crowley agus a choinsias.

202 Ó Tuama, *Déan Trócaire ar Shagairt Óga*, p. 2. Ní rabhas ach sé seachtaine fillte abhaile an uair seo. Taréis mo thréimhse i Swansea, is beag a cheapas gur i mbosca beag faoistine sa Ghaeltacht a bhainfí an leagadh is mó riamh asam. Is dócha go gcaithfeadh rud éigin mar seo a thitim amach dom uair éigin i rith mo shaoil . . . ach nuair fhéachaim siar anois air féachann sé go léir beagán dochreite . . . rud éigin a tharlódh i dtír i bhfad i gcéin . . .

203 Ibid., p. 3. Ní dhéanfaidh mé 'athair. Beidh gach ní go breá anois. Tá sé inste agam duitse . . . agus do Dhia, chomh maith.

204 Ibid., p. 8. Tá sé leachta ar fad ar leanaí óga.

205 Ibid., p. 9. Nuair a chonac mé féin arís ag leagadh lámh chomh ceanúil sin ar ghualainn ar Bhrian, caithfidh mé a rá gur baineadh preab asam . . . Bheartaíos go gcaithfinn luí isteach ar mo chuid oibre sóisialach: an club a bhunú, an lá a líonadh.

206 Ibid., p. 12. He says 'go mbeadh cailíní agus sciortaí gearra orthu ag promsáil ar fud an halla gach oíche, rith na háite fúthu féin, iad ag gabháil amach leis na buachaillí go tigh Connor ag ól *gins* –'

207 Ibid. Sea, ach cad fé ndeara don gcuid acu a fhanann anso a bheith iompaithe amach ina leath-dhaoine mí-nádúrtha?

208 Ibid. Tá sé ró-dhéanach, 'athair, don mbóthar idir-eatarthu.

209 Ibid., p. 16. Ní déarfainn go bhfuil an cailín ann a bheadh sásta liomsa, agus mise léi-sin, agus mar bharr ar an scéal í sin bheith sásta chomh maith mo mháthair-se a thógaint mar ualach uirthi féin.

210 Ibid. Bhíos chomh trí chéile gur chuimhníos tamall gur ag cumadóireacht a bhí sé nuair a inis sé a scéal dom sa bhfaoisdin. Ach nuair a chuas siar im

aigne air gach a ndúirt sé liom an uair sin bhí fhios agam nárbh fhéidir sin a bheith . . . Maidin Dé Domhnaigh nuair a chonac an taxi ag imeacht arís is beag nár thit mo chroí as mo chléibh.

211 Ibid. Bhuel, a Ghearóid, tá's agat féin an dlí . . . Faoi phéin pheaca maraitheach ní féidir ar aon chúis ar domhan séala na faoisdine a bhriseadh.

212 Ibid., p. 18. He says 'go measaim go bhfuil rud ann is bunúsaí ná aon dlí ná aon údarás . . . Do choinsias féin . . . Sa tslí má thagann an t-am go deo go ndeireann a choinsias le sagart gur chóir dó rún faoisdine a scaoileadh, ansan creidimse, ní hamháin go bhfuil sé ceadaithe aige, ach go bhfuil sé ceangailte air de réir dlí Dé, an rún sin a scaoileadh'.

213 Ibid., p. 22. Ach níor phósais-se ach an oiread, 'Athair.

214 An tAthair Tomás also tries to bribe him by saying that if An tAthair Gearóid does as he is told the parish social club he wants to establish will be approved.

215 Ó Tuama, *Déan Trócaire ar Shagairt Óga*, p. 30. An fíor go bhfuil báidh agat lena leithéidese?

216 This insinuation may well have a basis in fact.

217 Ó Tuama, *Déan Trócaire ar Shagairt Óga*, p. 31.

218 It is worth noting that apparently he has not yet done so.

219 Ó Tuama, *Déan Trócaire ar Shagairt Óga*, p. 33. Á sea. Ach an bhfuil cathú orm. Dúrt go raibh . . . ach dá mbeinn macánta liom féin d'admhóinn go ndéanfainn arís amárach é, dá mba ghá. Sé an t-aon chathú atá anois orm, dáiríribh, nár inseas an scéal dosna gardaí an chéad oíche chuala é sa bhfaoisdin . . . ansan bheadh buachaill beag amháin saortha ón mbás agam . . .agus buachaill eile – . . . Thugas móid dom féin . . . thugas geallúint fiú amháin sa bhfaoisdin . . . ná raghainn i mbun a leithéid go deo arís . . . Is é atá

á rá agam 'Athair go bhfuil an mianach céanna ionam féin ar deireadh is atá i Micheál a' Taxi. (De chogar) Homosexual mise chomh maith.

220 Ibid., p. 34.

221 Ibid., p. 35. Ach fanfaidh mé anseo . . . tamall éigin eile, féachaint an dtiocfaidh aon fheabhas ar an scéal. Ó Tuama offers a moving picture of the solitude of an elderly priest in his poem 'Sagart' (A priest) in *Saol fó Thoinn*, p. 33.

222 In his 1984 interview in *Innti*, he makes a passing reference to both his play about a homosexual priest and another one about a priest 'who failed and became an informer and so on' (ar theip agus a dhein spiaireacht agus mar sin de). Unless, as seems unlikely, he is referring to *Déan Trócaire ar Shagairt Óga* as if it were two separate plays, that means he wrote a second play with a priestly protagonist that has never been produced or published (*Innti* IX (1984), p. 41).

223 He may also have had doubts about the future of theatre itself. In answer to a question about whether Gaelic writers should in future put more emphasis on 'topical videos and things like that' (*videos* topiciúla agus mar sin), he stated: 'I don't know about plays themselves. Many people think plays are old-fashioned' (N'fheadar i dtaobh drámaí féin. Tá drámaí seanaimseartha dar le mórán daoine) (ibid., p. 35).

224 In his 1984 interview with *Innti* he pointed out that when he first began writing there was a need for new plays in Irish in Cork and thus to a certain extent his becoming a playwright was due to 'fate' (cinniúint) (ibid., p. 40).

225 Máiréad Ní Chinnéide, *An Damer: Stair Amharclainne* (The Damer: history of a theatre) (Baile Átha Cliath: Gael-Linn, 2008), p. 71.

CHAPTER FIVE
Questions of Conscience

1   Criostoir O'Flynn, *Consplawkus: A Writer's Life* (Cork: Mercier Press, 1999), p. 297.
2   Ibid., p. 58. See his poem 'Athrú Poirt' (A change of tune), in *Aisling Dhá Abhainn* (A vision of two rivers) (Baile Átha Cliath: Foilseacháin Náisiúnta Teoranta, 1977), p. 58.
3   Tá oiread sin taithí againn sa tír seo ar dhaoine a bheith roinnte i dhá champa chontráilte faoi cheist ar bith nach féidir linn glacadh leis fós go bhfuil dhá theanga againn agus nach gá do scríbhneoir cloí le ceann thar cheann eile acu má tá cumas liteartha aige iontu araon.
4   He had taken a more moderate attitude the previous year in 'Trí theanga na hÉireann' (The three languages of Ireland), *IP*, 18/7/72. He listed the three languages as Irish, English, and 'Anglo-Irish'.
5   An tÉireannach a scríobhann i mBéarla, féachann sé chuig margadh mór an domhain Bhéarla, féachann sé chuig Londain agus Nua-Eabhrac, chuig an British Arts Council agus an Guggenheim Foundation, ag tnúth le luach saothair agus pátrúnacht a fháil a chuirfidh ar a chumas lán a acmhainne a dhíriú ar shaothrú na litríochta . . . Ach tig leis a anam féin a shásamh go domhain leis an tsnaidhm a cheanglaíonn a shaothar cruthaitheach féin de dhúchas iomlán a chine
6   O'Flynn, *Consplawkus*, p. 58.
7   Ibid., p. 131.
8   He has written: 'I am also, I think, the most censored writer in Ireland, having had my work suppressed or rejected on moral or political grounds by the Abbey Theatre, the Department of Education, the Irish Book Club (An Club Leabhar), the Jesuits, and certain newspapers and magazines.' See ibid., p. 12. See also his account of this whole episode in his 'Eipileog' (Epilogue) in *Ó Fhás go hAois* (From growth to age) (Baile Átha Cliath: Sáirséal agus Dill, 1969), pp 71–92.
9   See Criostoir O'Flynn, *A Writer's Life* (Dún Laoghaire: Obelisk Books, 2001), p. 106. His original intention seems to have been not to write anything at all in Irish (*IP*, 24–26/12/69).
10   See Cian Ó hÉigeartaigh and Aoileann Nic Gearlait, *Sáirséal agus Dill 1947–1981: Scéal Foilsitheora* (Sáirséal agus Dill 1947–1981: a publisher's story) (Indreabhán: Cló Iar-Chonnachta, 2014), pp 351–3. The printer Browne and Nolan refused to allow its name to appear in the published text. See O'Flynn, *A Writer's Life*, p. 56 and 58.
11   See Críostóir Ó Floinn, 'Cor i gcúrsaí an oideachais' (A turn in educational affairs), *IP*, 11/3/75 and 'Leabhair don Nollaig' (Books for Christmas), *IP*, 30/11/78.
12   Sea, mar sin, scríbhneoir dá-theangach anois mé. Agus i mo scríbhneoir dom, tugaim aitheantas don litríocht, pé teanga ina gcumtar í. Tá mé bródúil as litríocht na hÉireann, as an scríbhneoireacht a dhéanann Éireannaigh i nGaeilge nó i mBéarla . . .
13   O'Flynn, *Consplawkus*, p. 18.
14   In 1969 his television play *Oileán Tearmainn* (Sanctuary Island), directed by Brian Mac Lochlainn and dealing with the same material as the title story of this collection was awarded the Jacob's Award for television drama (*CE*, 11/10/69). Reviewing the play for the *Irish Independent*, Brian Devenny called it 'a play in which the writer defied the conventions of tellydrama' and 'a worthwhile piece of experimentation which expressed a desire to explore beyond the safety of accepted norms in dramatic presentation' (*II*, 23/4/69). Writing in *The Irish Press*, Tom O'Dea called *Oileán Tearmainn* a 'witty, intelligent but rather slight play' that 'enabled the cast and the whole production team to give a fine account of themselves', adding that 'if it left questions unanswered, at least they are interesting ones' (*IP*, 26/4/69). The teleplay was broadcast again by RTÉ in March 1983 (*II*, 12/3/83).
15   O'Flynn, *A Writer's Life*, p. 262.
16   See here his poem 'Roth an Mhuilinn' (The millwheel), in *Seacláidí Van Gogh* (Van Gogh's chocolates) (Baile Átha Cliath: Coiscéim, 1996), p. 44.
17   See his discussion of both of the events in *Consplawkus*. In a 2014 piece in the *Limerick Leader*, he refers to 'my own crisis of faith, resulting from being twice sacked from teaching posts, directly by the Archbishop of Cashel in 1962 and indirectly by the Archbishop of Dublin in 1968' (*LL*, 12/4/14). For a discussion of his difficulties with Archbishop McQuaid of Dublin see *A Writer's Life*, pp 59–63. See also the first three stanzas of his poem 'Bean Zeibeidé', in *Ó Fhás go hAois*, pp 32–3. 'Mrs Zebedee', his version of this poem in English, was published in *The Woman Who Never Said 'Hello': Selected Poems* (Dublin: OriginalWriting Ltd, 2014), pp 51–2. See also the notes on this poem in *The Woman Who Never Said 'Hello'*, pp 177–9.
18   O'Flynn, *Consplawkus*, p. 37.
19   Ibid., p. 38.
20   Ibid., p. 104.
21   See, for example, Philip O'Leary, *Gaelic Prose in the Irish Free State 1922–1939* (Dublin: University College Dublin Press, 2004), pp 71–89; O'Leary, *Irish Interior: Keeping Faith with the Past in Gaelic Prose 1940–1951* (Dublin: University College Dublin Press, 2010), pp 43–9; and O'Leary, *Writing beyond the Revival: Facing the Future in Gaelic Prose 1940–1951* (Dublin: University College Dublin Press, 2011), pp 387–407.
22   In ainneoin mé a theacht ar an saol i ngealchathair Luimnigh cois Sionna . . . níor chuir prionsabal liteartha mo dhuine aon chorrbhuais ormsa mar údar; is amhlaidh a bhí trí dhráma Gaeilge de mo chuidse á léiriú an bhliain chéanna sin . . . See also O'Flynn, *Consplawkus*, p. 58.

23 Is oiriúnach an mhaise é gurb é áit ina bhfuilimid ag cruinniú chun na Féile seo ná an catacóm seo faoi thalamh. Cuireann an focal catacóm ag cuimhneamh sinn ar chúrsaí creidimh agus reiligiúin, ar ghéarleanúint, agus ar aiséirí. Tugann son chun ár gcuimhne gur thosaigh an drámaíocht sa seansaol mar ghné den reiligiún, agus gurbh í an Eaglais a rinne athbheochan ar an drámaíocht mar ghléas chun soiscéal agus teagasc an tslánaithe a léiriú don phobal.

24 Ach faoi mar a neartaigh an Creideamh go buacach sna catacómaí dó, gur aiséirigh chun buaghlóire i gcathair na Róimhe agus sa domhan uile, tiocfaidh an Ghaeilge agus ealaín an drámadóra slán. Tá siad ag neartú a chéile in imeachtaí ar nós na Féile Drámaíochta seo. Is le dúchas an chine agus le sprid an duine a bhaineann siad, agus is buaine an cine agus an sprid ná an impireacht nó an eagraíocht, ná an dúil san airgead.

25 Ó thaobh na drámaíochta de ní mór an tairbhe do chiste ealaíne an chine daonna é dráma nár léiríodh riamh ach atá ina bhurla de leathanaigh ag buíochan is ag lobhadh i dtrúnc a bhfuil an eochair dulta amú.

26 An mhórchuid agaibh, lucht leanúna dílis na Gaeilge, nach dtéann go dtí drámaí Gaeilge chor ar bith, bígí san airdeall le socrú a dhéanamh dul go dtí bingo an tsagairt nó cruinniú de Chumann Gaelach éigin an oíche a bheidh an dráma ar siúl. See also his comments on the four-night run of his own *Is É a Dúirt Polonius* in the Peacock the following May (*IP*, 15/5/73).

27 Sa bhliain 1968 ghlac an Gúm le trí dhráma de mo chuid. Níor foilsíodh fós iad – agus na cumainn drámaíochta ag lorg drámaí nua, Taibhdhearc na Gaillimhe ag léiriú aistriúcháin ar *Moll* agus *Big Maggie*.

28 Tá's agam, a chroí, tá's agam nach bhfuair tú seans ar é a fheiceáil. Cúig oíche a fhágtar an dráma Gaeilge ar siúl sa Phéacóg, i dtreo is go mbíonn sé á bhaint den stáitse faoin am go mbíonn a fhios ag an bpobal go bhfuil sé ar siúl (meastar nach gá fógraíocht roimhré do na fíor-Ghaeil).

29 Agus ó thaobh ealaín na scríbhneoireachta de, is dóigh liom gur ag cur ama agus spáis amú a bhítear nuair a fhoilsítear léirmheasanna ar shaothair nua litríochta; mar sin féin, is maith ann iad, óir tugann siad poiblíocht don saothar nuabheirthe agus cuidíonn siad leis an léirmheastóir a bheatha a thuilleamh . . . Feictear chuigesean, ach an umhlaíocht is an chúiléith bheith aige chuigesean, go bhfuil rúndiamhair san ealaín . . . Is é an bealach ina ndéanann an léirmheastóir dochar, dar liom, ná go bhfuil sé tagtha de chor sa saol gurb ar an gceird agus nach ar an ealaín atá an meas i bplás an mhargaidh, san áit mar a gcaithfidh an t-ealaíontóir a shaothar a reic lena bheatha a thuilleamh. See also Críostóir Ó Floinn, 'Lucht máirseála ar leathchois' (One-legged marchers), *IP*, 15/2/72; and 'An Dr Herrema sa Dáil' (Dr Herrema in the Dáil), *IP*, 18/11/75.

30 He was angered 'nuair a fheicim ar liosta leabhar a cheap coimisiún nó coiste scoláirí éigin don chúrsa Gaeilge san Ard Teastas, liosta a bhfuil dráma amháin air . . .' The play was Ó Tuama's *Gunna Cam agus Slabhra Óir*.

31 In *Consplawkus* (p. 69) and *A Writer's Life* (p. 58), he thanks Ní Ghráda for her assistance with the publication of his controversial play *Cóta Bán Chríost*.

32 Other of his radio plays are *Dónall Bán* (Fairhaired Dónall) (1953), *Naomh agus Ridire* (Saint and knight) (1954), *Oiche Shamhna i dTeamhair* (Samhain Eve in Tara) (1955), *Prionnsa na hÉigipte* (The prince of Egypt) (1955), *One Night Stand* (1974), *Tá Damascus i gCill Dara* (Damascus is in Kildare) (1976), *The Price of a Father* (1980), *Just Another Fairy Fort* (1981), and *Fear na gCrúb* (The man with the hooves) (1982). He also wrote scripts for Radio Éireann's serial radio drama *Harbour Hotel* for two and a half years in the 1980s. See O'Flynn, *A Writer's Life*, pp 224–6. His plays for television include *The Lambs* (1967) and *Oileán Tearmainn* (1968). He was asked to write for the popular soap opera *The Riordans*, but refused. See O'Flynn, *A Writer's Life*, p. 220.

33 O'Flynn, *Consplawkus*, p. 32. He lists it solely as a radio play in the list of his works in *The Woman Who Never Said 'Hello'*, p. 183.

34 O'Flynn, *Consplawkus*, p. 32. He states that he never attended the Abbey when he was a student in Dublin.

35 Ibid., p. 85 and 88.

36 He returned to the writing of entertainments of this kind in 1978 when he collaborated with Tomás Mac Anna and Gabriel Rosenstock on *Táinbócú* at the Peacock. See Críostóir Ó Floinn, 'I gcuimhne ar shár-aisteoir' (In memory of a superb actor), *IP*, 11/1/79.

37 There is no Irish-language version of this play. The play deals with the relationship – not sexual – between a female English artist and a mute young Irish man. Ó Floinn discusses this play with some plot summary in *Consplawkus*, pp 224–5. The text has been published in Criostoir O'Flynn, *Three Plays* (Dún Laoghaire: Obelisk Books, 2000), pp 1–92.

38 His opinion about this play has not changed, as he made clear to me in an email on 7 March 2016.

39 O'Flynn, *Consplawkus*, pp 294–5.

40 Ibid., pp 162–79.

41 Ibid., p. 86. See also pp 164–5.

42 Mar sin ba mhaith liom a chur in iúl go poiblí, mar chathróir agus mar scríbhneoir, go bhfuil sé in am . . . Amharclann na Mainistreach a dhúnadh. Aon duine agaibh nach dtuigeann faoin am seo cad chuige atáim, is duine é nach bhfuil feiliúnach fiú do ghnó an léirmheastóir amharclainne.

43 Ach ní ar mo shon féin atá mé ag labhairt nuair adeirim go bhfuil an Abbey imithe i bhfad ón gcuspóir a leagadh síos don Amharclann Náisiúnta. Agus tuigim cén fáth a gcuirfeadh sé míshásamh ar Stiúrthóirí an Abbey nuair a chuirim in iúl don phobal go bhfuil ag éirí go breá le drámaí áirithe de mo chuid féin ar dhiúltaigh Mac Anna agus a chairde dóibh go maslach. See also Críostóir Ó Floinn, 'Rudaí nach bhfuilim na bhfábhar' (Things I am not in favour of), *IP*, 13/10/70; 'Ceird na léirmheastóireachta' (The craft of criticism), *Comhar*, Dec. 1971, p. 8; and 'An drámaíocht faoi thalamh' (The underground drama), *IP*, 7/10/75.

44 O'Flynn, *A Writer's Life*, p. 155. See also p. 170.

45 O'Flynn, *Consplawkus*, p. 32. I have not found any references to such productions, but needless to say the work of small amateur groups is not always well publicised.

46 Ibid., p. 29.

47 Críostóir Ó Floinn, *Is Fada Anocht* (Tonight is long) (Baile Átha Cliath: Oifig an tSoláthair, 1968), p. 6. Ní mór dó greim a choinneáil ar an áit seo, seilbh Uí Chonchubhair a choinneáil slán go dtí go bhfaighimid ár gceart.

48 Ibid., p. 19. Tagadh sé anois, agus tógadh sé a chuid den saol.

49 Ibid., p. 17. Ar dheis leat ceithre chorpán ar an tinteán seo ná trí cinn? Agus tú féin d'fháil le cois an chlaí ar do theacht arís chun na dúiche seo, mar nach mbeadh aon neach beo romhat chun déirc a shíneadh chugat?

50 Ibid., p. 8. Is mór an trua fear chomh breá leis a bheith á chéasadh ag an dóchas.

51 This version of the play was published in O'Flynn, *Three Plays*, pp 97–183.

52 O'Flynn, *Consplawkus*, pp 291–2.

53 Ibid., p. 11.

54 In his review in the *Irish Times*, Seamus Kelly blasted 'an insensitive first-night Festival audience who came late, banged seats about, and giggled inanely', but noted that they gave the play and its performers 'a richly earned ovation at the final curtain' (*IT*, 3/10/67).

55 An rud is measa faoin argóint seo go léir ná go mbeidh leisce ar amharclann glacadh le drámaí ó Chríostóir Ó Floinn ar aon chor má cheapann siad gur deacair déileáil leis.

56 He gives examples of the changes he objected to in *A Writer's Life*, p. 43. See also pp 38–9.

57 Quoted in ibid., p. 34.

58 Abraim láithreach gur dóigh liom gurbh fhearr de dhráma é an t-aistriúchán ná an bun-shaothar sa chás áirithe seo . . . Ní shroicheann an léiriú sa Damer an doimhneas céanna: ní shroicheann sé, mar a déarfá, ifreann na tragóide. Tá sé fadálach foclach, go mórmhór sa chéad ghníomh . . .

59 An púca a chímse san amharclann, is é údar an dráma mhistéire é, an dráma nua-aimseartha seo nach léir d'éinne cad is bun, cad is barr nó cad is

bolg dó ach amháin – tá súil agam – don phúca a scríobh é . . . Is í an bheatha an mhistéir is rúndiamhraí ar bith, agus bhí an mhistéir agus an mhíorúilt ina mná cabhartha nuair a thug an Eaglais an dráma nua-aoiseach ar an saol ina cliabhán meánaoiseach . . . Más fíor go bhfuil an rúndiamhair san fhaisean in amharclann an lae inniu, ba chóir gur scéal áthais é sin leis an scríbhneoir Críostaí. Tá an mála nó an leabhar aigesean ag cur thar maoil le mistéir agus le rúndiamhair . . . Chífimid, b'fhéidir, an amharclann ag filleadh chun aiséirí ar [*sic*] an gcliabhán as ar fhás sí, an mhistéir agus an gcreideamh.

60 Expressions of his loyalty to the Church and to a nationalist reading of Irish history are frequent in his writings. For examples, see his poems 'Domhnach Fola' (Bloody Sunday) in *Aisling Dhá Abhainn*, pp 34–7; and 'An Chailleach Bhéara' (The hag of Beare), in *Seacláidí Van Gogh*, pp 52–4.

61 O'Flynn, *Consplawkus*, p. 291.

62 The director, Keith Darvill, said that the play would have run for four hours had cuts not been made (*MN*, 6/1/68).

63 Críostóir Ó Floinn, *Cóta Bán Chríost: Dráma Trí Ghluaiseacht* (The white coat of Christ: a play in three movements) (Baile Átha Cliath: Sáirséal agus Dill, 1968), p. 3. Ina shúile liatha is ea atá a shástacht, agus cé ná fuil aon rian den ragairne air, is deimhin nach bhféadfadh sé an lá mór seo a chur thairis gan braon éigin a bhlaiseadh ar thathaint an Chanónaigh. Tá bun thar an ngnách lena shástacht anocht – an chéad Nollaig dó ina shagart paróiste, agus bhí sé d'onóir aige bheith ina thíosach agus ina bhiatach do chléir shinsir na comharsannachta.

64 Ibid., p. 7. Tá an chuma chéanna orm a bhí ar an Maighdean nuair a cuireadh ó dhoras an tí ósta í. Agus is faoin treoir chéanna atá mé.

65 Ibid., p. 13. Mór an trua nach chuig fear stuama éigin a cuireadh tú, fear cáilithe, an Canónach, abair. Bheifeá amuigh ar an mbóthar aigesean sula mbeadh an deis agat do bhéal a oscailt in aon chor.

66 Ibid., p. 17. Mar sin bí i do shagart anois go hiomlán, agus bíodh do mhuinín agus do chreideamh gan staonadh sa Tiarna Ró-Ard sin a chuir chugat mé lena rá . . . 'Móraíonn m'anam an Tiarna / Agus rinne mo spiorad gairdeas i nDia mo Shlánaitheoir.' Ó Floinn's title for this first act, or 'movement', is 'Teachtaireacht' (Message).

67 Ibid., p. 18. Iarrann tusa ar an gcine daonna a leithéid a chreidiúint gach lá. Ba chóir gurbh fhusa duitse toil Dé a thuiscint.

68 Ibid., p. 23.

69 Ibid., p. 27. A Chroí Ró-Naofa Íosa, cad tá agam le déanamh? Cad tá i ndán dom? Mise, do shagart, gan uaim ach a bheith i mo shagart, do thoil a dhéanamh. An é atá á déanamh agam, nó an bhfuil mé i mo cheap magaidh ag slua ifrinn?

70 Ibid., p. 34. He envies those atheists who are 'gan amhras ar bith; chomh socair sámh is a bheadh

d'aigne, gan aon chur isteach ar do choinsias ó bheith ag géilleadh don Dia Uilechomachtach seo a bhfuil gach eolas aige agus grá aige do gach neach agus do gach ní'.

71 It is not explicitly stated the city is in England.

72 Ó Floinn, *Cóta Bán Chríost*, p. 67. Faigh bás, faigh *bás* a deirim, anois, ar an bpointe! Agus dá mbeadh ifreann ann, ba neamh liomsa tusa a fheiceáil á róstadh ann le saol na saol, tusa agus gach chluanaire salach eile sagairt atá ag bréanadh na cruinne seo ar an gcine daonna!

73 Ibid., p. 69. Bhuail mise bob ort. Bhuail mé bob ar an sagairtín cráifeach Dé. Agus caithfidh tú a admháil go ndearna mé go hálainn é.

74 Ibid., p. 76.

75 Ibid., p. 80.

76 Ibid., p. 96.

77 Ibid., p. 104. Chreid an bodach úd de shagart paróiste gach focal a dúirt an striapach óinsiúil sin leis; díbríodh mo dheartháir le mallacht na Róimhe, gan caoi aige ar é féin a chosaint ar na scéalta éithigh sin a chum na spiairí aontumha agus a gcuid Máiríní Maigdiléana.

78 Ibid., p. 111. Dar liomsa – dar liomsa bhí sé ina shagart a deirim . . . Sagart – sagart na híobartha, an t-aon chaomhuan fulangach Dé a mbeadh meas ag an gcine daonna air dá dtuigfidís; agus ba í mo mháthairse Máthair an Dóláis – mo mháthair – agus fág uaim an bhean sí Ghiúdach sin i do phictiúr meánaoiseach. This is a picture of 'Máthair na Dea-Chomhairle' (The mother of good counsel) – the Virgin Mary – that we first see on the wall of the priest's sitting room with a votive candle lit beneath it.

79 Ibid., p. 143. Is doimhne an ghairm shagairt ná an bóna cruinn agus an foirgneamh mar a ndéantar an íobairt. Leis an fhírinne a nochtadh duit, a chailín, ní féidir deireadh a chur le sagart. Sagart lá, sagart choíche. Nó b'fhéidir gur tháinig tú ar an ráiteas seo le linn duit bheith ag pulcadh na Scrioptúr: 'Tá tú i do shagart go deo, de réir ord Mheilcisideic' . . . Is é Dia na glóire ábhar gach beatha; is cuma conas a ghintear é. Émánuel – 'Dia inár measc' – is ea gach leanbh nua a thagann ar an saol . . . A Dhia – a Dhia – cén fáth ar thréig tú mé? The stage direction here states: 'His tears now, who knows that they are not tears of blood' (na deora atá leis anois, cá bhfios ná gur deora fola iad).

80 Ibid., p. 178. Is bean mé a thuigeann a fear.

81 Ibid., p. 182. Bhfuil a fhios agat, a Iúd, taibhrítear dom gur chosúil leatsa a bheadh mo dhearáir dá – dá mbeadh –

82 Ibid., p. 186. Má – má éiríonn leat post eile a fháil, d'fhéadfaimís leaba bheag a cheannach don seomra seo. Tá an tolg gránna sin – Iúd, an bhfuil tú – an bhfuil tú crosta liom?

83 Ibid., p. 188.

84 This production seems to have been ignored by critics.

85 Ó Floinn's short story 'Oisíní' uses this same material, but with a very different and considerably less effective ending. See Críostóir Ó Floinn, 'Oisíní', *Comhar*, Mar. 1968, pp 5–14. This story was also published in his 1968 collection *Oineachlann* (Retribution) (Baile Átha Cliath: Oifig an tSoláthair, 1968), pp 89–112.

86 For the venues on this tour, see 'Bringing theatre to Gaeltacht', *CT*, 7/7/72; and 'Aggiornamento sa Gaeltacht [*sic*]', *II*, 11/7/72.

87 For Ó Floinn's account of his dealings with RTÉ regarding this script, see 'Leabhar úsáideach do chách' (A useful book for everyone), *IP*, 10/10/72. See also O'Flynn, *A Writer's Life*, pp 146–7.

88 Tá féith na trua go láidir sa dráma agus tuiscint tráthúil don deacracht (síoraí?) cumarsáide idir na glúine . . . Ceapadh an lucht éisteachta uilig i ngaiste glic an údair.

89 D'fhaisc Ó Floinn an traigéide agus an íoróin leis an deisbhéalaí go healaíonta. Dáiríre, d'fhéadfainn liosta an fhada de nithe a thaitin liom maidir leis an dráma, [gan] an léiriú agus an aisteoireacht a lua.

90 An príomhlocht a bhí le fáil agam, áfach, ná a chosúla a bhí an léiriú seo leis an gceann a chonaiceamar in 1968. B'ionann iad, gníomh ar ghníomh, agus radharc ar radharc, geall leis. B'ionann an fhoireann, páirt ar pháirt . . . Agus an bhreith sin á thabhairt agam tuigim go maith gur thug an dráma pléisiúr dá lán dá raibh i láthair . . . Bhain mé féin taitneamh as chomh maith. Déarfaidh daoine nach mar dhráma ach mar chomparáid a thit *Aggiornamento* an turas seo. Ní déarfainn nach mbeadh cuid mhaith den cheart acu.

91 Trí bhliain ó shin léirigh Noel Ó Briain 'Aggiornamento' le Críostóir Ó Floinn sa Damer agus rinne sé éacht. Is dána an té a déarfadh nár dhein sé éacht chomh maith nuair a léirigh sé an dráma céanna ann aréir. Máiréad Ní Chinnéide agreed about the lack of originality in the revival in her review (*Inniu*, 15/1/71).

92 Quoted by John Cooney, in *John Charles McQuaid: Ruler of Catholic Ireland* (Syracuse: Syracuse University Press, 1999), p. 371.

93 In a clever nod to O'Casey's *Juno and the Paycock*, Máirtín often seems to be playing Joxer Daly to Seán's Captain Boyle.

94 Críostóir Ó Floinn, *Aggiornamento: Dráma Trí Mhír* (A play in three acts) (Baile Átha Cliath: Oifig an tSoláthair, 1969), p. 23. Tá mé chun a mholadh don easpag athnuachan iomlán a dhéanamh ar an áit seo.

95 Ibid., p. 26.

96 Ibid., p. 28. Tá sé beartaithe agam club a bhunú san áras seo, club do dhaoine óga an pharóiste seo, sea agus do dhaoine óga an bhaile go léir . . . Maith go leor, mar sin, a Athair, má tá fútsa an Chlub seo a chur ar fáil do na daoine óga céanna. Imígí oraibh, tú

féin agus na daoine óga céanna, agus déanaigí an áit sin daoibh féin, faoi mar ab éigean dúinne a dhéanamh nuair a bhíomar-na óg ar an mbaile seo agus áit de dhíth orainne . . .

97 Ibid., p. 43. B'fhéidir gur trua leis nach bhfuair Seán bás ar son na hÉireann, seachas an deartháir.

98 Ibid., p. 54.

99 Ibid., p. 99.

100 Ibid., p. 100.

101 In her review of the 1971 production Máiréad Ní Chinnéide found this ending 'clumsy' (liobarnach) (*Inniu*, 15/1/71).

102 Láimhsíonn Ó Floinn a théama go díreach simplí. Cruthaíonn sé cuid mhaith dá charactair le cruinneas . . . Thug an t-údar a théama leis ar aghaidh go díreach tríd an dráma, á smachtú féin taobh istigh de theorainn na téama.

103 Is geall le seanmóir é. Tá sé ró-shoiléir tríd an dráma nach bhfuil sna míreanna ach samplaí chun *thesis* an údair a chruthú . . . Bhraith mé uaim an choimhlint atá riachtanach in aon dráma den tsórt seo – an choimhlint idir maith, leath-mhaith, olc.

104 Ní foláir dom a rá gur chuir 'Is é Dúirt Polonius' díomá nach beag orm. Bhí an dráma féin tanaí ach níor chuidigh an léiriú pioc leis. He continued: 'It could be that it would have been more successful had the play been produced as a "straight" drama and had the tricks and the *geamaireacht* technique been left out' (D'fhéadfadh gur fearr a d'éireodh leis dá léireofaí mar dhráma 'díreach' é is go bhfágfaí na cleasanna is teicníc na geamaireachta ar lár).

105 Cuma cén cumas samhlaíochta a bheadh ag an léitheoir, ba dheacair dó dul faoi aisling léitheoireachta ar bith san agallamh anseo. Níl oiread is ráiteas amháin ann a mheallfadh é chun an 'unwilling [*sic*] suspension of disbelief' a chur ar fáil don údar.

106 He found 'an chaint mheicniúil chéanna i mbéal gach cainteora, canúint neodrach, nach Béarla í ná Gaeilge, nach beochaint mná í ná bladaireacht fhir, ná caibideal ar bith de bheochanúintí an chine dhaonna'.

107 'Typicalities' tanaí iad go léir, ainmneacha fidil, gan an smidín is lú de dhiabhlaíocht ná d'ainglíocht ná daonnúlachta le sonrú ar a mbéalra . . . Nuair nach bhfuil carachtair sa chaint chun dul i bhfeidhm ar an tsamhlaíocht is lú liom ná an sioc bán cad é an finscéal a fhéachtar lena ríomh ina dtaobh.

108 Damien Ó Muirí writes: 'Perhaps one would say that it is my imagination, but it is clear from the lay-out of the *dramatis personae* in *Is É a Dúirt Polonius* that the author is trying to make a study of kinds of people' (B'fhéidir go gcuirfeadh duine an tsamhlaíocht in mo leith, ach is soiléir ó leagan amach an *dramatis personae* in *Is É a Dúirt Polonius* go bhfuil an t-údar ag iarraidh staidéar a dhéanamh ar chineálacha daoine). See Damien Ó Muirí, 'Drámaí Chríostóra Uí Fhloinn' (The plays of Críostóir Ó Floinn), *Léachtaí Cholm Cille* X (1979), p. 94. For

Eugene McKendry, *Is É a Dúirt Polonius* is 'a classical tragedy', with its protagonist 'a classical hero, with the qualities and weaknesses identified with such a character'. See Eugene McKendry, 'Innovation and tradition in the drama of Críostóir Ó Floinn', in *Celtic Literatures in the Twentieth Century* (Moscow: Languages of Slavonic Culture, 2007), p. 175. He writes that *Cóta Bán Chríost* should also be read 'in the light of the classical tragedy tradition' (p. 177). In particular, McKendry sees the influence of Corneille and Racine on Ó Floinn's tragic plays (pp 178–9). For an Irish-language version of this essay, see Eoghan Mac Éinrí, 'Críostóir Ó Floinn agus traigéide ár linne' (Críostóir Ó Floinn and contemporary tragedy), *An tUltach*, Mar. 1993, pp 16–21. Antonia Ní Mhurchú traces what she sees as parallels between this play and Ibsen's *Et dukkehjem* (A doll's house) in '*Is É a Dúirt Polonius* agus *A Doll's House*', *IMN*, 1986, pp 43–84.

109 Críostóir Ó Floinn, *Is É a Dúirt Polonius: Dráma Trí Mhír* (What Polonius said: A play in three acts) (Baile Átha Cliath: Oifig an tSoláthair, 1973), p. 13. Dá mbeadh ceart le fáil, is tusa a bheadh i do Bhainisteoir, tusa a bhfuil céimeanna agus cáilíochtaí nach bhfuil a mboladh ag an slíbhín sin thuas.

110 Ibid., p. 30. Sin bainisteoireacht duit, a bhean bheag! Scaoileann siad liom ar feadh bliana, ansin ceithre huaire fichead chun rogha a dhéanamh idir toil an Lucht Stiúrtha agus mo thoil féin, idir an bhréag mhéith agus an fhírinne lom . . . Tá a fhios agam, a Eibhlín, a rún, mura nglacaim leis go mbeimid gan phost, gan bhia. Ach – beatha duine a thoil, deirtear freisin.

111 Ibid., p. 42. Tá an Feidhmeannach ina shuí ag a chrinlinl, é ag labhairt ar an nguthán, díreach faoi mar a bhí an bainisteoir rannóige nuair a chuaigh Diarmaid chun cainte leis sin . . . Tá post an Fheidhmeannaigh seo ar an leibhéal céanna cumhachta agus tuarastail is atá post an bhainisteora úd san eagraíocht eile.

112 See ibid., p. 59.

113 Ibid., p. 62. Ach má ghéillimse anois – a Eibhlín, a ghrá gheal, ní féidir liom géilleadh dóibh . . . Níl mé chun m'ainm a chur le clúmhilleadh orm féin agus glacadh le pionós nach bhfuil tuillte agam.

114 Ibid., p. 69. Déan do mhachnamh air sin leis, a Mhic Uí Rodaí. Cibé tairbhe eile atá sa ghairm seo againne, múineann sí dúinn go bhfuil coirpthigh mhóra mhallaithe faoi ghradam agus faoi onóir, fad atá daoine cneasta ag fulaingt éagóir agus céasadh . . .

115 Ibid., p. 83. Nach bhfuil sé cosúil leis na scéalta a chloisimis i dtaobh na dtíortha cumannacha . . . Ní aon ghnó suarach é, a Dhiarmaid, cearta agus ionracas an duine atá i gceist. Ní leatsa amháin a bhaineann sé, ach le gach duine sa tír, leis na glúine atá ag teacht, leis an gcine daonna.

116 Ibid., p. 84. Inseoidh mé duit an smaoineamh aisteach a tháinig chugam – gur dócha go mbíodh

amhras mar sin ar na fir a chuaigh amach ag troid in Éirí Amach 1916. . . Ó Floinn has great respect for the rebels of 1916, as is evident from his poetry collections *Éirí Amach na Cásca 1916* (Baile Átha Cliath: Sáirséal agus Dill, 1967) and its English version *The Easter Rising: A Poem Sequence* (Dún Laoghaire: Obelisk Books, 2004), and his play *A Man Called Pearse: A Play in Three Acts* (Baile Átha Cliath: Foilseacháin Náisiúnta Teoranta, 1980). See also his poem on Pearse, 'Oilithreacht' (Pilgrimage), in *Aisling Dhá Abhainn*, p. 49.

117 Ó Floinn, *Is É a Dúirt Polonius*, p. 85. Má dhéanann tú íobairt ar son an chirt, gabhann do chruatan – agus airím cruatan do chléithiúnaithe mar chuid dá mbeidh le fulaingt agatsa – gabhann sin leis an gcéasadh a rinne giollaí an diabhail ar chorp daonna Mhac Dé, moladh go deo Leis.

118 The letter does no good.

119 Ó Floinn offers a much lighter satirical take on an interview with a bureaucratic board in 'Comhluchtum postanna a líonadh: ar dhul faoi agallamh' (The company for filling positions: on going for an interview), *Comhar*, Aug. 1964, pp 15–16.

120 Ó Floinn, *Is É a Dúirt Polonius*, p. 97.

121 Ibid., p. 98.

122 Ibid., p. 103.

123 In his review of the play for *Inniu*, 'D. P. F.' wrote that this scene reminded him of Kafka (*Inniu*, 17/5/68).

124 Ó Floinn, *Is É a Dúirt Polonius*, pp 117–18. Arbh fhiú é –? B'fhéidir nach bhfuil ionam ach amadán mórchúiseach, dailtín stuacach; ciaróg faoi chosa na cinniúna. A ghealach agus a réaltaí, cad tá i ndán dom, dom féin, do mo bhean agus do na leanaí a thugamar ar an saol? Agus cad tá i ndán do shliocht ár sleachta?

125 See the stanza of his poem 'At Dún Laoghaire Lighthouse' beginning 'This kindly light above my head has beamed' in *Banana* (Baile Átha Cliath: Foilseacháin Náisiúnta Teoranta, 1979), p. 69.

126 Ó Floinn was very pleased with Stafford's work on the play, stating: 'His artistic method was the kind every playwright would wish for in a director, in that it consisted in the desire to create on the stage, as effectively as possible, what the author had imagined in his mind and transferred to the script.' See *A Writer's Life*, p. 143.

127 Ó Floinn has written that 'although promised a production by the Abbey, [it] was never produced anywhere . . . and several years later it was listed by a scholar in U.C.D. among the ten most important literary works in the Irish language written in the twentieth century.' See ibid., p. 188. I do not know who this scholar was or where the list appeared. *Cad d'Imigh ar Fheidhlimidh?* was published by An Gúm in 1978.

128 The story does not, however, end with this final battle in either of its two major recensions, but rather

concludes anticlimactically with a fight between two bulls representing the two warring provinces.

129 In the oldest version of the tale, that in the twelfth-century *Book of Leinster*, she kills herself by jumping from Conchobar's chariot and smashing her head against a rock. In one later version of the tale she leaps into Noísiu's grave and dies of grief; in others she stabs herself.

130 Críostóir Ó Floinn, *Cad d'Imigh ar Fheidhlimidh?: Dráma Trí Mhír* (What happened to Feilimidh?: a play in three acts) (Baile Átha Cliath: Oifig an tSoláthair, 1978), n.p. Ghlac mé leis an léiritheoir san amharclann mar scéalaí, atá ag cur scéalta i láthair a lucht éisteachta chomh taitneamhach, chom healaíonta agus atá ar a chumas. He added that in his opinion this theatre of the mind created by the storyteller was 'far stronger and more lively' (i bhfad níos beo agus níos treise) than formal productions in a theatre. In the event of a production, he did, however, wish to make use of the full resources of the modern theatre: 'If this play were being produced, I would seek the assistance of all the theatre artists for it, as well as the director and the actors . . . The music and the dance and the lighting would be just as important as the dialogue to present this story of stories truly artistically' (Dá mbeadh an dráma seo á léiriú, d'iarrfainn cabhair ealaíontóirí uile na hamharclainne chuige, i dteannta an léiritheora agus na n-aisteoirí. Bheadh an ceol agus an rince agus an soilsiú chomh tábhachtach céanna leis an bhfriotal chun an scéal seo thar scéalta a chur i láthair go fíorealaíonta).

131 Ibid.

132 Ibid.

133 Ibid., p. 1.

134 Ibid. Is dócha gur maith ann é, dá olcas; tá na drámaí Gaeilge chomh gann san.

135 Ibid., p. 2. Cá bhfuil Yeats na Gaeilge, a thabharfadh insint chorraitheach fhileata dúinn ar na seanscéalta áille?

136 Ibid., p. 3. Nach é bunús ár gceirde é go nglacfaidh an lucht féachana le rud ar bith ach é a chur ina láthair go healaíonta?

137 Ibid. Deirdre . . . Deirdre an bhróin. An áilleacht . . . an óige . . . an neamhurchóid . . . agus . . . an tuaigneas, an drúis, an grá . . . an Bás . . . Deirdre . . . ise . . . dhéanfadh . . . á, dá mbeadh an sgríbhinn againn! The ellipses are in the original.

138 Ibid., p. 13. Dheara fág uait Deirdre! Nach bhfuil sin ar an téama is spíonta díobh go léir – Yeats, Synge, AE, Samuel Ferguson – sea agus Donnchadh Mac Donnchadha, mac le Tomás a fuair bás ar son na hÉireann. There is also a reference to Yeats on p. 98.

139 Ibid., p. 3. Nach breá bog mar a thuill roinnt de na buachaillí sin go léir airgid ag cur balcaisí Béarla ar cholainn Ghaeilge! He refers again to the appropriation of the Deirdre story by Yeats and Synge on p. 26.

140 Ibid., p. 3. Dá mbeadh an lampa draíochta againn, nó an meaisín ama, a chasfadh siar sinn, siar . . . siar . . . conas a bhuailfeadh an eachtra linn? 'Bhfuil tosach an scéil ag duine ar bith agaibh, nó, 'bhfuil bhur gcuimhne millte ar fad ag cultúr reatha an lae seo againn?

141 Ibid., p. 4. Mise Feidhlimidh, scéalaí Chonchúir. Aithrisím scéalta oiriúnacha ar luach saothair.

142 Ibid., p. 5.

143 Ibid., p. 8. 'Bhfuil a fhios agaibh, bheadh sé ábhairín deacair don lucht féachana a leithéid sin a leanúint nuair atá taithí acu ar – bhuel, is binn béal ina thost agus bíonn cluasa ar na ballaí.

144 Ibid. Ba mhaith dúinn agus do chách an iarracht a dhéanamh. Ní haon bhearna réidh é eolas a chur ar chroí nó ar anam an duine, agus dá airde a ghradam is ea is casta a mheon agus a mhianta.

145 Ibid., p. 9. Ais. A: Cad is gá scríbhinn? Nach bhfuil gach aon chur amach agatsa ar *Stanislavsky* agus an *Actors' Studio*? Ais. B: Ar *Ionesco*, an *Commedia dell'Arte, Pirandello*? Ais. A: Músclaímis as ár n-anam féin é. Ais. B: As cianchuimhne ár gcine.

146 Ibid., p. 10. Thosóidís sin ag iomaíocht lena chéile, gach coilichín acu ag scairteadh óna charn féin. Níorbh fhada go mbeadh cruthú ar fáil duit . . . go raibh triúr nó ceathrar de Dheirdrí ann . . . Ó Floinn is here poking fun at the scholarly controversy over whether there had been two St Patricks.

147 Ibid., p. 26. A Mhuire, ach ar shlí ba mhór an faoiseamh dúinn a bheith ar ais ar an bhfeirm úd ag tnúth leis an mac óg ó San Francisco! . . . Ó gan amhras is fusa cócaireacht a dhéanamh ar an ispín ná ar an mbradán feasa. The 'salmon of knowledge' (bradán feasa) is a creature from Irish mythology the eating of which gives a person vast knowledge. The actors refer to the play they are rehearsing as 'a sausage' (ispín).

148 See Philip O'Leary, 'Honour bound: the social context of early Irish heroic *geis*', *Celtica* XX (1988), pp 85–107.

149 Ó Floinn, *Cad d'Imigh ar Fheidhlimidh?*, p. 45. Cinnte dá mbeadh do shaothar le léiriú san West End nó ar Bhroadway, bheadh ort gach gné den ghnéas agus den ainghnéas a chíoradh go scanrúil.

150 Ibid., p. 87. Anocht a thuigim. Ceist ealaíne é go bunúsach. Anocht a thuigim d'Iúil Caesar, d'Alastar Mór, do Napoleon, do Hitler . . . Tuigimís don chogadh adamhach atá chugainn, don chogadh idir reanna neimhe nuair atá an Chruinne seo séidte, tuigimís do Cháin ag ligean fola a dhearthár.

151 Ibid., p. 93. Ní dheachaigh mé ar an scoil riamh, ach casadh na mic léinn orm in áit an mhargaidh. Gach Ultach a cheanglaíos é féin leis an sais de chruachairte na cuimhne, cá bhfios ná gurb é oidhre Chúchulainn é?

152 Ibid., p. 95. Bhí tú ag teacht chun cinn go breá áiféiseach ansin ó chianaibh, ar mhodh an lae

amáraigh go buacach, agus seo anois tú de thuairt ar ais le hAnnála Ríochta Éireann.

153 Ibid., p. 87.

154 Ibid., p. 99. His being a storyteller 'on salary' (ar tuarastal) must be intended to sound more compromising than Feidhlimidh's telling his stories 'for pay' (ar luach saothair).

155 In an email of 3 June 2016, Ó Floinn informed me that this play was not an English version of his English-language radio play *Escape*, broadcast by Radio Éireann in June of that year (*II*, 26/6/53).

156 Críostóir Ó Floinn, *Éalú ó Chill Mhaighneann* (Escape from Kilmainham) (Baile Átha Cliath: Oifig an tSoláthair, 1968), p. 32. Má chabhraíonn tú linn na buachaillí seo againne a thabhairt slán ón gcroch, sábhálfaidh tú freisin na saighdiúirí a mharófaí in éiric orthu . . . A Tommy, dá mbeadh tusa mar a bhfuil Lloyd George, is fada ó bheadh síochán agus cairdeas bunaithe idir an dá thír seo againne.

157 In *A Writer's Life*, Ó Floinn states that he was 'depressed' by 'the poor quality of the production, and lists some of the liberties Ó Briain took with his script. The play was originally supposed to have been directed by Tomás Mac Anna for the Dublin Theatre Festival, but he had gone to America to teach and did not return in time to work on the production. As a result the play was not on the festival's schedule. See O'Flynn, *A Writer's Life*, pp 167–9.

158 There is a picture from the production in the *Irish Times*, 28/2/74. On 27 August 1978, a scene from the play, directed by Tris Nic Giollarnáth, was part of *Caoga Bliain ag Fás* (Fifty years a-growin'), a show celebrating An Taibhdhearc's fiftieth anniversary. See Ciarán de hÓra, *Na Drámaí a Léiríodh i dTaibhdhearc na Gaillimhe 1928–2003* (The plays that were produced in Taibhdhearc na Gaillimhe 1928–2003) (Gaillimh: Ollscoil na hÉireann, Gaillimh, n.d.).

159 The director for both productions was An Canónach Risteárd Ó hÓráin.

160 Is dócha gur thriáil sé an iomarca leis . . . An iomarca conspóideachta ann b'fhéidir le go gcomhdhlúthódh na gnéithe uile le chéile in aon ionad. Ach bhí giotaí ar fheabhas . . . See also 'Taibhdhearc stages Ó Floinn [*sic*] Raifteirí', *CS*, 19/2/74.

161 O'Flynn, *Consplawkus*, pp 49–50. See p. 52 for his problems with MacManus.

162 Damien Ó Muirí sees the influence of both Brecht and the absurdists in the play (*LCC* X (1979), p. 124). Ciarán Ó Coigligh calls it 'an epic tragedy with a strong trace of the absurd in it' (traigéide eipiciúil a bhfuil rian na háiféise go láidir air). See Ciarán Ó Coigligh, 'An teispéireas drámata: sracfhéachaint ar dhrámaíocht Chríostóra Uí Fhloinn' (The dramatic experience: a quick look at the drama of Críostóir Ó Floinn), in *Mangarae: Aistí Litríochta*

agus Teanga (Miscellany: essays on literature and language) (Cathair na Mart: Foilseacháin Náisiúnta Teoranta, 1987), p. 25.

163 Alan Titley writes of the play 'Ó Floinn manages to mix the story of blind Raftery with the cultural debates that took place at the turn of the 20th century and with our later literary wars ... This gives an idea of the range and scope of the work, but Ó Floinn, being the master he was, never lets the culture clog up the story, or history slow down the action. He never subordinates a "message" to the essential work of providing dramatic sustenance, and even if he did, then the theatre can survive and thrive on that too.' See Alan Titley, '"Neither the boghole nor Berlin": drama in the Irish language from then until now', in *Nailing Theses: Selected Essays* (Belfast: Lagan Press, 2011), p. 275.

164 In his dedication of the published text to the *Evening Press* journalist Terry O'Sullivan, Ó Floinn praises him for, among other things, his readiness to acknowledge 'that Irish is the foundation and the heart of the native tradition of the Irish people' (gurb í an Ghaeilge bonn agus croí an dúchais ag cine Gael).

165 See Críostóir Ó Floinn, *Mise Raifteirí an File: Dráma Trí Mhír* (I am Raftery the poet: a play in three acts) (Baile Átha Cliath: Sáirséal agus Dill, 1974), pp 188–9. Raifteirí is presented as a significant voice in the Irish tradition of resistance to British rule in *Éirí Amach na Cásca*, Ó Floinn's collection of poems about the Easter Rising (pp 11–12 and 23).

166 For this controversy see P. J. Mathews, 'Hyde's first stand: the Irish language controversy of 1899', *Éire-Ireland*, spring-summer 2000, pp 173–87.

167 Ó Floinn, *Mise Raifteirí an File*, p. 56.

168 Ibid.

169 Sean O'Faolain would have been an equally, if not more, appropriate target for Ó Floinn.

170 Ó Floinn, *Mise Raifteirí an File*, pp 15–16. Titeann an file ó neamh isteach sa saol; nuair a bhíonn a ré tugtha, scuabann an bás uainn an file, ach fanann an suaitheadh, an ghluaiseacht saoithiúlachta, a thiomsaigh sé, mar a bheadh tonn ar uisce an tsaoil, tonn a shnámhann amach i bhfad ó áit dúchais an fhile. Is amhlaidh a tharla sé gur buaileadh i m'aghaidh an tonn saoithiúlachta a thóg file bocht dall i gContae na Gaillimhe, file a fuair bás níos mó ná dhá scór bliain sul má chuala mise trácht air.

171 Ibid., p. 35.

172 Ibid., p. 37. She regrets that they were not contemporaries 'go bhfáilteoimis roimhe chun an tí seo, go scríobhfaimís síos gach focal de na dánta óna bhéal féin go díreach, go gcloisfimis a chaint uasal fhileata lenár gcluasa féin ...'

173 Ibid., p. 74. Tuigtear dom go bhfuil an dá chine i ngach áit sa tír seo, an dream in uachtar, na

Protastúnaigh Ghallda anall, na gadaithe a chuir muide as seilbh leis an lámh láidir, agus muide, na Caitlicigh, na hÉireannaigh, an daoraicme ina dtír féin. Raifteirí is also scathing about a Catholic priest who frequents the houses of the aristocracy, including Lady Gregory's Coole (p. 75).

174 Ibid., pp 154–5. A Raifteirí, a chara dhil, bíodh ciall agat! Ní féidir liom fáiltiú romhat chun an tí seo mura gcoinníonn tú smacht ar do theanga.

175 Ibid., p. 159 and 164. Sa teach seo anocht, ní Sasanaigh ná Éireannaigh muid, Caitlicigh ná Protastúin, ach aos ceoil is oirfide is éigse.

176 Ibid., p. 166. Chuala mé an ceol sin cheana, mura bhfuil dul amú orm. Bhfuil an Thomas Moore seo ag maíomh gur leis féin an chumadóireacht sin ar fad?

177 In one scene in the play, they discuss the need to develop a drama movement in Irish (ibid, pp 174–6).

178 Ibid., p. 230. Dá mbeadh an scioból sin ina sheasamh fós, is air a bheadh triall na ndaoine le homós do Raifteirí, agus ní ar Theach an Chúil ... Hyde tells of how Lady Gregory discovered Raifteirí's grave and had it marked with a monument.

179 Ibid., p. 241. Tá Béarla an National School agam ó na páistí, agus tá Béarla Mheiriceá agam ón telefisíon, agus tá Béarla Bhirmingham agam ó bheith ag dul ar cuairt gach samhradh chuig clann mo mhic atá fásta suas agus pósta sa chathair bhreá sin.

180 See ibid., pp 240–1.

181 Ibid., pp 7–8. Más cúis leis na saoithe a líofa a éiríonn Lady Gregory i labhairt na Gaeilge go luath sa dráma, tuigfidh na fealsaimh nach cín lae ná stair atá á scríobh agam ach dráma ... Is léir go mbeidh éifeacht an dráma mar shiamsa amharclainne ag brath go mór ar an bhfeidhm a bhainfear as dearadh, ceol, soilsiú agus an gcomhréir idir na gluaiseachtaí. Ó Floinn was disappointed with the production in the Peacock, which apparently did not use many of these elements, and much preferred the production in An Taibhdhearc, which did. See Ó Floinn, 'An drámaíocht faoi thalamh', *IP*, 7/10/75; and *A Writer's Life*, pp 168–170.

182 There is a picture from the production in *The Irish Press* (*IP*, 8/10/75).

183 The English version was published in O'Flynn, *Three Plays*, pp 185–260.

184 In 'Naomh Oilibhéar: lá mór sa róimh' (St Oliver: a great day in Rome), Ó Floinn wrote that at the performance of *Homo Sapiens* on the evening of Plunkett's canonisation, there were '[only] three examples of the same Homo Sapiens in the audience' (triúr sampla den Homo Sapiens céanna sa lucht féachana' (*IP*, 14/10/75). See also O'Flynn, *A Writer's Life*, p. 191.

185 Duine taobh amuigh de ráillí, leathdhuine istigh. Tosaíonn comhrá eatarthu. Bunsmaoineamh an-spéisiúil, ach ní tugtar in éifeacht é. Ní leor caint

abartha. See Ó Floinn's response in 'Dr Herrema sa Dáil', *IP*, 18/11/75. Ó Glaisne replied to Ó Floinn in *IP*, 28/11/75.

186 The Abbey rejected the play as 'too surrealistic'. See O'Flynn, *A Writer's Life*, p. 191. In a note in the published text, Ó Floinn states: 'It seems to the author, because this is an experimental play, that special attention needs to be given to the music and to the lighting that would be used as artistic support for the action . . . In any case, I do not think that pieces of music that are too familiar should be used' (Feictear don údar, toisc gur dráma turgnamhach é seo, gur gá aire faoi leith a thabhairt don cheol, is don soilsiú a d'úsáidfí mar thaca ealaíonta leis an ngníomhú . . . I gcás ar bith, níor cheart píosaí ceoil so-aitheanta a úsáid, dar liom). See Críostóir Ó Floinn, 'Nóta' (A note), in *Homo Sapiens: Dráma Dhá Mhír* (A play in two acts) (Baile Átha Cliath: An Gúm, 1985), n.p.

187 His original title for the play, which, according to his usual practice, he wrote in both Irish and English, was *Barraí/Bars*.

188 Ó Floinn, *Homo Sapiens*, p. 1.

189 Ibid., p. 2.

190 Ibid., p. 6.

191 Ibid., p. 12.

192 Ibid., p. 7. Na milliúin, na billiúin barraí, barraí iarainn, barraí adhmaid, an scuab do mo tharraingt gan aon staonadh, barraí, barraí ag siúl romham de shíor, barraí ag síneadh romham, timpeall an domhain . . .

193 Ibid., pp 17–18.

194 Ibid., p. 29.

195 Ibid., p. 39.

196 Ibid., p. 35. Among his new friends will be Napoleon, Karl Marx, Hitler, Quintus Horatius Flaccus, and the seventeenth-century Irish scholars known as the Four Masters.

197 Ibid., p. 38.

198 Ibid., p. 40. Tá cuma aerach air anois agus imeacht bhíogiúil.

199 Ibid., pp 41–2.

200 Ibid., p. 31. Cabhair do Jaic, cabhair do na barraí. De bhrí nach léir do Jaic ach a thaobh féin de na barraí, d'fhág sé máchail na meirge ina bruitíneach ar chnámh droma is ar cholpaí mánla anseo is ansiúd. Seo chun oibre tú ar maidin le neamhfhuadar ag cúlú, ag fógairt go bhfuil do scuab ag fí go peannaideach leis an bhforchóta a chur ina thaiséadach umpu. Ach níl an fóchóta fite fuaite i gceart ar a gcolainn chaomh. Éilímse, Billí, ceart do na barraí.

201 Ibid. Dheara, spota anseo is ansiúd ar an taobh sin agatsa. Ní fheicfeadh an Máistir iad sin.

202 Ibid. Feiceann na toir iad agus an lon dubh.

203 Ibid., p. 47. Trí lá eile gan tuarastal, gan toitín, gan chomhluadar ach an . . . an . . . á, maise, go bhféacha Dia an trócaire ort, a Jaic, a dhuine.

204 Ibid., p. 45.

205 Sílim gur thogh sé gréasán ró-mhór agus measaim go ndearna sé iarracht an iomarca tuinte 'de shaol ár muintire sa lá atá inniu ann' a fhíochán isteach le chéile. In his 'Réamhrá' (Preface) to the published play Ó Floinn writes: 'It seemed to me in the end, after bending and folding some of those subjects in a rough draft that the most appropriate thing for this occasion would be a comic entertainment in which there would be some insight into the life of our people today' (B'fhacthas dom i ndeireadh thiar, tar éis filleadh agus feacadh a bhaint as cuid de na hábhair sin ar bhonn dréachta tástála, gurbh é an t-earra ab oiriúnaí don ócáid seo siamsa grinn a mbeadh léargas á dhéanamh ann ar shaol ár muintire sa lá atá inniu ann). See Críostóir Ó Floinn, 'Réamhrá', in *Cluichí Cleamhnais* (Matchmaking games) (Baile Átha Cliath: Foilseacháin Náisiúnta Teoranta, 1978), n.p.

206 He felt 'go raibh an snas agus an chríoch-núlacht atá go sonrach i ndrámaí eile de chuid Uí Fhloinn ar iarraidh. Measaim go bhfuil an bun-smaoineamh go rí-mhaith ach is mór an trua nár ghiorraigh an t-údar a shaothar agus nár chuir sé teannas dlúithe sa ghníomhaíocht'. The result was 'go bhfuil iarracht den fhadálacht ag baint leis an dráma agus nach dtéann sé i gcionn mar a bhítear ag súil leis'.

207 Dráma grinn tá anseo mar adúras, ach tá níos mó abhfad ná áiféis agus greann ann mar tá tuairimí aibidh ar staid agus ar imeacht na tuaithe agus na tíre fré chéile . . . ann; creidim go mbainfeadh lucht féachana ar bith sásamh mór as. As 'Fríostóir Ó Cloinn', Ó Floinn is one of the many Gaelic literary figures Mac Amhlaigh pokes fun at in his satirical novel *Schnitzer Ó Sé*. See Dónall Mac Amhlaigh, *Schnitzer Ó Sé* (Baile Átha Cliath: An Clóchomhar, 1974), p. 62.

208 Ó Floinn, 'Réamhrá', in *Cluichí Cleamhnais*, n.p.

209 Ibid., p. 19.

210 Ibid., p. 30. Ní thuigeann siad dada faoi ealaín na hamharclainne.

211 Ibid., p. 39. Ní bheadh a fhios agat gur bean in aon chor í siúd mura mbainfeá di a bhfuil de sheanbhalcaisí a hathar uimpi.

212 Ibid., p. 51. Níl de shaibhreas agam go fíor ach mo ainm agus mo anam, mo shinsireacht uasal agus mo mhianta uaisle.

213 Ibid., p. 52. B'fhacthas dom gur glan amach as *Riders to the Sea* agus Jack B. Yeats a d'éirigh an fear óg álainn seo chugam.

214 Ibid., p. 61. A mhaithe agus a mhóruaisle Éireann, is mór an onóir domsa a bheith anseo in bhur láthair inniu . . . Ba mhaith liom anois, tar ceann Rialtas agus pobal na Seapáine, a dhearbhú daoibh cé chomh mór is atá ár meas ar mhuintir na

tire seo, tír ársa aoibhinn álainn a bhfuil meas ag tíortha an domhan –

215 Ibid., p. 63.

216 Ibid., p. 111.

217 Such behaviour could still be seen as comic in 1978.

218 One result of these marriages is that both the parish priest and the retired teacher lose housekeepers.

219 Ó Floinn, *Cluichí Cleamhnais*, p. 91.

220 Ibid., p. 92.

221 Ibid., p. 36.

222 Ibid., p. 99. Dhera nach túisce leo anois an teach breá, brat ar gach urlár, an carr agus an telefís agus laethanta saoire sa Spáinn, ná an gnó arbh chuige a cheap Dia na glóire an fear is an bhean. Inseoidh Sinéad daoibh faoi na piollaí agus na giúirléidí go léir atá ceaptha ag na heolaithe le go mbeadh an craiceann agus a luach ag daoine, mar a déarfá.

223 Ibid., p. 100. Agus níos measa fós, tá siad ag marú leanaí sa bhroinn thall sa Bhreatain agus i Meiriceá agus i dtíortha eile nach iad . . . Má tá, is anseo in Éirinn a ghintear go leor de na leanaí sin a mhúchtar thall sa Bhreatain.

224 A scene from the play was performed at An Taibhdhearc in the summer of 1983 as part of a show entitled *Fáilte* (Welcome) (*CS*, 12/7/83).

225 Críostóir Ó Floinn, *Lámh Dheas: Lámh Chlé* (Right hand: left hand) (Baile Átha Cliath: Oifig an tSoláthair, 1978), p. 8. Déanann sibh an-tairbhe, gan amhras, do na dílleachtaí úd, ach déanann sibh bhur leas féin chomh maith . . . agus bíonn poiblíocht agus moladh mór le fáil agaibh as gach leathphingin a chaitheann sibh ar son na carthanachta.

226 Ibid., p. 9. Níl an charthanacht chomh héasca ar an gcuma a leag ár dTiarna síos lena déanamh.

227 Ibid.

228 Ibid., p. 11. Rinne tú maitheas do m'anam, agus is ró-annamh a chuimhním go bhfuil anam agam.

229 Ibid., p. 27. Ó! Cad ina thaobh nár phós mé mac an táilliúra nó fear an bhainne!

230 See Miriam Hederman, 'Great success with "the Barrets of Wimpole Street"', *II*, 10/12/68.

231 O'Flynn, *Consplawkus*, p. 100.

232 Críostóir Ó Floinn, *Solas an tSaoil* (The light of the world), in *Solas an tSaoil/Mair, a Chapaill!* (Live, horse!) (Baile Átha Cliath: Oifig an tSoláthair, 1980), p. 12.

233 Ibid., p. 21. Nuair a d'fhéach sé orm, chuimhníos ar na focail a dúirt Maois leis an Ardsagart sa chúirt inniu. 'Is mise solas an tsaoil.' Tuigim anois é.

234 Ibid., pp 21–2. Ní fios d'aon duine againn cad atá i ndán dúinn, nó cén fáth a bhfuil na nithe seo ag tarlú. Ag Dia na Glóire atá gach fios.

235 Críostóir Ó Floinn, *Mair, a Chapaill!*, in *Solas an tSaoil/Mair, a Chapaill!*, p. 53. Agus cogar, a dhuine, ná ceap gur féidir leat bob a bhualadh orm le seandealbh de Naomh Pádraig!

236 The original title confused people, who apparently expected to see a straight adaptation of Ó Conaire's story. Ó Floinn felt compelled to clear up this confusion in a letter to the *Irish Times* in which he stated that 'it is in no way an adaptation, but an entirely original work' (*IT*, 17/11/78).

237 Críostóir Ó Floinn, *Taibhsí na Faiche Móire: Dráma Aonmhíre* (The ghosts of Eyre Square: a one-act play), p. 3. The play has not been published. I am using a typescript provided to me by the author. Mise an té arbh leis an t-asal beag dubh úd a bhfuil tusa ag inseacht do chuid bréaga dubha faoi le blianta fada anuas.

238 The mayor of Galway, Paddy Ryan, created some controversy in the city by speaking at what some felt was undue length in Irish at the ceremony welcoming Kennedy.

239 Ó Floinn, *Taibhsí na Faiche Móire*, pp 13–15.

240 Ibid., p. 19.

241 Ibid.

242 Ibid., p. 28.

243 Ibid.

244 Ibid., p. 30.

245 It was broadcast over Radio Éireann in April 1992 (*AC*, 9/4/92). In an email to me dated 7 June 2015, Ó Floinn wrote of this play that 'it was produced here and there' (léiríodh é anseo is ansiúd).

246 Ach cuirfidh mé geall nach raibh i measc an [*sic*] lucht éisteachta 'An Spailpín Fánach' i rith na seachtaine seo duine ar bith nár chuir lena thuiscint ar cheann de phríomh-údair na Gaeilge . . . Tar éis an dráma seo a fheiceáil ní bheidh duine ar bith nach dtuigfeadh an fear dearóil seo níos fearr.

247 I am using a photocopy of the script in the Taibhdhearc na Gaillimhe Papers in the James Hardiman Library at NUIG. In the script, p. 41 is missing. This copy was kindly made for me by Dr Louis de Paor of NUIG.

248 Críostóir Ó Floinn, *An Spailpín Fánach* (The wandering farm labourer), pp 5–6.

249 Ibid., p. 7.

250 See ibid., p. 28.

251 Ibid., p. 49. This scene is in English in the original. On p. 47, the Functionary is sharply critical of the way Ó Conaire deserted his wife and children.

252 Ibid., p. 28.

253 See Liam Ó Flaithearta, 'Ag casadh le Pádraic Ó Conaire' (Meeting Pádraic Ó Conaire), *Comhar*, Apr. 1953, pp 3–6.

254 Ó Floinn, *An Spailpín Fánach*, p. 30. O'Flaherty says he wants 'tusa a dhíbirt go dtí oileán mara i bhfad ó chomhluadar daoine is ón mbuidéal san atá do do mharú. Choineoinn bia do dhóthain leat agus flúirse páipéir agus peann agus ní ligfinn abhaile go hÉirinn thú go dtí go mbeadh an t-úrscéal mór seo scríofa agat a bhfuilim tinn de bheith ag éisteacht leat ag caint faoi. In the last years of his life, Ó Conaire was supposedly working on a novel to be

called *An Fear* (The man). See O'Flaherty, 'Ag casadh le Pádraic Ó Conaire', *Comhar*, Apr. 1953, p. 4.

255 Níl cead agamsa dada a scríobh ach leabhair do na páistí scoile, nó a bheith i mo Fhearfeasa Mac Feasa ag déanamh grinn do léitheoirí an 'Connacht Sentinel'. Ó Conaire felt that writers of Irish suffered from 'the tyranny of the schoolchild' as a result of the widespread belief that the only audience for books in Irish was in the schools. See, for example, 'Páistí scoile: an bhfuil siad ag milleadh nualitríocht na Gaeilge?' (Schoolchildren: are they destroying modern literature in Irish?), in *Aistí Phádraic Uí Chonaire* (The essays of Pádraic Ó Conaire), ed. Gearóid Denvir (Indreabhan: Cló Chois Fharraige, 1978), pp 80–1. This piece was originally published in *An Claidheamh Soluis*, 17/2/17. Ó Conaire's harmless comic tales about Fearfeasa Mac Feasa were collected and published posthumously in 1930.

256 Ó Floinn, *An Spailpín Fánach*, p. 33. Tá m'anam chomh seirgthe, chomh folamh, le blaosc an chnó chapaill úd a thit den chrann i lár na coille. Níl aon ní fágtha agam le rá . . .

257 Ibid., p. 43. Ach níl an ceart agatsa, ná ag aon Éireannach eile a thugann a dhroim le dúchas is le cultúr a chine féin ar mhaithe le hairgead nó le cáil.

258 Ibid. Dílis go bás, don tír is don teanga, an mar sin é? . . . Sin an ceacht a d'fhoghlaimíos ó mo shinsir, sin an dúchas atá mar oidhreacht agam ó Fhlaithrí Ó Maolchonaire agus an chuid eile acu a d'fhulaing céasadh nó imirce ar son chine Gael. Tá

dóchas agam as cine Gael. Fanann an aisling agam, go mbeidh Éire saor agus Gaelach lá éicint amach anseo.

259 Ibid., p. 44.

260 Ibid. Deirimse go mbeidh an Ghaeilge marbh ar fad faoin am sin. Ní bheidh Gaeltacht ar bith fágtha. Beidh scoláirí ollscoile ann, is dócha, ag plé le Gaeilge mar a bhítear ag plé leis an Laidin anois, ina teanga marbh.

261 Le blianta fada anuas is faoi Ghael-Linn agus an Damer a fágadh an drámaíocht Ghaeilge a chothú go seasmhach.

262 O'Flynn, *Consplawkus*, p. 300.

263 D'iarras go ndéanfaí iad a mheas lena léiriú in éineacht. Fuaireas litir ar ais ó dhuine éigin ón Bhord, á rá go gcuirfí na drámaí faoi bhráid an Stiúrthóir Ealaíne agus ag tagairt go cineálta do na drámaí eile úd dem chuidse a líon An Taibhdhearc sna blianta a d'imigh tharainn. Focal eile níor chualas ó shin.

264 Alan Titley, 'Contemporary literature', *The Crane Bag: Irish Language and Culture/An tEagrán Gaelach* V:2 (1981), p. 64. He has also called Ó Floinn the writer who comes closest to being 'an important writer in Irish . . . primarily known for his or her work as a dramatist' but added that 'he may have been too eclectic for his own career'. That, of course, may seem like praising Ó Floinn with a faint damn. See Titley, 'Neither the boghole nor Berlin', in *Nailing Theses*, p. 271.

Afterword

1 The Abbey did commission Tom MacIntyre's *Cúirt an Mheán Oíche* (The midnight court) and *Caoineadh Airt Uí Laoghaire* (The lament for Arthur O'Leary), both adaptations of famous poems from the eighteenth century. The former had its premiere by the Abbey in Coláiste Chonnacht in Spiddal, Co. Galway in 1998 with Michael Harding directing; the latter was first performed by the Abbey, with Kathy McArdle as director, at Taibhdhearc na Gaillimhe in 1999.

2 Another Dublin company performing in Irish is Mouth of Breath, founded in 2010 by Melissa Nolan and Cathal Quinn. This company has performed Irish translations of plays by Yeats and Beckett.

3 This production was enthusiastically received at St Brendan's Hall in Boston's Dorchester neighbourhood in 2004.

4 An Taibhdhearc also staged his adaptations of his own short stories 'An Fear a Phléasc' (The man who exploded) and 'Seacht gCéad Uaireadóir' (Seven hundred watches) in 2001 with Máire Áine Ní Chinnéide directing. Moreover, Ó Conghaile's translations of plays by Martin MacDonagh and Jimmy Murphy have been successful with audiences in Galway.

5 In an interview with the website The Wild Geese, co-founder and managing director Darach Ó Tuairisg defined 'fíbín' as 'explosion of joy and happiness'. See The Wild Geese website at: thewildgeese. irish/profiles/blogs/this-wednesday-community-chat-with-darach-o-tuairisg-of-fibin-teo.

6 Another Gaelic company in Galway is Branar (Fallow land), which produces plays in Irish for children. It was founded in 2001 by Marc Mac Lochlainn, who remains its artistic director.

7 Of course plays in Irish are produced from time to time in all of these places and many others by small amateur companies, Gaelic League branches, and school and university drama societies.

8 Aisling Ghéar developed from a group named Aisteoirí Aon Dráma (Actors of any play).

9 The company has also produced Irish translations of plays by Irish writers of English like Seán O'Casey, Brian Friel, and Tom Murphy.

10 *Scaoil leis an gCaid* was produced at Taibhdhearc na Gaillmhe in 2003, with Darach Mac Con Iomaire directing.

11 Titley has also written radio plays.

Selected Bibliography

PRIMARY SOURCES

I MANUSCRIPTS AND PERSONAL COMMUNICATIONS

An Comhar Drámaíochta, documents relating to, including letters, reports of the secretary and treasurer, etc., donated to the National Library of Ireland by Pádraig Ó Siochfhradha ('An Seabhac').

Ní Ghráda, Máiréad, *Rité: Dráma Aonmhíre*, script provided by An Comhlachas Náisiúnta Drámaíochta.

Ó Floinn, Críostóir, emails to author.

_____, *An Spailpín Fánach*, copy of the script in the Taibhdhearc na Gaillimhe Papers, James Hardiman Library, National University of Ireland, Galway.

_____, *Taibhsí na Faiche Móire: Dráma Aonmhíre*, copy of the typescript provided to me by Ó Floinn.

Ó Néill, Séamus, *Adhaint na Tine Beo* (1967), performed as *Spiorad na Saoirse*, unpaginated typescript of this pageant given by Ó Néill to Professor John V. Kelleher of Harvard, who gave it to me.

_____, *Rún an Oileáin*, script provided by An Comhlachas Náisiúnta Drámaíochta.

Ó Tuairisc, Eoghan, *Carolan*, script provided by An Comhlachas Náisiúnta Drámaíochta.

_____, *De Réir na Rúibricí: Coiméide Trighníomh*, script provided by An Comhlachas Náisiúnta Drámaíochta.

_____, *An Hairyfella in Ifreann*, script provided by An Comhlachas Náisiúnta Drámaíochta.

Ó Tuama, Seán, *Déan Trócaire ar Shagairt Óga*, script provided by An Comhlachas Náisiúnta Drámaíochta.

_____, *Iúdás Iscariot agus a Bhean*, script provided by An Comhlachas Náisiúnta Drámaíochta.

Taibhdhearc na Gaillimhe Papers, James Hardiman Library, National University of Ireland, Galway.

II NEWSPAPERS AND PERIODICALS

Aiséirghe
The Anglo-Celt
Ar Aghaidh
Ardán
Books Abroad
An Claidheamh Soluis
Comhar
The Connacht Sentinel
The Connacht Tribune
The Connaught Telegraph
The Cork Examiner

The Derry People and Donegal News
Éire: Bliainiris Ghaedheal: Rogha Saothair Ghaedheal mBeo
An tÉireannach
Evening Herald
Evening Press
Fáinne an Lae
Feasta: Reiviú don Litríocht, don Eolaíocht, do na hEalaíona, don Pholaitíocht is don Smaointeachas
       Éireannach
Fermanagh Herald
Galway Advertiser
An Glór
Hibernia
Inniu
An Iris
The Irish Booklover
Irish Bookman
Irish Independent
The Irish News
The Irish Press
The Irish Rosary
Irish Times
Irisleabhar Mhá Nuad
Irisleabhar na Gaedhilge
The Kerryman
Léachtaí Cholm Cille
The Leader
Leitrim Observer
Limerick Leader
Longford Leader
The Mayo News
Meath Chronicle
Misneach
The Munster Express
The Nenagh Guardian
Sinn Féin
The Southern Star
The Standard
Sunday Independent
The Tuam Herald
Ulster Herald
An tUltach
The Western People
Westmeath Examiner

Newspapers were accessed online via the Irish Newspaper Archive
(www.irishnewsarchive.com)

Selected Bibliography

III BOOKS AND ARTICLES

Annála Ríoghachta Éireann/Annals of the Kingdom of Ireland by the Four Masters, from the Earliest Period to the Year 1616, vol. 5, ed. and trans. John O'Donovan (Dublin: Hodges, Smith and Co., 1856), pp 1462–541.

Blythe, Ernest, 'Gaelic drama', in *The Irish Theatre: Lectures Delivered during the Abbey Theatre Festival Held in Dublin in August 1938*, ed. Lennox Robinson (London: Macmillan and Co., 1939), pp 177–97.

Carleton, Karen, 'Tomás Mac Anna in conversation with Karen Carleton', in *Theatre Talk: Voices of Irish Theatre Practitioners*, ed. Lilian Chambers, Ger Fitzgibbon, Eamonn Jordan, Dan Farrelly, and Cathy Leeney (Dublin: Carysfort Press, 2001), pp 277–89.

'Dónall Óg', in *Nua-Dhuanaire Cuid 1*, ed. Pádraig de Brún, Breandán Ó Buachalla, and Tomás Ó Concheanainn (Baile Átha Cliath: Institiúid Ardléinn Bhaile Átha Cliath, 1971), pp 73–4.

Du Bois, W. E. B., *The Souls of Black Folk*, ed. David W. Blight and Robert Gooding-Williams (Boston: Bedford/St Martin's, 1997 [1903]).

Eliot, T. S., 'Litttle Gidding', in *Four Quartets* (New York: Harcourt, Brace and World, 1977 [1943]), p. 51.

Gallagher, Frank, *Days of Fear: A Diary of Hunger Strike* (Cork: Mercier Press, 1967 [1928]).

_____, (as 'David Hogan'), *The Four Glorious Years* (Dublin: Irish Press Ltd, 1953).

Greene, David, ed., *Fingal Rónáin and Other Stories*, Medieval and Modern Irish Series XVI (Dublin: Dublin Institute for Advanced Studies, 1955).

Gregory, Lady Augusta, *Poets and Dreamers: Studies and Translations from the Irish* (Teddington: The Echo Library, 2006 [1903]).

Kearney, Colbert, *The Consequence* (Dublin: Blackstaff Press, 1993).

Mac Amhlaigh, Dónall, *Schnitzer Ó Sé* (Baile Átha Cliath: An Clóchomhar, 1974).

Mac Anna, Tomás, *Fallaing Aonghusa: Saol Amharclainne* (Baile Átha Cliath: An Clóchomhar, 2000).

Mac Liammóir, Micheál, 'Drámaíocht Ghaeilge san am atá le teacht', in *Ceo Meala, Lá Seaca* (Baile Átha Cliath: Sáirséal agus Dill, 1952), pp 225–40.

Ní Ghráda, Máiréad, *Giolla an tSolais: Duais-Dráma Trí Mír* (Baile Átha Cliath: Oifig an tSoláthair, 1954).

_____, *An Grádh agus an Gárda: Dráma Grinn Aon-Mhíre* (Baile Átha Cliath: Oifig Díolta Foillseacháin Rialtais, 1937).

_____, *Lá Buí Bealtaine: Dráma Aonmhíre* (Baile Átha Cliath: Oifig an tSoláthair, 1954).

_____, *Mac Uí Rudaí: Duaisdhráma Oireachtais na Bliana 1960* (Baile Átha Cliath: Oifig an tSoláthair, 1962).

_____, *Stailc Ocrais: Tragóid Stairiúil: Dráma Aonghnímh* (Baile Átha Cliath: Oifig an tSoláthair, 1966).

_____, *Súgán Sneachta: Geandráma Aon-mhíre* (Baile Átha Cliath: Oifig an tSoláthair, 1962).

_____, *An Triail/Breithiúnas: Dhá Dhráma* (Baile Átha Cliath: Oifig an tSoláthair, 1978).

_____, *An Udhacht* (Baile Átha Cliath: Oifig an tSoláthair, 1935).

_____, *Úll Glas Oíche Shamhna: Dráma Aonmhíre* (Baile Átha Cliath: Oifig an tSoláthair, 1960).

Ó Coileáin, Dáithí, 'Fíodóir na bhfocal: agallamh le hEoghan Ó Tuairisc', *Comhar*, Oct. 1974, pp 4–8 and 20.

Ó Floinn (O'Flynn), Críostóir, *Aggiornamento: Dráma Trí Mhír* (Baile Átha Cliath: Oifig an tSoláthair, 1969).

_____, *Aisling Dhá Abhainn* (Baile Átha Cliath: Foilseacháin Náisiúnta Teoranta, 1977).

_____, *Cad d'Imigh ar Fheidhlimidh?: Dráma Trí Mhír* (Baile Átha Cliath: Oifig an tSoláthair, 1978).

_____, *Cluichí Cleamhnais* (Baile Átha Cliath: Foilseacháin Náisiúnta Teoranta, 1978).

_____, *Consplawkus: A Writer's Life* (Cork: Mercier Press, 1999).

_____, *Cóta Bán Chríost: Dráma Trí Ghluaiseacht* (Baile Átha Cliath: Sáirséal agus Dill, 1968).

_____, *Éalú ó Chill Mhaighneann* (Baile Átha Cliath: Oifig an tSoláthair, 1968).

_____, *The Easter Rising: A Poem Sequence* (Dún Laoghaire: Obelisk Books, 2004).

_____, *Éirí Amach na Cásca 1916* (Baile Átha Cliath: Sáirséal agus Dill, 1967).

_____, *Homo Sapiens: Dráma Dhá Mhír* (Baile Átha Cliath: An Gúm, 1985).

_____, *Is É a Dúirt Polonius: Dráma Trí Mhír* (Baile Átha Cliath: Oifig an tSoláthair, 1973).

_____, *Is Fada Anocht* (Baile Átha Cliath: Oifig an tSoláthair, 1968).

_____, *Lámh Dheas: Lámh Chlé* (Baile Átha Cliath: Oifig an tSoláthair, 1978).

_____, *A Man Called Pearse: A Play in Three Acts* (Baile Átha Cliath: Foilseacháin Náisiúnta Teoranta, 1980).

_____, *Mise Raifteirí an File: Dráma Trí Mhír* (Baile Átha Cliath: Sáirséal agus Dill, 1974).

_____, *Ó Fhás go hAois* (Baile Átha Cliath: Sáirséal agus Dill, 1969).

_____, *Oineachlann* (Baile Átha Cliath: Oifig an tSoláthair, 1968).

_____, *Seacláidí Van Gogh* (Baile Átha Cliath: Coiscéim, 1996).

_____, *Solas an tSaoil/Mair, a Chapaill!* (Baile Átha Cliath: Oifig an tSoláthair, 1980).

_____, *There Is an Isle: A Limerick Boyhood* (Cork: Mercier Press, 1998).

_____, *Three Plays* (Dún Laoghaire: Obelisk Books, 2000).

_____, *The Woman Who Never Said 'Hello': Selected Poems* (Dublin: Original Writing Ltd, 2014).

_____, *A Writer's Life* (Dún Laoghaire: Obelisk Books, 2001).

O'Malley, Ernie, *On Another Man's Wound* (Dublin: Anvil Books, 1979 [1936]).

Ó Morónaigh, Seán, ed., *Drámaíocht ó Dhúchas ó Bhéalaithris Thaidhg Uí Chonchubhair* (Camas: An Comhlachas Náisiúnta Drámaíochta, 2005).

Ó Néill, Séamus, 'Agallamh le Séamus Ó Néill', *IMN*, 1962, pp 5–8.

_____, *An Tusa d'Fhoscail an Fhuinneog?*, *Feasta*, May 1953, pp 7–10.

_____, *Buaidh an Ultaigh: Dráma Nua* (Baile Átha Cliath: Oifig Díolta Foillseacháin Rialtais, 1936).

_____, *Colm Cille: Dráma i gCeithre Radharcanna* (Baile Átha Cliath: Oifig an tSoláthair, 1946).

_____, 'Cúlra stairiúil na críchdheighilte', *Comhar*, Apr. 1954, pp 6–7.

_____, *Díolta faoi n-a Luach: Dráma Cheithre Radharc* (Baile Átha Cliath: Oifig an tSoláthair, 1946).

_____, *Faill ar an bhFeart: Dráma Trí Ghníomh* (Baile Átha Cliath: Sáirséal agus Dill, 1967).

_____, 'An fhírinne fá Cholum Cille', *Iris*, Jan. 1946, pp 49–56.

_____, 'Gaelic literature', in *Dictionary of Irish Literature*, vol. 1, ed. Robert Hogan (Westport, CT: Greenwood Press, 1996), pp 17–62.

_____, 'The hidden Ulster: Gaelic pioneers of the North', *Studies*, spring 1966, pp 60–6.

_____, *Iníon Rí Dhún Sobhairce: Tragóid Trí Ghníomh* (Baile Átha Cliath: Sáirséal agus Dill, 1960).

_____, *Iníon Rí na Spáinne* (Baile Átha Cliath: Oifig an tSoláthair, 1978).

_____, *Lámh Dearg Abú!* (Baile Átha Cliath: Foilseacháin Náisiúnta Teoranta, 1982).

_____, *Máire Nic Artáin* (Baile Átha Cliath: Cló Morainn, 1959).

_____, '*Ní Chuireann Siad Síol' nó 'Poll Bocht'* (Baile Átha Cliath: Oifig an tSoláthair, 1952).

_____, *An tSiúr Pól: Dráma i dTrí Gníomha* (Baile Átha Cliath: Oifig an tSoláthair, 1961).

_____, *Tonn Tuile* (Baile Átha Cliath: Sáirséal agus Dill, 1947).

_____, *Up the Rebels: Dráma Grinn: Mír Amháin* (Baile Átha Cliath: Oifig an tSoláthair, 1954).

Ó Tuairisc, Eoghan, *Aisling Mhic Artáin* (Baile Átha Cliath: Clódhanna Teoranta, 1978).

_____, *Cúirt na Gealaí: Coiméide Trighniomh* (Baile Átha Cliath: An Gúm, 1988).

_____, *Dé Luain* (Baile Átha Cliath: Allen Figgis and Co., 1966).

_____, 'Fornocht . . . comhrá le hEoghan Ó Tuairisc', *Innti* VI (1981), pp 15–47.

_____, *Fornocht do Chonac* (Baile Átha Cliath: Oifig an tSoláthair, 1981).

_____, *Lá Fhéile Míchíl* (Baile Átha Cliath: Clódhanna Teoranta, 1967).

_____, *Lux Aeterna* (Baile Átha Cliath: Allen Figgis, 1964).

_____, *Na Mairnéalaigh*, in *Gearrdhrámaí an Chéid*, ed. Pádraig Ó Siadhail (Indreabhán: Cló Iar-Chonnachta, 2000), pp 109–31.

_____, *Religio Poetae agus Aistí Eile*, ed. Máirín Nic Eoin (Baile Átha Cliath: An Clóchomhar, 1987).

_____, *Sidelines: A Diary of Poems 1951–1974* (Dublin: Raven Arts, 1981).

_____, *The Weekend of Dermot and Grace* (Dublin: Allen Figgis, 1964).

Ó Tuama, Seán, *Ar Aghaidh linn, a Longadáin: Extravaganza Cheithre Ghníomh* (Indreabhán: Cló Iar-Chonnachta, 1991).

_____, *Corp Eoghain Uí Shúilleabháin: Dhá Ghníomh agus Dhá Eadarlúid*, in *Moloney agus Drámaí Eile* (Baile Átha Cliath: An Clóchomhar, 1966).

_____, *Faoileán na Bheatha* (Baile Átha Cliath: An Clóchomhar, 1962).

_____, *The Gaelic League Idea* (Cork: Mercier Press, 1972).

_____, *Gunna Cam agus Slabhra Óir: Dráma Véarsaíochta Thrí Ghníomh* (Baile Átha Cliath: Sáirséal agus Dill, 1964).

_____, *Is É Seo M'Oileán: Trí Ghníomh*, in *Moloney agus Drámaí Eile*.

_____, 'Love in the medieval Irish literary lyric', in *Repossessions: Selected Essays on the Irish Literary Heritage* (Cork: Cork University Press, 1995), pp 164–95.

_____, *Moloney: Dráma Aonghnímh*, in *Moloney agus Drámaí Eile*.

_____, 'Samuel Beckett, Éireannach', *Scríobh* III (1978), pp 37–41.

_____, *Saol fó Thoinn* (Baile Átha Cliath: An Clóchomhar, 1978).

_____, '"Slabhraí óir . . .": Comhrá le Seán Ó Tuama', *Innti* IX (1984), pp 28–54.

Ryan, Phyllis, *The Company I Kept* (Dublin: Town House, 1996).

Ryan, Vera, *Dan Donovan: An Everyman's Life* (Cork: The Collins Press, 2008).

SECONDARY SOURCES

Bradshaw, Brendan, 'Manus "the magnificent": O'Donnell as renaissance prince', in *Studies in Irish History Presented to R. Dudley Edwards*, ed. Art Cosgrave and Donal McCartney (Dublin: University College Dublin, 1979), pp 15–36.

Breathnach, Diarmuid, and Máire Ní Mhurchú, *1882–1982: Beathaisnéis a hAon* (Baile Átha Cliath: An Clóchomhar, 1986).

_____, *1882–1982: Beathaisnéis a Trí* (Baile Átha Cliath: An Clóchomhar, 1992).

_____, *Beathaisnéis a Naoi: Forlíonadh agus Innéacsanna* (Baile Átha Cliath: An Clóchomhar, 2007).

Byrne, Francis John, *Irish Kings and High-Kings* (London: B. T. Batsford, 1973).

Cassidy, John Gerard, 'Séamus Ó Néill: a shaol agus a shaothar', unpublished MA thesis, Queen's University, Belfast, 1983.

Comóradh Mháiréad Ní Ghráda: Drámadóir – Craoltóir – Gearrscéalaí, Cill Mháille, Co. an Chláir, 14–15 Meitheamh, 1997. Leabhrán Cuimhneacháin.

Selected Bibliography

Cooney, John, *John Charles McQuaid: Ruler of Catholic Ireland* (Syracuse: Syracuse University Press, 1999).

de hÓra, Ciarán, *Na Drámaí a Léiríodh i dTaibhdhearc na Gaillimhe 1928–2003* (Gaillimh: Ollscoil na hÉireann, Gaillimh, n.d.).

Fallon, Brian, *An Age of Innocence: Irish Culture 1930–1960* (Dublin: Gill and Macmillan, 1999).

Kiberd, Declan, *Inventing Ireland: The Literature of the Modern Nation* (London: Jonathan Cape, 1995).

_____, 'Seán Ó Ríordáin: file Angla-Éireannach', in *Idir Dhá Chultúr* (Baile Átha Cliath: Coiscéim, 1993).

Mac Aonghusa, Proinsias, *Ar Son na Gaeilge: Conradh na Gaeilge 1893–1993: Stair Sheanchais* (Baile Átha Cliath: Conradh na Gaeilge, 1993).

Mac Craith, Mícheál, '*Geineasas, Antigone* agus *Lá Fhéile Míchíl*', *Comhar*, Oct. 1985, pp 46–52.

McKendry, Eugene, 'Innovation and tradition in the drama of Críostóir Ó Floinn', in *Celtic Literatures in the Twentieth Century* (Moscow: Languages of Slavonic Culture, 2007), pp 157–82.

Mathews, P. J., 'Hyde's first stand: the Irish language controversy of 1899', *Éire-Ireland*, spring-summer 2000, pp 173–87.

Mercier, Vivian, 'Swift and the Gaelic tradition', in *Fair Liberty Was All His Cry: A Tercentenary Tribute to Jonathan Swift 1667–1745*, ed. A. Norman Jeffares (London: Macmillan, 1967), pp 279–89.

Morgan, Eileen, '"Unbroken service": Máiréad Ní Ghráda's career at 2RN, Ireland's first broadcasting station', *Éire-Ireland*, fall-winter 2002, pp 53–78.

Ní Bhaoighill, Caoimhe, 'An drámaíocht Ghaeilge 1954–89', *IMN*, 1991, pp 131–61.

Ní Bhrádaigh, Siobhán, *Máiréad Ní Ghráda: Ceannródaí Drámaíochta* (Indreabhán: Cló Iar-Chonnachta, 1996).

Nic Eoin, Máirín, 'Contemporary prose and drama in Irish 1940–2000', in *The Cambridge History of Irish Literature*, vol. 2, ed. Margaret Kelleher and Philip O'Leary (Cambridge: Cambridge University Press, 2006), pp 299–306.

_____, *Eoghan Ó Tuairisc: Beatha agus Saothar* (Baile Átha Cliath: An Clóchomhar, 1988).

Nic Giolla Bhríde, Áine, 'Drámaíocht i nDún na nGall', in *Scríbhneoireacht na gConallach*, ed. Nollaig Mac Congáil (Baile Átha Cliath: Coiscéim, 1990), pp 203–10.

Ní Chinnéide, Máiréad, *An Damer: Stair Amharclainne* (Baile Átha Cliath: Gael-Linn, 2008).

_____, *Scéal Ghael-Linn* (Indreabhán: Cló Iar-Chonnachta, 2013).

Ní Dhálaigh, Ursula, 'Máiréad Ní Ghráda oideachasóir', in *Comóradh Mháiréad Ní Ghráda ... Leabhrán Cuimhneacháin*, pp 3–9.

Ní Mhurchú, Antonia, '*Is É a Dúirt Polonius* agus *A Doll's House*', *IMN*, 1986, pp 43–84.

Ní Shé, Máiréad, 'Séamus Ó Néill: saol agus saothar', *IMN*, 1987, pp 62–101.

Nugent, Martin, *Drámaí Eoghain Uí Thuairisc* (Má Nuad: An Sagart, 1984).

Ó Ciosáin, Éamon, 'Máiréad Ní Ghráda agus a saothar liteartha', in Máiréad Ní Ghráda, *An Triail/Breithiúnas: Dhá Dhráma* (Baile Átha Cliath: Oifig an tSoláthair, 1978), pp 173–96.

_____, 'Tábhacht Mháiréad Ní Ghráda', in *Comóradh Mháiréad Ní Ghráda ... Leabhrán Cuimhneacháin*, pp 26–8.

Ó Coigligh, Ciarán, 'An teispéireas drámata: sracfhéachaint ar dhrámaíocht Chríostóra Uí Fhloinn', in *Mangarae: Aistí Litríochta agus Teanga* (Cathair na Mart: Foilseacháin Náisiúnta Teoranta, 1987), pp 18–35.

Ó Coileáin, Diarmaid, 'Drámaíocht na Gaeilge', *Inniu*, 31 Aug., 7, 14, 21, 28 Sept. 1979.

Ó Conchubhair, Brian, '"Twisting in the wind": Irish-language stage theatre 1884–2014', in *The Oxford Handbook of Modern Irish Theatre*, ed. Nicholas Grene and Christopher Morash (Oxford: Oxford University Press, 2016), pp 251–68.

Ó Cuimín, Seán, 'An áiféis agus an teiseachas i ndrámaí Sheáin Uí Thuama', *IMN*, 1988, pp 30–66.

Ó Dubhshláine, Tadhg, 'Drámadóir gan traidisiún: staidéar ar thrí dhráma le Seán Ó Tuama', *IMN*, 1971, pp 42–51.

Ó hÉigeartaigh, Cian, and Aoileann Nic Gearailt, *Sáirséal agus Dill 1947–1981: Scéal Foilsitheora* (Indreabhán: Cló Iar-Chonnachta, 2014).

O'Leary, Philip, *Gaelic Prose in the Irish Free State 1922–1939* (Dublin: University College Dublin Press, 2004).

_____, 'Honour bound: the social context of early Irish heroic *geis*', *Celtica* XX (1988), pp 85–107.

_____, *Irish Interior: Keeping Faith with the Past in Gaelic Prose 1940–1951* (Dublin: University College Dublin Press, 2010).

_____, 'Jeers and judgments: laughter in early Irish literature', *Cambridge Medieval Celtic Studies* XXII (winter 1991), pp 15–29.

_____, *The Prose Literature of the Gaelic Revival: Ideology and Innovation* (State College: Pennsylvania State University Press, 1994).

_____, 'Reasoning why after fifty years: the Easter Rising in Eoghan Ó Tuairisc's *Dé Luain* (1966)', *Proceedings of the Harvard Celtic Colloquium* XXXI (2011), pp 253–81.

_____, '"What would Willie say?": Lady Gregory and popular theatre in Irish', *Journal of the Galway Archaeological and Historical Society* LXIII (2011), pp 158–80.

_____, *Writing beyond the Revival: Facing the Future in Gaelic Prose 1940–1951* (Dublin: University College Dublin Press, 2011).

Ó Loingsigh, Domhnall, 'Mo chéad leabhar scoile!: na seoda litríochta a d'fhág Máiréad Ní Ghráda againn', in *Comóradh Mháiréad Ní Ghráda . . . Leabhrán Cuimhneacháin*, pp 19–21.

Ó Maoláin, Caoimhín, 'Baoithín a d'Fhill: staidéar ar dhán le Seán Ó Tuama', *IMN*, 1968, pp 71–88.

Ó Muimhneacháin, Aindrias, *Dóchas agus Duainéis: Scéal Chonradh na Gaeilge 1922–1932* (Corcaigh: Cló Mercier, n.d.).

Ó Muirí, Damien, 'Drámaí Chríostóra Uí Fhloinn', *Léachtaí Cholm Cille* X (1979), pp 92–130.

Ó Riain, Seán, *Pleanáil Teanga in Éirinn 1919–1985* (Baile Átha Cliath: Carbad, 1994).

Ó Ríordáin, Traolach, *Conradh na Gaeilge i gCorcaigh, 1894–1910* (Baile Átha Cliath: Cois Life, 2000).

Ó Siadhail, Pádraig, 'Drámaí Sheáin Uí Thuama', *IMN*, 1986, pp 7–42.

_____, 'An phrológ', in *Gearrdhrámaí an Chéid*, ed. Pádraig Ó Siadhail (Indreabhán: Cló Iar-Chonnachta, 2000).

_____, *Stair Dhrámaíocht na Gaeilge 1900–1970* (Indreabhán: Cló Iar-Chonnachta, 1993).

Ó Súilleabháin, Donncha, *An Cumann Scoildrámaíochta 1934–1984* (Baile Átha Cliath: An Clóchomhar, 1986).

_____, *Scéal an Oireachtais 1897–1924* (Baile Átha Cliath: An Clóchomhar, 1984).

_____, 'Tús agus fás na drámaíochta i nGaeilge', *Ardán*, Oireachtas 1971, spring and summer 1972.

Snyder, Gary, *The Practice of the Wild: Essays by Gary Snyder* (San Francisco: North Point Press, 1990).

Taibhdhearc na Gaillimhe 1928–2003, compiled by Fiona Bateman, Kieran Hoare, and Lionel Pilkington for the exhibit '75 Years of Taibhdhearc na Gaillimhe', which ran from 14 July to 8 August 2003 at the James Hardiman Library, National University of Ireland, Galway.

Titley, Alan, 'Contemporary literature', *The Crane Bag: Irish Language and Culture/An tEagrán Gaelach* V:2 (1981), pp 59–65.

_____, '"Neither the boghole nor Berlin": drama in the Irish language from then until now', in *Nailing Theses: Selected Essays* (Belfast: Lagan Press, 2011), pp 267–77.

_____, *An tÚrscéal Gaeilge* (Baile Átha Cliath: An Clóchomhar, 1991).

Uí Choileáin, Máirín Breathnach, *Aisteoirí an Spidéil* (Indreabhán: Cló Iar-Chonnachta, 2015).

Endnote

RESOURCES FOR THOSE INTERESTED IN READING OR PRODUCING ANY OF THESE PLAYS

Most if not all of the published plays discussed in this book are in the National Library of Ireland in Dublin. Many of them can also be found in the libraries of the various Irish universities. Finding these works outside of Ireland is far more of a challenge, though some are held by the Library of Congress, the Boston Public Library, the New York Public Library, or libraries at universities with a special interest in Irish Studies such as Boston College, Harvard, New York University, or Notre Dame.

Most if not all of the plays in print can be purchased at the Gaelic League's bookshop An Siopa Leabhar (www.cnagsiopa.com) in Dublin; An Ceathrú Póilí (www.anceathrupoili.com) in Belfast; Ruiséal Teo (www.lrbooks.net) in Cork; An Café Liteartha (www.ancafeliteartha.com) in Dingle; or online through www.litriocht.com. Used copies of the plays can sometimes be found in second-hand bookshops in Ireland, perhaps most notably Kennys in Galway (www.kennys.ie) or Naughton Booksellers in Dún Laoghaire (www.naughtonsbooks.com).

For those interested in producing any of these plays, there are two essential resources. Playography na Gaeilge (www.irishplayography.com) provides a searchable database of almost every original play staged in Irish since 1901. The site offers information on the first production, including the names of director and original cast, a brief synopsis of the play, as well as indicating the length of the work and the gender breakdown of the cast. An Comhlachas Náisiúnta Drámaíochta (The national drama association) (www.drama-gaeilge.com), based in Camas in the Conamara Gaeltacht in Co. Galway, maintains a library of, as it says, 'most of the plays in Irish staged around the country' (formhór mór na ndrámaí Gaeilge a chuirtear ar stáitse ar fud na tire). Moreover, it has copies of many of these plays, including unpublished scripts, available for sale. An Comhlachas also employs advisers to assist amateur groups as well as judges for drama competitions in addition to publishing the annual journal *Stáitse*. While this journal has not appeared since 2005, An Comhlachas is hoping to revive it in the near future.

Virtually all of the theatre groups mentioned in this book that are still active maintain websites of varying quality and timeliness. Many of them include archives and galleries in which one can see information about past productions and photos from shows past and present. The websites for four major companies are www.abbeytheatre.ie for the Abbey and Peacock Theatres;[1] www.antaibhdhearc.com for Taibhdhearc na Gaillimhe; www.aislingghear.com for Aisling Ghéar; and www.fibin.com for Fíbín Teo.

---

1   The Abbey website also provides access to an online performance database and information about the Abbey archives.

Index